Deep
Down
Things

D0862636

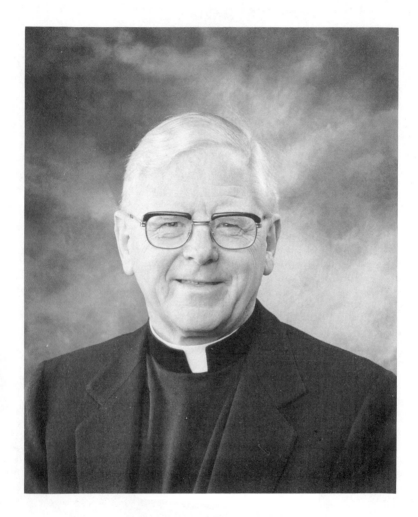

Richard McCullen, C.M.

Deep Down Things

Selected Writings

Richard McCullen, C.M.

New City Press

Published in the United States of America by New City Press
202 Cardinal Rd., Hyde Park, New York 12538
©1995 Vincentian Fathers

Nihil Obstat: Joseph Levesque, C.M.
             Delegated Censor
Imprimatur: W. Francis Malooly
             Vicar General

Library of Congress Cataloging-in-Publication Data

McCullen, Richard.
  Deep down things : selected writings / Richard McCullen.

  Includes index.
  ISBN 1-56548-033-3 (pbk.)
  1. Vincentians--Spiritual life. 2. Daughters of Charity of St.
Vincent de Paul--Spiritual life. 3. Sermons, English. 4. Catholic
Church--Sermons. I. Title.
BX3770.M33   1995
255'.77--dc20   95-2255

".... And for all this, nature is never spent;
There lives the dearest
freshness **deep down things**;
And though the last lights off
the black West went
Oh, morning, and the brown
brink eastward, springs—
Because the Holy Ghost over the bent
World broods with warm
breast and with ah!
bright wings."

"God's Grandeur" by Gerard Manley Hopkins, S.J.,
taken from the *Oxford Book of English Mystical Verse*,
Oxford University Press, London.

Table of Contents

1986

1987

1988

1989

1990

1991

1992

Preface

I am delighted to present to you this work, which contains many of the homilies and talks that Father Richard McCullen gave during his twelve years as Superior General.

Most members of the large Vincentian Family—priests, brothers, sisters, lay men and women—have had the pleasure of hearing Father McCullen speak. As someone who listened to him often, I can attest personally to the impact that his words, accompanied by the witness of his life, have had on me. This book brings together in a very well-organized and convenient form, a significant number of his talks.

I congratulate Sister Mary Ellen Sheldon and Sister Eleanor McNabb not only for placing this very useful work in our hands, but for winning the gentle battle they had to wage because of Father McCullen's reluctance to have his works published. Having enjoyed the sisters' presence here in Rome myself, and having benefitted enormously from their service to me as Superior General, I had no doubts from the start that they would prevail!

I encourage the reader to digest this book well by taking small daily bites. Father McCullen's talks were meant to be listened to one by one on separate occasions, not read back-to-back in a few sittings. They should be very useful to all of us who live in the Vincentian tradition as a source for meditation.

Finally, I want to express my deepest gratitude to Father McCullen for the gift of his writings, his preaching, and his example to the Vincentian Family. We are very much the richer for the beauty of his words and the depth of their meaning.

Robert P. Maloney, C.M.
Superior General
Rome
September 27, 1994

Acknowledgements

Sincere gratitude to all those who have assisted us so generously and competently in the preparation of this volume:

To Father Robert P. Maloney, C.M., Superior General, for his encouragement and for writing the Preface of this book;

To Father Joseph L. Levesque, C.M., Provincial Superior, and Father Stephen M. Grozio, Assistant, for their support during this entire project;

To Sister Virginia Ann Brooks, Visitatrix of the Province of Emmitsburg, for permitting us to work on the editing of the writings of Father McCullen;

To Father Miguel Pérez Flores, C.M., for his assistance with quotations from the Spanish edition of Coste;

To Father Paul Henzmann, C.M., Archivist of the Congregation of the Mission, Paris, for verifying so many quotations from the French edition of Coste;

To Father William W. Sheldon, C.M., for installing the equipment and for his many helpful suggestions;

To Father Joseph McClain, C.M. who read every word of the manuscript and whose comments were very helpful;

To the readers who have given us the benefit of their knowledge and skill: Sister Cecilia Connelly, Sister Aloysia Dugan, Sister Margaret Flinton, Sister Marie Poole and Sister Joan Marie Waters;

To Sister Maureen Beitman for the cover design;

To Sister Joan Marie Waters and Kitty Kessler for their assistance with the proof reading;

To all those Daughters of Charity, Priests of the Congregation of the Mission, relatives and friends whose prayers and support have made this work possible.

Editors' Note

In April, 1992 the Spanish Publishing House, CEME, of Salamanca published a volume containing selected works of Father Richard McCullen, Superior General of the Congregation of the Mission and of the Daughters of Charity from July 1980 to July 1992. The book was translated from English into Spanish by Father Luis Huerga, C.M.

We then asked Father McCullen if we could compile a volume with selected homilies, talks and letters which he had given during his term of office as Superior General. Father McCullen assented and Sister Virginia Ann Brooks, our Visitatrix, gave her consent. Father Levesque, Visitor of the Eastern Province of the Congregation of the Mission, agreed to sponsor this work.

From the more than 2,000 documents which we had conserved, we selected a variety which would include a wide range of topics. We were limited by the necessity of making the book in a size that could be conveniently used.

There are many quotations from the French edition of the fourteen volumes of the correspondence, documents and conferences of Saint Vincent de Paul by Pierre Coste, C.M., published in the 1920s. At this writing there are four volumes translated from the French and we have used this official translation in the quotations. For the quotes from volumes five through eight we have used Father McCullen's translation which he took directly from the French. Volumes nine and ten, conferences to the Daughters of Charity, were translated by Joseph Leonard, C.M. and published in four volumes by Burns Oates and Washbourne, Ltd., 1938-1940. The four volumes were republished in one book in 1979 by Collins Liturgical Publications. Quotations from volumes eleven through fourteen of Coste were again taken by Father McCullen directly from the French edition.

Quotations from the Spiritual Writings of Louise de Marillac were taken from the 1991 book, edited and translated from the French by Sister Louise Sullivan, D.C.

Quotations from the Constitutions, Statutes and Common Rules of the Congregation of the Mission were taken from the English Translation edition of 1989, published in Philadelphia. Quotations from the Constitutions and Statutes of the Daughters of Charity of St. Vincent de Paul were taken from the English edition of 1983.

The text includes many quotations from the Bible and Father McCullen used a variety of biblical translations. Most of the scriptural quotations are from the Revised Standard Version of the Bible, copyright 1946, 1952 and 1971 by the Division of Christian Education of the National Council of the Churches of Christ in the U.S.A., used by permission; from the Jerusalem Bible, copyright 1966 by Darton Longman & Todd, Ltd. and Doubleday, a division of Bantam Doubleday Dell Publishing Group, Inc., reprinted by permission of the publisher; from the Douay-Rheims Bible; and from the Knox Bible. When he quoted in English from a foreign Bible, Father McCullen did the translation himself.

Any omission of acknowledgment is unintentional and will be promptly rectified in any future edition.

We are deeply grateful to Father McCullen for permitting us to publish his writings and to all who have assisted and encouraged us in this work. May the book be as inspiring to those who read it as it has been to us.

Sister Eleanor McNabb, D.C.
Sister Mary Ellen Sheldon, D.C.

Abbreviations

A.I.C.   International Association of Charities
C.   Constitution
CLAPVI   Conference of Latin American Vincentian Provinces
C.M.   Congregation of the Mission
Conf. Eng. Ed.   Conferences of St. Vincent de Paul,
                    translated by Joseph Leonard
CR   Common Rules of the Congregation of the Mission
DC   Daughter of Charity
DCNHS   Daughters of Charity National Health System
Fr. Ed.   French Edition, Pierre Coste, C.M., St. Vincent de Paul,
                    Correspondence, Conferences, Documents
NASA   National Aeronautic and Space Administration
LA   Lines of Action
MEGVIS   Central European Vincentian Studies Group
SIEV   International Secretariat for Vincentian Studies
VSI   Vincentian Studies Institute

1980

First Talk as Superior General

20 July 1980   Paris, France

Mother Rogé, Father Richardson and Father Lloret,

I wish first to thank Father Lloret who, within two hours of my election, had written a long letter inviting me to come to Paris this weekend, and within the same period of time, Mother Rogé had sent me a very warm, sincere telegram assuring me of the prayers of all the Sisters here in the rue du Bac, to whom I would like to say from my heart this morning: *"Thank you very much!"*

There is nowhere in the world that I would like to have been yesterday more than here in Paris in the rue du Bac. Coming here to Paris and to rue du Bac has been for me always a visit to what I regard, since I came to the Community, as my favorite shrine of our Blessed Lady.

Last Friday after my election, telegrams came, not only from Mother Rogé, but from Daughters of Charity the world over, and it has been to me an enormous source of strength. I felt in the past ten days the real support of the prayers of the Daughters of Charity.

The morning of my election, I felt like a man who had gone out to sea for a swim and then got caught in a current which carried me away from all that was familiar to me, and to depths that I have never known. So your prayers and the prayers of my confreres have meant much to me, especially these past ten days. I have spoken to Father Richardson about it, and he said to me with his characteristic strength and honesty: *"Father, when the Sisters say they will pray for you, they mean it."* So, if I have nothing else to say to you this morning, I just want to say this: *"Thank you for everything you have given me!"* I say that to Mother Rogé and through her to the Daughters throughout the world.

Yesterday, shortly before three o'clock, we (Fathers McCullen, Richardson, Lloret) prayed together in the sanctuary of the chapel. I

1

want to tell you something that perhaps you have not heard before about the significance of this sanctuary to our Province of Ireland. Our Province was founded in 1833, and you recall how when Our Blessed Lady was talking to St. Catherine, she promised her that there would be a new increase of vocations to the Double Family of St. Vincent. Recently, I have been reflecting on that promise. The Province from which I come, Ireland, was not founded immediately by a confrere from France or from Italy. Our Province was founded in this way: about four or five students in the large seminary in Maynooth came together and began to talk about the need to preach missions in Ireland. They were not yet priests: they were ordained in 1833 and shortly after that time they were talking to the Archbishop of Dublin, who said to them: *"Why not join yourselves to some congregation in the Church that is interested in preaching retreats and missions?"* And so they did, but what is interesting is that almost the same year Our Lady was promising an increase of vocations to the family of St. Vincent in 1830, these four or five men, without knowing it, were starting to plan the beginning of what is the Irish Province today. So you understand how much the sanctuary of the rue du Bac chapel means to me! I mentioned this to our own confreres in Ireland.

Naturally, the thought of vocations to both our Communities is much on our minds in the last few years. I do not think that we should be too disturbed about it. Certainly, we must pray. Certainly, we must look to find workers for the harvest of souls, and it is encouraging for us all here in Europe to realize that while vocations may be few here in these parts, there are regions of the world where vocations are more plentiful. Did not St. Vincent say that he saw the time coming when the Church and many Christians might be found in the continent of Africa? And so it is happening. During this past week on 16 July, the first six Nigerian Sisters pronounced their vows for the first time. So there is room for hope and optimism for both our Communities. Perhaps we, living here in Europe, have too narrow a vision. We should be encouraged by the fact that the Church is growing in other parts of the world and by this vision that St. Vincent had in his time.

Last week after my election a Spanish confrere, a journalist, came to me with no less than fifteen questions to put to me about the

Community. I told him it was rather like an examination of conscience! Among the questions he had was: *"Would you have one word for the Daughters of Charity?"* I thought for a moment and then said: *"Well, I could say much but you only want one word, one sentence, and the one sentence I offer you is their motto: 'Caritas Christi urget nos.'* Then we went on to talk about the Daughters of Charity and I told him that I admired the Daughters of Charity (and I say this not because I am speaking to you this morning), because of their consistent devotion to the poor for Christ's sake.

It is important that we be devoted to and look for the poor to serve them, but we must also do so because of Jesus Christ: *Caritas Christi urget nos.* The first two words are most important, *Caritas Christi.* I also told him that I admired the Daughters of Charity because of their courage to give up works which they may have had for a number of years, because they were convinced that those works were not for the poor. Especially since the end of Vatican Council II, I have admired how your Community has managed to keep such uniformity among yourselves: uniformity, not only in devotion and in community practices of prayer, but also in dress. Yesterday, on the plane from Rome to Paris, Father Richardson and I were talking about this uniformity and we both agreed that it was something that St. Vincent impressed very deeply on the Daughters of Charity, and by the grace of God, you have been faithful to that since then. It is a uniformity that is born not just for good order's sake, but it is a uniformity that is born out of love for the person of Jesus Christ, Whom you wish to serve in the person of the poor.

During the past week I have been reflecting on how much my appointment has brought me closer to you. I have been reflecting, too, on the phenomenon of the work of the Holy Spirit, Who united St. Vincent and St. Louise three hundred years ago to do a spiritual work for the Church of that time. I have been reflecting, also, on how that spiritual unity between two persons here in this city of Paris has been perpetuated and lives on in the unity of the two Congregations to which by God's grace and favor, we here in this hall belong. It is a phenomenon. It is a work of the Holy Spirit, and I do believe that in the past ten or twelve years, the unity of the two Congregations, despite fewer numbers, has in fact been strengthened.

In our meditations on the life of St. Vincent and St. Louise we often think about what St. Vincent brought to St. Louise. We know very well how much she grew in holiness under the guidance of St. Vincent. Perhaps we men rather like to think that St. Vincent brought more to St. Louise than St. Louise brought to St. Vincent. We know from the very touching letters she wrote to him that she brought him many things. I remember reading a letter which she wrote to him when he was sick, and how she sent him some good things to eat and recommended some medicines to him. That spirit still lives on in the Community as we confreres, Vincentians, know only too well. It is true that St. Louise gave St. Vincent a great deal; perhaps you think of it more often than we do. St. Louise enabled St. Vincent to reach an enormous number of poor people whom otherwise he could not have reached.

These days, as Father Richardson and Father Lloret will tell you, we have been talking about and praying about how best we could serve the poor of the world and live our motto which St. Vincent gave us: *"Evangelizare pauperibus misit me."* I think that the Congregation of the Mission is still called to help the Daughters of Charity and the Daughters of Charity to help the Congregation of the Mission. Whatever I may be able to do during my term of office in helping the Daughters of Charity, I will look upon in this way, that in doing so I am being enabled to reach some of the poor of the present-day world whom otherwise I could not reach and whom, like you, I am called to serve. Our Congregations have this ideal in common. We can do it in different ways, but we have been called first to know and to love the person of Jesus Christ and then to bring some of that love and compassion and concern and spirituality to the poor of this world.

I wandered a little bit from the sanctuary of the rue du Bac about which I was speaking to you some minutes ago and which means so much to me. I would like to come back to it. Last evening Mother Rogé very kindly gave me some pictures of Pope John Paul's visit to the rue du Bac and Father Lloret pointed out to me the plaque which you have erected to commemorate that historic visit. As yet I have not had an opportunity of reading in the pages of *"La Documentation Catholique"* the words which our Holy Father spoke to you. I look forward to reading them in the future. I thought last night of what Pope Paul VI did at the end of one of the sessions of Vatican Council II. The Bishops of the Church had completed the work on the chapter on Our Blessed Lady and her place in the Church, and before the bishops left Rome to go back to their dioceses (and I recall reading this in the *"Documentation Catholique"*), he presented each of the two thousand bishops with a small gold Miraculous Medal. I often thought about this gesture of his. I do not know why he chose the Miraculous Medal for that occasion, but when we reflect on it we can see that it was a very fitting gesture, because in that Miraculous Medal we have the summary of everything that the Church teaches about Our Lady: the summary of all that the Church has taught and will go on teaching about Our Lady, about the power of her intercession; about her power over the evil forces of this world, about her union with her Divine Son, about the place of the Cross in our lives. The stars on the reverse of the Miraculous Medal, have they not taken on a new significance in the light of what the Church has been teaching us through Vatican Council II? Those stars suggest to us the future. If the Church advanced her teaching on our Blessed Lady in the course of the Vatican Council, she announced it in reminding us that what Mary is—now as ever, without spot, without wrinkle, without stain—the Church in time will come to be.

I have something else to say to you on this occasion. I told it to my confreres in Rome after my election. The idea was put into my own mind the night before the election when I became afraid of what might happen the following day. A confrere told me: *"No matter how unworthy you are, no matter what you have done in the past, no matter what you have failed to do in the past, if the confreres elect you tomorrow morning, it is a call to conversion."*

That is how I see it. You may smile but that is how I experience it. In the appointment we get in Community, whether we like it or whether we do not, it is a call to conversion. Perhaps we think the word *"conversion"* has something in relation to sin, and it has; but there is also a very rich positive meaning to that word of conversion. Each appointment we receive in Community is a call to turn to investigation and to discover the riches that are to be found in the heritage St. Vincent and St. Louise have left us. Every appointment we receive, whether it is according to our own feelings or not, is a call to appreciate and to give God thanks for the enormous wealth of riches and strength that are to be found in both our Communities. May that grace be given to us all here today, to be enlightened to see our appointments, no matter how surprised we may be about them, as a call to conversion, to become more like her who is the Mother of God and who was totally converted to Him because of the privilege of her Immaculate Conception; a call to appreciate and to rejoice in that beautiful word that Father Lloret used this morning in his homily, when he referred to the *"delicatesse"* of our Blessed Lady toward both our Communities.

Silence and Prayer

15 August 1980   Paris, France

Mother Rogé, a Happy Feast Day to you!

My dear Sisters,

In the Gospel which Father Lloret read for us this morning at Mass, we did not hear any word about the Assumption of Our Blessed Lady into heaven, but, of course, we believe that mystery with our hearts and minds because it is the teaching of the one, holy, catholic and apostolic Church. While we did not learn from this morning's Gospel anything about the Assumption of Our Blessed Lady into heaven, we did learn a great deal about Our Lady's prayer. I am sure that many times you have reflected on how little Our Lady spoke. If you read carefully the first two chapters of St. Luke's Gospel, you will notice that in those two short chapters, St. Luke twice makes the point that Our Lady pondered in her heart all the events of those early years of Jesus Christ. He portrays Our Lady as a very thoughtful, reflective, meditative person.

On the last occasion when I was speaking to you here, I said that I had not had the opportunity of reading what Pope John Paul spoke about in the Chapel of this house. Since then I have done so and I am sure you have reflected on and prayed that beautiful prayer which he addressed to the Mother of God. The very last paragraph must mean a great deal to the Daughters of Charity all over the world, and especially to the Daughters of Charity in this house. Let me pray again that last sentence of his prayer: *"We pray to You for those who dwell in this house and who welcome, in the heart of this feverish capital, pilgrims who know the price of silence and prayer."*

The Pope points up the contrast between the feverish activity of a city like Paris, or any modern city, with the atmosphere of silence and prayer that he experiences at the heart of the rue du Bac. When I read his words and reflected on them, the thought came to my mind that Our Lady, when she appeared in that sanctuary where we celebrated Mass this morning, has by her presence left behind her in the rue du Bac an aroma of silence and prayer. Silence and prayer are very much part of the character of Our Blessed Lady as we know her from the Gospels. When the Pope said that pilgrims come to the rue du Bac to find silence and prayer, I would venture to say that he was relying on you, as a Community, to preserve those two values: silence and prayer. They are features of the character of Our Blessed Lady. They are features also of the character of St. Catherine Labouré.

During these last few years there has been a renewed interest among old and young people in prayer. Perhaps we need to remind ourselves in our Communities that if we are to pray deeply we need silence. In that classic book *"The Imitation of Christ"* there is a sentence that goes like this: *"In silence the devout soul goes forward and learns the secrets of the scriptures."* It was in silence that Our Blessed Lady learned the secrets of the scriptures. St. Luke seems to indicate that when he twice reminds us that Our Lady pondered all these things in her heart. You cannot ponder unless you do so in silence. It is very difficult for us, modern people in this age, to create silence. Yet I think it is very necessary for all of us to have an oasis of silence in the desert of sound and noise where we can ponder and reflect as Mary did. That does not mean that we keep silence all the time; it does not mean that we abandon contact with the poor. The point I am making is this, that for all of us in Community at the present time, it is a continuing challenge to ponder as Our Lady did, while not neglecting the care of her Son and His members, especially the poor.

Two nights ago, when I went to my new house in Rome, after having been carefully looked after for eight weeks by the Daughters in the Via Ezio, I sat down at my desk to prepare, and to think about, this conference which I was to address to you this morning. I said to myself: *"I wonder did St. Vincent ever write a letter on the 15 August."* So I took the eight volumes of Coste. No, I did not read them all, but I picked a few volumes and looked for the month of August. Quite quickly, in the third volume of Father Coste, I came upon a letter which St. Vincent wrote in 1646, and the heading of the letter was: *"Paris, Vigil of the Assumption of Our Lady"*. The letter was addressed to St. Louise. St. Louise was not in Paris on the 15 August 1646; she was in Nantes. She had gone there to do business with some hospital administrators. St. Vincent was thinking about her and he begins his letter to St. Louise by remarking that he had not received any communication from her. He was just wondering how things were going, and so very early in the letter he had a little word of encouragement for St. Louise. In a paragraph of the letter he prayed: *"I beg His Divine Mercy to give you for this purpose an ample share of His Spirit, so that you can communicate it to your dear daughters, and together with them diffuse in souls the fragrance of holy devotion!"* (Coste III, Eng. ed., no. 833, p. 16).

Mother Rogé, on this your feast day, I cannot think of any better expression of a wish than to pray that prayer of St. Vincent for St. Louise which he prayed on the vigil of the Assumption in 1646.

However, as St. Vincent and St. Louise and Mother Rogé know so well, life is not all good wishes and just prayers with our lips. There are problems to be faced and many of them. In the next paragraph of the letter St. Vincent mentions a little problem that had arisen while Louise was away in Nantes. He writes: *"I have been able to see your assistants here only one time. I am supposed to see them today, please God. Everything is going rather well, except for a little restlessness apparent in a few Sisters, but your presence will set everything right again, as will perhaps the conference I plan to give them next week."* (Ibid.). I noticed that Father Coste remarks in a footnote that in fact St. Vincent did address the Sisters here in Paris while St. Louise was in Nantes. The conference is extant today. It is a rather long conference and I don't propose to read it in its entirety to you. The conference he gave was addressed to the Sisters four days later, 19 August, 1646, and it is entitled: *"On meekness and the practice of mutual respect."* Let the voice of St. Vincent, just for a few moments, be heard:

It was said in the first place that meekness and respect are most pleasing to God. Is not that true, my dear Daughters, and is there anything more pleasing to Him than the respect and meekness which are the virtues of the Son of God? As you have said very truly, He has taught us this Himself: 'Learn of Me,' He said, 'that I am meek and humble of heart.' That is to say, my dear Daughters: Learn of Me that I am meek and respectful because He interprets humility as respect, for respect proceeds from humility. Was there ever a man as meek and respectful as Jesus Christ? Oh no! He was meek and humble towards all . . . . You may be perfectly certain, my dear Daughters, that this is pleasing to God, and indeed most pleasing, and by this men will know you are really Daughters of Charity. For what is charity but love and gentleness? And if you do not possess this love and gentleness, you cannot be Daughters of Charity. And, as has been said, you would have no more than their name and habit, which would be a great misfortune. Oh! may God in His infinite mercy be pleased to avert it from your Company. Yes, my Daughters, you must know that a Daughter of Charity who is not on good terms with her sister, who saddens her, who vexes her and persists in that state without making any attempt to set things right by practicing these two virtues of respect and meekness, oh! from that moment she is no longer a Daughter of Charity. No, she no longer is. She should not be spoken of as such. It is all over as far as she is concerned. She has nothing now but the habit. Hold fast, therefore, to those two virtues, my Daughters. This will please God and will please Him so much that there will be scarcely anything else in the world more agreeable to Him."
(Conf. Eng. ed. 19 Aug. 1646, pp. 237-8).

After St. Vincent in this letter, written on the Vigil of the Assumption, had told St. Louise that there had been a little bit of disturbance, as happens in all our communities, he had another little piece of news for her. It is about her son: *"Your son is not feeling well . . . "* (Ibid.). Then immediately to allay St. Louise's anxiety he tells her that the boy is staying in bed at the doctor's house. Then comes this delightful little sentence: *"I offered him our house and anything we could do to make him feel better, or two Sisters to nurse him, in the event that he wanted to stay where he is. He preferred the help of the Sisters, who have been with him for several days now."* Then *"Monsieur Brin has just been to see him; he assures me that he is better and that there is nothing to fear."* (Ibid.).

I think you will pardon me if I make a little diversion here. Father Brin was a fellow countryman of mine. When two nights ago, rather late, I looked at the index of Father Coste's works to find out about Father Brin (I knew a little about him already), I found a very brief resume of his life. In his final sentence on Father Brin, Father Coste remarks that he was the best Irishman that St. Vincent had in his Congregation. I must tell you immediately that there were some other Irishmen that St. Vincent had in his Congregation who, as Father Lloret knows well, caused St. Vincent some acute headaches! It was also a little matter of consolation to me in that when St. Vincent tried to spell correctly the name of this Irish priest, he had as much success as I have when trying to speak French! That was a little morsel of consolation I had late a few nights ago, that we both understood each other in this question of languages. After that St. Vincent passes on to something else.

There was another little anxiety on his mind. It was this, that he was in trouble with the Ladies of Charity at the Hotel Dieu. It seemed that the Ladies were very annoyed that St. Louise had left Paris for Nantes and some of them carried on what St. Vincent in his own words, and you will see it in the letter, referred to as *une rude guerre*, precisely because he had consented to St. Louise's going away. St. Vincent was unperturbed and he remarks to St. Louise: *"If you return in good health, as I hope from God's goodness, peace will soon be made. So please take the best possible care of yourself. Take all the time you need so as not to rush anything or inconvenience yourself regarding your return. Our Lord will be pleased with this, since you will be doing it for love of Him."* (Ibid.). The letter ends there. There is a little postscript in which he adds that the letter she had written had just arrived.

The letter to which I have been referring is not the most profound of

St. Vincent's letters, but this thought came to me that the lives of St. Vincent and St. Louise were, for the most part, made up of little problems, little difficulties such as we in our lives experience today. Both of them accomplished magnificent work for the poor of Paris, of France and beyond France. The volume of the work which St. Vincent and St. Louise achieved can blind us to the meticulous attention which both of them gave to the small acts of consideration and charity of which, for the greater part, their lives, as ours, were made up.

That letter of St. Vincent written on the eve of the Assumption in 1646 does not mention Our Lady except at the heading of the letter, but it does breathe the spirit of the exquisite charity which we know to have been Our Lady's. That little word *exquisite* suggests detail. We speak of a tapestry, an embroidery; it is exquisite precisely because there is so much care and attention given to detail. Our lives become full of the love of God and of Jesus Christ and of His poor through our attention to the small acts of courtesy and mutual respect, first within our own communities. Our Lady, from what we know of her in the Gospel, showed such exquisite charity: her care of her Divine Son, her thoughtfulness in relieving the embarrassment of that bridal couple at Cana. This thought also struck me last night, her willingness and her generosity and her self-sacrifice, to be ready and willing to remain close to people who did not just irritate her and cause her annoyance, but who sapped the blood out of her life's work; who sapped the life blood out of Him Whom she knew so well to be the fruit of her loving womb, Jesus. For her there was no opting out of Community because of difficulties. One phrase in the Gospel of St. John, I think, speaks a lot to us of the strength of character of Our Blessed Lady: *"She stood by the cross of Jesus."* (Jn 19:25). There was no need for her to go to Golgotha but she went and witnessed with her own eyes the crucifixion of her Son. Our little difficulties of living together in communities pale into insignificance when we reflect on her strength of character to remain close to people who drove nails in the hands and feet of her Son, Jesus Christ, truly God and truly man.

Today we are not thinking and reflecting on her sufferings. Rather are we thinking of her glory. The Gospel this morning was one of thanksgiving, and I come back to what I said at the beginning of this talk: Mary spoke little, a lady of silence and prayer. But if you count up the words in the New Testament that Mary spoke, the Magnificat makes up the greater part of them and that is a hymn of thanksgiving. Today we are living in an age of protest, of violence. Every evening we sing or say that hymn of thanksgiving of Our Lady. My last thought to you is this, that in this age of protest, of marches, of violence, let thanksgiving be a prominent feature in your prayer as it was in Mary's prayer, and you will find that through giving thanks to God from your heart and counting your blessings, you will come to know that serenity and peace which you find in St. Vincent's writing and which the grace of God communicated to him. I think thanksgiving is a flower of that humility which is the foundation stone of both our Communities. It is thanksgiving and humility which enabled the grace of God to accomplish great things in St. Vincent and St. Louise for those who are our portion, the poor.

Let me end again with the words of St. Vincent spoken on that August day in 1646: *"May God in His goodness be pleased, my dear Daughters, to pour forth His Spirit on you in abundance, which is nothing but love, sweetness and charity, so that by the practice of these virtues you may do all things in the manner He wishes you should do them, for his glory, your own salvation and the edification of your neighbor. And I, although the most harsh and least mild of men, relying on the mercy of God, will not omit to pronounce the words of blessing, and I beseech with all my heart that as I utter them He may be pleased to replenish you with His holy graces. Benedictio Dei Patris . . . ."* (Conf. Eng. ed. 19 Aug. 1646, p. 248).

Abba—Amen

1 October 1980   Tollcross, Scotland

My dear Sisters,

The beauty of Autumn is the beauty of the trees and the beauty of the tree in Autumn is the beauty of her leaves. The beauty of the single tree in Autumn is the beauty and the variety of the colors that were once green and are now shading into brown and gold; leaves of the same tree, bearing the same shade, yet different in color, for one short week or two, before they fall to the ground; different in color, yet all belonging to the same tree.

The saint of the day bears the same spiritual shape as a Daughter of Charity, for St. Thérèse, as any Daughter of Charity, belongs to a branch of the same vine as Christ. But the spiritual coloration of the saint of the day, is slightly different from the coloration which St. Vincent and St. Louise consider as the spirit God has given to your Community. I say that the saint of the day bears the same spiritual shape, for ask any lay person about the Little Flower and, if they know anything at all about St. Thérèse of Lisieux, they would say, *"Well, she was simple, humble and charitable."* Taking the last quality first, her charity is very significant in the passage from her autobiography which the Church presents today in the Office of Readings. It is a very simple passage in which she made this spiritual discovery that while the Body of Christ had many members, it was all important that the Body of Christ should have a heart and that that heart should be love. So she saw herself, in her simple way, as being love at the heart of the Church, supporting all the other members of the Body of Christ, which is His Church. Love she saw as the center of her vocation. Love is at the center of your vocation. The coloration is different. Her love was asked to be expressed in the confines of a Carmelite Monastery. Your love is to find expression in your service and your constant seeking out of the poor of Christ. So I just offer you this thought about St. Thérèse's being *"love at the center of the Church."*

As the years take their toll of us, and we find the sphere of activity more and more restricted for us in Community through advancing years and the cross of diminished activity which falls on our shoulders, it would be very important for us to be able to see our vocation as being one of love at the heart of our Community. We will find that others come along, younger in years and greater in strength and energy, and we will be asked to lay down tasks that we held very dear to us in the service of the poor. It will be very important for us and I hope the grace will be given to us to see that, in those autumn years of our life, we will be like the center of our Communities.

As for simplicity, which St. Vincent recommended as a characteristic
quality to both our communities, St. Thérèse saw herself very much as
a simple person. The Church looks on her as a very simple saint, but
she made this discovery again through the grace of God that following
Him was everything. At times in her autobiography she tends to be
almost childish in her expressions, particularly those she uses about the
Fatherhood of God, but she lived the Fatherhood of God more and more.
She penetrated the heart of that little phrase, which made such a deep
impression on the early Christians and the early writers, which we find
in St. Paul's Epistle to the Romans, *"Abba, Father,"* (Rom 8:15) the
word that Jesus used in the Garden of Olives. St. Paul reminds us that
it is really the Spirit of God in our hearts which helps us to cry out *Abba*,
using the very Aramaic word that Jesus used, even though Paul was
writing in Greek.

Some years ago a very renowned English scholar, C.H. Dodd, wrote
a book on *The Central Message of the New Testament* which was widely
acclaimed, a small but very significant work. After years devoted to the
study of the Scriptures, C.H. Dodd came to the conclusion that the
Central Message of the New Testament was *"The Fatherhood of God."*
St. Thérèse of Lisieux lived this message, so much so that she remarks
in her autobiography that even if God condemned her to hell, she would
go on thinking of Him as a Father. How simply she tells us, too, of the
occasions when in Community she had to bite her lips to prevent herself
from crying out some word of rebellion. We who live in Communities
know how difficult it can be at times not to give way to expressions of
rebellion and anger in our pride and discouragement.

Reflecting on these two virtues of St. Thérèse of Lisieux and of your
Community, I thought of two words, which, as somebody said on one
occasion, could sum up the entire New Testament: *Abba, Father* and
Amen. The whole of the New Testament, you might say the whole of
Christ's life, is in those two words. All our spirituality is in them, too.
If, by the grace of God, I am able to say *Abba, Father*, I will also be
able to say *Amen*, let it be so, I accept it. A lot lies behind that little
word we say so often, *Amen*.

I remember visiting an old priest who was dying and I noticed that
every so often there would be a silence in our conversation, and he

would say *Amen*. On one of my last visits to him in the hospital, he was having his lunch and as he pushed his lunch tray away from him, he said, *Amen*. I said to him (very rashly!), *"That's a great prayer."* He paused for a moment and said, *"Yes, if you could mean it."* So I said no more.

I would like to offer you this other thought. If the whole of Christian spirituality is in those two words, *Abba, Amen*, the spirit of the Daughters of Charity lies in your Community's ability to pray *Abba* and *Amen*, in your Community's ability to live simply because you are the children of an all-providing God. If you are able to say as a Community, *Amen*, that will mean in practice fidelity in living out your vow of obedience. I have said, on more than one occasion, that I admire your dedication to the poor, wherever they are to be found in a changing society. You will continue to serve them if, in your individual lives and those of the Community, there is that simplicity and humility from which charity will flow. It was not without thought that St. Vincent gave those three virtues to you, and I see as the root of the flower of obedience in your Community that characteristic virtue of St. Vincent and St. Louise, humility of heart.

"As for myself," St. Vincent said, *"I don't know, but God has given me such a high esteem of simplicity that I call it my Gospel."* (Conf. Eng. ed., 24 Feb. 1653, p. 538). Today that Gospel is the Gospel of all of us here this evening so that we may be children of God, so that we may be able to cry with confidence, *"Abba, into your hands I commend my spirit."* Having lived in simplicity, in humility and in its flower, obedience, we will be able to say, even though at times very painfully, *Amen* and having said *Amen* and lived it in Community throughout our lives, we will be able to do what we have just done, that is, put the *Alleluia* in front of the *Amen*. That will be our hymn in eternity, *Alleluia, Amen, Amen, Alleluia.*

Our Lady of the Miraculous Medal

7 December 1980   Armagh, Northern Ireland

Your Eminence, Fathers, and my dear Brothers and Sisters in Christ,

Over in the cemetery of the Sacred Heart Convent there lie the remains of one of His Eminence's predecessors, Primate Dixon, whose name will always be associated with the recommencement after the famine years of the work of building this Cathedral, in which we are gathered this evening to honor Our Blessed Lady. Primate Dixon had the privilege of being in Rome on the occasion when Pope Pius IX defined the Dogma of the Immaculate Conception of Our Blessed Lady. During his days there, he kept a personal diary of the event. It is a small thing for a Primate to be concerned about the weather, but we do know that the Archbishop was concerned about the weather on the evening of the 7 December 1854. It had rained incessantly in Rome all day on the 7th and when His Grace was retiring to rest, it was still raining. In his simple style, he noted in his diary: *"Hence on retiring to bed on the night of the 7 December, it was rather an ardent desire which I felt for the coming of a fine day on the morrow. On account of this desire, I got up repeatedly during the night to look at the appearance of the sky, and when about four o'clock in the morning, I saw that my hopeful antici- pations for the great day were about to be fully realized, it delights me now to remember with what joy and thankfulness, I repeated the 'Ave Maris Stella.'"*

The sun did shine resplendently in Rome on the 8 December, 1854, as Pope Pius IX declared that by a special privilege of grace, Our Lady, Mary, the Mother of God, was preserved from the stain of original sin by the power of her Son's redeeming death.

While we have a detailed account from the Primate of the event and of the joyous mood of a fully-packed St. Peter's on the 8 December 1854, we know nothing of the reactions of a Sister of Charity in Paris, who was working in a geriatric hospital for poor men. Presumably she had assisted at Mass that morning, received the Body and Blood of Our Lord, and sang hymns to honor the Immaculate Conception of Our Lady. Then after breakfast she would have set about doing the work that has to be done in the morning in every hospital or geriatric home, whatever the feast day or occasion may be. One wonders did she say to herself, *"I have seen it already,"* for in a very real sense, Catherine Labouré had seen it already. She was now coming close to the Silver Jubilee of her entrance into the Daughters of Charity of St. Vincent de Paul. Twenty-four years earlier, in July 1830, during her novitiate year in the rue du Bac, Paris, this young, simple, practical, country girl had been awakened about midnight and led to the chapel by a young child where, after a short wait, Our Lady entered and, seating herself on a chair in the sanctuary, spoke with Catherine Labouré for two hours. Later that same year on a November evening during her evening prayer in the chapel, Catherine was shown by Our Lady the image of what we now know as the Miraculous Medal, but which was not given that title either by Our Lady or St. Catherine or the Church, but by plain, ordinary people who began to wear it, and to honor Our Lady by reciting the one-sentence prayer inscribed on the medal, *"O Mary, conceived without sin, pray for us who have recourse to Thee."* Apart from this prayer, all else on the medal was expressed in symbolic signs, which today are recognized to be a condensed catechism of the Church's teaching on Our Lady and her place in our lives.

It has been remarked that the Miraculous Medal is the catechism of the humble and the poor, put into their hands in order to safeguard imperishable riches that are ever threatened: grace, the Mystery of the Cross, the Incarnation and the Redemption. It is a catechism or compendium of the Church's teaching on Our Lady, for through sign and symbol is expressed her Motherhood of God, her loving association with her Son in His work, her concern for the suffering world, and the power of her intercession. The stars on the reverse side of the medal have taken on a new meaning for us during these last few years. With clearer insight since the Second Vatican Council, the Church has seen more deeply into the relation between Mary and the Church. Her insight has been that what Mary is now, *"without spot and without wrinkle,"* the Church is one day destined to become. Of that truth you will be reminded as you listen to the prayer of the Preface tomorrow at Mass: *"Father . . . You allowed no stain of Adam's sin to touch the Virgin Mary. Full of grace, she was to be a worthy Mother of Your Son, Your sign of favor to the Church at its beginning, and the promise of its perfection as the Bride of Christ, radiant in beauty. "* (8 Dec., Feast of the Immaculate Conception).

The chapel in the rue du Bac where Our Lady spoke to St. Catherine and showed her the model of the Medal of the Immaculate Conception could almost be described as undistinguished, except for the fact that more people visit it in a year than visit the Eiffel Tower or the Louvre in Paris. Last Thursday, 27 November, more than ten thousand people filed in and out of that relatively small chapel. The chapel is undistinguished, in that you could pass it by easily, standing as it does in the recess of a side street in the city of Paris. You will find no eye-catching sign outside it, not even a signpost at the top of the street to direct you to it. It is as undistinguished as the earthly life of St. Catherine herself. It was only after her death that her deep holiness was recognized and that her life was declared by the Church to have been one of heroic virtue. When, in the mid-1830s and later, people began to discover, through wearing Our Lady's medal and praying with confidence the little prayer on it, that their lives were changing for the better; when they began to find God's goodness and kindness breaking through like sunshine in all sorts of new and unexpected ways into their lives, speculation became rife about the identity of the Sister of Charity to whom Our Lady had appeared. Catherine, however, kept her secret for forty-six years, disclosing it only to her confessor, who for quite a time was very skeptical. She lived an outwardly undistinguished life in her Community, caring for the needs of those sometimes cantankerous old men in the wards of a geriatric hospital in the suburbs of Paris.

But it is not of Catherine Labouré that we are thinking so much this evening, as of Her to whom St. Catherine points, Mary, conceived without sin. Cardinal Newman, two months before he was received into the Catholic Church, decided in a simple gesture of faith to wear the medal of Our Lady. The Cardinal took Our Lady at her word when she said that all who would wear the Medal of the Immaculate Conception would receive abundant graces. Years later in a letter he was to pinpoint the exact day when he did so, implying that Our Lady had more than something to do with his reception of the fullness of the faith and his entry into the Catholic Church in October 1845. (Letter to Pusey, 22

August 1867). Years later, too, the Cardinal was to write a magnificent reflection on original sin which he described as *"some terrible aboriginal calamity,"* in which the human race is implicated. (*Apologia*, p. 242). From implication in that *"terrible aboriginal calamity,"* Our Lady alone was by a unique privilege of grace preserved. Tremors of that aboriginal calamity are still to be felt in the lives of mankind. The tremors of evil can be shattering in their power, laying waste in lives what has been painfully and patiently built up. Amidst the ruins Jesus Christ has given us a home and a hearth in His Church, and He has promised us a *"lasting city that is to come."* (Heb 13:14). He also points to Her who alone has not been touched, even momentarily, by evil, not been begrimed by sin. He presents Her to us as one who, in our greatest moments of disillusionment with ourselves and with others, can sustain our belief in the goodness of humankind. He presents Her to us as one who, if we are only humble enough to ask, can bring us more than first-aid for the wounds of body, mind and spirit that cause so much pain and suffering. *"Son,"* He has said in the last hour of His life, *"there is your Mother."* (Jn 19: 27). It may very well be a measure of our spiritual poverty, of the narrowness of our vision, perhaps of our egoism, if we cannot rejoice and be glad that God has graced one human being in such an unique way, a human being who is at once so fully His and so much ours.

Let me finish where I began, and where we all are this evening, in the Mother Church of this Archdiocese of Armagh. It can only be a source of joy and of hope that we are witnessing in this country, and particularly in this Archdiocese, a new stirring of devotion to Our Lady, a fresh recognition of her uniqueness and of her power, a new realization that Our Lady one hundred fifty years ago did not put a time limit to her promise. A number of parishes have lately begun almost spontaneously to honor Our Lady through what we know as the Perpetual Novena. In our consciousness we would seem to be recognizing anew and looking to Mary as a sign of hope for our own troubled land, the hope that because her own heart was never divided by sin, She will help us, her squabbling children, to put aside what is so sadly and tragically dividing the Family of God.

When Primate Dixon stood at his window in Rome in the dark hours of the early morning before the dawn of the 8 December 1854, and saluted Our Lady in the words of the hymn, *"Ave Maris Stella,"* he would have prayed these stanzas:

> *Gentlest of all Virgins,*
> *Let our love be faithful,*
> *Keep us from all evil,*
> *Gentle, strong and faithful.*
> *Show yourself our Mother,*
> *He will hear your pleading,*
> *Whom your womb has sheltered*
> *And Whose hand brings healing.*
> *Guard us through life's dangers,*
> *Never turn and leave us.*
> *May our hope find harbor*
> *In the calm of Jesus.*

In these dark hours for our country, when we are looking at the appearance of the sky and hoping that the heavy clouds of hate and vengeance will break up, may the gentlest of all Virgins, Mary, tame *"the cruelty of man to man which is making thousands mourn."* May the hope that she is presently holding out to us *"soon find harbor in the calm of Jesus"* Who is and always will remain the Fruit of her Womb, she who is the most clement, the most loving, the most sweet Virgin Mary.

1981

Cordial Respect

Mother Rogé and my dear Sisters,

When I came here to Paris on 15 August last for Mother Rogé's feast day and when I spoke to you here in this hall, I put myself back into an August day of 1645, when St. Vincent came across from St. Lazare to speak to the little group of Sisters who were the first Daughters of Charity. When a few nights ago I began to think of what I could offer you this morning, I took down again the volume of St. Vincent's conferences to the Daughters of Charity. On this occasion, I looked for the date, a New Year's Day, and I found that St. Vincent addressed the Daughters of Charity on New Year's Day 1644. (Conf. Eng. ed. 1 Jan. 1644, pp. 129-43).

The subject of the conference was: *On Cordial Respect*. I do not know if there was any particular reason why he should have chosen this subject. It was almost the same topic as that which two years later, on 19 August 1646, St. Vincent chose for reflecting on and sharing with St. Louise's Community, and which we in turn thought about on 15 August last. And while we know from St. Vincent's correspondence that there was a particular reason for choosing the subject in August 1646, we do not know why he chose *On Cordial Respect* as the topic for the conference on New Year's Day 1644. I began to think that it might have been the fruit of St. Vincent's own meditation on the mystery of the Incarnation, for what is the mystery of the Incarnation but the mystery of God's cordial respect for the humanity of man. The mystery of the Incarnation is God's vote of confidence in the goodness of mankind. One of the most beautiful prayers which you will find in the treasury of Christian Prayer is that which we pray at the third Mass of Christmas Day, a prayer which is prayed at every Mass, when the priest places a little drop of water into the chalice of wine: *"God, Our*

21

Father, our human nature is the wonderful work of Your Hands, made still more wonderful by Your work of Redemption. Your Son took to Himself our manhood; grant us a share in the Godhead of Jesus Christ Who lives and reigns forever and ever."

The prayer is a summary of the history of salvation. It is a prayer which is an exquisite miniature of the drama of human existence and its interplay with the grace of God:

Act 1: The creation of man by God: *"The wonderful work of Your Hands;"*

Act 2: The still more wonderful work of Redemption: the remaking of mankind;

Act 3: The sharing of our human life by God made Man;

Act 4: The sharing of God's life by man made divine.

The Incarnation is a vote of confidence passed by God in the essential goodness of humankind. God did not decide to start all over again after man spoiled His design through sin, through that mysterious aboriginal calamity which we call original sin. God took the broken pieces and remade humanity from within. He chose, as we so often remind ourselves, to be born lovingly of the Virgin Mary, taking life as He found it on this earth, being like to us in all things except sin. As a seventeenth century English poet, Crashaw, expressed the truth:

"'Twas once look up—'Tis now look down—To Heaven."

Yes, the Incarnation is God's gesture of cordial respect for broken, sinful but still living and lovable humanity.

When I think of the cordial respect which God has shown, and is showing, every human being by becoming one of ourselves, I think of what is perhaps most beautiful of all the parables that fell from the lips of Jesus Christ, the parable of the Good Samaritan (Lk 10:29-37). This parable could be described as the parable of God's cordial respect for man: the Good Samaritan finds the poor man on the road *"wounded and half-dead."* (Ibid.). The Fathers of the Church liked to see that poor man as a representative of humanity after original sin, lying weak and helpless on the road of existence. Then Jesus Christ, God made Man, comes along. He does not pass by. He shows interest and love. He pours oil and wine on the wounds of the poor man. The Fathers of the Church liked to think of the oil and the wine as the Sacraments of Christ. Then the Good Samaritan lifts the poor man off the road, places him on his own beast, and brings him to an inn, which the Fathers of the Church saw as an image of Christ's Church.

The parable, too, has been described as a self-portrait of Jesus Christ because it speaks of the love of the Good Samaritan for one poor man. The Good Samaritan helps the poor man on the road silently. Have you ever noticed when reading the parable that the Good Samaritan does not speak at all, except at the end to the innkeeper when he is making arrangements for the poor man's accommodation? It is a parable that could and should be the portrait of a Daughter of Charity: who has cordial respect for the poor, who is always looking out for the poor who are lying on life's road *"wounded and half-dead."* (Ibid.). A Daughter of Charity is one who tries not to pass by the poor, as she journeys along life's road. A Daughter of Charity is one who does her work for the poor silently in imitation of Jesus Christ, the Good Samaritan.

Before we are able to show profound cordial respect to the poor, we need to be convinced of the profound cordial respect which Jesus Christ has for each one of us. The people who today have most difficulty in loving others are those who through some mishap, some accident, some misunderstanding, have not had the experience in infancy and youth of being loved, of being appreciated. So many of you can testify to the truth of that from your experience of working with and among the poor. If we are to love others with the love of Christ, and it is the love of Christ which we bring to the poor, it is necessary that we should be always trying, with the grace of God, to deepen within ourselves this conviction: I am deeply loved, cordially respected by Jesus Christ for what I am. In my prayer and reflection I must try to think of Jesus Christ as re-making me all the time. He is all the time bending over me, tending my wounds, pouring in oil and wine, lifting me up off life's road, giving me new heart. He is all the time addressing to me those words which I hear addressed to me by His representative at Mass every day: *"Let us lift up our hearts."*

Perhaps I should refer here to the two Sacraments of the Eucharist and Penance. So often nowadays we hear people say of these two Sacraments: *"I do not get much out of Holy Communion. I do not get much out of the Sacrament of Penance."* What we should be wondering and thinking more about is what Jesus Christ, the Good Samaritan, wants to give us through these Sacraments. What we need is the grace to see things more from His point of view, and less from our own. Jesus Christ has such cordial respect for us that He will not force Himself upon us. To use a phrase from the Book of Revelation: *"Behold, I stand at the door and knock. If any one hears my voice and opens the door, I will come in to him and eat with him and he with Me."* (Rv 3:20). We must first open the door to Him. When we invite our friends to a meal in our houses, we do not calculate first what they are going to bring us. We invite them because they are our friends, because we have cordial, loving respect for them. *"If a man loves Me . . . My Father will love him and We will come to him and make Our home with him."* (Jn 14:23).

Every time we approach Jesus Christ in one of His Sacraments, we are at once showing Him cordial respect and growing in the experience of being loved personally by Jesus Christ. And it is from that experience of being loved personally by Jesus Christ that we are able in turn to show authentic love to one another in Community, and to the poor who are lying helpless on life's road, and who cry to us for help. It is from the experience of being loved personally by Jesus Christ that we are able to lift them up and bring them to the inn of God's Church, and prepare them in faith and hope to meet the Good Samaritan in person when He returns: *"And I on my return will repay thee."* (Lk 10:35).

It is New Year's Day, a day when the Church asks us to pray for peace and reconciliation among mankind. I once heard a confrere say at a General Assembly that St. Vincent was a magnificent example of the meaning of reconciliation. The confrere did not elaborate on his reasons for his statement.

If you think about it, however, you will find it is true. After his deep conversion during the fourth decade of his life, he devoted himself to bringing people, especially the poor, to experience the *"unsearchable riches of Christ"* (Eph 3:8), to share in *"the love of God which was in Christ Jesus."* (Rom 8:39). He tried also to bring the rich and wealthy closer to the needy and the poor. You yourselves as a Community are a living monument to the genius of St. Vincent, for the Daughters of Charity were the great mediators, the great reconcilers between the rich and the poor, the poor and the rich. St. Vincent brought the resources of the rich to the poor, and he did that in a loving way. Perhaps I should stress the word *loving*. In no line of St. Vincent's writings will you find a bitter, recriminating word against those who were wealthy. He could persuade a dying king to take some food when others had failed, and then return to St. Lazare to think and plan how he could provide more for the poor of the world. St. Vincent could reflect in his thought and action the Fatherhood of God in Whom is to be found no distinction between Jew and Greek, slave and free, male and female. I mention this facet of St. Vincent's spiritual portrait at a time when we could let ourselves be led, almost unconsciously, to identify ourselves with the poor only in order that we might despise the rich. Certainly your vocation is the poor, but let it be with the mind of Jesus Christ Who did not despise anyone, not even the Pharisees; let it be with the mind of St. Vincent who pitied and worked for the poor without dismissing and despising the rich and wealthy of this world.

I have almost come to an end without mentioning her whom the Church is honoring today, she who showed such cordial respect to her Son, even when she did not understand, she who in the chapel of this house showed such cordial respect to Catherine Labouré in entrusting her with a mission to the Church and to the world. I have come to an end, too, without allowing St. Vincent himself to speak to you. The conference which he gave on 1 January 1644 to the Sisters, taken down in writing by St. Louise herself, has a balance in it that is equalled only by the balance that is to be found in that Christmas prayer which I have quoted already. Let St. Vincent himself speak:

> *My daughters, you must know that one can show two sorts of respect to others. One is grave and serious, the other cordial and kind. Serious respect is often forced; it is the respect of inferiors to superiors; it is sometimes shown rather from fear than good-will, and hence is neither cordial nor genuine. My Daughters, the respect which you should show each other should always be accompanied by a sincere cordiality, that is to say, by a genuine sense of reverence . . . .But, my daughters, just as respect without cordiality would not be genuine respect, so cordiality without respect would not be strong and firm, but would occasionally give*

*rise to familiarities not in good taste, and would render such
cordiality valueless and liable to change. Now, this will
never happen if cordiality is combined with respect and
respect with cordiality. God, by His grace, has endowed
several of you with those two virtues which are the marks of
true Daughters of Charity, that is to say, Daughters of God.
I give thanks to Him for it.* " (Conf. Eng. ed., 1 Jan. 1644, p.
129).

My prayer for you on this New Year's Day is that you will show
cordial respect to one another; both words are important, as St. Vincent
reminds us; that you will first be a good reconciler within the Community. *"Blessed are the peacemakers."* (Mt 5:9). Be peacemakers, not
troublemakers, within the Community. Only then can you with security
go forth to be Good Samaritans to the poor, showing them cordial
respect, reconciling the rich with the poor and the poor with the rich,
until we all meet in the Kingdom of the God Who will be all in all. May
Mary, the Mother of us all, make us worthy of the promises of Christ
on this New Year's Day. May she show unto us the Blessed Fruit of her
womb, Jesus.

Accept People as They Are

3 March 1981   Rome, Italy

My dear Sisters,

The passage from the Gospel of St. Mark which we have just heard,
has not been chosen specially for this Mass which we are celebrating
on the first day of your Study Week. The passage is that which has been
assigned by the Church for the Tuesday of the eighth week of the year.
We have taken the passage as we have found it, what the Providence
of God provides for us today. From it I would like to draw the first
reflection for you, namely, the importance of accepting Sisters, other
people and things as we find them. It is what Jesus Christ did. He always
began to help people by first accepting them as they were. He took the
woman at the well as He found her, looking for water. He started to talk
to her about the water she had come to get. Only later did He speak to

her about her five husbands, expressing His conviction to her that she was not properly married.

For us who have been called in the Community to the service of authority, it is important that we first try to take people as we find them, before we try to help them grow in faith and hope and love, before we try to help them to give themselves more fully to God for the service of the poor.

To return to the passage of today's Gospel, Jesus touches on something that is fundamental to the consecrated life. He touches on what St. Vincent would call detachment. Peter began to say to Jesus: *"We have left everything and followed You."* (Mk 10:28). Then Jesus begins to talk of the vows of poverty and of celibacy. He speaks of the sacrifice involved in leaving family (consecrated chastity) and of leaving houses and lands (consecrated poverty). Speaking as I am to you who are Sister Servants here in Italy, I would like to offer you for reflection just one sentence from the Council document, *"Perfectae Caritatis."* You will find it in paragraph 12 of that document: *"Let all and especially Superiors, remember that chastity is preserved more securely when the members live a common life in true brotherly love."* The Church lays on us Superiors the responsibility of promoting charity within our Community as one of the principal safeguards of the consecrated chastity of each Sister.

All of you know, as Superiors, how difficult it can be to sustain the practice of charity within a community. I would like to encourage you today to promote and develop charity within the Community, not only because it is one of the two principal commandments, but because in doing so, you will be helping your Sisters to live their vow of consecrated chastity. Perhaps we do not sufficiently realize that if a person feels rejected in Community, or feels misunderstood, especially by us as Superiors, we could, without knowing it, make the living of the vow of chastity more difficult. As an animator of your local community, your first task is to animate the Sisters, not only with a love of God but of one another. How often in his conferences to the Daughters did St. Vincent stress the need for mutual charity within the Community. Before animating your community with a love for the poor, animate them with a love for one another. In doing so, you will be serving them and enabling them, without knowing it, to live more fully their vow of consecrated chastity.

While putting this reflection before you, I pray that you will not be discouraged, for I know how difficult at times it can be to help Sisters to love one another. May the grace of Our Lord Jesus Christ help you to keep alight at all times the flame of charity within the Community. I leave the last word to St. Vincent: *"The love of God is the summit; halfway down is the love of our neighbor and the poor; the foot is love of one another."* (Conf. Eng. ed., 4 Mar. 1658, p. 1046).

Easter Letter—Hope

19 March 1981   To Each Confrere

My dear Confrere,

May the grace of Our Lord Jesus Christ be with us forever!

I am writing this personal letter to you from our Mother House in Paris where I have been staying for the past three weeks. My room, as many of you know, is only a few paces away from the remains of the earthly body of St. Vincent. More than once during these weeks, while looking at the casket that contains St. Vincent's bones, I have reflected on God's question to Ezekiel: *"These bones, will they live?"* (Ez 37:3). For the Congregation of the Mission the answer to the question lies with us who are called to incarnate (the phrase is a daring one) the spirit of St. Vincent de Paul in the Church and the world.

First, let me wish you much joy this Easter. It so happens that the anniversary of St. Vincent's birthday falls this year in the octave of Easter. There could be much significance for us all in the fact that his birthday this year is associated with the Resurrection. The Resurrection is the feast of hope and in celebrating the birthday of St. Vincent within the octave of the feast of hope, all of us will be praying, not only with a sense of gratitude to God for what He has done for the world through Vincent de Paul, but also in and with the hope that He will continue to show mercy and kindness to mankind through the Communities which His servant Vincent has established.

In mentioning hope, I am reminded of the observation made about the Old Testament prophets. They have been described as men who had not optimism, but who had hope. The distinction is a valid one. Optimism is a human quality; hope is a spiritual one. A Christian may not always be optimistic about the world, but he need never be without hope, for Jesus Christ has risen and is with us. Perhaps at times you are not optimistic about the future of our community or your Province. At no time, however, should you be without hope for its future. It was one of St. Vincent's most profound convictions that the founding of the Congregation was entirely the work of God; that He had possessed it from the beginning; and still continued to do so. A diminishing number of vocations does not necessarily mean that the strength of God's hold on our Community has been weakened. We must resist the temptation, one to which David yielded, to measure our success before God by counting the number of our heads. More important is this: the hope which the Risen Christ has placed by His Spirit in our hearts should find expression in daily gestures of fidelity to what we once promised by vow to do for God in and through and with the Congregation of the Mission. *"My Confreres, let us ask of the Divine goodness that we may have a great confidence in the outcome of everything that concerns us. Provided only that we are faithful to Him, we will want for nothing. He Himself will live in us, and guide us, and defend us and love us."* (Coste XII, Fr. ed., pp. 141-42).

Pascal remarked that a stone cast into the sea heightens the surface of oceans everywhere. Do not stand on the shore, indulging a sense of pessimism or disillusionment with the Congregation, your Province, your particular community. Rather, humbly bend down and search for a stone which you can cast, not at the Congregation, but with the Congregation into the ocean of God's goodness, and you will be raising the level of the seas of His love which encompass the world. In the love of Our Lord, I remain, your devoted confrere.

Fragrance of Consecrated Lives

25 March 1981   Paris, France

My dear Sisters,

Two Sundays ago I spoke at Mass to you and to the Sisters from the Provinces of France, who had come here on pilgrimage to honor in a special way Our Lady and St. Louise. It so happened that the Gospel of that Sunday was an account of the Transfiguration of Our Lord. Since that time my mind has gone back to dwell on the experience of the three disciples on Tabor. This morning I am thinking of it again. Before the disciples had that marvelous vision of Jesus Christ on Tabor, they would have had a long laborious climb. Presumably, it was only when they had come to the top of the mountain that they had that vision of Christ, which so rejoiced their hearts and which made Peter eager to remain there always.

This morning all of us can look back on the long climb which the Community has had to reach the joy which we are celebrating here this evening. Some months ago each Sister after prayer and reflection presented to her Sister Servant her request to renew her Vows. The Sister Servant presented them to the Visitatrix, who presented them to Mother Rogé and her Council. Then on 2 February, Mother Rogé came to Rome and presented me with a book containing the requests and asked that the Sisters whose names were in it should be allowed to renew their vows today. Such has been the arrangement, which goes back to the time of St. Vincent and St. Louise and which has been continued unbrokenly since. Each year the Community, at the end of this long ascent of the mountain towards Renovation, receives from God a new vision of Christ and of His presence in the poor. So today the fragrance of so many lives ascends to God *"like incense in His sight."* (Ps 141:2). *"It is good for us to be here."* (Mt 17:4). *"This is the day which the Lord has made, let us rejoice and be glad."* (Ps 117:24).

I mentioned a few moments ago that your lives were like fragrant incense in the sight of God. This morning you will have noticed that we began Mass by incensing the altar, and later we incensed the offerings which you presented. The offerings at the Mass this morning had a special significance, because of the Renovation of your Vows which preceded the presentation of the gifts. Then the fragrance of incense filled the Chapel. And that too had much significance this morning. The fragrance that filled the Chapel was achieved by placing just a few hard grains of incense into a burning charcoal. When the hard grains of incense first contacted the fire, they resisted. Then they surrendered, and the result was the perfumed smoke that filled the entire Chapel. It is so with our lives. Our vows call for surrender to the fire of God's love. Our hard hearts protest at first, but when they have surrendered to the love of God, we become more closely united with Him, Who is Love. It is He Who sees to it that the fragrance of our consecrated lives fills not just a Chapel, but the Church which is the Body of Christ.A grain of incense is very tiny, but put it in contact with a little fire and see what is produced. So it is with you. The offering of yourselves to God for the service of the poor may seem a small thing to you, but God will see to it that what you have done this morning will bring fragrance to His Church and joy to His poor.

To come back to the mountain of the Transfiguration. St. Luke makes the point that it was while Jesus prayed there that the disciples had a new vision of Him. Your vocation is to bring spiritual and bodily necessities to the poor in whom you recognize a presence of Christ. It is from the experience of a vision of Christ that you go to the poor. For that reason we must always keep climbing the mountain of prayer.

Jesus Christ prayed at other times, as the Gospels tell us. The experience on the mountain of Tabor, as on another occasion on another mountain, emphasizes for us the depth and the prolonged nature of His prayer. Both St. Vincent and St. Louise have left us in no doubt about the importance of mental prayer or meditation. St. Vincent's phrase about leaving God for God to serve the poor is a celebrated one. With equal insistence, however, he emphasized the importance of daily meditation. In our own day, the present Pope has on more than one occasion told priests and religious that we can be so busy about the work of the Lord as to forget the Lord of the work.

All that you do for the poor must spring from your vision of Christ. In every gesture of love for the poor, you bring heaven down to earth, and you are preparing, getting things ready, so that Christ can come again, take possession of His kingdom and hand it over to His Father Who will be all in all.

On Tabor Jesus talked with the prophets Moses and Elias, and then Peter began to talk to Jesus about the possibility of remaining there always. Prayer is a loving conversation with God, we with Him and He with us. It is from the experience of talking with God that we talk to others. Since I came here to Paris, I have read the farewell address of Cardinal Marty, which he gave in Notre Dame. Speaking to the people of the city, he remarked on the loneliness which so many experience in a city such as this. *"Loneliness is our Parisian misery . . . .Deaf to the clamor of the city, but also the appeals of the neighbor. Break the silence. Look around you, listen and talk to one another."* It is not enough, however, just to talk to people to lighten their loneliness. We can only lighten their loneliness when we speak to them, not only with our lips but with our hearts. We can only speak to others with our hearts when we have spoken to God with our hearts in prayer. We can only listen to others when we have listened to God in the silence of prayer. It is St. Vincent who apropos of prayer reminds us: *"God is glorified as much by silence as by hymns which are sung in His honor."* (Coste XII, Fr. ed. p. 57).

There is a great need of silence in the lives of those who wish to bring joy and peace to others: *"O my Sisters,"* St. Vincent said, *"When we are silent, we can hear God speaking to our hearts."* (Conf. Eng. ed. 14 June 1643, p. 108).

As you go to the poor, think often of that pain of loneliness which so many experience in cities today. Indeed what the Cardinal said of Paris could sometimes be said of our communities. In some communities *"loneliness is our . . . misery."* Hence the importance of accepting the Cardinal's imperatives: *"Break the silence. Look around you, listen and talk to one another."*

Today we celebrate and honor Mary's unconditional surrender of herself to God. *"Most Holy Virgin,"* prayed St. Louise, *"you are our example in everything, but principally in what concerns our vows . . . make me honor you as my holy Mother and learn from you the fidelity which I owe to my God for the rest of my days."* (Sainte Louise de

Marillac, Fr. ed. 1961, pp 845-46). You know what a profound spiritual significance the feast of the Annunciation had for St. Louise. That is why we celebrate the fact that so many Daughters of Charity all over the world are trying, in the measure of their ability, to do the same today by renewing their vows.

Today you have come for the first time to give yourselves to the service of the poor. Today you can leave the failures of the past behind, as you start again to climb to God through His poor. Today you have promised to live according to the spirit of the Company. This is the spirit of the Company in St. Vincent's words: *"The spirit of the Company consists in giving itself to God to love Our Lord and serve Him corporally and spiritually in the person of the poor, in their own homes or elsewhere, to teach young girls and children and, in general, all those whom Divine Providence sends you."* (Conf. Eng. ed. 9 Feb. 1653, p. 525).

"You are the good fragrance of Christ" (2 Cor 2:15) to the Church, to one another, to the poor. May you be able to see today with fresh eyes the greatness of your vocation and, seeing it, may you rejoice and be glad. *"Lord it is good for us to be here."* (Mk 9:5). May Mary, the only Mother of the Company, win for us all this grace.

Our Heritage

15 April 1981   London, England

My dear Sisters,

Before all else, let me say how grateful I am to Sister Joan for her kind invitation to come here and speak to you. Let me say also how grateful I am to you all for the warm reception you have given me here this morning. I see all such expressions of welcome as expressions of faith in the office I hold. The devotion which you have, and I don't think the word *devotion* is too strong, to the office of Superior General is profoundly deep among you. I have more than once in the past few months wondered how it should be so. I think it is that, as you see it, the office of Superior General is the same as that which was held by St. Vincent himself. We know that St. Vincent was reluctant to assume this office and it was only after much prayer and quiet insistence on the part of St. Louise that he was prevailed on to accept it, and not only for himself, but for those who as Superiors General of the Congregation of the Mission would come after him as his successors. Recently talking to Mother Rogé, we both agreed that it was an enormous act of confidence in God and faith in His Providence that they should have agreed to this, for they had no idea what sort of men would be the successors of St. Vincent. More than once I have felt that your faith in the office of Superior General is not of the will of man but of God from Whom ultimately all good things come.

At another level, and a more human one, I am happy to be among you again. It is nice to speak publicly without being preoccupied with the proper pronunciation of open and closed vowels. It is nice to be speaking publicly again the Queen's English, even if with an Irish accent.

As far as I remember, I did not choose the title of this talk. I accepted the idea from Sister Joan that I would talk about St. Vincent, but the finalizing of the title was, if I am not mistaken, left to the organizing committee here in London. The title suggests two topics, our heritage and St. Vincent's devotion to and confidence in the Providence of God. The two topics are not unrelated because our heritage, which we enjoy today in the Community, would not be as rich as it is, had not St. Vincent been devoted to and confident in the Providence of God.

One of the most beautiful parables that fell from Our Lord's lips is concerned with heritage, or rather with the problems that heritage can bring. *"A certain man had two sons. The younger of them said to his father: 'Father give me the portion of substance that falleth to me.' And he divided unto them his substance."* (Lk 15:11-12). The remainder of that parable is a story of how a heritage may be received, destroyed and lost. However, that was not the main point of the parable. It is the warm, welcoming, accepting, forgiving attitude of the father towards the younger son that is the point of Our Lord's story. Such attitudes are spiritual values that money cannot buy. In his old age, I imagine the younger son thought more about the loving acceptance which he had experienced from his father than of the loss and squandering of the material part of his heritage.

These days in a number of provinces we see the closing of houses, the withdrawal of the Community from institutions where it has served for a hundred years and more. We must grow accustomed to considering well what is the principal heritage which we have received and enjoy. There is always the temptation to identify our heritage with material buildings or particular localities. Read the Conferences of St. Vincent and you will find that that is not what he wished to bequeath to the Daughters of Charity. Certainly he did not despise material buildings, nor did he minimize the importance of good administration of Community property. Needless to say, he would not endorse a policy of squandering money on purposeless projects. An independent observer, however, who could cast an eye down the list of topics of conferences which St. Vincent gave to the Sisters of his time, could only conclude that what this man, Vincent de Paul, was concerned about was the art of relating well to God, to Jesus Christ, to one another within the Community, and to the poor. I think that, important as the service of the poor was to St. Vincent and still must be to the Daughters of Charity, the richest part of our heritage lies in what St. Vincent has taught us of spiritual values, spiritual techniques, which will insure that we are abiding deeply in Christ without Whom we can do nothing.

It was only after he had lost all that the younger of the two sons of the parable came to know something of the depth of his father's love for him. I am not suggesting that the Community must recklessly divest itself of all its material assets, if it is to come to know how much it is cherished by God. What I am saying is that the painful experience of being parted from what we regarded as portions of our inheritance, may serve to purify the eyes of our minds so that we can see more clearly, collectively and individually, what lies at the heart of all service of the poor, and which must always remain the principal portion of the inheritance we have received from the Spirit of God through St. Vincent.

At the heart of the heritage which St. Vincent has left us is his devotion to the Providence of God. With all the limitations which any generalization has, it could be said that until the fourth decade of his life, St. Vincent liked to gallop ahead of Divine Providence, but that thereafter he became fearful that he might cut God's heel by walking too close behind Him. Francis Thompson's poem, *"The Hound of Heaven,"* has immortalized an experience which so many can share: how God pursued the poet down the nights, down the days until he is overtaken by God, the hound of heaven, and surrenders to Him.

> *Still with unhurrying chase,*
> *And unperturbed pace,*
> *Deliberate speed, majestic instancy,*
> *Came on the following Feet,*
> *And a Voice above their beat*
> *"Naught shelters thee, who wilt not shelter Me."*

The poem, as so many of you know, ends after the surrender with the loving invitation: *"Arise, clasp My hand and come."*

The same loving God caught up to Vincent, galloping ahead in search, now of a good parish, now of a debtor, and now of some indeterminate ecclesiastical honor. When Vincent had been overtaken by the Hound of Heaven and when he had begun to shelter Christ in the person of the poor, he seems to have decided only to venture forth when he was sure that he was being led through the thicket by the Hound of Heaven. How he came to be so deeply devoted to the Providence of God, we do not know. Which of his spiritual mentors was it who taught him to follow, rather than anticipate, God's Providence? Certain it is that the lesson was learned well. In his conferences to the Daughters, the Providence of God is mentioned no less than seventy times, while in his correspondence with his priests, it is a theme which is treated with many variations.

Thank God, St. Vincent had in his Congregation some men who were in a great hurry to get things done. It was these who called forth from St. Vincent his deepest convictions on devotion to the Providence of God. One such was Father Codoing whom St. Vincent sent to Rome to act as his agent to the Holy See. Father Codoing was a rather colorful character. When asked by St. Vincent to go to Rome, he was rather sluggish about taking up the appointment, and there is a letter extant in which St. Vincent reminds him that it was time he was thinking of moving from Annecy and doing God's will in Rome. Once Father Codoing arrived in Rome, he seems to have decided that, while Rome might be eternal, time was short and so all negotiations should be dispatched with a minimum of delay and all officials of the Roman Curia spurred into immediate action. This manner of procedure displeased St. Vincent, but happily for us elicited some magnificent gems on the place of the Providence of God in the conduct of affairs.

To Father Codoing on the 16 March 1644, he wrote: *"Grace has its moments. Let us abandon ourselves to the Providence of God and be on our guard against anticipating it. If Our Lord is pleased to give me any consolation in our vocation, it is this: I think it seems to me that we have tried to follow Divine Providence in all things and to put our feet only in the place It has marked out for us. "* (Coste II, Eng. ed. no. 704, p. 499).

And a month later to Father Codoing: *". . . by the grace of God, we have always tried to follow and not to anticipate Providence which knows how to conduct all things so wisely to the end Our Lord destines for them. "* (Coste II, Eng. ed. no. 707, p. 502).

And yet again to Father Codoing, this time in July of the same year: *". . . nor should you move so fast! The works of God do not proceed in that way; they come about of themselves, and those He does not create soon perish. "* (Coste II, Eng. ed. no. 715, p. 514).

In August St. Vincent wrote again to him: *"I have told you on previous occasions, Monsieur, that the things of God come about by themselves, and that wisdom consists in following Providence step by step. And you can be sure of a maxim which seems paradoxical, namely, that he who is hasty falls back in the interests of God. "* (Coste II, Eng. ed. no. 720, p. 521).

Six years later in 1650 the Confrere who was to be St. Vincent's first successor was Superior in Rome. St. Vincent wrote to him: *"I have been told that the Archbishop of Toulouse has been waiting for a long time for me to give him some indication that I would like the Company to work in his diocese, so he could establish us there and put us in charge of his seminary, but I have been careful not to give him the slightest sign of this. His brother was here a few days ago; he skirted the issue with me for a long time, but I deliberately refrained from discussing it. Providence must call us and we must follow it, if we are to go forward confidently. "* (Coste III, Eng. ed. no. 1178, p. 538).

This last quotation gives us an indication of the sensitivity of St.

Vincent to Divine Providence. It was not sufficient for him that by hearsay the Archbishop had expressed his desire that the Community come to his diocese. Even when the Archbishop's brother was trying to force St. Vincent to show his hand, so to speak, it was only the direct invitation of the Archbishop himself, seemingly, which would satisfy St. Vincent that the work would be of God.

St. Vincent's first biographer, Bishop Abelly, singles out his devotion to the Providence of God and imitation of Jesus Christ as the principal features of the Saint's spirituality. St. Vincent's devotion to the Providence of God could possibly be explained in terms of devotion to the Will of God. For him, the teaching of the Church was a clear manifestation of God's Will. When, in either of his Communities, Superiors expressed themselves in accordance with the Rules or Constitutions of the Company, then that, too, was a clear manifestation of God's Will for the individual. So much for the guidance we need for the present. God's Will, however, for the future, the immediate future, expresses itself slowly, unfolds itself like the dawn of day. One cannot hasten the dawn. One must wait for the dawn. *"My soul is waiting on the Lord. I count on His Word. My soul is longing for the Lord, more than watchman for daybreak."* (Ps. 129:5-6).

It was, I think, St. Vincent's profound respect for the Will of God that made him slow to presume that the decision to be made, the house to be established, the course of action to be adopted, was in fact in accordance with that Will which alone mattered. *"We see now in a dark manner"* (1 Cor 13:12) and one can advance only slowly in the dark if one is not to lose one's way totally.

Speaking to you as Daughters of Charity, I must refer you to the conference which St. Vincent gave your predecessors on the 9 June, 1658. Let me offer you an aperitif, drawn from what is vintage Vincentian teaching.

> *There are some who think their peace of mind depends on being with a certain Sister or not being with another, who is of such or such a disposition, or being in one place rather than another, and they place their confidence in that. Mark you, a Sister who has placed her confidence in God does not consider whom she is with. When you find it less easy to live*

with one Sister rather than another, you should get rid of that feeling for it is a temptation and will give rise to divisions amongst you, if it is not remedied in time. And, therefore, Sisters, a Daughter of Charity who trusts in Providence never asks: 'Who are you sending with me?' It is enough for her to know that it is God Who inspires Superiors to send her to that place. And so she goes, hoping that He will never abandon her. (Conf. Eng. ed. 9 June 1658, pp. 1080-81).

In the index to the volume of Conferences to the Daughters you will find a reference to Providence on page sixty-seven and on that page you will read two short paragraphs which are as realistic today as when they were first spoken by St. Vincent:

Do you know how to practice obedience to the most Divine Providence of God? When an occasion arises for you to go from one house to another, then, O my Sisters, be most exact in obeying its decrees, reflecting that Providence has so ordained it, and never say: 'It is such and such a Sister, such and such an event that has been the cause of my leaving here.' On the contrary, believe that Divine Providence is taking care of you . . . .O my daughters, you should have such great devotion to and such great confidence in and love for Divine Providence, that if Providence itself had not given you the beautiful name of Daughters of Charity, you should bear that of Daughters of Providence, for it was Providence that brought you into being. (Conf. Eng. ed. June 1642, p. 67).

I have suggested that St. Vincent's devotion to the Providence of God was rooted and founded in his devotion to the Will of God. His confidence in the Providence of God must have been strengthened by his reflection and meditation on that classic expression of the lovingness of God's Providence which we find in the Sermon on the Mount: *"The birds of the air neither sow nor reap nor gather into barns, yet your heavenly Father feeds them . . . Behold the lilies of the field . . . "* (Mt 6:26,28). His faith, however, must have been tried, as ours is, by the large number of people who seem to be outside that loving

Providence, the poor. When he said that your title could be Daughters of Divine Providence, could he have been thinking that your vocation was to be a sacrament of God's loving Providence to the poor and to those who are on the margin, or seem to be beyond the margin, of God's caring love? The sight of so many such people in a world of rapidly increasing population perplexes us and tries our faith and confidence in the Fatherhood of God which is the central message of the New Testament. I have not had the time to go more deeply into this question. Let me only say this, that it is paradoxical that, as St. Vincent became more acquainted with the vast needs of the poor of his day, his confidence in the loving Providence of God seems to have taken deeper and firmer root. That conviction is expressed, not in any hastily written letter, but in a carefully chiseled out paragraph of the Rule which he had printed two years before his death for the Priests and Brothers of the Congregation of the Mission. He wrote:

> *Christ said: 'Seek first the Kingdom of God and His justice; and all these things (which you need) will be given to you as well.' That is the basis for each of us having the following set of priorities: matters involving our relationship with God are more important than temporal affairs; spiritual health is more important than physical; God's glory is more important than human approval. Each one should, moreover, be determined to prefer, like St. Paul, to do without necessities, to be slandered or tortured, or even killed, rather than lose Christ's love. In practice, then, we should not worry too much about temporal affairs. We ought to have confidence in God that he will look after us since we know for certain that as long as we are grounded in that sort of love and trust we will be always under the protection of God in heaven, we will remain unaffected by evil and never lack what we need even when everything we possess seems headed for disaster.*
> (CR II, §2).

Perhaps that paragraph is for me the finest expression of St. Vincent's devotion to and confidence in the Providence of God. With Lacordaire, St. Vincent could say: *"All I know of tomorrow is that Providence will rise before the sun."*

The final word must, however, be left with St. Vincent himself, as he closed the conference on Divine Providence which he gave on the 9 June 1658: *"I implore God once more not to allow any one of you to leave here without making a firm resolution to abandon herself to the Providence of God. This is the prayer I offer up to Our Lord: 'Saviour of my soul, grant our Sisters this grace in virtue of Thy own submission to the orders of Thy Father and by the submission Thou hast bestowed on our Sisters; grant it by the Blessed Virgin's love of obedience; grant us the grace of not cleaving to anything by the conformity which Thou always hadst to the Will of God Thy Father.'"* (Conf. Eng. ed. 9 June 1658, p. 1088).

Thanksgiving

22 April 1981 Berceau, France

My dear Confreres,

I once heard of a man who made a voyage around the world in order to experience the joy of discovering his own home. This morning after a cycle of four hundred years, a small group of us are experiencing the joy of discovering, not only the home of Vincent de Paul, but in a sense the home of all who consider themselves to be members of the great Vincentian family.

In a real sense, this place is the home of that family. In our Community parlance, we call it *"The Berceau."* More often than not we do not qualify that phrase. It is our *berceau* (cradle). Grace builds on nature, and it was here that Vincent de Paul received his nature. It was here that he first learned to be aware of others and their needs. It was here that he first heard of and experienced the reality that the world was unequally divided: that there were rich and poor. It was here that, like the first stirrings of Spring in the soil, his heart would have begun to feel compassion for those who were less fortunate than he. Let us never forget that whatever conversion he would later experience, the nature of Vincent de Paul must have been a tender, compassionate one, and it was in this place that his nature was first formed. Let us give thanks this morning for the great things God has done for St. Vincent de Paul, for his nature as well as for the grace which built upon that nature, received here in the *pays des Landes.*

The Gospel passage to which we have just listened has been described as the best short story ever written. It commences with the sad disillusionment of the two disciples: *"We had hoped . . . ."* (Lk 24:21). Then they are joined by the unrecognized Risen Christ Who, through allowing them to talk, drains them of despair and disillusionment and sows in their hearts faith and hope. *"Ought not Christ to have suffered?"* (Ibid. v. 27). The story ends in the charity of the Eucharist: *"They recognized Him in the breaking of the bread."* (Ibid. v. 35). The Eucharist is carried forward into mission . . . *"The disciples returned to Jerusalem . . . and they told their story of what had happened on the road, and how they recognized Him in the breaking of bread."* (Ibid. vv. 33,35).

For all of us here this morning, I ask God to grant us three graces: 1. That our hearts be emptied of all discouragement about the Congregation of the Mission, so that the Risen Christ may fill them with faith and hope. 2. That all of us may be able to see more clearly Jesus Christ in the Scriptures, in the Eucharist and in the poor. 3. That in our recognizing Jesus Christ, we may all find again the sense of mission and a renewed zeal, so that we conceive the desire to start from here to announce the good news of the Gospel, above all to the poor, as the two disciples of Emmaus and as St. Vincent de Paul. *"Were not our hearts burning . . . .?"* (Ibid. v. 32).

> *"Let us love God, my brothers, let us love God, but let it be with the strength of our arms and with the sweat of our brows."* (Coste XI, Fr. ed., p. 40).

This is the day that the Lord has made; let us be glad and rejoice!

Jesus Christ in the Modern World

14 May 1981   Jamaica, New York

I am quite certain that if there is one human agent who has brought us all here this evening, it is St. Vincent de Paul who celebrated his four hundredth birthday three weeks ago.

First, there is His Eminence, Cardinal Oddi, who has received his priestly formation in one of St. Vincent's seminaries. That is a source of pride for us, Vincentians, and from what we hear, a source of joy to His Eminence. I hope St. Vincent will not mind my saying that his Congregation has had more success in the formation of future Cardinals than he had himself when he was on earth. One of the two young men he educated in the De Gondi household subsequently became a Cardinal and it suffices to say here that he must have been at times an embarrassment to St. Vincent in later life. Your Eminence, far from being an embarrassment to St. Vincent's Congregation, you can be considered a joy and a crown of it, so distinguished have been the services which your Eminence has given to the Church and to the world of our time. In the citation which was presented to us this evening by Father Newman, we have been given some insight into the qualities of your dedicated life. In the final months of his life, St. Vincent wrote a letter to his one-time pupil, Cardinal de Retz:

My Lord, I have reason to think that this is the last time I will have the honor of writing to Your Eminence because of my age and an infirmity which has come on me and which, perhaps, will bring me to the judgment seat of God. In this situation, I very humbly ask Your Eminence to pardon me if I have displeased you in anything. I am so spiritually weak that I can do so without willing it, but I have never done so on purpose. I am bold enough also to recommend to Your Eminence this little Company of the Mission which you have founded, maintained and favored and which, being the work of your hands, is also subject and grateful to you as to its Father and its Prelate. (Coste VII, Fr. ed. p. 436).

In the light and tenor of that letter, I feel that the only fault St. Vincent would find with Father Newman this evening is that he spent too much time talking about St. Vincent's successor, time which he could have devoted to telling us more about the Cardinal to whom the Church is so indebted today.

When I studied Canon Law in the Seminary, I recall our professor explaining at length the meaning of the term, "communication of privileges." It was a recognized legal way by which certain spiritual privileges which the Pope granted to one religious body could be communicated to another. When Father Cahill wrote to me and invited me to accept this honorary degree in the company of Cardinal Oddi, I came to the conclusion that the Law School here in St. John's had discovered some hitherto unknown legal principle which allows a simple priest to share, on occasion, the honors and privileges which a University accords to a Cardinal in recognition of his distinguished life. So, let me say at once how grateful I am to St. John's, not only for the degree they have given to me, but for this communication of privileges and, to use the parlance of the Royal Court in Britain, for making me a "Companion of Honor" with the Cardinal from Rome.

On one occasion I recall seeing a large poster with the image of St. Vincent on it. Underneath his picture was printed in capital letters, *"This man has a lot to answer for."* Beneath that sentence one could read in smaller print some details of the Saint's life, his achievements and the apostolates of his present-day Communities. It was an eye-catching poster for vocations. Certainly St. Vincent lived out his life in the conviction that he had a lot to answer for. His frequent references to his own personal unworthiness and sinfulness can be baffling to us. However, we read the poster slogan, not as St. Vincent would read it, but as the Church has read it, and has responded with a *thanks be to God* and then declared him a saint. What St. Vincent has to answer for are the multiplicity of apostolates we see clustering around his name today. It was Daniel Rops who remarked that St. Vincent's works surround him like a forest and that his humility envelops him like a fog. In that forest of works I have no doubt that he sees this University as a strong and sturdy oak tree. St. John's has remained unbowed by wind and storm and, what would please St. Vincent enormously, has remained firm in the ground of that truth which the Catholic Church possesses and offers to all mankind.

While the works of St. Vincent surround him like a forest, he himself was fond of saying, *"The works of God do themselves."* They do, when the grace of Our Lord Jesus Christ finds a partner in the heart and will of man. The grace of Our Lord Jesus Christ was everything to St. Vincent de Paul. Perhaps I should preface that remark by saying that Jesus Christ was everything to St. Vincent de Paul. *"Remember, Monsieur,"* he wrote, *"we live in Jesus Christ through the death of*

Jesus Christ, and we must die in Jesus Christ through the life of Jesus Christ, and our life must be hidden in Jesus Christ and filled with Jesus Christ, and in order to die as Jesus Christ, we must live as Jesus Christ." (Coste I, Eng. ed. no. 197, p. 276). Most of St. Vincent's letters, and he wrote some thirty thousand of them, began with the same greeting which in one of its forms opens our Masses today: *"May the grace of Our Lord Jesus Christ be with us forever!"* His letters treat of spirituality, finance, the poor, administration, the sick, the ransoming of hostages in Algeria, the religious and political condition of the Church in Scotland and Ireland and a host of other topics, but all these subjects are put under the grace of Our Lord Jesus Christ. I mention this facet of his spiritual outlook because ours is an anxious and a fretful generation, and perhaps we are anxious and fretful because we have come to rely too much on ourselves and have become forgetful of that which is the coefficient of all Christian action, the grace of Our Lord Jesus Christ. I knew a Seminary professor who, in the 1970s, was fond of reminding his students that the most insidious heresy attacking the Church today was Pelagianism. The vast forest of works which surround the name of Vincent de Paul today would not have been planted by human effort alone. More than anything else, I feel Vincent de Paul would point us today to the centrality, relevance and need of the grace of Our Lord Jesus Christ for all mankind and every human undertaking. For St. Vincent de Paul, each man was included in the Mystery of the Redemption. He saw Jesus Christ as uniting Himself to each one through this Mystery, a theme that has been so magnificently developed by Pope John Paul II in his first Encyclical, *"Redemptor Hominis."* In thus associating the vision of St. Vincent de Paul with the teaching of Pope John Paul II, I am suggesting that St. Vincent is a modern saint who speaks to the mind and to the heart of the Christian today. In a word, St. Vincent de Paul is four hundred years young. I like to think that he is happy to answer to God for everyone here tonight, even if in the Court of Heaven he is embarrassed, not by any Cardinal on earth, but by his present-day successor.

Christian Joy

15 August 1981   Paris, France

My dear Sisters,

Let me begin by saying what all of you would like me to say in your name and in the name of all our Sisters throughout the world: Mother Rogé, a very happy feast day!

A few months ago when I was planning a visit to Australia, I told the Confreres and Sisters there that I wished to be back here in Paris for the feast day of Mother Rogé on the 15 August. I thought it important that I should be here today for two reasons: first, because of my esteem for her person and for what she does for the Company and, second, because of my respect for the office she holds. To echo a phrase of St. Vincent : *"It is by Divine Providence that your souls are placed in her hands,"* and through celebrating the feast day of the Mother General we are acknowledging that fact and are rejoicing in it.

Feast days are given us by God so that we may come to experience more fully what He wishes us to have even in this life, Christian joy. It was Pope Paul VI in an exhortation on Christian joy who focused attention on how much Jesus Christ knew and appreciated and celebrated a whole range of human joys which are within the reach of everyone. Jesus admired the birds of the heaven, the lilies of the field. He drew our attention to the joy of the sower and the harvester, the joy of the man who finds a hidden treasure, the joy of the shepherd who recovers his sheep, the joy of the woman who finds her lost coin, the joy of a marriage celebration, the joy of a father who embraces his lost son, the joy of a woman who has brought a child into the world. *"For the Christian as for Jesus,"* wrote Paul VI, *"it is a question of living in thanksgiving to the Father, the human joys that the Creator gives him."*

The celebration of a superior's feast day is given us by God so that we may have an increase of joy. When a Community enters fully into the spirit of one of its feast days, tensions are relaxed, charity grows and, from charity lived, are born joy and peace. It is St. Thomas Aquinas who remarked that joy and peace are daughters of charity.

Through celebrating the feast days of our superiors in a simple, loving and humble way, we will not only be given a new experience of Christian joy, but also we will be doing something for our superiors which we often overlook. Much time, thought, prayer and consultation goes into the appointment of superiors at different levels in the Company. But we could almost say that it is one thing to appoint a Visitatrix or Sister Servant, it is another thing to make a Visitatrix or a Sister Servant. All of us may not have the responsibility of appointing Superiors, but all of us have a responsibility for making our superiors. What I mean is this: our attitudes towards our superiors can help or hinder them in their growth as superiors. It is a helpful exercise for us all when we find ourselves complaining that our superiors are lacking in sensitivity, in warmth, in consideration, to ask ourselves how much sensitivity, warmth and consideration we are offering to our superiors. It is sensitivity, warmth and consideration shown by us to our superiors which enable them to grow as persons in their office. Jesus Christ has said, *"As you wish that men would do to you, do you also to them in like manner."* (Lk 6:31). That rule guides you in your service of the poor. May it also guide you in the service that God asks you to do for your superiors, as you live out your vow of obedience in our Community.

A few days ago I returned from Australia where I visited our communities of Confreres and Sisters. I saw most of the works which our Sisters are doing for the poor and deprived people, who are to be found on that continent, as they are in the other four continents of the world. One community of our Sisters is working with the Aborigines, and I visited one of the settlements of these people. The Sisters explained to me that these Aborigines feel lost, dispossessed, and are unable to cope with life and especially with the products of a modern, western civilization that has flooded their lives. More seriously, they have little or no confidence in themselves or in the white man.

As I listened to the Sisters speaking of the slow patient work of building up bonds of trust and confidence between themselves and these confused and lost Aborigines, I thought of how the human race must have seemed to God when through original sin it lost Paradise and was forced to wander over the world, unable to cope with the products of creation. When I saw the patient sensitivity of the Sisters to these poor people, I thought of the Son of God Who emptied Himself and took the form of a servant in order to establish bonds of trust and confidence between poor, lost humanity and the loving goodness of God. The Sisters told me that results of their work among the Aborigines do not appear and sometimes end in apparent failure. I thought of Jesus Christ and His patience and unwillingness to break the bruised reed. I thought, too, of St. Vincent's instructions to the first Sisters and of his conviction that Christian service of the poor can only come from a loving, simple, humble heart which is closely united to Jesus Christ Who came that all might have life and have it more abundantly.

What I saw of the work of the Sisters with the Aborigines in Australia is only a tiny segment of work that is being done for the poor by the Company all over the world. I was going to say that faces of the poor differ from country to country, from province to province, but that is not fully true. The poor have only one face, that of Jesus Christ, and whether it be here in Paris or anywhere else in the world, what matters is that your service of them should not be done from a sense of condescension, but should flow from your heart, which has learned the melody of that hymn in the second chapter of St. Paul's letter to the Philippians: *"Let this mind be in you which was in Christ Jesus . . . .He humbled Himself . . . taking the form of a servant."* (Phil 2:5-7). I would venture to say that it was St. Vincent's favorite hymn.

What I have been saying to you this morning can be epitomized in the person of Our Lady, joy. She breathes and speaks of it in her Magnificat. Making Superiors: she it was who in a very real way made Jesus Christ, for she gave of herself totally to God and the working of His Holy Spirit. Service of fallen people: of all creatures she has been and still is most closely associated with God in lifting up poor fallen humanity.

May you feel her presence close to you today, Mother Rogé, and may the thought of her presence, body and soul in heaven, lift up our hearts in hope that the best for all of us is yet to come.

Advent Letter—Incarnation

15 October 1981   To Each Confrere

My dear Confrere,

May the grace of Our Lord Jesus Christ be with us forever!

From my room here in Rome, I can just see in the distant horizon the cupola of the dome of St. Peter's through the branches of some Roman pines. When my eye catches sight of it, I invariably think of the wealth of history that lies beneath that cupola and of the bones of Peter which shelter under it. Then my mind travels to the Lake of Galilee and across the hill country of Judea to Bethlehem, where Jesus Christ was born of the Virgin Mary. At times I find myself reflecting on the contrast between the massive magnificence of St. Peter's and the simplicity of life beside the Lake of Galilee and of the still starker simplicity that surrounded the birth of Jesus in a cave at Bethlehem.

Yet that contrast is pale in comparison with the contrast that is to be found within the Incarnation itself. In human experience there is no greater contrast than that there should be found within the dimensions of one frail human body *"the fullness of Him Who fills the whole creation."* (Eph 1:23).

St. Vincent in his day saw contrast between the rich and the poor, and what he brought to both was the fruit of his reflection on the mystery of the Incarnation. He had reflected on the fact that *"Jesus Christ, being rich, became poor for our sake."* (2 Cor 8:9). Then he decided to go and do likewise himself. The mystery of the Incarnation was the permanent inspiration of St. Vincent's life. It must be ours, too. We shall only fully see Christ in the poor when we have fully seen God in Christ. That is why all that we do and say will have meaning only if it is born of our relationship with Jesus Christ, truly God and truly man. What we bring to the poor must be more than a program for the betterment of their material and economic condition. We must bring something of the peace, the joy and the spiritual freedom which we ourselves have experienced from being present to Jesus Christ through prayer and the sacraments of the Eucharist and Penance.

I do hope that you will have a happy Christmas. The poor are never closer to the Christian than at Christmas time. I hope that through giving some time this Christmas to the poor and lonely—often a listening heart is of more value than money—you will have enriched the lives of some of those millions of people who have so much less to eat than we have, and so much less to live for.

I shall write again to you at the end of January. Meantime I commend the Little Company and myself to your prayers. In the love of Our Lord I remain, your devoted confrere.

Christian Family in the Modern World

27 December 1981   Naples, Italy

My dear Sisters and Confreres,

A little over two weeks ago the Pope published a rich pastoral exhortation on the role of the Christian family in the modern world. The exhortation is the fruit, not only of the Pope's own reflection on the Christian family, but also, as he reminds us, of the deliberations and discussions which the Synod of Bishops held on the topic for a month in Rome during October of last year.

Today we are reflecting on the Holy Family of Nazareth, which was an altogether unique family. Mary and Joseph were truly married, but their child, Jesus, as our faith teaches us, was conceived by the Spirit of God. Their life as a family together must also have been unique because Jesus and Mary were sinless. That, too, is a defined fact of our faith, and we cannot imagine that God would have entrusted the care of both Jesus and Mary to St. Joseph if he were not a man who would respect to the highest degree the sanctity of the persons for whom he was to provide, in St. Vincent's phrase, *". . . with the strength of his arm and the sweat of his brow"* for a span of years that the Gospels do not reveal to us.

The family of Nazareth was a family altogether different from other human families, from the family into which we ourselves were born. There came a point in our own lives when we left our human families and joined what we called the Vincentian family, one of the two Communities founded by St. Vincent de Paul. Later still, through our Vows of consecrated celibacy or virginity, we decided to forego being direct constructors of human families, but undertook instead to be indirect builders of Christian families through the intensity of the dedication of ourselves to the Person of Jesus Christ and to His interests through our Vows of Poverty, Chastity and Obedience in the Community.

I said that we are indirect builders of the Christian family in the world. It is important for us to reflect from time to time on the fact that the value of our consecration and its usefulness to the Christian family comes from Jesus Christ Himself. It is He Who uses us to strengthen Christian families in the world. For that reason, we should have confidence in the goodness of our own lives. What I mean is this: all of us have met married couples whose fidelity to each other or to their marriage promises has been a source of strength to us in the living of our own lives. Perhaps we do not realize it sufficiently enough—that married couples in their turn are strengthened in their fidelity by the witness of our consecrated lives. In the words of the Pope's recent exhortation: *"Virginity or celibacy keeps alive in the Church a consciousness of the mystery of marriage and defends it from any reduction and impoverishment."* (*Familiaris Consortio,* §16).

On this Feast of the Holy Family there is something else I would like to share with you. We speak of our Community in a broad sense as being a family. To our parents we owe an enormous debt of gratitude, as we do also to the other members of our family with whom we were brought up. So many of the good qualities we have, and let us not with false humility deny them, have come to us from God through the home into which we were born. But after our natural family, I feel it is our Community that has given us much more than anybody else in this world. It is the Community that has given us the spirit of St. Vincent and St. Louise. It is the Community that has helped us to form our spirituality. It is the Community that offers us an opportunity of working for the poor. It is the Community that has supported us in that work. It is the Community which in the end will support us in our old age, if we live that long. It is the Community which after our deaths will go on pleading to God for His mercy for us. Cultivate, my dear Sisters and Confreres, a sense of gratitude to our Community, whatever its failings may be, because all of us have received much from it and will continue to receive much from this family of St. Vincent into which, by God's Providence, we have been led. On occasions in our lives we may feel resentful, angry and impatient with authorities in the Community. My prayer for us is that such moods may not blind us permanently to the goodness and kindness of God which He is showing us daily through the family of St. Vincent.

What I have been trying to say has been expressed marvelously by St. Vincent himself in a paragraph which he wrote in the Rules for the Missionaries just two years before his death: *". . . we should think of other Congregations as being far worthier than our own, though we should have greater affection for ours, just as a well brought up child will have far greater love for his own mother, poor and unattractive as she may be, than for any others, even if they are outstanding for wealth and beauty."* (CR XII,10).

May that love, of which St. Vincent writes, be given to us all on this Feast of the Holy Family of Nazareth.

Divine Secrets

28 December 1981   Naples, Italy

My dear People,

First, I would like to express my thanks to all who have arranged this Mass here in Sant'Angelo this morning. I count it as a privilege to be with you on the Feast of the Holy Innocents. It is a privilege for me to be thinking of the innocent children who died at the time of the birth of Christ, and at the same time to be thinking of the innocent children and adults who died here on the 23 November 1980. The death of so many innocent children and adults here last year is, in a sense, a greater mystery than the death of the Holy Innocents at Bethlehem. It was the jealousy, the greed, the evil in the character of Herod that caused the death of the Holy Innocents at Bethlehem at the time of the birth of Our Lord. But to whom can we attribute the earthquake here in November 1980? More than the death of the Holy Innocents at Bethlehem, we could say that the death of so many innocent people here last year remains an even greater mystery of God.

In the country from which I come, and in the language of my country, the Gaelic language, the expression for Divine Mystery is always translated by the words, *"Divine Secret."* Mysteries of God are always thought of as so many secrets of God. Each of us has our secrets which for good reasons we do not tell to others. So, too, with God; He has His secrets which for good reasons He does not reveal to us now. He will tell us all His secrets later, and when He does, we will see that all His secrets were good ones and, furthermore, that He had good reasons for not revealing them to us during our lives. Some of His secrets are joyful, some are sorrowful, some are glorious, just as there were, in the lives of Jesus and of Mary, joyful, sorrowful and glorious mysteries, which we recall every time we pray the Rosary.

Here in Sant'Angelo you have lived through a time of great sorrow, suffering and pain. It has been a time of great mystery and the mystery has been a sorrowful one for you. God continues to keep His secret. He does not give us the reason why the earthquake happened, but He keeps His secret, for did He not say: *"You have sorrow now, but I will see you again and your hearts will rejoice, and no one will take your joy from you."* (Jn 16:22).

My prayer for you who live here in Sant'Angelo and in this region of suffering is that God will share all His secrets with those who died in the earthquake of last year. I pray, too, that you who still suffer the pain of the loss of your loved ones and the loss of your possessions, may be comforted by the thought that, while God does not reveal to us for the present all His secrets, Jesus Christ did say: *"Not a sparrow will fall to the ground without your Father's Will."* (Mt 10:29). Not only does God know that sparrows fall to the ground, but He has a reason for allowing them to do so. *"Fear not, therefore, you are of more value than many sparrows."* (Ibid., v. 31).

Every time we celebrate Mass we remind ourselves that we are waiting *"in joyful hope for the coming of Our Savior, Jesus Christ."* May God in His goodness give us the patience to wait with hope in our hearts until all His secrets will be revealed.

1982

Wonder in our Lives

1 January 1982   Paris, France

My dear Mother Rogé, my dear Sisters, and Father Lloret,

Let me begin by expressing a prayer that this New Year, which is but a few hours old, will be for all of us a year of grace. There was a time in past centuries when people qualified every year in the calendar with that little phrase, *"the year of grace."* Although we do not use that phrase so frequently now, it is true, nonetheless, that for us Christians the year that has just begun is *"the year of grace, 1982."* All our years are years of grace because the mercy of God endures forever. But just as each year has its seasons with their own particular beauty, so there are seasons of God's grace, each with its own particular beauty. For people living in some parts of the world, there are just two seasons, the rainy season and the dry season. For us here in Europe, there are four seasons. Each season, however, has its own particular beauty, just as each season or epoch in our lives has its own particular beauty. As a new year opens, each of us wonders if perhaps it might be the last one which God is giving us on this earth. The elderly amongst us are particularly preoccupied with this thought. Allow me just to say this to the elderly and infirm, that just as there is a peculiar quality of beauty about the dawn, and a magnificent clarity in the noon-day light, so too is there a particular beauty about the sunset. I hope that our elderly and infirm Sisters will receive the grace of being able to see that peculiar beauty which, however difficult it may be for us to see, God gives to the sunset of a long life dedicated to Him in the service of the poor.

This year of grace, 1982, will have its own special quality of beauty as God's grace reveals itself to the Church, to the Community and to ourselves as individuals. At the Community level we know there will be a special quality about the grace which God will offer us, because for a few months yet we will continue to celebrate the fourth centenary year of St. Vincent's birthday. Birthday celebrations are always a time of special grace, a time of special rejoicing. Birthday celebrations are occasions for the giving of gifts. I am certain that God is offering our own Communities some special gifts with which to celebrate the four hundredth anniversary of the birthday of his servant, Vincent de Paul. Of that there is no doubt, for we have had many proofs from the accounts we have received from the different provinces of the world. All of us are guests at this birthday celebration and one does not come to a birthday celebration empty-handed. So a good question for all of us who are celebrating St. Vincent's four hundredth birthday is this: What particular gift have I offered to his Community during this year of celebration? I do not mean gifts wrapped in fancy paper. The sort of gift I have in mind is the quality of my charity within the Community, the effort I have made to understand better those with whom I live, my spiritual contribution to the local community. In a word, can I truthfully say that I have brought such a gift to my Community, that I have enriched it and in that way have made it more easy for my Community to serve the poor?

It is the year of grace, 1982. The grace of God is a mystery. St. Thérèse of Lisieux used to say, *"tout est grace."* Everything is grace. Perhaps because everything is grace, it is all the more mysterious to us. Events in our lives, appointments that we received in the past, the composition of our communities that we are asked to accept, may strain our faith to see how these events, these people, are graces to us. But the perspective of the years very often does enable us, especially if we are sufficiently humble and pure of heart, to see that these events, these people, these Sisters, were, in fact, real graces to us and that everything, sin excepted, is grace. Even our sins, which we find difficult at times to admit and accept, can be transformed into occasions of grace. For has not God in His goodness provided us with a Sacrament to enable us to repent and to be reconciled with Him and with the members of His body, so that even our sins can become occasions of grace for us? *"Tout est grace."*

If we are to rejoice in the grace of God—and the grace of God is given to us in order to enable us to rejoice (doesn't the very word, *grace*, mean favor, gift, and gifts are given to us to rejoice our hearts)—we must have eyes that see and ears that hear. That in turn demands a reflecting heart, the sort of heart which Our Lady had and with which, according to St. Luke, she *"pondered all things in her heart."* (Lk 2:19). I often think that Our Lady must have had a marvelous capacity for wonder. The Magnificat bears that out, for the Magnificat is a song whose theme is wonder at *"the great things"* which God had done for her and for her race, and indeed for us all. There can be no wonder in our lives without silence, and the capacity or ability to be silent in order to be able to wonder is something which over the past decade or more, has slipped down, I feel, in the scale of values in our Communities. We are called to the service of the poor, but our service must come from a heart which resembles that of Our Lady who knew how to be silent, who knew how to wonder, who knew how to marvel at the grace of God, without which we can do nothing.

No conference or address of St. Vincent ever ended without some real, down-to-earth, practical advice, and so, following his own practice, could I suggest to you that you try to snatch more moments of reflection during the day, to cultivate silence of the heart, so that you may be able to wonder at the grace of God that is all around us, like the air we breathe. In large measure it is the use we make of silence and reflection that makes us the sort of persons we are becoming. To dig continually a well of silence in our lives is to have an assurance that the living water of God's grace will keep springing up, especially when we need it to help the needy who thirst for God's grace and kindness, and seek it from our hands and lips and hearts. Above all, my dear Sisters, try to reserve some moments of silence after Holy Communion, so that you can wonder at the great thing God has done and is doing to you. The experience of receiving the Body and Blood of Our Lord daily may have lost something of its wonder for us, precisely because we are not silent enough—and for long enough—after that great encounter has taken place. Moments of silence after Holy Communion enable us to deepen our capacity to wonder at what must be among the greatest of graces that a human being can enjoy, namely, to be fed by the living Body and Blood of the Risen Christ. In a very striking sentence St. Vincent said: *"Remember this, my daughters, the principal devotion of a Daughter of Charity is to make a good Holy Communion."* (Conf.

Eng. ed., 22 Jan. 1646, p. 212). And I, for my part, might dare to add that it is difficult to make a good Holy Communion without silence.

When St. Vincent spoke to the Daughters of Charity on the 1 January 1654 on *How to Behave when Living Away from the Mother House*, he made this observation: *"Make yourselves beloved by all by the example of a good life. The good odor you have given has led to your being asked for in several places. And why so? It is because a little flower of your charity has been observed."* (Conf. Eng. ed., 1 Jan. 1654, p. 593).

May that flower of charity, which I, too, have noticed everywhere I have visited your communities during the past year, grow stronger. In a word, in this year of grace, may we all be *"the aroma of Christ"* (2 Cor 2:15) Who came not to be served but to serve, especially those who have most need of His love, of His truth, and of His grace—the poor. But first may you all in your own lives and throughout each day of this year of grace have fresh experience of His love, of His truth. For all is grace, *"tout est grace"*.

How to Spend Lent Profitably

24 February 1982   Rome, Italy

My dear Sisters and my dear Confreres,

I know a priest who decided one summer to spend a good part of his vacation in the desert. He was a priest who was very busy at all times. He gave his days to counseling people, praying with people, dialoguing with people, advising people, and after a long experience of this type of life, he felt that he needed to get away from people and to spend time alone with God. So he decided to go into a real desert. He went to Tamanrasset and there after several hours of journeying, he reached a hermitage which the Charles de Foucauld Brothers have in that part of the Sahara Desert. The nearest person to him was a priest of the Charles de Foucauld Society who had spent twenty-three years in that part of the desert and he lived in a hermitage a kilometer away. My priest friend had decided to spend a month there in the hermitage in which was to be found the Blessed Sacrament, a small bed and some supplies of food to keep him alive. He took with him a number of spiritual books. All went well for eight days and then the sheer isolation of the desert overcame him. He told me that in a sudden gesture he threw his breviary down on the ground one day and rushed over to see the priest who was, of course, a counselor and a friend to him. After a discussion, he decided that it would be best for him to return to more normal conditions of living. The old hermit explained to him that living in the desert was not something that could be taken on easily. He told my friend that it would have been much wiser for him to spend maybe three days in the desert and thus gradually accustom himself to its silence and solitude. For it was precisely the solitude and silence that broke the nerves of this well-intentioned priest.

Jesus Christ spent forty days in the desert. We honor that mystery in His life each Lent. Physically we do not go into the desert, but we try by the grace of God to enter into the spirit in which Christ passed those forty days of His life. It was in the desert that He had His temptations, those temptations which one could say were related to the *"concupiscence of the flesh, the concupiscence of the eyes and the pride of life."* (1 Jn 2:16). Did Jesus Christ in the desert come to a more profound understanding of His poverty, of His celibacy, and of His obedience? Along those lines, I will find inspiration about the manner in which I ought to spend this Lent.

A desert is a silent place, a desert is a place where one does not find the ordinary amenities of life. God is not inviting me to do what my priest friend did, but He may, and almost certainly, is inviting me to have a little more inner silence in my life. He is probably inviting me to give more time to personal, private prayer this Lent. He is probably inviting me to have the experience of relying less on material things. As I look around my room, He is probably asking me quietly, *"Do you really need all these things? Can you manage on just a little less, so that you would be a little more free to think about and 'seek the things that are above, where Christ is sitting at the right hand of God,'* (Col 3:1) *to have a little more time for others, to have a little more to give to the poor?"*

Lent is above all a time when we reflect upon the mystery of the sufferings and death of Jesus Christ, so that we may be able to enjoy more fully now and after our death the fruits of the Resurrection. We have here in this oratory a simple set of the Stations of the Cross. Apart from admiring them, I could from time to time during this Lent make the Way of the Cross in the Presence of Jesus Christ in the Blessed Sacrament. With Jesus Christ in the desert, with Jesus Christ on the Cross, I ask myself: can I offer Him something that is definite and practical which I will do daily for Him and His Kingdom and my own conversion, something that will distinguish each of these forty days which I am now, by His grace, about to begin? *"O, that today you would hear his voice: 'Harden not your hearts as at Meribah, as in the day of Massah in the desert, where your fathers tempted me; they tested me though they had seen my works. Forty years I loathed that generation, and I said: They are a people of erring heart and they know not my ways.'"* (Ps 95:8-11)*"... Jesus came from Nazareth in Galilee and was baptized in the Jordan by John... .At that point the Spirit sent him out toward the desert. He stayed in the wasteland forty days, put to the test by Satan."* (Mk 1:9,12,13).

Lenten Letter—Stability

25 February 1982   To Each Confrere

My dear Confrere,

May the grace of Our Lord Jesus Christ be with us forever!

When I wrote to you in Advent, I promised that I would do so again in January, and I intimated to the Visitors that the subject of my next letter would be *Stability*. Perhaps it tells you something of the stability of my own resolutions that this letter is only being written now at the beginning of Lent. I had hoped to have made a deeper study of this topic along with the Council, but for a variety of reasons we were unable to find sufficient time to discuss the topic at length. So, rather than delay this letter further, I am setting down some reflections which I hope, by the grace of God, may strengthen you in your vocation in the Little Company.

During the final days of Lent we find a phrase in the liturgy which keeps recurring again and again. It is that of St. Paul, *"Christus factus est obediens usque ad mortem—Christ became obedient unto death."*

(Phil 2:8). When Jesus Christ on the eve of His death was looking beyond that event, St. Peter in his admiration of His Master exclaimed: *"Lord, I am ready to go with you to prison and to death."* (Lk 22:33). Just how far St. Peter was prepared to go, at least on that celebrated occasion, all of us know. On that night when Jesus was betrayed, Peter was anything but ready to go *"usque ad mortem—unto death"* for Christ. Events proved that a few challenging words from a portress at the gate were sufficient to show that Peter belied his name. He was anything but a rock of stability in his dedication to Christ.

All of us who have taken vows in the Congregation have, like Peter, made an *"usque ad mortem—unto death"* promise to Jesus Christ. Both in the traditional as well as in the more recent vow formulations, we will find the phrase, *"toto vitae tempore—for the duration of my life."* When we pronounced our vows, we promised that we would observe poverty, chastity and obedience according to our Constitutions, and that through our vow of stability, we would dedicate ourselves to the evangelization of the poor *"toto vitae tempore,"* or if you prefer the Pauline and Petrine expressions, *"usque ad mortem—unto death."*

For St. Vincent, stability was synonymous with fidelity to a vocation one had personally received from God. On the 16 October 1658, St. Vincent wrote to two Confreres living in the community at Troyes, both of whom had intimated to him that their stability in the Congregation was under strain. The letters, which St. Vincent wrote to each of them, merit reading and reflection, because they blend in an exquisite manner sympathy with encouragement and understanding with firmness. If I quote a few sentences from each of these letters, it is only to entice you to read both of them in their entirety: *"When we think about another state of life, we picture for ourselves only what is pleasant in it, but when we are actually there, we experience only what is troublesome in it and what runs contrary to nature. Remain in peace, Father, and continue your voyage to heaven in the boat in which God has placed you. That is what I hope from His goodness and from the desire which you have to do His Will. If you have succeeded in remaining for twenty years in the Company, you will remain yet another twenty or thirty years in it, since things will not be more difficult in the future than they were in the past. In binding yourself to God exactly as the others do, not only will you edify them, but Our Lord will bind Himself more closely than ever to you, and He will be your strength in your weakness; He will be your joy in your sorrow; and He will be your stability in your wavering.* " (Coste VII, Fr. ed., pp. 292).

If St. Vincent would think of the Congregation as a boat on a voyage to heaven, then we, as its crew members, have our responsibilities to keep it on a stable course. To keep a ship on a stable course does not mean to leave it stationary or static. In this context I feel that it is important that provinces keep themselves open to the appeals which the Spirit of God is now making to us through our new Constitutions and Statutes. He is inviting us to new apostolates for the poor; to new forms of sharing with one another in Community; to a new simplicity of life; to the adoption of new techniques for reaching the heart and mind of man. For that reason, it is important that communities be familiar with the content of our new Constitutions and Statutes. I feel that a revival in a new form and in a regular way of our Community spiritual conferences, based on our Constitutions and Statutes could do much to strengthen us in the living of our vow of stability.

In the boat of St. Vincent's Congregation, we are responsible for one another's safety and survival. More than we realize, it is not only our personal dedication to God through the Community, but our interest in one another's apostolates which can support Confreres in their living of the vow of stability. All of us in the Congregation are in a special way *"our brothers' keepers."*

Let me return once more to St. Peter and his crisis of stability. By the grace and graciousness of Our Lord, he surmounted that crisis. After the Resurrection, he was able to accept from the lips of the Risen Christ the forecast that his future would be a difficult one as leader and a member of the Christian Community. From the lips of Jesus Christ also, he was to learn not to be too preoccupied by what the future might hold for others, or what the pattern of their lives would be. *"Lord, what about this man? Jesus said to him, 'If it is my will that he remain until I come, what is that to you? Follow Me.'"* (Jn 21:21-22).

As with St. Peter, our stability will be tested. We may feel drawn to leave the Congregation; we may feel influenced by the decisions others have taken. To us all, however, Jesus Christ keeps saying with quiet insistence what He said to Peter: *"Follow Me."* (Ibid.). In those two simple words there lies an invitation to accept the mission which comes to us from Jesus Christ, through His Church, through the Congregation, through our Visitor. It is the acceptance of that mission which is at once the guarantee of our stability and the expression of the vow we made to serve Him in the Congregation *"usque ad mortem—unto death."*

The difficulties of the future did not deflect Peter from *"strengthening his brethren"* (Lk 22:32) for he did not doubt the love of Jesus Christ. My prayer for us all is that we will never doubt that Jesus Christ is loving us through the Congregation and thus enabling us to persevere in our vocation *"usque ad mortem—unto death." "Remain then in peace and continue your voyage to heaven in the boat in which God has placed you. That is what I hope from His goodness and from the desire which you have to do His Will."* (Coste VII, Fr. ed., p. 293). I am in the love of Our Lord, your devoted confrere.

New Year's Day in the Community
25 March 1982   Paris, France

Mother Rogé, my dear Sisters and Father Lloret,

It was on New Year's Day that I last spoke to you in this hall, and it was a feast day of Mary, the Mother of God. Although the official title of today's feast is the Annunciation of the Lord, it is very much Our Lady's day. Today we are honoring both the mystery of the Incarnation and the obedience of Mary that made it possible. Today, in a certain sense, is New Year's Day also. There was a time when in some Christian countries, the 25th March marked the beginning of a new year.

For you, Daughters of Charity, it is still very much New Year's Day. For today you have commenced a new era in your ascent to God. Through the renovation of your vows you have given yourself to God for the service of the poor, and I am certain that through this renewal, you are enabling the light of His love to shine more brightly in the darkness of this world. For that, all of us have reason to rejoice: the world, the Church, the Company and the poor.

St. John in the first chapter of his Gospel wrote: *"The light shone in the darkness, and the darkness did not comprehend it.''* (Jn 1:5). I believe St. John's word 'comprehend' could be taken in two senses: the darkness did not *understand* it, or the darkness did not *overcome* it. We must not be surprised if in a secularised society many people do not understand the meaning of the consecrated life or do not appreciate its value. We ourselves, however, must not become discouraged by that fact. Always remember that it is Jesus Christ Who gives value to your consecrated lives. It is true that we are invited to cooperate with His grace, and that cooperation is often costly. It is He, however, Who can take that little drop of water which is my life, and place it in the chalice bearing the rich wine of His life, sufferings, death and resurrection, and transform all into an offering *''for the glory of God and the salvation of the world.''* The darkness of this world will not be able to *overcome* the power that radiates from Christ and those who have hidden themselves and their lives in Him.

So, my dear Sisters, may this New Year's Day in the Community lift you up to new heights of devotion to God and His poor. May the grace of renovation make your hearts more pure in all that you do and say and think. May this New Year's Day lift your hearts up to new heights of confidence in the love which God has for you personally. In saying this to you, I feel I am echoing a thought which St. Vincent expressed on many occasions to your first predecessors: *''Mark this, my Daughters, your work is great. As it is great, so, too, are God's designs on it, and in order to cooperate with them it is essential for Daughters of Charity to perform actions that are in conformity with the name they bear. Has not God great designs in your regard since He wishes you to spend your life in following the maxims of His Son? Oh! Sisters, how happy you are.''*(Conf. Eng. ed., 2 Nov. 1655, p. 756).

Today is New Year's Day in the Company. It is also Our Lady's day, the day of the first Joyful Mystery of her rosary. These last few weeks I have looked often at the statue of Our Lady of the Globe in the chapel, that statue which was, to use St. Catherine's own words, "the cross" of her life. Looking at that statue of Our Lady which now surmounts the body of St. Catherine, I realized for the first time that there was not one globe, but two globes presented to us. Our Lady stands on one globe with the serpent crushed by her foot, and she holds another one in her hand, a golden one surmounted by a cross. The globes can be said to speak to us of the victory of the grace of Our Lord Jesus Christ, but also of the presence of sin in the world.

That statue speaks to you, not only of her whom it represents, but also of your own vocation as Daughters of Charity. You are called to work amongst the poor in the world that still feels the sting of a dying serpent. As Daughters of Charity, you are called to work, not for the coming of a utopia, but for the coming of the Kingdom of Jesus Christ. Do not let your vision be shortened by any purely temporal vision of society or of the world. You must not let your eyes rest solely on the globe on which Mary stands. Rather must you lift up your eyes and the eyes of the poor to that globe surmounted by a cross which Mary holds in her hands. There are many people today who are passionately working for a more just society, for the alleviation of the sufferings of the poor. That is not enough for a Daughter of Charity. Hers must be a longer vision, the vision of Jesus Christ Whose *"Kingdom was not of this world."* (Jn 18:36). A Daughter of Charity must fix her eyes on those tender loving hands which hold the globe surmounted by a cross, and must reflect the tenderness and love of Our Lady in all that she does for the poor.

Our Lady of the two globes has much to say to us on this New Year's Day in our Community. Our Lady's feet are fixed firmly on the globe on the ground. The Gospels show her to have been a practical woman, who recognized the needs of people as soon as she saw them. Of Our Lady you can say that she lived the prayer of her Son for His disciples: *"I am not asking that Thou shouldst take them out of the world, but that Thou shouldst keep them from evil."* (Jn 17:15). She was, as St. Vincent remarked, like the ray of the sun which penetrates into dark and murky places while itself remains unaffected in its purity. That could be said to be the vocation of a Daughter of Charity, to be in the world, but not of it, to be a beam of God's sunshine while remaining unaffected by the evil you encounter in your work of service.

The globe in Our Lady's hands, have you noticed the gesture of her hands which is at once one of love and detachment? Of love, for has she not been proclaimed Mother of the Church, and so must care for it as it continues to grow. Of detachment, because the throne of David was not given to her, but to her Son Whose Kingdom will have no end. (cf. Lk 1:32-33).

In all that you do, my dear Sisters, until the day of Renovation comes again, may you experience the power of Our Lady's caring intercession. May you work with her in the preparation of the world for the final coming of her Son Whose Kingdom will have no end. In St. Vincent's words: *"I implore the goodness of God to grant you His Spirit that you may carry out this good work according to His good pleasure."* (Conf. Eng. ed., 23 July 1654, p. 638).

Counsels to Sister Servants

14 April 1982 Beyrouth, Lebanon

My dear Sisters,

In speaking to you this morning, I am conscious that I am speaking to Sister Servants. Perhaps the most important task of any Superior, of any Sister Servant, is to assist the mystery of spiritual growth in the Sisters who are entrusted to her by the Providence of God. The principal task of any Sister Servant or Superior, according to St. Vincent's mind, is to help each member of her or his community to grow into the likeness of Jesus Christ. The principal task of a Superior is to assist each member of the community to grow in union with Jesus Christ and to accomplish the Will of our Father Who is in heaven.

Allow me to offer you two counsels, one negative and one positive. Negatively, do not force the growth too much. A farmer cannot force the growth of wheat in the field. We cannot force the spiritual growth of other people. It is important for a Sister Servant, as it is for everybody, to accept people as they are and to help them to grow, but not to force them to grow. It is significant that Jesus said: *"And I, if I am lifted up will draw all things to Myself."* (Jn 12:32). *"I will draw all things to Myself."* He did not say, *"I will force all to do as I want them to do."* As for the positive counsel, it is this: try to create around you the conditions that will help people to grow in faith, and in hope, and in love of God and the poor. The gardener can remove obstacles that prevent the growth of the seed in the ground. He can shelter, and when necessary water the ground, to assist the growth of the seed. So, too, with us, we should try to create around us the conditions that will enable people to come out of themselves into the light and sunshine of God's grace. I sometimes think that all of us underestimate what we can do to create within our Communities the atmosphere that will allow, not only myself, but others to mature in the love of the Community and of our vocation to serve the poor.

One of the most practical pieces of advice any of us in authority could receive is to start by taking things and people as one finds them, and not as one would wish them to be. Apropos of that, I think that one of the most practical pieces of advice in the New Testament is the letter of St. James. You will find much in it to help you in your task: *"My brothers, you will always have your trials, but when they come, try to treat them as a happy privilege."* (Jas 1:2). Yes, all of us know that Sister Servants have often much to suffer, precisely because they are Sister Servants. St. James speaks of suffering as a happy privilege. I think it is important that whatever our sufferings are, we try not to talk too much about them, at least to our communities. If we speak too much to our communities about our difficulties as superiors, our communities will not be happy ones. An air of gloom will settle down upon them. I am not saying that a Sister Servant should not confide her difficulties to a prudent person. This week should afford you an opportunity of talking in general about some of the difficulties that you experience in guiding your communities, always respecting the law of charity. St. James would say that whatever your sufferings are as Sister Servants, through them you are becoming *"fully developed and complete."* (Jas 1:4). To be a Sister Servant is to receive a vocation within a vocation and all this comes under the loving Providence of God.

Secondly, St. James remarks: *"If there is any one of you who needs wisdom, he must ask God Who gives to all freely and ungrudgingly."* (Jas 1:5) To a young Superior who asked him for advice, St. Vincent in his old age made this precise point: *"You will need wisdom as Superior: you will receive it in prayer."* In crisis situations that arise, often the last means we adopt to solve them is to spend fifteen minutes in quiet prayer before Jesus in the Blessed Sacrament, asking that wisdom which we need and which He is ready to give freely and ungrudgingly.

Finally, St. James observes: *"It is right for the poor brother to be proud of his high rank and the rich one to be thankful that he has been humbled."* (Jas 1:9-10). That is a variation of St. Paul's idea, so dear to St. Vincent, that God chooses weak things of the world to confound the strong. For all of us in authority, it will remain in this life a mystery why God should have chosen us for this office. In our weakness we can draw strength from St. Vincent's consoling words: *"As for your feelings of inadequacy regarding the duty you are carrying out, remember that Our Lord has enough competence for you and for all humble persons, and ask Him to have mercy on me."* (Coste V, Fr. ed., p. 463).

To deepen within us the virtue of humility, we can often reflect on the fact that authority is only one form of many services that can be offered to the Community. It will help us to keep our sense of proportion right, if we are sensitive and appreciative of the good qualities that lie in the members of our Community whom we are now called by God in this moment of our lives to serve.

Your vocation as Sister Servants and as Daughters of Charity is well summed up in the final verse of that first chapter of St. James' letter: *"Religion that is pure and undefiled before God and the Father is this: to visit orphans and widows in their affliction, and to keep oneself unstained from the world."* (Jas 1:26-27).

Love in Spirit and in Truth

21 April 1982   Dahr-es-Sawan, Lebanon

My dear Friends in Jesus Christ,

First, let me say how happy I am to meet you, members of the St. Vincent de Paul Society, and to have the privilege of praying with you our greatest prayer, the Mass. One of the truths which the Vatican Council emphasized again and again was that the Eucharist was the summit and the source of all Christian activity. It is from the Eucharist that we derive strength to do the works of charity to which Christ invites us. Our works of charity are a practical expression of our experience of participating in the banquet of the Eucharist, which is the Sacrifice of the Cross.

St. Vincent de Paul was a great inspiration to Frederic Ozanam in his life, work and writings. For Vincent de Paul, however, and for Frederic Ozanam, it was the charity of Christ which pressed them on to do what they did for the poor of their time. I have no doubt that the opening sentence of today's Gospel must have been written deep in the heart of Vincent de Paul and Frederic Ozanam. *"Yes, God loved the world so much that He gave His only Son so that everyone who believes in Him may not be lost but may have eternal life."* (Jn 3:16). *"God so loved the world that He gave His only Son."* One could say that this is the central declaration of the Christian faith. It is the heart of the Gospel, for the heart of the Gospel is not *God is love.* That is a precious truth, but it does not imply any divine act for our saving. But the words, *"God so loved the world that He gave,"* indicate the cost to the Father's heart. *"He gave."* It was an act, not just a continuing mood of generosity. It was an act at a particular time and place. That is why I say that we could consider the phrase, *"God so loved the world as to give His only Son,"* as the heart of the Christian Gospel.

These words must have meant much to Vincent de Paul and Frederic Ozanam, and indeed to any member of this Society. There are millions who watch pictures of poverty on our television screens and feel generous towards the poor. Their reaction, so often, goes no further than feeling. You, however, imitate God, our Father, in that you are not content to feel generous, but you show your generosity at a particular time and place. The St. Vincent de Paul Society has always been recognized for its practical charity. May you be continually strengthened, not only to love in word, but in deed and in truth.

It is a mystery how God could love mankind, disfigured by sin and infidelity. Likewise, it is a mystery of God that you, as members of the St. Vincent de Paul Society, are able to love people who are disfigured by the effects of poverty and injustice, and who are often so unattractive in their poverty. As you work for and visit the poor, take heart from the thought that you are reflecting into this dark world the light and the love of God, our Father, Who gave us His Son, the Light of the world.

Let me end by quoting some lines from St. Vincent de Paul. His vision of the poor is one, no doubt, which all of you share: *"I should not consider a poor peasant or a poor woman according to their*

*exterior, nor according to what seems to be the extent of their intelli-
gence; for often they do not seem to have either the face or the mind of
reasonable persons, so gross and earthly are they. But turn the medal
and you will see by the light of faith that the Son of God, who wished
to be poor, is represented to us by these poor. . . . "* (Coste XI, Fr. ed.,
p. 32).

Advice to Seminary Directresses

2 July 1982   Paris, France

My dear Sisters,

The time for saying goodbye to one another has come. There's
always a certain note of sadness when friends must say goodbye and
go their separate ways. Very many of you came here without knowing
anyone else in the group, and what a difference the month you have
passed together has made. You have not only discovered new riches of
spirituality in St. Vincent and in St. Louise, but you have discovered
new riches of spirituality in one another. I would like to think, too, that
you have not only discovered new spiritual riches in the Company and
in one another, but in yourselves also; that each of you is going back to
your Province greatly enriched by what she has received and discovered. Returning to your Provinces you are surely rejoicing that you are
members of this Company which is united throughout the world in its
love of God and in its service of the poor; rejoicing, too, that you have
been called to a very special task within the Company; rejoicing humbly
that by the grace of God, you are now a more adequate Directress than
when you came here a month ago.

As you go on your way rejoicing, some of you will return to
seminaries where the number of Sisters is sizeable. Others will go back
to seminaries where vocations are few in number. Let none of you be
discouraged. He whom St. Vincent liked to call *"our blessed Father,"*
St. Francis de Sales, used to say that one soul was sufficient for a
Bishop. In the practical order, it certainly makes life more difficult for
a Directress when there are only two or three in the Seminary than when
there are twelve or thirteen. However, let not our minds dwell too much

on numbers, but rather on the very rich inheritance which is ours now and which we hope to pass on to others—the heritage which was passed down to us by St. Vincent and St. Louise.

Our Lord remarked to the little group of disciples who were with Him at the well in Samaria, *"The harvest indeed is great and the laborers are few."* (Lk 10:2). The fact that He Himself felt that the numbers were few and the work was great, did not deflect Him from pressing on with the work of preaching the Gospel to the poor, of healing the sick, of giving sight to the blind. Nor did it deter Him from going up to Jerusalem to suffer and to die. So it must be with us. We should not allow the fewness of numbers to depress us, nor to deflect us from pressing on in faith, which enables us to see only in a dark manner, towards what St. Paul calls *"the prize of the upward call of God in Christ Jesus."* (Phil 3:14).

Speaking of harvests, we can say that they are not gathered in quickly, nor do they ripen quickly. Have you ever noticed how many parables of Our Lord center on the image of the growth of small seeds? These parables underline for us the need of patience. *"The kingdom of God is as if a man should scatter seed upon the ground and should sleep and rise, night and day, and the seed should sprout and grow, he knows not how."* (Mk 4:26-27). These parables of growth underline for us the point that we should not look for immediate results and that harvests do not ripen quickly. So it is with us as we try to direct others. In this age of instant results, it is difficult for us to be patient with the slow growth of virtue in ourselves and in others. On many occasions St. Vincent counsels Superiors to be patient with the defects and limitations of their subjects. Like his Divine Master, he did not wish to break the bruised reed nor extinguish the smoking flax. Certainly in the name of the Community, you must make demands on young Sisters. These demands must be carefully distinguished from those which may be motivated by reasons that border on the selfish. Live with the conviction that God is working through you in the souls of young Sisters in ways of which you are unaware. In future years you will be surprised to find one whom you had as a Seminary Sister who will gratefully recall some observation you made as Directress, when you yourself have long since forgotten it. At times, that can be embarrassing, at other times encouraging. Live, too, with the conviction that, according to Our Lord, it is one person who sows and another who reaps. Be content to think of yourself as a person who sows. If we, by the grace of God, gladly do some careful sowing now, God will give the increase in His good time. Above all, be confident in the special grace which God gives you by reason of your office. Take heart in what St. Vincent said to a member of his Community on one occasion. Quoting St. Francis de Sales, he said that *"when God calls a person to an office, He either sees that person already in possession of the necessary qualities, or He intends to give them to him."* (Coste XI, Fr. ed., p. 142).

I cannot close this Seminarium without expressing your thanks and mine to Mother Rogé and her Council for initiating and planning this meeting of Directresses of the entire Company. Our thanks also are owed to the Commission which under Sister Isabel began the work of organizing the details of this session more than a year ago. I am sure all of you are also grateful to the community of the Mother House who have hosted us throughout the past month. From what I observe here, the community of the Mother House seems to be receiving Sisters from provinces all the year round. Their cordial receiving of Sisters is indeed a very special form of giving. May the Lord reward them for their generosity. In your name, too, I would like to thank those who have performed the difficult work of translating. In the full sense of the word, they have been mediators among us, as they translated the thought of one mind into the language of another. May the Word of God be their enlightenment and recompense.

Let me end with a little prayer which fell one day from St. Vincent's lips: *"O my God, You have given me a soul redeemed by Your most Precious Blood and You will that I help it to draw profit from that Sacred Blood which was spilled forth, in order that it may be able at the universal judgment to say that I am its co-redemptor, together with You, my God."* (*Perf. Evan.*, Ital. ed., p. 873-74).

Spiritual Weapons

Mother Rogé, Father Lloret and my dear Sisters,

The instruction which St. Vincent gave to the three Sisters setting out for Nantes on the 12 November 1653 (Conf. Eng. ed., pp. 585-88) reveals him, not only as a man who placed great confidence in the power of God's grace, but who recognized that the grace of God must struggle with human wills that are so often stubborn and imperfect. St. Vincent's remarks to the Sisters are masterly. He barely conceals from them the difficulties which they are going to experience with those who administer the hospital and even with the Bishop of the locality. It is easy to read between the lines that the Sisters were going into a hornet's nest. But St. Vincent alludes to all these difficulties in such a way that he does not allow the Sisters to lose heart, even before they set out. He stresses for them the importance of *"the spiritual weapons of humility, meekness and deference. When you are armed with those virtues,"* he remarks, *"you will be armed from head to foot and prepared to go out and wage war against the enemy."* He stresses, too, the importance, quoting as he did so often, *"our blessed Father, the Bishop of Geneva,"* that we should try to comply with the will of others rather than seek to make others comply with ours. The instruction concludes with the imperatives which are printed on the program of today's Mass. There are six of them: *"Go . . . .Work for Our Lord . . . . Have a high opinion of . . . .Respect our dear Sisters . . . .Be very much on your guard against conceiving a bad opinion of anybody . . . .Make it apparent that you have the true spirit which God wishes you to have."*

In asking you to reflect on these final imperatives of St. Vincent, I am not suggesting that you are going back to your seminaries to find a situation similar to that which was to be found in Nantes in 1653. At the same time I recognize that as Directresses you do face difficulties which arise from the diversity of characters which you find, not only among the young Sisters, but among the Sisters of the community in which you yourselves are placed. The most important of St. Vincent's imperatives is the second one, *"Work for Our Lord."* That is an appeal for simplicity, an appeal that your eye be single. We can sustain much difficulty in our daily lives if we are intent on working only for the living Person of Jesus Christ. If I might be permitted to add something to St. Vincent's words, I would say: *"Labor for Our Lord; yes, and labor with Him."* Reflect often, my dear Sisters, on the words of today's Gospel: *"You have not chosen Me, but I have chosen you."* (Jn 15:16). He has chosen you through the authorities of our Community to do the work you are presently doing. Draw strength from the knowledge that ultimately your appointment as Directresses comes not from the General Curia here in Paris, but from Our Lord Himself.

Three of St. Vincent's imperatives can be grouped together: *"Have a high opinion of.... Respect our Sisters.... Be very much on your guard against conceiving a bad opinion of anybody...."* These three imperatives reveal the strength of St. Vincent's conviction that, if we are to change people, we must respect and love them for what they already are. There are no exceptions to the rule to which we have listened in today's Gospel. *"This is My commandment that you love one another as I have loved you."* (Jn 15:12). Our Lord does not say that we should show our love to others only when they show signs of accepting and responding to His love. The Sisters in our seminaries must first feel accepted by us before they will accept from us the formation which the Community asks us to give them.

Lastly, in the first imperative of St. Vincent: *"Go forth, then, my dear Sisters,"* the note of confidence is clearly to be heard. St. Vincent echoes the command Our Lord gave to the disciples before His Ascension into Heaven. *"Go, therefore, and make disciples of all nations."* (Mt 28:19). Allow me in turn to echo the voice of St. Vincent. Go forth, return to your Province, secure in the knowledge that you are, in St. Paul's phrase, *"... equipped for every good work."* (2 Tim 3:17). To you Christ is saying today, *"I will not call you servants. I call you friends."* (Jn 15:15). He is saying to you also: *"Whatever you ask the Father in My name, He will give it to you."* (Jn 15:16). My prayer for you is that you will have that joy of which Our Lord speaks in today's Gospel; that the joy of Our Lady's Magnificat will vibrate in you as you leave this house, which belongs to her in a special way, and that you will be enabled to communicate that joy to the Sisters in whom you are trying to perfect the image of Christ Jesus, Our Lord and Head.

Union and Collaboration

2 August 1982   Salzburg, Austria

My dear Mother Rogé, my dear Fathers and my dear Sisters,

When I received the program for these days of celebration, I was very glad to see that you had set apart one day in which you would honor St. Louise. I am very happy that we are honoring St. Louise this morning for two reasons; first, because she is the Co-Foundress of the Company. Because she is, she deserves from us the tribute of honor and thanksgiving. Second, I think it very fitting that we should be honoring her on this occasion when the theme of our celebration is union and collaboration. What was achieved one hundred years ago was principally a growth in union and collaboration. On those two themes St. Louise has much to say to us. In her lifetime she had come to understand the meaning of collaboration. Not only did she understand what collaboration meant, but she lived to see the rich fruits of humble collaboration with others.

There was first her collaboration with St. Vincent. That collaboration extended over a long period of years, beginning with her relationship with St. Vincent as her spiritual director. His clarity of vision which enabled him to see Christ in the poor, and St. Louise's confidence in his practical judgment was a work of collaboration. The fruit of that collaboration was not only the alleviation of the sufferings of the poor but the foundation of the Company to which we belong today. From her collaboration with St. Vincent there was born, too, the friendship between them. It was at once human and reserved, spiritual and practical. It was a friendship that still rejoices our hearts when we read of it in the letters which they wrote to each other. Let me choose just one short extract from a letter of St. Vincent to illustrate that beautiful friendship: *"I most humbly thank you for all the care and charity which you exercise towards me, for such good bread, your preserves, your*

apples, and for what I only now learned that you have just sent me . . .
God knows with what pleasure I receive your gifts; yet also, ever in my
mind is the fear that you are depriving yourself of necessities in order
to practice charity in this way. In the name of God, do not do it any
more. "(Coste I, Eng. ed., p. 220).

St. Louise was an artist of collaboration with the Ladies of Charity.
She herself moved at ease among the Ladies and was equally at ease
with the simple girls whom she gathered about her for service of the
poor. She succeeded in achieving excellent collaboration between the
Ladies of high society and those simple first Sisters who gave themselves to God for the service of the poor. In her writings and remarks
to the Sisters, one comes upon many sentences like this: *"I praise God*
with all my heart for the great peace that exists between you and the
Ladies of Charity. There is nothing more powerful to preserve this
peace than the respect and humility you must manifest toward them."
(*Spiritual Writings of Louise de Marillac*, ltr. 555, p. 580).

Of her collaboration with those first Sisters who are your predecessors in the company, we have ample testimony in those two conferences
at which St. Vincent was present in July 1660 and which were entitled:
On the Virtues of Louise de Marillac. The collaboration between St.
Louise and those early Sisters must at times have been difficult. Louise
was a cultured, highly educated and refined lady. Writing to three
Sisters at Nantes, she appeals to Sister Andrée as follows: *". . . for the*
love of God, learn how to spell so that I can read your letters easily and
answer you as you would wish." (*Spiritual Writings of Louise de*
Marillac, ltr. 566, p. 588). It is an indication of the cultural gap that
existed between those with whom St. Louise was working. Yet through
her patient collaboration with these Sisters, they served the poor effectively and humbly.

Humility was the secret of St. Louise's ability to collaborate with
those early Sisters in the service of the poor, and her successful
collaboration with the Ladies of Charity. It was the secret, too, of the
manner in which she, a talented person, could submit her judgment to
that of St. Vincent who, after a little time, discerned her strength, her
talents and her humility. This experience in turn for St. Vincent must
have deepened his own humility and in that way, as he would like to

remind us, brought down further blessings of God on the collaboration between himself and St. Louise. May the collaboration between the Daughters of Charity and the Priests of the Mission be deepened. May the collaboration of this Province with the Mother House in Paris be strengthened. May all this be brought about through the united prayers of St. Vincent and St. Louise in heaven.

Renewal

9 August 1982   Dublin, Ireland

When Sister Pauline asked me some months ago to speak at this meeting, I was happy to accept her invitation. At the time the subject matter of the talks was left undetermined and still is, but that is no fault of Sister Pauline's. Months ago the date for the party was fixed, but the menu left undecided. We knew who the guests were going to be—yourselves. I am not too sure that St. Vincent would approve of my looking at it this way, that Sister Pauline and I were to be the hosts and you the guests. For it is a remarkable feature of those conferences, which were held in the presence of St. Louise in the Mother House, how much St. Vincent gained from the reflections, the observations and the spiritual enlightenment which he elicited by questioning, from those first members of the Company.

The conferences are punctuated by exclamations of praise and thanksgiving to God for the light which the Spirit of God had given to those simple and, for the most part, uneducated Daughters of Charity. There is no doubt that St. Vincent used the conference as a means of instructing the first Daughters of Charity. But we must believe that he himself was also edified, *built up,* in his faith by the replies that the Sisters made when he asked them for their thoughts on the given subject of the Conference. The conferences were conferences, not just a monologue such as I have embarked upon now! Indeed, it could be a much more enriching experience for all of us here today, if, after some brief introductory remarks, I began to say like St. Vincent: *"And you, my Daughter, what do you think?"* and interrogated a number of you at random.

If I understood Sister Pauline rightly when she asked me to speak to you, I think she suggested that I might say something that would encourage you in your vocation and give the Province a new sense of hope. Not indeed that she or I have reason to think that the Province is flagging in its spirit. No! For my part, I am always happy when asked by Sisters of other Provinces in what parts of the world the Company is growing in numbers, to be able to cite the region of Nigeria as one among a number of countries where there are unmistakable signs of numerical growth. It is always gratifying to be able to observe that twenty years ago there were no Daughters of Charity working in Nigeria and that today there are fifty-five, among them thirty-five Nigerian Sisters. The growth of the Nigerian Region could only have taken place because of the healthy condition of the roots and trunk of that tree which so shortly will be celebrating the fiftieth year of its planting.

Whenever St. Vincent in his last years looked back on his life, or more particularly on the life of his Communities, his reaction was always predictable. He would protest that he had not planned the planting of the Company, or had anything to do with its expansion. All the planting, all the planning had been done by God. That, for St. Vincent, was *"something understood."*

"Something understood" at the end of his life was the real service of Christ in the poor. He had only come to understand that reality slowly, but when he had grasped it, it became like one of those immense turbo-prop jets that lifted him off the flat earth of mediocrity and thrust him upwards and forwards so that he had a panoramic view of the needs of the poor, while all the time *"bearing healing in his wings."*

"Something understood" was that such healing that he or the Company could bring to the hemorrhaging world of the poor could only come from Jesus Christ. Hence the importance of real personal contact with Jesus Christ through faith, through the Sacraments, through personal and community prayer. For St. Vincent, *"virtue went out of Jesus"* as it had done when He walked the roads of Galilee. Today, as then, it is necessary to touch Him if, like the woman in the Gospel, we are to experience His virtue, His strength in our lives.

"Something understood" by St. Vincent in his mature years was the importance in all apostolic work of not standing in God's light. He grew more and more convinced of the importance that his own life and the

lives of those whom he directed in his two Communities should have a transparency about them, a transparency that enabled God to pass through, on his way to reaching His poor, and a transparency that also enabled the poor to see and come to God. It was St. Vincent's conviction of the importance of such transparency in our lives that led him to stress so much for us those sister virtues of simplicity and humility.

Apropos of these two virtues which so distinguish the Company throughout the world, allow me to speak of a recent experience which for me has been *"something understood."* A fortnight ago I was visiting a number of houses of the Company in the north of Morocco. It is a mission which belongs to the Spanish Province of Granada. In most of the houses in which I visited or stayed, the Sisters were working among an almost entirely Mohammedan population. One of the hospitals suffers acutely during the summer season from a chronic shortage of water, although a tourist hotel in a more wealthy part of the town is never without an abundant supply. Two other hospitals administered by our Sisters labor under similar difficulties. While walking around each of these hospitals and noting how clean the Sisters managed to keep them, despite the lack or scarcity of such an elemental necessity as water, and noting at the same time that the patients were all poor and all Mohammedans, I found myself impatiently saying to myself, *"Why does the Company stay here?"* The following day we called to see three Sisters living in a three-room flat in a town of four thousand where there is not a single Christian. The Sisters have a tiny oratory where once a week they have the privilege of a Mass. They run a dispensary and also try to instruct women, not in the faith, for that is strictly forbidden, but in some elementary domestic and feminine skills. Again I found myself asking almost impatiently, *"Why stay here?"* Yet in all these communities there was a particular fragrance of joy among the Sisters. I am quite sure that there were hidden community tensions, as there always must be in this imperfect world, but there was a transparent joy among them nonetheless, that was not affected, a joy that was of the Lord.

The question, *"Why does the Company stay here?"*, became less persistent in my mind as the visit progressed. Certainly the poor were there and that was a reason why they should remain. But an equally powerful reason for remaining was the transparency of the lives of the

Sisters. In a hundred different ways the tender mercy of God was breaking in on the lives of these Mohammedan people like the dawn from on high. The people could see the beauty of that dawn because of the transparency in the lives of the Sisters. In their simplicity the Sisters looked up to God, to Him Who is the Light of the World, and through their humility they drew down grace and truth upon these people, because they themselves were trying to put up no resistance through pride or self-seeking. *"God resists the proud and gives His grace to the humble."* (Jas 4:6). Through such transparent lives, suffering was being alleviated, ignorance dispelled, the poor were being served. More than that, only God could tell us. What deep stirrings of His saving grace were silently taking place in the inner depths of the souls of those people who gazed through the transparent lives of the Sisters on the loving kindness of our God, on the grace and truth that comes from Jesus Christ, is God's secret. Some of these poor will get no further than articulating a word of gratitude. The rest is silence and must remain so until *"the secrets of all hearts will be revealed"* (1 Cor 14:25), when the Son of Man will come again in glory to render to each man according to his works.

Do I hear one of you say, *"Father, you are in Ireland now, not in Morocco"?* And so I am. Geographically there is an important difference between Ireland and Morocco, as there is between Nigeria and Morocco. Spiritually and within our Community, there is none. In suggesting to you that the virtues of simplicity and humility give a transparency to your lives, I am suggesting to you the qualities that give a particular distinction to you as Daughters of Charity in your service of the poor. Perhaps it might help you to think of your lives and vocations as rich stained-glass windows which, in the words of the song, are letting in *"God's heavenly light."* Any great stained-glass window is made up of myriad pieces of different colors, all combining to proclaim the message of God's word, the message of the faith. The great white light of the sun outside is transformed by the glass into rich reds and blues and golds. So it is with our lives as individuals and as a Community in God's Church. Within our Communities, each of us is unique. We are by nature and by grace of a certain hue and color through which the bright sun of God's goodness is shining and delighting the building which is the Church, which is the Body of Christ. As individuals we are part of our Community which has a message for the Church of God, and not only a message but a service for the poor, the handicapped, the brokenhearted.

As rich stained-glass windows in God's Church, stained by the Blood of Christ, we can as individuals and as Communities become smeared and smudged by the grime and dust of man's city, and that almost imperceptibly so. Thanks be to God Who has inspired you to be deeply devoted to that purifying process which is the annual retreat, the annual renovation of vows, to the monthly retreat and to seeking greater purity of heart in the regular experience of the Sacrament of Reconciliation.

One window is not the entire cathedral. It is part of an harmonious whole. The window, if it could think for itself, would have a sense of its proportion. It is indeed the architect's sense of proportion that gives beauty to a building. As windows in God's great building, which is the Church, we need to keep our sense of proportion. Certainly God, the architect, has a sense of proportion. It is we who at times lose our sense of proportion when we try to be or become something that He does not intend us to be or become. I have sometimes wondered if future historians of the Church will judge those first ten years after Vatican Council II as years when individuals and Communities within the Church tended to lose their sense of proportion.

We were invited by the Spirit of God to renew ourselves as Communities, to adapt ourselves and our apostolates to the needs of the modern world. Nearly all tried to respond. The trouble came when some, instead of being content to clean the windows, decided to dismantle them or enlarge or diminish them according to their taste. Let me say at once—and I think St. Vincent and St. Louise would not object to this—that by and large the Company throughout the world has, by the grace of God, kept its sense of proportion. Under the grace of God I attribute that not only to the intercession of St. Vincent and St. Louise and our large Community in heaven, but also to the eminently practical character of the spirituality which St. Vincent and St. Louise inculcated into your predecessors, the first Daughters of Charity. *"Give yourselves to God in order that you shall speak in the humble spirit of Jesus Christ confessing that your doctrine is not yours, but from the Gospel. And be particularly careful to imitate Our Lord in the simplicity of language He used and of the comparisons He drew when speaking to the people.* (Coste XI, Fr. ed., p. 346).

Whatever is simple and humble, keep these things, pursue these things. In so doing, you will be following the path of Vincent de Paul, for his spirituality is impregnated with simplicity and humility. *"Simplicity,"* he observed one day during a conference, *"is my Gospel."* His humility has been put forward by at least one profound student of his works as one of the two great dynamic forces that lay behind all that he achieved in his lifetime.

In praying that we will, as a Company and as individuals, keep our sense of proportion, we are asking something big of God, for proportion affects all aspects of our lives. We need proportion in allocating time for work and time for formal prayer; time for study and time for leisure; time for God and time for my community; time for my friends and time for the poor; time for reading and time for reflection. We need a sense of proportion even in evaluating our own personal difficulties and problems. Dr. Johnson, the writer and critic, used to say to his anxious and often troubled friend, Boswell, agonizing over some difficulty: *"Sir, consider its importance fifteen years hence . . . ."* That is a very wise thing to do. St. Peter's advice to *"bow down under the mighty Hand of God,"*(1 Pt 5:6) and *"to cast your cares upon Him"* (Ibid., v.7)—which is more difficult to do than we realize—would do much to help us keep our sense of proportion in the face of difficulties which at the present moment may loom large in our lives and in our thinking.

Proportion affects even our serving of the poor. The cares of the poor have become more insistent in our day. We have been urged to respond to them, and we have been trying—not without pain and sacrifice—to orient our works to where the needs of the poor of our society are greatest. If we do not have a sense of proportion, we may feel unconsciously that we must help all the poor. Then, when we cannot, a certain frustration and annoyance is born within us, a dissatisfaction with our particular community and the Province, which in turn breeds discontent with our vocation. That is why I say it is important that we keep a sense of proportion even in our service of the poor. This sense of proportion is touched upon by St. Vincent in his remark: *"The works of God have their moment; His Providence arranges that they take place then and not sooner or later. The Son of God saw the loss of souls, and nevertheless He did not anticipate the hour ordained for His coming."* (Coste V, Fr. ed., p. 596).

I imagine that St. Vincent would alert us to the danger of excessive zeal. *"It is true,"* he wrote, *"that zeal is the soul of the virtues, but most certainly, Monsieur, it must be according to knowledge, as St. Paul says; that means according to the knowledge of experience. And because young people ordinarily do not possess this experiential knowledge, their zeal goes to excess, especially in those who have a natural asperity."* (Coste II, Eng. ed., ltr. 460, p. 84).

Hopefully our Community and Provincial Plans will preserve our sense of proportion and save us from that excessive zeal which St. Vincent was realist enough to fear. Our Community and Provincial Plans are not green or white papers, nor are they merely results of human reason and human experience, ratified by the sum of the members who contributed to their production. They are rather the fruit of prayerful reflection on the part of the whole Community which humbly seeks the light of God so that it can marry its limited human and spiritual resources with the needs of the poor among whom it lives. *"Send forth Your light and Your truth. Let these be my guide."* (Ps 43:3).

"Something understood." That hints that there are many things which we don't understand. We have certain great securities in our lives, our faith which is as imperishable as gold, even when it is tried by the fire of doubt and depression. Even with our faith, we can see now only in a dark manner. The darkness somehow seems to keep deepening about us: the Ireland of the Eucharistic Congress of 1932 seems to have been a brighter country than the Ireland of 1982. Let us not delay too long in making comparisons. What is important for us privileged people—privileged by reason of our vocation in Christ Jesus—is that we should not go like Dylan Thomas, raging into the darkness of the night, but rather following the advice of St. Peter, advance into it with the flickering light of faith, secure in the knowledge that the light which we carry has been caught from Christ, the Light of the World, that this light shines in the darkness, and that the darkness, however deep it may seem to us, has not and will not overcome it.

Silent, Undeviating Loving God

9 August 1982   Dublin, Ireland

My dear Sisters,

Perhaps I should have begun this morning by saying something about the title of these two sets of reflections which I am putting before you today, *"something understood."* They are the two last words in a poem by the sixteenth century English poet, George Herbert. The poem is one on prayer, and he uses a number of short, pithy phrases to describe the experience of prayer. The final one is that simple expression, *"something understood."* It is not the most accurate nor the most attractive definition one could find of prayer, for it focuses rather on one of the results of prayer than on the heart of the experience itself. It is, however, true enough: it does suggest that God communicates something to us in prayer.

When we adore God at the beginning of prayer and allow ourselves to fall with our minds and hearts and wills into the depth upon depth of His power and wisdom and love, we do come to understand a little more clearly the meaning of some of those phrases which all too lightly we say with our lips: *All-powerful, ever-living God; All-wise, ever-loving God.* When in prayer we allow the glance of Christ to rest on our weaknesses and betrayals of Him, as it rested for a moment on Peter, we come to know more of the selfishness and immaturity of all sin and the silent, undeviating lovingness of God. Or again when in that childlike way, which Christ so much commended to us, we unfold the desires of our heart to Him in petition, we come to know ourselves better and at the same time know in a more experimental way the meaning of the Fatherhood of God. So, too, with thanksgiving. It is thanksgiving in our lives that helps us to understand something of the open-handed generosity of our Father in heaven, Who makes the sun shine on the just and the unjust alike. It is thanksgiving, too, that teaches us something about the meaning of generosity in our own lives and leads us to an appreciation of it in the lives of others.

So it is true that every lifting up of our souls to God in prayer does result in something being understood—about God, about ourselves, about our places and our apostolates in His world.

Let us turn our minds away from ourselves and towards St. Vincent, who certainly came to understand much through prayer. His first biographer, Bishop Abelly, remarked that St. Vincent in his humility tended to be reticent about his personal prayer. But the primacy of prayer in his own life and in the lives of the members of his Communities is plain for all to see. When reading the conferences and letters of St. Vincent, allow yourself to be distracted sometimes by the vividness of his imagination. In instructing people, he followed the example of Our Lord and used simple but very picturesque language to convey his convictions. Much of his teaching on prayer centers specifically on mental prayer. Here is a random selection of the images which St. Vincent uses, in instructing others on the centrality and importance of mental prayer in our lives. For St. Vincent mental prayer is the food of the soul: it is for the soul what air is for man or water is for fishes: it is a fountain of rejuvenation: it is an ornament of the soul: it is as the looking-glass by which we come to know ourselves.

What St. Vincent came to understand in prayer is expressed, at least partially, in his works. Our own Communities must be seen certainly as the work of the Spirit of God, but also as *"something understood"* personally by St. Vincent in and through his prayer. By the very nature of things and also because of his own humble reticence, much of what he did come to understand in prayer is known only to God. Very likely, too, he would tell us that he came to understand the things of God only slowly; that he was a slow-learner. For that reason, he needed much time to learn the grammar of God first and then to acquire the ability to read the purposes of God which more and more he discovered to be very loving ones, particularly for those to whom the Son of God had come to preach and to help in a special way, the poor. St. Vincent believed that the deep things of God were learned only slowly. Perhaps that was the reason why, with so much fidelity over so many years, he gave the first hour of his day to mental prayer, and encouraged his priests and Brothers to do likewise.

We can only penetrate a short distance into the inner courts of St. Vincent's castle of prayer. We might, however, learn something of what he himself came to understand in and through prayer by listing some of those words which were most frequently on his lips. Sometime in the future, I imagine, some enterprising Daughter of Charity or Confrere will feed the fourteen volumes, or fifteen with the discoveries made since the 1920s, of Coste's edition of St. Vincent's Correspondence, Conferences and Writings into a computer, and the computer will give us back all sorts of interesting information about St. Vincent's use of language and the most frequently occurring concepts and ideas of his mind. I was going to say, *"meantime, allow me to present you with a provisional list of such words,"* but that would be far too presumptuous on my part, for I have not studied deeply even the official index volume of Father Coste, a volume which, valuable as it is, is far from being an exhaustive index to the ideas and spiritual ideals which circulated so freely in St. Vincent's mind. What I have done is jotted down at random, and I invite you to do the same, just some of the words which I imagine were most frequently on St. Vincent's lips and which consequently may be an indication of *"something understood"* by him in prayer.

Those who watched St. Vincent die in the early morning of 27 September 1660, tell us that the last word which they saw shaping on his lips was *Jesus.* That Name had come to mean everything to him over the years. Of course, it would have been taught to him in his home at Dax by his mother some eighty years earlier, but it must have taken on a much richer significance for him when, in his late thirties or early forties, he had come to know Christ Jesus, not just with the mind of a theologian, but with the heart of a priest who had recognized Jesus as the Good Samaritan, Who had come into this world to lift up the poor and broken forms of sinful humanity, which were lying on the roads of this world half-dead. Something of the intensity with which St. Vincent loved and breathed the Spirit of Jesus Christ is to be caught in that celebrated quotation from a letter written to Father Portail: *"Remember, Monsieur, we live in Jesus Christ through the death of Jesus Christ, and we must die in Jesus Christ through the life of Jesus Christ, and our life must be hidden in Jesus Christ and filled with Jesus Christ, and in order to die as Jesus Christ, we must live as Jesus Christ."* (Coste I, Eng. ed. ltr 197, p. 276).

As St. Vincent matured in years, Jesus Christ became for him, to quote his own phrase, *"life of my life,"* and from that experience there sprang very frequently to his lips not only the name of Jesus Christ, but much more importantly, appeals to himself and to others to conform their way of acting to that of the mind of Jesus Christ. Not once, but several times in his conferences and letters, he counseled this to his confreres: *"Ask yourself how Jesus Christ would act in these circumstances. How would He preach to this people? How would He comfort this poor creature?"* The same ideal was put before the Sisters. You will never read many lines in any of St. Vincent's writings before he introduces you to the Person of Jesus Christ. It is that which distinguishes him from the purely social reformer and steers him away from all human ideologies. For St. Vincent, to quote his own phrase, *"All human action becomes the act of God when done in Jesus Christ and through Him."*

Jesus Christ was sent into this world by His Father. He had a mission from His Father in heaven. *Mission* is one of the central words in the New Testament. It is not surprising that for one like St. Vincent, who had impregnated himself into the mind of Jesus Christ and who would have us priests read a chapter of the New Testament each day, the word *mission* should be central in his life and in his spirituality. When it came to baptizing the Community of priests and Brothers which he had founded, the name that came to his lips was *mission*. For St. Vincent, the Sisters who came to him for a blessing before going to Nantes or to Calais were going on *mission*. For St. Vincent, such departures were occasions, not so much of farewell, for imparting some practical advice or bestowing a blessing, but a fresh enactment of that missioning of Christ, Who had said after His Resurrection, *"As the Father has sent Me, so also I send you."* (Jn 20:21).

For St. Vincent, such *mission* was a matter of urgency. He lived with the conviction that if people had not explicit knowledge of the Trinity and of the Incarnation, it would be difficult, if not impossible, for them to be saved. That understanding or particular interpretation of theology gave a burning urgency to his concept of *mission*. He saw his two Communities as continuing the *mission* of Christ, Who had come to save that which was lost.

Mission, then, must always remain a central concept in Vincentian thinking. The Community itself receives its *mission* from the Church, and each of us as individuals from the Community. That is why an ordinary appointment within the Community has a much greater significance than we often realize. Our vision is sometimes so short that we cannot see an appointment other than an administrative act which will facilitate the smooth running of the Province. It is much more. All appointments are a sending forth. Hence, the importance of being more passive than active when it comes to accepting an appointment. I am not saying that we should not enter fully into the consultative process that precedes the making of an appointment. St. Vincent would encourage us to make known in all simplicity the difficulties and the repugnances we may feel, while at the same time he would strongly urge us after that to accept the decision of our superiors as the manifest Will of God. When the consultative process is completed, it is important that then we should be more passive than active in order that we, through the Company and through the Church, can hear and accept what Christ is still saying, *"As the Father has sent Me, so also I send you."* (Ibid.).

Speaking to you as Daughters of Charity, I must single out a favorite word of St. Vincent's which he liked to employ when he was giving a conference to your predecessors. That word was *Providence*. In the volume of Conferences to the Daughters, you will find that he uses the word at least seventy times. On one occasion, he remarked to the Sisters that if they had not been called Daughters of Charity, they would be called Daughters of Providence. For St. Vincent, the Providence of God was *"something understood."* It was the central personal devotion of his life. In all that concerned his Communities, his great fear was that he or any of us would *"cut the heel, or tread on the heel of God's Providence."* We must keep a respectful distance behind the loving Wisdom of God. We do not rush in where angels fear to tread. But with equal conviction, St. Vincent would stress that when the loving Providence of God did indicate whither we should direct our steps, then we must not hang back; we must not drag our feet. Writing to one of his priests on the topic of an unfortunate accident which had happened, St. Vincent remarked: *"How will we react to that except by willing what Divine Providence wishes and not willing what Providence does not want. This morning during my very poor prayer, I experienced a great desire to will all that happens in the world, be it good or evil . . .*

because God wills it, because God sends it . . . .Let us study to have this disposition of will in regard to the Will of God, and among the very great blessings which will come from it, not the least will be tranquillity of soul. " (Abelly, Vol. II, Book III, p. 182: ed. 1843).

Writing in 1644, he said: _"Grace has its moments. Let us abandon ourselves to the Providence of God and be on our guard against anticipating it. If Our Lord is pleased to give me any consolation in our vocation, it is this: I think it seems to me that we have tried to follow Divine Providence in all things and to put our feet only in the place It has marked out for us._ (Coste II, Eng. ed., ltr. 704, p. 499).

High in the order of words most frequently upon his lips was that of the _poor_, and one would say almost in the same breath, the word _charity_ which should be shown to them; not any kind of charity, but the charity of Jesus Christ. Apropos of the charity of St. Vincent towards the poor, one hears nowadays an occasional voice raised about St. Vincent's concept of social justice. Did he have, it is asked, a sense of social justice? A critic has asked, through his charity did he retard the evolution of social justice in society? There is at least one reference in his correspondence to the need of putting justice before charity. What is remarkable in his writings and conferences is that, not withstanding his clear vision of the unequal distribution of wealth, never once does he denounce the rich and their possessions in bitter terms. He certainly worked in a practical way to make the rich distribute some of their wealth to the poor and in that way level, in however small a degree, the inequality that existed between the rich and the poor in the society of his time. I like to think of his refusal to criticize bitterly the rich for their unconcern of the plight of the poor because of his deep respect for the dignity of the individual person. It should not be forgotten that such respect for the dignity of any person is the first claim that justice makes upon us.

I have been digressing somewhat from those two words, the _poor_ and _charity_, which must have been almost hourly upon St. Vincent's lips. The poor of Jesus Christ and the charity of Jesus Christ were two of the great realities that preoccupied his thinking, his praying, and his planning during the last twenty years of his life. _"It is certain that charity, when it dwells in a soul, completely occupies all its powers._

There is no rest: it is a fire which is unceasingly active, keeping the person it inflames always keyed up and always in action." (Coste XI, Fr. ed., p. 215). That was a phrase St. Vincent used during a conference. You could almost say it was a pen-portrait of himself.

We could go on adding to this list of St. Vincent's favorite words. I have not mentioned *prayer*; how often exhortations such as this fell from his lips, *"And, therefore, Sisters, pray, because prayer is a most powerful means of obtaining from God that His work shall be accomplished according to His Holy Will."* (Conf. Eng. ed., 29 July 1655, p. 706). Nor have I mentioned faith, confidence, simplicity, humility, Holy Communion, the Blessed Virgin, words which must have been dear to him. What he himself once said of the ceremonies of the Mass could be applied to any one of St. Vincent's favorite words: *"They are only shadows, but they are shadows of great realities."* These favorite words of St. Vincent are shadows, but for him they were shadows of the great realities which he himself treasured, and which in his generosity he would share with others, and today with us.

I have spoken about some words which St. Vincent used very often in his daily conversation. Let me end with citing a word which I think appealed greatly to him, though he never said so. It is just a guess on my part. It is the word, *little*. His Congregation was the *Little Company*: the method which he advised us to use when preaching was the *Little Method* and his illnesses were his *little fever*. *Little* was a word which he liked to use to qualify his own and the collective talent of his Company: *"to the best of our little ability . . . ."* He liked the word, and he used it with affection. There is something at once both appealing and revealing in St. Vincent's fondness for the word, *little*. Appealing: this man surrounded by works of gigantic proportions with a heart that had room for human poverty of every kind, liked, in the intimacy of his heart and in the presence of His God, to think of what was closest to himself as *little*. Had he, like Julian of Norwich, seen a tiny acorn representing all things that are, resting in the palm of God's Hand? His fondness for the use of the word *little* is also revealing, for it suggests that virtue which appealed so much to him—humility.

St. Vincent's fondness for the word *little* was indeed for him *"something understood."*

Funeral Mass for Father William M. Slattery, C.M.

14 August 1982   Philadelphia, Pennsylvania

Your Eminence, Cardinal Krol; Your Excellencies, Bishop Graham, Bishop Lohmuller and Bishop Schulte; Mother Rogé, and my dear Brothers and Sisters in Christ:

A few months before St. Vincent died, he experienced the pain of losing through death two of his closest collaborators in the work of preaching the Gospel to the poor and of alleviating their sufferings. On the 14 February 1660 St. Vincent wrote: *"It has pleased God to deprive us of the good M. Portail."* Then, just a month later, God invited St. Louise de Marillac to enter into the joy of her Lord. Writing to one of his Confreres after the death of M. Portail, St. Vincent remarked: *"He died as he had lived—in the good use of suffering, in the practice of virtue, in the desire of honoring God, and of passing his days, as Our Lord, in the accomplishment of His Will. He was one of the first two Confreres to work on the missions, and he always contributed to the other apostolates of the Company to which he rendered notable services. The Company would indeed have lost a great deal by his death, were it not for the fact that God has arranged all things for the best, enabling us to find our well-being even when we thought we were suffering loss. There is reason to hope that this servant of God will be even more useful in heaven than on earth. I ask you, Father, to offer for his soul the usual suffrages."* (Coste VIII, Fr. ed., p. 248).

That restrained but warm tribute of St. Vincent to his closest collaborator and friend in the Community would sit very easily on him who was to become St. Vincent's nineteenth successor and to whom we are saying *farewell* today.

As St. Vincent watched Father Slattery drawing to the end of his days on earth, he must have nodded his head often in heaven and said: *"Yes, he is dying as he had lived, in the good use of suffering and in the practice of virtue."* For Father Slattery's sufferings in these last few months, and indeed these last few years, were plain to all. His stooped form, his failing eyesight, his arthritic pains and latterly his difficulty in breathing were sufferings of which he spoke little, but which required no medical eye to discern. What we did discern was his good use of them. *"Cheerfulness,"* wrote Cardinal Newman, *"is a Christian duty."* It was a measure of the deeply Christian character of Father Slattery that he remained unfailingly cheerful even when the weight of suffering stooped and bent him low.

A number of his Confreres will cherish the memory of him, sitting in the Community oratory here in Germantown with the Divine Office in one hand and a large magnifying glass in the other, laboriously praying the morning office before the arrival of the Community, because, as he would say with a cheerful smile, he was not able now to read as well as the Community. Some of the physical sufferings of Father Slattery these last few years and his uncomplaining acceptance of them were plain to see.

Perhaps not so evident, however, were the spiritual and moral sufferings of earlier decades in his life. These were not evident because he was not wont to speak of them. What we do know is that he rose magnificently to a call which St. Vincent sets forth in the Rule for his Congregation that all should be prepared to renounce one's attachment to one's country and offices and persons when obedience and the interests of the Community demand it. Father Slattery's obedience was what St. Paul would describe as *"the obedience of Faith."* (Rom 16:26). We know, too, that his was a gentle spirit and that the cost of such renouncement must have at times weighed heavily upon him.

Such suffering was not sustained, however, in any stoical way. Stoics are not cheerful, and Father William Slattery was. We observed in him what St. Vincent observed in Father Portail: *". . . a desire of honoring God and of passing his days, as Our Lord, in the accomplishment of His Will."* The accomplishment of God's Will was something central to Father Slattery's thinking and living. Some of us here will recall the intensity and sincerity with which in a few short phrases he spoke on this subject at the General Assembly in 1968. The question for him at that time was not whether he should or should not continue in the office of Superior General. Humbly he sought and serenely he accepted what to him was the manifest Will of God, and he was at peace. He became in the confessionals here a minister of God's peace and serenity to hundreds of people, until his physical strength would no longer carry him to this church which from the days of his youth he loved so much.

With the Perpetual Novena and the Novena Band his name will always be associated, so much did he encourage these two apostolates. The encouragement he gave to the Novena Band, which works under the aegis of Our Lady of the Miraculous Medal, was an indication not only of his devotion to St. Vincent's ideal of preaching the Gospel to the poor, but also of his personal devotion to the Mother of God and the Mother of the Church. It was at once touching and revealing, when visiting him these last few months, to find only one personal object on his little bedside table—his rosary.

No doubt his long association with the Mother House of the Daughters of Charity in the rue du Bac, Paris, must have deepened his attachment to her who was conceived without the stain of original sin. It was significant that he should have been elected Superior General of the Congregation of the Mission and of the Daughters of Charity during the very month when the Church canonized that faithful servant of Our Lady, Catherine Labouré. During the twenty-one years that were to follow that event, the Daughters of Charity throughout the world were to come to know something of the personal holiness of Father Slattery, who became for them as well as for his Confreres in the Congregation of the Mission a sign of charity and a stimulus to it. By the grace of God he was enabled as Superior General *"to act justly, to love tenderly and to walk humbly with his God."* (Mi 4:6). *"There is reason to hope,"* concluded St. Vincent, in his reflection on the life of Father Portail, *"that this servant of God will be even more useful to us in heaven than on earth. I ask you, Father, to offer for his soul the usual suffrages."* (Ibid.).

We recognized great spiritual strength in the ascetic life of Father Slattery. For many years now, both inside and outside St. Vincent's two Communities, a certain *"fama sanctitatis"*, or reputation for remarkable holiness, attached itself to the name and person of Father Slattery. Now he has been called to sustain what St. Paul in the second reading of today's Mass refers to as *"the eternal weight of glory"*—the *"pondus gloriae."* (2 Cor 4:17).

Even at the close of a long life distinguished by suffering uncomplainingly endured, and distinguished by fidelity to the ideals of Jesus Christ as presented by St. Vincent, a man may yet not be strong enough to sustain *"the eternal weight of glory,"* which the face-to-face vision of God brings with it. St. Vincent recognized that fact and appealed for the prayers of the Community, so that what might be lacking in the strength of one member could be supplied by the strength and prayers of the others. This is what we are now asking through this most efficacious of all prayers, the Mass, for this servant of God, Father William Slattery, who will undoubtedly be even more useful to us in heaven than he was on earth.

May this Province of Philadelphia, which gave him as Superior General to St. Vincent's two Communities throughout the world, be the first to experience the help of his prayers in heaven.

May God rest you, Father Slattery, may God rest you—and until we meet again—*Goodbye*!

Our Lady, Beautiful Spiritually and Physically
16 August 1982   Paris, France

Mother Rogé, Father Lloret, my dear Confreres and my dear Sisters,

When I was flying to Philadelphia for the funeral of Father Slattery, I spent part of the time reading a little book about Our Blessed Lady. The author devoted a paragraph to the consideration of the one Greek word which expresses the phrase *full of grace* in the salutation of the Angel Gabriel to Our Blessed Lady. It brought back to my mind an observation which a professor of Sacred Scripture made to me some years ago. He said that the Greek word, *Kecharitomene* or *full of grace*, could suggest not only spiritual beauty, but also physical beauty. It is not difficult for us to imagine that Our Lady must have been physically very beautiful as well as being spiritually perfect. The physical beauty of our bodies changes with the passing of the years. Even if it did not, death will change the physical beauty of our bodies, as we return to the dust out of which we were made.

Apropos of the beauty of our bodies, it is good to recall often St.

Peter's advice to the Christian women of his time: *"You should not use outward aids to make yourselves beautiful. . . . Instead your beauty should consist of your true inner self, the ageless beauty of a gentle and quiet spirit, which is of the greatest value in God's sight."* (1 Pt 3:3-4).

It is good to recall some of those wise counsels which St. Vincent gave to guide us towards a true appreciation of spiritual and physical beauty through our vow of chastity. We would be mistaken to think that the advice which St. Vincent and St. Louise offered us is no longer relevant today for the living of our chastity. We have heard and read much in recent years about the positive aspects of chastity. We would, however, deceive ourselves by thinking that there is no longer place for those essential negative safeguards which St. Vincent along with the saints of other ages have emphasized. Times may change, but human nature does not. Relationships which begin in the spirit can still end in the flesh. The beauty of the human body can and should lead us to God. It can, however, lead us away from Him, if our chastity is not rooted in the love of the Person of Christ and in a crucified life.

The physical beauty of Our Lady was not touched by the change or corruption of the grave, for when the course of her earthly life was complete, she was taken, body and soul, into heaven, so that she could fully share in the Resurrection of Him Whom she bore in her womb. *". . . Quia quem meruisti portare, alleluia; Resurrexit sicut dixit, Alleluia . . . ."*

In the Preface of today's Mass there is a lovely little phrase describing the present activity of Our Blessed Lady, assumed into heaven: *"She guides and supports the hope of your people still journeying."* Which of us here has not experienced in a tangible way in our lives the guidance and the hope which Our Blessed Lady offers to us all?

What Mary does for each of us, God wills that we should try to do for our fellow pilgrims. Within the limits of what St. Vincent would call our little abilities, our vocation is to guide and sustain the hope of the poor, in that humble and unobtrusive way which characterized all that Mary did, when she, like us, was a pilgrim in this life.

Today our thoughts are on Our Blessed Lady: on the beauty of her soul and on the beauty of her body. Today our thoughts are also centered on Mother Rogé on this, her feast day. We pray that in a special way she will experience in her life that guidance and that hope which Mary likes to give. We pray, too, that Mother Rogé will continue to be what she already is: a sure guide and an effective sign of hope to the entire Company, which is accompanying the poor on their pilgrimage to the Kingdom of God.

Centenary of the Foundation of the C.M.
1 September 1982   Panningen, Holland

My dear Confreres and Sisters,

Exactly one hundred years ago next Sunday, Father Antoine Fiat, Superior General of the Congregation of the Mission and of the Daughters of Charity, wrote from Paris to the Bishop of Breda, and in the course of his letter he remarked: *"Your Excellency, in the difficult times through which we are passing, it seemed useful to us to have a foothold* 'un pied à terre' *outside France, and we are thinking of buying the property of Wernhoutsburg in the diocese of Breda."*

This letter drew a very prompt reply from the Bishop, for only two days later he replied, authorizing the purchase of the property and welcoming the establishment of the Congregation in his diocese.

In the letter of Father Fiat, there is one little phrase which for all of us has a prophetic ring about it. He sees the new foundation in Holland as a foothold, *"un pied à terre."* Now a foothold is by definition something you take with a view to advancing further. We who now one hundred years later look back on the history of the Congregation in Holland can see the fulfillment of that prophetic little phrase. For Holland was to become a foothold from which the Congregation established houses not only within the borders of this country, but into countries thousands of times its size and thousands of kilometers away from Wernhoutsburg and Panningen.

In the Gospel passage to which we have just listened, St. Luke remarks that the seventy disciples were *"appointed by the Lord."* Hundreds of Dutch Confreres were by their vows or through ordination to the Priesthood *"appointed by the Lord . . . to go ahead of Him into towns and places where He Himself was about to come."* (Lk 10:1-2).

And these towns and places are to be found in all five continents of the world.

Each of the ten decades that has passed since September 1882 has been marked by the establishment of houses of the Congregation among peoples who for all eternity will salute our Dutch Confreres in the words of Isaiah, as *"ministers of our God . . . who brought good tidings to the afflicted and proclaimed the year of the Lord's favor."* (Is 61:1).

If I were to list in detail the missionary enterprises of this Province of Holland during the past one hundred years, I fear some of you would be distracted, for your mind would linger in one or other country, lost in admiration of what was achieved, and you would refuse to follow me on my missionary journey. Just allow me to choose one decade, or more precisely a span of eleven years, and let me list some of the footholds established by the Confreres of this Province:

1946 - Departure of a group of Dutch Confreres to Tientsin, China.

1947 - Departure of a group of Dutch Confreres to Denmark.

1951 - Departure of a group of Dutch Confreres to the United States.

1952 - Departure of a group of Dutch Confreres to Central America.

1954 - The first Dutch Confreres arrive in Taiwan.

     - the first Dutch Confreres arrive in Ethiopia

1955 - Departure of Dutch Confreres to Zaire.

1957 - Departure of first Dutch Confreres to Curaçao.

That is far from being a complete list of the missions established by the Province of Holland, but it is an indication of the vigor and zeal that has been so distinctive. Let me remind you that this year we will be commemorating also the sixtieth anniversary of the departure from Holland of the first two Confreres for Fortaleza in Brazil. One of them died very shortly after his arrival there. The seed, however, did not remain in the ground alone. It has brought forth fruit, so that fifteen years ago, Fortaleza became a fully established Province of the Congregation.

Speaking of anniversaries, I should mention here that this year marks the eightieth anniversary of the establishment of the first house of the Daughters of Charity in Holland, at Sustera. The Daughters of Charity must certainly feel pleased with what the Bishop of Ruremonde wrote a year after their coming and when permission to establish this house of Panningen was being sought: *"We know a proverb which says: 'When one has tasted a good apple, one wishes to have still another one of them.' Last year your Superior General gave us the Daughters of St. Vincent de Paul; yes, tell him to send his Sons this year . . . ."*

Perhaps, however, I should remind the Daughters that, whatever was said about the diocese of Ruremonde, other places in Holland had already for twenty years come to know the Sons of St. Vincent as *"bonnes pommes."*

Enough of the past. We give thanks to God for it. Today we sing a song of *"praise to the glory of His grace."* (Eph 1:14). What of the future? It is veiled from our eyes as it was from the eyes of Father Fiat and those Fathers who came to Holland one hundred years ago. We could speculate about the future, and among us there may be some prophets of gloom. Let us not give ear to their dark prophecies. Rather let us reflect on Our Lord's words about the pruning that His heavenly Father carries out on the vine, so that it *"may bring forth more fruit."* (Jn 15:2). Vocations seem to be non-existent. Note that I say "seem." Numerically Dutch Vincentians in the world will become fewer in the years immediately ahead. The vine will be cut back, but only that it may bring forth more fruit. As a thousand years are as one day with the Lord, we may not live to see the new fruit which in the future the vine will yield. Whether we see it or not is unimportant.

What is important is that each Dutch Vincentian establish for himself a foothold in the Gospel as lived and interpreted for us by St. Vincent. What is important is that all of us Vincentians be convinced of the relevance today of St. Vincent's spiritual teaching. What is important is that we maintain confidence in what he established in and for the Little Company. What is important is that we look first to St. Vincent's spiritual formulae and afterwards to his structures. What is important is that the Province here in Holland continues to support spiritually, morally and financially, as it has been doing, the Confreres of Holland who are scattered abroad to preach the good news to the poor. What is important is that the Province here at home remain a true *berceau* for all Dutch Confreres wherever they may be. What is important is that none of us lose hope that God will continue to use us Vincentians *"to comfort those who mourn in Sion, to give them the oil of gladness instead of mourning.* " (Is 61:3). What is important is that wherever Dutch Vincentians are to be found, the people whom they serve may be able to echo what the Bishop of Broda said to Father Fiat three months after becoming acquainted with the Confreres in 1882: *"You are men of peace and charity: do all the good that you can in the spirit of St. Vincent de Paul, which is humility and love of the poor."*

With St. Vincent, I pray today as he so often did in his letters to Confreres: *"May the grace of Our Lord Jesus Christ be with us forever!"*

Agape of Love

27 September 1982   To Each Confrere

My dear Confrere,

May the grace of Our Lord Jesus Christ be with us forever!

Before the close of this day which united us all in a special way around St. Vincent, I write to greet you and to join my prayer with yours to St. Vincent that we may all *"love what he loved and practice what he taught."*

This evening I spent a little time in prayer before the casket which contains St. Vincent's mortal remains. As always, what attracted my attention was not so much the waxen features of St. Vincent's face, but the little crucifix that has been placed in his hands. According to the tradition in our Community, it was that little crucifix which St. Vincent held before the eyes of the dying King Louis XIII in May 1643. That St. Vincent should have been called to the bedside of the King tells us much about the confidence that he must have inspired in people who felt themselves in need and about the length and breadth of his love. St. Vincent's love for the poor was not so exclusive that he could not assist a king in his dying hour. That should not surprise us, for the love that was in St. Vincent's heart, and in ours too, is but a created participation in that 'agape' of God, Who makes His sun to shine upon the just and the unjust alike. *"The 'agape' of God has been poured into our hearts through the Holy Spirit."* (Rom 5:5).

All this has significance for ourselves and for our Community apostolates. We are to be clearly identifiable as a Community of men who have been called to take a special interest in the preaching of the Gospel to the poor and in the formation and spiritual well-being of the clergy. Our apostolates, however, are not based on the shifting sands of any merely human or political ideology of the day. Rather they must draw their inspiration and their strength, as St. Vincent's did, from a practical reflection on Jesus Crucified Who broke down barriers, making peace by the blood of His Cross. (cf. Eph 2:13-18).

During my reflection this evening before St. Vincent's casket, I thought of him who in God's Providence was called to be his nineteenth successor, Father William Slattery. He died, as you know, on the 10th of August, *"full of days"* (Job 42:17) and full of merits. May his saintly and gentle soul now rest in the fullness of God's peace! For twenty-one years he guided our Congregation. More fitting than any words of mine as a tribute to his memory are those which St. Vincent penned a few days after the death of his closest friend and collaborator in the Community, M. Portail:

> *He died as he had lived—in the good use of suffering, in the practice of virtue, in the desire of honoring God and of passing his days, as Our Lord, in the accomplishment of His Will. He was one of the first two Confreres to work on the missions, and he always contributed to the other apostolates of the Company to which he rendered notable services. The Company would indeed have lost a great deal by his death, were it not for the fact that God has arranged all things for the best, enabling us to find our well-being even when we thought we were suffering loss. There is reason to hope that this servant of God will be even more useful in heaven than on earth. I ask you, Father, to offer for his soul the usual suffrages.* (Coste VIII, Fr. ed., p. 248).

Lastly, let me end this short letter with the assurance that I thought about you this evening and recommended you to St. Vincent's intercession. May you be strengthened in the conviction that in a certain but real sense you, too, are a successor of St. Vincent, for the Spirit of God has entrusted you with a share of his charism. Asking a remembrance in your prayers, I remain in the love of Our Lord, your devoted confrere.

Spiritual Role of Provincial Directors

29 September 1982   To the Provincial Directors

My dear Confrere,

May the grace of Our Lord Jesus Christ be with us forever!

For quite a while now, I have been thinking of writing to you, principally to express my appreciation of the work which, as Director, you are doing for the Daughters of Charity. It has been said to me on a number of occasions that, when a Confrere is appointed to be Director, he often experiences difficulty in seeing clearly what his precise task is, and that he would welcome more information than is available in the Constitutions of the Daughters or in the tradition of the Community as it is handed down from one Director to another. Perhaps in the future I may be able to place at your disposal some extracts from canonical studies that have been made on the *figura* of the Directors of the Daughters of Charity. For the moment let me just offer you some personal reflections on your office.

It is hardly necessary for me to tell you that the Daughters appreciate very much the help they receive from their Directors at a general, provincial, local and personal level. The institution of the Director goes back to the very origins of the Company, and the stability of the Company throughout the centuries, and especially during the last two decades, is due in no small measure to the help which the Directors have been able to give to Sisters in guiding them towards ever greater union with God and towards an ever more effective apostolate to the poor of Christ. The appreciation of the Daughters to their Directors is often expressed in prayer as well as in word and gift. Be assured that their gratitude to you goes even deeper than its expression. To their many expressions of gratitude to you, let me now add mine.

Reading the Constitutions of the Daughters, you will notice that the article which refers to the Director (C. 3.38) speaks of both responsibilities and faculties and that the responsibility which receives explicit mention is that of promoting with the Visitatrix and her Council the Vincentian spirit in the Province. The Constitutions immediately add the following sentence: *"To fulfill that mission, he collaborates in the organization of all that concerns the spiritual formation of the sisters, particularly that of the Sister Servants. "* (Ibid.).

One sometimes hears it said that the role of the Director has been changed greatly, particularly since 1968. The role may have changed somewhat, in that the Director is now less involved in administration of the Province than he had been in the past, but has there ever been a time when the central role of the Director was other than collaborating with the Visitatrix in the organization of all that concerns the spiritual formation of the Sisters, and in particular the Sister Servants? What has evolved since 1968 is to place in greater relief the spiritual and priestly role of the Director. For that we can only be grateful.

You exercise your responsibilities, first through collaboration with the Visitatrix and the Council. As in all work of human collaboration, it may at times be difficult for a variety of reasons. Any work of collaboration in apostolates in the Church calls for *kenosis*, self- emptying. More difficult than a difference of opinion is the *kenosis* that is demanded of you on many occasions during a Council meeting. It is often difficult to remain silent for a long time in order to allow full expression of differing viewpoints to take place. It is pleasant to be able to announce the last word in any discussion. It calls for *kenosis* on your part to leave that to the Visitatrix to whom belongs *"the immediate government of the province. "* (C 3.32).

Both inside and outside the Council, most appreciated in the Director is that he has a "listening heart." A good listener is not passive all the time. There is *"a time to keep silence and a time to speak. "* (Ecc 3:7). It is the Spirit of God alone who can give us both a listening heart and enlightenment on when we should be silent and when we should speak.

The Constitutions state that the Director makes those visits of the local communities which are required by the Church. An obligatory canonical visitation of each house in the Province is made by the Director every five years. At the end of the canonical visit it is customary that the Director set down in writing a short reflection which the Sisters of the community can read from time to time and which will recall for them the assistance he tried to give them. In addition to such canonical visits, he will create other opportunities to visit the houses of the Province so that he can promote by prayer and by word the

Vincentian spirit. Such visits, too, will give the opportunity to the Sisters of speaking with him.

It has been the custom now for a number of years that the Directors furnish a report to the Superior General annually on the state of the Province. A standard form for such reports was made available to the Directors to facilitate this task. I would like very much that the practice of making an annual report to the Superior General on the Province be maintained. It is not necessary, however, to use any particular form. What I would like to receive is an overall impression of how you see the Province, indicating to me any particular difficulties which you may be experiencing in your office or which you have observed in the Province. I would welcome, too, information on the number of canonical visits you have made in the course of the year. I would suggest that this annual report be made during the first three months of the new calendar year. As there will be a meeting of the Visitatrixes in Paris next May, you will appreciate that it will be very useful for me to have your next report here before the end of March 1983.

For some years now, Directors of a country, where there are a number of provinces of the Daughters, have met to discuss their work and to exchange ideas on how they could discharge their office more effectively. Such regional meetings can be of great benefit and they could possibly be extended to include a Director of a neighboring country. Reports on such meetings would be of help to me, for I could circulate them from time to time to other Directors who would appreciate very much the ideas and suggestions that were proposed and discussed.

This letter has been long enough. Its main purpose is to thank you and to encourage you in the work you are doing in an apostolate which gives glory to God and assistance to the Sisters, and through them to the poor of Christ. In His love I remain, your devoted confrere,

Parable of the Lost Coin

4 November 1982   Rome, Italy

My dear Sisters and my dear Confreres,

It has sometimes been said that St. Luke the Evangelist, besides being a writer, was also an artist. Whether he was or not, we do not know, but it is certain that, when he came to write his Gospel, he shows himself to have many of the qualities of a good artist. Take, for instance, the opening sentences of this morning's Gospel. He presents us with two pictures, Jesus in the midst of the poor and, close to Him but very much apart, the Scribes and Pharisees who criticize Him for associating with such poor and despicable people. In two verses St. Luke succeeds in presenting us with that striking contrast of attitudes. To answer the criticism, Jesus tells three simple but very profound parables which bring us right into the heart of God.

Have you ever noticed this contrast in this morning's Gospel? The Pharisees and Scribes think of sinners as just a group of people. Then Jesus answers their criticism by telling three stories which emphasize the importance of thinking in the singular. A man has one hundred sheep and he loses one. A woman has ten coins and she loses one. A man has two sons and he loses one. Jesus is saying quite clearly to the Pharisees: You think of the poor just as a group of unfortunate people, but God thinks of each of them as individuals. Before we come to the poor, it is important that we ourselves should often reflect on the fact that Jesus Christ is always thinking of us as individuals. In recent years we have been asked to think about the social responsibilities which flow from our celebration of the Eucharist. However, we must never forget that we receive all the Sacraments as individuals. We were baptized as individuals; we were confirmed as individuals; we are fed one by one with the Body and Blood of Christ every day. When we receive the Sacrament of Reconciliation, we do so normally as individuals, and when we will receive, please God, the Sacrament of the Sick, we will receive it as individuals. We need to reflect often on the fact that we are loved personally by Jesus Christ. To each of us He still says: *"I know mine and mine know Me."* (Jn 10:14).

When Our Lord told that story about the woman who lost one coin in the house, was He thinking of an experience which Our Lady had in the home at Nazareth? Thank God, it is not always a sin, or even an imperfection, to lose things, and I imagine Our Lady, like the rest of us, suffered from time to time the frustration of not being able to find something quickly, not being able to find something which by chance she had lost. Anyway, the woman in this parable is a poor woman, as Our Lady was a poor woman. The poor we meet have always a sense of loss. The poor with whom you are working have a sense of loss of opportunities or a loss of self-respect, or a loss of money, or a loss of friends or a loss of a sense of direction in life. All the poor we meet are suffering from some sense of loss.

This parable is also a parable of searching. The woman searches the house for the lost coin. A Daughter of Charity is always seeking the poor in affection and, as far as possible, in effect as well. Not only is the individual Daughter of Charity characterized by searching for the poor; so, too, are provinces. Provinces of the Company, and the entire Company itself, must be like the woman in today's parable, searching for those who are lost in life. Like the woman in the parable, we have to keep searching out the hidden corners of society for the poor who are lost.

This parable is also one of rejoicing. The woman rejoices when she finds the lost coin. We ourselves, our communities, our provinces and the Company, have a sense of joy when we are close to the poor. On a few occasions it has been remarked to me in the last two years that those communities are the happiest which are closest to the poor. You as Provincial Councils devote much time to studying and reflecting on the problems of individual communities in your provinces. Let me say just this: joy in a community is a sign that that community is close to the poor. The beauty of these parables is that they reflect the mind and the heart of God Who is always searching for our hearts and always rejoicing when He finds them. These parables illustrate the meaning of the Incarnation and we in turn are called to continue the work of the Incarnation. To the first Sisters St. Vincent said: *"You do that which Our Lord did. He went from city to city, village to village, and He healed all those whom He met. Sisters, does that not show you the greatness of your vocation . . . to do what God did on earth . . . yes, Sisters, should you not be angels in the flesh? O, pray to God to realize fully the splendor of your employments and the holiness of your actions. "* (Conf. Eng. ed., 2 Feb. 1653, p. 518).

Advent Letter—Loss and Gain

15 November 1982   To Each Confrere

My dear Confrere,

May the grace of Our Lord Jesus Christ be with us forever!

A little over a hundred years ago Cardinal Newman wrote a novel entitled, *Loss and Gain.* Although I have never read the work, I have often in these post-conciliar years reflected on its title. Your experience, I feel sure, has been like mine: during the past twenty years we have felt a certain sense of both loss and gain. Each of us could make his own list of what he would consider to have been losses and gains for the Church during these two decades. We would see the gains as clearly the work of God's Spirit, and the losses as liabilities stemming from man's sin and his weakness in understanding *"the deep things of God."* (1 Cor 2:10).

At the center of our lives is the Eucharist. Each of us can thankfully list some of the gains which have been ours in the celebration of that central act of worship of our faith: the provision of richer fare at the table of God's word; more active participation of the laity in the rite of celebration. And the losses? Perhaps failure to assimilate through silence the loving power of God's rich message; the loss of a sense of mystery.

It is difficult to define what precisely this sense of mystery is. Perhaps it is something that must be experienced before being defined: something that is caught rather than taught. Has the sense of mystery and of wonder at the reality of Christ's abiding presence in the Blessed Sacrament been one of the losses of these last two decades? It is certain that the presence of Christ in the Blessed Sacrament was central in St. Vincent's life and he meant it to be so in ours. On going out from the house and returning to it, he would have us salute Christ in the Blessed Sacrament. (cf. CR X, 20). That recommendation is a reflection of St. Vincent's own conviction that the starting and finishing point of our approach to Christ's presence in the poor must be His presence in the Eucharist. A high degree of sensitivity and reverence towards the presence of Christ in the Blessed Sacrament should make it more easy for us to be sensitive and reverent before His presence in the poor. Furthermore, without the gravitational pull of Christ's presence in the Eucharist, we could lose ourselves in life's empty spaces and become disorientated in our vocation and thus ineffective in bringing to the poor that which Jesus Christ wishes to give them through us.

When you receive this letter, you will be preparing to celebrate the mystery of Christmas. *"While all things were in quiet silence and the night was in the midst of its course"* (Wis 18:14), the Eternal Word of God broke into our little world as an infant, being brought forth from the womb of His Mother, the Virgin Mary. May you have joy this Christmas and may your joy be full.

Shortly after Christmas, your Visitor will be setting out for Bogota to take part in the meeting of all the Visitors of the Congregation between the tenth and the twenty-fifth of January. This pastoral meeting will be devoted to a reflection on our two basic ministries in the Church: the preaching of popular missions and our service of the clergy. In the course of these two weeks we will be thinking about and sharing our experiences on some of the losses and gains of recent years in these two primary apostolates of our Congregation. We will be trying to enrich one another through a humble exchange of views on the mystery of these two ministries which lie at the heart of our vocation in the Church, the Body of Christ. You, too, will be participating in this meeting through the support of your prayers on which, I need hardly say, we will be counting. For that reason I would appreciate it very much if, along with your superior and the other members of your local community, you prayed for an hour before the Blessed Sacrament on some agreed day between the first and the twenty-fifth of January. I cannot believe that such a concerted volume of prayer ascending to God from each community of our Little Company will not bring down both grace and truth on the Visitors in Bogota and on our Community mission of bringing to the poor *"good tidings of great joy."* (Lk 2:10).

I will write to you again at the close of the Visitors' meeting. Meantime, in the love of Our Lord, I remain, your devoted confrere. P.S. The four Assistants along with the Confreres and Sisters who work here in the Curia send you their greetings for Christmas and the New Year.

Die Between Two Pillows

26 November 1982   Tolagnaro, Madagascar

My dear Sisters,

St. Vincent had the privilege of being a personal friend of three people who were later to be canonized saints. They were St. Francis de Sales, St. Jane Frances de Chantal and St. Louise. The first of these three future saints whom he came to know was St. Francis de Sales. St. Vincent in his conferences to both his Communities often referred to St. Francis de Sales as our blessed Father and, when the Saint's beatification cause was introduced, St. Vincent was among the witnesses who testified to the holiness of his life. So, too, was St. Jane Frances de Chantal, and her sworn testimony was published in attractive book form some years ago.

Speaking of the hope which was evidenced in the life of St. Francis de Sales, St. Jane Frances remarks: *"He said one day to a great prelate, to the Bishop of Belley, in fact, who has since passed it on to us in a sermon, that we must die between two pillows: our humble confession that all we deserve is hell and our perfect trust in God's mercy which will give us Paradise."* (*Testimony*, edited by Elisabeth Stopp, p. 62).

I was reminded of these two pillows between which, according to St. Francis de Sales, we should die, by the readings of today's Mass. Instead of speaking of pillows, St. John in the Book of Revelation speaks about books: *"The Book of Life was opened and other books opened which were the record of what they had done in their lives."* (Rv 20:12) The books set forth the credit and the debit side of our lives. They remind us of the justice and mercy of God.

We may pass through the gates of death, resting on those two pillows of which St. Francis de Sales spoke, but when we wake up in eternity, I think what will cause us pain will be the realization of the intensity of the love which God—Father, Son and Holy Spirit—had for us from the very first moment of our existence, and our poor realization of it and reaction to it during our years on earth. Did you ever have the experience of causing pain to somebody and then only later discovering that that person had been enormously good to you without your knowing it? The experience can be a very painful one for us when we discover such goodness too late. By that I mean, when the person is already dead. The pain you experience is the pain of love you have failed to recognize. I think it will be that way after our deaths. It will not be so much the justice of God that will strike us first, but rather the burning intensity of His love which in so many instances of our lives we spurned and rejected. St. John, as an old man, said over and over again: *"God is love."*

Cardinal Newman wrote a very fine imaginary poem on the experience of dying. It is called, *The Dream of Gerontius.* The poem, a fairly long one, ends with the soul being ushered into the presence of God by its guardian angel. The soul gasps and then cries, *"Take me away,"* asking and pleading hopefully and peacefully to be lowered into the cleansing experience of Purgatory.

If it is the love of God for each of us that will pain us most after our deaths, we must still remember that His love endures forever and that His love will arrange all things for us, so that when we have been purified in Purgatory, we will be able to accept fully and without regrets the intense and everlasting love of God. The experience of Purgatory will be the experience of the psalmist in today's responsorial psalm: *"My soul is longing and yearning, is yearning for the courts of the Lord. My heart and my soul ring out their joy to God, the living God."* (Ps 84:3).

The experience of dying must not take away our hope. Even in the darkness of that experience Our Lord holds out hope to us in today's Gospel. *"Think of the fig tree, and indeed every tree. As soon as you see them bud, you know that summer is now near. So with you, when you see these things happening, know that the Kingdom of God is near."* (Lk 21:29-30). In countries where there is a season of winter, it is always a great thrill to see the first signs of spring coming in the trees. Spring is a time of hope. Our Lord is assuring us that even in the experience of dying, we should not lose hope.

As we go through the experience of dying, we will rest, as St. Francis de Sales has said, not on one pillow, thinking of the justice of God, but on another one also, thinking of His great *"mercy which will give us Paradise."*

1983

Mountain of Perfection

1 January 1983   Paris, France

Mother Rogé, Father Lloret and my dear Sisters,

In the early days of the New Year 1657, St. Louise wrote a letter to the Sister Servant at Angers:

My very dear Sister,

> *I imagine that it must have grieved you to go so long without receiving a letter from us. I have so little time because of my ailments and the sister who assists me has also been unwell. This has caused part of the delay. However, I was also waiting for the first conference of the year, so I could participate in the drawing for the holy pictures, in your place, after our Most Honored Father had blessed them. Enclosed are the ones that Providence has chosen for you. We wanted to allow each of you the consolation of drawing her own when they are distributed.*

> *The subject of the conference was the obligation we have of striving after our own perfection this year, even more intensely than we have in the past. The first point gave the reasons why we must strive to reach perfection; the second, the means at our disposition to attain it; the third, the obstacles that we might encounter as we seek perfection.*

> *If Monsieur l'abbé could spare you a little time, and if all our sisters were animated by a sincere desire to reach personal perfection, I think that you would profit considerably by a little conference on this subject. Believe me, Sister, it is more harmful to our sanctification than good to seek our own satisfaction by speaking privately first to one person then to another. However, the advice given to all, assembled in the name of Our Lord, which each one receives*

109

as coming from the hand of God and intended for her personally, is much more profitable.

But allow me to tell you what often prevents us from being better and more faithful despite all the instructions which are so charitably given us. It occurs when we do not reflect that it is God who is speaking to us, or when we say that such and such a thing is said for us personally because we are held in low repute. It also happens when, instead of being convinced that we need all that is being taught us, we are bold enough to say that it is being addressed to this sister or that one, or that another sister has indeed been told off.

Am I not mean to think this way? But do not believe, my dear Sisters, that I think such things of you. I point them out because I have observed such conduct in some sisters here, and each of us is capable of committing all the faults that others commit. I, therefore, allow myself to bring these obstacles to your attention while begging God to preserve you from them and urging you, during this new year, to renew your first fervor for the service of God, so as to obtain from His goodness the grace of fidelity and perseverance in fulfilling His holy will. If you realized how fortunate you are to be in a place where everything contributes to your sanctification, you would praise God continually for having chosen you for this work. (Spiritual Writings of Louise de Marillac, p. 531, ltr. 505).

These few paragraphs from one of St. Louise's letters reveal quite a lot about her. Her sensitivity towards others: letters unanswered can cause people pain. Her concern for the unity of spirit and of direction in the Company: the main points of M. Vincent's New Year conference are to be pondered upon by all the Sisters. Her insight into the workings of the human mind and of its weaknesses: the tendency to apply what one hears in conferences to others and not to oneself. Again her sensitivity to her correspondents: *"no, I'm not thinking of you."* Lastly, her concern that the New Year would bring to the Company two of those graces which she so often asked God for: fidelity and perseverance in fulfilling His Will.

But what of that New Year conference which St. Vincent gave on the 5 January 1657? The subject was *Striving After Perfection*. Perhaps your first reaction is that the title needs to be modernized. When you read the conference, you might feel tempted to say that it is negative in tone, for almost throughout the conference, St. Vincent speaks of the importance of mortification.

It is true that conditions of life, as we know them, have changed from those of the seventeenth century. To that extent, the words of our Founders call for some interpretation, and that interpretation we will find, for the most part, in our Rules and Constitutions. What I think all of us have to be on our guard against is being too selective in the way we read writings of St. Vincent and St. Louise. Some of us tend to be like children who pick the currants out of a cake and leave the rest uneaten, and that is not very complimentary to the cook!

We do not use the phrase, *"striving after perfection,"* quite as much nowadays as we did before. That, however, should not distract us from the truth of the fundamental reality, that the good we will do for the poor will be proportionate to the efforts we are making to acquire, in all things and at all times, the mind and outlook of Jesus Christ. It is rather significant that in the conference of the 5 January 1657, St. Vincent mentions the poor only once. At the very end of the conference, he asked God for the grace of striving after perfection so that the Company may be preserved *"for the good of the poor."* It is clear that St. Vincent believed that the source of a Sister's dynamism in her work for the poor came from her sincerity in seeking her personal perfection according to the Gospel; in seeking, as St. Vincent so often said, to conform her will in all things to that of God.

St. Vincent and St. Louise realized that the acquisition of what St. Paul calls the mind of Christ, the *"sensus Christi,"* was not achieved through a broad, general resolution to act and react as Christ would do. Not only was much reflection and prayer necessary, but one had to learn to say *no* many times to oneself in order to say *yes* to the deeper and higher call of Jesus Christ. In the New Year conference of 1657, St. Vincent touches on the importance of saying *no* to our senses, our will and our judgment, in order that we may respond more fully to God. It is clear that St. Vincent put a high premium on mortification, if our service of the poor was going to be according to the mind of Christ. What he was saying to the Sisters on that January day, 1657, was: look to your own spiritual perfection, look to the quality of your personal union with Christ, look to the mortification of your exterior and interior senses before you set out to help the poor. And if we are not just to pick the currants from the cake, we must accept, not only what St. Vincent said about the importance of serving the poor, but also what he said about the importance of striving after evangelical perfection in our personal lives and accept, too, the importance of mortification of senses, will and judgment in realizing that ideal. I have little doubt but that he and St Louise would say the same to us on this New Year's Day, 1983. St. Louise, for her part, would express the hope, as she did in her letter to the Sister Servant at Angers, that the beginning of this New Year would recapture for us all the first fervor of our vocation in the Community. Today, being a feast of Our Lady, she might recall for us the fact that at the end of her letter to the Sister Servant of Angers she asked her to tell one of the Sisters that she would pray to Our Lady for the intention which the Sister had confidently entrusted to the Mother of God.

May Our Blessed Lady, whom the Church honors in a special way on New Year's Day, obtain for us the graces of fidelity and perseverance. May she accompany us each day as we climb the mountain of perfection which is the mountain of the Lord.

Holy Year of Redemption

25 March 1983   Paris, France

Mother Rogé, Father Lloret, my dear Sisters,

I could begin this morning's conference by announcing to you that this is the year of *"The Open Door."* In a few hours' time, the Holy Father in Rome will knock three times on the door of St. Peter's which is known as the Holy Door, sealed by Paul VI at the closing of the last Holy Year, and the masonry will fall down. When the dust has subsided, the Pope himself will, as a humble pilgrim, enter through that Holy Door, to be followed in the course of the coming twelve months by thousands and thousands of other pilgrims, all of whom will be seeking God's pardon for their sins and the grace of reconciliation with the Church, which is the Body of Christ. The special grace which the Holy Father has requested us to ask of God is a deeper appreciation of that central grace in all our lives—the grace of the Redemption brought to us by Our Lord Jesus Christ Himself.

"The specific grace of the year of the Redemption is," he has written, *"therefore, a renewed discovery of the love of God Who gives Himself, and a deeper realization of the inscrutable riches of the Paschal Mystery of Christ gained through the daily experience of Christian life in all its forms. The various practices of this Jubilee Year should be directed towards this grace, with a continual effort which presupposes and requires detachment from sin and from the mentality of the world which 'lies in the power of the evil one' and from all that impedes or slows down the process of conversion."* (Jubilee of Redemption, §8, 6 Jan. 1983).

To turn your minds away from Rome for a moment and back here to France, I have been haunted these last few days by the scene of those four Daughters of Charity of Arras who in the course of the French Revolution gave their lives for the faith at Cambrai on the 26 June 1794. We are told that, as they were led to execution, they sang joyfully the stanzas of the Ave Maris Stella. The final line of the first stanza of that hymn, which should be so dear to every Daughter of Charity, is one where Our Lady is saluted as *"Felix coeli porta,"* the happy door of heaven. It is a most felicitous phrase for, not only was Mary the door through which the Word Incarnate came when He entered into this poor, sinful, distressed world of ours, but she is the door through which all of us, now become adopted children of God, our Father, through baptism, and co-heirs with Christ, make our pilgrim way back to God.

Mary is the open door of heaven. Her Son referred to Himself as the door, *"I am the door of the sheep,"* (Jn 10:9) and we are living in the year of the open door. As we contemplate the image of the open door—be it Christ Himself, Mary His Mother, or the great jubilee door which the Pope is opening today—try to live this year as an open door. Be a door that is fully open to others, especially to the poor. Be an open door to the members of your community, that is, be transparent, be simple in your relationships with one another in love. Be an open door to all: allow people to use you, to pass through you. Allow people to take you for granted. Be an open door by being humble. An open door does not discriminate, allowing some to pass and some not. In one word, open the doors of your hearts widely to all this year, and especially to the poor. Open the doors of your hearts widely to those who claim a little more understanding from you. Open the doors of your hearts more widely to the claims which obedience is making upon you in this year, so historic for the future of the Company. In a word, open the doors of your hearts so widely today that neither the poor, nor your Sister Servant nor your Sister companions will feel any hesitancy in coming to ask of you a simple service in the name of Christ, Who is ever standing at the door and knocking. (cf. Rv 3:20).

It is time, you may be saying, that I made some reference to the great feast which we are celebrating within our Community. So, let me congratulate you on the Renovation of your Vows which you have made here this morning. The Renovation made by so many thousands of Sisters today has a special character. The Renovation today is being made in the course of the three hundred-fiftieth Anniversary of the Foundation of the Company. The Renovation this year, too, is being made in the course of the three hundred-fiftieth Anniversary of the death of Marguerite Naseau, whose life and character have been so magnificently evoked by Mother Rogé in her letter of the 2 February. The Renovation this year is being made on the very day when the Holy Father is proclaiming a Jubilee Year in honor of our redemption by Our Lord Jesus Christ, through Whom all good things come.

The grace of Renovation is indeed a marvelous grace, but I am well aware how costly a grace it must be for some Sisters, how much humility its asking must call for. Let us not forget the measure of responsibility which rests on Sister Servants, Visitatrixes, Mother General and her Council in asking this grace for you. Let us not now look back, but rather forward: *". . . forgetting what lies behind and straining forward to what lies ahead, I press on towards the goal for the prize of the upward call of God in Christ Jesus."* (Phil 3:13-14). Yes, your vocation, my dear Sisters, is to press forward in all things lovingly towards Christ, lovingly towards Him in your service of the poor.

Allow me to single out one word which for all Christians, and especially for us during this Jubilee Year, should often be on our lips and in our hearts. It is a word to which I have already referred. It is *reconciliation*. It is a word which lies at the very heart of the Sacrament of Penance which has been and is such a constant concern of the present Pope. It is the theme of the Synod to be held by the Pope in Rome next October.

My suggestion to each Sister in each community on this Renovation Day is that this year she should strive to engrave that word, *reconciliation*, deep in her heart and in her consciousness. Let the Sacrament of Reconciliation find a new place in her life. Ask not what you may be getting out of the Sacrament of Penance, but rather ask what Christ, the Spouse of your soul, wishes to offer you through it. Secondly, reconciliation in the local community. There is hardly a community in the Company without its tensions, misunderstandings and the difficulties that come from the diversity of temperaments that compose it. But would it not be wonderful to think that during this Jubilee Year there would be no day when the sun would go down on the anger of even one Sister in our Community? Would it not be wonderful to think that at the end of each day of this Jubilee Year, each Sister in her local community would be reconciled one with the other?

Some time ago I was asked publicly what I thought of two Sisters who in the same community were not talking to each other for quite a long time and who were in that way a source of pain and of scandal to the Community. It did not take me too long to reply. *"What,"* I asked, *"would St. Vincent reply to such a question?"* Here is a typical reply of his: *"Now I recommend you, as you have this holy custom of asking forgiveness, never to fail to do so when you have given reason to anyone to feel annoyed, and at once, or at least in the evening, to ask her forgiveness for having mortified her. This is in conformity with the Word of God which says: 'Let not the sun go down on your wrath'."* (Eph 4:26). (Conf. Eng. ed., 4 March 1658, p. 1043).

He would motivate each of those Sisters to humbly ask pardon of each other. All of us are aware how difficult this is. All of us are aware, too, that there will be momentary periods when Sisters find it difficult to talk to one another because of some hurt, real or imaginary. There will be in some of our communities occasions when Sisters will lapse into what can only be described as 'wounded silence'. But let not such silences be for long. Let not the sun go down upon them. What I say to you, I am quite certain St. Vincent and St. Louise would address to communities this opening day of a year that is characterized by the joy of reconciliation. Jesus Christ wept over Jerusalem because it did not know the things that were to its peace. We must not allow Him to weep over even one of our communities because it does not know the things that are to its peace, through the practice of reconciliation. This is the year when we honor in a special way the fact that Christ reconciled us to Himself and gave us the ministry of reconciliation, entrusting to us the message of reconciliation. So we are ambassadors for Christ, God *"making His appeal through us."* (2 Cor 5:18-20). What a vocation is yours, my dear Sisters, to be *"ambassadors of Christ"* to the poor with His message of reconciliation and that with Him there is to be found *"abundant redemption."* (Col 1:14).

As you try to live this ideal of reconciliation in your local community throughout this year, be conscious of the gentle presence of Mary, the Mother of God, who, through her obedient generosity, brought it about that the Word was able to take flesh in her womb and become the *"Felix coeli porta"* for the millions and millions of sinful, squabbling children whom she is always trying to reconcile, so that she may present them to her son, Jesus—she who is the most clement, the most loving, the most sweet Virgin Mary.

Yes, Sisters, by the grace of God, just try to be in this Jubilee Year for the poor and for each other what Mary already is for each one of us—*"felix coeli porta"*—a happy door to heaven.

Generosity

4 April 1983   Rome, Italy

Dear Members of the Marian Youth Group,

Welcome to Rome! Let me first tell you about three people who once came to Rome and had an audience with Pope Leo XIII. The Pope asked the first person how long he would stay in Rome and the reply was, one

week. *"You,"* said the Pope, *"will see quite a lot." "And you,"* the Pope
said to the second, *"How long do you intend to stay here in Rome?"*
"A month," was the reply. *"Oh, you will see a lot,"* the Pope observed.
Then the Pope asked the third person how long he would stay and the
reply was, one year. *"You,"* said the Pope, *"will see nothing."*

So it seems the longer you stay in Rome, the less you see, and there
is truth in that because, when you live in Rome, you promise yourself
to visit all sorts of places, but somehow you keep postponing the visits.
So I hope that during your short stay here in Rome, you will see much
and that you will return to France very happy but very tired.

I do not know if you have yet visited the Church which is called San
Andrea delle Fratte. That is a Church which has a special connection
with the rue du Bac in Paris. Twelve years after Our Lady had entrusted
the Miraculous Medal to St. Catherine in Paris, a Jew named Alphonse
Ratisbonne, who was not a Catholic but who had consented to wear the
Miraculous Medal as a favor for a friend of his, stepped inside that
Church while his friend went into the sacristy to talk to a priest. Quite
suddenly Our Lady of the Miraculous Medal appeared to Monsieur
Ratisbonne and immediately he received the fullness of the Faith and
became a Catholic. He also became a priest and founded two Congregations whose principal work is praying for and helping the Jewish
people towards the full acceptance of Christ.

It was in this Church, too, that a young Polish priest celebrated his
first Mass and to which he often came to pray. His name was Maximilian Kolbe. The Pope canonized him last October. You will remember that St. Maximilian Kolbe freely took the place of a married man
who had been condemned to die in a starvation bunker in Auschwitz.
St. Maximilian Kolbe had a great devotion to Our Lady and he often
went to that Church to deepen his devotion to Our Lady. I think there
is an important point for us all here. You cannot be really devoted to
Our Lady without being at the same time generous to others. If you
want to know how devoted you are to Our Lady, don't count just the
prayers you say to her every day but also the acts of generosity you
show to others.

I do not know if you have the phrase which is in the English language:
All roads lead to Rome. The origin of the phrase may have been that,

when pilgrims were walking to Rome, it helped them to think that they would eventually arrive there, no matter what road they took. We know that all roads don't lead to Rome, but we can be sure of this: that all true devotion to Our Lady will bring you to her Son, Jesus Christ, and through Him to the home which He has prepared for us all in Heaven.

Lastly, I want you to pray especially for the Daughters of Charity of France, who are holding an important meeting in the rue du Bac these days. I will be going to see them tomorrow and I will bring your greetings to them and the promise that you will pray for them.

Now, if I go on talking much longer, a month will soon have passed and you will say to yourselves: Pope Leo XIII was right. We came to Rome and spent a month there and saw nothing. We saw nothing in Rome because Father McCullen talked too much! Thank you very much, Fathers and Sisters and leaders, for inviting me to meet you here this evening. May Our Lord and His Mother be with you all in a special way these days.

Listening Heart

6 April 1983   Paris, France

Mother Rogé, my dear Sisters and my dear Confreres,

The Emmaus incident, as recounted by St. Luke, could be described as one of the finest short stories in all literature. It is a story which begins in sadness and ends in joy. It is a story which begins in a mood of disillusionment and ends in one of hope. It is a story that describes how Christ gently put light where there was darkness and faith where there was unbelief. Above all, it is a story that speaks volumes about the humility, sensitivity and gentleness of Christ.

The incident opens in a mood of depression. The two disciples are walking away from Jerusalem, sad and disheartened. They are joined by the Risen Christ who, perhaps noticing their sadness, sympathetically asks them, *"What matters are you discussing, as you walk along?"* (Lk 24:17).

Often the best help we can offer a person who is depressed is to afford them an opportunity of talking. Jesus Christ does exactly that when He encounters the depression of the two disciples. So often depressed people seek only a listening ear, or rather, a listening heart. Jesus Christ offered to the two disciples a listening heart. By listening attentively and lovingly to them, he drained the depression out of them.

Many of you here have discovered in your work for the poor that, while their material needs are often great, their spiritual needs may be greater still. Many of you have discovered, too, that on many occasions, when the poor present a problem to you or seek your advice, you come eventually to realize that their real need is not your advice, but rather the sympathy of your listening heart. Often I feel that I have given advice to people when what they were really asking for was understanding and compassion. I have found words like *"What you ought to do is . . . "* come too easily to my lips when speaking to a poor person.

In the dialogue between Our Lord and the two disciples, did you notice the slight note of sarcasm used by the disciples? *"You must be the only person staying in Jerusalem who does not know the things that have been happening there these days."* (Ibid., v. 18). Jesus ignored the note of sarcasm and simply asked, *"What things?"*. It is always wise to ignore sarcasm and wiser never to employ it, for it is a very wounding weapon.

When Jesus had by His loving and attentive listening lifted the disciples out of their depression and thus given them joy, He went on to open the meaning of the Scriptures to them. The whole experience culminated in the Eucharist. *"They recognized Him in the breaking of the bread."* (Ibid., v. 35). But before that, did you notice the delicacy of the Risen Christ Who was unwilling to force His company on the two disciples. *"He appeared to be going further but they constrained Him, saying: 'Stay with us for it is toward evening, and the day is now far spent'."* (Ibid., vv. 28, 29). If Our Lord's ignoring of the sarcasm of the two disciples was an indication of His gentleness, then His unwillingness to force His company on the disciples was a manifestation, not only of respect for their persons, but of that humility of heart which He has asked us to learn from Him.

In our era we hear much about the need to respect individual persons in all that we do for them. That is not sufficient for a Daughter of Charity. In addition to respect for the person of the poor, the Daughter of Charity must manifest also in her attitude the humility of Christ. In the teaching of our Founders the work, whatever it is which we do for the poor, should be three-dimensional—simple, humble, loving. When you come to think of it, the Christ of the Emmaus Road was just that: simple and humble and loving in all that He did for His two disciples. They not only responded joyfully, but even their hearts began to burn within them. (cf., Ibid., v. 32). The beginning of all our service for the poor lies in being simple, humble and loving persons through our contemplation of Christ in prayer and through our intimate contact with Him in the Eucharist. *"And their eyes were opened . . . ."* (Ibid., v. 31). May He open our eyes to see more clearly and accept that truth as, like Him, we try to give new heart and new hope to the poor whom we meet on the road of life.

Fiftieth Anniversary of Priesthood

28 April 1983   Rome, Italy

The Acts of the Apostles is a book which is full of incidents of deep human interest. The opening phrase of the first reading of this evening's Mass is one such. Paul, Barnabas and John Mark had reached Perga and it was there that, to quote St. Luke, *"John Mark left them to go back to Jerusalem."* (Acts 13:13). What reason John Mark had for leaving them we do not know. It has been suggested that, as Paul was intent upon advancing into very difficult, mountainous country, John Mark did not feel up to it and decided that it would be better for him to return to his own country. Or again it has been suggested that perhaps John Mark just felt homesick and did not have the stamina which was needed, and which Paul had, to face an unknown situation that called for much physical and moral strength.

This evening we are happy to have Father Richardson here with us in the Curia and to join with him in thanking God for fifty years of his priesthood. I know that Father Richardson would like me to dwell upon the theme of thanksgiving for the millions of graces which he has received during that time. During the coming weeks he will look back gratefully on his first three years of priesthood here in Rome, when he studied, like so many of you, in one of the Roman universities. He will look back gratefully, too, on his twenty years of work in the formation of future priests for our own Community and for the Archdiocese of Los Angeles. He will recall with gratitude his years as Vice-Visitor in Los Angeles until his election as St. Vincent's twentieth successor in 1968. He will feel especially grateful for the innumerable graces bestowed on him during the years when as Superior General he guided the two Communities of St. Vincent towards a greater realization of their vocation to serve Christ in the poor. With him, Father Richardson would like us to say over and over again the response of today's psalm: *"I will sing forever of your love, O Lord."* (Ps 89:2).

What I would like to dwell on this evening and in the context of the first reading is Father Richardson's courage which prompted him to offer himself for the mission in Kenya. Perhaps St. Vincent would prefer me to use the word *zeal* instead of courage. Like St. Paul, Father Richardson had the zeal to face an unknown world, far from his own nation, and to dedicate himself to the work of the formation of future priests, a work which, in St. Vincent's view, could not be more noble. Far from seeking an honorable retirement on the occasion of his Jubilee, he intends to return once again to Kenya to resume his work of leaving a number of successors behind him in the priesthood in a continent that we know was very dear to the heart of St. Vincent.

When St. Paul and his companions had penetrated into the mountainous country of Turkey and reached Antioch, the presidents of the synagogue sent a message to Paul: *"Brothers, if you would like to address some words of encouragement to the congregation, please do so."* (Acts 13:15). Father Richardson, you do not have to speak one word here this evening. Your presence is an encouragement to us all. Your life is an encouragement for us to live the ideals of St. Vincent: of lifelong fidelity to the priesthood, of detachment of heart, of love for the Community and of zeal for souls.

In the synagogue service in which St. Paul participated in Antioch, he would have recited the Shema, the eighteen blessings. Father Richardson, we pray, not eighteen blessings but eighteen times eighteen blessings on your head and on your work in preaching the Gospel to the poor and in forming men to continue the work of Christ, our high priest.

Crisis of Faith in the World Today

9 May 1983   Louvain, Belgium

My dear Confreres,

The late Cardinal Heenan of London used to tell a story of how, when he was a young priest, he traveled into rural parts of England on a Sunday morning in order to celebrate Mass for Catholics who were isolated and far from any Church. On one particular Sunday he went to a very remote part of the country where there were very few Catholics. He parked his car and went off to a little hall where the Catholics had gathered for Mass. After Mass, he came back to his car only to find the four tires of his car slashed. It was a gesture of hostility against the presence of a Roman Catholic priest in a part of England which was very Protestant. The Cardinal used to say that his first reaction was one of great annoyance. In such a remote part of England, it would be difficult to find four new tires on a Sunday afternoon. However, when he had calmed down, the Cardinal said that he found himself beginning to thank God that the old religious spirit in England was not yet dead. His four slashed tires were proof that somebody was interested enough in religion to show that he disapproved of Catholicism. It is, in a sense, easier to put up with outright hostility to religion from people, than to live in a society that is indifferent and apathetic to religion and the Gospel.

I was reminded of this incident of which Cardinal Heenan spoke, by the phrase in this morning's Gospel. *"They will expel you from the synagogues and indeed the hour is coming when anyone who kills you will think he is doing a holy duty for God."* (Jn 16:2). That is not the situation here in Belgium or, indeed, in any of our western European countries. What can pain very many priests today is not the threat of persecution, but the fact of religious indifference and apathy. When, in times of persecution, there was a price on a priest's head, when he was, as the police today would put it, a "wanted" man, he was kept aware of the fact that he had in his possession a great treasure, namely, his faith. Today the priest, for many people, is far from being a "wanted" man. He is made to feel to be just irrelevant and that can be a very painful experience.

You will have noticed in today's Gospel passage that Our Lord said: *"I have told you all this so that your faith may not be shaken."* (Jn 16:1). That phrase recalls what earlier that night He had said to Peter: *"Simon, Simon, behold, Satan demanded to have you that he might sift you like wheat, but I have prayed for you, that your faith may not fail."* (Lk 22:31-32).

Whether it be persecution or the pain of suffering that comes from the religious indifference of society, the crisis will always be one of faith. The crisis at the present time for so many priests is not one of celibacy but of faith. Whatever the trial be, we have this assurance: that Christ has prayed for us and still prays that our faith will not fail, because He who now sits at the right hand of the Father is always living to make intercession for us.

Faith, as we tell our people, is a gift. If it is a gift, it is a grace. We know, too, from our theology that the economy of God's grace has its laws. There are some graces that only come to us when we ask for them. Incidentally, it was one of the points that Our Lady made clear to St. Catherine in the rue du Bac: the diamonds, from which no rays came forth, were those graces for which Our Lady had not been asked.

Because we are members of the Congregation, there are also graces which will only come to us through being full, active members of the Congregation. There are graces which will only come to us when we gather with Confreres, as we are today, to ask God as a body, for the graces which not only the Congregation needs, but which each one of us needs in his own particular ministry. It was St. Vincent's vision that men went forth from Community to preach the Gospel to the poor and his vision of Community was one in which men shared a life of prayer and drew from each other the strength that true community life can give. As our Constitutions put it: *"The Vincentian Community is, therefore, organized to prepare its apostolic activity and to encourage and help it continually."* (C. 19).

What I am trying to say to you, my dear Confreres, is that, if we are not to be discouraged and disheartened by the religious indifference that surrounds us, our faith needs to be strong. Our faith can only be strong if we put ourselves in full contact with Christ Who has prayed that our faith will not fail. And we are only in full contact with Christ when we have more than a superficial contact with the Community which He has raised up through His servant, Vincent de Paul.

Yes, it is important that we do not lose faith in Christ, that is clear. It is important also that we do not lose faith in the Congregation which, as St. Vincent saw it, was the little ship in which we go to heaven. It is important that we do not forget that vow of stability by which we promised God that we would work for Him in and through the Congregation *"toto vitae tempore."* In a word, it is important that we do not break faith with God. *"I am bound by the vows which I have made."* (Ps 56:13).

"To this end we always pray for you, that our God may make you worthy of His call and may fulfill every good resolve and work of faith by His power, so that the name of Our Lord Jesus may be glorified in you and you in Him, according to the grace of our God and the Lord Jesus Christ." (2 Thes 1:11-12).

Hospitality

19 June 1983   Livorno (Leghorn), Italy

My dear Friends in Jesus Christ,

My first words today must be words of appreciation and thanks to the Bishop of Livorno, Bishop Ablondi, who has kindly invited us all to rejoice with him in the celebration of the first Mass offered in this Church, dedicated to St. Elizabeth Ann Seton. Many of us have come from different countries, especially from that country beloved by St. Elizabeth Ann, and what we are experiencing here today is the hospitality of Bishop Ablondi and of the Diocese of Livorno. So let me, in the name of all of us who have come from dioceses near and far, offer to Bishop Ablondi, to his priests, to the people of the parish and to the people of the diocese, our thanks for the hospitality we are receiving from you this day.

Hospitality is one of the virtues singled out by both St. Peter and St. Paul as one which should distinguish a Christian community. *"Practice hospitality ungrudgingly to one another,"* wrote St. Peter (I Pt 4:9), while St. Paul in the second reading of today's Mass exhorts the

Christians in Rome to *"contribute to the needs of the saints. Practice hospitality."* (Rom 12:13).

When we read the biography of St. Elizabeth Ann and in particular the history of her relations with the bishops, priests and people of this diocese, it is a story of hospitality generously shown and of hospitality graciously received .

In 1803 it was the sensibility of the Filicchi family that prevailed on the authorities of Livorno to shorten the period of quarantine required by law to enable St. Elizabeth Ann and her sick husband to enter this city. It was hospitality that prompted the Filicchi family with marvelous delicacy to visit St. Elizabeth Ann and her husband daily. And it was in this city that the mortal remains of St. Elizabeth Ann's husband, William, received the hospitality of a final resting place after his death on 27 December 1803.

It was the hospitality of Livorno that enabled St. Elizabeth Ann to have that significant experience in the Sanctuary of Montenero, an experience which was to have a transforming effect on her life, and through her on the members of her Community in the United States, the Daughters of Charity, who this year are celebrating the three hundred-fiftieth anniversary of their foundation. It was the hospitality of Our Lady at Montenero that showed her the fruit of her womb, really present in the Eucharist, which is at once *"the source and the apex"* of all charitable work.

It is touching to read how St. Elizabeth Ann reciprocated the hospitality she received here by the welcome she gave to Antonio Filicchi when he spent a year in the United States. From the flower of hospitality given and received, there grew up that garden of charitable works which delights us still today. As that garden grew, Livorno through the years continued to show hospitality to members of her own family, and to the new spiritual family which God was raising up through her.

The latest gesture in this series of being generous *"in offering hospitality"* is our celebration today. Seventeen years have passed since Bishop Emilio Guano announced his intention of making St. Elizabeth Ann feel more at home in this diocese and city by dedicating one of the parishes to her, and placing it under her special patronage. Bishop Ablondi has over the years enthusiastically supported that project of making St. Elizabeth Ann welcome in this city, while since 1968 Father Gino Franchi has watched the building of this church grow, and has watched, too, I am certain, the people of this parish grow in *"grace before God and men."* (Lk 2:52).

Today, then, we are celebrating hospitality, given and received by the spiritual family of St. Elizabeth Ann, who through their generosity have helped to make this church a permanent place for St. Elizabeth Ann in this city which must in heaven still hold a special place in her interest and in her affection.

Gathered in this church today we are a very diverse group of people. There is a diversity of nationalities among us and a diversity, too, of languages. St. Paul would express it in his own profound way and remind us, as we heard in the second reading, that *"though many we are one body in Christ and individually members one of another. We have gifts that differ according to the favor bestowed on each of us."* (Rom 12:4-5). It is that diversity of gifts, that diversity of nationalities along with a consciousness of being one in Christ, that is the secret of the growth of that beautiful flower of hospitality whose fragrance we are enjoying today. It has been *"planted by the Lord to show His glory."* (Is 61:3). Let us, then, rejoice and be glad, for this is the day which the Lord has made.

Liberation Theology

15 July 1983   Fortaleza, Brazil

My dear Friends in Jesus Christ,

The author of a short book of the Bible, that of Ecclesiastes, takes a special delight in reminding us that there is nothing new under the sun. If he were alive today and heard us talking about the importance of liberation theology, he might shake his head and say: *"Did I not tell you more than two thousand years ago that there is nothing new under the sun?"* Liberation theology is not new. One of the most important books of the Old Testament is taken up largely with that idea. The Book of Exodus is an account of how the Israelite people were liberated from the Egyptians, and one could say that the remainder of the Bible is a celebration of that liberation, which was repeated again and again throughout their history. The Old Testament is in great part a celebration of liberation, and the theology of the Old Testament has as one of its most profound themes that of liberation. The first reading of today's Mass gives us the account of how the people were instructed to celebrate that liberation. For centuries they celebrated it faithfully each year in the Feast of the Passover. The Feast of the Passover will always remain significant for the Christians, for it was in the course of celebrating the Passover, or the great liberation from Egypt, that Our Lord instituted the Sacrifice of the Mass. Our Lord's own sacrificial death is the great liberation of mankind and each Mass is a celebration of that event.

When we speak of liberation today, our minds center upon the poor. We think, not only of the sufferings of the poor, but in a special way of sufferings that are caused to them through the injustice of others. When we think about how they can be liberated, we think in a particular way how we could achieve greater social justice in our society.

All of us here are aware of the immense work which in his lifetime St. Vincent de Paul accomplished to liberate the poor of his day from their sufferings. It must be said that explicit references to injustice, as being the cause of their sufferings, are few in his writings. He was a man of his time and the demands of social justice, as well as the responsibilities of ownership, had not been spelled out as clearly as they have been in our day. If St. Vincent de Paul was a man of his time, it must not be forgotten that he was also a man of the Church. Listen to this: *"The sort of liberation we are talking about, knows how to use evangelical means, which have their own distinctive efficacy. It does not resort to violence of any sort or to the dialectics of class struggle. Instead it relies on the vigorous energy and activity of Christians, who are moved by the spirit to respond to the cries of countless millions of their brothers and sisters."* (Puebla, §486). Take out the word *dialectics* from that quotation and it would sit quite easily in almost any of St. Vincent's letters. It is, in fact, a quotation from the document of Puebla. St. Vincent would be the first to agree that *"whatever the miseries or sufferings that afflict human beings, it is not through violence, power plays or political systems, but through the truth about human beings that they will find their way to a better future."* (Ibid. §551).

St. Vincent de Paul was a man of his time and a man of the Church. He was, above all, a man of the Gospel and in his correspondence, in his conferences, in his contacts, he was never far from the Person of Jesus Christ. The pages of his correspondence and of his conferences are penetrated by the Gospel. It is for that reason that it can be confidently asserted that on the theme of liberation, he would remind us, as the document of Puebla does, that *"we must try to read the political scene from the standpoint of the Gospel, not vice versa. "*(Ibid. §559).

May the Lord of the Sabbath, Who is the Lord of history, be in our hearts and on our lips, so that we may worthily proclaim the Gospel, in the name of the Father and of the Son and of the Holy Spirit.

Lost Sheep

9 August 1983   Sao Paulo, Brazil

My dear Sisters and Confreres,

The Gospel passage which the Church sets before us today is in part about numbers. There are a number of disciples surrounding Jesus and for a moment He takes his eyes off them and looks at one small little child, addresses an invitation to the child to come close to Him, and then invites all His disciples to look at this child. *"I assure you, "*Jesus says, *"unless you change and become like little children, you shall not enter the Kingdom of heaven. "*Today at the end of the Gospel passage, Jesus talks about the man who had a hundred sheep and loses one. He leaves the ninety-nine and goes off to find the one sheep that was lost.

As I speak to you, I am conscious that I do so in the most populous city of your country, and one of the largest cities of the world. I imagine that at times you must feel that it is not a question of leaving ninety-nine sheep and looking for one that is lost, but rather of leaving one sheep and searching for the ninety-nine that are lost. You live daily with the problem, or rather the challenge, *"How can we reach the millions of this city with the good news which in the Name of Christ the Church wants to bring to them?"*

To me it is always a clear manifestation of God's grace that in the face of so many millions who are not in direct contact with the Church, priests and religious and lay leaders do not lose confidence in the task of trying to reach the crowds with the message of Christ. So often the visible results of your dedication to God's people and especially to His poor are very meager and unspectacular.

There is much encouragement for us in the final phrase of today's Gospel: *"It is no part of your heavenly Father's plan that a single one of these little ones should ever come to grief."* (Mt 18:14). We make our plans: our pastoral plans, our Provincial plans, our Community plans with a view to reaching the ninety-nine. We do well. Let us not forget, however, the allusion which Our Lord makes today to *the plan* of His heavenly Father. That is the plan which matters most, and all our pastoral plans must take account of that great plan which in this life remains for us in large measure hidden from our eyes. *"Who has known the mind of God? . . . O the depths of the Wisdom of God."* (Rom 11:33).

It should be a source of confidence to us that God has His own plans for reaching the ninety-nine, that everything does not depend on us. Certainly He seeks and counts on our cooperation in reaching the ninety-nine. The truth is that God's grace, God's love, God's wisdom is not exhausted, when I myself reach the point of exhaustion, frustration and failure in what I try to do for Him in the salvation of souls, in the search for the ninety-nine.

To return to the opening incident of today's Gospel, I must at all times think of myself as a child. *"Unless you become as little children . . . ,"* (Lk 18:17) as simple as a child in the confidence which I have in the power and goodness of God. *"Simplicity,"* remarked St. Vincent to the Daughters of Charity, *"is my gospel."* (Conf. Eng. ed., 24 Feb. 1653, p. 538). It is part of God's plan that simplicity should clearly characterize all of us who are members of St. Vincent's Community and in all that we do for the poor who *"are lying like sheep without a shepherd."* (Mk 6:34).

Four Dimensions of Human Existence

15 August 1983   Paris, France

Mother Rogé, Father Lloret and my dear Sisters,

On 5 July 1642, St. Louise wrote a letter to Sister Jeanne Lepintre in which, speaking about another Sister, she remarked: *"I believe that she will also return to the city around mid-August so as to celebrate fittingly this holy feast and to strengthen herself in virtue. Pray for all our Sisters who share her intention."* (*Spiritual Writings of Louise de Marillac*, ltr. 64, p. 77).

For St. Louise it was not necessary to spell out what feast would be celebrated in mid-August. For, shining like the sun at midday, the feast of Our Lady's Assumption into heaven marks the middle of August each year. As we here in Paris celebrate it, it could be said that, like the Sister to whom St. Louise alludes, the whole Company comes, at least in spirit, to the Mother House to celebrate it. For it is on that day that we honor her who by her example and work continues to do what St. Louise did for the first generation of Sisters. Mother Rogé, in the name of the whole Company, I wish you a very happy and peace-filled feast day.

Year after year we celebrate our feast days in the Community. We do so with gratitude and joy. The lengthening shadows of the years bring us all to the realization that, however good our intentions have been, there is much work which we have left undone, much unfinished business. I recall a saintly priest saying, as he was dying, that it was not what he had done during his life that troubled him, so much as what he had failed to do. It is significant that when the Confiteor of our Mass was being revised some years ago, a phrase about our sins of omission was inserted into it. Which of us at the end of our cycle of years on earth will not want to call upon the mercy of God for our failures to do the good He so often invites us to do?

On the night before He died, Our Lord prayed to His Father: *"I have finished the work which You gave Me to do."* (Jn 17:4). Only one other person of the human race, as far as we know, could pray that prayer with utter certainty, and that person was Mary, the Mother of God. *"I have finished the work you gave me to do."* (Ibid.). We know only the great moments in Mary's work for her Father in heaven. We reflect upon them each time as we pray the joyful, sorrowful and the first three glorious mysteries of the Rosary. When we reach the fourth glorious mystery of the Rosary, we do not think so much of the work which God gave her to do, but rather of the recognition by God of the perfection of her work, and of the cooperation she gave at every moment of her life to the grace of God for the accomplishment of His Will.

The mysteries of our faith are not conundrums or puzzles given to us to exercise or to tease our intelligences. The mysteries of our faith come and present themselves to us like the Person of Christ Himself. He came that we might *"have life and have it more abundantly."* (Jn 10:10). So, too, with the mystery of this day's feast. It is presented to us by Christ and His Church that we *"may have life and have it more abundantly."* (Ibid.).

If the mystery of the Immaculate Conception could be said to focus our minds on the beauty of Mary's soul, the mystery of her Assumption into heaven could be said to direct our attention to the present beauty and perfection of her body. The two mysteries must be taken together: they mark the beginning and the end of Mary's earthly existence. Indeed, when Pius XII defined the Assumption of Our Lady in 1950, it was remarked that he was but completing the work of Pius IX who, a hundred years earlier, had defined the Immaculate Conception.

The apostolates of the Company are directed towards both the souls and bodies of the poor. Our Founders in their work for the poor moved easily from the care of the bodies of the poor to the care of their souls, and back again. Our Founders lived their lives with a heightened consciousness of the four dimensions of human existence on this earth, namely, body and soul, time and eternity. Some of us lesser people can, even in our service of the poor, become so absorbed in one of the four dimensions that we almost lose sight of the other three. Today's feast reminds us of the importance of all four dimensions in our service of the poor.

At the moment of the Incarnation, it could be said that eternity penetrated into time in a new way. At the moment of the Assumption, it could be said that time penetrated into eternity in a new way. On the feast of the Incarnation, we say, with St. Leo the Great, that Mary conceived her Son first in her mind and then in her body, while on the feast of the Assumption our thoughts are centered on the beauty of her body as an expression of the unique beauty of her soul.

In all that you do for the poor, you are penetrating their lives with rays of eternity. In providing for the simplest needs of their bodies, you are lifting up their minds to the God Who created their souls. Perhaps in the monotonous round of your daily work, it does not always seem like that to you. But then, who other than God could have assured Mary of Nazareth that in what she was doing in the home, she was preparing her Son for His Resurrection and herself for her Assumption, body and soul, into heaven. In moments of discouragement, reflect on the theological fact that the vocation of Mary, the Virgin Mother of Nazareth, comes from the same living God Who today calls you to be a servant of the poor in the Company of the Daughters of Charity.

What St. Louise calls "the feast of mid-August" is indeed a mystery of God, but a mystery that gives new life to us, for on this day we, in the words of your new Constitutions, look at Mary *"to make of their lives, 'an act of worship of God as She did, and to make their worship a commitment of their lives'."* (*Marialis Cultus*, §21; C. 2.16).

With love, then, let us celebrate this feast and be joyful and glad.

Hound of Heaven

22 September 1983   Costa Rica

My dear Confreres,

At the beginning of this century there was a Catholic poet, Francis Thompson, who lived in London. He was a very poor man and had once been a candidate for the priesthood. He wrote a celebrated poem called *The Hound of Heaven*. The poet envisages a hunt in which God is the hound in pursuit of the poet himself. The poem begins like this:

I fled Him down the nights and down the days;
I fled Him down the arches of the years.

At the end the poet is overtaken by the hound and surrenders himself into the loving arms of God, realizing at last that everything in life betrayed him except God Who pursued him with such love.

All things betrayest thee who betrayest Me.

I thought of this poem when I reflected upon the first reading of today's Mass. One could say that the history of the Old Testament is a history of the Hound of Heaven pursuing lovingly His chosen people. The history is an account of how the Israelite people tried to escape from that pursuing love.

It was during the period of the exile that the Israelites realized in a new way the love which God had for them. They experienced His love in a new way also when they were brought back to Jerusalem again and began to rebuild the temple. It was not long seemingly before they began to escape from God's love. They became absorbed in their own personal interests and left aside the task of rebuilding the temple. In today's reading Haggai gently reminds them: *"Is it a time for yourselves to dwell in your paneled houses, while this house lies in ruins?"* (Hg 1:4). The prophet Haggai reminds them that the interests of the Lord must be placed before their own personal comfort: *"Go up into the hills and bring wood, and build the house that I may take pleasure in it and that I may appear in my glory, says the Lord."* (Ibid., v. 8). Equivalently, Haggai was reminding the people that their peace and their freedom could only be guaranteed if they surrendered themselves to the Hound of Heaven.

What the Israelite people were probably facing then was a problem that arose from their new-found affluence. Haggai speaks of paneled houses, something that the Israelites had not known when they were in exile in Babylon. I hardly think that affluence is as great a threat to the Church in Central America as it may be in other parts of the Western world. In my own country there is an old phrase which goes: *"Wooden chalice, golden priest; golden chalice, wooden priest."* The meaning is clear. When the Church falls upon hard times and is poor, the great qualities of the priesthood shine out more clearly than when the Church is comfortable and well-off. In times of prosperity the priest, as Haggai expresses it, can settle into paneled houses and forget about the building of the temple which is the Church of God. I suppose you could say that

St. Vincent was on his way to settling into a paneled house when he went out to seek what he called an honorable retirement.

Happily for us and for millions of others, he heard the call of God to *"go up to the hills and bring wood and build the house"* (Ibid.) of the Lord. I cannot speak for others, but I can speak for myself and say that I can feel the bias towards affluence in my own life. I can testify to a desire to escape from the Hound of Heaven. I can testify to a desire to settle in a paneled house, rather than to go up in the hills and bring wood and build the house of the Lord. I am aware of a desire to escape from the Hound of Heaven Who is pursuing me with His love.

Towards the end of his life, St. Vincent was concerned that the Congregation's failure to live the ideal of evangelical poverty would be the cause of its ruin. There is much food for thought in this observation which St. Vincent made earlier in his life to Father Codoing: *"In the name of God, Monsieur, let us abandon ourselves to the direction of God's loving Providence, and we shall be safe from all sorts of inconveniences that our haste may draw down on us. We are not sufficiently virtuous to be able to carry the burden of abundance and that of apostolic virtue and I fear we may never be, and that the former may ruin the latter."* (Coste II, Eng. ed., ltr. 718, p. 517-518).

More than three centuries have passed since St. Vincent penned those words. His psychological insight remains valid today. Affluence and apostolic virtue, or zeal, do not make good traveling companions. May God give us the grace to keep our hearts detached from all that could weigh heavily upon us and prevent us from going up to the hills to bring wood to build the house of the Lord.

Although the writings of the Old Testament prophets are at times obscure and at other times are what St. John the Evangelist would describe as *"hard sayings,"* still the prophets were essentially men of hope. It could not be otherwise, because if they were, as we believe, inspired by God in their writings, then their writings must breathe hope. Our God is a God of hope. How often do we read in the psalms: *"In you, Lord, do I place my hope . . . .You are my rock and my salvation."* If the prophets could be men of hope, how much more must we be men of hope, we who believe that God took a body like ours and Who died, but is now risen and is *"always living to make intercession"* (Heb 7:25) for us in heaven.

For the Congregation here in Costa Rica, there are new signs of hope. New shoots are beginning to appear on the tree of the Congregation here in Costa Rica. That should give us all new hope. It is also a new appeal from God to us to be faithful to our Constitutions and Statutes which interpret for us today the mind of St. Vincent. Let me end by offering you St. Vincent's own words uttered in a conference to his confreres on 21 February 1659: *"If we do God's Will, He will do ours. Let us seek His glory and be concerned about that, and let us not be worried about anything else. Let us be intent on having God reign in ourselves and in others by all the virtues, and all other temporal things, let us leave to Him. He wills it so. Yes, He will provide us with food and clothes and even with knowledge . . . .Admire (His) confidence. He does not trouble himself about what will happen. Why cannot we have the same hope, if we leave to God the care of all that concerns us and prefer that which He commands? . . . "* (Dodin, pp. 556-557,559).

"My good Jesus teach me to do it and bring it about that I do it . . . " (Ibid. p. 565).

Death of St. Vincent de Paul

27 September 1983   Guatemala

My dear Friends in Jesus Christ,

It was on this day 323 years ago that Saint Vincent de Paul died. He drew his last breath at the time of the day when he was accustomed to rise and to give himself to prayer for an hour before he celebrated the Sacrifice of the Mass. He died, sitting in his armchair, surrounded by a few of his priests and Brothers, shortly before dawn broke over Paris on the 27th of September, 1660.

Among those who watched Saint Vincent die was Father Jean Gicquel. He has left us a detailed account of those last few hours because Father Gicquel kept a diary. There are entries into his diary for the early days of June, and then no more until early September. Perhaps the intervening months have been lost, or perhaps Father Gicquel took a long vacation that year. Anyway, he resumed his diary entries in September and we have a pretty clear picture of what St. Vincent was doing during the last two weeks of his life. Until a few days before he died, he was doing routine business. Then he grew weaker, and Father Gicquel was in and out of his room, and was present with St. Vincent when he died.

St. Vincent's death was not dramatic. What he said of the death of his faithful associate and Confrere, Father Portail, who had, like St. Louise, predeceased him some months earlier, was true of St. Vincent. *"He died as he had lived . . . . "* St. Vincent lived in faith and hope and love, and at the end his faith and hope and love surfaced. *"Credo". . . "Confido."* These words were on his lips during the last hours of his life. And his love, well, there were demands on it to the end: *"Do you bless the confreres?" "Yes." "And the benefactors?" "Yes." "And the Daughters of Charity?" "Yes." "And the Foundlings?" "Yes."* Then when those around him were pushing in prayers to his ear, there is a delightful touch. *"That's enough, "* (Coste XIII, Fr. ed., pp. 190-191) the Saint said with that practicality that characterized his life. You can have too much of a good thing, even of such a good thing as vocal prayer. Silence. In the silence was he reflecting on that passage of the Gospel to which we have listened? *"When did I see Thee hungry . . . As long as you gave it to one of these least of My brethren, you gave it to Me . . . . "* (Mt 25:44). The last word they saw shape on his lips was that of *Jesus.*

What happened after that we can only guess, for we see now in a dark manner. We do know that years later the Church gave us an infallible assurance that Vincent de Paul enjoys today the vision of God. And that means that he possesses and is possessed by the Source of all that is good and true and beautiful. We know, too, that he shares intensely with Jesus Christ His prayer that *"where I am now, you also may be."* (Jn 14:3). Meantime, we live on to express the quality, the tint, the tone of the love of God which was in the heart of Vincent de Paul and which found such deep expression in his love for the poor. Our vocation is to preserve for the present-day world the quality of that love which graced the person of St. Vincent de Paul.

During his long life St. Vincent could never have imagined that three centuries later a very popular film would be made about his life. In that film there is a marvelous scene towards the end of it, where Queen Anne of Austria is talking to St. Vincent. He is an old man and the Queen is reminding him of all that he achieved during his lifetime. St. Vincent keeps shaking his head and saying that he has done nothing. The Queen insists further and St. Vincent repeats again: *"I have done nothing."* Finally the Queen gets somewhat impatient with the Saint and says to him: *"If you say you have done nothing in your lifetime for God, what must we do?"* St. Vincent's eyes light up and he turns to the Queen and looks directly into her eyes and speaks one word: *"More."*

If St. Vincent were speaking here tonight and he had just time to say one word to this large, representative gathering of people who draw inspiration from his life, he might just pronounce that one word to us all: *More.* Not more for ourselves, but more for the poor, more justice for the poor, more time for the poor, more food for the poor, more medicine for the poor, more education for the poor. The reason why St. Vincent would ask us to give more to the poor is because he himself recognized the presence of Jesus Christ in the poor. He would ask us, not only to give more to the poor because of Jesus Christ, but he would also ask us that, in all we would do for the poor, we would do it after the manner and with the gentleness of Jesus Christ. Let us never forget that, in all that St. Vincent did for the poor, he was motivated, not by political or social theories but by the love which he had for the person of Jesus Christ. One of his most celebrated sayings is: *"Nothing pleases me but in Jesus Christ."*

When St. Vincent died in September 1660, he was in his eightieth year. Ten years earlier he made this reflection on his life which may very well have been his reflection on 27 September 1660. *"All our life is but a moment which flies away and disappears quickly. Alas, the seventy years of my life which I have passed, seem to me but a dream and a moment. Nothing remains of them but regret for having so badly employed this time. Let us think of the dissatisfaction we will have at our death, if we do not use this time to be merciful. Let us then be merciful, my brothers, and let us exercise mercy towards all in a way that we will never find a poor man without consoling him, if we can, nor an uninstructed man without teaching him in a few words those things which it is necessary to believe and which he must do for his salvation. O Saviour, do not permit that we abuse our vocation. Do not take away from this Company the spirit of mercy, because what would become of us if You should withdraw Your mercy from it. Give us, then, that mercy along with the spirit of gentleness and humility. "* (Coste XI, Fr. ed., p. 342). May St. Vincent, the father of the poor, the light of the clergy, the hope of the abandoned, pray for us all now and at the hour of our death.

Guardian Angels

2 October 1983   San Salvador, El Salvador

My dear Sisters,

If this were not a Sunday, we would be celebrating in the liturgy the feast of our Guardian Angels. Because our faith is based on the Resurrection of Christ—has not St. Paul reminded us that, *"if Christ be not risen, our faith is in vain. "* (1 Cor 15-17)—the Church always likes to celebrate Sunday as a little Easter day. It is for that reason that this year no explicit mention is made in today's liturgy of our Guardian Angels. That does not mean, however, that we should not salute them today and other days throughout the year. St. Vincent had a profound devotion to the Guardian Angels and recommended to Sisters that, before they entered a city, they should salute the angel that God had assigned to protect it. Living as you are amidst many dangers here in El Salvador, you probably call upon the protection of your Guardian Angels more frequently than if you were living in circumstances that were altogether safe. Perhaps when we were young, one of the earliest prayers we were taught was a prayer to our Guardian Angel, and after we have died, when the Church is saying an official goodbye to us before our bodies are taken to the grave, she will pray: *"And may the chorus of angels come to greet you. "* So today we breathe a prayer of thanks to those messengers of God who accompany us day and night, as we try to strengthen, help and console the poor who cross our paths.

Speaking about prayers, I imagine you must have no difficulty in making your own that prayer in the opening lines of the first reading in today's Mass: *"How long, O Lord, I cry for help but you do not listen. I cry out to you, 'Violence!' but you do not intervene. Why do you let me see ruin? Why must I look at misery? Destruction and violence are before me. There is strife and clamorous discord."* (Hb 1:2-3). From your experience each of you could comment on the misery and violence and ruin and strife and discord that meet you daily in your lives. To your protests which you make to God about the violence you see, there comes, as there came to Habakkuk, only a partial answer. Have you remarked upon the answer which Habakkuk received? *"Then the Lord answered me and said: Write down the vision clearly upon the tablets."* (Hb 2:2). The Lord's answer to violence was vision. We can say that His answer to the problem of violence in society today is still vision. Not the vision of any kind, not the vision that springs from the heart of man for, as the prophet Jeremiah remarks: *"The heart is deceitful above all things and desperately corrupt. Who can understand it."* (Jer 17:9). The vision which God offers us is the vision that springs from faith, and faith is a created participation in the knowledge that God has of Himself and of all that He has created. Faith is an authentic vision of God even if, as St. Paul remarks, *"We see now only in a dark manner."* (I Cor 13:12). We can, however, improve the quality of our vision and of our faith. Like the Apostles, we must ask of God an increase of faith, for faith is a gift of God. More than this, we can improve the quality of our faith by purifying our heart, as far as possible, of its corruption. *"Blessed are the pure of heart, for they shall see God."* (Mt 5:8).

I sometimes think that the emphasis which St. Vincent put on the importance of the virtue of simplicity has much to do with purity of heart. For St. Vincent, acting with simplicity meant acting with God alone in view.

Simplicity or purity of intention in carrying out the tasks of our daily lives, may seem a very small thing to us in a world where we feel so powerless in the face of so much violence and misery. Yet it has been said that a stone can change the surface of the ocean. Be confident in that goodness which comes from simplicity, from trying to act always with God alone in view and out of love for Him. Through your simplicity, God is using you—often unknown to yourselves—to bring down from their thrones those who are working against the coming of His Kingdom. Take heart from the words with which St. Paul addresses us today in the second reading: *"God did not give us a spirit of timidity, but a spirit of power and love and self-control."* (2 Tim 1:7). Take heart from the thought that in the midst of so many dangers you are not alone. Your Guardian Angel is *"bearing you up, lest you dash your foot against a stone."* (Mt 4:6).

For all of you here who care for the sick, who assist the poor, who receive the homeless, I pray with St. Vincent: *"O my Saviour and my God, give us the grace to look on all things with the same eye as You look upon them."* (Coste XII, Fr. ed., p. 88) *"How long, O Lord, I cry for help, but You do not listen. I cry out to you, 'Violence!' but you do not intervene. Then the Lord answered me and said: 'Write down the vision clearly upon the tablets'."* (Job 19:7). *"The Apostles said to the Lord: 'Increase our faith'."* (Lk 17:5).

Parable of Good Samaritan

3 October 1983   San Salvador, El Salvador

My dear Confreres,

Of all the parables that fell from the lips of Our Lord, I think the parable of the Good Samaritan, along with that of the Prodigal Son, must be considered the most tender and appealing. You will notice how it was a professional person, a lawyer, who stood up to pose the problem to Jesus. *"Teacher, what must I do to inherit everlasting life?"* (Lk 10:25). It was a question put by a professional man to One Who all the world knew had not done any professional studies in law. As all good teachers will do from time to time, Jesus answered the question by asking another. *"What is written in the law?"* (Ibid., 26). To that the lawyer replied: *"You shall love the Lord your God with all your heart, with all your soul, with all your strength, and with all your mind, and your neighbor as yourself."* (Ibid., v. 27). This reply, especially when it was given with others present, must have caused the lawyer to lose a little bit of face. So, as St. Luke remarks, *"to justify himself,"* he said to Jesus: *"And who is my neighbor?"* (Ibid., v. 29). It was that question which brought forth the parable of the Good Samaritan.

Whenever I reflect upon this parable, I think of the Fathers of the Church who liked to see the poor man, who was wounded and half-dead on the road, as representative of humanity after original sin. Then Jesus Christ, God made man, comes along. He does not pass by. He shows interest and love. He pours oil and wine on the wounds of the poor man. The Fathers of the Church liked to think of the oil and the wine as Sacraments of Christ. Then the Good Samaritan lifts the poor man off the road, places him on his own beast, and brings him to an inn, which the Fathers of the Church saw as an image of Christ's Church.

So this beautiful story is descriptive of the whole work of our redemption. It is descriptive, too, in a special way of the work of Jesus Christ. Did you ever notice, when reading the parable, that the Good Samaritan only speaks at the end to the innkeeper, when he is making arrangements for the poor man's accommodation? We think of St. Vincent's expression: *"Let us love God, but let us love Him with the strength of our arms and the sweat of our brows."* (Coste XI, Fr. ed., p. 40). The Good Samaritan did just that.

There are scripture scholars who say that there is a very subtle twist to the end of the parable. Jesus asks the lawyer: *"Which of these three, in your opinion, was neighbor to the man who fell in with robbers?"* (Lk 10:36). The answer came, *"The one who treated him with compassion."* (Ibid., v. 37). It would seem that in asking the lawyer that question, Jesus was saying equivalently to him, *"You asked Me 'who was my neighbor?'. That was not a good question. The question you should have asked me was: 'To whom can I be neighbor?' And the answer to that question is, 'the first poor person you meet on the road.'"*

In speaking to you, I am conscious that here in El Salvador you are daily finding people, like the man in the parable, *"lying on the road half-dead."* The parable of the Good Samaritan for all its beauty and tenderness is also a parable about violence. Goodness and violence live side by side in this world. At a repetition of prayer one day, St. Vincent gave expression to the pain of his heart as he contemplated the sufferings of poor, innocent people. I am certain you here in Salvador can appreciate fully what he said: *"I renew the recommendation which I made and which cannot be made too often to pray for peace . . . .For twenty years there has been war. If the people sow the crops, they are not sure that they will reap them. The armies come and plunder and carry away . . . . What is to be done? What is going to happen? If there is a true religion . . . .what have I said, wretched man! . . . .If there is a true religion . . . .I speak in a materialistic way . . . .It is among the people, it is among the poor that true religion is preserved and the faith lives. They believe simply, without being critical . . . the poor vineyard keepers who give us their work and ask that we pray for them, while they spend themselves to nourish us . . . .The poor nourish us. Let us pray to God for them. Let no day pass that we do not offer them to Our Lord, so that He will grant them the grace to make good use of their sufferings."* (Coste XI, Fr. ed., pp. 200-202).

As in St. Vincent's day, goodness and violence live side by side. Need I remind you of St. Paul's conviction that evil will not be conquered by evil, but by goodness. *"Do not be overcome by evil, but overcome evil with good."* (Rom 12:21).

I pray that you will not be disheartened by the violence you witness almost every day. I pray that in opposing violence you will be enlightened to use, as the document of Puebla expresses it, *"evangelical means which have their own distinctive efficacy . . . ."* May you rely on what Puebla calls *"the vigorous energy and activity of Christians who are moved by the Spirit to respond to the countless millions of their brothers and sisters."* (Puebla §486). In a word, may each of you be imitators of Jesus Christ, Who is for all mankind the good and reconciling Samaritan.

Pray With Heads and Hearts

6 October 1983   Santiago de Veraguas, Panama

My dear Confreres,

A child could understand this morning's Gospel without a word of explanation from its parent, teacher or priest. It is a marvelous feature of the parables of Our Lord that most of them could be understood by a child and, at the same time, the most profound of theologians will not exhaust the depths of riches which they contain.

Our Lord's words in today's Gospel are an encouragement to us to persevere in prayer and not be discouraged because God seems to be slow in answering our prayers. Perhaps the reason we become discouraged in prayer is that we feel in a vague sort of way that God is not taking us seriously. The fact is, of course, that it is we, very often, who are not taking God seriously. I remember meeting a person once who had become a member of a prayer group. At the first meeting the group prayed for one of his intentions and afterwards he obtained his request. This happened a second time a little later, and on the third occasion my friend exclaimed to the group: *"I had better be careful in what I ask because God is taking me seriously."* In saying this, my friend revealed that up to that time he didn't believe profoundly that God took him seriously when he asked for some grace or favor in prayer.

The truth is that it is not God Who fails to take us seriously when we pray to Him, but rather we fail to take God seriously. I do not mean that we are disrespectful towards God when we pray, but rather that in our heart of hearts we pray without full confidence that He is going to give us what we ask. I wonder if God is slow in answering our prayers at times in order to perfect the confidence which He wishes us to have in Him Who is our Father.

Sometimes I imagine that the reason of God's delay in answering our prayers is that He wants to make us ready to accept what He desires to give us. Often we ask God for favors with our heads but not with our hearts. At other times we ask God for favors with our hearts but not with our heads. He desires us to ask with both our hearts and our heads. *"You shall love the Lord, your God, with your whole heart and with your whole mind and with your whole strength."* (Mk 12:30). Prayer must always be an expression of the love that is in us for God, for His world, for His Church and for those who have so much less than we have, namely, His poor.

Today's Gospel centers on the prayer of petition. Ten or fifteen years ago there were some who discredited the prayer of petition. It was a consequence of the death of God theology. The death of God theology has lost much of its credibility in more recent years, and we have seen a revival of interest in prayer all over the world. Groups of people come together to pray because they believe more deeply than they did, in the power and efficacy of Christian prayer.

You may recall a passage from the writings of St. Augustine, which is presented to us in the Divine Office on this subject of petitionary prayer. In a letter to a lady called Proba, St. Augustine wrote: *"God does not want our wishes to be made known to Himself, since He cannot be ignorant of them; but He wants our desire to be exercised in prayer, thus enabling us to grasp what He is preparing to give."* In St. Augustine's view, a petitionary prayer is releasing from our hearts some of those thousands of desires that are locked up within them. St. Augustine would seem to say that God has too much respect for that inner sanctuary of our hearts to enter it unasked. So He invites us to present those desires to Him so that He in turn can fulfill them.

In my heart I know there is a desire to possess God. There is a desire to do His will. There is a desire to help my friends, a desire to help the poor. Every simple prayer of petition is a releasing from my heart of one of these desires in order that God may be allowed in His goodness to fulfill it. Community prayer can be seen as a presentation to God of some of those fundamental needs which we experience in Community in order that God Himself may fulfill them.

"Let your requests be made known before God," was St. Paul's advice to us. (Phil 4:6). St. Augustine adds: *"Not in order that they may become known to God, but that they may become known to us in the sight of God."*

I seem to have come to the end of this homily without drawing from the riches of St. Vincent's teaching on petitionary prayer. Let us leave the last word to him. To a Sister who had become discouraged because God had not apparently listened to her prayers, he wrote: *"You say that you have already shed tears and offered prayers and novenas. All that is good. Our Lord has said, 'Blessed are those who weep' and that those who ask shall receive. He has not, however, said that as soon as we will pray, we will be heard, and the reason for that is that He does not wish us to cease from praying. That is why, my Sister, you should not have said that word which escaped from you, that the more you pray, the less you obtain. That shows that you are not well resigned to the Will of God and that you do not trust sufficiently in His promises. Often through refusing us what we ask of Him, God actually gives us more grace. We ought to believe that, since He knows better what is good for us, He sends us the best, even when it is disagreeable to nature and contrary to our desires . . . .I greet you with affection and I pray God that He will give you His holy strength and an abundance of blessings."* (Coste VII, Fr. ed., 240-241, 243).

Frederic Ozanam

16 October 1983   Ballsbridge, Dublin, Ireland

Your Excellency, The Nuncio, My Lord Bishops, Reverend Fathers, Brothers and Sisters in Christ,

There is a little phrase in the second reading of today's Mass which captures the spirit of what all of us are experiencing here today. The phrase is a short, pithy piece of advice which the aging St. Paul wrote to the young Timothy: *"Remember who your teachers were."* (2 Tim 3:14). All of us can remember who our teachers were and, when we have long forgotten many of the details of grammar, science or whatever else they imparted to us, we can remember what manner of people they were. It is that, I imagine, which St. Paul is evoking for Timothy. In as many words, St. Paul is saying to him what he said to others on different occasions: *"Become imitators of us and of the Lord."* (1 Thes 1:6).

The particular teachers whom we are evoking today are two. They are separated from each other by two hundred years or so and, although they shared the same nationality, they came from very different backgrounds: one from the land, as we might say, and the other from the professional or business world. One was to die young, leaving a wife and a child; the other was to live into old age as a priest, until the end an active mediator of God's love for the world. The contrasts between St. Vincent de Paul and Frederic Ozanam are many, but what is more striking still is the depth and intensity of the vision both men shared. To each of them was given a penetrating insight into the mystery of Christ and His presence in the persons of the poor.

"We must not consider," wrote St. Vincent de Paul, *"a poor agricultural worker or a poor woman according to their external appearance, nor according to their apparent intellectual abilities . . . .Turn the medal and you will see by the light of faith that the Son of God, Who wished to be poor, is presented to us through these poor people."* (Coste

XI, Fr. ed., p. 32). The life and work of Frederic Ozanam was an endorsement of that reflection of St. Vincent de Paul.

"Remember who your teachers were." Neither of our teachers could be described as a *"remote, intellectual don,"* for even if Frederic Ozanam held with great distinction a professorial chair in the Sorbonne University of Paris, he still could find time, along with the other founding members of the Society, to climb the stairs of high tenements in Paris to visit, talk with and assist the poor families who eked out their existence in them.

Not only the poor of Paris, but of other European cities as well, touched the heart of Frederic Ozanam. In 1851 he was persuaded to visit the great exhibition which was being held in the Crystal Palace in London. It was during his visit to the Crystal Palace that Frederic Ozanam became quite distracted, not by what he saw there, but by the poverty of the Irish immigrants who were to be found, some fourteen to a room, in buildings only five minutes' walk from Regent Street. It was not the exciting discoveries of the scientific world of the time that riveted the attention of the brilliant professor from the Sorbonne, but the sufferings of the poor of Christ in the heart of the British capital. What captured the admiration of Ozanam in the London of 1851 was the work of some English members of the Society, who were able, as Ozanam expressed it, to *"rise above the prejudices of their birth"* and come to the help of some poor Sicilians and Irish people, who were showing so clearly the effects of poverty in their bodies, and which, to a man of Ozanam's spiritual insight, was a revelation of the features of the suffering Christ.

Of our other teacher, St. Vincent de Paul, and his concern for the poor of this country three hundred years ago, we know more. Into the dioceses of Limerick, Cashel and Emly, he sent priests of his Community at a time when to be a priest in Ireland was to live dangerously. Because of that danger, many Irish priests had become refugees in the city of Paris, and we know for certain that St. Vincent de Paul commissioned one of his Community to seek them out and to offer them some financial help in order to save them the embarrassment of having to beg their bread in the streets of the capital.

"Remember who your teachers were." The memory of Timothy's

teachers is evoked by St. Paul, not in any nostalgic way, but rather as a stimulus to become, as St. Paul himself expresses it in the final phrase of today's second reading, *"fully equipped and ready for any good work."* (2 Tim 3:17). In evoking our teachers, St. Vincent de Paul and Frederic Ozanam, we do so, not only to allow our wonder to grow as we reflect on their monumental lives, but also that in some small way we may be able to go and do likewise.

These two teachers of ours will not object if at this point we recall with gratitude some of those other teachers which the Society of St. Vincent de Paul has known since its foundation some one hundred fifty years ago in Paris. There is the illustrious line of International Presidents that culminates for us today in the person of M. Amin de Terrazzi, men who have inspired the Society and have given its members a sense of unity throughout the world in their work of lifting up some of the broken forms of humanity that are lying on life's road. Besides the International Presidents, each of us here today would like to honor the memory of the Irish National Presidents of the Society, predecessors of Don Mahony. Perhaps they, as well as many other members of the Society, would lay no claim to being teachers. However, their devotion to the Society and to the poor of Ireland is a demonstration lesson to us on the meaning of the two great commandments of the law, on which in the evening time of our lives we will be examined. *"At evening time, I will examine thee on love."* By the grace of God, they have made themselves, in St. Paul's phrase, *"fully equipped and ready for any good work"* (Ibid.) that would lighten the burden of those whom St. Vincent liked to call *"our lords and masters,"* the poor.

Yes, we have had many teachers in the Society whose memory we treasure today, and whose work is a stimulus for us not only to seek out the poor (did somebody say that 25% of Ireland's population could be classified as poor at the present time?), but also to engage the interest, or I should say, the love of the young to work in the Society for the poor, who are always with us. In this large classroom where this afternoon so many pupils or disciples of St. Vincent de Paul and Frederic Ozanam are gathered, what would our teachers say to us today?

Would Frederic Ozanam find us so engrossed in the great exhibition of affluence, that we have become a somewhat depersonalized society?

Perhaps he would marvel at the phenomenon that while the five continents of the world can become present to us in the intimacy of our homes through a television set, loneliness and depression in our society has reached almost epidemic proportions. Would he, picking up the title of a present-day film, *The Loneliness of the Long Distance Runner*, have a pertinent word for us on the importance of giving generously of our time to those who are the long-distance runners on life's road, the aged in our society? Frederic Ozanam might remind us that the Society of St. Vincent de Paul is rooted and founded in the experience of the Eternal Word of God, Who came, in St. John's phrase, *"and pitched His tent"* among us and visited His people, especially the poor, in person. In person—yes, what has characterized the Society from its beginnings, and must continue to do so, is its determination to be more than an agency of relief. Its members are called to be not only dispensers of food and fuel and clothing to the poor—both obvious and not so obvious—but dispensers, too, of the love and compassion of Christ, which has been poured into their own hearts by the Spirit of God. The Society recognizes that if *"The whole earth is our hospital endowed by the ruined millionaire,"* then personal contact, patient listening, a profound acceptance of the individual will be a very effective therapy in healing the wounds which poverty or injustice has left in the hearts of so many today. *"The hint half-guessed, the gift half-understood, is Incarnation."*

Perhaps St. Vincent de Paul in addressing us might begin by protesting at the publicity which the Society has given to his name, for he would vigorously assert that he was not the founder of it. However, he would pardon the Society for the publicity, if he could be persuaded that it was done so entirely in the interests of God and His poor. With a smile and a little touch of irony, he might add: *"At least in the matter of publicity, the two Communities which I did found have been much more successful in respecting my wishes to be unknown."* Of St. Vincent de Paul, it could be said that he had a hard head and a soft heart. I say he had a hard head, for at a time when there was no organized government social assistance, he succeeded in providing it, principally through the Ladies of Charity and the Daughters of Charity whom he founded, along with a network of other organizations which he set up to make the basic necessities of life available to the poor. He was not a politician, but he had no fear of going to the rich, influential people of his day to obtain help with his projects for the poor, and in doing so, sensitizing their consciences to their social obligations. For such planning and courage, a man needs a hard head. He had, however, a soft heart and, in his approach to those who held authority or enjoyed prestige, there was nothing shrill or aggressive. His respect for the individual person was too deep to allow him to adopt tactics that were faintly menacing or remotely violent. The sufferings of refugees, one-parent families, dropouts, victims of violence, hostages and prisoners, all tore his heart out, because in their cries of pain, he could hear only the voice of Jesus Christ on His cross.

"Remember who your teachers were." Perhaps we should, on this occasion when we are celebrating here in Ireland the one hundred-fiftieth anniversary of the foundation of the Society of St. Vincent de Paul, leave the last word to our two distinguished teachers. In 1651 St. Vincent de Paul addressed a letter to a city council in France that had shown an unusual degree of sensitivity to the needs of the poor in its society. The Council members had written to St. Vincent, expressing the hope that he might be able to assist them in the work of alleviating distress. Characteristically, the Saint replied that he would do what he could, and then added a few words of encouragement (did he think that State agencies, such as they were at that time, needed encouragement as much as goading if they were to be more just and generous to those whom we today rather clumsily call the *"underprivileged"*?). For St. Vincent de Paul, the poor were not names in a register or, had he been living nowadays, cards to be fed into a computer. For him, the poor were the open and raw nerves of the suffering Body of Christ. So he wrote to the city council: *"Gentlemen, how pleased Our Lord is with your concern for the relief of His suffering members! I ask Him to be your reward for this, to bless you and your government, to give peace to the kingdom, and to deliver His people from the evil they are enduring . . . and I am, in the love of Our Lord, Your most humble and obedient servant, Vincent de Paul, unworthy priest of the Mission."* (Coste IV, Eng. ed., ltr. 1360, p. 202).

Now for Frederic Ozanam's last word. On a spring day in 1853, looking out on the Mediterranean Sea, Frederic Ozanam began to feel the tide of life ebbing from his body, so he wrote what he called a *"codicil of gratitude"* to his will:

> *I commit my soul to Jesus Christ, my Saviour . . . . I die in the bosom of the Catholic, Apostolic and Roman Church. I've known the misgivings of the present age, but all my life has convinced me that there is no rest for the mind and the heart except in the faith of the Church and under her authority . . . . I implore the prayers of my friends of the Society of St. Vincent de Paul and of my friends in Lyons. Let not your zeal be slackened by those who say, 'he is in heaven.' Pray unceasingly for one who loved you all much, but who has sinned much. Aided by your supplications, dear kind friends, I shall leave this world with less fear. I firmly trust that we shall not be separated and that I shall remain in the midst of you until you rejoin me. May the blessing of God, the Father, and of the Son and of the Holy Spirit rest upon you all. Amen.* (J.P. Derum, *Apostle in a Top Hat*, p. 265).

Advent Letter—Humility

14 November 1983   To Each Confrere

My dear Confreres,

May the grace of Our Lord Jesus Christ be with us forever!

Some of you who will read this letter, will have had the grace and the joy of having visited the Church that has been built over the spot where, according to tradition, Christ was born. You will remember that the entrance to the Basilica of Bethlehem was very low. In fact you had to stoop to enter it. It would seem that the low entrance dates back to the Middle Ages and was constructed in order to prevent horsemen from galloping up to the entrance and riding right into the interior of the Basilica. The low entrance is a curious relic of earlier centuries, but for all that, it is a permanent reminder that the mystery of the Incarnation is essentially one of stooping. He *"through Whom all things were made*

. . . " (Jn 1:3) emptied Himself and stooped so low that He was to be found in the womb of the Virgin Mary. Even when the Word of God made flesh had grown to full physical stature, must not His experience have been one of stooping, for *"who is able to build Him a house since heaven, even the highest heaven, cannot contain Him?"* (2 Chr 2:5).

The mystery of God's stooping is at the heart of the Incarnation and very central, too, to St. Vincent's vision of the Congregation, which must always remain *"humble and hidden in the Lord."* (CR XII, 10). Perhaps we find it difficult to reconcile the call to be *"humble and hidden in the Lord"* with the appeal that comes to us from so many quarters, to speak up and take action for the poor who are stooped because of social or political oppression. Only by prolonged and prayerful reflection on the mind of Christ will we resolve the difficulty, for Jesus Christ preached the Gospel to the poor and liberation to the captives out of a heart which He Himself assured us was gentle and humble. (cf. Mt 11:29).

The justifiable emphasis which our age has been putting on the importance of human rights must not allow us to overlook the importance of sharing with Christ His experience of stooping. His experience of stooping did not end with his entrance into the womb of the Virgin Mary. It was a lifelong one, living and working as He did within the limitations of time and place, and accepting patiently the human limitations of those with whom He worked and to whom He preached. And all for what? To lift up mankind to the height of becoming adopted sons of God, *"who are born not of flesh nor of the will of man but of God."* (Jn 1:13).

We who are called to continue the mission of Christ can take no other way than that which He took. There is no bypass. If we wish to lift up the poor for Christ, we must share in His experience of stooping. We must be ready to accept such limitations as working within an imperfect Community, of foregoing personal preferences in the interests of the Community and of being ready, too, to cauterize the many personal sensitivities that make us at times stand on our dignity and thus prevent us from stooping, as Christ did when He washed the feet of His disciples. This humility is the foundation of all evangelical perfection and the essential thing in the spiritual life. *"If a person has this humility everything good will come along with it. "* (CR II,§7) In a word, can we ever lose sight of the fact that when God chose to come into this world, He did so by entering it under our feet?

Allow me to use this occasion to propose something to you on which I have been reflecting now for quite some time. Christmas is the feast of the home. If St. Vincent can be said to have an earthly home, it is where his mortal remains are resting. The Chapel of the Mother House in Paris belongs in a certain sense to us all. It is in need of some restoration at the present time. When last January in Bogota, I mooted the idea to the Visitors of making an appeal to the Provinces and to individual Confreres to contribute to the project, I received much encouragement. So, for that reason I now invite Provinces and Confreres, who may wish to do so, to send me here in Rome contributions towards the work of beautifying this Chapel which houses, not only the body of St. Vincent but the mortal remains of our Blessed, John Gabriel Perboyre and Francis Regis Clet. The Province of Paris has undertaken to contribute as much as it can to the fund, but the cost of the restoration will be in excess of that figure. Should there be any surplus money available when the work is finished, it will be distributed to the poor.

In restoring our Chapel in the rue de Sèvres, I would hope that it would become more attractive as a place of spiritual pilgrimage and reconciliation with God for all who love what St. Vincent loved and who are trying to put into practice what he taught.

Let me end by citing what St. Vincent himself said one day to his community apropos of the reception of the relics of some saints into the Church of St. Lazare: *"We will so dispose ourselves to receive these precious relics as if we were receiving the honor of a visit from the saints themselves. In this way we will honor God in His saints. We will ask Him to make us sharers in the graces which He so abundantly poured into their souls. "* (Coste XI, Fr. ed., 49-50).

I do hope your Christmas will be a happy one and that your joy will be full. That wish is shared by the four Assistants as well as by the Confreres and Sisters who work here in the Curia. We all send you our greetings and commend ourselves to your prayers. In the love of Our Lord I remain, your devoted confrere.

1984

Incarnation

1 January 1984   Paris, France

Mother Rogé, Father Lloret and my dear Sisters,

On this New Year's Day, let me speak to you about gifts—for Christmas and the New Year is the season of gifts—of gifts given and of gifts received. It is so because of the great exchange of gifts that took place when the Word of God took flesh in the womb of the Virgin Mary; when, as we recall at every Eucharistic celebration God became a partaker of our human nature, so that we might become sharers in His Divinity.

Gifts. Think about some of the best gifts you have received at Christmas time over the years. You will find that, like so much else in life, there is an art in giving gifts. In the recipe for the giving of good gifts, you will find quite a number of ingredients that do not always appear at first sight. First of all, to give a good gift you must first give much thought to it. The reason why thought is the most important ingredient in a recipe for a good gift is because you wish your gift to meet a need in the person to whom you offer it.

A second element in the giving of gifts is surprise. Gifts are carefully wrapped at Christmastime in fancy paper, and is it not one of the joys of life to spend some moments of guessing before opening a gift, wondering what it might be? Surprise is always an excellent condiment for any gift, given or received.

It goes without saying that the exchange of gifts between friends is an expression of the love that unites them. As love is spiritual, our gifts are but tokens of what we want to say or express in our giving of them.

Only one gift in the world has been an adequate expression of the love that lay behind it. *"God so loved the world as to give His only-begotten Son."* (Jn 3:16). Who can measure the thought that lies behind the Incarnation? *"In the beginning was the Word and the Word*

153

was with God . . . and the Word was made flesh. " (Jn 1:1,14). For centuries God's chosen people played guessing games, so to speak, about the Messiah and His coming. In their wildest dreams they did not guess that God's gift to them would be His Son. If surprise is an element in the giving of a gift, has the world ever been given a greater surprise than that the God who swung the stars into motion should be found as a new-born Infant lying in the manger?

The shepherds were surprised by the multitude of angels who broke the silence of the night as they sang: *"Glory to God in the highest and peace to those who are God's friends."* (Lk 2:14). The wise men from the East were surprised by a star that led them to Bethlehem.

What of the wrapping of the gift? It was Mary, the Virgin Mother, who according to St. Luke *"wrapped the child in swaddling clothes and laid Him in a manger."* (Lk 2:7).

In preparing for the feast of Christmas, the Church in one of her Eucharistic prefaces makes us pray for the gift of *"wonder and praise."*

I can think of few more useful graces for any of us at the beginning of this New Year than that of wonder and praise for the gift of the Incarnation and its prolongation in the Eucharist, in the Church and in the poor. Each day of this New Year will bring to us a new gift of God's grace. It is because we have lost to some degree the capacity to wonder like children, that we cease to be surprised at what God is working in us and through us. What a gift and what a surprise is our daily Holy Communion, not to mention the thought that God has put into it so that it would meet the needs of our hearts and our lives. Like Martha, however, we are so busy and anxious about other less important experiences in our lives that we fail to wonder and praise Our Lord for that gift which makes every day a Christmas Day for us. Each morning we begin our prayer with: *"O Lord open our lips."* We would do well to ask Him also to open our eyes, as He opened Mary's eyes to see *"the great things"* that He is doing for us day by day. *"And of His fullness we have all received . . . grace upon grace."* (Jn 1:16).

Your vocation is, as St. Vincent so often reminded the first Sisters, a gift of God. Not only that, you yourselves are God's gift to the poor. Reflect often on the manner of God's giving in the Incarnation. Could anything be more simple and self-effacing than the appearance of an infant in a manger? Be simple and self-effacing in the manner in which you offer yourselves to the poor. Do not force yourselves on the poor. The Infant Jesus did not force himself on the shepherds nor on the wise men from the East nor indeed on humanity today. Allow yourselves to be led to the poor through the Community as Mary allowed herself to be led by others toward Bethlehem. Do not be disheartened if your own plans for serving the poor are not realized as you would like them to be. Mary's and Joseph's original idea was that the child should be born in the inn. But then there was no room there, and he was born in a stable which became a sign for the shepherds.

All that I have been saying has been expressed marvelously by St. Louise in a letter which she wrote a few days after Christmas 1659: *"You will learn from Jesus, my dear Sisters, to practice solid virtue, as He did in His holy humanity, as soon as He came down upon earth. It is from the example of Jesus in His infancy that you will obtain all that you need to become true Christians and perfect Daughters of Charity."* (*Spiritual Writings of Louise de Marillac*, ltr. 647, p. 666).

My dear Sisters, may 1984 be a year when you will see with fresh eyes and with wonder and gratitude the gifts that the Incarnate Word of God is silently offering to you through the Community. May it be a year in which you yourselves become pure gifts for the poor who, whether they know it or not, are God's friends. May it be a year when the printed articles of your Constitutions will be translated faithfully into living realities in your personal and community lives. May it be a year when with deeper conviction *"you will honor Our Lord Jesus Christ as the source and model of all charity, serving Him corporally and spiritually in the person of the poor."* (Common Rules of the Daughters of Charity, I:I; C.1.3). May it be a year that will bring you many surprises through the gifts of grace which Our Lord in His personal love for you is already preparing to give you, for *"He is able to do immeasurably more than we ask or imagine—to Him be glory . . . forever and ever. Amen."* (Eph. 3:20-21).

Sanctification Continues

15 February 1984   Budapest, Hungary

My dear Confreres and Sisters,

On Monday I had the joy of celebrating Mass for a number of Daughters of Charity, and today I am very happy to be celebrating Mass surrounded by my own Confreres of this Province of Hungary. Let me begin by thanking you all for honoring me in this way, and welcoming the Sisters who have come again this morning to join us in offering that most efficacious of all prayers, the Holy Sacrifice of the Mass.

It is only since I have come here to Hungary that the full impact of the history of your Province during the past thirty-four years has forced itself upon me. It was a very moving experience for both Father Wypych and myself to have been able to visit those places which were once the chapels of the two houses of formation for this Province. On Saturday we visited the chapel of the house at Menesio and on Sunday evening we visited the chapel of the Internal Seminary at Pipisesaba. We not only visited those two chapels, but we prayed in them. In both places the words of the *"Expectatio Israel"* came to my lips. *"Quos autem vocasti serva eos in nomine tuo et sanctifica eos in veritate."* Yes, that prayer is valid for us all today.

No matter how things have changed, no matter how men have worked against us, no matter how many obstacles men place in the way of the Church, the work of God's sanctification of us will continue to go on. No man can stop God from sanctifying those whom He has called to be members of St. Vincent's Community. Houses and property may be taken away from us, but no one can interfere with Our Lord's call to us to do His Will. No one can interfere with Our Lord's power to give us His grace in all circumstances and at every moment. That is why I say that no matter what has happened to the property or structures of our Community here in Hungary, Our Lord is continuing to sanctify you. I have seen clear proofs of that since I have come here last Friday.

When I think of you and how you have been dispersed, I think of some of those Confreres whom St. Vincent sent to Scotland and to my own country of Ireland. To be a priest or a Brother in those countries at that time was to live dangerously. These men were unable to live in Community in the same way as St. Vincent and his Confreres were living in Community at St. Lazare. Yet, because they lived according to their vows and in the spirit of the five virtues, St. Vincent regarded them as very precious members of the Little Company. They wrote letters to St. Vincent, and he wrote letters to them. That is why I think it is so important for you to keep in contact, as far as is possible, with the Visitor and with each other. I am very pleased to know that you come together from time to time in order to strengthen each other in the spirit of our Vincentian vocation.

We know the past of our Community. We do not know what designs God has for the future of this Province of Hungary. St. Paul said, *"When I am weak, then I am strong."* (2 Cor 12:10). When the Province may feel that it is weak and its future uncertain, that may be the moment which God will use to bring about a change of which we have not even dreamt. For us all I would like to read two of my favorite pieces of St. Vincent's writings. The first is from the Common Rules, and the second is the advice St. Vincent offered to priests and a Brother who were setting out in 1646 for Ireland where persecution was raging against the Church:

> *Christ said: 'Seek first the kingdom of God and His justice, and all these things which you need will be given you as well.' That is the basis for each of us having the following set of priorities: matters involving our relationship with God are more important than temporal affairs; spiritual health is more important than physical; God's glory is more important than human approval. Each one should, moreover, be determined to prefer, like St. Paul, to do without necessities, to be slandered or tortured, or even killed, rather than lose Christ's love. In practice, then, we should not worry too much about temporal affairs. We ought to have confidence in God that He will look after us since we know for certain that as long as we are grounded in that sort of love and trust, we will be always under the protection of God in heaven, we will remain unaffected by evil and never lack what we need even when everything we possess seems headed for disaster.* (CR II, 2).

*Be united . . . and God will bless you, but let your union be
through the charity of Jesus Christ . . . .A union not cemented by the blood of this divine Saviour cannot last. It is
. . . in Jesus Christ, by Jesus Christ and for Jesus Christ you
must be united. The spirit of Jesus Christ is a spirit of peace
and union; how could you draw souls to Jesus Christ if you
were not united to one another and to Him? It could not be
done. So, then, be of one and the same mind, one and the
same will . . . .It would be rather as if horses were yoked to
the same plough, and one started to pull in one direction and
the other in another; they would spoil and ruin everything.
God is calling you to labor in His vineyard; enter it then,
having only one and the same heart, one and the same
intention in Him, and by this means you will return with fruit
from His vineyard.* (Coste, *The Life and Works of St. Vincent
de Paul*, II, pp. 30-31).

Lenten Letter—Unity

15 February 1984   To Each Confrere

My dear Confrere,

May the grace of Our Lord Jesus Christ be with us forever!

In Advent I wrote, telling you of the decision that had been made to
redecorate our Chapel in the rue de Sèvres, which houses the mortal
remains of St. Vincent and two of our Blessed. Among the reasons for
this decision was our desire to make the Chapel a tangible expression
of our concern to keep alive in the Congregation a sense of that unity
of mission and of spirit which God, through St. Vincent, has given it.

The unity, and indeed uniqueness, of the Congregation's vocation in
the Church is a gift of God which all of us wish to be preserved, and
the Confreres who have participated in the General Assemblies that
have taken place since the end of Vatican Council II can testify to the
strength of that desire. The resolution passed at the General Assembly
of 1980, that there be adopted throughout the Congregation a common

"Ratio Formationis," is indicative of a concern that the unity of the Congregation be preserved in the future. What recent Assemblies have formulated is the ideal of unity in diversity: a unity of vocation that finds expression in a diversity of cultures, needs and traditions. *"We are,"* observed St. Vincent, *"missioners, and we make up one body only."* (Coste XI, Fr. ed., p. 120).

The unity of the Congregation is a treasure, however, which is carried in an earthen vessel, and St. Vincent clearly recognized this fact. For how else can we explain the emphasis he has given in our Common Rules and Conferences to the importance of uniformity. Uniformity would be, to quote his own phrase, *"the safeguard of good order and of the holiness which comes from being together."* (CR II, 11). No line of his writings, however, suggests that he saw uniformity as identical with unity. His penetrating mind and breadth of vision would make it easy for him today to accept the fact that in the diversity of cultures and subcultures of our modern world, the model of uniformity, which he proposed in the seventeenth century, would need considerable modification. What would not be negotiable for him would be the unity of vocation which God gave to the Congregation at its very beginning and which is expressed in the first part of our present (1980) Constitutions.

"Only one thing is needed for this uniformity to be maintained constantly among us, namely, the most exact observance of our Rules and Constitutions." (Ibid.). Let these two truths be engraven on our minds: first, that the ideal of unity in diversity, to which the Church has called the Congregation in our time, is a delicate flower which the cold winds of individualism can easily wither and destroy; and second, that it is only when the Congregation is making its Constitutions and Statutes a point of reference and guidance in all its apostolates at international, provincial and local levels, that it can fully serve the universal and local Church.

If unity in diversity is a delicate flower, it is for all that a *"many-splendored thing."* Meeting a group of Confreres recently in an eastern European country, I was deeply impressed, not only by their loyalty but by the breadth of their interest in the Congregation world-wide. The fact that these Confreres have been dispersed now for thirty years or more, and communication with the center made difficult for them, did not weaken their attachment to or belief in the vocation of the universal Congregation, its mission and its spirit. It is the unity of the Congregation's vocation in the Church which gives a special color to the union that Our Lord wishes to exist among us.

Union amongst ourselves is, in St. Vincent's vision, a starting point for our mission to the poor. The English writer, G.K. Chesterton, remarked on one occasion that, while we make our friends and our enemies, God sends us our neighbors. We preach the good news of Christ to the poor and thus become their friends. We must do so, however, without forgetting or neglecting the neighbors God has sent us in our community. Our local community, as well as the poor, has a claim on our gifts of nature and of grace, on our understanding and on our time. It is only when each of us is making a personal contribution towards union amongst ourselves that we can securely preach to the poor in the way envisaged by St. Vincent. It is for that reason that I make my own the wish and practical advice which St. Vincent offered on one occasion to a Confrere who was experiencing the difficulty of working for unity both outside and inside his community:

> *I pray Our Lord that He will give you the fullness of His grace and of His guidance, so that you may correspond fully to the intentions of the Bishop and so that you may maintain peace in your own house without which it would be difficult to do the rest. I pray the Holy Spirit, Who is the union of the Father and the Son, that He will also be yours everywhere. You ought to pray for that intention unceasingly and, in addition to your prayers, to pay great attention in trying to unite yourself with heart and deed to each one in particular and to all in general. The evil of communities, especially of a small community, is ordinarily rivalry. The remedy for that is humility. You ought to try to advance in that virtue, as well as in those other virtues which are necessary to bring about this union.* (Coste V, Fr. ed., p. 582).

I hope to write to you again when our Constitutions and Statutes will have received definitive approval from the Holy See. There is good reason to believe that this approval will not be long delayed. In the meantime we can reflect on what St. Vincent wrote to M. Alméras, who was Superior in Rome. *"What does not get done at one time gets done at another, particularly in Rome."* (Coste III, Eng. ed., ltr. 1119, p. 459).

With warmest greetings from all of us here in the Curia, and recommending myself to your prayers, I remain in the love of Our Lord, your devoted confrere.

Martyrs of Angers

20 February 1984   Rome, Italy

Mother Rogé, my dear Confreres and my dear Sisters,

I invite you to join me in a coach which is traveling from Angers to Paris on the 2 February 1640. One of the passengers is Mademoiselle Louise Le Gras. She is looking somewhat pale because during the past few weeks she has been quite ill. She has spent almost three months in the city of Angers and her principal preoccupation has been the negotiation of a contract with the Administrators of the long-established Hospital of St. Jean. According to the terms of the contract, the Daughters of Charity would undertake the nursing of the sick poor in that hospital. It was only the day before, the first of February, that she signed the contract. The Company, she thought to herself, is but six years established and it has now for the first time taken over the care and the nursing of the poor in a hospital.

The negotiations over the hospital have been tiring and protracted. It is true that she has in her satchel a number of letters which Monsieur Vincent had written to her during the past three months. In them he had given her great support and expressed his concern and that of the Sisters in Paris for the health of Mademoiselle. She begins to nod off to sleep, thinking about the first of February. The years begin to pass by, like the kilometers on the road, and it is now the 1 February 1794. She sees to her amazement two of the Sisters with their hands tied together, being led out to a field on the edge of the city to be executed by a firing squad. The contract, which she had signed the previous day, did not envisage such an eventuality. She finds herself protesting: *"The contract, the contract; it is against the contract.*" Then she seems to hear the two Sisters reply to her: *"But who shall separate us from the love of Christ ... shall persecution ... or peril ... or the sword ... .No, in all things we are more conquerors through Him Who loved us .... Neither death, nor life, nor anything else in all creation will be able to separate us from the love of God in Christ Jesus, Our Lord."* (Rom 8:35-39).

"They must be going to be martyrs then," Mademoiselle concludes. *"Christian martyrs,"* she reflects, *"do not think in terms of contracts. The weeks of negotiation before the signing of the contract were weeks of calculation. But martyrdom is outside all calculation. What enables Christians to accept martyrdom is the love of God which has taken possession of their hearts, and who can measure or calculate what is infinite, as is the love of God."*

"Could it be," Louise asks herself, *"that these martyrs would one day be honored by the Church at a time when Christians needed to be reminded that in the service of God, in the service of the poor, we can be too calculating? Could there come a time in the future when Sisters would measure out too carefully what they would give to God through their Vows of Poverty, Chastity, Obedience and Service of the Poor? Although it is not according to the terms of the contract I signed, that two of our Sisters should suffer such a violent death, still God could strengthen Sisters of other generations through the fortitude which they are now displaying."*

Mademoiselle moves forward to speak a word of encouragement to Sister Marie-Anne and Sister Odile as they stand bound together in that field outside Angers, awaiting the moment of death. She reminds them that Our Lord had prayed for them. *"Keep them in Thy name, that they may be one as We are one."* (Jn 17:11) She just has time to say that to them before they offer their lives to God, not calculating the cost.

It was then that she awoke. It is still the 2 February 1640. She is still on the road back from Angers to Paris where she will report to Monsieur Vincent all that has happened. What she would write some seventeen years later to two of the Sisters at Angers is already taking shape in her mind: *"... the Daughters of Charity of Angers have been singularly blessed by God for the service of the sick poor of the hospitals. May He be forever blessed! One of the practices of all our Sisters strikes me as*

*excellent and I beg them and you also, my dear Sisters, to continue it.
It consists of informing the Sister Servant of everything that occurs in
the hospital. She is to be the only one to render any account to any of
the numerous people involved, after she has learned from you the state
of affairs in the matters for which you are respnsible. If you always
respect this custom, you may be certain that all will go well. You will
be respected by those outside the Company, and the union and cordiality prevalent among you will be so strong that it will form an impregnable rampart against the devil."* (*Spiritual Writings of Louise de
Marillac*, ltr. 554, p. 578-579).

Yes, it was impossible for the devil to break the union between Sister
Marie-Anne and Sister Odile on the 1 February 1794, a union which
was, to quote a phrase of St. Vincent, *"cemented by the blood of the
Divine Saviour."* (Dodin, *Entretiens*, p. 93). Their union with each other
and with God, cemented by the blood of Jesus Christ, was on a February
morning in 1984 proclaimed by the Vicar of Christ to be shining out in
the heavens because, although in the sight of the unwise they seemed
to die, they were, and are, *"in the hand of God Who watches over His
holy ones."* (Wis 3:1).

New Nazareths

24 March 1984   Paris, France

Mother Rogé, Father Lloret and my dear Sisters,

Towards the end of the last century there died an English Jesuit priest
who earlier in his life had been converted to Catholicism. He lived his
religious and priestly life with great dedication and suffering. He gave
expression to the intensity of his experience as a religious and as a priest
in poems which during his lifetime he never published. Some twenty
years after his death his poetry was published and the excellence of
some of his religious poetry was acclaimed by literary critics who
neither shared the priest's faith nor understood the meaning and significance of the consecrated life.

One of the poems this Jesuit wrote (his name was Gerard Manley
Hopkins) centered on the person of Our Lady and her experience of the

Incarnation. In one line of that poem the priest makes this request of God: *"Make new Nazareths in us."*

The little prayer comes to my mind this morning when I think of the new Nazareths that are being made all over the world as the Daughters of Charity renew their vows. Each of you this morning has tried to say *yes* to the messenger of God who has invited you to surrender your-selves to God and to His Will anew, so that you can serve his poor. Each of you has echoed this morning the words of Our Lady: *"Be it done unto me according to Thy Word."* (Lk 1:38). Because there are new Nazareths this morning, Christ, Our Lord, is breaking into the world in a new way, and particularly into that world which is so close to His heart, the world of the poor.

You are new Nazareths and your concerns must be those of Mary. It is not difficult for us to imagine what must have been one of her preoccupations when she had renewed her dedication to God by giving her consent to the Incarnation. She must have been concerned that she would not only safely bear the Holy One of God in her womb, but also would bring Him forth to the world. As a new Nazareth today, your primary concern must be to bear the Lord Jesus in the intimacy of your own heart and then to bring Him forth to the poor of the world. The first gift we can offer to the poor is something of the holiness of Jesus Christ. The poor, whether they articulate this request or not, are asking you to introduce them to Jesus Christ. They are saying to you what the Greeks said to Philip on Palm Sunday: *"We wish to see Jesus."* (Jn 12:21). What those Greeks wanted from Jesus Christ, we do not know. Of this we can be certain, that before they received anything from Him, the holiness of His person would have touched them. I have often reflected on this observation of W.H. Auden: *"I have met in my life two persons, one a man, the other a woman, who convinced me that they were persons of sanctity. Utterly different in character, upbringing and interests as they were, their effect upon me was the same. In their presence I felt myself to be ten times as nice, ten times as intelligent, ten times as good-looking as I really am."*

Over the Nazareth of the Gospels there lies a great silence, and in that silence *"the Child grew in wisdom and in stature and in favor with God and man."* (Lk 2:52). As new Nazareths, try to secure times in the day when silence will lie upon your heart and mind. When St. Vincent said that the street must be your cloister, I like to think that he was inviting you to bring the silence and recollection of the cloister into the street. In his conference on Holy Communion, St. Vincent remarks: *"The most Blessed Virgin went out to provide for the needs of her family and to solace and console her neighbors, but she always did so in the presence of God . . . .Ask her, my Daughters, to obtain for you from God this interior recollection by which you will prepare yourselves for the most Holy Communion of the Body and Blood of her Son, so that you will be able to say: 'My heart is ready, O my God, my heart is ready.'"* (Conf. Eng. ed., 18 Aug. 1647, pp. 303-304).

It is over twenty years now since Paul VI made his historic visit to the Holy Land. When he reached Nazareth, he told the people that Nazareth was a school where, even as Pope, he had much to learn. In describing Nazareth, he used a very daring phrase. *"It is,"* he said, *"the school of the Gospel."* The first of the three lessons, which he felt should be learned in this school of the Gospel, was silence. What he said on silence was brief and to the point. *"May esteem for silence, that admirable and indispensable condition of mind, be revived in me, besieged as we are by so many uplifted voices, the general noise and uproar in our seething and oversensitized modern life."* (cf. Office of Readings, Feast of the Holy Family). For us, who live busy lives, it is difficult to provide for silence in our lives. In large measure, however, it is the use we make of silence and reflection that forms us into the sort of persons we are becoming. To dig continually a well of silence in our lives is to have an assurance that the living water of God's grace will keep springing up, especially when we need it to help the needy who thirst for God's grace and kindness and seek it from our hands and lips and hearts.

In consenting again this morning to become servants of the Lord and servants of the poor, it is good to think of your vocation as something simple and humble, as simple and as humble as those things which Mary did for the Child of her womb in the home of Nazareth. Perhaps it might help us in the living of our vocation to think of ourselves as servants of the Lord, rather than as in the service of the Lord. Many people give service to others; much fewer, however, think of themselves as servants.

Yet it was as a servant that Our Lady thought of herself when she consented to become the Mother of God. Indeed, the word Our Lady used, according to St. Luke, was "slave." *"I am the slave of the Lord."* In an age in which much is said and much is being done for human rights, such language seems old-fashioned and out-of-date. Still, this great reality remains: that the Incarnation took place because a simple, humble, loving Virgin in Nazareth could think of herself as the slave of the Lord. Your Constitutions do not use the term "slave," but they do reflect, if we prayerfully meditate on them, the mentality of Mary: *"Authority and obedience commit them (the Sisters) to both a common seeking and a humble, loyal acceptance of God's Will . . . .The obedience that the Daughters of Charity have freely chosen entails sacrifices. Far from diminishing the dignity of the person, however, obedience enhances it by increasing the freedom which belongs to the children of God."* (C. 2.8).

"Make new Nazareths in us." Perhaps in some countries we hear voices like Nathanael's saying, *"Can anything good come out of Nazareth?"* (Jn 1:46). There are people who see no point in there being "new Nazareths" in the world and who question the value of the consecrated life. Let us not spend too much time arguing the point. Rather, let us take a hint from St. Philip who did not argue with Nathanael, but simply replied: *"Come and see."* Let your lives be of such dedication and love that they will be an invitation to all to come and see Jesus Christ, to Whom this morning you have surrendered yourselves with all your strength, with all your heart and with all your mind. Draw confidence from these words of St. Vincent: *". . . if God bestows a blessed eternity on those who give only a cup of water, what will he not give to a Daughter of Charity who has left everything and makes an offering of herself to serve them all the days of her life? . . . She has good grounds for hoping to be of the number of those to whom He will say: 'Come, blessed of My Father, possess the kingdom which has been prepared for you.'"* (Conf. Eng. ed., 13 Feb. 1646, p. 224).

May the Lord make new Nazareths in us, morning, noon and evening, until the time of Renovation comes around again.

Last Supper Continues

10 May 1984   Mexico

My dear Sisters,

A few years ago on a journey I met a layman who was unmarried and who, during our journey together, began to talk about religion. In the course of the conversation the topic of the Blessed Eucharist came up, and with great simplicity and sincerity he told me that he would find it very difficult to live if he could not receive Holy Communion daily. He spoke a little bit about the suffering that he endured when he was hospitalized on occasions during his life and when he could not receive Holy Communion each day. He frankly admitted that he had caused trouble in hospitals by asking insistently for Holy Communion. Then he told me how at times he would walk great distances in order to receive the Body and Blood of Christ to strengthen him to live. It was a remarkable revelation to me, for the man was not a religious fanatic, though I got the impression from him that he was a very sensitive man. He was somebody, I thought afterwards, whose heart and mind and whole being had been burned by the truth of Our Lord's words in today's Gospel: *"I am the Bread of life. I Myself am the living Bread come down from heaven. If anyone eats this Bread, he shall live forever."* (Jn 6:48,51).

On another occasion I recall talking to a Daughter of Charity who told me that she had brought a non-Catholic lady to one of our hospitals and into the Chapel. The Sister explained the significance of the Chapel and of the Blessed Sacrament. The non-Catholic asked Sister, did she really believe that Jesus Christ was present there in the tabernacle under the appearance of bread. The Sister, of course, replied *yes*, to which the non-Catholic lady said: *"If I believed that, I would never be able to tear myself away from this room."*

Like so many of God's graces and blessings, which we receive from Him daily, we take them too easily as something as ordinary as the light of day. I don't imagine that there are many Sisters in this Province who can remember the time when it was customary for people to receive Holy Communion on Sundays and on feast days. It was St. Pius X who flung open the doors of the tabernacles of the world. In St. Vincent's day there was a movement to close the doors of the tabernacles of the world. The Jansenists of France persuaded people that they were unworthy to receive Holy Communion. It was one of St. Vincent's great achievements in his life that he succeeded in persuading authorities in Rome that this was a dangerous doctrine. St. Vincent saw the value of frequent Holy Communion, even if the Church did not encourage people to receive it with the frequency that it does today.

The challenge for all of us, who have the joy and the privilege of receiving Communion daily, is to keep in our souls a sense of wonder that the Bread of Life which we eat each day is the same as was distributed by Our Lord to his apostles at the Last Supper. The Last Supper is going on still. Just before we receive the Body and Blood of Christ in Holy Communion, the Church reminds us that we are happy to be called to the table of the Lord. *"Happy are those who are called to His supper,"* for at this supper it is no ordinary bread. When the Host is placed in our hands or on our tongues, Jesus Christ is saying to each one of us in particular: *"I am the living Bread, come down from heaven. If you eat this Bread, you shall live forever. The Bread I am giving is my flesh for the life of the world."* (Ibid., v. 51).

To keep alive the sense of wonder at this daily miracle in our lives, we need to create a certain silence and moments of reflection in our lives. Before the reform of the Liturgy, we used to spend ten minutes, perhaps, in thanksgiving when the priest had left the altar after Mass. That is not so common now because the Church encourages priests especially to create a little period of silence after Holy Communion before the final prayers. Should a priest not do that, I think it is important for all of us to try to find some moments of quiet and personal thanksgiving for the gift of the bread that has come down from heaven to be the life of our souls. Without such reflection, the experience of Holy Communion will become stale, superficial and perfunctory. Let me end with a few phrases from a prayer which St. Louise used to recite before receiving Holy Communion: *"Most Holy Spirit, the Love of the Father and of the Son, come to purify and embellish my soul so that it will be agreeable to my Savior and so that I may receive Him for His greater glory and my salvation. I long for You with all my heart, O*

Bread of Angels. Do not consider my unworthiness which keeps me away from You, but listen only to Your love that has so often invited me to approach You. Give Yourself entirely to me, my God. May your precious body, your holy soul and your glorious divinity, which I adore in this Holy Sacrament, take complete possession of me. Amen." (*Spiritual Writings of Louise de Marillac*, A. 49, p. 834).

Lord, What Do You Want Me to Do?

11 May 1984   Guadalajara, Mexico

My dear Confreres,

Three times in the Acts of the Apostles the story of Paul's conversion is recounted. We have just listened to one of those accounts. In another of them St. Luke tells us that, when St. Paul was knocked off his horse and had recognized the hand of God in the experience, he said: *"Lord, what do you want me to do?"* (Acts 22:10). Those are the words which I would like to write on the walls of every seminary in the world. *"Lord, what do you want me to do?"* When we come to a seminary or to a Community like ours, we come with the intention of becoming a priest or a Brother. Before we come at all to the seminary, we have done much reflection and have taken advice. Even after all that, there will remain an element of doubt about our vocation. So it is for that reason that I suggest the prayer of St. Paul to you as one which should often be on your lips and in your hearts. *"Lord, what do you want me to do?"*

A seminary is a place where we become more certain of our vocation or we come to realize that we would be better Christians outside the seminary and as lay persons. A seminary is a place where we find our vocation. It is for that reason that I think any man who is earnest about his life in the seminary should have no regrets if he should come to the conclusion that he would serve Our Lord better in lay life. For many, of course, their vocation is strengthened and confirmed in the seminary. For all, then, in the seminary, the prayer of St. Paul is very appropriate. *"Lord, what do you want me to do?"*

The prayer, *"Lord, what do you want me to do?"* will be answered in time. What is important is that you give yourself fully to the life of the seminary as it is proposed to you. The answer to the prayer, *"Lord, what do you want me to do?"* will be given with assurance if you dedicate yourselves fully to the work of studying, praying, visiting the poor, and to participating fully in community life. Our Lord said on one occasion: *"He who does what is true comes to the light."* (Jn. 3:21). Reflect often on that advice of Our Lord. If we do what is true, that is, if we dedicate ourselves fully to the task of the present moment, we will come to the light. Our minds will be enlightened about what we should do with our lives. *"Lord, what do you want me to do?"* He who does what is true, comes to the light. As I celebrate this Mass with you, I pray that each one of you will come to the light and see clearly what Our Lord wants you to do.

Did you notice in the reading how St. Paul was told to go into the city of Damascus to a certain house and to a man called Ananias? Wasn't it strange that Our Lord did not tell him immediately what he was to do? Our Lord used another man to make known His Will to St. Paul. That is something else which we should often reflect upon in our lives, especially when we are seeking light about our vocation, or when we are finding some appointment difficult. Our Lord makes known His Will to us in all sorts of ways, but in a special way by those, to quote St. Vincent, in whose hands our souls are placed by Divine Providence.

St. Paul does not seem to have undertaken any great missionary journey immediately after his experience on the road to Damascus. In fact, he would seem to have undertaken a very long retreat. The time we pass in the seminary is one of the most valuable periods of our lives for this reason, that you are given an opportunity of coming to know Our Lord better, to know His Church better, and to know St. Vincent and our Community better. All this is accomplished under guidance by the Director and other Confreres who already know our Community, but also through your own reflection. That is why it is so important that you try, not only to acquire knowledge about Our Lord, the Church, St. Vincent and the Community, but to reflect and pray quietly about your experience of life here in the seminary. Cultivate a humble attitude of mind, in order that you may draw fully from the riches of spirituality which St. Vincent's Community offers to each one of us. As St. Vincent himself expressed it in a letter to a Confrere: *"Let us learn from the*

Saint of Saints to be gentle and humble. These are the virtues which you and I ought to ask Him for unceasingly and to which we ought to pay a great deal of attention so that we will not be surprised by the contrary vices; the vices which produce so many effects and destroy with one hand the spiritual building which the other hand has constructed. May Our Lord animate us with His infinite gentleness which will permeate our words and our actions to make them so that they may be agreeable and useful to our neighbor . . . ." (Coste VI, Fr. ed., pp. 387-388).

May Our Lord, through the intercession of Our Lady and of St. Vincent, give us that grace and all graces we need, so that we may do what He wants us to do. *"Lord, what do you want me to do?"*

Sick and Elderly Sisters

1 June 1984   Madrid, Spain

My dear Sisters,

Whenever I have the privilege of visiting one of our infirmaries, I always come away feeling a little more humble and, at the same time, a little stronger in my vocation. I come away feeling a little more humble because in our infirmaries I meet living biographies of great people: of Sisters and Confreres who have been serving the poor for years, who have been preaching the Gospel to the poor for years, and who have been devoted to the Community all their lives. I see them as people who over decades have been trying to be genuine disciples of Jesus Christ Who came, not to be served, but to serve.

In our infirmaries I meet Sisters and Confreres who have devoted years, and often in very difficult circumstances, to serving Christ and the poor, and now they find themselves in a situation where they feel almost imprisoned and often in a condition of being served. For when we grow old or are sick, we are obliged to allow others to do things for us which formerly we did for ourselves. That experience can be for some people a very painful one. In our infirmaries I see people who are experiencing the pain of diminishment which comes from weakness and age. Visits to our infirmaries make me feel a little more humble because I see lives, that have been much richer in work and in suffering for Christ than mine has been.

I always go away from our infirmaries feeling also a little stronger in my vocation. Our infirmaries are the hearts and the capitals of our Provinces. From our infirmaries there ascends to the throne of God, like fragrant incense, a great volume of prayer and suffering, and there is no doubt that there then descends upon our Provinces a wealth of graces for those who hold authority and for each member of St. Vincent's two Communities.

One day St. Vincent went to comfort a Brother of his Community who was very sick. He reminded the Brother that one of the greatest honors that we can render to God is to hope in the goodness of His heart and to take courage from the fact that God builds His throne of mercy on our weakness. It was also on that occasion that St. Vincent used the celebrated phrase: *"Love is inventive to the point of infinity."* (Coste XI, Fr. ed., p. 146). May you find it consoling in your weakness that God all the time is seeking ways to express His love for you. *"Love is inventive to the point of infinity"* even in old age and sickness.

St. Louise for her part thought and wrote much about the care that we must give to our old and sick. In regard to a sick Sister she wrote: *". . . look upon her as the first among your patients and as the dear companion God has given you to help you grow in holiness. Do not scruple to omit one or other of your exercises either to assist your Sister or for the service of the poor. You do this for the love of God and this is what He asks of you. Remember that the thing that we must have most at heart, and the greatest honor that we can receive, is to satisfy the wishes of our Divine Master."* (*Spiritual Writings of Louise de Marillac*, ltr. 547B, p. 526).

Living here, you must often feel impelled to use the words of the Gospel: *"Master, do you not care that we are perishing?"* (Mk 4:38). My prayer for you is that you may hear the voice of Jesus Christ Who says to us all in our moments of agitation what He said to the winds of the sea: *"Silence, be calm, and the wind ceased and all was again calm."* (Mk 4:39). May the grace, peace and serenity of Our Lord Jesus Christ be with you today and forever.

Hardening of Spiritual Arteries

8 June 1984   Tardajos, Spain

My dear Confreres,

Is there any of us here who has not a certain fondness and understanding of Peter, the Apostle? One of the twelve whom Our Lord chose, he is the one who in the Gospels is portrayed as the most human and the one whom we can understand most easily. Perhaps we feel close to Peter because in the story of his vocation and of his life's experience we can see fairly clearly a reflection of our own experience since we answered the call of Our Lord to come to the Community and to devote ourselves to Him and His poor.

In the first pages of the Gospel we admire his generosity. Maybe a fishing boat and some nets were not a great deal to give up. Still with great generosity he left them there at the lakeside and joined the little Community which Our Lord was gathering about Him. The spectacular must have enchanted Peter for a time. The blind began to see and the lame to walk, and Peter was right in at the center where the action was. When miracles were happening every day, you would cease to wonder at them. Besides, where was it all leading? Jesus had been giving dark hints about the state of unpopularity into which He would soon fall, and not only that but also hints of the shameful and humiliating death He would suffer on the Cross. It was time to ask a searching question, and it is recorded in this morning's Gospel. *"Peter began to say to Jesus: 'What about us? We have left everything and followed You.'"* (Mk 10:28).

All of us here remember the definitive decision we took to enter the Community. It cost us quite a bit. But then we were young and we were generous. We were surprised at times by our own generosity in those early years in the seminary and before vows. Then came our vows and we were still generous. Perhaps after that some of us may have fallen into Peter's frame of mind: *"What shall we have?"* Not that we were looking for millions. We were just doing a little bit of calculation. Sometimes I feel our middle years in the Community can become years of calculation.

Then came Peter's dramatic fall and denial of Christ, but how marvelously he recovered. How sensitively Our Lord helped him in the process of rehabilitation. In this evening's Gospel what delicacy Our Lord shows in not referring to Peter's fall. Then there is the depth of Peter's sincerity: *"Lord, You know all things. You know that I love You."* (Jn 21:17).

Peter's rehabilitation was the ability to accept the failures of the past, even when everyone knew about them, and to press on with the work of being a good shepherd and feeding the flock of Christ. The success of Peter was to recapture in his middle years something of the enthusiasm he had for Our Lord when he was young.

May the prayers of St. Peter, St. Vincent, and all our Community Saints save us from any hardening of our spiritual arteries, so that we may remain young and generous in heart until the end. *"I wish you a young heart,"* wrote St. Vincent, *"and a love in its first bloom for Him Who loves us unceasingly and as tenderly as if He were just beginning to love us."* (Coste I, Eng. ed., ltr. 288, p. 408). That wish of St. Vincent, my dear Confreres, is also mine for you.

Presence of God

15 June 1984   Granada, Spain

My dear Friends in Jesus Christ,

Many years ago I remember reading a short detective story about a murder that had been committed in a house on a city street. The police came to make investigations. They asked witnesses, who lived on the same street, if they had seen anybody entering the house. Nobody had. After a long time one witness came forward and said that he now recalled the fact that the postman had called at the house, where the murdered man lived, on that particular morning to deliver a parcel. It was the postman who had committed the murder. When the other witnesses were asked if they had seen the postman in the street on that particular day, almost all of them said: *"Why, yes."* Nobody mentioned the postman because the postman was on the street every morning. The point which the writer of the detective story wanted to make was that we do not see with our eyes what is commonplace and ordinary. No one had thought of the postman because the postman had been taken for granted.

I was reminded of this little story when I reflected on the first reading of this evening's Mass. Elijah had gone outside to stand on the mountain and was told that the Lord would pass by. First, there was a strong wind, but the Lord was not in the wind. Then there was an earthquake, but the Lord was not in the earthquake. Then there was a fire, but the Lord was not in the fire. Elijah, naturally thinking about the majesty and the greatness of God, would have expected the Lord to manifest Himself in the strong wind, in the earthquake, in the fire, but no. When the Lord did pass by, He made Himself known by *"a still, small voice."* (1 Kgs 19:12).

Our experience of the presence of God in our lives will be very similar to that of Elijah. God makes Himself known to us by the *"still, small voice"* of our conscience. The voice of our conscience is small and delicate, as small and delicate as a child. A child needs care and attention. So, too, with our consciences; we need to give them care and attention. That is why it is good at the end of each day to take a few moments to be silent in order to hear what the small, delicate voice of our conscience is saying to us about the day that has ended. Before we receive the Sacrament of Penance, it is good to give time in order to pay attention and give care to the still, small voice of our consciences.

Elijah found God, not in the strong wind nor in the earthquake nor in the fire, but in the still, small voice which he heard. God speaks to us in all sorts of ways: through the Scriptures, through His Church, but also through all the events, great and small, that happen to us. Since most of our lives are made up of very ordinary tasks which we must do each day, it is in these especially that the voice of the Lord is to be heard. We make the mistake so often of expecting God to speak to us through some great event or happening when, in fact, all the time He is speaking to us in all the small events of each day. You will remember how after the Resurrection Peter and John were fishing on the Lake of Galilee. Day was breaking and in that twilight, John saw Our Lord on the shore. *"That disciple whom Jesus loved said to Peter: 'It is the Lord.'"* (Jn 21:7). For all of us here, it would be a very great grace if, in all the circumstances of our lives, in all that we do, in accepting all that happens to us, pleasant and unpleasant, we could say, *"It is the Lord."* St. Vincent de Paul recommends that we accept all things *"when something unexpected happens to us in body or mind, good or bad, we are to accept it without fuss as from God's loving hand . . . ."* (CR II, 3). If we could live that ideal of St. Vincent, we would have great peace in our lives. Elijah only heard the voice of the Lord when he went forth and stood upon the mountain. May all of us here be strengthened to go forth every day and to stand upon the mountain of our daily work, so that we may hear and be consoled by the presence of the Lord passing by.

May all of us here be given the grace to find, in the words of St. Teresa of Avila, *"the Lord amidst the pots and pans."* May we be given the grace to give loving care to the voice of our conscience, which is the still small voice of God within us. Finally may we all be given the grace, through the intercession of Our Lady and of St. Michael of the Blessed Sacrament whose feast we celebrate today, of finding Christ in the Blessed Sacrament and in the poor.

We Die as We Live

21 July 1984   Buenos Aires, Argentina

My dear Sisters,

I remember hearing of an episode in the life of St. Ignatius of Loyola, in which the Saint, at this time an old man, was passing through a house where he was staying and where some novices were sweeping the corridor. He stopped to greet them and they began to talk. The novices held St. Ignatius in great veneration and, thinking of him as a very old man, (novices always think that their Superiors and Directors are of immense age!) and looking for an easy formula that might bring them to holiness quickly, they said to him: *"Father Ignatius, what would you do if you learned now that you were going to die tonight?"* Some of the novices thought that he might recommend an intense retreat for the hours that remained, others that he might suggest an immediate general confession, others yet again that he might counsel assistance at as many

Masses as possible during the few hours that remained to him. After a little pause, St. Ignatius looked at them and said: *"I would go on sweeping the corridor."*

The answer which St. Ignatius gave was brilliant. It expressed this great spiritual truth, that if we are doing the work which God wants us to do at this particular moment, we can be doing no better work, and if we can be doing no better work than the work we are presently performing, then that would be the best preparation for meeting Our Lord in judgment. To pray when one ought to be working is as much a sin, as to work when one ought to be praying. Quite clearly St. Ignatius saw that truth and impressed on the novices that, when they are working at the time and in the place where God wants them to be, they are offering a most acceptable prayer to God.

When I was in the seminary, there was a little Latin phrase which was often quoted to us. It was: *"Age quod agis."* Translating that freely, it could be rendered as: *"Do with your whole heart that which you are meant to be doing at this particular moment."* It is one of the most valuable lessons we can learn, by the grace of God, during our days in the seminary. By learning that lesson, we are slowly and perhaps painfully acquiring that precious gift of purity of intention or purity of heart.

When Our Lord said that we should not be thinking too much about tomorrow and that the problems of today are sufficient for us, he was revealing the truth that the grace of God, without which we can do nothing, comes to us moment by moment. The grace of God is to be found only in the present moment. Most of our anxieties in life come from trying to fight tomorrow's battles with the grace of today. When we learn to give ourselves fully to the task of the present moment, whether it be assisting at Mass, praying the rosary or sweeping the corridor, we are placing ourselves in the full light of God's grace. It is only when we are standing and allowing rays of God's grace to shine fully upon us that Our Lord can look on us and say in the words of today's Gospel: *"Here is my servant whom I have chosen, my loved one in whom I delight."* (Mt 12:18).

The ability to devote ourselves fully to the task of the present moment, and thus arrive at purity of intention and purity of heart, is a very precious grace. For people who have a lively imagination and who like to think of themselves in situations different from the ones in which they are at present, this grace is won with difficulty. The months we spend in the seminary are an excellent opportunity for schooling ourselves to acquiring the art of giving ourselves fully to the task of the moment, however small and insignificant it may be. In doing so we are loving God with our whole heart and with our whole soul and with our whole mind, and that is the first great commandment of the law.

Sweep the corridor with purity of intention. Enter into recreation with purity of intention. Serve the poor with purity of intention. Meet Christ in the Sacraments with purity of intention, and imperceptibly you will grow in the love of God and of the poor.

> *Purity of intention*, asks St. Vincent, *how can one practice it better than by doing the Will of God? Is there anyone who has a more perfect purity of intention than that of wanting to do all that God wants and in the manner in which He wants it done? In comparing all (spiritual exercises), you will find that God is more glorified in the practice of His Will than in all others, and that there is no one who honors Him more than he who gives himself fully to this holy practice.* (Coste, XII, Fr. ed., pp. 152-153).

To all of you St. Louise would say, as she wrote to one of her Sisters: *"The Sisters must often renew their purity of intention which causes them to perform all their actions for the love of God. This will enable them to preserve the spirit which true Daughters of Charity must possess."* (*Spiritual Writings of Louise de Marillac*, ltr. 400, p. 432).

May St. Vincent and St. Louise obtain that grace for us.

Transfiguration

6 August 1984   Cochabamba, Bolivia

My dear Sisters and my dear Confreres,

Six years ago today Pope Paul VI died in Rome. His predecessor, John XXIII, remarked a few days before his death that any day in the year was a good day to die. When Paul VI died on the feast of the

Transfiguration, people felt that there was something appropriate that he should have died on that day, just as they did in 1963 when Pope John XXIII died during the Octave of Pentecost. Pope John XXIII spoke much about the Holy Spirit and thought of the Council as a new Pentecost. Pope Paul VI worked to implement all that the Council had decided, so that the Church would be transfigured and would shine more brightly as the *Lumen Gentium* in the darkness of this world. He was, then, a Pope of transfiguration.

The experience of the three disciples on the Mount of the Transfiguration was an experience of seeing the inner glory of Jesus Christ. After His Resurrection, those disciples would discover that the experience which they had on the Mount of Transfiguration would be continued in a new, but no less real, way through the reality of Baptism. Over and over again, St. Paul kept reminding the Christians of his day that even now they were participating in the glory of the Resurrection. St. John who was on the mountain of Transfiguration would write years later: *"As many as received Him, He gave them power to become sons of God . . . and we saw His glory . . . and of His fullness we have all received, grace upon grace."* (Jn 1:12,14,16). Grace, it has been said, is glory away, and glory is grace at home.

In the monotony of daily life, it is difficult to realize that through Baptism we are already sharing in the inner glory of Jesus Christ. Listen to St. Paul's way of expressing it. *"The charity of God is poured forth in our hearts by the Holy Spirit Who is given to us."* (Rom 5:5). That is the foundation of our love for the poor. The smallest service we do for the poor is a releasing of the love of God which is already in our hearts. It is a manifestation of the glory of Jesus Christ. By the smallest act of love shown to the poor, we are reenacting the Transfiguration in our own little lives. Just as the Transfiguration of Christ rejoiced the hearts of Peter, James and John, so, too, when we manifest authentic and selfless love to the poor, their hearts are warmed and they rejoice.

All that calls for faith. St. Vincent expressed it marvelously when he said: *"I must not consider a poor peasant or a poor woman according to their exterior, nor according to what appears from their behavior. Very often they have not really the appearance nor intelligence of rational beings, so gross and earthly are they. But turn the medal and you will see in the light of faith that the Son of God, Who wished to be poor, is represented to us by these poor people . . . .It is beautiful to see the poor if we consider them in God and with the esteem which Jesus Christ had for them.* " (Coste XI, Fr. ed., p. 32).

When the disciples came down from the mountain of the Transfiguration, they saw Jesus alone. When St. Vincent invites us to love and serve the poor, he invites us to see in them Jesus Christ: *"Turn the medal and by the light of faith you will see the Son of God."* (Ibid.).

St. Luke makes the point that while Jesus prayed there the disciples had a new vision of Him. Your vocation is to bring spiritual and bodily necessities to the poor in whom you recognize the presence of Christ. It is from the experience of a vision of Christ that you go to the poor. For that reason we must always keep climbing the mountain of prayer.

St. Vincent's phrase about leaving God for God to serve the poor is a celebrated one. With equal insistence, however, he emphasized the importance of daily meditation. In our own day, Pope John Paul II has on more than one occasion told priests and religious that we can be so busy about the work of the Lord as to forget the Lord of the work.

All that you do for the poor must spring from your vision of Christ. In every gesture of love for the poor, you bring heaven down to earth. You are preparing, getting things ready so that Christ can come again and take possession of His kingdom and hand it over to His Father Who will be all in all.

When Pope Paul VI was dying on this evening six years ago, his final prayer, which he repeated over and over again, was the opening phrase of the Our Father: *Our Father, Who art in heaven.* This great Pope who loved the Church so much recognized that the final graces of his life would come from the Father Whose voice was heard on the Mount of the Transfiguration: *"This is My Son, My chosen one."* (Mt 17:5). May we come to understand more deeply the Fatherhood of God and imitate more closely Him Who makes the sun to shine on all alike.

Wait on the Lord

8 August 1984   El Trompillo, Bolivia

My dear Sisters,

A few years ago I recall seeing a very touching film about an orphan boy who was trying to survive in the world. He had as his motto in life: *Do not take no for an answer.* I thought of this film when I was reflecting on this Gospel to which we have just listened. On this particular occasion Our Lord was outside His own country, and the woman, who approached Him to ask a favor, was not an Israelite. Our Lord refused her request. She was determined that she would not take *no* for an answer. She persisted. There is a slight suggestion of humor in this Gospel passage. Our Lord said it was not right to give the bread of the children to the dogs (I wonder, was there a suggestion of a smile on Our Lord's face when He spoke about children, surrounded as He was by His strong, healthy Apostles who wanted to get rid of this woman). It is possible, too, that the woman picked up Our Lord's humor when she replied: *"Yes, Lord, yet even the dogs eat the crumbs that fall from their master's table."* (Mt 15:27).

Picking up that phrase of the woman in today's Gospel, allow me to reflect on the Saint of the day whose name means *"the dog of the Lord."* St. Dominic is often represented by a star and a dog with a torch in its mouth. Whenever I pass by the Basilica of St. John Lateran in Rome, I think of St. Dominic and St. Francis of Assisi. Both these Saints are said to have met each other in that Church during the Fourth Lateran Council. In a little book, called *The Flowers of St. Francis,* which is associated with the great Saint of Assisi, the soul of the faithful Christian is compared to a dog who is attached to its master. A faithful dog will lie for hours outside a house into which his master has entered, waiting patiently for him to come out again. The image is a very useful one. It reminds us of that line in the psalm: *"My soul is waiting for the Lord; I count on His word."* (Ps 130:6). If we could absorb the spirituality of that single line of the psalm, there would be much more peace in our lives. We spend so much time fretting about the future because we have not learned to wait on the Lord. The darkness and dryness we experience in prayer at times is all the more painful because we cannot lie patiently, like dogs, waiting for the return of Our Lord. St. Vincent's insistence on the wisdom of taking decisions slowly and of not anticipating the Providence of God was the fruit of knowing how to wait on the Lord. *"My soul is waiting on the Lord; I count on His word."* (Ibid.).

The grace of waiting on the Lord, and of acting only when we have clear signs of the direction that He wants us to take, can bring much peace and serenity to our souls. Of St. Dominic his first biographer remarked that nothing disturbed the even temper of his soul except his quick sympathy with every sort of suffering. All that was built on the foundation of humility, poverty of spirit and confidence in God. When he lay dying in Bologna on the 6 August 1221, St. Dominic said to his friars: *"These, my much loved ones, are the bequests which I leave to you as my sons: Have charity among you; hold to humility; keep willing poverty."* We can only wait on the Lord when we have come to think of Him as our all. *"My God and my all,"* exclaimed St. Francis of Assisi. God can only be our all when we have stripped our hearts of all desires that are inordinate, whether these desires be for the affection of others or for the material things of this world. And if we must go to the bedrock of all spirituality, be it Dominican, Franciscan or Vincentian, we arrive at the foundation of faith. It is only when we have faith in the person of Jesus Christ that we can surrender ourselves to Him, making the sacrifice of our desires which that surrender demands. All that brings me back to the point from which I started, the Gospel of today. Our Lord yielded to the woman who would not take *no* for an answer, because her faith was great. *"Woman, you have great faith."* (Mt 15:28). May our faith be great, so that we will not take *no* for an answer when there is question of surrendering ourselves to Christ in order that we may be servants of the poor. *"O my God, we give ourselves entirely to you. Grant us the grace to live and die in true poverty . . . to live and die in chastity . . . to live in a perfect observance of obedience. We also give ourselves to you, my God, to honor and serve our Lords the poor, all our lives."* (Conf.Eng. ed., 5 July 1640, p. 22).

Pilgrim Status

9 August 1984   Rio de Janeiro, Brazil

My dear Sisters and my dear Confreres,

Exactly a year ago to the day I celebrated Mass here in Rio with you at the end of my visit to this vast country of yours. Here I am again, this time passing through San Paolo and Rio on my way back to Rome from visiting some other countries of Latin America. As we meet each other briefly this evening, I stand before you very much as a pilgrim. My stay is a short one, just a stopover. Let me say, however, that I am very happy to greet you once again and to have this opportunity of offering with you the Mass, that sacrifice which, in the words of one of the Eucharistic prayers, brings salvation to the whole world.

Like all pilgrims I am torn between the desire to reach my destination and another desire to settle down and remain in those places which attract me. However, true pilgrims never lose sight of the fact that it is arrival at the goal of their pilgrimage which gives sense to the whole pilgrimage. So the desire to settle down in one particular place must be resisted, and that often costs a lot. The vows we take in Community could be said to have as one of their purposes the keeping alive in us of the mentality of a pilgrim. Pilgrims, while on their journey, lodge in places that are not their homes: we have our vow of chastity, we do not establish homes of our own. Pilgrims usually travel light, as we say: we have our vow of poverty. Pilgrims keep on the move: we have our vow of obedience that places us now in one house and now in another. Pilgrims are not unmindful of their fellow travelers: so Sisters have their vow of service of the poor and Confreres their vow of stability, that is, their engagement to the preaching of the Gospel to the poor.

It is good to see our vows in this light from time to time, because in that way we are helped to remain detached from all that could either make us forget what we are supposed to be doing with our lives, or distract us from the ideals set before us in the Gospel and in our own particular Constitutions.

You could say that the temptation to which we are continually exposed, namely, of losing sight of our pilgrim status, was one to which

St. Peter succumbed. In the Gospel of today's Mass St. Peter wanted Our Lord to bypass the pilgrim route that took Him through Calvary. Our Lord rejected with considerable force that suggestion of Peter's. On another occasion at the beginning of Our Lord's public life, St. Peter wanted Our Lord to settle down in Capernaum where one evening He had great success in curing and healing a multitude of people. Our Lord turned down Peter's suggestion: *"Let us,"* He said, *"go on to the next towns that I may preach there also, for that is why I have come."* (Mk 1:38).

To St. Peter's credit it must be said that by the light and strength of the Holy Spirit he learned the lesson well. St. Peter passed from Jerusalem to Antioch and from there to Rome. Peter made his pilgrimage to Rome where, sharing in the passion and cross of his Master, he entered into the heavenly Jerusalem which is the terminus of the pilgrimage for us all.

So as a pilgrim on my way to Rome, allow me, my dear Sisters and my dear Confreres, to offer you a word of encouragement, you who are companions of mine on that more important spiritual pilgrimage which we are making together to the place which Our Lord Himself has personally prepared for us. May we all be given deeper insight into the importance of the vows we have taken in our Communities. May we see these vows, not as mere legal obligations but as gifts of grace, offered to us by God to facilitate and lighten our journey to God. May the Virgin Mary, who in the words of the document, *Lumen Gentium,* is *"a sign of certain hope and comfort to the pilgrim people of God,"* (§68) give special hope and comfort to us who are dedicating our lives in our Communities to the service and to the evangelization of the poor.

Nature of Pilgrims

15 August 1984   Paris, France

Mother Rogé, Father Lloret, and my dear Sisters,

When you pray the Rosary and reflect on the words, actions and experiences of Our Blessed Lady, perhaps you have found yourself impressed by the number of times Mary made the journey from Nazareth to Jerusalem and back. There is, first, the journey from Nazareth into what St. Luke calls *"the hill country to a town of Judea"* (Lk 1:39) to visit her cousin, Elizabeth. The Gospel passage to which we listened at Mass this morning opens with noting that fact, and it closes with the observation that Mary made the return journey three months later. The third joyful mystery of our Rosary is celebrated at the end of the journey which Mary with Joseph made from Nazareth to Bethlehem. The fifth joyful mystery also marks the beginning of the journey back to Nazareth from which Mary, Joseph and the child Jesus had earlier set out. Whether she returned, like the disciples, into Galilee after the Resurrection, we do not know, but if she did, we know for certain that she was again in Jerusalem when the Spirit of God came upon the Church at Pentecost.

These journeys of Mary from Galilee to Judea tell us something of the physical strength and endurance of the Mother of God. We have only to look at present day photographs of the type of country that separates Galilee from Judea to realize what physical effort and endurance must have been called for. More important for us, however, is the inner spiritual strength that sustained Mary in these journeys, for these journeys which Mary made had the character of pilgrimages. Pilgrimages are more than journeys, because pilgrimages have a special inner quality which faith in the living God gives to them. It was quite clearly faith in the living God that prompted Mary to make those journeys or pilgrimages from the humble town of Nazareth to the city of Jerusalem, the special dwelling place of the God of Sion.

In the years since Vatican Council II, we have come to appreciate the insight which the Spirit of God has given us on the pilgrim nature of the Church. It could be said that the Constitution *Lumen Gentium* presents Our Lady as the pilgrim who has already reached the heavenly Jerusalem and, because she is glorified both in body and soul in heaven, can be a special source of hope and encouragement to us who are still on the pilgrim's road.

A pilgrim must resist the temptation to settle down, however attractive the countryside may be through which he passes. The vows we take in Community can be seen as means to help us from putting our roots down too deeply into what the passing scene may offer. A pilgrim does not set up his own house and home along the road he travels: so, we have our vow of Chastity. A walking pilgrim will travel light: so, we have our vow of Poverty. A pilgrim on the road will ask and accept directions; so, we have our vow of Obedience. A pilgrim will have an eye and a hand and a heart for the weak and wounded he may meet on the road: so, a Daughter of Charity has her vow to serve the poor of Christ.

Our vows have as one of their purposes to counter our innate tendency to settle down too comfortably on the road of life and not to press on. Perhaps it is for that reason that St. Vincent had so much to say on the importance of what he called indifference or detachment.

When we make our meditation on indifference or detachment, it is important to allow the Community to enter into the sanctuary of our hearts. By that I mean that it may be relatively easy to offer the total gift of myself to God in the intimacy of my prayer. It is much more difficult to offer the total gift of myself to God through my Community. It is through the Community that I receive my apostolate, my house, my office. To none of these, however, must I be so attached that the Community finds it very difficult or even impossible to ask me to give them up. A pilgrim on the road does not build walls around himself. Neither must we surround ourselves, nor even our apostolates, with walls that make it difficult for our Superiors to approach us with the suggestion that we move forward in a direction that we may not have thought of, or even which may not appeal to us.

Perhaps the quality, or rather gift of God, which I am thinking about, is availability; that is, a readiness, a facility, almost an agility, to move in any direction which obedience may indicate or suggest. Devotion to Jesus Christ present in the poor is indeed central to the vocation of a Daughter of Charity, but it must always be understood as only to those poor whom the authorities in the Company present to the individual Sister to be served. The attachment of a Daughter of Charity to her poor must never be so great that she makes it difficult or almost impossible for her Superiors to ask her to accept in exchange another group of poor to be served in place of those whom she is presently serving. True dedication to the service of the poor goes hand in hand with the gift of availability.

It was precisely because she had this gift of availability, this spiritual agility, that Mary was able to go *"with haste"* into the formidable hill country of Judea to visit and assist her cousin Elizabeth in giving birth to John the Baptist. In one word, the gift of availability enables us to walk on the pilgrim way with lightness in our step.

The pilgrims on their way to Jerusalem had their songs, as they walked along the road. No doubt Mary knew them well. We still have some of them in our book of psalms: *"They are happy whose strength is in you, In whose hearts are the roads to Sion. As they go through the bitter valley, they make it a place of springs."* (Ps 83:6-7).

During almost two decades of years, as Councillor and Mother General, Mother Rogé has been a pilgrim to the Provinces of the Company. By her presence, by her words and, above all, by her life she has made our valleys *"places of springs."* On this, your feast day, Mother Rogé, may, in the words of the pilgrim's psalm, your *"heart and soul ring out their joy to God, the living God."* (Ps 83:3). Mother Rogé, a very Happy Feast Day!

Vocation of Vincentian Brothers

18 August 1984   To Brothers on Retreat

My dear Confreres,

May the grace of Our Lord Jesus Christ be with us forever!

Two days ago Brother Camille Harmond wrote to me, asking if I would join you during your annual retreat. Regretfully I am unable to do so, as I will be spending almost the entire month of September with our Confreres of the Province of Poland. So I write these few lines to greet you, to pray God's blessing on your retreat and to ask your prayers for the needs of the Congregation and for mine.

Let me say how happy I am that you are making your retreat together. I congratulate you on supporting this initiative which has been taken by yourselves. I am sure that the experience of praying together and of sharing your spiritual insights with each other will deepen in you the love and appreciation of the vocation which God has given you.

A grace that I hope God will give to each of you is to see with clarity of vision that the vocation which you have as a Brother is a special one. Too often we look only to what our eyes can see and our hands accomplish, and we judge the value of our lives by our external achievements. The truth is otherwise. What gives value to our lives is the quality of our personal relationship with Jesus Christ. That relationship arises from the vocation He has given to each one of us. The Church of Jesus Christ has authoritatively told us through our Constitutions that to some men Jesus Christ has given the grace of being Brothers in the Congregation of the Mission, and who are thus called to preach the Gospel to the poor through their prayer and the work which they daily do.

One of the graces that I received from God in the past two years was to meet a Brother in one of our Provinces in the United States who is blind, but who asks daily to be led out into the grounds of the house so that he can, by his sense of touch, trim the grass under some of the trees. When I arrived at the house where this Brother lives, the priest Confreres pointed him out to me as a blind Brother whom they looked upon as a very saintly confrere. Talking with this Brother for a little while later in the evening, I found myself agreeing fully with what the priests had said to me about him earlier. I mention this fact to illustrate the truth which we all know; namely, that it is not the position that we occupy in the Congregation that matters most in God's eyes, but the quality of our personal relationship with His Son, Jesus Christ.

Today I read the following few lines in a letter of St. Vincent to Brother Martin Baucher on 27 July 1659. I make St. Vincent's sentiments my own as I greet you individually in my heart: *"Continue, my dear Brother, to give to God all the affection of your heart, the application of your spirit and the works of your hands, and hope for great blessings from His divine goodness. Ask Him for mercy for me who am in His love, my dear Brother, your very affectionate Father and servant."* (Coste VIII, Fr. ed., p. 56).

Blessed John Gabriel Perboyre, C.M.

11 September 1984   Poznan, Poland

My dear Sisters,

This evening we are celebrating the feast of Blessed John Gabriel Perboyre, the missionary who at thirty-eight years of age and after only thirty-eight months of work in China, endured extremely painful tortures and was finally executed by strangulation.

In 1982 I met in the United States a young Vincentian priest who is firmly convinced that he was cured of cancer through the intercession of Blessed John Gabriel Perboyre. He was a patient in one of the hospitals of the Daughters of Charity in Chicago, and during his serious illness there, he began, at the suggestion of a Daughter of Charity, to make a novena to Blessed John Gabriel Perboyre. Shortly after he finished the novena, he got better quickly. Today he enjoys good health and the doctors confess that his cure is to them a mystery.

On the other side of the world, in China, you will find another type of miracle. From time to time, Mother Rogé receives letters written with great discretion from Sisters in the heart of China. They write to her to assure her that they are devoted to St. Vincent and St. Louise and are loyal to the Company here on earth. They live lives of great poverty and treasure the teachings of our Founders and the traditions of the Company. After so many years of persecution of the Church in China, that is a miracle, and I am certain that the prayers of Blessed John Gabriel have something to do with it. Let us remember often in our prayers the two Communities of St. Vincent which are still alive in the Church of Silence.

Today we join with the entire Vincentian Community throughout the world in celebrating the feast day of one of St. Vincent's outstanding disciples. The Gospel of today's Mass tells us that *"Jesus went out to the mountain to pray, spending the night in communion with God."* (Lk 6:12). Only prayer and constant union with Christ, especially in the Holy Eucharist, enabled Blessed John Gabriel Perboyre to lay down his life for Christ, and enabled the Church some fifty years after his death to proclaim him Blessed.

It is from the Eucharist that we, too, draw the strength to withstand the storms of temptation that beat from time to time on the house of our souls. It is from the Eucharist that we draw strength to be martyrs, that is, witnesses to Christ present in His poor in our daily lives. It is from the Eucharist that we draw strength to be sacraments ourselves, that is, signs of Christ's love to each other in Community. I pray that you will never lose confidence in the power of the Mass and that you will never lose faith in His living Presence in the Blessed Sacrament. Let me end by quoting part of a prayer composed by Blessed John Gabriel: *"May my hands be the hands of Jesus. May my tongue be the tongue of Jesus . . . .I pray You to destroy in me all that is not of You. Grant that I may live only in You, by You and for You, so that I may truly say with St. Paul: 'I live, now not I, but Christ lives in me.'"*

Judgment

13 September 1984   Slubice, Poland

My dear Sisters and my dear Confreres,

When I was a young boy, a lady who held very high principles about life lived near our home. When she had an opportunity, she would express some of these principles to us over and over again. One of these sayings was: *"Life will give you back what you put into it."* I think the lesson she was trying to teach us young people was that, if we wish others to be generous with us, we must be generous with them. That was an important lesson for young people who, like all people, have a tendency to be selfish. I was reminded of this lady and the teaching she used to impart to us by a little phrase in this evening's Gospel. Jesus said, *"The measure you give will be the measure you get."* (Lk 6:38). Perhaps you are saying to yourself that you have been generous to people who have not shown kindness and generosity to you. That indeed may be true. It was the experience of Our Lord Himself, Who gave to people without counting the cost and received in return crucifixion and death. On occasion, when we give to the poor, our kindness and our generosity are not acknowledged, are taken for granted, and that hurts us. Even if we are not repaid in kind for what we give to others, we do receive mysteriously a measure of peace and joy which comes, not from those to whom we give but from our Father in heaven from whom all good things come. It is the Spirit of God Who assures us that *"God loves a cheerful giver."* (2 Cor. 9:7). The peace and joy that God gives us in our hearts is the first installment of the peace and joy which He will give us when we enter into the fullness of life with Him after our death. Our lives are springtime when we sow the seed in the ground which will be reaped later, when the harvest time comes at the end of our lives.

The time of harvest will be the time of judgment. To secure a favorable judgment, Our Lord offers us a simple assurance and recommendation. *"Judge not, and you will not be judged."* (Lk 6:37). Recently I read about a priest who started his homily at a funeral, saying: *"I am going to preach about judgment."* There was dismay in the congregation. Then he went on. *"Judgment is whispering into the ear of a merciful and compassionate God the story of my life which I had never been able to tell."* Many of us have a story, or part of one at any rate, about which we have never been able to speak to anyone. We are afraid of being misunderstood. We are unable to express ourselves fully, or we fear the darker side of our hidden lives. Our true story is not told, or only part of it. When we meet our merciful and compassionate judge, Jesus Christ, we will start to tell Him the full story about ourselves, and He will begin that process of healing and preparation which we call Purgatory.

In a sense, all our lives we are preparing and choosing the sort of judge we will have at the end of our lives. It is the compassionate and understanding judgments which we make about others which are fashioning the judge we ourselves will meet at the moment of death. If our judgments have been harsh and unsympathetic towards others, then the judge we are choosing for ourselves at the end of our lives will be a harsh and unsympathetic one. We must draw that conclusion from Our Lord's own words: *"With the judgment you pronounce you will be judged."* (Lk 6:38).

Speaking to the first Daughters of Charity, St. Vincent quoted his friend, St. Francis de Sales, who remarked that if a person's action presented a hundred different possible interpretations, we should choose that which is the most favorable one. In offering this counsel to the Daughters of Charity, we can safely assume that it was St. Vincent's own practice. In all that he said and wrote, it is remarkable how careful St. Vincent was to avoid passing categorical judgments on people he met and to whom he wrote. The charity that was the inspiration of so much of St. Vincent's works sprang from a heart that was kind and compassionate and a mind that had reflected on the words of Christ: *"Has no man condemned you . . . neither will I."* (Jn 8:10-11).

Judge not and you shall not be judged. Rather, *"bear one another's burdens."* (Gal 6:2). It was while reflecting on these words of St. Paul that St. Vincent exclaimed in a conference: *"My Lord, henceforth I wish only to fix my eyes on my own defects. Grant that from now on, enlightened by the splendor of Your example, I will carry in my heart all mankind and support them with Your help. Grant me the grace of working in that way and enkindle in my heart Your love."* (Coste XI, Fr. ed., p. 270).

Discipline

19 September 1984   Krakow, Poland

My dear Seminary Sisters,

When visiting the different provinces of the Company, I always like to have a short meeting with the Seminary Sisters, and this for two reasons. First, I regard the Seminary Sisters as especially privileged people because of the fact that it was during the time she spent in the seminary that St. Catherine received from Our Lady the Miraculous Medal. It is something very remarkable that, of all the people in the Company of the Daughters of Charity, it should have been a simple Seminary Sister who received that medal which the Community and the world have treasured since 1830. Whenever I reflect upon it, the words of St. Paul to the Corinthians come to my mind: *"The weak things of the world God has chosen that He may confound the strong."* (I Cor 1:27). Until the end of time this fact will remain unchanged: that it was to a Seminary Sister that Our Lady entrusted the theology and the practical message of the Miraculous Medal. That is why I think that

Seminary Sisters in all the provinces of the world are and will always remain for us, special people.

The second reason why I like to talk to the Seminary Sisters is that I am convinced that the days we pass in the seminary are very valuable ones. It is during this time that we acquire habits which will remain with us until the end of our lives. It is true that we will not always do things in exactly the same way as we did in the seminary, but you will find that some of the most useful suggestions you will get for your lives will be offered to you during these months.

The months we spend in the seminary are very valuable because we try to deepen in ourselves two very important virtues, humility and silence. In our seminary days especially, and indeed throughout our lives, we try to become more humble people. That costs us a lot. It is only through growth in humility that we come to know ourselves better and to draw closer to Jesus Christ. The Directress and others will help you to come to know yourselves better. At times that will cost a lot and will bring you almost to tears. Take heart, however, and reflect often on St. Augustine's prayer: *"Lord, may I know myself so that I may come to know You."* In the seminary we learn more about discipline, not only in theory but in practice. Another name for discipline is mortification. That is not a popular word in the world today. When you find it difficult to be disciplined or mortified, think of the fact that to be a close disciple of Christ, it is necessary to be disciplined. The two words are almost the same: *disciple* and *discipline*. We cannot be disciples of Christ without being disciplined.

There are many other things I would like to say to you about your seminary life, but there is one final suggestion which I would like to offer you. Have great confidence in the traditions of the Community. Some of our traditions are very old and they have enabled thousands of Sisters to become loving servants of the poor and very holy people. Be slow to reject what is presented to you as our way of doing things, as our way of serving the poor. Other Communities will do things differently. Let us, however, accept humbly the way the Directress and others in the Community suggest we do things. Acting in that way, we will be accepting the traditions of our Community, which in the main go back to St. Vincent and St. Louise. May these two great Saints be the inspiration of your lives.

Your new Constitutions state: *"Formation is, above all, the work of God living and acting in the heart of those whom he calls. Next, it is the work of the sister herself, prompted by the desire for increasing fidelity to her vocation. In this discovery of God's design upon her, a Daughter of Charity is not alone; the Company is at hand to help her to become a servant of the poor."* (C. 3.5).

Poverty and Riches

26 September 1984   Zakopane, Poland

My dear Friends in Christ,

In the first reading of today's Mass there is one of the most beautiful prayers of the entire Bible. Let us listen to it again. *"Give me neither poverty nor riches. Feed me with the food that is needful for me, lest I be full and deny Thee and say, 'Who is the Lord?' or lest I be poor and steal and profane the name of my God."* (Prv 30:8-9). What a wise prayer it is, for when we have too much money, too many good things, we tend to forget God, and when we have not sufficient to live upon and our stomachs are empty, we blame God and, as the author says, profane His name.

Most of the people of the world must live out their lives in great poverty. It is said that two-thirds of the world's population go to bed hungry every night. So, if we do not go to bed hungry, we have a lot to be thankful for. We must be considered as part of that one-third of the world which is not considered to be hungry. Perhaps we are not hungry, but we are not rich. Take comfort from the thought that, when God Himself decided to come into the world, He chose to be among that group of persons among whom we find ourselves. It is true that Our Lord said that He had not where to lay His head. When we consider the strenuous life He led when He was preaching in various parts of Palestine, and the long journeys He took on foot, we must conclude that He was a physically strong man. He would not have been a physically strong man if His mother, Mary, and Joseph had not fed Him well as an infant and as a young and growing boy. So, we can conclude that He was not poor to the extent that, as an infant and as a boy, He had not sufficient to eat; nor was He rich. We know that He was born in a stable, because there was no room for Him in the inn. If Mary and Joseph had been wealthy people, they would have been able to buy their way into the inn. We must conclude that Joseph was a conscientious tradesman and that he earned sufficient money to keep his wife, Mary, and her Son, Jesus, in sufficiently good circumstances to enable Jesus to grow into the strong man portrayed in the Gospels.

Jesus Christ was not rich. He chose to live poorly and there is not a shadow of doubt but that He died in abject poverty. They even took the clothes from His back and cast lots for them. When He died, He had no money to leave, no property, not even a shirt on His back. We may not be considered to be rich people nor are we considered to be extremely poor, thanks be to God. What we as Christians have to watch could be expressed in one word, and that word is *more*. We always seem to want more money, more pleasure, more power, and it is desiring more that can draw us away from Christ and make us unhappy people.

There is a little story told about a poor man who was talking to a king one day. The king had much land. The king said to the man: *"I will give you as much land as you can run around between the rising of the sun and its setting."* *"Agreed,"* said the poor man. So the next morning when the sun rose, he started to run around one field and then another and then another, and so on through the day. When the sun was setting, he had accumulated quite a large amount of land, though before the sun disappeared he saw one other field he would like. He had to run up a hill to reach it. So he ran up the hill and, just as he reached the top of the hill, he dropped dead. Friends came to the king and said: *"What will we give this poor man?"* The king thought for a moment and replied: *"Give him six feet. That is sufficient ground to bury him."* It was the man's desire to have more that brought about his death. So all of us have to guard against greed of every kind. *"Jesus said to them: 'Take heed and beware of greed of every kind.'"* (Lk 12:15).

So if we have sufficient food for ourselves, our families, and reasonable comfort in our homes, let us be content. Let us spare a thought and some money for those who, unlike us, are suffering from extreme poverty which tempts people, in the words of the reading in today's Mass, *"to profane the name of the Lord."* (Prv 30:9). A very great

English Saint who lost all his property and his life in the end, because he was unwilling to deny the faith, used to pray: *"Thanks be to You, Lord Jesus Christ, for all that you have given me. Thanks be to You, Lord Jesus Christ, for all that you have taken from me. Thanks be to You, Lord Jesus Christ, for all that You have left me."* May those sentiments of St. Thomas More, the English Saint and martyr, be ours today and always.

Abraham

12 October 1984   Cagliari, Sardinia

My dear Confreres, Sisters and Friends in Jesus Christ,

If you asked St. Paul to write down the names of the people who influenced him most in his life, there is little or no doubt that, after Jesus Christ, he would write down the name of Abraham. Not only was Abraham a hero, but he was looked upon as the founder of the nation. We can be certain, too, that in the little home of Nazareth, Mary and Joseph often spoke to the Child Jesus about Abraham who was, not only the founder of their nation, but more than that, a man of faith and obedience. Religious Communities look back to their founders and admire them. The little family community of Nazareth looked back to Abraham and admired him for many things, but principally for his faith and obedience. In his writings Paul constantly asked Christians of his day to imitate the faith of Abraham, as he did in the second reading to which we have listened this evening.

Abraham's faith was tested when God said to him: *"Go from your country and your kindred and your father's house to a land that I will show you."* (Gen 12:1). The invitation which God gave to Abraham has been uttered by Him over and over again. When Jesus Christ called the twelve Apostles to leave all things and follow Him, He was speaking as God spoke to Abraham. It was that same call which fifty years ago this month was heard by the three men we are honoring in a special way this evening, Father Eugenio Pomatto, Father Giovanni Cau and Brother Luigi Ursic. Rejoice with them that they listened to the call of Jesus Christ: that they left their families and entered the Congregation of the Mission; that they allowed themselves to be led by God into those places and into that work which He appointed them to do. Two of them, Father Pomatto and Brother Ursic, dedicated many years to the life of the College, while Father Cau was called to devote many years of his life to the preaching of missions. We rejoice with them and we thank God for what He has given to them through St. Vincent's Congregation. We pray God that He will give them much peace tonight and during whatever span of years is left to each of them. May they continue to walk in faith until their faith gives way to vision and they enjoy the fullness of light, happiness and peace in seeing God face to face in Heaven.

"Those who believe," writes St. Paul in the first sentence of this evening's reading, *"are sons of Abraham."* (Gal 3:7). Yes, we are all spiritual children of Abraham. It was Abraham's faith that enabled him to venture out into the unknown. It must not have been easy for him to leave the security of his home and family and set out for a land about which he knew nothing. We have a natural fear of the unknown. We seek for security in our homes, in employment, in life and in health. The truth is that everyone who accepts a vocation to be a priest or Brother or Sister, is venturing out into the unknown. When St. Vincent de Paul was writing to one of the first priests he was sending to the mission of Madagascar, he said: *"You will need generosity and sublime courage. You also need faith as great as Abraham's and the charity of St. Paul."* (Coste III, Eng. ed., ltr. 1020, p. 279).

Such qualities are still required of those whom God calls to the priestly or religious life. To those whom He calls, God gives these qualities, but like the seed of wheat in the ground, they are not always visible to us immediately. It is time and the sunshine of grace that makes them sprout and grow.

To the young men and girls who may be listening to me and who may feel some stirrings of a religious vocation, I say: Do not think that you don't have the qualities of generosity, faith and love about which St. Vincent speaks. Very likely Abraham did not realize the strength of his faith and the extent of his generosity, until he had left his father's house. So it is with us today. It is only when we have made the first sacrifice of offering our lives to God that He will cause our faith and generosity and love to grow and fit us for the tasks that a priestly or religious vocation demands.

It was along the two great highways of faith and charity that St. Vincent led St. Louise to the heights of sanctity. He first taught her to have faith in the Providence of God Who could provide much better for her son, Michel, than she could. Then he taught her how to cast out her fears for the future by caring for the sick poor.

It is along those two roads also that St. Vincent would like to lead us to God, as he has already done with so many Missionaries and Daughters of Charity. In these days when so many things seem uncertain and so many dangers threaten our little, fragile lives, when we have so many fears in our hearts, St. Vincent would say to us: *"Have faith in the living God. Live one day at a time. God will provide."* At the same time St. Vincent would urge us as individuals and as Communities to go out and to help the poor in a simple, humble way. Firm faith in God's Providence, and humble helping of those who are in greater need than ourselves, are the most certain means we have of casting out fear from our hearts, of increasing our faith, and of making room for the peace of Christ which surpasses all understanding.

There have been many Abrahams born in this island of Sardinia. Priests and Brothers and Sisters have left their homes and are now working in other continents. They are creating new spiritual descendants of Jesus Christ. While we thank God for our three Confreres who this evening are celebrating fifty years of their vocation, we thank God for that very large number of Missionaries and Daughters of Charity who, like Abraham, have left their homes and have gone forth into the land which God has shown them. May the light of faith in their hearts continue to burn brightly amidst the darkness of this world, and may God in His mercy continue to raise up new Abrahams in this island, to make Jesus Christ known and loved in the world and to lighten the sufferings of the poor.

Mortification

17 October 1984   Paris, France

My dear Sisters,

It is a little late in the month to be welcoming you to this city of St. Vincent and St. Louise, seeing that you are now on the point of leaving it. This house, in which you have spent the month, is for all of you your spiritual home. Our homes are the places in this vast world where we should always feel welcome, always and not just at the moment of arrival. So I would like to think that throughout this month you have felt at home here. I am certain that during the month you have been provided with rich spiritual fare from the tables of St. Vincent and St. Louise, served to you by those who know well in what order to offer the courses of the banquet, so that you can savor them best and draw the greatest nourishment and refreshment from them. I am certain, too, that you have not been without the good wine of one another's company which has brought new cheer and a new joy to your hearts. For all these good things we say, *"Thanks be to God and to her who is the Mediatrix of all graces."*

Much as you may have enjoyed this month, each of you must soon return to your local community which is your everyday home. There is a saying that goes, *"Home is the place where we grumble the most but are treated the best."* It is true of our spiritual homes. From time to time we do our share of grumbling about our local communities. But if there comes a crisis in our lives, most of us will come to a new realization that it is the Community that has our spiritual and temporal good deeply at heart. Perhaps our communities do not always succeed in showing that love and concern in the way that they should. Our communities resemble somewhat that portrait which St. Paul sketches in the first reading of today's Mass. Within our communities there is a running battle between what St. Paul calls *"the desires and the deeds of the flesh and the manifestation of the fruits of the spirit."* (Gal 5:17). It is our human condition. Thank God that the grosser forms of the deeds and desires of the flesh, of which St. Paul writes, are not to be found in the Company. However, all of us have seen the weeds of *"strife, jealousy, anger, selfishness, dissension, party spirit, envy"* (Gal 5:20) spout up from time to time in our communities and in our provinces. St. Paul's words are strong and a little intimidating. *"Those who do such things shall not inherit the Kingdom of God."* (Gal 5: 21).

That is the unpleasant side of our home life. There is, however, another more attractive side of it. *"The fruit of the Spirit,"* remarks St. Paul, *"is love, joy, peace, patience, kindness, goodness, faithfulness, gentleness, and self-control."* (Ibid. v. 22). Is there any of us here who has not seen the fruits of the Spirit maturing and ripening in the lives of our Sisters and in the lives of the poor?

I think it is important that we train our critical senses to see the fruits of the Spirit being manifested in the lives of others. In that way we will save ourselves, and this is particularly relevant for young Sisters, from falling into the pit of disillusionment and bitterness which can deprive us of the joy and hope which we had when we first entered the Seminary.

If the fruits of the Spirit are to ripen in our own lives, it is important that we do not pass over an important condition which St. Paul mentions in this passage from his letter to the Galatians: *"Those who belong to Christ Jesus have crucified the flesh with its passions and desires."* (Ibid. v. 24). Let no one persuade us that the crucifixion of our senses, interior and exterior, by mortification is outmoded. The truth is that we have *"passions and desires"* that run contrary to the law of Christ's life. It is humility to acknowledge them and it is charity to crucify them. Only thus can we *"belong fully,"* to use St. Paul's phrase, *"to Christ Jesus."* (Ibid.).

As you prepare to journey back to your provinces and to your communities, I make my own the sentiments which St. Vincent expressed to Sister Nicole Haran: *"From God I ask only two things for you and for your Sisters. The first is that He give you a great concern for the salvation and for the relief of the poor, and the second, that He give you the grace to love one another and to bear with one another; for if you have one and the other, you will practice the virtues Our Lord recommended most to us. You will give edification to everyone and you will enjoy great peace."* (Coste VII, Fr. ed., p. 52).

May that peace, of which St. Vincent speaks, be yours and may you bring it back with you to your communities and to the poor who are your *"joy and crown."* (Phil 4:1).

First and Second Commandments

28 October 1984   Murguia, Spain

My dear Sisters,

Let me begin by offering you two statistical facts. First, of the millions of people on this globe at the present time, only about eighteen or twenty percent have heard of Jesus Christ and accept His message. Secondly, every moment of the day about three people die and enter into the presence of God for judgment.

While we know that God wills every human being to be saved, and that He is infinitely just and merciful, we often find ourselves wondering how those millions, who have never heard of Jesus Christ or His Church, much less of Vatican II, are saved. We do know that God has written into every person's conscience and heart the commands that enlighten everyone who is born into this world. For the millions who know the Old Testament, the two great commandments of the law are clear: love God with your whole heart and with your whole soul and with your whole mind. That is the first commandment, and the second is like it: You shall love your neighbor as yourself. These two commandments of the Old Testament found their fullness in Jesus Christ. By His life, death and resurrection He has thrown light on the meaning of these two commandments and how they should be interpreted in a human existence. We here are further privileged. We are the direct heirs of the teaching of St. Vincent de Paul and St. Louise on how these two commandments can be fulfilled best in a life dedicated to the service of the poor.

Have you ever found yourself wondering about the reason for the success of the Company or of the spiritual formula which St. Vincent and St. Louise have left the Daughters of Charity? The secret of that success is known fully to God alone, but I like to think it is the marvelous manner in which St. Vincent and St. Louise have proposed a way in which we can fulfill the two commandments of the law that accounts for this distinction which your Company has of being the largest single Community in the Church. There is an admirable equilibrium in the teaching of our Founders. They proposed a very dedicated service of the poor, while leaving us in no doubt that the source of the strength to serve the poor can only come from the strength of a Sister's personal love of God in Christ Jesus.

The dynamism, the energy, the love which St. Vincent de Paul manifested to the poor did not come from any doctrinaire views on politics or sociology. The source of his energy and the clarity of his spiritual vision came from his contemplation of the words and actions of Jesus Christ in the pages of the Gospel, and from his daily contact with Jesus Christ in the quietness of prayer. He became convinced that once men and women are made new through their personal dedication to Jesus Christ, a new world will follow.

When you listen to St. Vincent speaking in his conferences to the Sisters, you will find him alternating between talking now about the first commandment of the law and now of the second. He marries these two commandments in a union which brings forth the fruits of the spirit, of which St. Paul speaks in his letter to the Galatians. Through her fidelity to the teaching of St. Vincent, expressed in his conferences and in the present Constitutions, a Daughter of Charity will bring to the poor *"love, joy, peace, patience, kindness, goodness, faithfulness, gentleness, and self-control."* (Gal 5:22). What all of us who are heirs of the spiritual riches of our Founders must remember is the observation made by Henri Bremond of St. Vincent; that it was not his charity that made him a saint, but his sanctity which made him truly charitable.

Yes, the two great commandments of the law are closely united. However, we must never forget in practice that there is a first commandment and a second commandment and that we can go to Jesus Christ in the poor with security only after we have met Him in the intimacy of prayer and the Sacraments. *"Teacher, which commandment of the law is the greatest? Jesus said to him: 'You shall love the Lord, your God, with your whole heart, with your whole soul, and with all your mind. This is the greatest and first commandment. The second is like it: You shall love your neighbor as yourself. On these two commandments the whole law is based, and the prophets as well.'"* (Mt 22:36).

With St. Vincent I say: *"So then, my Daughters, be modest, I beseech you, and labor earnestly to be perfect. Do not rest content with doing good, but do it in the way God wishes, that is to say, as perfectly as you can, making yourselves worthy servants of the poor.*" (Conf. Eng. ed., 19 July 1640, p. 21). May the Virgin Mary, Mother of the Company, obtain for us this grace from her Son.

Gratitude

10 November 1984   Saragossa, Spain

My dear Sisters,

Of all the letters that St. Paul wrote, for many people the one that is the most personal is that which he sent to the Christians at Philippi. There had grown up between St. Paul and the Philippian Church a friendship closer than that which existed between him and any other Church. It was St. Paul's proud boast that he had never taken help from any man or from any Church and that he had provided for his needs by the work of his hands. It was from the Philippians alone that St. Paul agreed to accept a gift. When he had left them and gone to Thessalonica, they sent him a present (cf. Phil 4:16), and when he had arrived in Corinth, the Philippians had sent him more gifts (cf. 2 Cor. 11:9). So in his letter to them it is not surprising that he addresses them as *"my brethren whom I love and long for, my joy and crown."* (Phil 4:1). In the first reading of today's Mass, St. Paul expresses his sense of gratitude to the Philippians. The gratitude which is in his heart flows out from it like a pure mountain stream. Gratitude, when it comes from the heart, is as refreshing as water from a mountain stream. Two months ago when I was in Bolivia, I came out of the Provincial House of the Sisters and, as I did so, a woman passed by pushing a small wooden cart with what looked like all her possessions on it. She was accompanied by two small children. As she passed, the articles on the cart fell off. For fifteen seconds or so I helped her put them back on again. I will never forget the depth and the warmth of the way she said, *"muchisimas gracias, Padre."* It was a lesson to me on gratitude. The service I gave her was tiny, but her expression of gratitude was as profound as if I had given her a thousand dollars.

Gratitude is a good barometer of our spiritual condition. If you find that you are giving thanks to God frequently in your prayer, for big things and small; if you find yourself showing gratitude to others, your spiritual life is probably in a healthy condition. To give thanks is a sign of humility. Failure to give thanks is a sign of pride and self-sufficiency. It is St. Vincent who remarks in one of his letters that *"ingratitude (is) the crime of crimes."* (Coste III, Eng. ed., ltr. 850, p. 42). Gratitude is a sign of humility. If we are humble, we will certainly be in God's favor, and His love, the most valuable gift we can offer to the poor, will be in our hearts.

Perhaps it was St. Paul's profound sense of gratitude for everything that enabled him to have what St. Vincent used to call the virtue of indifference. Listen again to the words of the first reading: *"I do not complain of want, for I have learned, in whatever state I am, to be content. I know how to be abased and I know how to abound. In any and all circumstances I have learned the secret of facing plenty and hunger, abundance and want. I can do all things in Him Who strengthens me."* (Phil 4:11-13). If we have a grateful heart, we will see everything as gifts of God. We will give thanks, as St. Paul so often reminded the Christians of his day, in all things and in all circumstances. There is a beautiful prayer of St. Thomas More who, when he was rich and enjoyed much favor from King Henry VIII, always kept his heart detached from the things of this life. The prayer goes: *"Thanks be to You, Lord Jesus Christ, for all that You have given me. Thanks be to You, Lord Jesus Christ, for all that You have taken from me. Thanks be to You, Lord Jesus Christ, for all that You have left me."*

May God give us the grace to be grateful for everything He has given us and to show that gratitude by generosity to others and to the poor. May He give us also the grace to be detached in heart from all things and the grace to be content in our vocation. With St. Louise I say: *"I praise God with all my heart for the grace His goodness has granted you to be a source of edification where He has seen fit to place you. However, be sure to thank Him for it through the practice of the virtues He asks of you, especially great cordiality and mutual understanding among you."* (*Spiritual Writings of Louise de Marillac*, ltr. 276, p. 314).

Advent Letter—Gentleness

20 November 1984   To Each Confrere

My dear Confrere,

May the grace of Our Lord Jesus Christ be with us forever!

Of the Christmas gifts of a lifetime, perhaps the ones we remember the best are those which came as a surprise to us. The Incarnation is God's greatest gift to humankind. While the prophets foretold the coming of the Messiah, no one dreamt that the gift would be God Himself in person. Then in Bethlehem one night God revealed the gift. The story of the event has never lost its freshness, at least for those who have become, or are trying to become by the grace of God, as little children. The gift God gave was a child. Is that the reason why it is only those who have become as little children, who will enter into His Kingdom?

God broke into time gently. *"When all things were in quiet silence and the night was in the midst of its course, Thy almighty Word leaped from heaven, from the royal throne . . . ."* (Wis 18:14-15). There is a gentle and poignant pathos in St. Luke's observation that the Virgin Mary brought forth her Child and laid Him in a manger *"because there was no room for them in the inn."* (Lk 2:7). The statement is devoid of harsh criticism. There is gentleness, too, in the call of the shepherds and the Magi to come and adore the newborn Child. The wrapping around the gift of the Incarnation is gentleness. In God's remaking of humanity, gentleness as a value can never be discounted.

Of that value St. Vincent has reminded us in our Common Rules. *" . . . by gentleness we inherit the earth. If we act on this we will win people over . . . .That will not happen if we treat people harshly . . . ."* (CR II, 6). It is gaining the hearts of men, in order to lead them captive to the obedience of Christ, which is central to all work of evangelization. The ultimate citadel that must be captured is the heart of man, which will never surrender to force but only to the power of gentleness. The weapon of gentleness (St. Vincent compares it to one of the five smooth stones of David) is offered to us by Christ. His gentleness is a controlled strength, and it is that controlled strength which can tame our natural aggressivity, hold back the bitter and sarcastic word and temper the rawness of criticism. It is not a virtue to be uncritical. However, let growth in the power of criticism be matched by a growth in gentleness. A bruised reed (and who is not a bruised reed?) must not be broken, much less felled with axes.

In our work of evangelization we may change the convictions of others through discussion and argument. We will, however, only bring about their conversion of heart when we can give evidence to them that we ourselves have through grace and prayer learned from Christ *"to be gentle and humble of heart."* (Mt 11:29).

It is the strength of gentleness that calms the noisy turbulence of activism within ourselves and makes us dispensers of the mystery of God's peace. It is the strength of gentleness that creates a certain space around us in which others can feel at ease to grow and in which they can feel accepted. To an anxious and fretful generation there are few gifts we can offer that would be more acceptable than the serenity and peace which are the flower of the sturdy root of evangelical gentleness. *"Continue, Monsieur,"* wrote St. Vincent, *"to be very docile to the guidance of God and to conform your own way of acting to that of Our Lord. He was always humble, gentle, attentive, and most accommodating to the moods and weaknesses of others, having in view the glory of His Father and the welfare of souls in general and in particular."* (Coste IV, Eng. ed., ltr. 1611, pp. 556-557).

I hope that your celebration of Christmas will bring you a new measure of serenity and peace, which you can share with the poor to whom you are bringing the news that *"the goodness and loving kindness of God, our Saviour, has appeared."* (Tit 3:4). Joined by the four Assistants and all who work here in the Curia in greeting you, I remain in the love of Our Lord, your devoted confrere.

1985

God's Questions

1 January 1985   Paris, France

Mother Rogé, Father Lloret and my dear Sisters,

Every New Year that dawns in our lives comes in with a large question: *"What is this year going to hold for me?"* In trying to answer this question, we spend time in guessing and hoping and fearing. In the end we have to leave the question largely unanswered. It is well, perhaps, that it should be so, for our very inability to answer the question throws us again into the arms of Him to Whom all time and ages belong. It is yet another invitation, as St. Vincent might express it, to surrender ourselves trustingly into the arms of God's loving Providence, knowing that for those who love Him, *"all things work together unto good."* (Rom 8:28).

Each New Year's question, *"What is this new year going to hold for me?"* can only be answered by God. Instead of raising questions ourselves, we would do well to allow God to raise some questions which only we can answer. His questions are of a different order from ours. They are addressed to our hearts, for it is into the locked citadel of our hearts that He wishes to enter, and it is only we who have the key in our hands.

The Gospels offer us many of God's questions. When Jesus Christ met His first disciples, He put the simple question to them: *"What do you seek?"* (Jn 1:38). That question is as relevant and fresh today for me as it was for the first disciples. My reply: Why, of course, I wish to serve You in the poor and through the Community. Allow Christ to repeat the question. *"What do you seek?"* Considering it a second time, I might feel inclined to use modern terminology and say: I seek self-fulfillment in my vocation. Reflecting on that second reply, I must admit that my terminology is not fully evangelical, for nowhere in the Gospel does Our Lord, speaking of His own mission, think of it as self-fulfillment. Rather is it the opposite. In Gethsemane He prayed that

His Will would not be done but that of His Father, and earlier He had stressed for His disciples the importance of denying oneself and of losing one's life. So that first question of Jesus Christ, _"What do you seek?"_ needs more reflection on my part before I answer it. My motivation needs the x-ray of the light of Christ, if only to prove to me that it is not as healthy as it might exteriorly appear. To use the terminology of St. Vincent and St. Louise: Is my seeking of Christ in the poor distinguished by that simplicity which at all times makes me act with God alone in view?

Let us allow Jesus Christ to put to us another of His questions on this New Year's Day. _"What were you discussing on the way home?"_ (Mk 9:33). The day Jesus put that question to the twelve, they were unable to answer it, or rather, they were ashamed to answer it. They could only hang their heads and be silent because they had been discussing on the way which of them would be the greatest. It was on that occasion that Our Lord used a visual aid to impress upon the twelve the importance of being humble. Setting a child amongst them, He said: _"Truly I say to you, unless you turn and become like little children, you will never enter the Kingdom of Heaven. Whoever humbles himself like this child, he is the greatest in the Kingdom of Heaven."_ (Mt 18:3-4). Our love of Jesus Christ and the supernatural value of our service of the poor is directly related to the humility of our hearts and minds, for, to quote St. Vincent: _"Humility is the source of all the good that we do."_ (Conf. Eng. ed., 15 Mar. 1654, p. 599).

Maybe on this New Year's Day we are conscious of the fact that time is running out for us, and that we have little to show for the years we have spent in Community. Across the years, as across the waters to the disciples in the darkness of the night, comes His question, addressed to Peter: _"O man of little faith, why did you doubt?"_ (Mt 14:31). The greatest tragedy that could befall us in this new year is that we would lose confidence in Jesus Christ and in His power to save us from ourselves as He saved the disciples on the lake on that stormy night. He is close to us in the Eucharist and in the Sacrament of Penance. To our doubting hearts He addresses the question which He put to the Apostles on the evening of His Resurrection: _"Why are you troubled and why do questionings rise in your hearts?"_ (Lk 24:38).

Perhaps the answers we can give to these questions of Jesus Christ may not be particularly flattering to ourselves. That does not matter too much. What matters is that the answers we try to give be true and, above all, that they be simple and humble. *"Suffer us not to mock ourselves with falsehood,"* prayed the poet (T.S.Eliot). It is only when we are not mocking ourselves with spurious reasons for dispensing ourselves from accepting the demands of being simple and humble and loving, both inside and outside the Community, that we can begin to answer that supreme question that Our Lord addressed to St. Peter and which He will address to us at the moment of our deaths: *"Do you love Me?"* (Jn 21: 16). May it be given to us at the end of our years on earth to reply: *"Yes, Lord, You know that I love You."* (Jn 21:16). At the beginning of the last year of her life St. Louise wrote to St. Vincent: *"Permit me to greet your Charity very humbly at the beginning of this new year, and at the same time, to ask for your blessing to help me to be faithful to God for as long as it pleases His goodness to leave me on earth."* (*Spiritual Writings of Louise de Marillac*, ltr. 649, p. 670).

We have no record of the reply that St. Vincent gave to this request of St. Louise, but we do know that three years earlier at the beginning of a new year he wrote to one of his missionaries: *"I pray Our Lord that this New Year will be a year of grace and that He will make your heart and your community abound in spiritual fruit and that He will preserve these fruits to eternity."* (Coste VI, Fr. ed., p. 153). These sentiments of St. Vincent, my dear Sisters, are mine for you today.

Lenten Letter—Silence

1 February 1985   To Each Confrere

My dear Confrere,

May the grace of Our Lord Jesus Christ be with us forever!

You have probably noticed that in the three-year cycle of readings for Sundays, we are invariably led into the desert with Christ for the first Sunday of Lent. Our minds dwell on the mystery of the three temptations He experienced there. Perhaps we reflect less on the silence of that desert where He spent those forty days of prayer and fasting.

The silence of a desert, is an experience we may sometimes wish for, especially when we feel our lives to be overcrowded with people and overcharged with work. Experience, however, has shown that the majority of men cannot sustain more than a few days of the absolute stillness of a desert.

To live the life of a hermit in a desert is not our vocation. But it is from a desert that we must come, as did Jesus Christ, to preach good news to the poor. He began His work of preaching and healing after having had the experience of the profound silence of a desert. St. Vincent was aware of a missioner's need to come from a desert of silence to preach the Gospel, when he reminded us in our Common Rules that it is impossible for any Community to persevere in virtue for a long time if there is no provision made for silence in its life. (cf. CR VIII, 4).

Conditions of life in our modern world are not in the main conducive to creating and achieving such silence which, to judge from the example given us by Jesus Christ, is a prerequisite to a life of apostolic activity. Too easily we make excuses when the Lord, Who is our Shepherd, sets about leading us to restful waters to revive our drooping spirits. (cf. Ps 23:2). The truth is that too much company, too much conversation and excessive dependence on radio and television can invade that desert of silence which God wishes to create within us, so that He can speak to our hearts in secret. In our more reflective moments we realize that our communication to others of God's word is shallow because we ourselves have not sufficiently reflected on it in the silence of prayer. We can identify with the sentiments of a modern Christian poet who wrote that *"the endless cycle of idea and action, endless invention, endless experiment, brings knowledge of speech but not of silence, knowledge of words and ignorance of the Word."* (T.S. Eliot).

It is the personal acquaintance which we have made with the Word of God in silent prayer that the poor most look for in us when in homily or conversation we speak to them. *"Give back, Lord, to the Little Company of the Mission, this holy virtue (of silence),"* prayed St. Vincent towards the end of his life. (cf. Coste XII, Fr. ed., p. 62). His prayer, I imagine, is unchanged today. In an age of noise and bustle he would wish that each of us would find more time to be still and silent in the presence of God; to make provision in our day for one hour's personal prayer, as our recently approved Constitutions propose (cf C. 47, §1); and to secure that the days of our annual retreat be marked by a desert-like silence that would prepare us for a revitalized preaching of the Good News of Jesus Christ. *"In silence and in hope shall be your strength."* (Is. 30:15).

So my prayer for us all this Lent is that we may live less on the noisy surface of things but through conscious cultivation of silence in our lives, we may penetrate more deeply into that silent mystery which we know as God in Whom we live and move and have our being. With kindest greetings from all of us here in the Curia and recommending myself to your prayers, I remain in the love of Our Lord, your devoted confrere.

Fragile Gifts of God

2 February 1985   Paris, France

My dear Sisters,

I do not know how far back in the history of the Community the tradition goes that the Mother General on the 2 February presents to the Father General the requests of the Sisters who wish to renew their Vows on the 25 March. Whoever first thought of it saw deeply into the significance of the vocation of a Daughter of Charity, for the 2 February is at once a feast of presentation and dedication. Mary brought her infant Son to the temple in Jerusalem to present Him to His heavenly Father and also to dedicate Him to the fulfilling of whatever the Father might ask of His Son, Jesus Christ, in the course of His earthly life. On her humble and obedient journey to Jerusalem, with Joseph and the Child, the thought of the presentation and dedication would have been uppermost in Mary's mind.

For us in the Company, the 2 February is also a feast of presentation and dedication. The presentation of your requests by Mother Rogé to renew your Vows is an expression of the desire of your hearts to dedicate yourselves once again to the fulfilling of the Will of God. His Will in your lives is expressed to you in and through the Company which the Spirit of God called into existence for the spiritual and physical service of the poor.

Mary's humble presentation and dedication of her Child to His heavenly Father was done by the light of faith and in obedience to the religious constitutions by which as a Jewess she lived her life.

Faith and obedience: they are fragile gifts of God, as fragile as the flickering light of a candle. The fragile light of a candle contrasts with the artificial light of electricity to which we are accustomed. Yet even in this age of electricity the Church has not abandoned the candle. At the ceremony of Baptism a lighted candle is used to symbolize faith. At the celebration of the Eucharist a lighted candle greets the coming of the Lord on our altars. At our funerals the Paschal Candle proclaims our faith in the Resurrection.

So, too, in our lives we must not abandon the light of faith and obedience which underpins our dedication to Christ and His poor. If we allow the light of faith and obedience, which guided Mary with her Child to the temple, to be weakened in our lives, then cold, calculating reasoning will take over. Your Constitutions state that *"In a spirit of faith the Sisters obey their superiors who accept the obligation of guiding them and of making final decisions."* (C. 2.8). Should the light of faith and obedience weaken in our lives, bitter, harsh winds will begin to sweep across our souls. The promise that marked our years in the seminary and our first sending on mission will be blighted, leaving us shrivelled, spiritually immature and undeveloped.

At the beginning of this reflection, I said I did not know at what point in the history of the Company the 2 February was established as the day for the presentation of the Sisters' requests to renew their vows. Perhaps it had its remote beginnings in this letter which St. Louise wrote to St. Vincent on the 1 February 1659: *"This letter is a consolation for me since I can . . . ask for your blessing for all our Sisters, especially Sister Marie of the Hôtel-Dieu, Sister Anne from Angers who has been in the Company for eighteen years, and Sister Geneviève from near Maule. After their recent retreat, they expressed to Monsieur Portail their desire to be allowed to renew their vows tomorrow. The Sister who came from Brienne with Sister Catherine very humbly asks for the simple habit of the Daughters of Charity. Several persons request your prayers for a matter of great importance for the glory of God and the salvation of souls redeemed by the blood of His Son. You are aware of how greatly I need your prayers and that is sufficient for me since I am, my Most Honored Father, your very humble daughter and most obedient servant, Louise de Marillac. (Spiritual Writings of Louise de Marillac*, ltr.609B, p. 630-631).

So my prayer for us all this morning, my dear Sisters, is that the light of faith and obedience will burn brightly in us; that our lives will be like the soft glow of candlelight in the darkness of a harsh world; that we may be a light for revelation to the Gentiles and for glory to the Israel of God.

Voice of Conscience

20 March 1985   Lerida, Spain

My dear Friends in Jesus Christ,

First of all, let me say how happy I am to be able to celebrate Mass here in your parish church at the invitation of Father Provincial and the priests of your parish. I would like also to thank you for the continual support you give the missionaries of St. Vincent who live and work among you. Without your generous assistance and your cooperation, they could not do the task for which they were ordained; namely, to make Jesus Christ known and present and loved by their preaching and by their celebration of the Eucharist and the Sacraments of Christ's Church.

When I saw from the program that your parish church is dedicated to St. Augustine, I began to wonder if the priests of your parish in their sermons quote from the book which this great Saint wrote some fifteen hundred years ago and which is still a best-seller today. The book is a very special spiritual autobiography, because St. Augustine writes about himself and his sins and failings with an honesty that few men could do.

His autobiography is known as *The Confessions of St. Augustine*. St. Augustine tells us in this book that, when he was a small boy, there were some pear trees in the garden of his home. There were also pear trees in his neighbor's garden. One day he and some companions decided to steal some pears from his neighbor's garden. It was not necessary, he tells us, to do so because the pears in his own garden were just as good, if not better than those in his neighbor's garden. Still, he wanted to steal because he found a certain pleasure in doing something which was forbidden.

This is a very old story but not, however, a very original one. That also was the experience of Adam and Eve. They had all they wanted in the garden, where God had placed them, but, because there was prohibition to eat the fruit of one particular tree, they wanted the pleasure of doing something which was forbidden to them.

The experience of Adam and Eve, the experience of St. Augustine, has also been ours. Have we not often done something that we knew to be wrong, simply because we wanted to get the maximum amount of pleasure that life could give us? When we are challenged about some action of ours that the Church or others condemn as wrong, we are quick to make excuses. Like Adam and Eve, we are quick to find reasons for justifying our action. Adam justified his eating of the forbidden fruit because Eve had offered it to him. Eve, for her part, justified her eating of the fruit because the serpent persuaded her to do so.

We are more than halfway through Lent. Perhaps that has not made any difference to our lives and perhaps we are already justifying ourselves for not doing anything special during this season. Could I suggest to you that Lent is a time when we decide to reduce the number of occasions when we try to justify ourselves before God, before the Church, before society and before our friends for what they say is wrong in our lives? Adam and Eve tried to justify themselves. They were wrong. Pilate tried to justify himself, and we all know that he was wrong. During this Lent take a little time to look on the Crucifix in your church or in your home and ask yourself the simple question: What does He think of my action and of my life as I am living it today? Don't turn away your gaze from the Crucifix too quickly, for if you do, you will begin to justify yourself in all that you are doing and saying in your home, in your office, in your business. Jesus Christ could have said a great deal more to Pilate during the course of His trial, but He didn't. He was silent, as the Evangelist remarks, so that *"Pilate wondered exceedingly."* (Mt 27: 14). During this Lent silence the voice of self-justification within you, so that you may be able to hear more clearly the authentic voice of your conscience, which is the voice of God Who created you and loves you.

You have heard often in this church that God loves you, but no priest could put this truth to you more forcefully than the prophet Isaiah does at the end of the first reading of this evening's Mass: *"Can a mother forget her infant, be without tenderness for the child of her womb? Even should she forget, I will never forget you."* (Is 49:14,15).

Through the prayers of Mary, the Mother of God, St. Vincent de Paul and St. Augustine, may we never forget that God's love for us is infinitely more tender and more enduring than the love of the tenderest mother for her child.

Lenten Season Thoughts

22 March 1985   Figueras, Spain

My dear Friends in Jesus Christ,

There is a Negro spiritual which some of the Christians in the southern part of the United States like to sing at this time of the year. The first line of the song goes: *"Were you there when they crucified my Lord?"* The answer that immediately comes to us is *no.* That was nearly two thousand years ago. Then, when you think a little bit more on the question, *"Were you there when they crucified my Lord?"* you feel as a Christian that you must say *yes.* Although I may not be able to see exactly how, as a Christian I believe that my sins had something to do with the death of Jesus Christ. As a Christian, each of us believes what St. Paul said, that Christ *"loved me and gave Himself up for me."* (Gal 2:20). We may not be able to see it clearly, but the truth is that each of us has said with the crowd of Good Friday, *"Crucify Him. Crucify Him."* (Jn 19:6). Every deliberate sin is a loud or a whispered cry, *"Yes. Crucify Him. Crucify Him."* (Ibid.).

"Were you there when they crucified my Lord?" No, I was not physically present, but suppose I was. What would I have done? Hammer the nails into His hands and feet? No, I could not bring myself

to do that, nor could I bring myself to mock and jeer Him, as did the Pharisees. One does not hit another when he is down, much less a man who is gasping and dying. I think I would have drawn close to the group of women who stood some distance from the cross, among them the Mother of the young man being executed. But would I? I think I might have said: *"I do not know these people. I can't do anything for them. I don't want to intrude on their sorrow."* So, taking one more look at the man on the cross, I might have said: *"This form of execution should be abolished. It's too grisly. Anyway, I had better get home. There's no point in wasting time here, for there's nothing I can do."* The attitude which I have just described was taken up by many people, as St. John remarks, who read the title on the cross of Jesus, for He was crucified not far from the city.

"Were you there when they crucified my Lord?" Suppose I was there and suppose I stayed to see the end. I think I would have been changed in my outlook, for I would have heard Jesus say: *"Father, forgive them for they know not what they do . . . .There is your Mother . . . .This day you shall be with Me in Paradise . . . .Into Your hands I commend my Spirit."* (Lk 23:24,43,46). Such words, coming from a dying man on a cross, would have set me thinking.

These weeks of Lent are invitations to me to stay at the scene of the Crucifixion and to ponder the words spoken by Jesus. In these words you will find what the first reading of this evening's Mass calls *"the secret purposes of God."* (Wis 2: 22). *"Were you there when they crucified my Lord?"* No, but you can think long and hard about the words spoken on the cross: *"Father, forgive them."*(Lk 23:24). Is there anyone who is openly or secretly asking me for forgiveness? *"Son, there is your Mother."* (Jn 19:26). Do I really believe that and speak tenderly and with appreciation to Mary daily, as I would to my Mother? *"Into Your hands, Lord, I commend My Spirit."* (Lk 23:46). Am I always taking things out of God's hands and into my own, wanting to do things my own selfish way and not His?

"Were you there when they crucified my Lord?" No, but Jesus saw me there and He asks only that I think more about Him these days and about His words when they crucified Him. Keep thinking of Him on the cross and of His words. If you do, they will slowly influence your

life and you will find that you won't want to hurry away. You will find, too, that you will not answer quite so quickly with a *no* to the question: *"Were you there when they crucified my Lord?"*

Vows A Wall of Fire

25 March 1985   Paris, France

Mother Rogé, Father Lloret and my dear Sisters,

There was once a very wealthy man who had a large family and, because he was wealthy and loved his family greatly, he gave them all that they needed to make them happy and content. When his wife was giving birth to their last child, she died. The child was born severely handicapped. Because the father was a loving man, he gave his handicapped child much time and attention. He would care personally for this, the youngest of his family, an autistic child. The other members of the family, however, were not in the main greatly interested in their youngest brother. Some wanted him put away in a State institution, while others, on growing up, left the home, became preoccupied with their affairs and lost interest in the child. The father continued to love his handicapped child, giving generously of his time so that he might penetrate into the closed world of his autistic son. One of the man's daughters, beautiful and talented, admired so much the loving devotion of her father that she decided to give her life to help him in looking after the needs of her youngest brother. Time passed and the father grew old. In his latter years he would repeatedly seek assurance from his daughter that, when he was gone, she would continue to do as he did, loving and caring for that child who could make little or no response to love and care. For years after her father's death the daughter continued to do exactly as he had done, attending the needs of the helpless child who was her brother.

That, my dear Sisters, is a parable. The father in the parable is your heavenly Father, and you are the daughter who promised Him to take care, even at great cost to yourselves, of the handicapped child who is for you the poor. It is your heavenly Father Who through the Community has entrusted the poor to your care.

In the parable only one of the family could share their father's vision of the condition and need of his youngest child. It is only a tiny minority of the world's population who share the vision which Christ had of the poor, and you are privileged to be among them. The father in the parable repeatedly asked his daughter for assurance that she would continue for the rest of her life to give the same devoted care as he did to the handicapped member of the family. This morning your heavenly Father asked a similar assurance from you and, thanks be to God, you gave it to Him with all the generosity of your heart. This morning you renewed your desire and intention to devote yourself to serving the poor, handicapped children of God. You did so because of the vision of the poor which God has given you, the vision of the poor which He has already shared with St. Vincent and St. Louise. That vision has been communicated to us through the traditions of the Community and through the Constitutions and Statutes of the Company. Once again this morning you have responded to your caring Father in heaven, promising to dedicate yourself to the service of the poor through your vows of chastity, poverty and obedience. Just as the daughter in the parable loved and admired her father and wished to follow his example in caring for his son, so, too, your vows are firstly an expression of love and admiration for your caring Father in heaven, Who has manifested Himself through His Son, Jesus Christ.

In the parable the father asked his daughter to continue to love and care for the handicapped child in the way that he did. It is so with us. God has given us through the Community a particular vision of how the poor should be served. In the care of the handicapped child, love had to be structured by regularity. Feeding and bathing had its regular hours. For us, too, in our vocation structures, however much at times we may like to abandon them, are necessary if we are to mediate the particular love which our heavenly Father wishes to show the poor He asks us to serve. In pronouncing our vows we freely accept a structured way of life. Our vows could be said to throw up a wall around us, but it is like the wall of which Zechariah, the prophet, wrote: *"I will be to her a wall of fire round about, says the Lord, and I will be the glory within her."* (Zec 2:9). Our vows are a wall of fire and the fire has its origin in the love which God has for us and for the poor whom He wishes us to serve. Ask often from God the grace of keeping alive His love in your heart so that you may be faithful to your vows. Reflect often on the joy of your heavenly Father as He sees you caring for the handicapped child He has entrusted to you.

To you, my dear Sisters, on this day of rejoicing, I offer you the sentiments which St. Vincent expressed to Sister Françoise Menage who had told him how she valued the vows she had made in the Company: *"My Sister, I praise God for the good dispositions He gives you to make yourself more and more agreeable in His eyes. You will reach this happy state if you practice well humility, gentleness and charity towards the poor and towards your Sisters. I pray Our Lord, Who has given us the example of these virtues, to gift you with this grace."* (Coste VII, Fr. ed., pp. 454-455).

Resurrection of Our Lord

14 April 1985   Ljubljana, Yugoslavia

My dear Friends in Jesus Christ,

It is a great joy for me to have this opportunity of celebrating Mass with you on what St. John in today's Gospel calls *"the first day of the week."* (Jn 20:1). Today our Orthodox brethren are celebrating Easter Sunday. Perhaps it would be nice if all of us who believe that Jesus Christ rose from the dead celebrated Easter Sunday every year together on the same Sunday. Perhaps some time in the future that may be agreed upon. Meantime, however, we can all agree on this truth, that every Sunday is a little Easter Sunday. For on every Sunday, *"the first day of the week,"* whether it be in winter or in smmer, in Lent or in Advent, we recall in a special way that it was on a Sunday, *"the first day of the week,"* that Jesus Christ rose gloriously from the tomb. In doing so He has given us, who believe in Him, an assurance that we, too, will, by His power, rise from the dead.

When we have an argument with a person, we like to win; we like to have the last word. Jesus Christ had an argument with death, and He not only won the argument and rose from the dead, but He also had the last word. His last word to us was that He would be with us always, that we would see Him again, that our hearts would rejoice and that no one would be able to take that joy from us. *"I will come back,"* He said, *"and take you to be with Me so that you also may be where I am."* (Jn 14:3).

There are people who say that there will be no resurrection, that there is nothing after death. There are atheists who go around trying to convince others that all this talk about another life is a fairy tale. When next you hear an atheist talking in that way, think of springtime. During the long hard winter that you have experienced, you probably said to yourselves: *"Will spring ever come this year?"* The ground was frozen hard for a long time. There was not a sign of life in the fields or on the trees. But now everything is changing. Flowers are appearing, the wheat is growing in the fields, the leaves are beginning to appear on the trees. No human power can keep back springtime. The winter may seem for a time to have had the last word, but no, each year winter is conquered by spring.

The winter of atheism may seem long. It may seem to be having the last word. But no, since the day Jesus Christ rose from the dead, the first signs of an eternal springtime have begun to appear. Each of us has met Christians who, despite great suffering that cannot be explained, have continued to believe that death is not the end. These people are signs for us that Jesus Christ has really risen. They are convincing arguments that the winter of atheism is breaking up. Many elderly people died during the cold of this last winter. If you asked them before they died, if spring was going to come, if they believed that spring would come after their death, they would say, *"Yes, of course."* So, too, a Christian who dies is convinced that he or she, despite death, will rise again, because Jesus Christ has said so. On the day when man can stop springtime coming, that will be the day when Christians will cease to believe in the Resurrection from the dead.

So, my dear people, I say to you what Jesus Christ said to His disciples on the first day of the week, *"Peace be with you."* (Jn 20:19). When I say, *"Peace be with you,"* I say it in the name of Jesus Christ, Who has risen from the dead and Who is present here this morning among us. May His peace cast out from your hearts all fear, as it did from the hearts of the disciples. May you be strengthened, through the intercession of the Virgin Mary, to leave this church and go out and share that peace with others by doing the things that you think Jesus Christ would do, by saying the things that you think Jesus Christ would say. For to all of us He has said what He said to the disciples: *"As the Father has sent Me, so I send you."* (Jn 20:21). My dear people of this parish of St. Jakob of Savi, *"May the peace of the Lord be always with you and with your families."*

Suffering for the Faith

17 April 1985   Ljubljana, Yugoslavia

My dear Confreres,

When I visit the various provinces of the Congregation, I am often asked if I have any news of the Confreres in China. It is always a little pain for me to have to reply that I have not. In the past five years I have only received one short letter from an elderly Brother who signed himself Joseph, saying that he was still loyal to St. Vincent and to the Congregation. I do know, however, of another Confrere in China who spent twenty-three years in prison because of his faith and his priesthood and his loyalty to the Congregation. Has there ever been a year since the Apostles first went forth to preach the life, death and resurrection of Our Lord Jesus Christ that there has not been someone in prison because of his convictions about our faith? We are only in the second week after the Resurrection and already as we have seen in the first reading of today's Mass, the Apostles are in prison because of their preaching of Jesus Christ crucified and risen. So it has been ever since. Wherever the Gospel has been preached in the world, there men and women have suffered for the faith as they have here in your own country.

To die for the faith is to die for something which one treasures more than life. To suffer for the faith is to suffer in order to preserve something that one recognizes as a very special and precious gift given by God. If the light of faith is to be kept alight in our minds and our hearts, it needs to be cared for. We who have taken vows of celibacy must never lose sight of the connection that exists between our faith and our celibacy. *"Blessed are the pure in heart,"* said Our Lord, *"for they shall see God."* (Mt 5:8). Should we celibates begin to experience difficulties with the faith, it could be that the reason lies in our living of celibacy. In our time there has been much discussion on celibacy. It could very well be that the crisis of the priesthood today is not so much one of celibacy but one of faith. Intensify our living of celibacy, remove from our lives compromises which we may be making with our vow of celibacy, and we may very well find that the light of faith will begin to burn more brightly in our minds and in our hearts. *"He who acts in truth,"* remarks Our Lord in today's Gospel, *"comes into the light to make clear that his deeds are done in God."* (Jn 3:21).

What I am trying to say to you, my dear Confreres, is that, if we are not to be discouraged, disheartened, in our vocation, our faith needs to be strong. Our faith can only be strong if we put ourselves in full contact with Christ, Who has prayed that our faith will not fail. We are only in full contact with Christ when we have more than a superficial contact with the Community which He has raised up through His servant, Vincent de Paul. It was St. Vincent's vision that men went forth from Community to preach the Gospel to the poor, and his vision of Community was one in which men shared a life of prayer and drew from each other the strength that true Community life can give.

St. Vincent wrote to one of his priests in 1647: *"Her (the Church) great need is evangelical men who work to purge, enlighten, and unite her to her Divine Spouse. This is what you are doing through His Divine Goodness."* (Coste III, Eng. ed., ltr. 960, p. 204). I have no doubt that St. Vincent would address the same words to us this morning and he would end, as he ended the letter which I have quoted: *"Let us labor at that with all our might, confident that Our Lord, Who has called us to His manner of life, will give us a greater share in His spirit and, in the end, in His glory."* (Ibid., p. 205).

Centenary of the Province of Great Britain

21 April 1985   London, England

My dear Sisters,

On the 21 April 1647, which happened to be Easter Sunday that year, St. Louise wrote a letter to St. Vincent. Among other requests she made to him was that he would be kind enough to write a letter to all the Sisters of the community at Nantes. There had been some considerable tension and division within the community and St. Louise thought it would be appropriate if St. Vincent were to write a letter to all the Sisters, manifesting what she called *"a little displeasure,"* while at the same time asking him that he would also encourage them. The formula was to be a little scolding blended with a little encouragement.

Were I to adopt the formula of St. Louise, I must confess that I would be at a loss to know what I should scold you about. Besides, you would respectfully suggest that such a scolding was not an appropriate subject for a Centenary celebration. Allow me, however, to say that, in the words of Our Lord in this morning's Gospel, one can detect the suggestion of a scolding, perhaps not so much a scolding as a reproach. Appearing to His disciples after His resurrection, He greets them with His peace. They are frightened. Our Lord seeks to calm them. There is a note of reproach in His words: *"Why are you so agitated and why are these doubts arising in your hearts?"* (Lk 24:38). If there is a reproach in Our Lord's words, it is not for something the disciples have done in the past. It is because of their present disbelief. Their friendship with Him before His sufferings and death, His own clear prediction, not only of His death but of His resurrection on the third day; all this should have banished their agitation and their doubts. The past should have prepared the minds of the disciples to accept the reality of the resurrection. In fact, however, it did not. Because of that, there is a note of reproach to be detected in the words of Our Lord in today's Gospel. It was the Jesus of yesterday Who had prepared the disciples for the Jesus of the day of the resurrection. The Jesus of yesterday is the Jesus of today. *"Jesus Christ is the same today as He was yesterday and as He will be forever."* (Heb 13:8).

There have been one hundred years of yesterdays in this Province, and all of them have been lived in and with Jesus Christ. There has been no day in the past one hundred years that Jesus Christ has not gathered Sisters about Him and renewed the offering of Himself to the Father in the Sacrifice of the Mass. There has been no day in the past one hundred years of this Province that Sisters have not at the end of Mass heeded the imperative to go forth to love and serve the Lord in the person of the poor.

We of today have certainly no reason to reproach the Sisters of the past for what they have passed on to us: apostolates, spirituality, fidelity to ideals of St. Vincent and St. Louise, loyalty to Superiors. But have the Sisters of the past anything for which to reproach us of the present? Rather, has Jesus Christ, Who is the same yesterday, today and forever, anything to reproach us for? Knowing St. Vincent's profound devotion to Divine Providence, I like to think that St. Vincent himself might suggest that we find an answer to that question in the Gospel which the Church, guided by Divine Providence, has asked us to reflect upon today. *"Why are you so agitated and why are these doubts rising in your hearts?"* (Lk 24:38). Have we tended to fret too much these last few years, to become disturbed and agitated because the Province has been forced to yield some of its works, to close houses? Have we become a little less Christocentric in our spirituality? Not for a moment am I suggesting that we do not believe in Christ, but is Christ the point of reference for us in all things, for our thoughts, our words, our deeds, our projects, as He was for St. Vincent? *"Look at My hands and feet; yes, it is I indeed. Touch Me and see for yourselves."* (Lk 24:39). Have we ever so slightly set aside some of the very valuable counsels of our Founders because we may consider them irrelevant today? Have we these last few years centered our lives less on the reality of the presence of the Risen Christ in the Blessed Sacrament, Christ Who is our *"still point in a turning world?"*

A little scolding, blended with a little encouragement; what of encouragement? Each of us here this morning will admire the tree that has sprung from the mustard seed that was sown here one hundred years ago. It is a mighty tree that has sent out branches or roots to Ireland, Australia, Ethiopia, Nigeria. It is a great tree in which a fraction of the poor of these countries now find shelter. But the territorial expansion of the Company is not the principal source of encouragement for us, impressive though it may be. What gives us encouragement is the intensity with which Sisters live their lives in Christ Jesus. What gives us encouragement is the single-minded devotion which they give to Jesus Christ in the persons of the poor. What gives us encouragement, too, are the new insights we have been receiving these last few years into the charism of our Founders and the enthusiasm with which these insights have been received and shared in our Community. What gives us encouragement is the continuing search that has gone on in this Province to find new ways of helping and serving some of the casualties of a society that has a broad system of social assistance but has yet to learn that man does not live on bread alone. What gives us encouragement is the deep faith, the serene hope and the unaging love of our elderly Sisters. I like to think that there is not one Sister here this morning who could not offer to the Province her own personal word of encouragement, mindful as she must be of what Jesus Christ has done through the Community in all the yesterdays of this first century of the British Province.

To return to St. Louise's request which she made on this day in 1647, did St. Vincent write that letter to all the Sisters, blending a little scolding with encouragement? He did, a letter of seven pages no less, written on the 24 April which was his sixty-sixth birthday. It is a letter woven with golden threads of spirituality and silver ones of practical advice. Characteristically St. Vincent does not commence with a little scolding, but rather with a little encouragement. So let me end by reading the opening sentences of that letter: *"I never think about you and the happiness you have to be Daughters of Charity and the first to be engaged in assisting the poor where you are, without feeling consoled. However, when I hear that you are living as true Daughters of Charity, which is to say, as true daughters of God, my consolation is increased to the extent that only God alone can make you realize. Keep this up, dear Sisters, and strive more and more toward perfection in your holy state ... a state which consists in being true daughters of God, Spouses of His Son, and true mothers of the poor."* (Coste III, Eng. ed., ltr. 939, p. 181).

Yes, my dear Sisters of this Province of Great Britain, may you continue to be true Daughters of God, true Daughters of Charity and mothers of the poor.

Blessed Sacrament

2 July 1985   JH's Hertogenbosch, Holland

My dear Sisters,

Some of the most terrifying pictures of our time are those which were taken of the cities of Hiroshima and Nagasaki in Japan after the dropping of the atomic bomb on them. The pictures came to my mind after reading and reflecting on the description of the destruction of the city of Sodom, which is recounted in the first reading of today's Mass. The scene was one of utter devastation, possibly caused by a combination of natural disasters. The destruction of Sodom was, according to the author of the book of Genesis, caused by the sinfulness of man. So, too, in the last analysis must we say that the destruction of the cities of Hiroshima and Nagasaki was caused by man's sinfulness. However frightening the destruction of Sodom was in the eyes of the author of Genesis, it was not as frightening as what happened to the two Japanese cities in 1945. The great mushroom cloud, that has become so familiar to us, has continued to grow so that we now all live under the threat that, not just two cities could be destroyed in an instant, but that man has it in his power for the first time in history to extinguish virtually all life on our planet. It is terrifying to think that the greed and selfishness and malice of man could bring this about. It is terrifying to think that man, who is so tiny in this universe, has it in his power to destroy so much of the beauty of God's work on this planet and also destroy what God in partnership with man has built up.

What effect all this must have on the collective consciousness of the human race I do not know. Millions of people feel powerless in the face of it. However, as concerned Christians, we ask ourselves if there is anything we as individuals can do to save humanity from such a disaster. Unlike Lot, who could escape from Sodom, we cannot leave the cities that are threatened and go into the country, for it is the entire globe that lies under the threat of extinction.

At the end of today's reading it is suggested that Lot was saved because of the goodness of Abraham. *"Thus it came to pass: when God destroyed the Cities of the Plain, he was mindful of Abraham by sending Lot away from the upheaval by which God overthrew the cities where Lot had been living."* (Gn 19:29). God's saving power was mediated to Lot through Abraham. Today God's saving power is mediated through His Son Jesus Christ. It is through His Son Jesus Christ, as we are reminded at every Eucharist, that all good things come. When the Church asks God, the Father, for anything, she always does so in the name of Jesus Christ. All her official prayers are addressed to God, our Father in Heaven, through Jesus Christ. How familiar to us are these words: *"We ask this through Our Lord Jesus Christ, Your Son, Who lives and reigns with You and the Holy Spirit, one God forever and ever."*

The most efficacious prayer that is addressed to the Father through His Son Jesus Christ is the Mass. The sacrifice of Jesus Christ on the cross is made present on our altars through the Mass. It is a sacrifice that is much more powerful than the life and sacrifice of Abraham, much more eloquent than the blood of Abel. The truth is that, whether the world knows it or not, it is through the Mass that all good things are coming to humanity today. The Mass is that sacrifice which, as the phrase in the fourth Eucharistic Prayer reminds us, *"brings salvation to the whole world."*

The Mass in its essence will not change until Jesus Christ comes again. The externals of the liturgy, however, do change and in our time rather dramatically so. Readings in the vernacular and greater participation of the laity in the celebration of the Eucharist are two of the most important external changes that we have seen in our lifetime. The question we can ask is: Has our attitude towards the Mass changed? Is the Mass as central to our days as it was twenty or thirty years ago? Is our attitude of reverence towards the Mass the same as it was before the liturgy was revised? These questions must be put first by us priests to ourselves, before we put them to the faithful, because the sheep will always follow the shepherd. If we must say that our convictions about the Mass have changed, that they are less strong, less deep, then we must humbly ask for the grace of not only being interested in saving this world from total destruction, but also of having confidence in that first means of doing so, namely, through a daily and personal union of ourselves with Jesus Christ in the sacrifice of the Mass, that sacrifice which *"brings salvation to the whole world."* The world is on the cliff edge of total destruction. It is for that reason that we cry out with the Apostles in today's Gospel: *"Lord, save us. We are lost."* (Mt 8:25). It is through the Mass that Jesus Christ still commands the winds and the waves of man's agitation to be still. It is through the Mass that a great calm can be won for the world, for our own lives and the lives of the poor we serve.

Before ending this brief reflection on the importance and value of the Mass for the world today, let me appeal to you to keep alive among you devotion to the Presence of Jesus Christ in the Blessed Sacrament. *"The Blessed Sacrament,"* wrote Karl Rahner, *"is the Mass held in meditation."* When we visit Our Lord in the Blessed Sacrament, we play again the four great movements of the symphony of the Mass: adoration, thanksgiving, repentance and supplication. If we wish to have stability in our lives, we need to cultivate personal devotion to Our Lord in the Blessed Sacrament. If we are to find Jesus Christ in the poor, we must first find Him in prayer and in the Blessed Sacrament. If we are to have a center for our hearts, a center-point to which we can refer all our apostolates, all our activities, all our needs, that center can only be Jesus Christ present in the Blessed Sacrament. There certainly would be less agitation in the Church, in our communities, in our lives, if all of us were more devoted to the real presence of Jesus Christ in the Blessed Sacrament. It is a grace for which I ask God for each of us here today.

To the first Daughters of Charity St. Vincent said: *"Go to Holy Mass every day, but do so with great devotion. Conduct yourselves in Church with great modesty and be an example of virtue to all who may see you . . . .It is not only the priest who offers up the Holy Sacrifice, but also those who are present and I feel sure that, when you have been well instructed, you will have great devotion to the Mass, for it is the center of devotion."* (Conf. Eng. ed., 31 July 1634, p. 4).

May the Mass, my dear Sisters, be just that for us, *"a center of devotion."* May the Virgin Mary, Mother of God, St. Vincent, St.

Louise and all our Community saints in heaven obtain from God for us this grace.

Conquer Evil with Good

6 July 1985 Eefde, Holland

My dear Friends in Jesus Christ,

Let me begin by saying how happy I am to be celebrating Mass with you here in this Vincentian center this evening. When this building was constructed some twenty-seven years ago, it was built with a view to the education of missionaries for St. Vincent de Paul's Congregation. I like to think that, although the work of educating Vincentian missionaries is no longer carried on in it, it retains its missionary character.

That word *mission* was a word very dear to St. Vincent. It was a word which, from his conferences and correspondence, we know to have been very often on his lips. He called the Congregation which he founded, the Congregation of the Mission. He wished that his priests would move from parish to parish, preaching missions to the people. He also wished that his priests would be missionaries in countries where the good news of Christ had not yet been preached. He sent priests to Madagascar and also to Scotland and Ireland where during his lifetime priests were few on account of religious persecution. When I think of St. Vincent and his strong desire to help the missions, I would like here to pay tribute to the large number of Vincentian priests who are presently working in missionary territories in Asia, Africa, and Latin America. There are close to ninety Dutch Vincentian priests working at the present time in various mission countries of the world. For that, I give thanks to God and express the hope that in the future (and who can say that this will not be so?) many more priests from Holland will go forth to share the riches of the Catholic Faith with peoples who have not yet heard of Jesus Christ and His Church.

Listening to the first reading of this evening's Mass, I wonder if you felt mildly shocked or scandalized. Jacob is one of the great figures of the Old Testament, but he does not appear in a very favorable light in this evening's reading. To put it bluntly, this evening's reading shows him up to be a man of deceit and sharp practice. He deceived his aged and blind father about his identity. He pretended to be his brother, Esau, in order to obtain that special blessing which the father reserved for his eldest son, a blessing which, when once given, was considered to be irrevocable.

We are somewhat shocked to see this corruption in the character of a man whom the Israelite people of subsequent centuries and Christian peoples today look upon as one of the great characters of the Old Testament. Perhaps we should ask ourselves if we should be surprised, when we see the sort of men Jesus Christ chose to be His Apostles when He came on earth. Who would choose St. Peter today to be Pope? We would say that, while he was a very generous man, yet we would not consider him to have the strength of character necessary in a Pope. Yet Jesus Christ chose him, notwithstanding his glaring weaknesses of character. So it was with the rest of the Apostles. They were ordinary men with the ordinary weaknesses of character that characterize Bishops and priests today. Yet it was on such a foundation that God chose to build His Church. It is through such ordinary men that Jesus Christ continues to guide His Church today.

The truth is that God is greater than the limitations of our human characters. He can achieve His purposes, despite the obstacles we place in front of Him. God's plan for the coming of Jesus Christ among the Israelite people was not stopped because of the dishonesty of Jacob. The Church, which Jesus Christ founded, survives today, notwithstanding the infidelities, the mistakes, the imprudences of Popes, Bishops, priests, religious and laity. That does not mean that we should not strive to cooperate with Jesus Christ and with His Church. Our vocation is to establish the Kingdom of God within ourselves first, and after that to work humbly and patiently with others for the coming of the Kingdom of God in their souls and in the world. In all that we do with others and for others, the ideal of St. Paul, which he expressed in his letter to the Romans, will always be relevant: *"Do not be conquered by evil, but conquer evil with good."* (Rom 12:21). That is the way of God. He did not reject Jacob because of his deceit. He did not write him off, and that is often what we do when others fail or deceive us. We allow ourselves to be conquered by evil instead of starting afresh to conquer evil with good.

"We should help and support one another," wrote St. Vincent to a missionary, *"and strive for peace and union among ourselves. This is the wine which cheers and strengthens travelers along this narrow path of Jesus Christ. I recommend this to you with all the tenderness of my heart."* (Coste IV, Eng. ed., ltr. 1414, p. 265).

May God in His mercy, through the intercession of the Virgin Mary and St. Vincent de Paul, give each of us the strength to overcome evil with good and never to lose heart.

Speak, Lord, Your Servant is Listening

27 July 1985   Benagalbon, Spain

My dear young People and Friends of Jesus Christ,

When I was a young boy, there was a popular song, the opening words of which were: *I hear you calling me.* The song was made popular by a tenor singer who became internationally famous because of the excellent quality of his voice and the depth of feeling he could put into everything that he sang. Some years after he died, his wife, who survived him for many years, wrote a book about her husband's success and she entitled the book: *I hear you calling me.* If the song to which I have referred existed thousands of years ago, it might well have been sung by the young Samuel. Samuel was a youth who was serving his apprenticeship under a man named Eli, an Old Testament priest. One night Samuel thought he heard Eli calling him. Three times during the night he got up, but Eli said that he had not called him. Then Eli suspected that the voice was that of God and he suggested to the young Samuel that, when next he heard his name being called, he should reply by saying: *"Speak, Lord, your servant is listening."* (1 Sam 3:9). Samuel did just that and he immediately received from God a clear message about what he was to do.

If you or I had the experience of Samuel, we would probably be frightened out of our wits. We all have dreams, but we do not hear the voice of God speaking to us at nighttime. However, when you come to think of it, God is speaking to us all the time. He is speaking to us through His word in the Bible, through His Church, through the

Sacraments, and through all the events, pleasant and unpleasant, of our lives. We sometimes fail to recognize the voice of God, just as Samuel did, or we choose to ignore it and sleep on. To God, Who is listening to us attentively night and day, we are unable to sing the first line of the song: *"I hear you calling me."*

To each of you young people God is speaking in a special way, for during these years of your youth He is speaking to you about your future. That is why the years of youth are so important. It is in youth that we set about choosing the highway that is going to take us into the heart and into the happiness of God for all eternity. What is so remarkable and marvelous is that there is not just one highway. God in His goodness has planned and constructed a highway for each one of us and which He would like each of us to take. For one person the route will be marriage, for another the priesthood; yet another will reach God by serving Him in the poor as a Sister or as a Brother. Many of you are now on the approach roads which will lead you into the highway which God wants you to take. That is why it is so important that at this point in your lives, you should listen carefully to the directions which the Spirit of God is giving you quietly and lovingly. Yes, the young person's song to God must be: *"I hear you calling me."*

If you wish to hear the voice of God clearly, you must give much attention to the little choices that you are making every day. Every day and every minute we are making choices, not big choices, just little ones. From the moment we awake in the morning we make choices. The decision to get up, although we hardly think about it at times, is a choice. We choose to get up or to remain in bed. We make choices about the food we eat, though it is good to recall that there are many poor people in the world who cannot make that choice. There is no food for them to eat, or there is no alternative to the little bit of rice which is at hand. We make choices about the work we will do and the way we will do it. We make choices about the people who will be our friends. Some choices we can change, others we cannot. The choices we make shape us into particular kinds of people. We can make a nice garden from a piece of ground or we can make it a refuse dump.

Often, in the course of the day, ask the Spirit of Jesus Christ to help you make wise choices, even in small things. In doing so you will be honoring Jesus Christ. You will be bringing Him closer to yourself, and your friendship with Him will be deepened.

If we make right choices in small things, then we will make right choices in big things. If we allow the Spirit of God to assist us in making small choices every day, He will not leave us at the moment when we must make a big choice, such as a decision about the vocation we will choose in life.

I have said that we all go to God by different routes. What is important is not so much whether we are married persons or priests or Brothers or Sisters. What matters is that we are on the particular route which God has selected for us. Our choices are important because they concern not only us, but Jesus Christ Who loves each one of us with an intensity that we cannot begin to imagine. When you find yourself perplexed about what you should do with your life, whether you should choose marriage, or whether you should choose to be a priest like St. Vincent de Paul, or a Daughter of Charity like St. Catherine Labouré, stop and reflect on what Jesus Christ has said: *"You have not chosen Me, but I have chosen you."* (Jn 15:16). We make our choices in life only after God has made a choice for us about the way He thinks we should go to Him so that we can plunge ourselves into the sea of His goodness, His truth and His beauty for all eternity.

The challenge all of us face is to find the true highway that will lead us to the heart of the God Who loves us. Listen to these words of Pope John Paul II, which he addressed to the youth of the entire world at the beginning of this year which is dedicated to youth: *"The world needs young people who have drunk deeply at the sources of truth. You have to listen to the truth and for this you need purity of heart—you have to understand it, and for this you need a deep humility; you have to surrender to it and to share it, and for this you need the strength to resist the temptations of pride, selfishness and manipulation."*

It is Jesus Christ Who has said: *"Happy are the pure of heart for they shall see God."* (Mt 5:8). We know that His Mother, Mary, lived this beatitude perfectly, for she was conceived without sin. If you wish to see the way ahead clearly in life and make a right choice about your vocation, then, like Mary, cultivate purity of heart, of mind and of body. In one word, give depth to the sincerity with which you pray the prayer of Samuel: *"Speak Lord, for Your servant is listening."* (1 Sm 3:10). Then you will be able to sing with joy and with security to God the song: *"I hear you calling me."*

Mountains Speak to Us of God

3 August 1985   Pallanza, Italy

My dear Sisters,

Before I leave here at the end of my retreat, I am happy to celebrate Mass with you and join you in your principal apostolate at the present time, and indeed at any time during your lives as Daughters of Charity, and that is praying for and in the name of the poor. It is good to reflect often on that sentence in your Constitutions which states: *"Praying for the poor and in their name remains the Sisters' primary obligation."* (C. 2.9).

You live your lives here, my dear Sisters, surrounded by mountains. Mountains speak to us of God. Mountains are beautiful in their majesty as God is beautiful in His majesty. Mountains are unchanging as God is unchanging. Mountains are always there as God is always present. Mountains are strong: they stand up to storms over thousands of years and show no signs of breaking. So, too, is God: He is strong. The wickedness of man can do his worst, but God goes on existing. As you pray the Psalms, note the number of times the psalmist speaks of mountains. Mountains make the psalmist think of God: *"You set the mountains in place by Your power."* (Ps 65:7). *"Let the mountains shout for joy at the presence of the Lord."* (Ps 98:8).

The mountains then speak to us of the beauty of God and of His strength and constant care. It is not easy, when we are sick or feeling the weight of years pressing upon us, to think of beauty or to see beauty in ourselves. Yet as God looks at us, He sees each of us as a particular reflection of His beauty, and that reflection He sees in no one else. It is St. Paul who reminds us that each of us is *"God's work of art."* (Eph 2: 10). It is St. Paul, too, who reminds us that, even when age is attacking and breaking down our physical bodies, there is an unseen life within us that is growing and developing. *"Though this outer man of ours may be falling into decay, the inner man is renewed day by day."* (2 Cor 4:16).

The mountains speak to us of the strength of God, and St. Vincent on a number of occasions reminded priests and Sisters who were feeling weak and without strength to face difficulties, that *"Our Lord has enough strength for Himself and for you."* So He has. That is why the Sacraments of the Eucharist and Penance are so important for us. It is through the Sacraments principally that Jesus Christ communicates His strength to us. Psalm 121 begins: *"I lift up my eyes to the mountains"* and then the Psalmist puts the question: *"Where shall come my strength?"* (Ps 121:12). The Psalmist knows that the mountains themselves will not bring him strength. We, as friends of Jesus Christ, know Who the source of our strength is, as St. Paul assures us: *"I can do all things in Him Who strengthens me."* (Phil 4:13).

Lastly, the mountains speak to us of God's constancy and care. God does care for us. We may feel old, but He loves and cares for us as a mother loves her infant child, only infinitely more so. Perhaps the greatest shock we will receive after our deaths will be to discover the intensity of God's love for us when we were young, middle-aged and old.

I conclude with a reflection of St. Vincent in his old age:

> *All our life is but a moment which flies away—disappears quickly. Alas, the seventy-six years of my life which I have passed seem to me but a dream and a moment. Nothing remains of them but regret for having so badly employed this time. Let us think of the dissatisfaction we will have at our deaths if we do not use this time to be merciful. Let us then be merciful, my brothers, and let us exercise mercy towards all in a way that we will never find a poor man without consoling him, if we can, nor an uninstructed man without teaching him in a few words those things which it is necessary to believe and which he must do for his salvation. O Saviour, do not permit that we abuse our vocation. Do not take away from this Company the spirit of mercy, because what would become of us if You should withdraw Your mercy from it? Give us, then, that mercy along with the spirit of gentleness and humility.* (Coste XI, Fr. ed., p. 342).

Nothing is Impossible with God

15 August 1985   Paris, France

Mother Duzan, Father Lloret and my dear Sisters,

A little less than two weeks ago I was returning to Rome by plane. The last passenger to enter the plane was a lady, and she sat in the vacant seat beside me. She had scarcely done so when she asked me if I was a Catholic priest and, on learning that I was, she asked if she could talk to me. She told me that she was an American Jewess and had two sons, now grown up, both mildly handicapped. She was a teacher of French, was separated from her husband and was visiting Italy. During the interval of an orchestral concert she had met a man with whom she struck up a casual acquaintance which very quickly developed into friendship and love. She admired the man for his gentleness, his refinement and his intelligence. Her desire now was to bring him to the United States and to marry him. He was also married and separated, and had one grown son. That is a brief synopsis of a very long conversation or rather soliloquy, for it was clear that the lady was not really seeking advice from me, but rather a listening ear. As the plane touched down at Rome, she repeated a few times: *"I hope I will be able to handle the situation."* Then she thanked me for listening and vanished into the crowd to catch a connecting flight .

As I listened to the lady talking, I found myself reflecting on the fact that she was a Jewess, like Mary of Nazareth. She attended the synagogue, like Mary of Nazareth, though perhaps with less regularity. The law and the prophets meant something to her, though not what they meant to Mary of Nazareth. This Jewess was an intelligent woman, like Mary of Nazareth. She was also a mother, like Mary of Nazareth. What, I began to wonder, would Mary of Nazareth have to say to the lady who, like her, was a descendant of Abraham? What word of advice would she have offered to the lady as she repeated: *"I hope I will be able to handle the situation"*?

Knowing the reticence of Mary of Nazareth, who kept all things in her heart, she would have said little. *"I, too, have had a Son, but they executed him. Envy, jealousy and the vested interests of religion con-*

spired to have Him removed from the scene. He was innocent, totally innocent, and His innocence has been established in a way that could only have been done by God. Although He died, He is now risen . . . and His body is the Church. I continue to love and serve Him in the Church which is His body. I do so because of my word that I gave to God before the power of the Holy Spirit overshadowed and came upon me."

In such an imaginary conversation between the American Jewess and Mary of Nazareth, all would have centered on their understanding of fidelity. For Mary of Nazareth, fidelity was something deep, lasting, permanent and penetrating into eternity. For the Jewess whom I met, well-intentioned as she was, fidelity was conditioned by emotional needs, changing circumstances and cultural tastes. Fidelity, as the Jewess saw it, was for years but not necessarily for life. Mary, the Virgin Mother of Nazareth, on the other hand, understood her vocation as one to which she had pledged herself for the duration of her life. She lived it to the end from the Nazareth of the Annunciation to the Jerusalem of the Crucifixion, yes, and beyond it in fidelity to the Church of which her Son had made her Mother. *"All these with one accord devoted themselves to prayer, together with the women and Mary, the Mother of Jesus."* (Acts 1: 14).

"I hope I will be able to handle the situation." In one form or another we formulate that expression often during our lives. There are moments of crisis in our lives, moments of difficulty, moments when we feel pulled away from surrendering ourselves to God and His Will as it is expressed to us through our Superiors and the daily events of our lives. In such moments of crisis and difficulty we hope that we *"will be able to handle the situation."* What we need in such moments is the capacity to take a long view of our situation. The Jewess had a shorter vision. She could see life as only so many individual episodes that were unrelated to each other. Life for her had no fixed center. For us there can only be one center, constant as the northern star, the living Person of Jesus Christ. Over and over again amid the changing circumstances of life, we must keep surrendering ourselves to Him and to His Will as did Mary, the Virgin of Nazareth.

Perhaps you have noticed in St. Vincent's correspondence with his Confreres and Sisters his fondness for using the imperative, *Continue,* when he wished to encourage them in fidelity: *"Continue for your part, my dear Sister, to practice well the virtues which are proper for you. Continue to go on growing from day to day in the love and imitation of Our Lord. Be very faithful to Him in your exercises. In that way you will make yourselves more and more lovable in His eyes and in the eyes of the poor, for you are as a mother to the poor. It is that which I hope for from His infinite goodness."* (Coste VI, Fr. ed., p. 42).

Let no current opinion convince you that it is impossible over a lifetime to give daily evidence of obedience, chastity, poverty and service of the poor. We wonder and hope that we will be able to handle the situation. However often we may diffidently say to ourselves, *"I hope I will be able to handle the situation,"* we must remember that we are not alone. Mary, the Jewess and Virgin Mother of God and now assumed into heaven, assures us by her life that fidelity to a vocation over the span of a lifetime is possible. I wonder how often she made her meditation on that single sentence spoken to her by the Angel Gabriel: *"With God nothing will be impossible."* (Lk 1:37). They were the final words of Gabriel's message to Mary. They must have given her strength to reply: *"Behold, I am the handmaid of the Lord. Let it be done to me according to your word."* (Lk 1:38).

From her uniquely privileged place in heaven, Mary's message to us who find difficulty in handling the situation of fidelity to our vocation day after day must surely be: *"With God nothing will be impossible."* Lifelong fidelity to one vocation is like a high mountain peak. It stands out. It is something from which one can take one's bearings. The Church on its pilgrimage has need of such high mountain peaks. Have confidence, my dear Sisters, in the value of fidelity to the vocation which is yours. Have confidence in the goodness of your own lives. It is fidelity to your vocation which can be, and so often is, a silent source of encouragement to others who are striving to be faithful to God in and through the Sacrament of Marriage. *"Those who trust in the Lord are like Mount Sion which cannot be moved but abides forever."* (Ps. 125).

"I hope I will be able to handle the situation." On this, your first official feast day, Mother Duzan, let me express in the name of the Community the confidence which we have that, with the grace of God

and the grace of office, you will competently handle the situation into which the Spirit of God has led you. It is our prayer today that with Mary, the Jewess and Virgin Mother of Nazareth, your spirit will rejoice in God, your Saviour, for He who is mighty has done great things for you, and holy is His name. Mother Duzan, I wish you a very Happy Feast Day .

Greatness of the Priesthood

2 September 1985   To Each Confrere

My dear Confreres,

May the grace of Our Lord Jesus Christ be with us forever!

I write to greet you for the feast of St. Vincent, which this year should have a special significance for us, for it is now just one hundred years ago since Pope Leo XIII declared St. Vincent to be *"the special Patron before God of all associations of charity."* The Pope who gave the Church the first of the great encyclicals on social justice in modern times, was also a profound admirer of St. Vincent, who animated with charity all his projects so that justice and peace might embrace each other in the interests of the poor. So, may your celebration of St. Vincent's feast day this year bring you a new measure of that joy which is the fruit of charity.

Four days before he died, St. Vincent celebrated the sixtieth anniversary of his ordination to the priesthood. Father Jean Gicquel, who chronicled some of the words and decisions that St. Vincent took during the final weeks of his life, makes no allusion to the Diamond Jubilee. We have no way of knowing what St. Vincent's personal sentiments were on this sixtieth anniversary. It is likely that they would not have been very much different from those he expressed earlier in one of his letters to a priest: *"For me, if I had known what the priesthood was when I had the temerity to enter into it, as I know it now, I would have preferred to work on the farm than give myself to such a tremendous state in life. I have said this a thousand times to the poor people of the countryside . . . and indeed, the older I get, the more I am confirmed in this opinion, because I discover every day how far I am from the perfection which I ought to have as a priest."* (Coste V, Fr. ed., p. 568).

The years had quite clearly given St. Vincent a vision of the greatness of the priesthood that he did not have when he knelt before the aged Bishop of Périgueux on the 23 September 1600. However unworthy of the priesthood St. Vincent may have felt himself to be, he could not have denied that it was his participation in the ministerial priesthood of Christ that had largely enabled him to do so much for the poor. His sermon at Folleville would never have been preached, had he not been a priest, nor would the Charity at Châtillon-les-Dombes have been established, if he had not been priest and pastor there on that August Sunday in 1617.

St. Vincent's participation in the ministerial priesthood of Christ was a constant reference point for him in the direction he gave to the dazzling panorama of his projects of charity and mercy. The Church herself makes the point clear for us in the prayer that she asks us to pray over the gifts on his feast day: *"God, You gave to St. Vincent, as he celebrated the Sacred Mysteries, the gift of imitating what he handled; grant by the power of this sacrifice that we also may be transformed into an offering pleasing to You." "To imitate what he handled . . . ."* The phrase is an echo of that used in the ordination rite which St. Vincent himself would have heard the ordaining Bishop pronounce.

The apostolic vitality of the Congregation will depend in large measure on the depth of appreciation which all of us in the Congregation have for the priesthood, and on the intensity with which it is lived by us priests. It is sometimes said that our era is the era of the layman. New horizons in theology and in the apostolates of the laity have been opening up for us. Within our Congregation some of our Brothers have been assuming new responsibilities that correspond with a new vision of the layman's vocation. However, if the layman is to be fully a layman, the priest must be fully a priest. The layman will only live his vocation fully if we priests are living fully the mystery of our participation in the ministerial priesthood of Jesus Christ.

To live intensely the mystery of the ministerial priesthood of Jesus Christ was for St. Vincent *"to exercise the two great virtues of Jesus Christ, namely, religion towards His Father and charity towards men."*

(Coste VI, Fr. ed., p. 393). In St. Vincent's vision of the priesthood, an equilibrium must be achieved between religion towards the Father and charity towards men. In our day preaching the Gospel has been emphasized as the primary task of the priest, and for us in St. Vincent's Community it is to the poor that we must go. That emphasis, however, should not deflect us from our work of participating with Christ in His mediation with the Father. Neither time nor circumstances can change this eternal truth that a priest is *"a man chosen from among men and is appointed on behalf of men in relation to God, to offer gifts and sacrifices for sins."* (Heb 5:1).

We rejoice that in our day the Church has in so many fine documents called us to be active in the pursuit of justice and charity for the poor. It is the same Church that asks us priests, not only to celebrate the Eucharist but also to pray day in and day out the prayer of the Divine Office which is the prayer of Jesus Christ Himself. As priests it would help us to reflect often on the words of St. Augustine: *"Jesus Christ prays for us as our priest. He prays in us as our head. He is prayed to by us as our God. So we must recognize our voices in Him and His voice in us."* (St. Augustine, Divine Office, Lent, Week 5, Wednesday).

The Bishop who ordained St. Vincent was almost blind. If we are to believe St. Vincent, he himself was suffering at that time also from a certain blindness of the spiritual order, a failure to see the greatness of a vocation to be a priest. Time was to cure St. Vincent of this ailment. May St. Vincent on his feast day enlighten the eyes of our minds to see and to live *"the two great virtues of Jesus Christ, namely, religion towards the Father and charity towards men."* (Coste VI, Fr. ed., p. 393).

Joined by all the Confreres of the Curia in wishing you a Happy Feast Day, I remain in the love of Our Lord, your devoted confrere.

Burning Love for the Poor

13 September 1985   Concepcion, Panama

My dear Brothers and Sisters in Jesus Christ,

How happy I am to be celebrating Mass here in what is a very Vincentian group. We have present here this evening members of St.

Vincent's two Communities. We have also members of the Society of St. Vincent de Paul, that Society which through Frederic Ozanam takes its inspiration from the life and work of St. Vincent de Paul. We all have a special love for Mary, the Mother of God and our Mother. That reminds us of the rue du Bac in Paris, for it was there in the Mother House of the Daughters of Charity that Our Lady appeared and gave to the world the medal which God's people have called *miraculous*. Certainly during his lifetime, St. Vincent could not have envisaged such a representative gathering as this. In a film of his life that was made three decades ago, there is a marvelous scene towards the end, where Queen Anne of Austria is talking to St. Vincent. St. Vincent is now an old man and the Queen is reminding him of all that he achieved during his lifetime. St. Vincent keeps shaking his head and saying that he has done nothing. The Queen insists further and St. Vincent repeats again: *"I have done nothing."* Finally the Queen gets somewhat impatient with the Saint and says to him: *"If you say you have done nothing in your lifetime for God, what must we do?"* St. Vincent's eyes light up and he turns to the Queen and speaks one word: *"More."*

St. Vincent's name will always be associated with charity. Those of us who have had the privilege of reading and reflecting on his life, can see that there is much more to the man than a very competent organizer of relief for the poor. Perhaps he would say that after his devotion to the Person of Jesus Christ and His Mother, what was most important for him was humility. He believed that if a person was truly humble before God and man, God would do great things through him or her. It is interesting to note that on one occasion when St. Vincent was talking about humility to his close collaborators, he quoted a remark of the Saint whom the Church is honoring today, St. John Chrysostom. He said: *"God has sent us to serve and evangelize the poor . . . in a humble, gentle and familiar way. That is why we can apply to ourselves what St. John Chrysostom said in one of his homilies that as long as we remain sheep by a true and genuine humility, not only will we not be devoured by wolves but we will even convert them into sheep. On the contrary, once we abandon this humility and simplicity . . . we will lose the grace which is attached to it."* (Coste XI, Fr, ed., pp. 61-62).

Hundreds of years separate St. Vincent de Paul from St. John

Chrysostom, but both of them read the same Gospels, celebrated the same Mass, recited the same Creed, and both of them had a burning love for the poor. Listen to St. John Chrysostom as he preached one day to his people:

> *Would you honor the body of Christ? Do not despise His nakedness. Do not honor Him here in Church, clothed in silk vestments, and then pass Him by unclothed and frozen outside. Remember that He Who said, 'This is My Body' and made good His words, also said, 'You saw Me hungry and gave Me no food . . . insofar as you did it not to one of these, you did it not to Me.' (Mt 25:42, 45) God has no need of golden vessels but of golden hearts. I am not saying that you should not give golden altar vessels and so on, but I am insisting that nothing can take the place of almsgiving . . . .Consider that Christ is that tramp who comes in need of a night's lodging. You turn him away and then start laying rugs on the floor and draping the walls, hanging lamps on silver chains on the columns. Meanwhile the tramp is locked up in prison and you never give him a glance. Well, again, I am not condemning munificence in these matters. Make your house beautiful, by all means, but also look after the poor, or rather, look after the poor first . . . . Adorn your house, if you will, but do not forget your brother in distress. He is a temple of infinitely greater value.* (Homily Brev., Sat., Week 21, Office of Readings).

Of the two saints, Vincent de Paul and John Chrysostom, St. John Chrysostom was called upon to suffer more for the faith. Twice as Bishop, plots were made against him and his enemies forced him into exile. On the first occasion it was the Empress at the time who was responsible. Shortly after she had succeeded in banishing him to a remote place, an earthquake took place. She took fright, seeing it as a sign of God's anger, and she called John Chrysostom back, to the delight of all the people. However, other enemies plotted against him, and he was abducted and brought to an even more remote place. The rigors of the winter weakened his health and he told his captors that he was going to die. He requested the Sacraments and then asked to be

clothed in priestly vestments. When that had been done, he continued
to pray. His final words were: *"Glory be to God for all things."*

The message which St. Chrysostom would have for us today would
be the same as that which he preached sixteen hundred years ago. Be
attentive to the poor. Hold on to your convictions about Jesus Christ,
His Church and the Faith. Do not yield to the pressures of people who
would turn you away from the Pope and the Bishops and from caring
about the poor. To the message which St. John Chrysostom would offer
us today on his feast day, St. Vincent would say from his heart, *"Yes.
Amen."* May St. Vincent and St. John Chrysostom keep us all devoted
to Jesus Christ, devoted also to Mary, the Virgin Mother of God and
our Mother, and generous at all times to His special friends, the poor.

Three Ways to Look at Christ on the Cross

14 September 1985   Los Angeles, Chile

My dear Brothers and Sisters in Jesus Christ,

Supposing this beautiful world of ours was destroyed by a number
of nuclear bombs and after hundreds of years someone from another
planet came to walk the burned surface of this earth, what would they
find most frequently among the ruins? There is little doubt but that in
one form or another that person would find the cross. For there are
crosses of all shapes and sizes scattered all over this globe. There are
crosses on our churches and on our altars. Our Bishops wear crosses.
There are crosses on our vestments, in our homes, on our rosaries and
in a thousand other places.

The cross holds a place of honor among us, but that was not so
always. Imagine if your friend started sending you a piece of rope with
a noose tied at the end of it, or that you began to see the noose of a rope
in all sorts of unexpected places. You would not care for it, because it
would remind you of the execution of criminals. You would consider
such a sign as rather bad taste. At one time the cross was just like that.
A person who was nailed to a cross was considered to be cursed by God.

Then after Our Lord had suffered on the cross and risen from the
dead, Christians began to honor, not only the place of His death and

resurrection but also the means by which He was put to death, namely, the cross. They built churches at the sites of Our Lord's death and resurrection, and it is the dedication of those churches more than sixteen hundred years ago that the Church is recalling today.

When St. John, who was present at Our Lord's crucifixion, saw Our Lord on the cross, he thought of some words in the Old Testament which had been written long before Our Lord was born. The words were: *"They shall look on him whom they have pierced."* (Zec 12:10). St. John was convinced that, if we can look in the proper way at Jesus Christ on the cross, we will not only draw strength for ourselves in all the circumstances of our lives, but it will help us to become more like Jesus Christ in thought, word and deed. Let me suggest to you three ways in which you can look at Christ on the cross. I say *look*, not just glance, at the cross. Many times when we look at our crucifixes, we do not look deeply into them. We see the outer appearances of the cross. We are only glancing at the cross. We are not really looking at Him Whom they have pierced.

First, there is the Mass or the celebration of the Eucharist. Our Lord Himself has guaranteed us that as often as the Mass is celebrated, there is made present for us the offering which He made to His Father as He hung on the cross. Do you wish to adore God? Then pray the Mass. Do you wish to express to God your regret for sin and to ask His mercy on yourself and on the world? Then pray the Mass. Do you want to thank God for all the good things of life? Then pray the Mass. Do you wish to ask God for good things for yourselves, your families and your friends? Then pray the Mass. For on the cross Jesus Christ did all these things. At the Mass He invites you personally to join Him in praying as He prayed on the cross.

The second way we can look at Jesus Christ on the cross is to look at the weak members of our society. If you want to honor Jesus Christ on His cross, do something for the sick or the poor or the aged or the handicapped. Do not just glance at the poor and suffering. Look at them and help them as best you can, and you will see Christ on His cross. The poor and people who are suffering do not look attractive, but then neither did Jesus Christ look attractive on the cross. Keep looking lovingly at those who have less than you have or are suffering more, and you will see Jesus Christ Whom they have pierced.

Third, in most churches of the world you will find hanging on the walls fourteen scenes from Our Lord's way to the cross. We call them the Stations of the Cross. Many artists have designed beautiful pictures for the Stations of the Cross. It is not enough to admire the art of the fourteen Stations of the Cross. The Church invites us to make the Way of the Cross, to move from one picture to the other, reflecting on the experience of Jesus as He went painfully to His crucifixion and death on the cross. Making the Way of the Cross frequently will help you to look on Jesus Whom they have pierced and through that experience to become more like Jesus Christ crucified and now risen.

Looking at and not just glancing at Jesus Christ on the cross, we will draw strength and healing from it, as did the Israelites of old when, obeying Moses, they looked at the bronze serpent which was a symbol of God's healing power. Through our reflection and contemplation of Jesus Christ on His cross, we will more easily accept and carry out His Will for us. St. Vincent de Paul, writing to one of his priests, remarked: *"Our perfect happiness consists in doing His Will in the true wisdom of desiring nothing than that. God often wants to build lasting benefits on the patience of those who undertake them; that is why He tries them in many ways . . . .I ask Our Lord . . . to fill your hearts with faith, hope and love."* (Coste IV, Eng. ed., ltr. 1435, pp. 290, 292).

Simon, the Pharisee

19 September 1985   Lima, Peru

My dear Confreres and Sisters,

When I was a boy growing up, there was a man in our neighborhood who, when he wanted to describe a house where he felt he was not welcomed, would say: *"I was served with a marble heart and cold shoulder."* It was an apparent allusion to an item on the food menu, but what he was really saying was that the people were cold and inhospitable.

I thought of this little phrase when reflecting on the Gospel to which we have just listened. Our Lord was certainly served with a marble heart and cold shoulder. It is hard to judge exactly the intentions of Simon, the Pharisee. Perhaps he was a collector of celebrities and with a half-patronizing contempt had invited the young Galilean to have a meal with him. There is a strange combination of a certain respect with the omission of the courtesies which the occasion demanded. Silence is golden, and Our Lord seemingly made no comment on the chilly reception for a time. Then, when this woman, who was seemingly a prostitute in the locality, came and began to treat Our Lord with great respect, He used the occasion to speak gently and kindly to Simon. *"Simon, I have something to say to you. And Simon answered, 'Master, say it.'"* (Lk 7:40).

I have often asked myself, did it cost Simon a good deal to say those words? Had he any fear that Jesus would say something disagreeable and hurtful to his pride, or ask of him some heroic sacrifice? The truth is often bitter and it takes courage to listen to it. At the end of a day it is good to allow Our Lord to say those words to us: *"I have something to say to you,"* and to add immediately, *"Master, say it."* When we allow those words to sink deeply into our minds, it is not to torture our consciences. It is important to be simple and sincere with God and important to ask God to be simple and sincere with us. Perhaps that strikes you as rather strange, for God is by His very nature simple and sincere. He is, but often He cannot get through to us or often we do not allow Him to be simple and sincere with us. Perhaps we are like Simon at the beginning of the meal. Our Lord saw clearly that Simon was omitting the elementary courtesies which were due to a guest, but He said nothing. Possibly He felt that He would not get through to Simon, or that Simon was not strong enough at that particular moment to perceive a simple and sincere observation of Christ about his lack of courtesy. So, often in prayer, sit still and allow Christ to say gently to you: *"I have something to say to you."* When we have listened to Him for a little while, ask Him for the grace to say from your heart: *"Master, say it."* If we did this more often, perhaps we would find that He would ask us to give up something, some practice, some pleasure, something we may be clinging to as our very life. He may be wanting to say to us that we do not deny ourselves, that we do not take up our cross, that we do not follow Him. We can trust Him, for if He asks anything, He will help us to do it.

When reflecting on this incident in the life of Our Lord, I have often thought that Simon was probably a smug and self-sufficient man. For that reason he had little time for the poor woman who came to show her respect and reverence for Our Lord. Self-sufficiency and smugness, or pride, fill our hearts in such a way that we have no room for Christ or His poor. Perhaps that accounts for the importance which St. Vincent gave to the two virtues of humility and detachment. Humility has a way of emptying our hearts of ourselves and of exaggerated ideas about our worth. Detachment will empty our hearts of the desire for material things and inordinate pleasures. If we are to love Our Lord, if we are to make room in our hearts and in our minds for Him, then we must ask Him for the grace of humility and detachment of heart. If we are to make room for the poor, if they are to feel at home with us, as the poor woman did with Christ, then we must first ask for the grace of humility and detachment of heart.

> *What a happiness*, exclaimed St. Vincent one day to the Sisters, *to seek nothing but to please God, to despise all the comforts that one might have, and to look upon all that savors of this world as nothing, for that is what Daughters of Charity do. Continue then, Sisters, and act in such a way that your Company may ever go on increasing and becoming more and more perfect in the grace of God, and that it may render more and more services to Our Lord by the observance of Rule . . . . Mark, if you do so, there is nothing else needed to make you saints. I told you before that Pope Clement VIII asked for nothing but that to canonize a person.* (Conf. Eng. ed., 9 Dec. 1657, pp. 988-989).

"Simon, I have something to say to you. He replied, 'Master, say it.'" (Lk 7:40).

Earthquakes

21 September 1985   Lima, Peru

My dear Confreres:

For a few minutes yesterday evening when talking to Father Rigazio about the earthquake in Mexico and the possibility of making contact with our Confreres there, we both began to reflect upon the mystery of this terrible happening over which man has no control. Why does God allow this to happen? We know for certain that He has His own reasons, but they are above and beyond our limited minds. An earthquake shakes not only the earth and all who stand on it. It shakes also our minds and forces us to admit that however deep man may probe into the secrets of the universe, he will never master them all. An earthquake brings man back to earth.

An earthquake brings man back to the realization that he is creature and not Creator. An earthquake brings a man into the heart of the psalmist who said: *"O God, how difficult I find your thoughts, How many of them there are! If I counted them they would be more than the grains of sand. When I awake, I am still with you."* (Ps. 138:17-18).

There are earthquakes of another order than the physical one, and one such was the call of Levi or Matthew, which is described in today's gospel. Looked at from our point of view, Matthew was not a suitable candidate for the priesthood, much less for the episcopacy.

To begin with, he was a man who had become rich on oppression. All the world knew that and thoroughly despised him for it. Matthew, for his part, had probably long ago become accustomed to being despised, which probably made him all the more avaricious and greedy. It was when Jesus Christ passed by and looked at him with His penetrating eyes that the earthquake happened in Matthew's life. Jesus Christ seemingly spoke only two words: *"Follow Me,"* (Mt 9:9) and Matthew rose up and followed, *"leaving everything,"* (Lk 5:28) according to St. Luke, except, we can presume, that pen with which he was to write that book which we know as his gospel and which will be a best-seller until the end of time.

What stirred Matthew to follow Jesus is his secret and God's. However, we can be certain of this; namely, that the glance of Jesus was one of love. That caused an earthquake in Matthew, for he was so used to receiving glances of hate from people, that the glance of love from Jesus Christ brought his world of money crashing to the ground, as buildings do in an earthquake.

The story of Matthew's conversion could be a salutary earthquake for us. It is very easy for us to label people and put them into categories of our own making, and especially to categorize unfavorably people who are different and who act differently from us. The story of Matthew's conversion is a forceful reminder to us that it is only God Who can fully read the human heart, and that the human heart will respond to love, when all other means fail. No change was wrought in Matthew until he felt the warmth of the love which Jesus Christ showed him. It remains true for us today. If we want to change the poor, if we want to change oppressors, the only way is that of Jesus Christ, Who changed Matthew by making him feel that there was goodness in his heart, not withstanding his grasping hands. Earthquakes of conversion only happen when there is movement of love from one individual heart to another.

In an era when there was much bitterness between Protestant and Catholic, St. Vincent saw clearly that no change would be achieved unless there was profound respect for the individual person, whatever his theological views might be, and unless the spoken and the written word sprung from a loving heart.

Let us listen to St. Vincent describing his personal experience: *". . . God has been pleased to make use of this wretch to convert three people; but I must admit that meekness, humility and patience in dealing with these poor misguided people was the essence of this good work."* (Coste I, Eng. ed., ltr. 30, pp 57-58).

May the Virgin Mary and St. Vincent obtain these virtues for us, which will make our neighbors feel that they are understood and loved by God.

Evangelical Poverty

25 September 1985   Arequipa, Peru

My dear Sisters,

When we read the New Testament, we have to be jolting our minds constantly back to the conditions of life as Our Lord, His Mother and His disciples would have known them. In those days there was only one way of sending a message abroad and that was by word of mouth. Newspapers did not exist; books had to be handwritten, and a book the size of the New Testament would have cost about $40 to produce. TV and radio, upon which we depend so much for ready news, had not even been dreamed of. So to spread the message which He had come to give to humanity, Jesus, Who was under the limitations of time and space, chose Twelve and, as St. Luke remarks in this morning's Gospel, *"sent them forth to proclaim the reign of God and heal the afflicted."* (Lk 9:2).

The Twelve were to travel light. Perhaps that was because the man who travels light can travel far and fast. The more material things a man possesses, the more he is tied to one place. However, there was probably another reason, a deeper and more spiritual one. If the messengers of Our Lord were to be seen traveling with all sorts of possessions, it could create in the minds of their hearers the impression that the messengers were making a lot of money from proclaiming the reign of God. Our Lord wished that it be made abundantly clear that these men were but spokesmen for Jesus, the Son of the living God. The message they proclaimed belonged to God and the Twelve were to be seen as men who were glad to be privileged with communicating that message without any self-interest on their part.

It is the same today. As priests or sisters we are sent out by Jesus Christ to proclaim the coming of the Kingdom of God and to heal the suffering. Should we be encumbered with too many possessions, should we show ourselves to be interested more in our own comfort than being selfless agents of Jesus Christ, we will not be credible to the poor. That same power of Jesus Christ through the Twelve will work through us, provided we keep the windscreens of our hearts clean. That is why St. Vincent and St. Louise insisted so much on the importance of evangelical poverty and the practice of the virtue of detachment in our lives. Your Constitutions put the ideal clearly: *"Only by a personal and collective practice of this kind of poverty will their witness be authentic. With great trust in Divine Providence, the Sisters live simply and are content to spend only what is necessary for their apostolic works and for their life as servants."* (C. 2.7).

In the Gospel passage, to which we have just listened, there is an interesting phrase at the beginning and at the end. St. Luke remarks that Jesus sent the Twelve out *"to preach the Kingdom of God and to heal."*

(Lk 9:2). After they had received their instructions from Our Lord, St. Luke makes the same point again. *"And they departed and went through the villages, preaching the Gospel and healing everywhere."* (Lk 9:6). So, on the Twelve Jesus laid two tasks, preaching and healing. They were to care for the bodies and for the souls of those whom they would meet. The message was not only one in words, however comforting, it was also one in actions. It was a message which was not confined to news of eternity, but it also proposed to change conditions on earth. It was a message for mankind in his temporal condition, as well as in his eternal condition.

The spiritual genius of St. Vincent could be said to have consisted in his ability to marry the task of preaching the Gospel to the poor with the task of healing their minds and their bodies. One of the most marvelous achievements, and perhaps the most fundamental, of St. Vincent, was to find and make explicit a formula of action which would help his two Communities to achieve the double task of enlightening the minds and hearts of the poor about Jesus Christ and His message, while also manifesting a very practical concern for the welfare of their bodies. The Christian could be said to be like a person who is walking on a tightrope. If he leans too much to one side, he will fall into a false spirituality which takes no account of the practical needs of the poor at our doors. If he leans too much to the other side, he can lose his balance and become so engrossed in political action for the poor as to forget that the poor are not intended to have a lasting city here on this earth, but with all other Christians are on pilgrimage to the city of the new Jerusalem whose maker and builder is God. If we absorb and live the spirituality of our Founders, we will keep our balance on the tightrope and by the grace of God make Jesus Christ and His message known to the poor and at the same time give them the practical assistance which the Good Samaritan gave to the wounded man he found on the road from Jerusalem to Jericho.

With St. Vincent then, I say to you, my dear Sisters: *"Hold fast then to the state in which God has placed you; always try to preserve your primitive spirit of humility and simplicity. As God has chosen you, as He chose St. Francis, to honor Him in your poor and lowly condition in the eyes of the world, hold fast to it and He will bless you . . . .So then, my daughters, you have been chosen by God to be predestined, if you are faithful to the observance of your Rules; it is not you who have chosen yourselves, but God Who has elected you. You are the apostles of charity . . . . Let us pray to the Blessed Virgin that she may pray to Her Son for us all . . . .O Blessed Virgin, who speak for those who have no tongue and who cannot speak for themselves, we beseech Thee, these good Sisters and myself, to assist this Little Company. Continue and perfect a work which is the greatest on earth."* (Conf. Eng. ed., 8 Aug. 1655, pp. 722-723).

Led by the Spirit

11 October 1985   San Francisco de Macoris, Santo Domingo

My dear Friends in Jesus Christ,

It will be just a year ago tomorrow since the Pope set foot here in your country and spoke to a vast crowd in the Olympic Stadium. One of the nine years of the novena that leads up to the five hundredth anniversary of the arrival of Christianity in the continent of Latin America has passed. I imagine you can still hear the Pope expressing his hope that the new Latin America will be, to quote his own words, *"free and fraternal, just and peaceful, loyal to Christ and to Latin American man."* You will recall, too, how the Pope quoted the prayer which Columbus' seamen recited at dawn: *"Blessed be the light and the holy true cross and the Lord of truth and the Holy Trinity. Blessed be the dawn and the Lord who sends it to us. Blessed be the day and the Lord who sends it to us."*

It is a year ago tomorrow since the Pope was with you. Let me recall another anniversary which we are celebrating today. If you were in Rome on this day twenty-three years ago, standing in the great square in front of St. Peter's, you would have seen filing past you an immense procession of Bishops, about two thousand of them. At the end of the procession came the Pope of that time, John XXIII, and they were all making their way into the huge basilica of St. Peter's to celebrate Mass and to begin Vatican Council II. In the hearts and minds of those Bishops on the 11 October 1962 were the sentiments of Columbus' seamen: *"Blessed be the day and the Lord who sends it to us."*

We never know at the beginning of a day what the Lord is going to send to us. We do not know what the day will bring us. So, too, the Pope and the Bishops of the world on this day twenty-three years ago did not know what the Lord would bring to them during their long meeting. The Pope and the Bishops, who commenced the work of Vatican Council II, were a little like explorers. They did not know what continents of new theology they would discover during their reflections and discussions. Or, to express it in another way, they invoked the Spirit of God on the 11 October 1962, but they did not know where the Spirit of God would lead them. This should not surprise us, because Our Lord said of the Holy Spirit that He is like the wind. *"The wind blows where it wills,"* said Our Lord, *"and you hear the sound of it, but you do not know whence it comes or whither it goes. So it is with everyone who is born of the Spirit."* (Jn 3:8).

At Vatican Council II the Bishops were led by the Holy Spirit into new discoveries about the Church. It was not that they made new theology. Rather they discovered new truths which lie hidden in the Creed. Before Latin America was discovered by Columbus and his men, it existed. Latin America is as old as Europe, but the people in Europe knew nothing about it until Columbus brought back the news that it was there. It is a little like that with theology. The truths which Jesus Christ gave to His Apostles are like a rich mine. It is only gradually that the wealth of the mine can be brought to the surface. Our Lord told His Apostles many things about the Church, and He promised, when He was about to leave them, that *"when the Spirit of truth comes, He will guide you into all truth."* (Jn 16:13). The work of a General Council and of the years that follow it is to discover new riches in the mine of the truth which Our Lord has left to His Church.

Since Vatican Council II, the Spirit of God has continued to reveal truths to the Pope and the Bishops of the Church. Next month once again the Pope will surround himself, not with all the Bishops of the Church but with a representative group of them, so that together they can listen to the voice of the Holy Spirit and see more deeply into the truths which the Spirit of God communicated to the Bishops of Vatican Council II twenty years ago.

One of the messages which the Church received from the Spirit of

God at Vatican Council II was that it should do more for the poor of the world. Over the past twenty years the Church has increased her interest in the poor. Not only has the Church tried to lighten the sufferings of the poor, but she has tried also to be more efficient in bringing the Good News of Jesus Christ and His Church to the poor. When the Pope was here with you last year, he made many important statements. One of them has impressed me greatly. The Pope said to you here in Santo Domingo: *"He who lacks material resources may be poor, but he who does not know the way which God marks out for him is even poorer."*

Perhaps the reason why this statement of the Pope impressed me so much is that it expresses in one sentence the ideal by which St. Vincent de Paul lived. St. Vincent was interested in feeding the hungry, visiting prisoners, caring for the sick, educating the poor, and he founded Communities and groups to continue his work. But he was also intensely interested in helping people, particularly the poor, to be reconciled with God, to cherish their faith, and to be loyal to the Church. In one word, St. Vincent de Paul was interested not only in the bodies of the poor, but in their souls also. There are some people who are only interested in improving the material conditions of the poor. That is important, certainly. Without any doubt it is important to keep searching for peaceful ways of securing greater justice for the poor. However, that is only half the work. Every poor person has a soul. Every poor person has a responsibility to save his soul. Every poor person has need of help in that task. It was St. Vincent de Paul's great achievement that he worked to save both the bodies and souls of the poor. He worked to save the whole person. *"What does it profit a man,"* asks Our Lord, *"if he gains the whole world and suffers the loss of his soul?"* (Mk 8:36). What, my dear friends, will it profit us if we gain the whole world for the poor, but do not help them to find the way which will lead them to God and the happiness of heaven?

Let us listen once again to the last words which the Pope spoke to you a year ago tomorrow: *"With the torch of Christ in your hands and full of love for man, go forth, Church of the new evangelization. Thus you will be able to create a new dawn for the Church and we shall all glorify the Lord of truth with the prayer which Columbus' seamen recited at dawn: 'Blessed be the light and the holy cross and the Lord of truth and the holy Trinity. Blessed be the dawn and the Lord who sends it to us. Blessed be the day and the Lord who sends it to us.'"*

Advent Letter—Divine Goodness
15 November 1985   To Each Confrere

My dear Confrere,

May the grace of Our Lord Jesus Christ be with us forever!

Visiting our Provinces during the past five years, I have often found myself in almost breathless admiration of the natural beauties of the countries I have seen from a plane or journeying with you in a car from one community to another. Mountains and oceans, forests and great plains, all speak of the grandeur and beauty of their Maker. Often my reflections have been brought to an abrupt end on entering the periphery of one of our great cities. Miserable and crowded housing: poor people on pavements with anxious expressions speak of man's greed and selfishness, contrasting sharply with the generosity and love and goodness of God.

That same contrast is to be found in the Christmas mystery as it is presented to us in the Gospels. The tenderness of the newborn Infant and His Mother Mary, the simplicity of the shepherds, the humble searching of the Magi, are in strong contrast to the indifference of the people to Mary's condition and to the duplicity and cruelty of Herod.

The Bethlehem of Christmas night is still with us and it could be said that our vocation is to live and work in the awareness of the contrast between the depths of God's love, beauty and generosity that lie at the heart of the Incarnation, and the sufferings of the poor that result from the selfishness, ugliness and injustice of humankind.

Our vocation is to move from the City of God to the City of Man with a lived message that will speak to the poor, not only of *"justice and mercy and faith"* (Mt 23:23), but also of one that will bring a measure of joy into their lives. Sometimes I have wondered if the poor, listening to us preaching the *Good News*, hear it as such. After all, good news always brings joy to people's hearts and it is the joy that is in the heart of Christ that those who listen to us preach seek so often to experience. Through us Jesus Christ wishes to say to the poor: *"These things I have spoken to you, that My joy may be in you and that your joy may be full."* (Jn 15:11). His words are a good test of the value of any program of evangelization, any homily, any argument we may use to convince another of the truths of our faith.

We live at once in the City of God and in the City of Man. Even in the City of Man there is much beauty, if we have eyes to see it, for the features of Christ are to be seen in the faces of all whom we meet, particularly of those who suffer through poverty. If we are to bring to the inhabitants of Man's City the Good News that Jesus Christ, truly God and truly man, is closer to them than they are to themselves, then we ourselves must be profoundly convinced of the goodness and the love of God towards just and unjust alike. Reading a number of St. Vincent's letters recently, I noticed how fond he was of the little phrase, *the Divine Goodness,* and how often he used it. Clearly St. Vincent did not limit the horizons of his thought and action to the sufferings of the poor and how they could be alleviated, but in his prayer and reflection moved into the immensity of that Divine Goodness, which gave us the Word made flesh and Who still dwells among us *"full of grace and truth."* (Jn 1:14).

I will end, but not before wishing you much joy this Christmas, a wish that is shared by all of us who live and work here in the Curia. Asking a remembrance in your prayers, I remain in the love of Our Lord, your devoted confrere.

Alpha and Omega

22 November 1985   Jamaica, New York

The two passages to which we have just listened could be described as a study in contrasts that meet at a focal point. In the first reading from Maccabees, we were given a description of the spirit of joy and exultation after the victory won by Judas. The reading pulsates with a sense of enthusiasm and of hope. The Israelites had found a new sense of purpose in their lives, which generated a deep sense of gratitude to God. All that culminates in the dedication of the temple. Perhaps you noticed that the word *joy* occurs no less than four times in that first reading of this evening. In the second reading there is a marked contrast. Jesus discovers that the Temple is being profaned. There is buying and selling. There is, quite clearly, a loss of a sense of direction, a loss of a sense of purpose, a loss of vision, and the mood is not of joy, but of anger. The focal point for these two events is the same, the Temple, which was that same Temple where Judas and his men rejoiced, that Jesus and His disciples entered and found the scene that is described in this evening's Gospel. There is a time difference of some one hundred seventy or one hundred eighty years.

What had happened in the meantime that there should have been such loss of vision? Nothing very dramatic; the years had passed; the Romans had annexed Judea, but they respected the religious convictions of the people. There seemed to have been an imperceptible contraction of vision. The sense of genuine religion had weakened, or rather had been warped. You remember how Our Lord reminded the woman at the well that a time would come when people would worship God in spirit and in truth. It would seem that many who entered the Temple in Our Lord's day worshiped God with their lips but their hearts were far from Him.

What of the Temple of the Church as we know it today? In the span of the lifetime of all of us, we can see a great contrast in the Church as we know it today and the Church as we knew it twenty years ago. Some will look back nostalgically to the past and feel that the Church has suffered much loss in those two decades. Others will see the past twenty years as a time when a great cleansing of the Temple of God's Church has taken place. Most will see it positively and realistically. There have been gains and there have been losses. The attitudes of all of us have been, and still are being, challenged by the Spirit of God.

We, according to our different points of view, like to speculate about the Church and the direction it has taken, and the direction it should take. What about the Temple of my own life as priest? Here, too, we note the great contrast. Take the vision of the priesthood we had on the day we were ordained and the vision of the priesthood as we see it today. None of us but will note the contrast between our first year in the priesthood and the priesthood as we live it today. Undoubtedly there have been gains over our years in the priesthood, resulting from the greater maturity which the years have brought us and also from the experience we have had as priests in serving and seeing the grace of God at work in others. All of us will resemble St. Peter. The Peter of the Gospels is a Peter different from the Peter we meet in that first letter which he addressed to the Christians of his time. There are also, however, shadows in the priesthood that we live today; the growth of selfishness, sluggishness and perhaps laziness which, according to St. Vincent, is the besetting sin of the priesthood. Maybe it was because of that, that he gave us as our fifth characteristic virtue, zeal for souls.

But this varying contrast must not stop there. We must move on to the point where the contrasts converge, and that point is the living person of Jesus Christ Who is our Alpha and our Omega. How much is Jesus Christ a point of reference for us in all things great and small? We talk about Him, but do we speak to Him in the quietness of prayer and personal affection about what is happening in our life and what He, or rather the Holy Spirit, is trying to accomplish daily in us? There is a world of difference between talking and speaking. Do we by constant, daily, almost hourly reference to Jesus Christ, the still point of our priesthood, prevent that hardening of our spiritual arteries which make us, as St. Vincent remarks in our Common Rules, *"insensitive to God's honor and our neighbor's salvation"*? The only antidote that we have to that disease of aging spiritually in the priesthood is the centering of all things on Jesus Christ, our great High Priest.

Let me end, my dear Confreres, by offering you St. Vincent's reflection on the experience of his priesthood in the last years of his life. On one occasion, when giving a repetition of prayer in St. Lazare, he remarked: *"All our life is but a moment which flies away. Alas, the seventy-six years of my life which I have passed seem to me to be a dream and a moment. Nothing remains of them but regret for having so badly employed this time. Just think of the dissatisfaction we will have at our deaths if we do not use this time to be merciful. . . . Let us then be merciful, my brothers, and let us exercise it towards all, in such a way that we will never find a poor man without consoling him, if we can, nor an uninstructed man without teaching him in a few words those things which it is necessary to believe and which he must do for his*

*salvation. O Saviour, do not permit us to abuse our vocation. Do not
take away from this Company the spirit of mercy because what would
become of us if you should withdraw your mercy from it. Give us, then,
that mercy along with the spirit of gentleness and humility."* (Coste XI,
Fr. ed., p. 305).

A Sense of Thanksgiving

28 November 1985   Emmitsburg, Maryland

My dear Sisters, my dear Confreres,

St. Vincent was exactly forty years of age when, in 1621, the first
Thanksgiving Day was celebrated here in America. Thanksgiving Day
had been celebrated for exactly two hundred years when St. Elizabeth
Ann left this Valley in 1821 for heaven. What St. Vincent's sentiments
might have been, had he been told about Thanksgiving Day, we do not
know. We have no extant letter of St. Vincent for the year 1621. We do
know, however, that many years later he would observe to a Confrere
in one of his letters that *"ingratitude is the crime of crimes."* (Coste III,
Eng. ed., ltr. 850, p. 42). That, from the pen of St. Vincent, is a strong
statement. Even if St. Vincent had never expressed that sentiment, we
can safely surmise that he would have heartily endorsed the idea of
Thanksgiving Day, for is there any canonized saint who is not a
profoundly grateful person? It is almost a definition for a saint that he
or she is a person who celebrates Thanksgiving, not one day in the year,
but every day, and many times every day. There is no canonized saint
who did not center his or her life on what the Second Vatican Council
calls *"the source and summit of all apostolic activity"* which is the
Eucharist. Eucharist, as we were taught when we were young, means
thanksgiving, and if Eucharist means thanksgiving, then living the
Eucharist, living an apostolic life, must mean living lives of thanksgiving.

There was an atheist philosopher in the last century who liked to
taunt Christians by saying that if they were a redeemed people, the
expressions on their faces did not give that impression. He might
equally have said if there is at the center of a Christian's life a mystery

which they call Eucharist or thanksgiving, they do not give the impression of being very grateful people. The truth is, however, that we are a Eucharistic people who are meant to cultivate consciously thanksgiving, not one day, but every day, for everything, for all things, great and small.

Recently in one of our Latin American Provinces, a group of young Sisters asked me if I had any advice to give them. I had no prepackaged reply to that question. I could have recommended them to read and ponder well every paragraph and every line of our Constitutions and Statutes. I could have suggested to them that if they really wanted some up-to-the-minute advice, they would find some excellent suggestions in the final document of our recent General Assembly. All this was what I could have said to the Sisters and did not say. What I did say to them was just this. *"Cultivate, my dear Sisters, a sense of thanksgiving."* If we cultivate a sense of thanksgiving, we will be people of joy. We will be conscious of the many good things we have received from God. Becoming more deeply conscious of the many good things we have received from God, we will wish to share them with those who are so much less fortunate than we. If we cultivate a sense of thanksgiving, we will be joyful persons and it is joy that generates energy and enthusiasm. It is thanksgiving that cuts back the weeds of cynicism and bitterness, which can at times make us hypercritical of the Church and of our Community. It is the weeds of cynicism and bitterness that blight the growth of our souls into deeper union with Jesus Christ. It is these weeds that prevent the opening out of ourselves to the sunshine of God's grace. It is thanksgiving that gives us hope. It is thanksgiving that keeps our hearts young, even when we are beginning to feel the weight of years. When, in the old rite of Mass, the priest came to the foot of the altar, he began with the words of a psalm, *"I will go to the altar of God,"* and according to one version of that psalm, the line continues to read: *"to the God who gives me back the joy of my youth."* (Ps 43:4).

If here in the United States Thanksgiving Day has been for some centuries a very special day, in recent years it has taken on a significance that is more important than ever. We are living in an age of protest. We are children of an angry generation. How many prophets of protest we have in our countries and in our cities today. We have true prophets of protest and false prophets. Some protest, such as the denial of human rights and the oppression of the poor, is justified. There are other forms of protest that are sinister or ill-advised, but I often ask myself, where are the prophets of thanksgiving? A Christian is called to be a thanksgiving person. Even more so are consecrated persons called to be prophets of thanksgiving. People who have dedicated themselves through vows are conscious of the fact that they have been specially called by God to witness to His generous love. They are people who live in the awareness that *"He who is mighty has done great things"* (Lk 1:49) for them. Do the laity think of religious today as prophets of humble thanksgiving? Do they think of religious in this country or in other countries as being Eucharistic persons? I venture to think that religious and people like ourselves are not always seen as prophets of thanksgiving.

On this Thanksgiving Day, may I remind you that thanksgiving has two other sisters. The first sister is giving. It was G.K. Chesterton who remarked that the highest form of giving is thanksgiving. Thanksgiving has another sister. She is called forgiving. If thanksgiving is the highest form of giving, then forgiving is the most difficult form of giving. These three sisters meet each time we gather together to do that great action which Jesus Christ asked us to do in memory of Him. Our Mass begins with forgiving: asking the forgiveness of God, and it is to forgiveness that the Liturgy returns when, before Holy Communion, she asks us to forgive each other by exchanging the sign of peace and reconciliation, *"Let us greet each other with a sign of peace."* What is our offertory procession but an outward expression of our desire to give ourselves wholly to God with all that we have and are? Then our little giving is swept up in the great Eucharistic Prayer, in the great act of thanksgiving which Jesus Christ makes with us in the unity of the Holy Spirit to the glory of the Father.

These great movements of giving and forgiving and thanksgiving find expression in the second reading which you have chosen for today's Mass. *"You must forgive one another as the Lord has forgiven you . . . everything you do or say should be done in the name of the Lord Jesus . . . give thanks to the Lord Jesus and to the Father."* (Col 3:13,17).

May Our Lady, whose spirituality is so marked with thanksgiving, make us truly Eucharistic people. May St. Catherine, who took to heart our Lady's words, *"Come to the foot of this altar; throw yourself there and open your heart,"* win for us on this, her Feast Day, the grace of being grateful people, Eucharistic persons, who center our lives reverently on the mystery of God's giving and forgiving and thanksgiving, which is our Mass.

Foundation of the Daughters of Charity

29 November 1985   Emmitsburg, Maryland

My dear Sisters,

The first line of this morning's responsorial psalm was *"Mountains and hills, bless the Lord,"* (Ps 148:4) and which of us does not think of mountains and hills when we think of Emmitsburg. We think of the valley that St. Elizabeth Ann loved so much. How can you have valleys without mountains and hills? Mountains speak loudly to us of God. It has been so since the psalmist wrote his psalms and long before that. Mountains are great and majestic, as God is great and majestic. When man looks at the massiveness of the mountains, he thinks of God, and how small is man by comparison. *"What is man that You should be mindful of him?"* (Ps 8:5). Mountains are imperturbable and unaffected by storms and the changing seasons. So, too, is God. He is unchanging. *"O Lord You live forever. Long ago you created the earth and with your own hands, You made the heavens. They will disappear, but you will remain."* (Ps 101:26-28). Or to express the same sentiment in Our Lord's words of today's Gospel, *"The heavens and the earth will pass away, but my words will not pass."* (Lk. 21:33). The mountains are always there. Generations and generations of people have looked at the mountain close by us. They have passed away, while it remains. So, too, God is always there, and, like the mountain, suggests permanence and strength. How often in the psalm does the psalmist say, *"The Lord is my strength"*? So, my dear Sisters, when you raise your eyes and look out at the mountain, think of God, His strength and His permanence. As the years pass, we become more and more conscious of the changing

nature of all things in this world. Friends die and we feel how imper-
manent all things are. The mountain reminds us that God remains and
will not abandon us. It was that thought that prompted the psalmist to
pray in psalm 71 (a most appropriate psalm to read when you feel you
are growing old and weak), *"I have relied on You all my life. Now that
I am old and my hair is grey, do not abandon me."* (Ps 71:18).

But let me come down from the mountain and walk along that street
in Paris, where on this day St. Louise gathered the first Daughters of
Charity about her, and began to speak to them of the love which Jesus
Christ had for them, and of how He wanted them to help Him in caring
for His special friends, the poor. This is a Thanksgiving Day in the
Company. There is a line in the psalms that speaks of the marvel of how
one day after another speaks of the glory of God: *"Day unto day takes
up the story."* (Ps 19:3). Yes, since the 29 November 1633, Sisters have
been taking up the story of St. Louise and the work which, with St.
Vincent, she began on that day, and have been passing it on to succeeding generations of Sisters. The Sisters are doing things today in Community and for the poor, because of what St. Louise said to those first
Sisters. One generation of Sisters has been passing on to the next the
traditions of the Community, and some go back to the very beginning
of the Company. Yes, *"day unto day takes up the story."* (Ibid.). What
can we say but *"Thanks be to God for His mercy is from generation to
generation."* (Lk 1:50). Now that I have sounded the note of thanksgiving, let me continue the peal of bells ringing out thanksgiving. I want
to thank you for all that you do for the Company, for the prayers and
sufferings and acts of patience you offer to God on behalf of the poor
and on behalf of the Company and, I must add, on my behalf. A
thousand thanks! I know you will not forget that phrase in your
Constitutions which states that praying in the name of the poor is the
first duty of a Daughter of Charity. We count on your silent intercession
with God and His mother that this Valley of Mother Seton will be
blessed by vocations, so that until the end of time *"Day unto day may
take up the story"* (Ps 19:3) of the great things God has done through
Jesus Christ for His people.

Now I would like to quote for you a thought of St. Vincent. Unfortunately, I forgot to bring the text of his words with me, so let me

paraphrase his thought. He was a man of seventy-six years of age when one day, during a repetition of prayer in St. Lazare, he reflected on how quickly his life had passed and how little he had accomplished during it. He asked God for the grace to use well what time God was going to leave him. *"Let us,"* he said, *"be merciful, my brothers. Do not let us abuse our vocation. Do not take away from the Company the spirit of mercy."* (Coste XI, Fr. ed., p. 305). Yes, that is my prayer for us this morning. May God not take away His spirit of mercy from the Company, may we continue to show mercy and kindness to the poor whom the Community asks us to help and to serve. May we continue to show mercy to each other in day-to-day living in the Community. May we take up the story of God's mercy from day to day and by our lives tell each other of the greatness of God's mercy, this mercy which is above the mountains and above all His works.

The World of Youth

28 December 1985   Rome, Italy

My dear Sisters and Confreres,

What was Herod's motive in massacring the children of Bethlehem? Jealousy, yes; insecurity, yes; possibly the deepest motive of all was fear. Fear is the foundation of all jealousy and the foundation, too, of insecurity. Herod was a man who was utterly strong but was suffering from fear, a fear so great that it led him to massacre the infants of Bethlehem. It seems strange, doesn't it, to find an adult so afraid of children, or of one child.

Here is the first question I would like to pose to you who have gathered for this meeting to discuss what you can do for youth. Are you afraid of the youth of today? Our immediate reaction is to say *no*. Perhaps, however, there may be a little more fear of youth in our adult hearts than we might think. The fear of youth that might be in our hearts does not give rise to jealousy, perhaps, but rather to a certain insecurity, the insecurity that arises when we are confronted with what we do not know or understand. However we may feel about youth, there are many adults today who distance themselves from young people because they fear they do not understand them. There are adults who keep saying: *"Youth is different today."* That gives them the excuse to keep away from youth. Often it is fear which puts up a barrier between adults and youth today, and both are losers because of that. Youth is different today but let us not exaggerate the difference.

When the Pope visited my country in 1979 and was speaking at a shrine of Our Lady, he said: *"Each generation is like a new continent which has to be won for Christ."* The world of youth is like a new continent. There are many natural riches in that continent, some clearly visible, others hidden. The continent of youth has to be won for Christ, and His way is not one that relies on force but rather on love and respect for the individual person. Because youth is a new continent, we should not be surprised that the continent will have new needs. That is why it is so important to listen to youth as they speak about their needs. Youth today will speak about their need to share with others in community, about their need of doing something to secure greater justice in their society and in the world. It is only after we adults have listened to youth that we should try to draw forth something from the treasure house of our own experience to help them.

Youth almost always will respond to challenge. People like yourselves, who are engaged in the apostolate to youth, must be continually asking the question: What challenge must I put to the young, and how? The challenges that we put to youth must come from Jesus Christ. So we will challenge youth to face the question which Jesus Christ posed: *"Who do you say that I am?"* (Mk 8:27). We will challenge youth to be open to accept forgiveness; to recognize Jesus Christ in the breaking of bread; to watch and pray to be saved from deceptions. Perhaps one of the most difficult challenges facing youth today is that of seeing and accepting the Church as the great Sacrament of Jesus Christ in the world. We know that many young people will accept Jesus Christ but reject His Church. How can we lead youth to accept and to participate in the life of the Church? How can we lead young people to experience the Church as a community of welcome and participation? How can young people be made to feel like partners with adults in the work of Christ in His Church today?

To these questions I cannot give any easy answer, particularly because I do not know minutely the circumstances in which you work. I would, however, like to make one final recommendation. Do not lose heart in the task of trying to conquer this new continent for Jesus Christ. You are not alone. Jesus Christ is with you. He is our *way*. The words, *"Do not fear,"* were often on His lips. So, do not fear to share your convictions with youth, but do so after the manner of St. Vincent, simply, humbly, gently. Young people respect (even if they do not always say so) the personal convictions expressed courageously by adults. Take heart, too, from the fact that, as Paul VI said: *"People today are less impressed by what they are taught than by what they witness."* When discouragement threatens you, or the pace of change seems too fast and provokes a sense of panic, stop and recall Our Lord's rebuke to His anxious disciples: *"Why are you fearful, O you of little faith?"* (Mt 8:26). Whatever failures you may experience in your approach to youth, do not cease to love them, for *"It is love,"* wrote St. John, *"that casts out fear."* (1 Jn 4:18). It is love which is the bridge between generations. Love is the language which both adults and youth must study together during life's pilgrimage, for it is the only language which has been taught to us by the Son of God and the only language which is spoken in His Father's house.

1986

Radiance in the Features of the Poor

1 January 1986   Paris, France

Mother Duzan, Father Lloret and my dear Sisters,

On this New Year's morning, made so fragrant for us by the celebration of a feast in honor of the Mother of God, let me introduce to
you a man who in today's language might be described as one of
society's dropouts. He was born in England and in his younger years
thought of becoming a priest. He spent some time in a seminary, but
then decided that instead of becoming a physician of souls, he would
become a physician of bodies. So he commenced studies for the
profession of medicine. A little later he abandoned these studies and
for a time he made his living selling newspapers and matches on the
streets of the capital. Then he turned his hand to writing and he tasted
success, not financial success but a success that brought him a few kind
and interested friends who cared about this rather lonely, sensitive
Catholic poet. Almost eighty years ago he died, a lonely figure, in a
London hospital at the age of forty-eight. His name was Francis
Thompson.

In his poverty this poor man was compelled, as so many are today,
to sleep under the arches of railway bridges in the city of London, close
to the river Thames. In the shivering cold of the night the arches
reminded him of Jacob's ladder and of what Our Lord had said about
the angels of God descending upon the Son of Man. The nearby waters
of the Thames reminded him of the Lake of Genesareth and of Christ's
walking upon it in the darkness of the night. From this poet's sensitive
soul came these few lines: *Yea, in the night my soul, my daughter cry:
clinging Heaven by the hems: And lo, Christ walking on the water, Not
of Genesareth, but Thames. (In No Strange Land)*.

Amid all the failures and poverty of his life, to this poor man was given the grace of seeing the radiance of Christ in his surroundings. It was a grace not unlike that which is offered to a Daughter of Charity. To her is offered the grace of seeing the radiance of Christ, not so much in physical surroundings as in the features of the poor. To a Daughter of Charity, Jesus Christ lends His eyes, but first she must sit, like the beggar on the roadside, and humbly proclaim to the Son of David that she is blind and has need of the gift of sight. The gift of sharing with Christ His eyes is one of the most fundamental graces in the vocation of a Daughter of Charity, and that gift is sought and humbly found in prayer and contemplation. No matter how sharp our perception of the needs of the poor, no matter how penetrating our analysis of the social conditions of the poor may be, it is of little or no avail to us, if we are not sharing in the vision of Christ. That is a grace which only God can give. We cannot talk ourselves into seeing Christ in the poor. Like the dew that falls silently on the ground, the grace of sharing the eyes of Christ is a gift that our Father in Heaven drops into our hearts and minds when they are open to Him in the silence of humble prayer.

The poor London poet had almost nothing on which to live, but he could see the angels of God descending on the Son of Man, and Jesus Christ walking on the waters of the river Thames. That vision of Christ he could share with others. The poor we often say preach the Gospel to us. As we listen to the poor preaching the Gospel to us and reflect upon their condition, it is good to remind ourselves that our basic desire to live in solidarity with them must spring, not from the fact that they are poor but, as St. Vincent so often insisted, because such was the lifestyle which the Word of God chose to adopt on coming into this world. In all things Christ is the Rule of the Company.

We share the eyes of Jesus Christ and those eyes are the eyes of a poor man. *"The eye is the lamp of the body. So if your eye is sound, your whole body will be full of light."* (Mt 6:22).

That observation was made by Our Lord, that our hearts will be where our treasures are. It may be that my heart is not free with the freedom of Christ's heart because it is cluttered up with vain and foolish desires. At the end of a day it is good to ask oneself: *"What engaged my heart today?"* God, the poor and the Community, yes; but what of all those desires that stole in or have been long squatting in my heart, taking more possession of it than perhaps I might be ready to admit? It would be salutary from time to time to allow the poor themselves to question the desires of my heart and some of the lines of action I take in order to be of service to them. We might be surprised to hear the poor describe our motives, or at least some of them, as masks for vanity and self-interest. We might even hear them quote, without their knowing it, St. Vincent's words: *"So there, my dear Sisters, is the enemy unmasked. I have shown him to you: be on your guard and make good resolutions now. If you are faithful to them, the Company will be the Company of Our Lord Jesus Christ, and you will become His spouses."* (Conf. Eng. ed., 15 Mar. 1654, p. 604).

It is New Year's Day, and although Jesus Christ shares His eyes with us, we cannot see the future nor what this New Year holds for us. *"All I know of tomorrow,"* wrote Lacordaire, *"is that Providence will rise before the sun."* On this New Year's Day St. Vincent would encourage us to cast ourselves into the arms of Divine Providence and to be in peace. May the peace of Christ, my dear Sisters, dwell in your hearts, that peace which comes after an unconditional surrender of ourselves to God in the particular community in which His Providence has placed us. May it be given to us all to see Jesus Christ *"lovely in limbs not His."* May we see Him under the arches of our city bridges and walking on the rivers of our lands.

Lenten Letter—Language of the Cross

1 February 1986   To Each Confrere

My dear Confrere,

May the grace of Our Lord Jesus Christ be with us forever!

It was Advent when I last wrote to you, and at that time the Synod of Bishops was meeting here in Rome. Since then the final report of that meeting has been published and I would like to focus your mind on one of the ideas that the Pope and the Bishops of the Synod proposed for our reflection. The entire document merits more than one reading, for not only is it profound, but it is very delicately nuanced. The document emphasizes for us certain truths which in the course of these past few years may have suffered a certain eclipse in our minds. One such truth is the theology of the cross. Let me quote a few significant sentences from the document: *"We assert the great importance and great actuality of the Pastoral Constitution 'Gaudium et Spes.' At the same time we are aware that the signs of the times now are somewhat different than those existing at the time of the Council, with an increase of problems and pains . . . . In today's difficulties it seems to us that God wants us to teach at a deeper level the value, importance and centrality of the cross of Jesus Christ."*

If we in the Congregation are to teach *"at a deeper level the value, importance and centrality of the cross of Jesus Christ,"* we ourselves must study what St. Paul calls *"the language of the cross."* (1 Cor 1:18). During these days of Lent we could set ourselves the task to revise the grammar of that language of the cross. The study will take us past the contemplation of the physical sufferings of Christ and deep into the mental attitude adopted by Jesus Christ throughout the experience of His trial and His sufferings and death on the cross. *"Let this mind be in you,"* wrote St. Paul, *"which was also in Christ Jesus."* (Phil 2:5). Into that mind St. Paul plunged and, when he did so, he came face to face with the humility and obedience of Jesus Christ. *"He emptied Himself, taking the form of a servant . . . . He humbled Himself, becoming obedient unto death, even to the death of the cross."* (Ibid. 7:8). As Christians and as men with a vow of obedience, we have accepted the invitation of Christ to share His experience of being humble and obedient. For Jesus Christ the test of His humility was an acceptance of being called into question, and His obedience was an intense desire not to have His own way. Can it be different for us? Do the people, we may ask, to whom we preach the cross and resurrection of Christ, see us as humble and obedient men? Each one of us can make and apply to his own life this reflection of the Synod: *"The Church becomes more credible if it speaks less about itself and more and more preaches Christ crucified* (cf. 1 Cor 2:2) *and witnesses to him by its life."*

Now let me speak to you of our forthcoming General Assembly. It will commence, as you know, on the 18 June. St. Vincent has remarked: *"If we persevere in our vocation, it is thanks to prayer. If we have success in our tasks, it is thanks to prayer. If we do not fall into sin, it is thanks to prayer. If we remain in charity and save our souls, all this is thanks to God and to prayer.* " (Coste XI, Fr. ed., p. 407).

To these words of St. Vincent we could add: *"and if our General Assembly is a success, it will be thanks to prayer."*

Let me make a suggestion to you. In the Ordo of the Congregation you will notice that the feast of Corpus Christi is celebrated on the 29 May and the feast of the Visitation of Our Lady on the 31 May. I ask each local community to set aside some special period of time during these three days when the community will gather before Our Lord in the Blessed Sacrament and ask Him to plead with His Father, *"from Whom all good things come"* (Mt 7:11), to bless our Assembly with an abundance of graces. Likewise, I would ask each community to commend in some special act of devotion our Assembly to the intercession of Mary, the Mother of God and Mediatrix of graces. For, as St. Vincent remarked: *"Every time the Mother of God is invoked and taken as Patroness in matters of importance, it is impossible that things will not go well, impossible, too, that they will not redound to the glory of Jesus, her Son."* (Coste XIV, Fr. ed., note p. 126).

It is my conviction that the Congregation will progress more securely on the path of its renewal and adaptation to serving the needs of the Church and the poor today, when it deepens its devotion to the presence of Christ in the Eucharist and to Mary, the Mother of God and Mother of the Church.

It will be close to Easter, or perhaps after it, when you read these lines, so may your celebration of the Resurrection bring you an increased measure of that joy and peace which Jesus Christ wishes to share with those who are His friends. In His love I remain, your devoted confrere.

Secrets of God

14 March 1986   Bikoro, Zaire

My dear Confreres,

Let my first word to you be one of appreciation and thanks to you for coming here to celebrate this Eucharist with me. I see in the presence of each of you here this morning a manifestation of faith in the office which I presently hold. Our Constitutions state that the Superior General is the center of unity for the Congregation. The fact that we are celebrating the Eucharist together this morning must be interpreted as a desire on the part of each one of us to deepen the unity that already exists among us. This Vice-Province is what I might call one of the growth-points in the Congregation. It has a growing number of indigenous vocations. It is evolving towards the status of a full Province. If it is to continue to grow, it will do so only if there is deep unity among its members.

In the first reading of today's Mass there is a little phrase which struck me forcefully. The author speaks of people who *"did not know the secrets of God."* (Wis 2:22). In the language of my own country, the Irish language, we have a rather special word for mystery. The word we use for mystery is *divine secret*. Mysteries are divine secrets. Each one of us has his secrets and we wish people to respect our secrets. We have a right to keep secrets to ourselves. So, too, with God. He has His secrets, and He asks us to respect them.

The priesthood, or our vocation to Community, is one of God's secrets, one of God's mysteries. During the past twenty years, we have heard discussions about the priesthood and religious life that leave us with the impression that the vocation to the priesthood or religious life is not a mystery, is not one of God's secrets. *"They do not know the secrets of God."* (Ibid.). If we want to preserve our vocation to the priesthood or to the religious life, we must continually and consciously accept our priesthood as a mystery, as one of God's secrets. We can only do that by giving time to silent and conscious reflection on the mystery of our vocation.

When I visit the missions of our Congregation, I am impressed by the volume of work which the Confreres do in circumstances that are often very difficult. More than once, however, I have come away with the impression that the Confreres are too busy, excessively active. I have sometimes thought that many of us in the Congregation have, what I might call, *the Martha Syndrome*. We are not working in such a way as to be able to enter into the secrets of God. *"They do not know the secrets of God."* (Ibid.).

There is one other little phrase in this morning's reading that merits some reflection. The phrase that follows the one which I have quoted reads as follows: *"... and they did not count on a recompense of holiness."* (Ibid.). Sanctity will only be rewarded and recognized fully in heaven. The question I ask all of us this morning is this: *"How convinced are we that genuine personal holiness is effective in our apostolate?"* In a general way we accept that a priest should be an authentically holy man. But do people recognize us as men of God, men who are on very intimate terms with God? Or do they see us as good men, but not as priests who can talk with deep conviction about God, and Him whom He has sent, Jesus Christ? The holiness I am talking about is not only integrity of life. The holiness I have in mind is a gift of God. We must humbly seek it and accept it from Jesus Christ through prayer and reflection, and which then expresses itself in action which we call apostolic. *"Lord, You are holy indeed, the fountain of all holiness."* (Eucharistic Prayer, n. 2).

To you, my dear Confreres, who are bearing the burden of the heat here in Zaire, I would say what St. Vincent so often said to Confreres: *"Courage."* That was one of his favorite expressions. Perhaps if he were here today in Zaire, he would add the word, *"Patience."* I was told a few days ago that to work in Zaire, the first, second and third virtue is patience. When I listen to you speak about the work that remains to be done before the Gospel will be preached to all peoples, I become more convinced that the second coming of the Lord is still a long way off. We are still probably in the epoch of the early Church. So let my final words to you this morning be those two simple verbs which St. Vincent used on one occasion and which I have written on the little picture which I leave with you: *"Wait ... but work."* Cultivate an attitude of waiting on the Lord. As St. Vincent once wrote to a Confrere: *"The works of God have their moments. His Providence brings them about at one particular point in time, neither sooner nor later."* (Coste V, Fr. ed., p. 396). At the same time we must act, expressing our love for God, as St. Vincent said in a memorable phrase, with *"the strength of our arms and the sweat of our brows."* (Coste XI, Fr. ed., p. 40).

May God in His goodness give us all the grace to follow the advice which St. Vincent gave to Father Jean Dehorgny, Superior in Rome: *"We must have confidence in God, be faithful to our duties, and entrust the rest to Providence."* (Coste IV, Eng. ed., ltr. 1486, p. 360).

Displaced Persons

22 March 1986   Paris, France

Mother Duzan, Father Lloret and my dear Sisters,

This year the shadow of the cross falls across the Feast of the Annunciation of Our Lord. This year Jerusalem is allowed to displace Nazareth in our meditations on the 25 March. This year the first joyful mystery of the rosary, which we celebrate traditionally on the 25 March, is displaced by the five sorrowful mysteries. For us such a displacement is not a great inconvenience, but there are millions in the world at the present moment who live daily and indeed hourly with an experience of displacement which cuts like a sword painfully into the very heart of their lives. One of the many forms of new poverty today is the rising number of displaced persons in our world. Immigrants, legal and illegal, in increasing numbers have been forced to leave their countries because of political or social pressures, and it is only those who work among them who can tell us something of the depths of the hidden suffering and anxiety which lie beneath the surface of their lives. There are other groups of displaced persons in our societies, the children who have been abandoned, husbands or wives deserted, workers displaced from their employment, the homeless in search of a home.

Jesus Christ knew what it was to be a displaced person. St. John, meditating upon the experience of the Word made flesh, reflected sadly that *"the Word was in the world and the world was made by Him and the world knew Him not. He came unto His own and His own received Him not."* (Jn 1:10-11). Jesus Christ was displaced at His birth. There was no room for Him in the inn (cf. Lk 2:7), and He was displaced at His death, for He was crucified outside the walls of Jerusalem. The experience of being a displaced person at His birth and at His death, and often throughout His life, was shared by His Mother, Mary. She could not but have read, as so many did, the words which were written in three languages above His head on the cross: Jesus of Nazareth, King of the Jews. From the sixth to the ninth hour on Good Friday as she watched Him die, the word, *Nazareth*, must have brought back many memories to her. Her mind would have gone back to the day when the Angel Gabriel greeted her with the words, *"Hail, full of grace; the Lord is with thee. Blessed art thou among women."* (Lk 1:28), and of that dialogue which ended with her own words, *"Be it done unto me according to your word."* (Ibid., 38). It was as a displaced person that she was forced to flee with the Infant in her arms to Egypt. She would have witnessed, too, the crowd in Nazareth who, when they listened to her Son preaching, decided not only to displace Him from their town, but to kill Him. Now her Son was dying on the cross, displaced from Nazareth, displaced from Jerusalem, and in the minds of those who plotted His death, displaced from the world and from the memory of His people. Was it, one might ask, to alleviate the pain of being a displaced person that Jesus asked St. John to give a place in his home to His Mother, Mary?

Happily there are many Sisters in our Company who are serving Jesus Christ in the displaced persons of our society and who today through the renovation of their vows are, like St. John, making a home for them in their hearts. When you come to reflect on it, however, every Daughter of Charity chooses to share the experience of those who are displaced. In living our vows we enter into the experience of being in a certain way displaced persons. To live the vow of Obedience is to be ready at any moment to move from one apostolate to another, from one house to another, from one office to another, when those in authority ask us to do so. Our vow of Poverty keeps reminding us that, when Jesus of Nazareth died as a displaced person on the cross, He had nothing. His very clothes became a prize in a lottery among those who crucified Him. Our vow of Chastity recognizes that, as displaced persons, we experience what the Constitutions call *"a certain loneliness of heart."* (C 2.6). In living our vow of Chastity we are enabled by the grace of God to transcend that loneliness, so that our hearts become free to assume *"the dimensions of the heart of Jesus Christ."* (Ibid.).

Our choice to live with Jesus and Mary as displaced persons is a deliberate one. We do so for the same reason which moved the Word of God to take flesh in the womb of Mary and to live among us. With Him we try to bring His good news to the poor. With Him we try to heal hearts that are broken. With Him we try to bring freedom to those who suffer and groan under any form of captivity. To express these ideas in the succinct words of the Constitutions: *"The Sisters' primary concern is to make God known to the poor, to proclaim Jesus Christ as their only hope and to tell them that the kingdom of heaven is at hand and that it is for them."* (C 1.7).

The renewal of your vows this morning is a proclamation to the world of your willingness to bring the strength and the joy of Christ to the poor and the displaced of the world. The renewal of your vows this morning is a proclamation to the world that you are intent on keeping close to Jesus Christ crucified and risen. The renewal of your vows this morning is a response, to quote the words of the final report of the recent Synod, to *"an invitation to a profound conversion of heart, to a share in the life of God, one and trinity, something that signifies and surpasses the fulfillment of all man's desires."* (1,4).

May the sentiments of St. Louise, my dear Sisters, on this day of Renovation find a home in your hearts: *"Let us live, therefore, as if we were dead in Jesus Christ. Henceforth, let there be no further resistance to Jesus, no action except for Jesus, no thoughts but in Jesus! May my life be solely for Jesus and my neighbor so that, by means of this unifying love, I may love all that Jesus loves, and through the power of this love which has as its center the eternal love of God for His creatures, I may obtain from His goodness the graces which His mercy wills to bestow upon me."* (*Spiritual Writings of Louise de Marillac*, A. 23, p. 786).

It is the Lord

13 April 1986   Milan, Italy

My dear Friends in Jesus Christ,

There is a marvelous freshness about the passage from St. John's Gospel to which we have just listened. To begin with, the whole event occurs in springtime, for Our Lord's Resurrection took place when spring was breaking in Palestine. Second, it is the dawn of a new day.

St. John makes the point that they had been fishing all night and had caught nothing. It is easy for us to imagine the beauty of that lake on a spring morning. Then there is the fire, the warmth of the fire which Our Lord seems to have lit Himself. *"When they got out on land, they saw a charcoal fire there with fish lying on it and bread."* (Jn 21:9). There is the freshness, too, of a picnic with Jesus Christ as host. *"Come and eat your meal."* (Ibid., v. 12).

Notwithstanding the freshness of the scene and the warmth and tenderness of Christ, the disciples had a little difficulty in recognizing Jesus Christ, and even when they did, they seem to have had a certain reluctance to address Him as they did before His death and resurrection. *"None of the disciples dared ask Him, 'Who are You?'"* (Ibid.). It is a remarkable fact that in all the appearances of Our Lord after His resurrection, His disciples and friends had a certain difficulty in recognizing Him. Yet that difficulty did not conflict with the assurance which eventually dawned upon them all, that Jesus Christ had indeed truly risen from the dead. That should be a source of encouragement to us. We, too, have the joy of living our lives after the Resurrection of Our Lord. We do not see Him with our physical eyes and He Himself has said: *"Blessed are those who have not seen and yet believe."* (Jn 20:29). We should not allow ourselves to be discouraged by the fact that we must now, as St. Paul remarks, *"see Him now dimly and in a dark manner."* (1 Cor 13:12). With those first disciples of Our Lord, we share the difficulty of seeing Him clearly in the ordinary events of our lives.

Speaking of the ordinary events of our lives, I never read this Gospel passage without thinking of a celebrated spiritual writer called Dom Marmion. Some of you may have read some of his books years ago before the second Vatican Council. This Benedictine Monk went to Rome on one occasion and had an audience with St. Pius X. At the end of the audience, Dom Marmion offered the Pope a little holy card and asked the Pope to write a sentence on it. St. Pius X took his pen and wrote: *"In all circumstances of your life say: 'It is the Lord.'"* That phrase, *"It is the Lord,"* (Jn 21:7) is found in today's Gospel. St. Pius X's application of it is very profound and, I might add, very Vincentian. St. Vincent was deeply devoted to the Providence of God. He recommends us to accept all things: *"when something unexpected happens to us in body or mind, good or bad, we are to accept it without fuss as from God's loving hand;"* (CR II, 3). If we could live that ideal of St. Vincent, we would have great peace in our lives. *"In all circumstances, say: 'It is the Lord.'"* (Jn 21:7).

There is something delightfully human about the incident recorded in the end of St. John's Gospel. Our Lord had just given to St. Peter a little glimpse of the future that awaited him. In veiled terms Jesus had indicated to Peter that his death would be that of a martyr. Possibly the fact that Jesus had foretold the future to Peter caused him some excitement. In his impetuosity—and how much impetuosity there was in the character of Peter—he asks Jesus to do a favor for his friend, John, by telling him about his future. *"Jesus said to him, 'If it is My Will that he remain until I come, what is that to you. Follow Me.'"* (Jn 21:22).

St. Peter's curiosity about John's future is very understandable. After all, John was a very good friend of Peter. For all that, Our Lord emphasizes for St. Peter the importance of keeping his eyes on Jesus Christ and not allowing himself to be too distracted by what happens to other people. Certainly it is important that we have and show interest in the spiritual and temporal welfare of others, particularly of our friends and of the poor. However, our interest in others must always be subordinated to the doing of God's Will in our own lives. Our interest and concern for others must grow out of our personal interest and love for Jesus Christ. When St. Paul wrote his letters to the early Christians, he was very fond of using the phrase, *"in Christ Jesus"*, over and over again. In the letters of St. Paul you will find that phrase used by him more than two hundred times. It is important for us in our concern and work for others to see them in Christ Jesus. We must try to do for them what we think Christ Jesus would like us to do for them. Our friendships with others must always be referred back to Christ Jesus. If we do not make Christ Jesus the reference point for all that we do for others, self interest or merely human satisfaction will enter into our relationships with others and we will not be instruments of that peace and joy which Christ would like to give them through us.

It is just over one hundred years since Pope Leo XIII declared St. Vincent patron of all works of charity in the Church. We will honor that centenary best by making positive efforts to support those movements of charity that have been inspired by his life and spirituality. May the Institute of St. Vincent, which this year celebrates the Silver Jubilee of its foundation, grow from strength to strength. May it be given to us to keep our eyes and our hearts centered upon Jesus Christ, so that His Will may be accomplished in us and through us for the glory of His Father Who is in heaven. *"Peter said to Jesus: 'Lord, what about this man?' Jesus said to him: 'If it is My Will that he remain until I come, what is that to you? Follow me.'"* (Jn 21:21-22).

Youth Vibrate with Inquiry

20 April 1986   Rome, Italy

When Sister Maddalena Graziuso wrote to me over a month ago, asking me to speak to you this morning, she suggested the following topic: *"The task of youth in the Church, in Italy and in the other nations known to you; in what areas are the contributions of youth more urgent today."*

St. Vincent recommends the virtue of simplicity very strongly to all of us who are part of the Vincentian family. Let me say with all simplicity that I feel inadequate to speak authentically on this subject. To begin with, I am no longer young! It is a little consolation to know that I was born in the same year as the present Queen of England and, if I am not mistaken, she celebrates her sixtieth birthday today. I am not quite as old as she is, for she was born in April and I was born in July, and that is another small consolation. Seriously, however, as we get older, we tend to feel that there is a big gap between us and the young and that for reasons of security, it is better not to risk trying to cross the gap. Hence comes the temptation not to risk talking to young people. There is a natural tendency to want to remain with one's own age group and leave the young on their own. That is a mistake, for the young have much to tell the old about the new world that is emerging and the old have much to tell the young about values that will never change, however much the scenery and society of life may change. When we discuss the question of what should be done for youth in the Church today, we tend sometimes to make a too rigid division of the tasks. At one moment we will concentrate on what adults should be doing for the evangelization of young people and at the next moment we will be emphasizing what youth should be doing for each other in the work of evangelization. We must not forget that these two sets of activities are not opposed, but rather they must go together. Adults and young need to learn much more how to give and receive at the same time. It was the present Holy Father who said during his visit to England some years ago that *"new expressions of wisdom and truth can be fashioned from the meeting of experience and inquiry."* Adults have experience. Youth vibrate with inquiry. It is important that youth meet adult, that experience meet inquiry.

If youth is to listen to age and age to youth, there must be a climate of confidence. That is where we fail more often than we realize. We, and by *we* I mean young and old, enter into dialogue with each other. Too often we have a hidden intention of making our particular point of view prevail. Without realizing it, we have not sufficient confidence in each other. Age thinks youth will ruin everything and youth tends to think that age does not know the new world that is emerging. What is vitally important is to have confidence that each one, be he old or young, has not only his own particular vision of the Church and of the world, but that it merits serious consideration. Without such a climate of confidence it will be difficult for youth to make its contribution to the life of the Church and for age to find a place for that contribution.

What I have been saying so far could be interpreted as a reflection on the first topic that was assigned to me: *"The task of youth in the Church."* But you ask me to comment more. You ask me to speak about the task of the young in the Church of Italy and of the other countries that I know. To this invitation I must reply by saying that you have manifested excessive confidence in my age and in my experience. I cannot claim to know the Church in Italy profoundly, nor in the other nations which in the past six years I have had the joy and experience of visiting. Here in Italy, as in other countries, I have met small groups of Marian and Vincentian Youth who impressed me with their enthusiasm for working together to convince their own age group and older people of the values of the Gospel. I might mention Spain as a country where Marian Vincentian Youth Movement is sizeable in number and cohesive in its structure. What grows in Spain may not flourish in Italy. However, the Movement, in my opinion, merits study and reflection.

The second topic which you have asked me to comment upon is: *"In what areas are the contributions of youth more urgent today?"* When I visit schools or educational institutes today, I often find classrooms with twenty-five or thirty computers where students are trained how to use them. For many of us older people this branch of modern science was unimaginable forty years ago. The world of the computer is a normal world for the young. It is one of many worlds a young person lives in today. Another world, a more painful one, is the world of unemployment. Many young people face the prospect of unemployment for life. All these worlds are the worlds a young person enters. It is into these worlds that the young must bring the Gospel. It is the young who will have to learn how to prevent technology from becoming the master of humanity, rather than the servant of human values.

The world, however, which is most important for the young is that of the young. It is now twenty-one years ago since the Bishops of the world expressed the conviction that, and I quote, *"The young should become the first apostles of the young in direct contact with them, exercising the apostolate by themselves among themselves."* (*Apostolicam Actuositatem*, §22). That is the ambit where the contribution of the young is most urgently needed today. It is the urgency of that contribution which gives meaning and significance to the Marian Youth.

For those of us who are no longer young, there remains the challenge of, not only trusting the young, but of creating opportunities which will allow them to be active apostles in the Church. How can we older people help younger people to discover the truth that they are as much members of the Church as priests and religious? How can we older people convey to the young that we are not trying to bury and suffocate their power to be effective communicators in word and action of the message that Jesus Christ has left to pope, bishop, priest, religious and to the young? Perhaps I should stop here, lest I myself be found guilty of suffocating you, the young, with words and words and words.

Interceding and Sending

11 May 1986   Rome, Italy

My dear Confreres,

When the first Russian astronaut had gone into space and had successfully returned to earth, he said: *"I have been out in space and I found nothing there. God is not there. So that proves that there is no God."*

We are a little amused at the naivety and at the crudity of the theology, but it does at least make you wonder if the Russian atheists have been reading the account of Our Lord's Ascension into heaven, or even some of the psalms. The psalmist always speaks of God living above the clouds and of walking on the wings of the wind. To an atheist, the first words of reply could very well be a phrase from the first reading: *"Men of Galilee, why stand you looking into heaven?"* (Acts 1:11).

We do not expect to meet God in space, because, as Jesus said, *"God is spirit."* (Jn 4: 24). When we meet a person in the street or in a room, he stands there before us to see. Within him there are several sanctuaries into which he can admit those whom he wills. A man and woman in love admit each other into sanctuaries which they keep closed to all others. The experience of admitting others into the sanctuaries of one's heart can be enriching, all the more if the persons are warm, loving persons. However intimately two human persons love each other, they can never succeed in penetrating into the ultimate sanctuary of the human heart. It was Cardinal Newman who said that the nearest star is closer to us than the heart of the person dearest to us.

The mystery of the Ascension is that not just a spirit, but a human body has been received into the innermost sanctuary of that Spirit whom we call God. The human soul and the human body of Christ is living in *"light inaccessible"* (1 Tim 6:16) in the innermost sanctuary of the Godhead. It is from that innermost sanctuary of the Godhead that Jesus Christ keeps coming back to humanity on earth. How else can we explain His words: *"I go away and I am coming to you."*? (Jn 14:28). Jesus Christ with His humanity lives in the innermost sanctuary of the

Godhead, or, as the formula of the Creed expresses it, *"He is sitting at the right hand of the Father."* He is coming to us all the time. He is radioactive, not dangerously so, but lovingly so. We may well ask: if a tiny particle of matter, such as an atom, can be made to release incalculable energy into the world, what energy must be capable of being released into the human heart by the experience of one Holy Communion or one meeting with Jesus Christ in the Sacrament of Penance? Unfortunately, we in our blindness keep putting up protective shields against the radiating heat of Christ in His sacraments and in His Word, and so, as St. Paul remarks, *"Many are weak and ill."* (1 Cor 11:30).

What is Jesus Christ doing now that He has ascended into Heaven? Two activities come to mind immediately: interceding and sending. The author of the letter to the Hebrews assures us that Jesus Christ, now that He has gone beyond the veil, is *"always living to make intercession for us"* (Heb 7:25) with the Father. The Christian is invited to participate in that activity at Baptism. A priest is plunged more deeply into that mystery by Christ's intercession when he is ordained. It is that fact which underpins the theology of a priest's duty.

Besides interceding, Jesus Christ is engaged in a work of sending. Ceaselessly He is sending the Holy Spirit so that we will not feel as orphans in this vast universe. The challenge for us is to have the antennae of our minds and hearts sensitive enough to receive the signals that the Spirit of Jesus is transmitting. That sensitivity is created by purity of heart.

"Men of Galilee, why do you stand looking into heaven?" (Acts 1:11). We, like the men of Galilee, keep looking for the spectacular. The fact is, however, that everything in life, sin alone excepted, is grace, for *"God has blessed us with every spiritual blessing of heaven in Christ."* (Eph 1:3). Everything is grace, because Jesus Christ, Who is now sitting at the right hand of the Father, has already through His Incarnation blessed and consecrated every human experience that is not sinful.

"Men of Galilee, why do you stand looking into heaven?" (Acts 1:1), for this Jesus has said, *"I go away and I am coming to you . . . . (Jn 14:3). Today, yes, even now, this Scripture is fulfilled in your hearing."* (Lk 4:21).

Walls Protect and Divide

22 May 1986   Berlin, Germany

My dear Sisters,

Who can think of Berlin without thinking of its wall? The wall that divides this city speaks to us and to the world of war and of peace, of division and of unity, of love and of heroism, of suffering and of death. If the wall of Berlin could speak, what stories could it not tell. Each one of you listening to me could tell stories about many human dramas that you have seen or heard about, which were enacted on the wall that divides the city.

When St. Paul was reflecting on the meaning of the life of Jesus Christ, and particularly on His redeeming death, he wrote to the Ephesians: *"Christ Jesus is our peace, Who has made us both one and has broken down the dividing wall of hostility."* (Eph 2:14).

Between the Jews and the Gentiles St. Paul saw a wall which divided them. It was Jesus Christ through His death Who dismantled that wall which was a sign of disunity. There is another expression of that same truth to be found in the Gospel of St. John who remarks that Jesus died *"not for the nation only, but to gather into one the children of God who are scattered abroad."* (Jn 11:52).

A wall can be built to protect or to divide. Think of the parable of Our Lord Who compared His people to a vineyard around which in His love He built a wall. But a wall can also be built to divide people. The wall of Berlin was built, sadly, to divide people. In the hearts of all of you there must live the hope that some day some Messiah-like figure will come and have the wall of Berlin dismantled. Meantime you must live in its shadow.

A wall can be a sign of protection or division. The Christian must build walls that will protect people and values. A Daughter of Charity will build walls of protection around the poor people she is asked to serve. By the care, the love, the sympathy, the interest you show in the people you serve, you are building walls of protection. Because you are building walls of protection around the poor, Jesus Christ addresses to each of you the opening words of today's Gospel: *"Any man who gives you a drink of water because you belong to Christ will not, I assure you, go without his reward."* (Mk 9:41). To many people every day you are giving much more than a drink of water. Every day Jesus Christ assures you that He personally will reward you for your work. Draw confidence from that assurance. Continue to build walls of protection around the people who look to you in a thousand ways to be saved from the harshness of existence and the insecurity of life.

Besides the walls of protection that we are building, there are also walls of division and these must be pulled down. Perhaps we do not design walls of division, but it is easy to lay bricks on walls of division that are already there. Within our communities it is easy to erect walls of division, little walls, but walls nonetheless. At the end of the day Jesus Christ quietly asks us (if we make time to listen to His quiet voice), what walls of division did you raise today within the community by your words, acts or omissions? At the end of each day He asks us to reflect on the sentiment of St. Paul: *"Christ Jesus is our peace. He has made us both one, and has broken down the dividing wall of hostility."* (Eph 2:14).

Whether we build protective walls or pull down dividing walls, it is from the Eucharist that we will get our strength. Bread gives us strength to build protective walls around the needy or those who come to us for help and support. Everything in the Eucharist speaks to us of unity. *"Because there is one bread,"* wrote St. Paul, *"we who are many are one body."* (1 Cor 10:17). At each Holy Communion Jesus Christ asks us to accept Him in His totality, in His body, blood, soul and divinity, and He also asks us to accept the members of His body. In each Holy Communion, using a phrase of St. Paul, He asks us, *"Is Christ divided?"* (1 Cor 1:13).

Let me end, my dear Sisters, by quoting a few sentences from two letters of St. Vincent. To one of his missionaries he wrote: *"I pray the Holy Spirit, Who is the union of the Father and the Son, that He will also be yours everywhere. You ought to pray for that intention unceasingly and, in addition to your prayers, to pay great attention in trying to unite yourself with heart and deed to each one in particular and to all in general. The evil of communities, especially of a small community, is ordinarily envy. The remedy for that is humility. You ought to try to advance in that virtue, as well as in those other virtues which are necessary to bring about this union.* " (Coste V, Fr. ed., p. 582).

"We should help and support one another and strive for peace and union among ourselves. This is the wine which cheers and strengthens travelers along this narrow path of Jesus Christ. I recommend this to you with all the tenderness of my heart." (Coste IV, Eng. ed., ltr. 1414, p. 265).

Our Lady, Help of Christians

24 May 1986   Berlin, Germany

My dear Sisters,

In a few hours Father Paul and myself must leave you. Within this Eucharist, which is our great thanksgiving sacrifice, I wish to thank you all for the kindness you have shown both of us during these days when we had the happiness of being with you.

In some parts of the world today Mary, the Mother of God, is being honored under her title of Help of Christians. The Catholics of Australia have chosen Mary, Help of Christians, as Patron of their country, and St. John Bosco in his lifetime wished that all members of his Communities would honor Mary under this title of Help of Christians.

Mary has been Help of Christians ever since that afternoon when, before He died, Jesus asked John to take her as his mother. Can you think of any worthy mother who does not want to help her child? After Good Friday the only glimpse of Mary on earth that we are given is when she is together with the Apostles, awaiting the coming of the Holy Spirit. St. Luke remarks that the Apostles were united in prayer. We must conclude, then, that one of the first ways Mary helped Christians was with their prayers. That should not surprise us, for is it not the desire of any good Christian mother to want to teach her child to pray? Mary, Help of Christians, has gone on helping her children to pray down through the centuries. We do not think of Mary as present to us in the same way as is the Spirit of God Who, as St. Paul assures us, assists us in the formulation of our prayers. (cf. Rom 8:26). When the Christian thinks of Mary and prayer, he or she will think of the power of her intercession. She helps Christians by lending her own voice to their feeble cries to God for help.

Intercession should not be the only melody in our repertoire of prayer. In the first reading of today's Mass you will notice how St. James encourages us to pray when we are suffering hardship. He also reminds us that praise and thanksgiving should find a place in our prayer. *"Is anyone among you cheerful? Let him sing praise."* (Jas 5:13). There is the prayer, too, of our work, of our power of influencing people to turn to God and away from sin. *"If anyone among you wanders from the truth,"* remarks St. James, *"and someone brings him back, let him know that whoever brings back a sinner from the error of his way, will save his soul from death and will cover a multitude of sins."* (Ibid., vv. 19-20). There is the prayer, too, of blessing, which is prominent in today's Gospel. *"Jesus blessed the children, placing His hands on them"*. (Mt 11:25). Blessing is not simply a question of raising hands and pronouncing a formula. Before blessing them, Jesus asked that the little children come to Him. He first received them and then He blessed them. The prayer of blessing is an acceptance of people because they are children of our Father Who is in heaven. We cannot call down God's blessing on people without first accepting them as Jesus did. We must make room for people in the homes of our hearts before we can call down upon them the kindness and the goodness of God. That acceptance is more difficult than perhaps we imagine. It is easy to pronounce a blessing with our lips. It can be more difficult to pronounce it from our hearts, showing people that we accept, value, respect and love them, even when they are different from us in a hundred ways.

A good mother is capable of loving each of her children. A good mother can accept all her children, even when in character and temperament each is different. It is so with Our Lady. It is because her children are so different that she has been given so many titles by them. All her children see her as Mother of God and Mother of us all, but because a Catholic in particular thinks of Mary as Mother in a special way, she is addressed by an immense variety of titles. Mary, Help of Christians, Mary conceived without sin, Mary, the only Mother of the Company, are but three in a long litany of titles with which the children of God address their Mother.

May Mary, the Help of Christians, continue, dear Sisters, to be close to you as you try each day to resemble more and more the likeness of her Son. May she be continually at your side, helping you as you lovingly serve the weaker and more needy members of God's family. In the words of St. Louise: *"Let us implore Mary to help us to render to God the service we have promised Him and to be as submissive as she was in accomplishing His holy Will."* (*Spiritual Writings of Louise de Marillac*, M. 33, pp. 785-86).

God's Will at Every Moment

1 August 1986   South Bend, Indiana

A little over two weeks ago I went into the Chapel in Paris which houses the mortal remains of St. Vincent de Paul. High above the main altar of the Church is the silver and glass casket that contains the body of St. Vincent. As I entered the chapel, I noticed in the distance a solitary figure kneeling in front of the glass casket. She was a young lady and she was deep in prayer. She had her two arms raised and resting on the glass of the casket, close to the head of the Saint. I remained some time in the Chapel and, when I left, the lady was still in prayer with her hands resting on the glass, earnestly asking the intercession of the Saint for some particular grace or favor.

What grace, I kept asking myself, is this lady seeking through the intercession of St. Vincent? The healing of a sick child? The obtaining of employment for her husband? Breaking away from drug addiction? Strength to forgive someone who had injured her? What her prayer was I do not know and did not dare to ask, but the intensity of it was clear and impressive. Clear also was the lady's conviction that the Saint, who has been given so many titles by God's people: Father of the Poor, Apostle of Charity, Protector of Orphans, could, by his influence over the mind and heart of God, do something for her. As I watched the lady in prayer, I could only guess what she might have been asking for. I could not help thinking that she was asking for one single grace. What that grace was remained a secret she shared with God and His servant, Vincent de Paul.

What one grace would you ask from St. Vincent de Paul this

weekend? Perhaps another question should be posed first. Have we sufficient faith in his intercession to ask him for one single grace, or must Our Lord pass the rather sad verdict on us that closes this evening's Gospel: *"And Jesus did not work many miracles there because of their lack of faith."* (Mt 13:58)?

The name, Vincent de Paul, will echo through the halls of Notre Dame throughout this weekend. How many of us, however, will at the end of it have spoken to the Saint with something of the intensity of that Parisian lady? How earnestly do we talk to him, who is the Patron of us all here, about the poor of our time? Does he, I wonder, find us theorizing much about the poor in a doctrinaire way? Is his name being used rather than his person being invoked in discussions about the poor and poverty in the world of our time? After all, it was Frederic Ozanam himself who observed that: *"A patron saint should not be a mere signboard to a society, like St. Denis or St. Nicholas over the door of a tavern. A patron saint should be regarded as a type on which we should try to pattern ourselves as he patterned himself on the Divine Type which is Jesus Christ."* (J.P. Derum, *Apostle in a Top Hat*, p. 112).

Supposing, however, we are convinced of the Saint's power of intercession with God, what one grace would you ask from God through his intercession? Would it echo one of the titles of the excellent topics that are being discussed here at this convention during these days: A greater readiness to respond to the cries of the poor? An eagerness to collaborate with others in hearing the cries of the poor? A clearer understanding of the Vincentian charism? These are all certainly very valuable graces. Perhaps, however, we would do better if we asked, not what we would like to obtain from God through the intercession of St. Vincent, but what St. Vincent himself would like to obtain for us from God. What might that grace be? It must remain a matter of conjecture. But if one is to judge from St. Vincent's voluminous writings, that one grace would not be more effective service of the poor, nor greater commitment to securing social justice, nor even a more generous response to the appeals of the Third World. The one grace would be quite a simple one: a more attentive, sensitive and personal response to what the living God is asking at this moment from each one of us. The formula, *"doing the Will of God,"* may seem to be almost trite. It might even sound in some ears as faintly suggesting an outmoded spirituality. The truth, however, is that St. Vincent de Paul was led to the poor and was able to lift the poor out of their wretched conditions because he himself lived with a profound consciousness of the importance of doing at every moment what he thought God wanted him to do.

Perhaps the Saint might at this point like to add a word of qualification to what I have just said. *"It is true"*, he might say, *"that I did reflect much upon the Will of God and its place in my life and in my work. It would, however, be more accurate to say that after the year 1617, I rarely thought of the Will of God without thinking of Jesus Christ. The reverence and the love which Jesus Christ had for the Will of His Father impressed me profoundly. I began to consciously submerge my plans and projects into the mind of Christ Jesus, to have them x-rayed by Him. Can you think of Jesus Christ without thinking of His reverence at all times, His constant referral of all His activity to the Will of His Father in heaven? Indeed on one occasion I recall speaking to the Community of priests and Brothers with whom I lived and saying to them: 'It is not enough to do what God wants, but I must do it for the love of God. We must do the Will of God according to the Will of God, that is, to do it in the way Our Lord did the Will of His Father when He was on earth.'* (Coste XI, Fr. ed., pp. 435-436).

"The world in which you are living has changed greatly since my time. There are millions more poor people on the face of the earth than there were three centuries ago. It is a grace of God that you have not allowed yourselves to become discouraged by the sheer numbers of poor who need help, millions more than in my time. Political systems seem so much more complex now than they did in the Europe I knew. My attempts to mediate between politicians of my time were not successful. When we have done everything in our power to mediate between people, we should preserve our tranquillity and peace, whether we are successful or not. It is only when we have emptied ourselves of self that God will fill us with Himself. Do not give up in the face of difficulty. 'Christ's teaching,' I remember writing two years before I died, 'will never let us down, while worldly wisdom always will.' (CR II:1). Do not lose your nerve, but make sure that you refer all your projects, great or small, to Jesus Christ and to the Will of His Father.

Don't forget that it is the earth which revolves around the sun, not the sun around the earth. Christ is the center, not we, however dazzling our projects may appear. Christ is the Light of the World. We must allow that Light to penetrate the crevices of our minds so that we may at all times do, as He did, the things that are pleasing to His Father in heaven. I recall some words I spoke towards the end of my life: 'Let us galvanize our wills to deal, to say and to accomplish the divine words of Jesus Christ, 'My food is to do the Will of Him Who sent Me and to accomplish His work.' (Jn 4:34). That has been your pleasure, Savior of the world . . . Since we cannot do it of ourselves, it is from You that we hope for this grace, confidently and with a great desire to follow You.'" (Coste XII, Fr. ed., p. 164).

To come back to the Chapel in Paris and that silver and glass casket. It was a coincidence that two weeks ago I should have entered that Chapel just at a moment when a lady was praying with upraised arms to St. Vincent de Paul. It is a coincidence today that we should be celebrating Mass with Bishop Murphy in this Church of the Sacred Heart on the First Friday of August, a day that brings to our minds devotion to the heart of Christ, the symbol of God's personal love for poor, broken humanity and of His personal love for each one of us. If St. Vincent de Paul was able to do so much for the poor of his day, it was because with his mind and heart he had come to know something of the length and breadth, the height and depth of the love of God that reposed in the Heart of Christ Jesus. As children of God, we must constantly be convincing ourselves in prayer of the excessive love with which God has reached out and is still reaching out to us each day and each moment of the day. If we are not convinced that God loves us as we are, even with our frailties, it will be very difficult for us to show the love of God to the poor. It is the work of humble prayer to come to know oneself as a person who is loved by God. It is the work of humble prayer to share that experience with the poor who are God's special friends.

May the thought of God's personal love for each of us, symbolized by the Heart of Christ, give us a new awareness of our value in His eyes. May it stimulate us to go forward and convince the poor that God does care for them. May we ourselves become sacraments of God's love for the poor. It is the love of God that presses us.

Our Lady Of Victories

10 August 1986   Emmitsburg, Maryland

My dear Sisters,

Going to and coming from the White House over the last few days I have stopped many times at the statue dedicated to Our Lady of Victories and have spoken there to the Mother of God. What an amount of history that statue has to tell!

There are well over one hundred thousand pilgrims coming here each year to the Shrine of St. Elizabeth Ann. Imagine some ten thousand less coming here on one day, ninety thousand, and not only spending a few hours here but encamping on the grounds. Imagine these pilgrims to be soldiers, and we have a faint idea of what it seemed like in 1863, when ninety thousand troops pitched camp here in preparation for a very bloody battle. The White House itself was occupied by the commanding officers planning the strategy of the war.

The group of Sisters here at that time must have been terrified. Did they, I wonder, make their meditation often during those days on the words of this morning's gospel: *"Fear not, little flock"?* (Lk 12:32). We do know for certainty that they prayed intensely to the Mother of God and in the simplicity of their faith promised that if the battle was averted, they would erect a statue to Our Lady of Victories. Plans were changed, and the army, the Union troops, took, as the little plaque tells us, the dusty road to Gettysburg, where one of the bloodiest battles in the history of your country was fought.

After the event, the Sisters faithfully erected the statue to Our Lady of Victories. There she stands today, holding the Infant in her arms with her left, graceful arm stretching out to support and protect her Divine Child. The gesture of faith of the Sisters is a magnificent commentary on the first sentence from the second reading of today's Mass: *"Faith is confident assurance concerning what we hope for and conviction about things we do not see."* (Heb 11:1). Those Sisters had assurance that Our Lady of Victories would not abandon them. They lived with the conviction that the troops who dotted the grounds would move and that they would be spared the horrors of war. So the statue stands today, speaking to us of the power of her whom we greet as Our Lady of Victories.

It must have been a great moment of tension in the history of the community here. Although we do not experience this particular type of tension in our lives today, we do speak about tension in our lives. We invoke many modern means to eliminate tension. We have discussions in our communities; we use consultation; we try to reach a consensus about decisions that are to be taken. These are all good means to reduce tension. The question, however, we must ask is: do we rely too much on natural means to dissolve and reduce tension within our communities? What about our faith?

I am reminded here of a difference between a problem and a mystery. By definition, a problem is something that can be overcome. There is a solution to the problem of a crossword puzzle. A mystery is, as we were often told, a revealed truth that our minds cannot comprehend. Do we, when we speak about obedience, find ourselves talking a great deal about the problems of obedience and very little about the mystery of it? Do we talk about the problems of poverty and scarcely at all of the mystery of our poverty? It is the mystery of the obedience, the chastity and the poverty of Jesus Christ that we are called to live and imitate.

Perhaps we have to think more about victories of grace in our lives. Perhaps we have to think of the importance of saying *no* to ourselves in order to say *yes* more fully to Jesus Christ, poor, chaste and obedient. Each *no* that we say to ourselves is a purifying of the windscreen of our minds so that we can see more clearly the road ahead in following Jesus Christ.

It is important for us to remember that faith is very much an affair of the heart. We recall Our Lord's words: *"Blessed are the pure of heart, for they shall see God."* (Lk 5:8). If we are having problems with faith, if we are having intellectual difficulties, it could be that the root of those difficulties does not lie in our heads but rather in our hearts. Faith is the capacity to see God and the things of God. If our hearts are not pure, then it is difficult for us to see God and the things of God. *"Blessed are the pure of heart, for they shall see God."* (Ibid.).

I recall on one occasion talking to a young man who rather aggressively attacked me because, as he said, the Pope had thirteen Cadillac automobiles in Rome. He was very vehement about this and could not reconcile it with the Church of the poor. He spoke so vehemently that I almost felt as if I was responsible for the Pope's having thirteen Cadillacs (which I am certain he does not have). However, I listened to him for a long time and, as he unwound, I came to realize that he had a serious moral, personal problem in his life. His dissatisfaction, it was clear, was not so much with the Pope as with his own manner of life. So true is it that difficulties of faith may have their roots in a lack of purity of heart. I do not mean to say that at times in our lives we may not have to walk through the valley of great darkness, such as has been described by some of the saints and mystics. But it is always worthwhile examining the foundations of belief, not in my head, but in my heart. *"Blessed are the pure of heart, for they shall see God."* (Ibid.).

Passing by the statue of Our Lady of Victories, I have thought many times of those words in St. John's letter: *"This is the victory that overcomes the world, our faith."* (1 Jn 5:4). How truly that was verified in the life of Mary! It was her faith that sustained her and gave her a victory. If the world is to be conquered today for Christ, the victory will come from faith. We talk much about secularism and the inroads it has been making in our religious lives. How can it be stemmed? *"This is the victory that overcomes the world, our faith."* (Ibid.). We need to live and to show the world of today that we have *"confident assurance concerning what we hope for and conviction about things we do not see."* (Heb 11:1). We nourish such an assurance and such conviction in the silence of prayer, but we must show them forth by the manner and simplicity of our lives.

Lady of Victories, by your faith you shared the victory of your Son over eternal death. Lady of Victories, you gave victory to this community in sparing it from the ravages of war, and you became protectress of this valley. Lady of Victories, win for us the gift of purity of heart that leads to faith, so that as we walk the dusty road of life, we may have assurance about what we hope for and conviction about things we do not see. *"Turn then, O most gracious advocate, thine eyes of mercy towards us, and after this our exile, show unto us the blessed fruit of thy womb, Jesus."*

Grace of Compassion

28 September 1986   Paris, France

My dear Sisters,

Some time during the past year a Confrere of mine, who was working in a Third World country, told me how difficult he found it to explain to a group of young men that he had a vow of poverty. He told the group that he had little personal money and that he had left his own country, which was more comfortable, in order to come and live among them, who were poor. My Confrere failed to convince them that he was poor. *"And why,"* he asked them, *"do you say that I am rich?"* There was silence for a moment, and then one of the young men said: *"You have shoes and you have a watch."*

To these young men a missionary of St. Vincent was seen to be Dives, simply because he had shoes and a watch. Now it is not very comforting nor consoling to think that perhaps more than two-thirds of the world would consider me to be a Dives today. But that is how I must seem to the starving millions who must lie down at night, gnawed by hunger. When on plane journeys the food I am served is not to my liking and I leave it there to be taken away, I find myself often reflecting on the fact that some of the families living in the territory over which I am flying would find enough to keep them going for a day, from what I leave on my plate to be thrown out by the airline companies. There are many Lazaruses who would like to get what I leave, to eat the crumbs that fall from my table.

Is there any difference, then, between the Dives of today's Gospel and myself? Can I avoid the fate of Dives? Must we say that it was the fact of being rich that condemned Dives? Or what precisely was Dives' sin for which he received such a severe sentence?

Dives' sin was not one of commission, but rather of omission. Dives did not commit any sin of violence: he did not attack Lazarus. Indeed he seemed to have allowed him to sit on his doorstep. Dives was a tolerant man. The sin of Dives seems to have been his failure to notice Lazarus with the ulcers on his body. Or if Dives did notice the pitiable condition of Lazarus, he did not lift a finger to help him. Lazarus was, according to the parable, in need both of food and medical attention, and Dives did nothing. Dives seems not to have had an eye for the poverty of Lazarus' condition nor a heart for his suffering.

We, of St. Vincent's Communities, profess to have both an eye and a heart for the suffering poor. We profess and proclaim to show the effective compassion of Jesus Christ towards those who are Lazarus in today's world. To have an eye and a heart of compassion for the poor is a grace of Jesus Christ. We cannot turn on the compassion of Jesus Christ, as we would water from a tap. We must humbly ask that grace of compassion from Jesus Christ.

There is one other grace which today's parable would suggest. Dives was condemned because he neglected to show effective compassion for Lazarus who sat at his door. Lazarus could hardly get closer to Dives, yet he received nothing from him. We who live in Community can never forget that the first person who has claim on our compassion and love is the person on our own doorsteps. Who knows if Dives might not have been very kind to poor people who lived far away from his house. The fact is that he was condemned for neglecting Lazarus on his doorstep.

Today's parable says something to me about the importance of the world of personal suffering in which my own local community members may be living. The Charity of Christ presses us to alleviate their sufferings before I leave the house to serve the poor and after I have returned to it. *"Be charitable,"* exhorts St. Vincent, *"be kind, have the spirit of forbearance and God will abide in your midst; you will be His cloisters, you will have Him in your home, you will have Him in your hearts."* (Conf. Eng. ed., 22 Oct. 1646, p. 259).

Stress in the Priesthood

7 October 1986   Bettystown, Ireland

Four years ago one of the commissions of the U.S. Episcopal Conference issued a report entitled *The Priest and Stress*. I was reminded of it by the content of the two readings which the Church offers us today for our reflection. Some of the biographical details which St. Paul presents in the first reading were occasioned by a stressful situation. There were those who questioned his credentials as an authentic apostle and disciple of Jesus Christ. Even within that story, as St. Paul recounts it, there are many stress vibrations, as there are throughout the corpus of St. Paul's writings. If we accept what St. Paul tells us, he seems to have been bounced from one stressful situation into another as he went through his life preaching Jesus Christ crucified and risen to Jew and Gentile alike.

The gospel passage to which we have just listened throbs with stress and tension. It seems clear that Jesus himself felt the stress of his ministry, not merely the drain which it made on his physical strength, but on his moral and spiritual resources as well. In the home of Martha and Mary he could *unwind*, as we say, and St John also in his gospel corroborates that fact. Jesus Christ was subject to human stress as we are, because he was both truly and perfectly God and truly and perfectly man.

On this particular occasion, when he went to relax in the home of Martha and Mary, he found himself caught up in a stressful situation. Reading the narrative, you can almost feel the tension rising in Martha until it boils over, and then she vents her frustration on the wrong person. Have you noticed that she attacks, not Mary, but Jesus himself? *"Lord, do you not care that my sister has left me to serve alone?"* (Lk 10:40). How authentically human is Martha's behavior. So often we work out our frustrations on the wrong people. The reaction of Jesus was not what mine would be: *"Why blame me?"* No, Jesus diffuses the tension, and reduces the stress by calmly addressing Martha. Note how He twice calls her by name: *"Martha. Martha . . . "* (Lk 10:41). How calming that must have been and conducive to helping Martha to regain her composure. Have you noticed that there is no rejection of Martha, no suggestion that she should not have been engaged in preparing the meal? Jesus merely underlines a truth that St. Luke records earlier, namely, that they are blessed who hear the word of God and keep it. He was putting an emphasis on a sense of attention to the word of God, if we are to offer that service to others which is the fulfillment of the second great commandment of the law. Hearing the word of God in prayer through reflection is a condition for true selfless loving service of the body of Christ.

Because the Bishops of the United States recognized the prevalence of unnecessary stress in the lives of their priests, they thought it worthwhile to study the phenomenon and to make some helpful recommendations. Although the Bishops' document does not say so explicitly, there can be a healthy and normal degree of stress in our lives, as there was in the life and experience of our great high priest, Jesus Christ. But there is another kind of stress which is undesirable, and which impairs our effectiveness as priests. It has its source not so much in our temperament as in our way of life or our way of thinking. *"Respect,"* we are advised by the Bishops' Commission, *"the four quadrants in which a healthy life is lived: prayer, work, friendship and leisure . . . .Define clearly what are the priority needs in your apostolates and how many of them you can attend to without bringing upon yourself unreasonable strain . . . .Do not forget that the quality of your work is more important than the quantity. What people are looking for in you more than anything else is a spiritual guide and one who will help them come to know the Lord and find his peace."* The Bishops, not of the 1950s but of the 1980s, reminded their priests of the old truth that *"regular time each day for prayer, meditation and spiritual reading is a 'sine qua non' for the unfolding in a priest's life of an authentic Christ-centeredness."* For the priest in Ireland, there is another subtle agent of stress. Not one of us is unaware that a certain corrosion of the sacred is taking place in the Ireland of today. We priests stand for the sacred, and which of us is not feeling the force of some of those strong winds of secularism which are blowing across our land. Let us by the grace of God stand our ground. Let us preserve and preach our values, Christ's values, the Church's values, in season and out of season, while being watchful that our own lifestyle is not in open conflict with those values. Above all, let us, priests of Jesus Christ, not forget that, however isolated and lonely we may feel at times, we are not alone. It is to us priests first that Jesus Christ gives the assurance that He is close to us. It was almost at the end of our ordination (according to the old rite) that the bishops said to us in the name of Christ: *"I will no longer call you servants, but my friends, for you know all that I have done in your midst."* (Jn 15:15). No sociological change, no shift of emphasis in theology can alter the fact that we are special friends of Jesus Christ by ordination, and that as far as He is concerned, we will remain so until the end. *"Tu es sacerdos in aeternum."*

May the Virgin Mary, who lived the stress of the sorrowful mysteries, win for us the peace that comes from becoming more worthy of the promises of her Son, so that we may be brought to the glory of His resurrection. We ask this through Christ our Lord.

A Priest's Spiritual Odyssey
7 October 1986   Bettystown, Ireland

When Bishop Eamonn wrote, asking me to join you today and to speak to you, the theme he suggested was: *A Review of the Spiritual Changes in a Priest's Spiritual Odyssey in Thirty-five years.* Now let me say straightaway that to escape from the raw fact that already we have passed three and one-half decades in the priesthood and that we have all reached or passed or are at least on the borders of the sixties, I found refuge and shelter in the odyssey dimension of the theme-title. One of the definitions given in the Oxford dictionary of the word *odyssey* is that it is an *adventurous journey*. What man among us here has not had an adventurous journey since he left the ordination sanctuary thirty-five years ago? Our lives, in their outward appearances anyway, could hardly be described as adventurous journeys. Most members of the class have lived out their lives within the confines of one diocese. You may have moved up and down, and over and across the diocese, but you would hardly claim that each move, each change was *"an adventurous journey."* Irish priests do not dramatize their lives, and with their sense of humble realism would be reluctant to present their lives in the priesthood as great adventures or themselves as particularly venturesome.

Yet each one of us here has had within the vast territory of his own heart an adventurous journey over the past thirty-five years, a journey which merits the title of *odyssey*. We will never get around to recounting in full the experiences of that adventurous journey, which is the spiritual odyssey of our priestly lives. We have not the insights into our own personalities and characters nor the powers of expression nor perhaps the humility nor the courage of a St. Augustine or a Thomas Merton to "go public" on our personal experience of being a priest for thirty-five years. However, there is not a man of us here but has had, spiritually speaking, an adventurous journey during the past three and a half decades as a priest of Jesus Christ. During these few days together I imagine that what you are doing is trying to heed the advice of Jeremias the prophet: *"Halt at the crossroad, look well, and ask yourselves which path it was that stood you in good stead long ago. That path follow, and you shall find rest for your souls."* (Jer 6:16). The halt is a brief one, and the crossroad is not perhaps a particularly significant one, or at least not as significant as that halt which you made here ten years ago and hopefully—at least for a remnant!—will make here fifteen years hence.

What you have asked me to do this morning is to reflect on certain experiences that we have shared together during our odyssey of thirty-five years, and which have affected our spiritual lives as priests. My reflections are random ones, and I cannot claim to be reading the map correctly as we look back over thirty-five years of journeying. It is for you to make the necessary corrections and adjustments, and what you will have to say may help all of us to move on with greater confidence and lighter step from this crossroads—which we will call thirty-five— at which we have decided to halt briefly.

I can recall very vividly the beginning of the priestly odyssey of this class. I am not thinking of that very first evening in Maynooth in September 1944, although that is still a very vivid memory in my mind. Rather am I thinking of the first steps you took as you moved out of the Maynooth sanctuary after your ordination in June 1951. You kindly invited me to be present at the class ordination. I was there as an observer in the choir stalls, having lost a year through "defecting" to the Vincentians. The steps you took as you moved down through the stalls at the end of the Ordination were very measured ones. The pace of the procession down the center of the chapel was, I can see it still, particularly slow. The steps may have been slow, but they were firm and confident ones on that ordination Sunday. The steps were firm and confident because you were moving out to a people who in every sense of the expression looked up to the priest. The people lifted up their eyes to the mountain of the priesthood. It was from there that help would come. So let us say that the odyssey of our priesthood began on a mountain. Life in the priesthood in the 1950s may not have been without its rough hours (when was it ever without its difficulties?), but it was studded with stability and security. We knew who we were, and it was good. The priest was a man set apart by God, and books such as Cardinal Manning's, *The Eternal Priesthood,* underscored the dignity and the elevation of the priesthood. The priest, too, was the Ambassador of Christ, who like Moses descended from the mountain to explain the law of God to the people, and to return to the mountain in order to offer gifts and sacrifices for the sins of the people he represented. The newly ordained priest of 1951 was reminded daily of the mountain of God as he began Mass praying Psalm 43, *"Send forth Your light and Your fidelity; they shall lead me on and bring me to your holy mountain, to your dwelling place. "* (Ps 43:3). Because of his dignity and because of his ambassadorial status, the spirituality of these years heavily under-scored the importance of a strong personal relationship with God in Christ. Our dignity as priests rested, too, on a deep consciousness of the powers of the priesthood. We came down from the mountain of God with power to make Christ present in the Eucharist, to pardon sins in His name, to baptize, and administer the sacrament to the sick. The consciousness of our dignity and of our priestly powers lifted us above the people, and the people looked up to us, even in our youthful rawness and inexperience.

Think back for a moment on some of the features of that mountain's spirituality; weekly or fortnightly confession, thanksgiving after Mass, visits to the Blessed Sacrament, the recitation of the Divine Office, lengthy, by today's standards, and in Latin. While we lived with the basic conviction that the breviary was the prayer of Christ, and accepted it as such, we would be less than honest if we did not admit that the shadow of the opinions of the moral theologians lay heavily over us, reminding us that the deliberate and inexcusable omission of a small hour constituted a mortal sin. For spiritual reading we were nourished on the works of authors such as Dom Marmion, Dom Chautard, Dom Van Zeller, and Dom Boylan. You will have immediately noticed that each of these authors was a monk. Their writings made strong emphasis on what was called *the interior life.* It would be unjust on our part to disparage or devalue the worth of the writings of these authors. They carried then and still do, much valid and profound theology that can still serve as pabulum for our priestly lives. I only invoke their names here to highlight the orientation given to the spirituality which was presented to us. The priest on the mountain was a consecrated man of God. There was a very forceful emphasis given to the importance of being holy. Can you still hear Father Tom Cleary in a rather high-pitched voice, somewhat excited, telling us that *"a holy priest makes a holy people"*? As you emerged from the college chapel in June 1951, you knew who you were, and so did the people of the parish into which you were going. There is lodged in my mind an observation which Cardinal Dalton made on a Union Day in Maynooth sometime in the early 1950s. He reminded the newly ordained priests that they were going out to a people who were second to none in the world in their devotion to, appreciation of, and love for the Catholic priesthood. Yes, we knew who we were, and it was good.

Down To The Sea In Ships

From the mountain fastness of the 1950s we began towards the end of that decade to go down to the sea in ships. We had just passed the ten-year mark in the priesthood when, from one of the slopes on the mountain range, our eyes caught sight of what seemed to be an immense ocean, clouded in a haze. A mist prevented us from seeing it clearly at first, but the prospect of it was enchanting. Vatican Council II can be likened to an experience of discovering the sea after a long trek across a range of solid mountains. The sea always calls forth adventure. The spirit of adventure was in the air in the early 1960s. It was not that the sea was healthier than the mountain, but there was a quality in the ocean air that was very gratifying and, above all, the sheer expansiveness of the ocean opened up within ourselves a new sense of freedom.

The Council launched us out into deep waters very quickly. New horizons opened up before us and new depths in theology were plumbed. In the exhilaration of the sea voyage we came to see ourselves a little less as *"other Christs,"* and a little more as *"servants of the servants of Christ."* We began to hear a little less about the dignity of the priesthood, and a good deal more about the people of God. If I recall rightly, it was the voice of the Irish bishops, with the late Cardinal Conway as their spokesman, that made a special plea at the Council that the priesthood be not overlooked in the documents that were being written. While welcoming the completion of the work of Vatican II on the role of the bishop in the Church, and rejoicing at the prospect of the development of the full potentialities of the lay person, the bishops underlined the centrality and the excellence of the order of priesthood in the Church.

It is noteworthy that the second sentence of the decree on the *Ministry and Life of Priests* remarks that *"a most important and increasingly difficult role is being assigned to this order in the renewal of Christ's Church"*. The fact is that a renewed vision of the Church was being presented to us in the Constitution *Lumen Gentium*. Because the concept of priesthood is inextricably linked with the theology of the Church, certain shifts of emphasis in the theology of the priesthood were inevitable. Central in the Constitution *Lumen Gentium* is the concept of the People of God, a concept already well accepted and lived by the Irish people as the term *Phobal De* clearly shows. However, down from the mountain and sailing across this new sea, we found ourselves closer than ever before to the laity. It was not that the Irish priesthood was ever distant from the laity, but we were beginning to turn our altars around. The laity were being given a different view of us, and we were seeing them in a different light. The placing of the chapter on the People of God before that on the hierarchy in the Constitution *Lumen Gentium* was not without its significance, nor the decision to treat the universal call to holiness before presenting the theology of the religious life.

It was during these years, too, of our spiritual odyssey that new riches in the theology of marriage were being discovered. Did we during those years begin to feel that the sacrifices we had made to become celibate priests were being ever so slightly devalued? Had the discovery of the new riches in the theology of marriage and presented in *Gaudium et Spes* made us feel in some inexpressible way less secure in our priesthood? Whether this be so or not, these were the years when we began to be told that celibacy was an eschatalogical sign of the coming of God's kingdom. They were years when we embarked on a search of finding new ways of living our celibacy at greater depth. Side by side with the question, *What is the meaning of celibacy?*, priests were raising the deeper question, *What meaning can I give to a life of celibacy?*. Some priests found the questions profoundly disturbing or realized that the charism of celibacy had not been theirs in the first instance and left the priesthood. These were the years, too, when the vernacular first inched its way into the liturgy and then after a short time, the Latin language virtually surrendered to it unconditionally. We found ourselves speaking less of "my Mass" and a little more about the people's Mass. No longer was there the same awesome silence at the consecration as there was in the days of the Latin Mass, to be followed by widespread coughing on the part of the congregation when the final consecration bell had been rung. The sense of mystery was diminished and we priests, too, were becoming less sacralized.

It was in the second decade of our priesthood, that we began to hear about the new Christology. The humanity of Christ, His knowledge about Himself and His mission became focal points of discussion among us. How much did Jesus Christ know? and when? Did He know that He was God? These were questions that were scarcely raised, or not at all in the manuals we knew, such as those of Van Noort or Tanquerey. The renewed Christology was emphasizing the deep human love of Christ, His compassion, especially for the poor, His appreciation of humanity, both His and ours. However, a consequence of emphasizing the humaneness of Christ was an almost imperceptible diminishment of reverence before the uniqueness and mystery of the Incarnation. Throwing into relief the richness of the theology of the Resurrection seemed to draw us away somewhat from the way of the Cross and the preaching of Christ crucified. Was it about this time that we noticed a weakening of the sense of sin among our people and the thinning out of the file of people outside our confessionals? As for ourselves, we seemed to be frequenting less the Sacrament of Penance or Reconciliation, as it was beginning to be called. It was not that we had lost faith in the absolving words of a fellow priest, but rather that we were not seeing things with the sharpness of Peter's faith when he felt compelled to cry out on his knees in the boat: *"Depart from me, O Lord, for I am a sinful man."* (Lk 5:8). The Council years saw us relegate Marmion and Vonier and Chautard to the shelves in the visitor's bedroom in our rectories, in order that we might make room for Quoist and Evely and Boros.

A Desert Place

We can say that in the years immediately following the close of Vatican Council II, we ran into some turbulence. I would prefer to suggest that we reached land again in 1965, but found the terrain very different from that from which we had set out in 1962. We moved inland again on our adventurous journey, after the bracing airs of the Council. Before long we found ourselves in a terrain that was very different from the one from which we had set out on our sea voyage. If the truth must be told, the late 1960s and early 1970s were years when it seemed to many that the Church had moved into a desert. Like the Israelites of old, there were those who began to question why God had led them out into a desert place. Why had He, if He cared for His people, taken away from them some of the old securities? These were the years when some theologians were speaking about the death of God. Perhaps a consequence of the death of God theology was the questioning of the validity of prayer. I have heard it said that at the turn of the decade, from the 60s to the 70s, Pope Paul VI became somewhat depressed by the thought that the Church was weakening in its conviction about the validity and efficacy of prayer. No, we did not give up prayer; we still celebrated Mass with the people and for them. We held on to our breviaries, somewhat relieved that at least now we could understand what was on the page before us. They were the years of the Interim Breviary, the Blue Book, rushed out rather hurriedly, it was said, lest the priests of this country would lose the habit altogether of praying the prayer of the Church. These were the years, too, when dispensations from priestly celibacy continued to be granted. The *Tu es sacerdos in aeternum* that had been sung in majestic polyphony at your ordination ceremony, no longer seemed to have the awesome finality that it had some twenty years earlier. For the laity the newly-granted dispensations from priestly celibacy were tolerantly and with understanding accepted, even if many of them remained bewildered and a little sad.

The wilderness situation of the late 60s and early 70s was characterized, too, by a feeling of not knowing what direction the people of God with their priests should be taking. Recently I heard of a French bishop, now retired, referring to these years as an era when it was forbidden to forbid.

It would not be fair nor true to speak in totally negative terms of these years which could be described as the wilderness experience. In the history of Israel, the wilderness experience of the Exodus had some profound spiritual effects on the Israelite people. In retrospect, our wilderness years did much for us priests. Somehow there seemed to be a new awakening in our consciences, that we were called to be our far distant brothers' keepers. The Irish diocesan priest was giving thought to the needs of dioceses far beyond our shores. Vocations to Mission Societies, Religious Orders and Congregations continued to drop. Yet almost systematically, individual Irish dioceses began to establish their own missions in third world countries. The numbers sent to such missions by individual dioceses may have been small, token forces, but they pointed to an awareness on the part of the priesthood in our dioceses, of the centrality of the priest's role in the extension of the Kingdom of God. These newfound missions did much for our people, calling forth an unsuspected generosity for their support. It would be idle to deny that we in turn were not moved by it.

The partnering of the two themes, the priesthood and justice, at the Synod of 1971 was also significant. The horizons of our minds were being widened, so that we began to feel responsibility for the poor and the oppressed of the third world. The 1950s saw a strong reaffirmation of charity in moral theology, in the writings of men such as Spicq and Haring. It was welcome emphasis. Then later, with the Popes themselves giving the lead, justice became the contemporary name for charity. Action on behalf of justice and participation in the transformation of the social order impinged more on our consciences. We were ordained for men in the things that appertained to God; our God was a just God, and we must consider ourselves as being among his privileged agents of justice. With the heightened awareness of the extreme poverty in two-thirds of humanity, we as priests came to a new realization that Jesus Christ had come to give the good news to the poor, that He had shown a particular interest in the poor, and that as men who shared in His ministerial priesthood, we should reflect that concern.

Deserts are often trackless, and sands shift. In deserts it is notoriously difficult to find direction for the onward journey. Confidence can be shaken. Each of us in the early 70s did feel a little confused about

direction at times. We were finding it difficult to present to our people
the old theology in its new dress. For some perhaps the weakening of
confidence accentuated the loneliness of the desert. Were these the
years when, with many familiar landmarks gone, we as celibates felt
most acutely the loneliness of the desert?

And Into A "Plain Place"

Imperceptibly after the publication of the masterly document, *Evangelii Nuntiandi*, by Pope Paul VI in 1975, which gave expression to
some of the difficulties of communicating the deep things of God to
mankind, we seemed to move into new terrain. It was a slow journey.
New vegetation gradually appeared. In paragraphs 25-39 of *Evangelii
Nuntiandi* Paul VI touches on the content of a priestly spirituality which
takes account of the two dimensions, the contemplative and the apostolic. Taking their cue from this document, authorities and writers will
throw into relief now one dimension and then the other, but always
stressing the intimate link that binds the contemplative with the apostolic in the life of the priest; not contemplation alone nor pastoral action
alone, but both working together without dichotomy, in the life of the
priest.

It was when Pope John Paul II was elected Pope in 1978 that he drew
attention to a range of mountains on the horizon. As the anniversary of
the institution of the priesthood on Holy Thursday came around each
year, Pope John Paul recalled for us the truth that a priest must be a man
of the mountains and a man of the sea, a man of the desert and a man
of the marketplace. He is called to be a man of prayer, and a man of
action. A priest must not spend so much time on the mountains that he
does not descend to the plains to interest himself in the struggle of God's
people for justice and peace. Nor must he be a man who never lifts up
his eyes to the mountains whence shall come his help. Nor must he be
a landlubber. Like his fellow priest, Peter of the Gospels, he must be
ready to obey his Master's command to launch out into the deep and to
let down his net for new catches. He is a man who has a strong sense
of tradition in his heart, but with his eyes wide open for what is emerging
before him.

At the present time two features mark spirituality in general and
priestly spirituality in particular. First, there exists a desire or a need

for more prayer, personal and community. Groups coming together to reflect on the apostolate, support groups, prayer groups are familiar features of life in the Church at the present time. Second, personal and community prayer is not looked upon as an evasion of the world, but rather as an encounter with God that will result in a more practical solicitude for the needs of contemporary society and mankind. An incarnational spirituality and a spirituality of service are consequences of a more intimate contact with God. The apostolic mission of the priest with all its implications is seen as flowing from the fact that he has in fact been chosen *"from among men and ordained for men in the things that appertain to God."* (Heb 5:1).

"To live is to change," wrote Cardinal Newman, *"and to live perfectly is to have changed often."* We have lived through changes and we ourselves have changed and have been changed for the better, if for no other reason than that for those who love God *"all things work together for the good."* (Rom 8:28). For all our limitations, failures and compromises in the priesthood, there runs like a golden thread through these thirty-five years an unbroken and deep desire to love God, to become less unworthy of the vocation to which we have been called. So for that reason we can be confident that the changes and emphases in priestly spirituality have in the mysterious design of God's Providence been working for our good.

At the end of this rapid, generalized and cursory review of some of the spiritual changes in a priest's spiritual odyssey in thirty-five years, let me stop and fix our sights on what has not changed. What has not changed is the fact that Jesus Christ has not gone back on His choice, a personal one, of us to be priests. Again, I can still hear Tom Cleary citing over and over again Our Lord's words: *"You have not chosen me, but I have chosen you, and I have appointed you that you should go and should bring forth fruit, and that your fruit shall remain."* (Jn 15:16). Whatever changes may have taken place, the Mass still remains central to our personal lives and those of our people. So do the sacraments and, above all, the deep need of our people to hear from us about God, His life, His love, His commandments and the eternal truths. *"What this parish needs is a minister who knows God more than by hearsay,"* was an observation made by a Protestant who was engaged in a process of selecting a new minister for the parish. More perhaps than ever do the people wait to hear the authentic voice of a priest who has climbed the mountain of God in prayer. For all the changes in these past thirty-five years, the priest does remain a man of power, power given to him by Jesus Christ through the imposition of the hands of the bishop who ordained him. Sound unchanging priestly spirituality will make a priest live daily in an awareness of that theological fact.

The word *change* is a vogue word today, because it corresponds to the reality of change with which and within which we must live our lives. Let not change unsettle us unduly. The church's ministry from first century Israel to twentieth century Ireland is a story of change: varying emphases, new ways of serving and caring for the Body of Christ. Draw comfort from this observation of Cardinal Bernadin of Chicago to his priests:

> *People are not looking for religious leaders who can solve all their problems or answer all their questions. Often they know the answers already or they know their problem has no immediate solution. More than anything else people look to us who minister to them for our presence as loving, caring and forgiving people. They want our help in their efforts to handle pain and frustration. They look to us for understanding; they seek a sensitive and consoling response to their hurt feelings; they need the spiritual comfort we can bring through our ministry of word and sacrament. They want someone who will pray with them, whose presence will remind them that no matter what their difficulties might be, God really loves them and cares for them. They want assurance that God will never abandon them. This is the preferred style of spiritual leadership in our day.* (Origins 1982, Vol. XI pp. 65 ff.)

As a parting word at this crossroad thirty-five, could I just say that, whatever changes have taken place in the world and in the Church, and whatever adaptations we priests must make in our ministry to our people, the most persuasive apologetic for Christian belief remains the phenomenon of holiness. Have we in these last few years been too preoccupied with the need for relevance? A preoccupation with relevance can be unsettling, not to say dangerous. It is required of us who are dispensers of the mysteries of God that we be found faithful, not that we be found relevant. Relevance, however, may be very well one of those things that will be added onto us if, in our lives, we first seek God and His justice. *"No, Father,"* wrote St. Vincent de Paul, *"neither theology nor philosophy, nor discourses can act upon souls; it is necessary for Christ to intervene with us or we with Him: that we act in Him and He in us, that we speak as He does and in His spirit."* (Coste XI, Fr. ed., p. 343). The holiness that we seek goes beyond moral rectitude and integrity. The holiness that we seek is a growth into the likeness of Christ. It is our most urgent necessity as we leave this crossroad thirty-five. The point has been made clear for us in the final document of the recent Extraordinary Synod: *"Throughout the whole history of the Church, in its most difficult circumstances, the saints, men and women, have been the primary sources of renewal. We badly need saints today and we should earnestly pray to God for them."* (Synod Doc. sect. 2, a.4). The visit of the Holy Father these days to Ars is a confirmation, if we needed it, that a holy priest does make a holy people in 1986 as in 1951.

Advent Letter—Openness of Mind and Heart

15 October 1986   To Each Confrere

My dear Confrere,

May the grace of our Lord Jesus Christ be ever with us!

It is now a little over a month since the Pope, along with the leaders of the world religions, gathered in Assisi to pray for peace. It was an event of historic significance, for it was the first time in human history that so many religious traditions came together to pray about a concern that was close to all their hearts. For us of the Christian and Catholic tradition it was a visible expression of one of the messages which the Spirit gave to the Church during the Second Vatican Council. It was then that the Spirit of God invited the Church to open its arms in a more expansive way to the whole of humanity. No other Ecumenical Council in the history of the Church has addressed such explicit messages of respect and comprehension to the other world religions as did the Second Vatican Council.

The gathering of the heads of the world religions around the person of the Pope took place significantly in the town of Assisi. It became a sort of *open city* for the occasion. The differing and sometimes conflicting religious traditions could agree to declare Assisi an *open city*, because of the respect the world has for St. Francis whose name evokes peace, humility, joy, detachment of heart. It was an appropriate setting to express the Catholic Church's new openness to the world.

How open is our Congregation to the world? Our particular and specific mission within the Church is to announce to the poor the good news of Christ's coming. It is towards the poor that we must direct the thrust of our love and zeal. We must, however, do that in such a way that we do not give people of other creeds or of other social classes an impression that we have no time for them. Read the correspondence of St. Vincent. His face is set towards the poor: his energies directed towards them. Yet on his way to the poor all passersby are respectfully greeted in the Lord and are humbly and graciously invited to join him on his pilgrimage to the City of the Poor. What an assortment of people accepted his invitation! The nobility, the clergy, the bourgeois, the poor themselves fell in behind St. Vincent on his pilgrimage to find Christ, not in Bethlehem, but in the suffering minds and bodies of the poor of his time. Would St. Vincent have magnetized such a variety of men and women if his mind and heart had not been an *open city*?

It is lack of openness of heart and openness of mind that gives so much pathos to the narratives recounting the birth of Our Lord. The innkeepers, Herod, the religious authorities in Jerusalem all suffer in one way or another from having closed minds and closed hearts. *"He came to His own home and his own people received Him not."* (Jn 1: 11). By contrast the shepherds, the Magi, St. Joseph and Mary, the Virgin Mother of Jesus, shine forth in the narratives as open characters, who received the word of God into *"a good and perfect heart."* (Lk 8:15).

For us, as for St. Francis of Assisi and St. Vincent, such openness of heart and openness of mind will be the fruit of humble, silent contemplation of the Word Incarnate in the Christmas Crib. If we are to walk with St. Vincent on his pilgrimage to the City of the Poor, we must check that the word *Poor* is not just a slogan word for us. To preach the gospel to the poor with the authentic accent of Jesus Christ, we must first have preached the poor Christ to ourselves. We can be at ease with the poor and be effective communicators to them, only if we have learned from Our Lord in prayer something about his own experience of being poor, that is, being detached in mind, in heart and in will, not only from material things, but from all that impedes us from a humble and loving accomplishment of God's will in our lives.

Allow me to suggest this Advent that you:

-Open your mind, by making room for those whom you tend to ignore or pass by because they are members of another social class or hold a different creed. Is there some one person, man or woman, rich or poor, whom you might persuade to join St. Vincent's pilgrimage to the open City of the Poor?

-Open your heart, by some gesture of generosity to a poor person or family who until now have been outside the circle of those you help. Have you some one in mind who before Christmas will feel less hungry, less alone, less unloved because of some gesture on your part?

I hope your Christmas will be a joyful one, and that wish is shared by all of us who live here in the Curia. What St. Vincent wrote in a letter a few days before Christmas in 1656 is apropos: *"Here we have nothing new except the mystery (of Christmas) which is drawing near and which will make us see the Saviour of the world reduced almost to nothing under the form of an infant. I hope that we will be gathered together at the foot of His Crib to ask Him to draw us after Him in His abasement. It is with this desire and in His love that . . . "* (Coste VI, Fr. ed., p. 150). I remain, your devoted confrere.

1987

Story of our Lives

1 January 1987   Paris, France

Mother Duzan, Father Lloret and my dear Sisters,

New Year's Day is like the opening of a new volume in a series of books in which we are writing the story of our lives. How many volumes we will write is not known to us. On average, says the psalmist, there will be seventy or eighty. *"Our life is over like a sigh. Our span is seventy years, or eighty for those who are strong.* (Ps 90:9-10)

We do not know if the volume we are commencing today will be the final one in the series. We know that the contents of volume 1987 are already known to God. *"Before ever a word is on my tongue,"* exclaimed the psalmist, *"You know it, O Lord, through and through."* (Ps 139:4). Before us this morning there lies a volume of 365 blank pages, on which God invites us to write with Him the continuing story of our lives.

The story of each of our lives is altogether unique and God, even more than we, wants that story to be a success story. In the fairy tales that were told to us when we were young, there was always a happy ending. The prince and princess always *"lived happily ever after."* We know for certain that God wishes that the end of our life's story will be but the beginning of a life in which we will be happy with Him ever after.

The latest volume of our lives, which we have just completed, that of 1986, is a volume which contains many pages which have brought joy to the heart of God. It is a volume that tells the story of many intimate contacts with Jesus Christ in the Sacraments, of kindness done to members of our Community, of sacrifices generously made to serve the poor. Volume 1986, like indeed previous volumes of our life's story, has been illuminated by the conviction that our lives are lived in partnership with Christ. For did not Jesus Christ say: *"I am the vine and you are the branches. He who abides in Me and I in him, he it is that bears much fruit, for apart from Me you can do nothing.* " (Jn 15:5).

In volume 1986 there are pages that have been stained by personal sin. These read as so many episodes when we took the pen from God's hand and decided we would write our own story—alone. It has been so from the time when Adam and Eve decided that they would take things fully into their own hands and so brought upon humanity that calamity, the consequences of which we are all aware, and from which we are delivered only by the grace of Our Lord Jesus Christ. *"Who will deliver me from this body of death?"* cried St. Paul. Then he immediately answered: *"Thanks be to God, through Jesus Christ, Our Lord."* (Rom 7:24-25).

The story of our lives must then be continually coauthored with Jesus Christ, Who is in love with us and wishes us to be in love with Him. Of two people genuinely in love, it is said that they do not so much live their lives looking into each others eyes, as looking in the same direction. So it must be for us in our relationship with Jesus Christ. Because we are in love with Him, and He with us, we will not begrudge Him time to be with Him in prayer, so that we can both look in the same direction. For the Daughter of Charity, that direction is clear. The eyes of Jesus Christ look towards the poor, those people whose lives, at least humanly, are stories of tragedy, with pages moist with tears shed in the bitterness and pain caused by injustice and poverty. As we look with Jesus Christ towards the world of the poor, the appeal which the Pope made during the Assembly of 1985 is still in our ears: *"My Sisters, do the impossible to go to the poorest."*

As we look at volume 1987 of our lives, the first page of which lies open before us, perfumed by the feast of the gentle and tender presence of the Mother of God, some days in this new year already begin to stand out. For us of St. Vincent's Communities, 1987 will be significant in that we will commemorate the two hundred fiftieth anniversary of the canonization of St. Vincent. It was on Sunday, 15 June 1737, the feast of the Blessed Trinity, that Pope Clement XII in the Basilica of St. John Lateran in Rome declared St. Vincent de Paul to be a saint. In this year when we will be reflecting on his sanctity, the observation of Henri Bremond on St. Vincent is very apposite: *"It is not his love of mankind,"* wrote Bremond, *"which led him to sanctity. It is rather that sanctity made him truly and efficaciously charitable. It is not the poor who gave him to God, but God Who gave him to the poor."* (H. Bremond, *Histoire du Sentiment Religieux en France*, Vol. 3, p. 219).

The holiness of St. Vincent and of each one of us is in the last analysis a gift of God. Each time we pray the second Eucharistic prayer, we are reminded that God is the fountain of all holiness. The holiness of a saint is a sharing in the holiness of God Himself, and we recognize holiness when we see the fruits of the Spirit in the life of a person. *"The fruit of the Spirit,"* writes St. Paul, *"is love, joy, peace, patience, kindness, goodness, faithfulness, gentleness, self-control."* (Gal 5:22). The love and goodness that appears in the life of a saint is but the flower of a root that reaches into the life of the Trinity, Father, Son and Holy Spirit. *"Your life is hidden with Christ in God."* (Col 3:3). To judge from the writings of our Founders, the mystery of the Trinity was very much in the forefront of their minds. St. Vincent's desire to preach the Gospel to the poor was fueled greatly by his conviction that knowledge of the mystery of the Trinity was necessary for salvation, while in the writings of St. Louise it is clear that she proposed to the Sisters the life of the Trinity as the ideal of union within the Community.

For us today who live rushed lives, we could profitably devote more time in our prayer and in moments of recollection to recalling the stupendous fact that the eternal and omnipotent God has loved us with an everlasting love and is living within us. *"If anyone keeps My word, My Father will love him and we will come and make our home in him."* (Jn 14:23). God took flesh of the Virgin Mary and dwelt among us. That was the first act in the drama whose second and third acts would be His dwelling in the Eucharist and in the souls of those who hear the word of God and keep it.

On this New Year's Day and throughout the year, when we will reflect on the holiness of St. Vincent, I invite you to journey often inward into the depths where reside within you the Father, Son and Holy Spirit. Such pilgrimages will strengthen you all the more to serve the poor, for the first gift you bring to the poor is God Himself. *"It is,"* wrote St. Paul, *"no longer I but Christ who lives in me."* (Gal 2:20). What the poor experience in our service of them is the life of God pulsating within us. Perhaps the poor will never express it in that way to us, but it is the reality, and we for our part must try to live our lives in an awareness of the three Divine Persons Who have made their home in the depths of our beings.

For us who live our lives in apostolic Communities, there exists always the risk of neglecting the contemplative dimension of our vocation. In doing so we risk living our lives on the surface of things. The journey outward to the poor can only be made with security, after we have made the journey inward to God Who lives within us. *"Do you not know that you are God's temple and that God's Spirit dwells in you?"* (1 Cor 3:17). Making that inward journey often will throw light, not only on the meaning of your vows, but will also bring you a new awareness of the presence and activity of God in your lives. It will bring you to a new awareness of the God Who has shared all things with us, even His beloved Son, and Who wishes daily to share the experience of our lives and the writing of its story.

Of the presence of God within the human soul, no one has been more conscious than the Virgin of Nazareth whose name was Mary. May she on this New Year's Day gift us all with a new awareness, not only of the God she brought forth from her womb, but of the God Who temples Himself in our hearts. May she help us to continue the writing of the story of our lives during this year of 1987, and to make more room on the pages of it for Him Who, as we are reminded on Holy Saturday, *"is the beginning and the end, Who is Alpha and Omega, and to Whom belongs all time and all ages."* (Rv 22:13).

Questions to the Magi

4 January 1987   Paris, France

My dear Sisters,

On this evening as we begin to celebrate the feast of the Epiphany, I invite you to go to Bethlehem and to interview the Wise Men from the East who have just now arrived in the town and have found Mary, the Mother of Him who is born to be the Savior of the world. The Wise Men are tired, and you are asked not to weary them further by too many questions. You will have time to put four questions to them and you begin now:

Question 1: Why did you come here?

Reply: We came only because we wanted to find the King of the Jews. Our journey was long, but we were helped greatly, and we must say mysteriously, by the strange star that guided us to Jerusalem. It disappeared for a while, but it reappeared and led us to Bethlehem where we happily found the Child with His Mother.

Question 2: Did you experience any special difficulties on your journey and during your stay here in Judea?

Reply: Yes, we experienced many difficulties. It would take too long to enumerate them. Perhaps the greatest difficulty we experienced was a cultural one. You see, we are not Israelites. Our culture, our language, our traditions are very different from those we have found here in Judea. The people we have met have in the main been very helpful. Still, we are very much aware of the fact that we are far from our own country and, although we are adults, each of us has had our moments of nostalgia as we recall and remember our own family and our own friends.

Question 3: Have your hopes been realized?

Reply: Yes, but not in the manner we had expected. We thought we would find the new-born King—His name is Jesus—in much more ornate and richer surroundings than we did. Still each of us has been rewarded with a deep sense of that peace which comes from doing what the God of our consciences has told us to do. Besides all that, it was an inexpressible joy for each of us to meet and talk with that gracious, humble lady who is the Mother of the King. Her name is Mary and she comes from a place called Nazareth.

Question 4: Will you tell us something about the gifts which we heard you brought to the young King?

Reply: The gifts we brought made us feel a little foolish at first. You see, we thought that the King would be living in a palace. We brought gifts that we considered suitable for one who would live his life in a palace. On arrival here we found the Infant King living in an ordinary, common house. However, His Mother graciously accepted the gifts from us and said that they would be useful now and in the future. We did not see how, but the depth of her sincerity convinced us, and now we are glad that we brought these gifts, and we have left them with the King and His Mother.

Although the Magi, my dear Sisters, are tired from their journey, they are interested enough to ask us if we would mind giving our answers to the questions we have just put to them. So they begin to interview us:

Question 1: Why did you come here, Sister?

Reply: In answer to a call from God. True, I had not a star in the sky to guide me here to Paris, but I am convinced that the same Divine Providence which led you to Bethlehem has brought me to Paris. I am equally convinced that it is here I will find that same Child with His Mother, whom you found in Bethlehem. The star of Divine Providence occasionally hides itself from me, as it did from you, and I am at times perplexed and confused. Still I keep trusting in God's loving Providence, and I know that all will be well in the end.

Question 2: Have you experienced any special difficulties on your journey to and during your stay in Paris?

Reply: Yes, my difficulties are, like yours, cultural ones. I live my life among Sisters who come from nations and cultures very different from mine. Like you, I am at times nostalgic for home and the poor whom I used to serve directly.

Question 3: Have your hopes been realized?

Reply: Yes. There comes a peace from knowing that, however difficult my present work at times may be, it is the task which God wants me to do today. It has been a special grace, too, to pray in that place where the Virgin Mary promised St. Catherine that she would find all the strength she needed to live her vocation as a Daughter of Charity.

Question 4: Will you tell us something about the gifts you have brought to the rue du Bac?

Reply: You embarrass me by asking about my gifts. I could not bring gifts such as yours to the new-born King and His Mother. My talents are few and my limitations are great. I am humbled daily by the knowledge of the imperfection of my motives in what I offer to God. Still, I do believe, even if I only see in a dark manner, that Christ, the Saviour, along with His Mother, are using my mind and my hands, my head and my heart, to bring comfort and strength to poor people whom I will come to know only at the end of life's journey. With St. Paul I keep saying: *"This life that I live now, I live by faith in the Son of God Who loved me and gave His life for me."* (Gal 2:20).

My dear Sisters, did Mary say thanks to the Magi? Who can doubt it? So do I say thanks to you for all that you do for the Company. Be assured that I am reflecting upon what you said to me during the visit I made in November and that I will communicate to the Mother General those recommendations which I consider helpful for improving the quality of your Community life and of the service you offer to God and to the Company. For the rest, my dear Sisters, continue to seek that star which will lead you to a more perfect doing of God's Will, while not forgetting that each of us is at each moment of the day called to be a star that will light the way and guide others towards discovering *"the Child with Mary, His Mother."* (Mt 2:11).

Little Lights Shining in the Darkness

18 January 1987   Maikodai, Japan

My dear Sisters,

In the little home of Nazareth one of the books of the Bible which Jesus, Mary and Joseph would have most talked about would have been the book of Isaiah, the Prophet. Certainly Jesus, when He had grown to adulthood, would have reflected much in His prayer on the writings of Isaiah. You will recall how, when on the first occasion He preached a homily in the synagogue of Nazareth, it was some words from this prophet that He quoted to describe the work He would do. He would bring good news to the poor, freedom to the captives and consolation to the broken-hearted.

I wonder, did Our Lord often make His prayer on the final words of today's reading from the prophet Isaiah: *"I will make you a light to the nations, so that my salvation may reach to the ends of the earth."* (Is 49:6).

Certainly Jesus spoke often about light. Indeed He said one day to the people who were listening to Him: *"I am the light of the world."*

(Jn 9:5). He asked His close followers to be light to the world. *"Let your light so shine before men, that they may see your good works and give glory to your Father Who is in heaven."* (Mt 5:16). There is also an echo of the words of Isaiah about salvation reaching to the ends of the earth in Our Lord's final words to the Apostles: *"Go, make disciples of all nations."* (Mt 28: 19).

Last night, my dear Sisters, when my plane was approaching Osaka, I looked out of the window and there below me was a beautiful carpet of dark black velvet, studded with little lights of white and gold and red and blue. That is how your great city of Osaka looked in the darkness of the night as seen from the height of a plane. I said to myself, *"I have reached the ends of the earth,"* for to a man who was born on a little island on the extreme west of Europe, Japan seems to lie at the other end of the world. It is all relative, because to you Europe lies at the other end of the world. For the little family at Nazareth, your country and my country would certainly have been thought of as *"the ends of the earth."* For the Holy Family of Nazareth, *"the ends of the earth"* would have been Persia and the Mediterranean Sea.

As I looked down on Osaka in the darkness last night, I reflected on the marvelous truth that here in Japan, so far away from the country where Jesus lived and died, there are to be found people who believe in Him and in the Church which He founded upon the rock of Peter. Yes, it is true, *"salvation has reached to the ends of the earth."* (Is 49:6). With the psalmist I say, *"By the Lord this has been done, and it is marvelous in our sight."* (Ps 118:23).

Osaka looked beautiful last night. What made it beautiful to me was the panorama of the specks of light which were shining in the darkness. The darkness was immense, but the little specks of light which I could see from the altitude of the plane were a delight for my eyes.

That is how you and I must seem to God. We are little dots of light shining in the darkness of this world. By our lives we give joy to the heart of God. Of us God the Father is saying, to quote freely the final phrase of this morning's Gospel, *"This is My chosen one."* (Jn 1:34). We are little points of light which can guide people to salvation and to God. The little points of light on the runway of the airport, which guide the pilot as he brings his plane safely down to earth, are not conscious of what they are doing for the safety (shall I say salvation?) of so many people in the plane. So, too, you, my Sisters. By the goodness of your lives, by what you do for the poor, by your love for each other, you are little points of light shining in the darkness. God is using you, and you hardly know it, to guide others, who hardly know it, safely to their destination and to the terminal building of heaven. *"I will make you a light to the nations, so that my salvation may reach to the ends of the earth."* (Is 49:6).

At the end of each day I pray this little prayer of Father Teilhard de Chardin: *"O God, grant that at all times You may find me as You desire me, and where You would have me be, so that You may lay hold on me fully."*

If we are in that place where God wants us to be, if we are doing that work which He through our Superiors asks us to do, we can be certain that He will take hold of us fully. He will use us. We will be little lights shining in the darkness. We will bring His salvation to the ends of the earth.

Obedience and Peace

19 January 1987   Maikodai, Japan

My dear Sisters,

How do you explain to people who know nothing about Christianity, the meaning of our crucifixes, such as the large one that hangs over this sanctuary? Would you begin by saying that the Man Who is hanging on the cross was learning the meaning of obedience? I hardly think so. Yet that is what the author of today's first reading states. *"Christ learned obedience through what He suffered."* (Heb 5:8). Yes, although He was God, He came to a new knowledge of the meaning of obedience through what He suffered on the cross. It is a very daring thing to say, yet that is what God tells us through the word which He addresses to us this morning.

It is remarkable that, when St. Paul reflects on all that happened in the life of Jesus Christ, his greatest wonder and admiration are reserved, not so much for the miracles Our Lord did, but for the humility and obedience which He showed during His life and particularly in His sufferings and death. We all know what St. Paul wrote in his letter to the Philippians: Jesus, although He was God, humbled Himself to become human; He was obedient all His life and was obedient until He died, even when His death was the humiliating one of execution on a cross. (cf. Phil 2:8).

Sisters, our vocation is not only to serve the poor, but also we are invited by God to be like Our Lord, through the experience of being obedient until our deaths. We, like Our Lord, must learn obedience, and that at times will cause us suffering.

However, it is our obedience that will make our work for the needy and the poor fruitful. The author of the letter to the Hebrews says that, because Our Lord was obedient, *"He became the source of eternal salvation"* (Heb 5:9) for others. So, too, with us: if we are truly obedient, our lives, wherever they are lived, will be a source of joy and peace to others.

I often think of Pope John XXIII. When he was appointed bishop, he took as his motto: *"Obedience and Peace."* It was an extraordinary choice for a bishop. Then the Pope sent him as Nuncio to Bulgaria where there were very few Catholics. Archbishop Roncalli, as he then was, had not much work to do, and the Pope left him there for ten years. He tells us in his writings that he was tempted many times to ask for a change, but that he always decided not to do so, after he had meditated on his motto, *"Obedience and Peace."* Because Archbishop Roncalli *"learned obedience through what he suffered,"* (Heb 5:8) he would later become a source of joy, peace and confidence, not only to the Church, but to millions of other people who do not share our faith.

So, my dear Sisters, may God, through the intercession of Our Lady, St. Vincent and St. Louise, strengthen us to live lives of obedience, so that we can be a source of strength and peace to others. In St. Vincent's words, spoken at a conference, I say to you: *"With all my heart I beseech Our Lord Jesus Christ . . . to implant in your hearts a true desire for perfect obedience, the true spirit of obedience which He Himself possessed . . . . I implore the Eternal Father by the Son and the Son by His holy Mother, and the whole Blessed Trinity."* (Conf. Eng. ed., 2 Feb. 1647, p. 273).

Lenten Letter—Holiness and Humility

10 February 1987   To Each Confrere

My dear Confrere,

May the grace of Our Lord Jesus Christ be with us forever!

Perhaps you have already heard the news that the Holy Father has graciously accepted an invitation from us to celebrate a Mass in St. Peter's Basilica on Sunday, 27 September, to commemorate the two hundred fiftieth anniversary of the Canonization of St. Vincent. It was on Trinity Sunday, 16 June 1737, that Pope Clement XII declared Vincent de Paul to be a Saint. If every canonization is, as Pope Paul VI remarked, a celebration of holiness, then our anniversary celebration of St. Vincent's canonization must be seen principally as the celebration of his personal holiness. The point cannot be too often made that, the forest of charitable works that grew up around St. Vincent in his lifetime and that still cluster around his name today, are there because of his personal holiness. In one of his conferences St. Vincent asked himself the question: *"What is holiness?"* He answered it himself, saying: *"It is the cutting off and the withdrawing from earthly things and, at the same time, an affection for God and union with His Divine Will."* (Coste XII, Fr. ed., p. 300). All of us have met living incarnations of that definition. Let me, however, pass on to you an observation of a modern Anglican poet who wrote: *"I have met in my life two persons, one a man, the other a woman, who convinced me that they were persons of sanctity. Utterly different in character, upbringing and interests as they were, their effect upon me was the same. In their presence I felt myself to be ten times as nice, ten times as intelligent, ten times as good-looking as I really am."* (D.W.H. Auden).

Would a meeting with St. Vincent in the final years of his life produce such an effect on us? I feel quite certain it would. To begin with, his personal holiness would make him accept us fully for what we are, and undoubtedly his own profound and living conviction about the importance of humility in his own life would cause him to look up to, rather than to look down on, us. It is so in the pages of the Gospel. The Samaritan woman, the woman taken in adultery, the good thief and so many others who, for a variety of reasons felt themselves to be at the bottom of life's ladder, could feel fully accepted and valued when they were in the presence of Jesus Christ, Who was humble of heart. It is this humility of heart that opens windows onto God's world and allows the light of His holiness and the warmth of His love, which is in our hearts through Baptism, to stream into the dark world of sin and infidelity.

It is holiness and humility that are at the heart of all evangelization. Evangelization is something greater than a transmission of the good news about the Kingdom of God. Evangelization is an event by which something of the holiness of Christ is appropriated by and passes through the one who evangelizes. We think of evangelization as being a work *ad extra*, directed to others. That is so. Let us, however, never forget that evangelization is also a work *ad intra*. While thinking about our *Lines of action* that will make our evangelization of the poor more effective, let us not neglect the acres of territory in our own hearts where the Gospel of Christ has yet to be preached, those desert areas of our hearts which have yet to be touched by the holiness of Christ.

Let me make one practical and simple suggestion to you this Lent and for this year when we are honoring in a special way the holiness of St. Vincent. Our Congregation could be said to have been founded on the experience of a simple confession in Folleville in 1617. The Sacrament of Penance has, since then, been a very marked feature of our preaching, particularly during our popular missions. On the landscape of our personal lives, is the Sacrament of Penance and Reconciliation a prominent and regular feature? Ask not what you are getting from the Sacrament of Penance; rather ask, what does Christ, the Holy One of God, wish to give you. There is a special efficacy and power in the word of Christ, spoken to us in the Sacrament of Penance, that helps us to shed our false illusions about ourselves and become more *"alive with a life that looks towards God through Christ Jesus."* (Rom 6:11). The truth is that Jesus Christ wishes to make us not only feel ten times holier than we are but really make us so.

Sometime after Easter I will be in touch with you again, when I will send you a document on the unity of our Congregation. It is the fruit of a study made by the General Council on the subject. Meantime I ask

Mary, the holy Mother of God, to pray that through our Lenten obser-
vances and reflection on the sufferings and death of Her Son, we may
be allowed, even now, to share a little more in the glory of His
Resurrection. In His love I remain, your devoted confrere.

True Dialogue

20 February 1987   Rome, Italy

My dear Sisters,

For those of us who travel around the world, visiting our missionaries
and Sisters, the first reading of today's Mass is a constant topic for
meditation. How often do I not find myself reflecting on the first
sentence of today's reading and saying to myself that it would be
wonderful if we could get back to the situation when, as the author of
Genesis states: *"The whole world spoke the same language, using the
same words."* (Gn 11:1).

Certainly communication would be easier, but how much easier? I
knew two priests in my own province who were brothers. They were
both very good priests, but very different in temperament and character.
When they used to meet each other—and it was not very often—they
would usually start to argue over some opinion or other. One of these
brothers used to say to us that the only thing that the two of them could
agree upon was the Creed. They were of the same family, belonged to
the same Community and spoke the same language. Yet for all that,
communication between them seemed to have been difficult.

So language is not the only barrier which prevents us from understanding and communicating with each other. Important as language is,
it is not the only means we use to transmit the thoughts of our minds.
Before we can speak effectively with our tongues to our communities,
we must speak to them with our hearts. Before we open our mouths to
speak to our communities, we must first open our hearts to them. Our
Lord has said that *"out of the abundance of the heart, the mouth
speaks."* (Lk 6:45). The hearts we must open to our communities must
be pure hearts. That is why in prayer and through the Sacraments,
through the Sacrament of Penance particularly, we must allow the Lord

to cleanse our hearts and to purify our motives of all that we say and do. That is why, too, we must often ask God with the psalmist *"to set a guard over my mouth, O Lord; keep watch over the door of my lips."* (Ps 141:3).

It is not difference of language that makes communication difficult within the Community. It is the diversity of character, of temperament, of experience, of upbringing, which confuses our communication with each other, and it is that confusion which causes tension among us. St. Vincent was realistic enough to know that within our communities all tension could not be eliminated. He did, however, recognize that the charity of Christ, which presses us, can be a strong force in helping us to live with tension. Furthermore, while we cannot change our temperament and cannot eradicate totally our weaknesses, we can often stop and ask ourselves if there is anything in our manner of living, in our manner of acting, in our manner of exercising authority which is an unnecessary source of tension to those with whom we live. While being conscious of your responsibilities as Sister Servants to lead your Sisters along the road of continual conversion, reflect from time to time on that prayer which, no doubt, you have seen: *"Grant me, O Lord, the courage to change the things I can change, the patience to accept the things which I cannot change, and the wisdom to see the difference."*

Before the experience of Babel, it would seem people were able to dialogue easily. I wonder, was it as easy as the author of Genesis suggests? It is one thing to use the same language in speaking to a person; it is another to really dialogue with a person. It is Vatican Council II that emphasized the importance of true dialogue in our communities. True dialogue should characterize all our communities. As Sister Servants, the gift and grace of being able to dialogue with your community is an important one. To dialogue is to invite others to speak of what the Holy Spirit has communicated to them and, at the same time, to genuinely welcome what the Spirit may have said to them. To dialogue is to humbly offer others what the Spirit has given to us. The key to all dialogue is acceptance, acceptance on the part of the Superior and acceptance on the part of the community of the decisions made by the Superior. Where there is true dialogue, there will be a life of communion. Where there is true dialogue, there will be an authentic missionary community. When a Sister Servant has succeeded in creating good dialogue, she will have gone a long way in fulfilling her essential function as Sister Servant. That essential function, according to the Directives, is, and I quote: *"to work for union among the Sisters and to foster the growth of charity."* (Directives Section: *The life of Charity*). As Pope Paul VI wrote in his first encyclical: *"Dialogue is a way of making spiritual contact. In a dialogue well conducted, truth is wedded to charity and understanding to love."* (*Ecclesiam Suam*, §81-82).

May He Who is love itself, give to us all, through the intercession of His Mother and of our Founders, the grace to speak the same language that is spoken in Heaven, the language of love.

Current of Change in the Church

23 March 1987   Amiens, France

My dear Sisters,

The name of this great city of Amiens evokes childhood memories for me. It was not that I visited this city as a child, but rather that this city gave its name to a small street in Dublin, the capital of my country. In that small street was located a rather imposing railway station which was the terminus for trains coming from the North of Ireland. When I was a child, Amiens conjured up in my mind excitement and adventure, for it was one of the simple joys of my childhood to be brought to the capital for a day, and it was in the station of Amiens Street that I got my first impression of our capital city.

What child is not impressed by its capital city? There is much evidence in the Gospels that Jesus Christ was not an exception. His parents would have brought Him to Jerusalem every year, and undoubtedly Our Lord's love for the Holy City would have developed during those early years of His life on earth.

Amiens Street still remains in the city of Dublin, but they have changed the name of the Station to that of a patriot. For me, however, the railway station will always remain Amiens Street Station.

Now that I have seen bigger railway stations in many other cities of the world, the railway station that was such a colossal place to me as a boy seems relatively small and insignificant. I now see the railway station of my youth in perspective. That suggests a little point for reflection, namely, the importance of seeing all things in perspective. The Christian is invited to see everything in the perspective of eternity. The reward for serving the poor is, as Our Lord reminds us in chapter twenty-five of St. Matthew's Gospel, an eternity of happiness, while the penalty for neglecting the poor in this life is an eternity of misery and unhappiness. Certainly the builders of your great Cathedral here in Amiens were able, if we are to judge from the scenes of the Bible represented in stone, to see things in perspective.

When one reflects on it, we would have much more peace in our lives and much less tension, if we could place our daily difficulties in proper perspective. Think of some of the incidents and people that used to annoy you in Community fifteen or twenty years ago, and ask yourself how you feel about them today. Probably you feel a little ashamed about some of your reactions ten or fifteen years ago. The annoyances do not seem quite as great now as they did then. Why? Because you see them in a better and clearer perspective. So may God give us the grace to keep putting all things in perspective. We will do that with more assurance, if through meditation and prayer we try to see things through the eyes and mind of Jesus Christ.

When I return to the Amiens Street Station of my youth, I feel a little sad to see how certain things have changed. Perhaps more than any other generation of people, we have had to live with the idea and the reality of change. The current of change has also touched our two Communities. For some, the current has caused such a shock that they seem paralyzed by the experience. For others the current of change has given new force and energy to the Community. Perhaps all of us are wondering what will be the long-term effects of this current of change which has touched all our lives, particularly during the past two decades.

As we look forward to the future, there are some attitudes of mind which I believe it important to adopt. First, let us acknowledge it is God who has released this current of change into the Church. He, as St. Vincent frequently liked to say, does all things according to His wise

Providence. In adopting that attitude we are not being asked to admit that every change that has been made is for the better. Some changes that have been made may have to be remade. Human error and imperfection exist even in a Divine institution.

Second, it is important that we realize that we live in two cities, the city of God and the city of man. We must be sensitive to the claims and needs of both. With our limited vision it is too easy for us to accept as absolute the standards of the city of man. *"Be not conformed to the pattern of this world,"* (Rom 12:2) St. Paul exhorts us. In his letter to the Ephesians, he reminds his readers that *"There must be a renewal in the inner life of your minds."* (Eph 4:23) The city of Man must not be allowed to dictate all policy for the city of God.

Lastly, try, my dear Sisters, to be a sign of hope. Hope can defeat such discouraging phenomena as scarcity of vocations, closure of houses, a rising median age. The vocation of a Daughter of Charity is in itself an expression of hope, for a Daughter of Charity by her life gives hope to the poor by lifting up their hearts. You will draw hope, my dear Sisters, as St. Louise did, from the contemplation of Our Lord on the Cross. A Daughter of Charity can make her own the sentiments of St. Vincent who wrote: *". . . where shall we hide ourselves at the sight of so much kindness from God? We shall place ourselves in the wounds of Our Lord . . . "* (Coste II, Eng. ed., ltr. 475, p. 119).

Not Afraid, Just Ashamed

25 March 1987   Paris, Mother House

Mother Duzan, Father Lloret and my dear Sisters,

An English Catholic lady, who was a poet, wrote at the beginning of this century a short poem in which she imagined that the end of time had come. The hour for the general judgment had struck, and all humanity was gathered together in readiness for the enactment of that scene which is recorded in chapter twenty-five of St. Matthew's Gospel. The Son of Man is about to come to separate the good from the evil, the just from the unjust, those who cared for the poor from those who did not. A moment before the Great Judge arrives we learn that there were people on other planets and that before the first sentence is passed, each planet will be called upon to tell the story of how God dealt with it. We listen to several other planets as they tell their story, and then it is our turn to speak, the turn of the tiny planet earth. We begin with those great phrases of our Creed: *"I believe in one God . . . . God from God, light from light . . . through whom all things were made."* These resounding phrases pass, and then the stupendous truth is enunciated to the other planets, *"Who for us men and for our salvation came down from heaven and was incarnate of the Holy Spirit and born of the Virgin Mary . . . "* There is an awesome silence among the people of the other planets, for God has not dealt thus with them. We, of the planet earth, however, cannot hold our heads high for long, as we go on to tell the tragic story of how the Word of God came to His own people, as St. John wrote, *"but His own received Him not."* (Jn 1:11). Our story has a happy ending as we go on to recount the Resurrection, the sending of the Holy Spirit, the gift of the Eucharist and the other Sacraments, as well as the kind gesture by which the Eternal Word of God left His Mother to us to be also ours as we make our way back to Him, *"mourning and weeping in this valley of tears."*

At the end of our account of God's dealings with us, our sentiments would be ones of honor mixed with shame. We would feel honored by the intense personal love shown to us by God, and shame that we had responded so feebly and so ungenerously to such love. Such mixed sentiments are often ours in moments of deep reflection. I often think of a Daughter of Charity who was dying and who was asked if she was afraid. She replied: *"No, I am not afraid. I just feel ashamed."* The Sister could only think of the unmeasured personal love God had shown her during her lifetime, and the very measured and half-hearted response she had given to God's loving invitations. *"No, not afraid, just ashamed."*

This Renovation Day is a day neither for fear nor for shame. For today God has given you the strength to respond with a *yes* to His invitation to love Him as a young bride might her husband. Renovation Day is the day when our Prodigal Father runs to us, clasps us in His arms and kisses us tenderly. (cf. Lk 15:20). It is the day when we once again ask our loving Father to take us at our word and to make us servants in His house, and servants, too, of His poor.

For many Sisters this Renovation Day is the latest in a long series of such days that stretch back through the years. Perhaps that thought is a little disconcerting, bringing a little blush of shame to your cheeks. There have been so many new beginnings and such little progress made on the road of holiness. Do not be disheartened. The truth is that there are immense deposits of love within your heart. Does not St. Paul assure us that *"the love of God has been poured into our hearts by the Holy Spirit Who has been given to us?"* (Rom 5:5). Just as the earth unfailingly brings forth each year a new harvest of fruits, so, too, does your heart bring forth those fruits of the Spirit of which St. Paul speaks: *"love, joy, peace, patience, kindness, goodness, forbearance, gentleness and self-control."* (Gal 5:22). It is an annual miracle that the dark earth can yield up such riches year after year to delight the sight and taste of humanity. Renovation Day is no less a miracle, when so many silent and hidden hearts of Sisters bring forth fruits of tenderness and love to console and delight so many thousands of the world's poor. Your vows, my dear Sisters, are a way of living. More importantly, they are a way of loving. At first sight your vows may seem limiting rather than liberating. But your own experience will testify that your vows are something that must be felt as limiting before they become liberating. Your vows follow that law of Christ Who said that we must lose our lives if we wish to find them. The cheerful acceptance of the limitations, at times very painful, which chastity, poverty, obedience and service of the poor impose on you, must be seen as the condition of liberating the energies of love that lie hidden in the depths of your hearts.

A secularized society will tend to concentrate its sight on the limiting, rather than on the liberating, effects of your vows. Neither must we be surprised if in a secularized society many people do not understand the meaning of the consecrated life nor see its value. For that reason it is important that we do not allow society to impose all its standards on us. A vowed life is a different life, and the difference comes from the mind and lifestyle of Jesus Christ Himself. Be convinced that it is not society but Jesus Christ Who gives value to your consecrated lives. It is He Who takes the little drop of water, which is your life, and places it in the chalice which bears the rich wine of His life and death, and transforms all into an offering for the glory of God and the salvation of the world.

Were we to discover at the end of time that there were people on other planets, there is one line in the psalms which would spring to our lips, and which would be taken up by all the peoples of the universe, after we had finished telling the story of the Incarnation and of all that followed upon it. The psalmist exclaimed: *"God has not dealt thus with every nation."* (Ps 147:20). His words must find an echo in the heart of every Daughter of Charity this morning, for to give oneself to God through your four vows is a privileged way of responding to the love God has shown in the Incarnation. Yes, indeed, *"God has not dealt thus with every nation."* (Ibid.). To the psalmist's exclamation let me add a few sentences from a letter of St. Vincent, written to one of his priests. The sentiments are particularly appropriate on this happy day of Renovation: *"Her (the Church) great need is evangelical men who work to purge, enlighten and unite her to her Divine Spouse . . . .let us labor at that with all our might, confident that Our Lord, Who has called us to His manner of life, will give us a greater share in His Spirit and, in the end, in His glory."* (Coste III, Eng. ed., ltr. 960, p. 204-205).

Golden Jubilee of Vincentians

23 June 1987   Chicago, Illinois

My dear Confreres,

When Father James Richardson was Superior General, he introduced the custom of writing to Confreres and Brothers who were celebrating the Golden Jubilee of their vocation to the Community or of their priesthood. We have often remarked in the Curia how much Confreres appreciate receiving a short letter of congratulations on their Jubilee from the Superior General. Many of the Confreres who receive these letters of good wishes, of greetings and congratulations, reply with letters that are invariably a joy to read, so full are they of appreciation and gratitude to the Congregation for what it has meant and done for them. Invariably these letters end with the expression of hope that the Lord will continue to support them until, in Cardinal Newman's words: *"the shadows lengthen and the evening comes and the busy world is hushed and the fever of life is over, and our work is done."*

I have often wished I could publish for the Congregation some of these letters, for they are vibrant with humble gratitude to God and to the Community. Living among an angry generation, we have more need than we realize for the refreshing breeze of thanksgiving during the long hot summers of angry protest that we have all experienced. Authentic thanksgiving is always born of humble wonder. It is the sort of loving, humble wonder of Jeremiah who, in trying to respond to his vocation, could only exclaim: *"Ah, Lord God, I know not how to speak. I am too young. But the Lord answered me: 'Say not, I am too young.'"* (Jer 1:6-7). It is not that protest, wonder and thanksgiving cannot live in harmony together. It was G.K. Chesterton who wrote: *"The voice of the rebels and prophets recommending discontent, should, as I have said, sound now and then suddenly like a trumpet, but the voices of the saints and sages, recommending contentment, should sound unceasingly, like the sea."*

Even if the hearts of our Jubilarians today are full of contentment, they would be hesitant to number themselves among the saints and sages of the Congregation or of the Province. Their sentiments are similar to those of St. Vincent which he expressed to his Community when he was seventy years of age and had just passed the Golden Jubilee of his Ordination:

All our life is but a moment which flies away and disappears quickly. Alas, the seventy years of my life which I have passed, seem to me but a dream and a moment. Nothing remains of them but regret for having so badly employed this time. Let us think of the dissatisfaction we will have at our deaths if we do not use this time to be merciful. Let us then be merciful, my brothers, and let us exercise mercy towards all in a way that we will never find a poor man without consoling him, if we can, nor an uninstructed man without teaching him in a few words those things which it is necessary to believe and which he must do for his salvation. O Savior, do not permit that we abuse our vocation. Do not take away from this Company the spirit of mercy, because what would become of us if You should withdraw Your mercy from it? Give us, then, that mercy along with the spirit of gentleness and humility. (Coste XI, Fr. ed., p. 342).

Is it true that as we advance in years in the Congregation, we feel more keenly the need of God's mercy? Not a few priests feel after their middle years that they are going to appear before God with empty hands and the thought can be frightening. For us in the Congregation it is consoling to think that the very last sentiment expressed by St. Vincent in our Common Rules is that *"we must get it firmly into our heads that when we have carried out all we have been asked to do, we should, following Christ's advice, say to ourselves that we are useless servants . . . "* (CR 12,14). To have the experience of feeling oneself a thoroughly unprofitable servant is a great grace because of it is born that attitude of mind which for St. Vincent was the kernel of his spiritual life: humility. *"If a person has this humility,"* writes St. Vincent, *"everything good will come along with it. If he does not have it, he will lose any good he may have and will always be anxious and worried."* (CR II, 7).

When our Jubilarians were ordained twenty-five or fifty years ago, the rite of ordination was different from that of today. Among the final words which the ordaining Bishop, according to the old rite, addressed to the newly ordained priest were those words of Our Lord to which we have just listened in the Gospel: *"I will not now call you servants, but friends."* (Jn 15:15). Today we speak much about ministry, old ministries and new ministries; ministry means service. Being a servant is a key concept in any theology of the priesthood, as it must be for any person baptized into Christ Jesus. But at its deepest level, the priesthood is friendship. To share in the pastoral priesthood of Christ is to share in a special way in the friendship of Jesus Christ. The initiative for that friendship was taken personally by Jesus Christ: *"I will not now call you servants but friends . . . .You have not chosen Me, but I have chosen you. Go forth and bear fruit."* (Ibid. vv. 15-16). Of all the possible failures in my priesthood, perhaps the greatest is to question the reality or the sincerity of Jesus Christ's willingness to share His life with me, a fragile priest of His own choosing, to question the reality and sincerity of His invitation to me to share my life with His. I could pray for no more perfect gift for our Jubilarians than that of giving, not just a notional but a real assent to Our Lord when He addresses them today, as He did on their ordination day: *"I will not now call you servants, but friends . . . .You have not chosen Me, but I have chosen you.* " (Ibid.).

In the context of this Eucharist, let me thank our Jubilarians for the work they have done for the Congregation and for this Province. May they continue to hear the word of God and, like Mary, the Mother of God and of us all, keep it in their hearts. May they, like Mary, continue to nourish the Body of Christ, which is the Church, and may she, when their work is done, show unto them the blessed fruit of her womb, Jesus.

Meantime, to each of the Jubilarians I address these words which St. Vincent himself wrote to a priest: *"Remain steadfastly in your state and 'walk in the vocation to which you are called'* . . . (Eph 4:1) *and 'do not swerve either to the right or to the left.'* (2 Cor 34:2). *You can be sure that your vocation will bring about your sanctification and, in the end, your glorification."* (Coste III, Eng. ed., ltr. 931, p. 174).

Challenges Facing Us

26 June 1987   Chicago, Illinois

A few years ago, when I was flying to Australia in a plane belonging to Qantas Airlines, I had much time to study a map of the world with which the company had provided their passengers. For one who had often heard English and Irish people refer to Australia as 'down under,' it struck me forcefully that on the map the Australian continent was placed firmly in the center of the world's land masses. To the left were Asia and Europe and to the right were the Americas. I said to myself, *"I have never seen the world like that before."* As a European my eye had been trained to see Europe at the center of the world with the Americas to the left, Asia to the right and Australia down under. After a time on the plane journey to Australia, I realized that the airline Qantas was an Australian company and that naturally Australians would put their continent on center stage. Were I to fly with an American company, I would find the Americas in the center of the map with Europe and Asia in the wings. It is perfectly understandable and to a point very reasonable. One starts a journey from where one is, though I did hear of a farmer in my own country who, being asked by a traveler for some road directions, began by saying: *"Well, if I were going to where you are going, I would not start from here . . . ."*

We must, however, start from where we are and move forward. That is what you have been doing here during this week. You have been looking at yourselves and where you are, and you have been planning, or at least trying to see the way ahead into America's heartland. Today you invite me to speak to you and, to quote from a letter that Paul Golden wrote to me, he interprets your wishes as follows: *"We felt it important to end our week together by offering the Confreres a global perspective rather than focusing solely on our little provincial world."*

Now, I feel that the Confreres of your province, who have participated in the last General Assembly, have already, by their contributions to this morning's program, lifted your sights above your provincial world. One of the great values of a General Assembly is to do just that. If the delegates bring to a General Assembly an open and receptive mind, it can be an immensely educative experience for them. One's land masses are moved around. One's province ceases to be the center of the Congregation. At a General Assembly we are forcefully reminded that St. Vincent and his Congregation are for all seasons and for all continents. The spirit of St. Vincent cannot be encapsulated in any one culture. It is true that we must try to give expression to St. Vincent's charism in the context of the culture in which we live, but we do well to reflect from time to time on the fact that our Congregation girdles the globe. I choose the verb carefully, for it suggests those spiritual links that bind together Confreres from north and south and east and west, welding them into one body, one spirit in Christ.

You have asked me for some reflections on, to quote Paul Golden, *"trends in the Congregation"* and *"challenges we face."* Looking at the Congregation in the world, it can be said that it has achieved *"a greater closeness to the world of the poor, that is, to the people themselves and to the environment they live in."* There can be noted, too, *"a sharper sensitivity to the unjust situations existing in a large part of the world."* There has sprung up, *"a more intense desire to concretize St. Vincent's work and his thoughts about the contents and methods of evangelization."* On the other hand, it must be recorded that in the Congregation *"there is considerable indifference in regard to our Vincentian lay movements and that there has been little interest in creating new forms of service to the clergy. There has been lacking a serious analysis of the causes of poverty, injustice and violence as well as consciousness of the need to commit ourselves to work against those evils.''* Among Confreres one can detect *"a searching for new ways of living the Gospels and preaching the good news together, as well as a desire to strengthen our communion by founding it upon common agreement concerning the content and methods of evangelizing the poor today.''* However, we must admit that in the Congregation there are many Confreres now *"who live together without knowing each other well enough, who have not time to listen to one another, and who look outside the Community for the dialogue and support which they do not find within it or to which they themselves fail to contribute.''*

How have you been reacting to what I have just said? Perhaps you are thinking that my evaluation is a highly personalized one, or perhaps somewhat familiar to you. If you think it is a too personalized view, you are, if I may respectfully suggest, mistaken and a little out of touch. If, on the other hand, you think what I have said is somewhat familiar to you, you are on the right track. For what I have offered you is not my evaluation of the Congregation, but the Congregation's evaluation of itself in the Church, an evaluation which was made by the participants of the General Assembly a year ago. What I have offered you are but a few of what I might call straight-from-the-shoulder statements that you will find in the *Lines of Action* (LA).

I could continue to highlight some of the practical challenges that the last Assembly's document contains, but let what I have taken from it serve as an aperitif which will, I hope, stimulate an appetite for those courses that the provinces, through their approval of the document, have pledged to provide, in accordance with their means and in the course of the years immediately ahead.

Besides inviting me to offer some reflections on the *Lines of Action*, Paul Golden, as your program indicates, asked me to speak, too, on the challenges facing the Congregation. In a sense there are no challenges facing the Congregation today. There are only challenges facing you and me as individuals in the Congregation. More than once in these last few years I have found myself thinking of St. Pius X who, on one occasion, speaking of his program for renewal in the Church, broke off quite suddenly when he was sharing his vision of what should be done by the Church, and said: *"Well, I suppose it all begins with me."* It is so easy for us all to project onto the Congregation or onto the province the challenges which, as individuals, we have been slow to face. Some personal challenges, of which we become aware, can be costly. We find ourselves reluctant to try them in the laboratory of personal experience, and so we pass them on as suggestions to a provincial council or a provincial commission. The challenges that face each of us as individuals in the Congregation, are many. Let me just list some of the more urgent and fundamental ones as I see them. I have already touched on some of them when I gave to the General Assembly a reflection on the state of the Congregation last year, as I saw it at the end of six years as Superior General.

There is, first, the challenge of continued conversion. It is very significant for us all that the General Assembly chose this as the first of the lines of action. *"We must move towards a conversion that will renew in each of us the spiritual experience of St. Vincent."* (LA §7). In this conversion there is inherent the challenge to incarnate in our personal lives, and in a clearly visible way, the vows we have taken.

I see a particular challenge facing us in the vow of obedience. If the Congregation is to adapt itself to the demands of its mission in the modern world, it needs a certain mobility. But how can a province be mobile, if the men themselves are not mobile, and I am not referring to means of transport! Consultation is a very necessary and useful process for discerning God's Will. Used, however, without sensitivity it can become a weapon for defending one's personal and at times selfish preferences. And so the faculty of mobility, that is intended to result from obedience, becomes atrophied. We take up entrenched positions and the advance of the province into new territory, new apostolates, is retarded or impeded.

There is a challenge, too, that comes from our vow of poverty. I doubt if there has been any period in the history of the Congregation when the word 'poor' has been so much on the lips of Confreres. The poor have certainly impinged much on our thinking and on the drawing boards of provincial projects. We go to the poor because Christ sends us to them, but it is a poor Christ who gives us that mission. There is a perennial challenge for us to close the gap between talking about the poor, even evangelizing the poor, and manifesting in our personal lives that spirit of detachment and poverty with which Jesus Christ lived His. We have spoken much in these last few years of the importance of simple life-style. It is an issue, but it is not the most profound one. The deeper one is to acquire personally the mind of Christ Jesus Who willingly became poor in His personal life that we might become rich.

Next, there is the challenge facing the Congregation of being able to speak to the poor and to all whose lives we touch, with firsthand knowledge of God. Such firsthand knowledge can only be received in deep and personal prayer. Many young people have frequently known difficulty in getting teachers or clergy to discuss, let alone answer, their most important and ultimate questions. Put more bluntly, the idea can be expressed in the words of a member of a Protestant committee that was selecting a candidate to be their minister: *"What this parish needs,"* one member said, *"is a minister who knows his God more than by hearsay."* There is the challenge, too, to promote vocations. It is not the challenge of vocation propaganda that I have in mind. Rather the challenge of letting young people see in our lives, in our houses, that we are men who, not only have a concern for the poor but who can pray together, recreate together, and submerge personal differences in the interests of the apostolate, thus presenting to the world of today, not only the image but the reality of being one body, one spirit in Christ.

The litany of challenges is unending. There remains, however, the challenge of faith, of hope and of charity. The challenge of faith which is, to quote Solzhenitsyn in his letter to the Patriarch of Moscow: *"Our readiness to be mocked publicly by ignoramuses."* The challenge of hope is no shallow invitation to be optimistic. Optimism does not go beyond the horizons of this life, while hope springs eternal. There is the challenge of not limiting our vision to the city of man, but of stretching it to that everlasting city to which we and our people are journeying. The greatest of all challenges is charity or agape. In an epoch that has seen so much discussion on celibacy, there is the daily challenge for us, both within and outside the Community, to make of our celibacy, to quote a conciliar phrase, *"a sign and a stimulus to charity."*

You will notice that the second part of the input I have been asked to present to you this morning, is entitled, *"Significant Trends in the*

Works of the Mission. " As I remarked last year to the Assembly: *"Throughout the Congregation there are notable signs of a desire to draw closer to the poor, so that as a Community we could break the bread of God's Word for them . . . .Some provinces have shown new awareness of the injustices suffered by the poor and have in a variety of ways been seeking practical and peaceful means of dismantling the structures of injustice in society. "* (Reflection on the State of the Congregation 1986).

However, it is true to say that, while Confreres have been greatly moved by the injustices suffered by the poor, many are perplexed as to how they can move from compassion to effective action in securing greater justice for the poor. One can notice in the Congregation, too, a new consciousness of the important place popular missions should hold in the apostolates of a province. There is, too, a very significant trend in some provinces to find new ways of expressing its charism of preaching the Gospel to the poor.

Let me at this point focus on an apostolate which I would like to see holding a place of greater significance in the Congregation's works. In the course of this week we have rejoiced with Confreres who have celebrated twenty-five and fifty years in the priesthood. Four days before he died, St. Vincent celebrated the Diamond Jubilee of his ordination to the priesthood. We have no way of knowing what St. Vincent's personal sentiments were on the sixtieth anniversary of his ordination to the priesthood. It is likely that they would not have been very much different from those he expressed earlier in one of his letters to a priest:

"For me, if I had known what the priesthood was when I had the temerity to enter into it, as I know it now, I would have preferred to work on the farm than give myself to such a tremendous state in life. I have said this a thousand times to the poor people of the countryside . . . and indeed the older I get, the more I am confirmed in this opinion because I discover every day how far I am from the perfection which I ought to have as a priest. " (Coste V, Fr. ed., p. 568).

However unworthy of the priesthood St. Vincent may have felt himself to be, he could not have denied that it was his participation in the pastoral priesthood of Christ that had largely enabled him to do so much for the poor. His sermon at Folleville would never have been preached had he not been a priest, nor would the charity at Châtillon-les-Dombes have been established if he had not been a priest and pastor there that August Sunday in 1617.

St. Vincent's participation in the pastoral priesthood of Christ was a constant reference point for him in the direction he gave to the dazzling panorama of his projects of charity and mercy. The Church herself makes the point clear for us in the prayer she asks us to pray over the gifts on his feast day: *"God, You gave to St. Vincent as he celebrated the Sacred Mysteries the gift of imitating what he handled; grant by the power of this sacrifice that we also may be transformed into an offering pleasing to You."*

The apostolic vitality of the Congregation will depend in large measure on the depth of appreciation which all of us in the Congregation have for the priesthood and on the intensity with which it is lived by us priests. In making that assertion I am not devaluing in any way the vocation of our Brothers in the Congregation who, because they are members of St. Vincent's Community, pursue with the priests the same end which the Spirit of God has given to the Congregation. What I do wish to say is that the lay person cannot and will not realize the full potential of his or her vocation as a lay person, if the priest is not realizing the specific potential of his.

In our *Lines of Action* we read: *"The Provinces will make creative efforts over the next six years to find those contemporary means by which our ministry on behalf of the clergy, which St. Vincent considered almost equal to that of the missions, might be revitalized."* (LA 11.2).

There is a profound challenge in those two words, *creative* and *revitalize*. The fact that in many provinces we have yielded up administrative and teaching positions to the diocesan clergy does not mean that our ministry to the clergy is at an end. Rather must it be interpreted as an invitation on the part of Divine Providence to revitalize those ministries which we still hold and create and innovate new ones. The task is all the more urgent in the light of the difficulties and doubts which are the experience of quite a number of priests today. A year ago I read an article by one of your own Bishops and it was entitled: *"Is there a NASA syndrome among today's priests?"* Archbishop Hurley of Anchorage, writing to his priests, remarked:

"From outside the National Aeronautics and Space Administration (NASA) there is much criticism; from within much introspection, soul-searching and calls for redesigns. Questions swirl around everyone: Are there basic flaws in the system? Have NASA personnel lost their common vision, their spirit of mutual support, their team work? . . . Much will depend on people within NASA itself, how true they will be personally to their high calling. So with the Catholic priesthood. At times its luster is tarnished or, because it is a countersign to the world, it is not attractive. That does not diminish its greatness. We know it is the priesthood of Jesus Christ. Its heroes and holy men, both of the past and present, remain heroes and holy men." ("Origins" 1986, vol. 16, no. 5).

The Congregation has an inbuilt power to counter the NASA syndrome among priests. It has had a long tradition of forming heroes and holy men for the diocesan priesthood. Most importantly, the Congregation itself must not succumb to the NASA syndrome. It must be alert to and receptive of the new ministries which the Spirit of God may be revealing among the priestly people. It must foster, encourage and develop in the laity those gifts which the Spirit of God has given to the baptized and confirmed for the building up of the body of Christ which is the Church.

The Congregation will respond to this challenge all the more effectively if it is convinced that, and I quote from the Council document, *Optatam Totius*: *"The wish for renewal of the whole Church in great part depends on the priestly ministry, animated by the Spirit of Christ."* (Introduction).

It was part of the creative genius of St. Vincent that he could link the movement towards the evangelization of the poor with that of the formation of the clergy. Has the Congregation in the centuries since his death tended to separate these two movements, setting them, as it were, on parallel lines—the seminary-college Confreres versus the rest? As a Congregation we should, by virtue of our charism and through reflection on the genius of our Founder, be able to fuse more effectively these two traditions for the advantage of forming laity for fuller participation in the life of the Church to which the Spirit of God is calling them today. Did such an idea, which I have just outlined, lie beneath this sentence in the letter which Pope John Paul II addressed to us in 1981, on the occasion of the fourth centenary of the birth of St. Vincent: *"Does not St. Vincent today call all priests to live their priesthood in fraternal teams, indissolubly united in prayer and the apostolate, at the same time very open to collaboration with the laity and penetrated with the meaning of their ministerial priesthood which comes from Christ for the service of the Christian community?"* (Pope John Paul II, Letter to the Superior General, 12 May 1981).

Even when the forthcoming Synod on the Laity will have provided us with fresh insights on the vocation of the baptized and its relationship to the vocation of the pastoral priesthood, there will remain for us these two questions:

"First, does the Congregation do enough, particularly in its parishes, to promote movements that are specifically Vincentian?

Second, is the Congregation in its Vincentian movements advancing towards or retreating from the world of youth today? (Reflection on the State of the Congregation, General Assembly 1986).

There is one final significant trend in the Congregation which I hope will receive a special impulse from the last General Assembly, and that is unity. Recently the General Council sent to the Provinces a document on the unity of the Congregation. It is the fruit of a prolonged reflection of the General Council on that topic. I hope the document will be read, reflected upon and discussed. The experience of the past week has certainly been an exercise in building unity within the Province. So let me at this point congratulate Father Hugh O'Donnell and his Council who fathered the idea of holding this Convocation. Let me also congratulate the commission who over a protracted period of time have organized it. I am quite sure, too, that the new Visitor has put some last minute touches to the program, and I thank him, as I thank you all, for the welcome you have given me.

Speaking of new Visitors, I recall an occasion in my own Province when a new Visitor was being installed. The patent of office was read and afterwards, at a lunch in the presence of the Provincial Council and some former Visitors, one speaker remarked that, not only had we here present today the present Visitor, but we had also in the persons of his predecessors, the past, the perfect and the pluperfect Visitors among us! I am happy to greet Father Hugh O'Donnell as the past Visitor, Father Cecil Parres as the perfect Visitor and Father Jim Fischer as the pluperfect Visitor. How can I not tell you also about my happiness in meeting Father Jim Richardson to whom the Curia in Rome, and the entire Congregation and the Daughters of Charity throughout the world, owe so much for what he did for us during the twelve years that he held the office of Superior General.

With the unity of your Province now deepened through the experience of this week, you will move with a more confident step into the many apostolates of your Province, which are all subsumed under that mission which the Congregation has by the Spirit of God received from the Church. That one mission is being lived out on all five continents of the world. We do well from time to time to reflect humbly and gratefully on the fact that the sun never sets on the Congregation. At any hour of the day there are Confreres rising to go forth openly or secretly, as in some Communist countries, to proclaim the good news of Jesus Christ, to celebrate the Eucharist and to help spiritually and corporally the poor to whom we have all been sent.

At the end of this week let us leave the last word to St. Vincent, as recorded in the celebrated conference of the 6 December 1658:

> *Let us give ourselves to God, Gentlemen, so that He may grant us the grace to stand fast. Let us hold fast for the love of God. He will be faithful to His promises. He will never abandon us as long as we remain fully obedient to Him for the fulfillment of His designs. Let us remain within the bounds of our vocation. Let us labor to become interior men. Let us do the good that presents itself to be done . . . .We are His and not our own. If He increases our work, He will also increase our strength . . . .That is what we hope for and that is what we ask of His Divine Majesty. And now let us all render Him infinite thanks for having called and chosen us for such holy functions, sanctified, as they have been, by Our Lord Himself Who first exercised them. What graces have we not reason to hope for, if we exercise them in His spirit for the glory of His Father and the salvation of souls. Amen.* (Coste XII, Fr. ed., pp. 93-94).

Independence Related to Jesus Christ

4 July 1987   Rome, Italy

My dear Sisters,

Today you celebrate Independence Day in your country. As a nation you have been celebrating it now for more than two hundred years. Independence is more in the air today than it was in 1776. Only yesterday I was reading an article in which it was stated that at the present time there are more than one hundred seventy official heads of States. In 1776 there would not have been that number. There is in the world today a great movement towards independence. Nations want to be independent and, even within nations, groups of people and regions want to be independent of central authority.

In the Church, too, one can note a movement towards greater independence. One could say that after Vatican II more autonomy was granted to the local Church. We have spoken much about decentralization in the past twenty years. Within religious Orders and Congregations also independence has been in the air. If we want proof of that, we have it in our Constitutions and in the recognition of the value of consultation in our Communities.

However much we in Community may talk about independence, it is very important that we relate it to Jesus Christ. If movements to greater freedom and independence in Communities are not rooted in Jesus Christ, some strange aberrations will appear. Jesus Christ Himself was passionately interested in independence. As an Israelite, the greatest feast in the year would have been the celebration of the Passover, which was the celebration of independence gained by the Israelite people from the Egyptians. It was during a meal celebrating independence that Our Lord left us His greatest gift, the Sacrifice of the Mass and the Eucharist. It was during that meal that He announced the winning of a new independence for those who believed in Him. The Sacrifice of the Cross was a war of independence. It was on Calvary that He overcame those mysterious forces of darkness which the human race has been battling since its original fall. They are the forces of greed, of pride, of lust, of anger, of gluttony, of envy, of sloth. In our catechisms we called them the seven deadly sins. Christ conquered them, but they still wage a sort of guerilla warfare in each one of us. We do well to recognize their presence within us, while, at the same time, we are confident that Christ has won the war for us, even if we have some battles yet to fight. Christ has won the war of independence for us and we are, to use a phrase from St. Paul, *"alive with the life that looks towards God in Christ Jesus."* (Rom 6:11).

The difference between a mature Christian and an immature one, between sanctity and mediocrity, is the ability to understand the true meaning of the independence won for us by Christ by His Cross and Resurrection. In the living of our lives we have constantly to choose between a true and a false independence. Our vows are weapons for securing independence or freedom with which Christ wants to make us free. Our vows are certainly restricting, but they are also liberating. If we wish to experience the liberating effects of our vows, we must first experience their restrictions. Live your vow of poverty with Christ and you will be free. Live your vow of chastity with Christ and you will be free. Live your vow of obedience—and this, perhaps, is the greatest paradox of all—and you will be free. What I have been saying stems from that great principle which Jesus Christ gave to His followers: *"Whoever saves his life will lose it, but whoever loses his life will save it."* (Mt 16:25).

It is Independence Day. Thanks be to God for the independence of the United States. Now for more than forty years it is the independence of the United States that has been able to guarantee independence to so many other nations in the world. For that let us rejoice and be glad. Thanks be to God for the independence which He has won for us through the life, sufferings, death and resurrection of Jesus Christ and which He continues to win for us through the celebration of the Sacrifice of the Mass. Thanks be to God for the freedom and independence that is ours through the vows. Let us be convinced that real independence will come to us through humble dependence upon God. That was the secret of Mary's freedom. She recognized that God had put down the mighty from their thrones and had given His victory to the lowly of heart. It was because of this that she could proclaim: *"My soul glorifies the Lord and my spirit rejoices in God, my Savior."*

Sense of the Transcendent

6 July 1987   Paris, France

My dear Confreres,

The personality of the liturgical week is Jacob. It is he who dominates the first reading in the Masses throughout this week. For the Israelites Jacob was one of the great heroes of their race. Along with Abraham and Isaac they numbered him among the immortals of their nation. Jacob was a founder whose dream or vision is recounted in the first reading of today's Mass. He was a founder to whom was given a promise for the future. His descendants would be numerous. They would spread out to all the points of the compass and they would bring with them a blessing for all the nations of the earth. Jacob, too, was assured that God would be with him. *"I will protect you wherever you go and bring you back to this land."* (Gn 28:15).

The lines of a great spiritual founder are to be found in the story of Jacob, even if some of his actions in the acquisition of property would lead us to believe that he held rather broad views on the subject of what moral theologians call *occult compensation*. Because Jacob was a great spiritual founder, we will find some of the lines of his history traced out also in St. Vincent. St. Vincent may not have had a dream such as Jacob had, but he was nonetheless a man of vision. Great promises about the future of his two Communities were not made to him, as far as we know, but St. Vincent's spiritual descendants are to be found today on the five continents of the world. The descendants of spiritual founders will always come back to their place of origin. *"I will bring you back to this land,"* (Ibid.) God tells Jacob. In this era more than ever, the spiritual descendants of St. Vincent come in pilgrimage to the places in France which were the theaters of his birth, growth and apostolic action. That is a healthy sign, for it reveals a desire in the hearts of Confreres *"to seek after,"* to quote Pope Paul VI, *"a genuine understanding of the original spirit, so that it can be preserved faithfully when deciding about adaptations."* (*Ecclesiae Sanctae*, §15.3).

Whatever faults of character Jacob had, he was gifted with a refined sense of the transcendent. In today's reading Jacob's sense of the transcendent is very forcefully presented. *"Then Jacob awoke from his sleep and said: 'Surely the Lord is in this place and I did not know it.' And he was afraid and said: 'How awesome is this place. This is none other than the house of God and this is the gate of heaven.'"* (Gn 28:16-17).

Were Jacob living in our world today, he might very well take us to task for allowing our sense of the transcendent to become weak. A loss of the sense of the transcendent has been one of the casualties of the years since the end of Vatican Council II. Reflecting upon the twenty-five years since the opening of Vatican II, the Synod of 1985 brought that loss to our attention. At the same time the Synod remarked on what it called *"the new hunger and thirst for the transcendent and the divine."* (Synod Report A. 1).

Our God is at once transcendent and immanent. We put much emphasis on the importance of finding God in the neighbor, in the poor, in the events of human history. We do well. At times, however, we tend to forget that He is the Lord of history, the Lord of the poor, the God Who is to be adored in His immensity, in His truth, in His goodness, in His beauty, in His love, and in His compassion. We must seek God in His transcendence and in His immanence.

When St. Vincent in our Common Rules wrote about the importance of our missions and of the work of forming the clergy, he reminded us to attend to the one without neglecting the other. That is a principle which could be applied to our reflections on the immanence and on the transcendence of God. We need to reflect in our prayer on the transcendence of God, while not neglecting reflection on the Incarnation and on the truth that what we do to one of the least of our brethren, we do to Christ, the Incarnate Word of God. The two readings of today's Mass present us with a very balanced picture. The first reading portrays the awe and the reverence of Jacob in the presence of the mystery of God, and the Gospel the nearness of the compassion of God, as He gives back life to a young girl and joy to her grieving parents.

If we fail to cultivate in ourselves the sense of transcendence in our worship, our concern with the pressing needs of our human contemporaries will be doomed to frustration. We can become so involved with human welfare that the basic justification for this involvement can fall out of view. For the Christian, radical action must always begin with radical contemplation.

The spirituality of St. Vincent is one of equilibrium. He could recognize and love the God of Abraham, Isaac and Jacob, as he saw Him on the mountain of contemplation, while he also could recognize and love God with the tenderness of a mother in the broken forms of humanity which he found in the market places of this world. St. Vincent, either in the silence of prayer or standing before a poor person, could say with the conviction of Jacob: *"This is none other than the house of God and this is the gate of heaven."* (Gn 28:17). May he obtain for us all the grace of the Church's invitatory psalm of bowing and bending low in His presence (cf. Ps 94:6) before we set out to find Him on the road from Jerusalem to Jericho.

Wrestling with God in Prayer

7 July 1987   Paris, France

My dear Sisters,

I have not had time to read any scriptural commentary on the first reading of today's Mass, the episode of Jacob's mysterious wrestling with God. It is a mysterious episode, but I would venture to say that all of us here have had a similar experience. Which of us has not wrestled with God in prayer? Which of us has not wrestled with God when some great suffering or sorrow comes to us or to those whom we know and love, or some great tragedy happens in the world? Yes, all of us have wrestled with God. Every time we say to ourselves, *'Why did this happen?'* we are wrestling with God.

When we wrestle with God, we want, like Jacob, to win, to overcome God, to be given a full explanation of events. And, as with Jacob, God refuses to make everything clear to us. You will have noticed in the reading that Jacob wanted to know the name of the person or the power he was wrestling with. And God refused to say who He was. Names were very important to the Israelite people. You will remember how, after God had created man, He gave him power to name the animals and the plants. In doing so, He was giving him power over creation. In refusing Jacob his request to know the name of the person he was wrestling with, God was telling him that he, Jacob, could not dominate God. Jacob could wrestle with God, and as a souvenir of the experience, he was given a wound in his hip.

Now the experience of prayer is a wrestling with God. When we pray, we try to enter into the mystery of God's wisdom, of His beauty, of His goodness, of His mercy, of His eternity, of His immensity, of His compassion. In prayer we wrestle with the great mystery that is God, Father, Son and Holy Spirit. And we emerge from prayer wounded by His love. The mystics of the Church speak very much of the experience of being wounded by God's love. We may not think of ourselves as great mystics, but the truth is that the more we come to know God, the more we come to love Him in Himself and in the poor, we will experience a sort of pain that comes from love. Think of any human person whom you loved greatly in life, and the memory of it causes a pain that has a certain sweetness about it. God is love, St. John tells us, and when we draw close to Him in prayer and in the accomplishment of His Will, He wounds us with His love, as He did Jacob.

St. Thomas Aquinas said on one occasion that prayer is an *"unfolding of the desires of our hearts, so that God can fulfill them."* Our hearts are full of desires; some of them are good, some are not, and some are a mixture of good and evil. In prayer we bring out from our hearts the desires that are there. We bring them into the light of God's truth and God's love. He purifies our desires in prayer and then fulfills them. However, we must first bring out from our hearts the desires that are present in them. God wrestles with us about these desires and we wrestle with Him. It can be strenuous and painful work, but in the end He fulfills our purified desires. We say, as Jesus said, *"May Your Will, O Father, be done."* (Lk 22:42).

Jacob said to God: *"I will not let you go, unless you bless me."* (Gn 32:28). And God said to Jacob: *"Why do you ask My name? And God blessed him."* (Gn 28:30). In those two phrases we find what our attitude in prayer should be. Humble perseverance, and acceptance that God is a mystery, but a mystery of wisdom and of love. Provided we are open to the Spirit, God will bless us and give us every good gift. He will wound us with His love. So, my dear Sisters, in the words of St. Vincent:

"Continue to give to God all the love of your heart, all the activity of your mind, and the work of your hands, and you can hope for great blessings from His divine goodness." (Coste, VIII, Fr. ed., p. 56).

Grace of Serenity

14 July 1987   Avila, Spain

My dear Sisters,

St. Vincent would say that it is the Providence of God that has brought it about that I should be celebrating Mass this evening in one of the many hospitals in the world where St. Vincent's Daughters are to be found. Today is the feast of St. Camillus de Lellis, and it was in 1930 that Pope Pius XI proclaimed him, along with St. John of God, patron of all who work in hospitals.

It was just two years before St. Vincent was born that St. Camillus dedicated himself to working in one of the hospitals in Rome. The hospital is still there today but it is a very different place from what it was in the sixteenth century. St. Camillus himself had no medical or nursing qualifications. When he started to work in the Roman hospital, he decided that he would do the most humble and simple tasks which would make the patients more comfortable. He brought to his work no profound skills, but as he left his own small house each day, he brought with him a heart that was centered on God and on the love which he found in Christ Jesus. Soon he was joined by a few other volunteers and in that way was born the Congregation which still lives in the Church today and which has for its apostolate the care of the sick and of the dying. St. Camillus lived to see his Congregation grow, but he himself had to carry the cross of misunderstanding, caused by some of his own confreres and by authorities outside his Community. He was living in Rome when St. Vincent visited there as a relatively young priest, and so one wonders if the two priests ever met. We do not know, but we do know that the two Saints shared the same fundamental vision, namely, that Jesus Christ lives in the poor and the suffering, and that in serving the suffering we draw very close to Christ and Christ to us.

Hospitals are very different places today from those which our

Founders knew. In Spain as in other western countries, the State is assuming more control of hospitals. More and more religious Sisters are less in evidence in hospitals of the modern State. Because the modern State commands great financial resources, hospitals can purchase equipment which would be beyond the means of a religious Community. That is a gain. But the withdrawal of Sisters from hospitals, however inevitable it may be, is a loss to the sick.

We can never forget, or should never forget, that the patients of the twentieth century are essentially no different from those of the seventeenth century. Every patient in a hospital is a displaced person, and displaced persons are lonely persons. Behind every patient's eyes there is a world of loneliness and fear. It was so in the time of our Founders and it is so today. A Daughter of Charity who is a nurse can offer her professional skills to patients, but the greatest gift which she can bring to any patient is love, assurance, understanding, tenderness and a capacity to enter into that world of fear and anxiety in which a hospital patient lives. These are gifts which she receives from the compassionate Christ with Whom she must be in daily contact through the Eucharist and reflective prayer. St. Vincent and St. Louise might be puzzled by all the science of our modern hospitals, if they were to come back today. St. Louise especially would have to revise radically all those remedies which she used to suggest to St. Vincent in his illnesses. But our Founders would not have to change a syllable of the advice which they gave on the subject of showing tenderness and love to all who were sick and suffering, particularly the poor.

To you, my very dear Sisters, who work in this hospital, St. Louise, were she addressing you tonight, would not change a word in a sentence which she wrote in a letter to a Sister who was working in a hospital in Nantes: *"My dear Sister, your great trials and mental turmoil in all this confusion do not arise so much from the uncertainty of events, opposition and conflicting reports, as from the fact that you have no one reliable to comfort you and give you advice. But, please believe me, my dear Sister, if I were in your place, I would ask God to grant me a great spirit of indifference and the realization that it is not up to us to act in this situation; rather I would ask Him to put us in the disposition to listen and to endure all that it said for or against us so that none of it troubles us." (Spiritual Writings of Louise de Marillac, ltr. 284, p. 320).*

May Mary, the Virgin Mother of God, and our Founders obtain for us the grace of being serene in all circumstances, so that we may bring to the sick and to the poor the joy, the peace and the love of Christ.

Our Lady in the Mystery of Life

18 July 1987   Segovia, Spain

My dear Sisters,

A few nights ago I was returning to our house in Avila, walking with Father Garcia. Darkness had fallen and we were passing the majestic building of the Cathedral. High up on one of its side walls I noticed two electric lights. They framed a cavity in the wall within which was a statue of the Virgin Mary with the Infant Jesus in her arms. The rest of the Cathedral building stood in comparative darkness. One could see the outline of the massive tower of the Cathedral. It was clear that the statue of the Virgin Mary was small in comparison with the massiveness of the rest of the Cathedral. Nevertheless in the darkness it was very clear that the statue of the Virgin Mary with her Child had a special place of honor in the building and that modern man had emphasized that fact by placing two electric lamps on each side of the statue so that the Virgin Mary with her Child could be seen.

Some time later I was reflecting on what I had seen as I passed along the street in the night, and I said to myself: Does not that Cathedral in the darkness with its illuminated statue of the Virgin tell us many truths about our lives and, above all, about our faith?

To begin with, the great Cathedral in its massiveness reminds us of the mystery of God, of the mystery of Christ Who lives in the Eucharist within it. The Cathedral has stood there for centuries and has looked down upon succeeding generations of people passing along the streets. For some the Cathedral has been a place of worship and still is. For others it is only a historical monument that has little or no relevance to life today. For some people God and Christ are the center of their lives; for others, God, Christ and His Church have no meaning or relevance.

Those to whom God, Christ and His Church are central to their lives, will easily recognize the special place the Virgin Mary has in the mystery of life. The fact that she is a creature means that she is small, and she herself was the first to recognize that truth. *"God has looked,"* she said, *"on the lowliness of His handmaid."* (Lk 1:48). The statue of the Virgin Mary in the wall of the Cathedral is small, but when you look up, you cannot fail to see it. So it is with us who have the gift of faith. When we raise our eyes to God and His beloved Son, the Word made flesh, we cannot miss seeing His Mother, Mary, from whom He took flesh. Her place in our lives, as in the life of her Son, is very special. For us she has been appointed Mediatrix of graces, as we make our way along the paths of our lives in the darkness of this world.

The two lights which modern man has placed on each side of the statue could suggest to us the two great truths about Our Lady which have been infallibly confirmed for us by the Popes during the past one hundred thirty years: first, the truth that Mary was conceived without sin, and second, the truth that at the end of her life on this earth she was taken body and soul into heaven. This truth we honor in the fourth glorious mystery of the Rosary.

We in the Vincentian family have a special vocation to honor the first truth, the Immaculate Conception of Our Lady. It was an honor for us that a Daughter of Charity should have been chosen to prepare the way for the infallible definition of Our Lady's Immaculate Conception in 1854. We can never forget that, nor the fact that it was one hundred fifty-seven years ago this evening that St. Catherine made her way down to the Chapel of the rue du Bac to receive the assurance from Our Lady that she greatly loved the two Communities of St. Vincent.

My dear Sisters, our vocation is not only to make the sinlessness of Mary known to others. Our vocation is not only to honor Mary in her Immaculate Conception. Our vocation is to present her to others through the goodness, the purity and the detachment that is evident in our lives. That is what she asked of St. Catherine and that is what she asks of us. In every sense of the word we must look up to Mary, so that she can guide us safely through the darkness of this world into the great Cathedral of Heaven where she will show us the blessed fruit of her womb, Jesus, Who is the light of the world.

Red and White Martyrdom

1 August 1987   Paris, France

My dear Confreres,

   On an April day in 1655 St. Vincent communicated to his Community some news about Father Francis White, one of his Confreres who was working in Scotland. Father White, or Father Le Blanc as St. Vincent knew him, was living dangerously at a time when being a Catholic in Scotland was to live dangerously. To be a Catholic priest in that country at that time was to live even more dangerously. Father Le Blanc had been working in the mountains of Scotland, but was taken prisoner along with a Jesuit Father and brought into the city of Aberdeen. The heart of St. Vincent went out to his Confrere because, as he remarked in the news that he gave the Community, there were few Catholics in that part of Scotland who would come to the defense of Father Le Blanc and encourage him to stand strong in the faith. As St. Vincent reflected on the courage of Father Le Blanc, the figure of St. John the Baptist came to his mind:

> *You know,* he said, *there are different types of martyrs. Apart from the one of whom we have just been speaking, there is another, that of mortifying incessantly our passions, and still more another type of martyrdom, which is to persevere in our vocation in the accomplishment of our duties and our practices of piety. St. John the Baptist, for having had the courage of reproaching a king for the sin of incest and adultery which he was committing, was put to death for that reason. He is honored as a martyr, although he did not die for the faith. He died rather for the defense of that virtue against which the incestuous king had sinned. It is, then, a kind of martyrdom to allow oneself to be consumed for the sake of virtue. A missionary who is thoroughly mortified and obedient, who carries out perfectly his duties and who lives according to the rules of his state, makes it clear by this sacrifice of his body and of his soul that God merits to be totally served and that He must be completely preferred to*

all the advantages and pleasures of this life. To act in such
a way is to proclaim the truths and maxims of the Gospel of
Jesus Christ, not by words but by conforming our lives to
that of Jesus Christ, and giving proof of His truth and
holiness to believers and unbelievers alike. Consequently,
to live and die in such a way is to be a martyr. (Coste XI,
Fr. ed., p. 175).

For St. Vincent, martyrdom was more than shedding one's blood for
the faith. In the language of my own country the distinction is made
between what is called *red martyrdom* and *white martyrdom.* St.
Vincent saw both red and white martyrdom in St. John the Baptist. What
white martyrs have in common with red martyrs is a deep, personal love
for Jesus Christ and His Church. *"No one,"* wrote Cardinal Newman, *"is a martyr for an opinion. It is faith that makes martyrs."*
("Discourses of Mixed Congregations," p. 182). We would do well to
ponder the Cardinal's words in the context of this Vincentian session.
It is not the opinions, it is not the conclusions of this Vincentian month,
that are of primary importance. It is the faith that each of us has in Jesus
Christ and in the particular appeal which St. Vincent so confidently
makes to us in the name of Jesus Christ. We are in no doubt about that
appeal: it is to respond to Jesus Christ by preaching Him to the poor,
by serving Him in the poor, by loving Him in the poor.

On this final day of the Vincentian month it is the red martyrdom of
St. John the Baptist which is presented to us in the Gospel. Long before
he suffered red martyrdom, St. John the Baptist had been a strong white
martyr. His austerity of life gave force to his white martyrdom, as the
Gospels testify.

Distant though St. John the Baptist may be in time from us, he is a
contemporary figure because of his prophetic stand against Herod. St.
John the Baptist may have lived in the desert, but he was not unaware
of the social conditions of his time. He was forthright in what he said
about justice. He denounced hypocrisy in high places. In a word, he
spoke with the accents of an authentic prophet. An authentic prophet
knows his place. He knows that he is only a voice and that his voice
must sometimes appear to him to be but one crying in the wilderness.
He is aware that his voice may well go unheeded. For all that he does

not lose his peace of mind. An authentic prophet is always a humble man, for he knows, as John the Baptist knew, that he was not the light but he was giving testimony to the light. (cf. Jn 1:8).

There is a difference between a social reformer and *"a prophet of the most High."* (Lk 1:76). The credentials of God's prophets are charity and personal humility. Our credentials as witnesses of the truth of Jesus Christ and His Gospel must at all times be ready and open to inspection. Charity and humility must shine out in our prophetic words and actions, as they did in St. Vincent's. The fire of anger must never be allowed to extinguish our charity and humility. It was St. Vincent himself who said that on the two or three occasions during his life, when he corrected Confreres in anger, he discovered that he failed miserably. For us today St. Vincent would underline the importance of St. Paul's ideal of always *"doing the truth in charity,"* (Eph 4:15) and I feel he might add, *"Yes, let it be done also in humility, for such was the way of John the Baptist and, more importantly, such was the way of Jesus Christ, Who yesterday, today and forever is our Way, our Truth and our life."*

Assumption of Our Lady

15 August 1987   Paris, France

Mother Duzan, Father Lloret and my dear Sisters,

One day within the last few months I was leaving this house, and while passing by the door of the chapel I was stopped by a man and his wife who had come from Sri Lanka. They had strayed into the alley leading to the chapel, and they seemed a little lost, at least to judge from the expressions on their faces. Hesitantly they asked me: *"What is this place?"* I asked them if they were Catholics, and they said *"No."* *"Are you Christians?"* *"No. We are Buddhists."* Where do I start, I said to myself, to explain to these two well-intentioned people the apparitions of Our Lady to St. Catherine.

Clearly 1830 was not the starting point. One must go back to Nazareth and to the stupendous event that took place when Mary gave her consent to God to become His Mother. After that something would have to be said about the life, death and resurrection of Jesus Christ, something, too, about the Holy Spirit, about the Church and its mission. How could one omit a word about the very prominent place Mary, the Mother of God, has held in Christian thought, and what an inspiration she has been to succeeding generations of those who believe in the divinity of Christ. Only after all that had been said could one properly situate the meaning and significance of the Chapel of the rue du Bac.

As I tried to explain very briefly to these two sincere Buddhists the mystery of the Incarnation and then the background to what happened in 1830, I became conscious of how difficult it can sometimes be to move into the mental world of people who know little or nothing of the person of Christ and His saving work. The experience was like carrying on a dialogue on a mountain with people who were far below in a valley and who were interested in knowing the best path by which they could reach the point on the mountain where I happened to be standing.

To those who have received the gift of faith is given a panoramic vision of life which is not enjoyed by those who are walking in the valleys of unbelief. Not indeed that all things are clear to the person gifted with faith. For all the certainty that faith brings to us, we still only see things, as St. Paul reminds us, *"in a dark manner."* (1 Cor 13:12).

However high we may be standing on the mountain of faith, we have not yet reached its highest peak. Throughout our lives we are engaged in climbing what the psalmist calls *"the mountain of the Lord."* (Ps 48:1). Far above the highest peak of the mountain is to be found the sanctuary of the Lord into which has entered Jesus Christ, risen from the dead, He who is, to quote the phrase of the author of the letter to the Hebrews, *"the pioneer and perfecter of our faith."* (Heb 12:2). Into that sanctuary, too, entered Mary, when the course of her life was ended, with her body, like her Son's, glorified.

Towards that sanctuary we also are making our way. There are days on our pilgrimage when we halt to rest and rejoice. Today is such a day. It is a day when we try to hear Mary's voice from a height far above us. Her message in today's gospel is one of thanksgiving and joy to us: *"My soul glorifies the Lord and my spirit rejoices in God, my Savior."* (Lk 1:46-47). In this Marian year we could perhaps give greater prominence to prayers of praise to God for Mary, and express to Mary herself greater gratitude for what she has won for us, she who is the Mediatrix of all graces.

In the volume of prayer that we address to her, do we allow begging to displace thanksgiving? True, Christian theology from earliest times has presented Mary to us as our most powerful human advocate before God. What, however, we must not forget, is that as a Mother she loves us for what we are, even before we ever breathe a prayer to her. She recognizes in each of us who have been baptized the likeness to her Son, however much we may have disfigured that likeness by personal sin. In that most frequently recited of all prayers to the Mother of God, the *"Hail Mary,"* the first half of the prayer vibrates with joy and thanksgiving, and only after that do we remind her of our weak, needy and sinful condition.

While we look up to the greater heights of God's mountain which we have yet to scale before we enter into our rest, we are encouraged by our conviction of faith that our bodies, like that of Mary, will at some future time be refashioned so that they too can rejoice *"in the courts of the Lord."* (Ps 84:11). What is still more encouraging for us is the truth emphasized by Pope John Paul II in his recent encyclical that *"the glory of serving,"* which was Mary's in her lifetime, continues to be hers today. *"Assumed into heaven,"* the Pope writes, *"she does not cease her saving service which expressed her maternal mediation."* (Redemptoris Mater, §41). That sentence of the Pope could also be taken as a summary of your vocation as Daughters of Charity. For is not your work, wherever obedience has placed you, a *"saving service"* for the poor? Are you not also by your simple, humble and loving manner of service expressing your *"maternal mediation"* for those who look to you to share with them your spiritual and material resources? If part of Mary's happiness today is still *"the glory of serving,"* then your humble serving of the poor, both inside and outside the Community, will bring her closer to you. Whether you are engaged in the direct service of the poor, or whether age, infirmity or the needs of the Community itself have removed you somewhat from direct contact with the poor, each day will bring you from God Himself and from His Mother an invitation to rise to *"the glory of serving."* There can be no authentic devotion to the Mother of God without a readiness and willingness to serve her Son at all times in the least of His brethren.

We are all pilgrims on God's mountain. Today we pilgrims are rejoicing in the light of that faith which tells us that, at the end of her pilgrimage on earth, Mary, the humble Virgin of Nazareth, was honored by God in a unique way. Today we can hear her voice, wafted down into the valleys of this world by the breath of the Holy Spirit, giving us instructions about climbing the mountain of the Lord, *"Do whatever He tells you."* (Jn 2:5). Today we rejoice in the truth that Mary's exaltation has not diminished, but rather enhanced her *"glory of serving."*

Today, too, we rejoice as a Community in honoring Mother Duzan on her feast day. In her many visits to the Provinces, far and near, she must have gained in these last two years new insights into what it means to be a pilgrim. May the Lord continue to enlighten and strengthen you, Mother, and may He continue to guide your steps into the way of peace. A very happy feast day, Mother.

Pilgrimage to Knock

12 September 1987   Knock, Ireland

My dear Friends of Jesus Christ,

How many pilgrimages did Mary, the Mother of God, make, I wonder, during her lifetime? One can easily count twelve for certain, for does not St. Luke in his Gospel refer to that annual pilgrimage which she used to make with her husband, Joseph, and her Child, Jesus, to Jerusalem? *"Now His parents,"* writes St. Luke, *"went to Jerusalem every year at the feast of the Passover. And when Jesus was twelve years old, they went up according to custom."* (Lk 2:41-42). Mary herself would seem to have kept up that custom of going every year on pilgrimage to Jerusalem, for twenty or twenty-one years later we know that she was in Jerusalem for the feast of the Passover. Presumably she had made the pilgrimage to Jerusalem from her home town of Nazareth. That was the pilgrimage which ended in tragedy, for it was when she was in Jerusalem that year that she learned of the arrest of her Son, and some hours afterwards watched Him put to death on a cross outside the walls of the city. As had happened twenty years previously, she lost her Son for three days, but was to find Him again in the glory of the Resurrection.

Mary's pilgrimage to Jerusalem that year would seem to have been prolonged, for we know that seven weeks later she was still in Jerusalem. With her Son's Apostles she was waiting to be endued once more with power from on high through the coming of the Holy Spirit on Pentecost Day. That was the day when a new sort of pilgrimage was inaugurated. The starting point of the pilgrimage was Jerusalem and its destination was the ends of the earth. From Jerusalem the Apostles set out, making their way through Judea and Samaria, as they had been asked to do by Jesus, and beyond that to the most distant nations of the world.

That particular pilgrimage is not over yet. It has not yet reached its destination. More importantly, you and I are making that pilgrimage and, as the Pope some months ago reminded the Church in his Encyclical on Our Lady (*Redemptoris Mater*), Mary, the Mother of God, is accompanying us on that pilgrimage. From her place in heaven she is, in the words of the Preface for her feast of the Assumption *"a sign of hope and comfort for the Christian people on their pilgrim way."*

Within this great pilgrimage which the Church is making to the nations of the world, with Mary as a sign of hope and comfort, we make our little pilgrimages, as we are doing here today in Knock. In her lifetime Mary made pilgrimages other than those she made to Jerusalem. What about that pilgrimage she made to her cousin Elizabeth? It was not a pilgrimage which was made in the comfort of a plane or an air-conditioned bus. On foot or in caravan she had to make her way across what St. Luke calls *"the hill country of Judea,"* (Lk 1:39) some ninety miles of rough, stony terrain. When we make pilgrimages, we pray along the way. All of us pilgrims here today have already prayed the rosary. Of the prayers Mary prayed on that pilgrimage, at least one of them is known to us and it can serve as a hint to all pilgrims. Mary's *Magnificat* is the prayer of a pilgrim at the end of a pilgrimage, and it is a prayer of thanksgiving. In these days when we hear and read so much about protest and experience so many forms of anger, could we not make a little more room in our conversations with God to express our gratitude for so much that He has given to the world, to the Church, and to ourselves? That is what Mary did at the end of her pilgrimage to the home of Elizabeth. Mary, the pilgrim of Nazareth, through her prayer of thanksgiving, suggests to us that we be prophets of thanksgiving, and St. Vincent de Paul reminds us that the crime of all crimes is ingratitude. (cf. Coste III, Eng. ed., ltr. 850, p. 42).

The pilgrimage of Mary to her cousin Elizabeth was one also of service. Can you imagine Mary in the home of Elizabeth doing nothing to help Elizabeth as she approached the term of her pregnancy? A pilgrimage for Mary did not mean just a journey with prayers recited all along the way and a hymn of thanksgiving at the destination. It meant also lending a helping hand to a person in need. A pilgrimage for Mary was an experience of not only intensifying her union with God, but also of drawing closer to those in need.

Our Vincentian pilgrimage to this sanctuary of Mary here in Knock will bring us closer to God and to His Mother. It will also bring us all closer to those people who are Jesus Christ's special friends, the needy, the poor, the suffering. A pilgrimage like ours is not a one-day-in-the-year event. For St. Vincent de Paul there was a pilgrimage to be made, not once a year but every day in the year. For St. Vincent de Paul the features of any poor, sick or suffering person were a sanctuary in which Jesus Christ was to be found. No day would pass but he would meet the needy and the poor. To these sanctuaries, where Christ in the poor was to be found, pilgrimages had to be organized. One did not go on these pilgrimages emptyhanded. One brought along that sort of offering of practical assistance which the Good Samaritan provided for the wounded and distressed man whom he found lying on the road, as he went down from Jerusalem to Jericho. St. Vincent de Paul's pilgrimages to the poor are still being organized. The activities of the Ladies of Charity, of the Daughters of Charity, of the Society of St. Vincent de Paul, of the Vincentian priests and Brothers, are group pilgrimages to the 10,000 places in our country where Christ is to be found in the poor.

Here in Knock today in Mary's house, we who admire the practical love and the genius of St. Vincent de Paul, have met and paused so that we may renew our strength for those daily pilgrimages to the needy which we will make in the year that lies ahead. By sharing together today the Bread of Life, which is the Body of Mary's Son, we will find new vitality and new heart for bringing Christ's strength and Christ's light to the problems and the suffering that the social conditions of our country have created.

Show unto us, Pilgrim of Nazareth, the blessed fruit of your womb. O most clement, O most loving, O most sweet Virgin Mary.

Advent Letter—Restore All Things in Christ
15 November 1987   To Each Confrere

My dear Confrere,

May the grace of Our Lord Jesus Christ be with us forever!

On a few occasions over the past three years I have given some thought to writing to tell you about the work of restoration that is being carried out in the Chapel of the Mother House in Paris. The response of the Confreres to the appeal which I made for financial help in 1984 was most generous, and it can only be interpreted as an expression of the love you have for St. Vincent and for what he means to all of us. Some of you on the occasion of a visit to Paris will have seen what has been so far achieved. The work is essentially one of restoration. There have been some adaptations made in the Chapel to reconcile its original design with the ideal of facilitating fuller participation of the laity in the liturgy, in accordance with the wishes of Vatican Council II. The work has been slow, painstaking and costly, and it will be a little while yet before it is completed. Meantime, thought is being given to how the Chapel can be made more attractive as a center of devotion to St. Vincent, with special prominence being given to the apostolate of the Sacrament of Reconciliation. Can our Congregation ever forget that it owes its origin in a sense to St. Vincent's own experience of reconciling one poor peasant with God in the year 1617?

The seasons of Advent and Christmas each year serve to focus our minds afresh on the mysterious and historical coming of God into our world of human experience of suffering, joy and love. The Incarnation is God's great work of restoration. As a work of restoration it has, from

God's point of view, been costly, slow and painstaking. Its cost is not to be reckoned in the currency of silver or gold but *"with the precious Blood of Christ."* (1 Pt 1:18). The work of restoration of humankind has been slow: almost twenty centuries after the Word of God came to dwell among us, less than 20% of the world's present population acknowledges Jesus Christ to be the Divine Artist that we know Him to be. The first to acknowledge and to welcome Him into the world was the Virgin Mary of Nazareth. She became, and still is, God's primary partner in the work of the restoration of humanity, but all of us who have become through baptism adopted sons of God are called to share in the delicate work of restoring to every human being, already marred and smudged by original sin, the image and likeness of Christ, Who is for all humanity the second Adam. (cf. 1 Cor 15:45).

As a Community in the Church and as individuals in St. Vincent's Congregation, we have been commissioned by the Spirit of God to devote our energies to restoring those most damaged parts of the Body of Christ, namely, the deprived, the poor, the neglected, those who are most in need of being convinced that they have been specially created to beautify with their individual lives the temple of the living God.

At a time when so much thought is being given to defining the diversity of roles in the Church, we would do well not to lose sight of the great overall design of God, which is *"to restore all things in Christ."* (Eph 1:10). Our Lord Himself began the work of restoration by taking the form of a servant, enclosing Himself in the womb of the Virgin Mary and becoming obedient unto death, even to death on a cross. (cf. Phil 2:6-8). The beginning and the end of Christ's life on earth are enveloped in the profound mystery of humility and obedience. The ongoing work of God's restoration must then continually return to those central theological facts, be the frequent subject of our reflections in prayer and be accepted as conditions, if our own personal contributions to restoring all things in Christ are to have meaning and value. *"The only wisdom we can hope to acquire,"* wrote a modern Christian poet, *"is the wisdom of humility."* (T.S. Eliot).

The work of restoring all things in Christ is a highly delicate one. Each of us is called to be an artist of the supernatural for the people to whom by the Providence of God the Community sends us. We can only be artists of the supernatural if, to quote St. Vincent, *"Our Lord imprints His mark and character on us and gives us, so to speak, the sap of His Spirit and grace . . . being united to Him as the branches are united to the vine."* (Coste XI, Fr. ed., p. 344). In working to restore all things in Christ we are not alone. God is with us: Emmanuel. His poor also are close to us. May we never forget that the ultimate source of hope and joy for the poor lies in our sharing with them our own deep personal conviction, born of prayer, that with the birth of Christ the Kingdom of God has come; that it is, like the mustard seed, growing; and that it is a kingdom of justice, of love and of peace.

May your celebration of Christmas be a joyful one, and may you *"be transformed by the renewal of your mind, so that you may discern what is the Will of God, what is good and pleasing and perfect."* (Rom 12:2).

The Confreres and Sisters who work here in the Curia join me in sending you their warmest greetings. In the love of Our Lord I remain, your devoted confrere.

1988

Bear the Beams of God's Love

1 January 1988   Paris, France

Mother Duzan, Father Lloret and my dear Sisters,

An English Christian poet, who lived three centuries ago, wrote that
we mortals were placed on this earth for a few short years, in order, as
he said, *"to learn to bear the beams of love."* In the poet's vision of
existence God is a consuming sun, blazing from all eternity, blazing
with the fire of love. We humans are small and fragile beings who have
been called into existence to share and to participate in that intense fire
of love for which, however, we must first be prepared. If you spend a
long time in a dark room and come out suddenly to the full light of day,
your eyes blink for a time before they can absorb the light. It is so with
our experience of God's love for us. The intensity of the heat of God's
love for each of us as individuals is beyond our imagining, and the years
of our lives are given us so that we can reach that point when we can
bear the light and the full heat of God's love. Our lives on earth are a
preparation, a sort of novitiate for the experience of living in the
presence of that sun which is God. *"And God,"* wrote St. John, *"is
love."* (1 Jn 4:8).

If the few years we pass on this earth are a preparation for bearing
the beams of God's love in eternity, what other purpose had the
Incarnation but to assist us in the experience of learning to bear those
beams of love. Years after Our Lord had ascended into heaven, the
author of the letter to the Hebrews, reflecting on the personality and
work of Christ, wrote: *"He is the radiant light of God's glory."* (Heb
1:3). All that Our Lord did for the poor and the sick and the marginalized, the encouragement that He gave to the repentant thief, the pardon
He granted to Peter, were so many beams of that radiant light which
not only brought joy and peace to hundreds of people of His time, but

367

also told us so much about that radiant light and love which is the life of God.

That is why it is so important for us in our meditations never to be far from the open pages of the Gospel, for they have so much to tell us about how the beams of God's love penetrate into the darkness of this world and how we can help others to bear them.

Learning to bear the beams of God's love, as they shine through the personality of the living Christ, is the work of our lives. His experience of suffering and dying on the Cross is there to remind us that, for one who lives in a world that is enveloped by the clouds and fog of sin, the learning process will at times be a painful one. How else can we explain that mysterious cry from the Cross: *"My God, my God, why hast Thou forsaken Me?"* (Mt 27:46).

I recall many years ago hearing of a non-Catholic lady who would walk into one of our churches from time to time and move around it, looking at the Stations of the Cross, and then leave the church immediately. On a particular occasion one of our Fathers spoke to her when she was leaving the church and remarked to her that he had noticed her admiring the Stations of the Cross. *"No,"* she replied, *"it's not a question of admiring the art of the pictures. From experience I have learned that, when things have not been going well for me, I come into this church, walk round and look at those fourteen pictures on the wall, and somehow when I finish, I feel stronger to face my sufferings."* Unknown to herself, that non-Catholic lady was learning *"to bear the beams of love."*

What shall I say of her who was conceived without sin and of her experience in learning *"to bear the beams of love."* Even for her, learning to bear the beams of love was costly. The radiance of God's love shone upon her at the Annunciation and momentarily perplexed her. The Annunciation was a form of catechesis which God presented to her, first for her acceptance and then for her implementation. The beams of God's love shone upon her when for three days she lost her Son Who was occupied, as He said, *"with My Father's affairs."* (Lk 2:49). The beams of God's love bore down very strongly upon her as she watched life ebbing out of the naked body of her Son on the cross. From His dying lips she learned that the beams of God's love would pass through her to every person who through baptism would become part of that body which is the Church. Because of her privileged calling to be Mother of the Church and Mediatrix of graces until the end of time, the beams of God's love are refracted by her, as the atmosphere surrounding the earth refracts the white light of the sun into many colors.

We, like Mary, are called to bear the beams of God's love in our personal lives. The events of our lives, so inscrutable, so perplexing, so painful at times, are slowly strengthening us, if we could but see them with the eyes of faith, to look steadily one day at the open face of God, Who is a consuming fire of love.

We, like Mary, are called also to refract the beams of God's love for the poor. We are called, not to stand immobile before the mystery of so many poor, hungry, lonely, homeless, wandering people, but to break down for them through our service of them, the strong light of God's love so that they, too, can learn, as is their vocation, *"to bear the beams of God's love."*

Because we are frail and fearful humans, we draw back from exposing ourselves to the sun of God's love. The saints are those who walked out fearlessly into the sunlight of God's love and drew others after them. We lesser people tend to stay indoors and warm ourselves at the fires of our own making which, compared with the sun outside, are pathetically inadequate for us who are called to live one day *"in inaccessible light."* (1 Tim 6:16).

So, my dear Sisters, every day of this new year, every hour and minute of it, is an invitation to come out from our tents of self-preoccupation and learn, like Mary, to bear the beams of God's love. Every day of this new year, every hour and minute of it, will present itself laden with the goodness and kindness of God, our Saviour. Each day of it will bring its gilt-edged invitation delivered to us in a variety of ways. The invitation on the card is to come out into the sunshine of God's love. Coming out into the sunshine of God's love means opening ourselves to Him fully in Holy Communion, accepting the indications of His Will which He gives us through our Constitutions, our Superiors, and what He allows to happen to us in the course of our day. On each invitation card, presented personally to us each day of this new year, you will find, discreetly inscribed in the corner, R.S.V.P. Please reply. Yes, our silent God and Host awaits eagerly our reply to His invitation to learn to bear the beams of His love.

To that invitation may we reply promptly and cheerfully and never yield to discouragement in trying to bear the beams of God's love, and in sharing our experience with the poor who so often have taught us about the healing power that they find in the rays of God's love.

From the resplendence of God's light and love in which she now lives, St. Louise would still address us in 1988 in the words of a letter she wrote to a Sister in January 1647: *"At the start of this new year rededicate yourselves to His service with the fervor that you had at the beginning when you first knew what He desired of you."* (*Spiritual Writings of Louise de Marillac*, ltr. 168, p. 190).

Centenary of Philadelphia Province

24 January 1988   Philadelphia, Pennsylvania

It is the way of old men to look back and to muse on the significant events of their lives, and St. Vincent was no exception. It was only in the last decade or less of his life that we find the most frequent references to the event of the 25 January 1617.

Unlike old men, however, who often look back on the past with nostalgia, St. Vincent looked back at Folleville, not with nostalgia but with wonder and gratitude for what the grace of God had done on that particular day. Being a man who loved to share with others, St. Vincent wished that his Community would share in his wonder and his gratitude by celebrating in a special way each year the 25 January, the feast of the Conversion of St. Paul. So it is that when the 25 January comes around, we find ourselves in the Community dividing our attention between St. Paul falling off his horse on the road to Damascus and St. Vincent mounting the steps of the pulpit in the little chapel at Folleville.

It is a very significant fact that on the 17 May 1658, when he distributed to his Confreres the only work he had printed in his lifetime, the Common Rules, he spoke during the conference that evening of the experience which he had on the 25 January 1617. The 25 January was to be, above all, a day of special thanksgiving for the mercy which God had shown to him over his lifetime and also to the members of his Community.

St. Vincent's concern that this day would be a day of thanksgiving tells us much about St. Vincent's character. It is a very healthy sign of anybody's spirituality that he or she is always disposed and always wants to say *thanks*, to give thanks to God. So it was with her whom we salute as *"full of grace and conceived without sin."* Her *Magnificat* is essentially a song of thanksgiving. Thanksgiving itself is an expression of that fundamental virtue of humility. I think the measure of our gratitude to God is the measure of our humility.

This evening throughout your Province you are deepening the dimension of thanksgiving as you celebrate the Centenary of the foundation of your Province. Eternity will not be long enough to express adequately the gratitude your Province owes to God for the great deeds He has wrought through the Confreres who have gone before you, marked with the sign of faith, and for what you yourselves are now, by the grace of God, accomplishing for the building up of His Kingdom. The formation of the clergy, the mission in China and presently in Panama, the preaching of popular missions, the deepening of people's devotion to the Mother of God through the propagation of the theology of the Miraculous Medal, the pastoral care of people in parishes, your Universities which touch the lives of so many young people, what a variety of apostolates with which God has gifted your Province. As we list each one, we can only respond with the refrain of the psalmist: *"His love endures forever."* (Ps 136:1).

Centenary celebrations, however, must not be limited to casting a backward glance on the hundred years that have passed. They must give us new impetus for the future. While we are aware of St. Vincent's conviction that we must not anticipate the Providence of God or, to use his own phrase, we must not *"cut the heel of God's Providence,"* at the same time we must be equally convinced that the Providence of God is actively appealing to us now to keep moving. For are we not part of a pilgrim Church? Pilgrims do not settle down permanently in the places through which they pass. They keep moving. So must we. New highways are being opened up for us, in order to lead the people, particularly the poor, to that city whose maker and builder is God. The Province as a pilgrim group is being invited to use them. The highway toll may at first sight seem high, but if it is God Who calls us to new forms of the apostolate, will He not strengthen us with His grace and direct our steps into the way of His justice and His peace?

This evening's celebration recalls the conversion of St. Paul and the foundation of our Congregation. The first reading is the story of how one man heard God's call. God is continuing to call young men to the Province, not in the dramatic way that He did Saul of Tarsus. He is calling young men to be priests and Brothers of the Province through us. As a Province and as individuals, allow me to make this suggestion to you, that each Confrere in the Province during this Centenary year would try to leave behind him a successor in the Province, a resolution that will be backed up by daily prayer for vocations to the Community and supported, too, by the example of a life that is authentically Vincentian.

I feel sure this evening that St. Vincent would like to repeat to us what he said about the Folleville sermon to the community of St. Lazare on the 6 December 1658: *"See, I beg you, the many reasons we have for praising God . . . and the reasons, too, for kindling in our hearts love for the work of helping the poor and of doing that work wisely and well because their needs are great and God is counting on us."* (Coste XII, Fr. ed., p. 82).

My dear Confreres, I rejoice in spirit with all of you this evening. *"Let us rejoice and be glad, for this is the day which the Lord has made."* (Ps 118:24). Yes, with the Virgin Mary you can rejoice with her for the great things He has done for you. For the future of the Province can I pray a better prayer than that of St. Paul that *"with the eyes of your hearts enlightened you may know what is the hope to which He has called you."* (Eph 1:18).

Presentation of Our Lord in the Temple

2 February 1988 Rome, Italy

Mother Duzan and my dear Sisters,

St. Luke has just told us how, forty days after Our Lord had been born, Our Lady and St. Joseph went up to the Temple in Jerusalem to present Him there. It was a sort of christening celebration. It was primarily a joyful occasion and then the old man Simeon comes along and spoils everything. He is like a ghost at the feast, for he foretells suffering for Our Lord and, turning to Our Lady he says: *"And your own soul a sword shall pierce."* (Lk 2:25). There was an Irish poet who wrote: *"Lord, Thou art hard on mothers; they suffer in our coming and in our going."* The Lord was certainly hard on His own mother. She suffered in His coming. To listen to that sad forecast about her Son forty days after His birth was hard. She suffered in His going: *"There stood by the cross of Jesus, Mary, His Mother."* (Lk 19:25).

Simeon spoke of one sword. In reality there were seven, and we can count at least seven occasions when sorrow entered Our Lady's soul. There was a possible eighth sorrow, and that was living with the fear of what was to come. That can be a heavy cross. It is often more painful to sit waiting in the dentist's waiting room than to sit in the dentist's chair. What I would like to think of as Our Lady's eighth sorrow was living with the sword, Simeon's sword, hanging over her. Yet, and this is what is most admirable, that did not deter Our Lady from going on with the business of living and caring for the home in Nazareth, from following Our Lord in His preaching journeys and from making her way to the spot where He was executed. She lived with fear, but was able with the strength of God to prevent it from immobilizing her. May Mary obtain for each of us the grace of surmounting those fears which occupy a place in the hearts of every one of us and sometimes paralyze us in showing love to God and to our neighbor.

With Our Lord and with His Mother this morning some of you are completing your annual spiritual exercises. Every retreat that we make is at once an end and a beginning. St. Vincent said on one occasion that a person is never the same after a retreat: one is either better or worse. At the end of a retreat we have closed one chapter in the book of our lives, and we are opening a new one. The end of a retreat is a new beginning to our lives. We may not be taking up a new appointment at the end of our retreat, but we do resolve to draw closer to Jesus Christ in prayer. We resolve to show more love and understanding to those with whom we live in Community. We resolve to give ourselves more fully to Christ in the person of the poor. All that is definitely a new beginning.

During your retreat, you have experienced in a new and intimate way *"the goodness and tenderness"* (Ti 3:4) of Our Lord for you personally. That experience is intended to be the beginning of a new manifestation on your part of goodness and tenderness to all whose lives you touch, both inside and outside the Community. *"Goodness and tenderness"* (Ibid.): St. Louise expressed that idea in one word, *cordiality*. In her writings to the first Sisters, it was a word that she loved to use. It is for that reason I pray for all of you that God may give you the grace of cordiality. To ask for the grace of cordiality is to ask God to enable us to externalize the love that He has poured into our hearts. So, I pray, as St. Vincent once did: *"I beseech God with all my heart to animate you all with His true and holy love, to give us the infallible marks of it and to grant us the grace always to grow in it more and more so that, aided by this grace, we may be able to begin in this world what we shall do in the next, to which may the Father, Son and Holy Spirit conduct us."* (Conf. Eng. ed., 19 Sept. 1649, p. 429).

Lenten Letter—Obedience

17 February 1988   To Each Confrere

My dear Confrere,

May the grace of Our Lord Jesus Christ be with us forever!

Perhaps you have had the experience during the course of your life of acting as a guide to a non-Christian who had strayed into one of our

Churches. In any Catholic Church or Chapel the crucifix or cross holds a prominent place. How would you go about explaining the significance or the meaning of this most widely recognized of all our Christian symbols? Would you dare say to the tourist, coming from a country where the Gospel has not yet been preached, that the Man hanging on the cross, was in the process of learning obedience through one of the most painful of all forms of death, crucifixion? I hardly think so. Yet the author of the letter to the Hebrews did not hesitate to make the daring statement that *"Christ learned obedience through what He suffered."* (Heb 5:8). The mystery remains that, although Jesus Christ was God, He came to a new knowledge of the meaning of obedience through what He suffered.

I am sure that in your reflections and meditations on St. Paul's writings, you have been struck by the fact that he reserves his greatest wonder and admiration, not so much for the miracles that Our Lord did (if we exclude the Resurrection), as for the humility and obedience which He showed during His life, particularly in His sufferings and death. *"He was,"* reflected St. Paul, *"obedient until His death, even to that excruciating death on the Cross."* (Phil 2:8).

Our Constitutions remind us of our own personal involvement in the *"saving action of Christ Who became obedient unto death,"* (C. 36) and for that reason we will try under the inspiration of the Holy Spirit to obey freely the Will of the Father as it is manifested to us in diverse ways. Our Constitutions also give importance to *"open and responsible dialogue"* (C. 37, §1) in the process of discovering at community or personal level, the things that are pleasing to the Father.

The introduction of greater dialogue and consultation in the Church and in the Congregation has been inspired by the Spirit of God. However, dialogue and consultation must always be seen in the light of the mystery of Christ's obedience to the Father which is the great saving action in the world. Our obedience is a contribution to that saving action. Dialogue and consultation are but means to that end. They must not empty our vow of obedience of its reality which is, to quote our own Constitutions, *"to participate in the mystery of the obedient Christ."* (C. 37). The problem of living our vow of obedience (at times so painful) must not so absorb us as to blind our vision of its mystery.

Obedience for us is the highway to mission. *"I did not come of My own will: it was He Who sent me."* (Jn 8:42). Obedience and mission are inextricably bound together for us as they were for Jesus Christ. There can be no true authentic mission for any of us without obedience. It is for that reason that provincial and local community projects, as well as our individual apostolates, must not only be missionary in character, but be regularly authenticated by our Superiors in the light of our Constitutions and Statutes and in the light of the obedient Christ Who, as St. Vincent reminds us, is the Rule of the Mission.

The suffering which you, as an individual Confrere, may be presently bearing, I do not know nor can I imagine. Perhaps your greatest suffering does not come from the vow of obedience you have taken in the Congregation. The suffering you are enduring, mental or physical or spiritual, is an invitation to enter more deeply into Christ's experience of learning obedience through the things which He suffered. It is through reflection on the theology of the Cross that we will draw strength for a more perfect fulfillment of the Will of God in our lives. *"Our perfect happiness,"* remarked St. Vincent, *"consists in doing His Will in the true wisdom of desiring nothing other than that. God often wants to build lasting benefits on the patience of those who undertake them, and that is why He tries them in many ways ....I ask Our Lord ... to fill your hearts with faith, hope and love."* (Coste IV, Eng. ed., ltr. 1435, pp. 290, 292). In the love of Our Lord and of His Mother I remain, your devoted confrere.

God's Surprises

25 March 1988   Paris, France

Mother Duzan, Father Lloret and my dear Sisters,

Some fifty years ago G.K. Chesterton wrote a play entitled, *The Surprise*. In the first act of the play there are no actors on the stage, just puppets. The puppets do exactly what the author of the play wants them to do. The author is not satisfied, for he realizes that, since puppets are lifeless things, they are carrying out exactly what he, the author, wants them to do. They have no wills of their own. So in the second act real people appear on the stage with instructions from the author about the play. They are asked to do what the puppets have been doing in the first act. The actors, men and women, behave in ordinary human fashion. However, they put their own interpretation on the plot of the play and in doing so, ruin the drama. Then the author can stand it no longer. He cries out suddenly from the wings: *"What do you think you are doing? Stop. I am coming down."* At that point the curtain falls.

The play, *The Surprise*, is a parable on the history of salvation. At the Incarnation God invaded the stage of human history. In His love He came down in person to visit His people and to reveal His purposes. *"Descendit de caelis, et incarnatus est de Spiritu Sancto ex Maria Virgine, et homo factus est."*

God's play did not end with the coming down on the stage of the Author and Creator of the universe. The final curtain will not fall until the moment when Jesus Christ at the end of time will return to hand over His kingdom on earth to His Father and when, as St. Paul assures us, God will be all in all. In the meantime the play goes on. Each of us has his or her part to play under the direction of Christ, or rather under the direction of the Spirit of Christ Who lives in our hearts.

God's play did not end with the Incarnation. There were many more acts to follow after Mary had said to the Angel: *"Be it done unto me according to your word."* (Lk 1:38). You and I are part of the cast. You and I are on the stage with our parts to play for a little while. We may not feel that we have major parts in the drama of life and history. That does not greatly matter. What is important is how much attention we give and how close we remain to Him Who is the author and director of the drama. He is with us on the stage, for did He not say that He would remain with us always, even to the end of the world?

We could say that men and women who take vows promise to be particularly sensitive to Christ Who is, in St. Peter's words, *"the shepherd and guardian of your souls"*. (1 Pt 2:25). Those who take vows in the Church are particularly intent on allowing Jesus Christ to write the script of their lives. He has assured us how to play our parts, for did He not say, *"I am the way"* (Jn 14:6) and again, *"I have given you an example, that you also should do as I have done to you?"* (Jn 13:15). Jesus Christ said also, when He was on the stage of life in Palestine, that *"the Son of Man has not come to be served but to serve."*

(Mk 10:45). His life, from His entrance onto the stage in Bethlehem to His exit off the stage on the Cross of Golgotha, was marked deeply by obedience. He lived out His life, as He so often said, in obedience to His Father in heaven, and it is St. Luke who makes the point that for many years in Nazareth He was subject, or as the nuance of the word might suggest, regulated by Mary and Joseph in Nazareth. Jesus Christ passed before the audience that saw Him in Judea and Galilee as a man detached from what money could buy and distinguished by that freedom which comes from a pure and chaste heart.

It is by leading such a life that we will draw closer to Jesus Christ and through Him find our way to our Father's house, where He wishes us to pass our eternity. Has not Jesus Christ assured us that *"I will take you to Myself, that where I am you also may be."* (Jn 14:3).

The play is rightly entitled, *The Surprise.* The Old Testament built up hope among God's people for the coming of a Messiah. What a surprise it is for us, in opening the pages of the New Testament, to discover that the Messiah is none other than God Himself. What a surprise that a virgin, whose name was Mary, was asked to bear in her womb the eternal Word of God. As the drama of His life continued, one surprise followed another: the surprise that He showed such favor to the poor, the surprise of His miracles, the unpleasant surprise of His cruel death, and the joyful surprise of His resurrection.

The surprises still continue for us who are now playing our parts in the drama of life which is directed by the Spirit, Whom Jesus Christ sent us after His resurrection. Each day brings its surprises. Some are unpleasant and, of the unpleasant surprises we meet, many of them come from the flawed nature of the actors who share the stage with us, not to mention the flaws, the imperfection and the pride which lie so deep in our own characters. Had we but eyes of faith, we would see that each day we are being surprised by joy. What shall we say about the joy of His daily coming to us in the intimacy of Holy Communion? Perhaps we are tempted to say that this is not a surprise. If so, it means that we have come to take the Author of life for granted and, taking Him for granted, we take so much else that is good in life for granted. Is not your call to serve the poor in your vocation a surprise, seeing that so many others on the stage are so imprisoned in themselves that their hearts remain untouched by the sufferings of the poor whom you are serving?

Your vocation as a Daughter of Charity is one of God's surprises. Your unselfish service of the poor is for the poor themselves a surprise. Perhaps they will not express their surprise to you. Some of them will, as we ourselves do with God, take your goodness for granted. But take heart from the fact that you are, to quote St. Paul, *"the good fragrance of Christ."* (2 Cor 2:15). With Christ on the stage of life you are giving glory to His Father in heaven. You are rejoicing His Church on earth and you are bringing the joy of Christ onto the stage of human history. Through the joy and peace of Christ, which you are radiating in your daily offering of yourselves to Him Who is the author and director of your lives, you are mitigating the sadness of the tragedy that you encounter in the lives of so many people.

The greatest surprise is yet to come. We hope the final surprise at the end of our lives will be one of indescribable joy. It will be a surprise for us to discover a moment after our deaths the fullness of the truth that, when we visited the sick, when we clothed the naked, when we fed the hungry, when we visited the prisoners, we were serving the person of Christ Himself, the Son of God. When, after all selfish and unworthy tendencies will have been purified in us, there will be the surprise of joining that community of Father, Son and Holy Spirit, Who throughout eternity will rejoice our hearts and minds with the unending surprise of Their life and Their love.

On this day when we are celebrating the surprise of God's entry into human history, you, my dear Sisters, here in Paris and on all the continents of the world, have renewed your vows. For that, to quote St. Louise: *"May God be blessed and eternally glorified for all the graces He bestows on His creatures, especially the graces bestowed on our little Company in general and on each of its members in particular."* (*Spiritual Writings of Louise de Marillac*, ltr. 244, p. 280).

To each of you I address the words of St. Vincent, which he wrote to the community of the Sisters of Nantes on his sixty-sixth birthday: *"I never think about you and the happiness you have to be Daughters of Charity and the first to be engaged in assisting the poor where you are, without feeling consoled. However, when I hear that you are living*

*as true Daughters of Charity, which is to say, as true daughters of God,
my consolation is increased to the extent that God alone can make you
realize. Keep this up, dear Sisters, strive more and more toward
perfection in your holy state . . . a state which consists in being true
daughters of God, spouses of His Son, and true mothers of the poor."*
(Coste III, Eng. ed., ltr. 939, p. 181).

St. Jeanne-Antide Thouret

23 May 1988   Paris, France

My dear Sisters,

Let us this morning greet a saint who is a newcomer to our Vincentian
liturgical calendar. It is now almost three years since the Holy See
suggested to us that we honor St. Jeanne-Antide Thouret on 23 May.
St. Jeanne-Antide Thouret would feel quite at ease and at home were
she participating in this encounter. For, like you, she was called by God
to the Community of the Daughters of Charity. Like you she had the
experiences of the Seminary. Like you she cultivated the three characteristic virtues of a Daughter of Charity and lived the four vows of the
Company. Like you she knew the spiritual teaching of our Founders
and accepted the traditions of the Community.

Her Community life was shattered in pieces by the turbulence of the
Revolution here in France some two hundred years ago. Jeanne-Antide
Thouret was forced to return to her native locality and soon became, as
she remarked, an exile on the roads of Europe. She continued to live
according to the spirituality of her vocation, and because every Daughter of Charity is also a Daughter of Divine Providence according to the
mind of St. Vincent, after some years Jeanne-Antide Thouret became
the instrument of Divine Providence in the establishment of a new
Community, which came to be known as Sisters of Charity of St.
Jeanne-Antide.

The fact that St. Jeanne-Antide Thouret tried to follow the lead of
Divine Providence did not spare her from intense sufferings. Because
of a difficult political situation and the small-minded action on the part
of an archbishop, St. Jeanne-Antide had the painful experience of not

being allowed to enter the first house of the Congregation which she had founded in Besançon, France. She accepted the cross without recrimination and returned to Naples, Italy, where she died in the sixtieth year of her age on the 24 August 1826.

I do not need to tell you, my dear Sisters, that her life was distinguished by service of the poor, and that the Rule she gave her Community (which today numbers eight thousand) comprised all that she could remember of the Rule of the Daughters of Charity, with which she became acquainted in her Seminary days in the Mother House here in Paris.

St. Jeanne-Antide Thouret lived her days in great perplexity, a perplexity caused by the upheaval of the Revolution, by the dispersal of the Community she had come to know and love, and by the conflict with the Bishop of Besançon. Perplexity can be destabilizing, and part of the greatness of St. Jeanne-Antide Thouret lay in her ability to be stable in the midst of perplexity. For that reason she is a saint for our times, and I may say, a saint for the Visitatrixes of today. The poor increase in numbers, while, at least in many Provinces, the number of Sisters declines. Social and political situations are more complex. You, as Visitatrixes, are called to give direction to a Province in this perplexing situation. At times you must feel, as St. Jeanne-Antide Thouret did, like an exile on the roads of the world. Where can one find stability? Only in the person of Jesus Christ: only in what I might call the seven special gifts of the Spirit to the Community, the three virtues and the four vows: only in recourse to the Mother of God, whom we greet as the Morning Star. *"O my merciful Jesus,"* prayed St. Jeanne-Antide Thouret, *"You have all power over hearts. You can convert them . . . . Make me know Your will and Your plans and all that You wish that I do . . . .I commit everything to Your Fatherly goodness in which I trust perfectly and always."* (Office of Readings for the feast).

May we be given, through the intercession of St. Jeanne, stability amid perplexity and the grace of being content to live our entire lives without the satisfaction of smoothing out the creases in God's great tapestry.

The Most Holy Trinity

29 May 1988   Paris, France

My dear Sisters,

On a hot summer's Sunday in 1653, here in Paris, St. Vincent left his house to do a little catechetical work with some poor children. Somebody had the good idea of taking notes during St. Vincent's catechesis, for we have a brief summary of the simple, charming lesson which he gave. Probably conscious of the heat, and we know it was very hot at that time, St. Vincent thought of the sun, and he used it to expound the mystery of the Trinity. Let us listen for a moment to M. Vincent:

> *My children, I am going to give you a comparison which was used by St. Augustine. It is that of the sun. Just as in the sun there are three things, and these three things do not make up three suns, so in the Blessed Trinity there are three persons who make up one God. There are three things in the sun: the sun itself, the light, the heat. The sun itself is a beautiful star which we see in the heavens. The light makes all things clear, dissipates the darkness of the night and rejoices the world . . . .The third thing in the sun is its heat, a great heat which comes from the sun's mass and from the light. It is this great heat which matures the fruits and other things which are on the earth. When there is hot, suffocating weather, as we are experiencing here now, it is from the sun that all this proceeds. From this comparison you can understand that there is no more than one God, and that there are three persons in God, Who are inseparable one from the other, just as the sun is inseparable from the light and the light from the heat.* (Coste XIII, Fr. ed, p. 159-160).

It would be interesting indeed to know how St. Vincent might have developed the mystery of the Trinity in relation to our own lives but, like a good teacher, he breaks off after that point to question his audience in order to find out if they have followed him.

What would St. Vincent have said about the mystery of the indwelling of the Trinity in the souls of the just? Were he alive today, he might very well have gone on to illustrate the marvel that is within each one of us by appealing to atomic physics. It was only when the scientists of our own day succeeded in splitting the atom that they discovered the wonders of the movement of protons and electrons that are to be found within the smallest particle of matter. So, too, with the marvel of the indwelling life of the Trinity in each one of us. Our eyes, my dear Sisters, like those of the two disciples on the road to Emmaus, are held. We can only dimly see the wonder and miracle of housing within the temple of our fragile bodies the eternal Father, Son and Holy Spirit. We read, but only weakly grasp the meaning of the simple words of Our Lord: *"If a man loves Me, he will keep My word, and My Father will love him and We will come to him and MAKE OUR HOME with him."* (Jn 14:23). Perhaps our experience at the moment of death will be not so much of going out to God, but of God rising up from the depths of our being into our full consciousness. The astounding truth is that within us there is the harmony of the living and loving God, but because of our absorption in the material world, we cannot hear the beauty of the music.

There is another dimension to today's feast, and it is St. Louise who repeatedly highlighted it for the first Sisters. Community life is rooted in the life of the Trinity. It is from the Trinity that the Community draws its dynamism. The practical consequence of that truth is that we keep striving to sacramentalize in our Communities the love, the understanding, the union which exists in the Trinity. *"Remember me to all our Sisters,"* wrote St. Louise, *"and tell them always to remember the advice of Monsieur Vincent, especially forbearance and cordiality, so as to honor the unity and the diversity of the Persons of the Blessed Trinity."* (*Spiritual Writings of Louise de Marillac*, ltr. 248, p. 289).

In the Church's prayers for the dying, the work of the Holy Trinity in each one of us is marvelously expressed in a single sentence: *"Go forth, O Christian soul, in the name of the Father Who created you, in the name of the Son who re-created you, and in the name of the Holy Spirit Who sanctified you."*

The work of creation and re-creation is over. It is the work of sanctifying that continues, and the agent of that work is the Spirit of God. But He does not act without reference to the Father and the Son, as today's second reading reminds us: *"... You have received the Spirit of sonship. When we cry, 'Abba, Father!', it is the Spirit Himself bearing witness with our spirit that we are children of God, and if children then heirs, heirs of God and fellow heirs with Christ."* (Rom 8:15-17).

Glory be to the Father through the Son and in the Holy Spirit, as it was in the beginning, is now and ever shall be world without end. Amen.

The Blood of Christ

5 June 1988   Paris, France

My dear Sisters,

When passing down the rue de Sèvres some mornings ago, I noticed a large van with the words *DON DU SANG* written on it. There was a notice inviting people to come inside and to donate some of their blood. We have become quite familiar with the practice of being a blood donor from time to time. What a marvelous reality it is, that I can give a pint of my blood today, which tomorrow or a year later may save the life of someone who has been involved in a road accident, or has been gunned down by a man of violence, or to a woman who is giving birth to a child. It is a reality we take for granted, but to one who lived a hundred years ago, it would pass for a miracle.

Whether we live in the twentith century after Christ or in the twentieth century before Christ, blood speaks of life. In the twentieth century before Christ as today, people died when all their blood was poured out. The miracle of modern medical science is that by giving blood to a person, even when that blood is not his own, his life can be saved. Life can almost be given back. The language of blood is the language of life.

All three readings of today's Mass speak of blood, and in each of them the language of blood is also the language of life. For an Israelite of Old Testament times, contact with the blood of an animal that had been ritually sacrificed was considered to be a very close contact with

God, the giver of all life. It is thus easy for us to see how momentous for the disciples must have been Our Lord's words recorded in St. John's Gospel: *"He who eats my flesh and drinks my blood abides in me and I in him,"* (Jn 6:56) or his words spoken at the Last Supper and recorded in today's Gospel: *"This is my blood, the blood of the covenant; which is poured out for many . . . and they all drank of it."* (Mk 14:24).

The tremendous reality of our lives is that each day we receive a blood transfusion, and the blood is the blood of God. Each day we receive a new transfusion of life, and the life is the life of God. The bleeding ulcers of sin and selfishness drain us of spiritual energy, and we lie on life's road wounded and half-dead. But each day the Good Samaritan, the living and risen Christ, passes by and pours into our veins a transfusion of His own blood, and with the new life received we are able to continue on our journey. Moreover, when we have been strengthened by the body and blood of Christ, we are enabled to share that life with others. What is your vocation, my dear Sisters, but to give new life to the poor? What you do for the poor is an expression of the life of God that is within you, and which is strengthened by your daily experience of Holy Communion. When you serve the poor in whatever way your vocation indicates to you, what are you doing but transfusing divine life to another suffering member of the Body of Christ?

Custom stales the daily miracle in my life that I am nourished with the body of Christ, the Son of the living God and of the Virgin Mary, and that I am energized by the gift of His blood. It would be a great grace indeed if God would give back to each one of us something of the wonder we once had when we received the body and blood of Jesus Christ for the first time. It would be a real grace, too, if on this feast of Corpus Christi our eyes would be opened in wider wonder at the miracle which is the Blessed Sacrament in our tabernacles. What a loss it has been for many in the past two decades that the abiding presence of Christ in the Blessed Sacrament is not the source of strength and energy that it once was for them, and which Our Lord would wish it to be. *"Sweet Jesus! Gentle Jesus!,"* prayed St. Louise, *"My God and my All! Have mercy on all souls redeemed by Your precious blood. Inflame them with the arrow of Your love in order to make them grateful for the*

love that urged You to give Yourself to us in the Blessed Sacrament."
(*Spiritual Writings of Louise de Marillac*, A. 49, p. 834).

*"The cup of blessing which we bless, is it not a participation in the
blood of Christ?"* (1 Cor 10:16). *"How can I repay the Lord for his
goodness to me? The cup of salvation I will raise, I will call on the
Lord's name."* (Ps 11:12-13).

The Messiah Among Us

5 June 1988   Paris, France

My dear Sisters,

Once upon a time there was a monastery which had fallen on hard
times. Vocations were few and the monks were living in a building
which had become far too big for them. There were many empty rooms
and the monks, only a handful of them, were all over seventy years of
age. Everything about the monastery spoke of past glory that had
vanished. Surrounding the monastery was a large woods and in the
middle of the woods there was a little hut to which a local Jewish rabbi
used to go to spend a few hours from time to time. The rabbi made a
sort of retreat in the woods when he felt the need of spiritual refreshment.

On one occasion when the rabbi was in his hut in the woods the abbot
decided to go and speak with him. The two men met in the rabbi's hut.
The abbot told the rabbi of his great anxiety for the future of the
monastery. *"We are dying out,"* said the abbot, *"We are all old and we
have no young vocations."* The rabbi replied that things were somewhat
the same among his people. The young were not coming to the synagogue
as they used to do. The materialism of modern society was killing the old
religious spirit. The old abbot and the rabbi wept a little and they prayed
a psalm or two together. Then they felt better and they embraced each
other. Before parting the abbot asked the rabbi if he had any suggestion
he could make about the future. *"No, I am sorry,"* the rabbi replied. *"The
only thing I can tell you is that the Messiah is one of you."* When the abbot
returned to the monastery, the monks gathered around him to ask, *"Well,*

what did the rabbi say?" "He could not help," replied the abbot. *"We just wept, and we read some psalms together. The only thing he did say, just as I was leaving, and it was rather puzzling, was that the Messiah is one of us. I do not know what he meant."*

In the days and weeks that followed, the old monks pondered this and wondered what significance the rabbi's words might have. The Messiah is one of us. If that is the case, which one? Could it be the abbot? Probably yes, for after all he has been our Superior and spiritual leader for years. But then it could be Brother Pacificus. Everyone knows that Brother Pacificus is a man of great prayer. It could not be Brother Dyscolus because everyone knows that Brother Dyscolus is touchy and impatient and rubs everyone the wrong way. When you come to think of it, however, Brother Dyscolus has a way of speaking the truth at community meetings and very often he is right, and almost prophetic. Maybe the rabbi did mean Brother Dyscolus. It certainly cannot be Brother Passivo. Sometimes one wonders if he has two ideas in his head. He rarely says a word at a community meeting, except when everyone is asked for a *yes* or *no* to a proposal. Brother Passivo's *yes* is *yes*, and his *no* is *no*. However, he has the gift of always being around in the community, and ready to fill gaps when someone else is sick or absent. Maybe, after all, Brother Passivo is the Messiah.

As they reflected in this manner the old monks began to treat each other with new respect, on the off chance that one of them might be the Messiah. And because each monk began to think of himself as possibly being the Messiah, he began to have a new respect for himself. On Sunday afternoons in the summertime, people would often come to the grounds of the monastery to have a picnic and to visit the rather dilapidated abbey church. As they did so they would meet the monks, and they would experience the warm glow of acceptance, respect and love which radiated in different ways from each one. People began to come out to the monastery not just to walk in its grounds, but also to speak with the monks. They told their friends about the monks, and then some young people came along. After a time one young man asked if he could join them, then another and then another. Within a few years the monastery had become a vibrant center, an authentic *"fraternal community in view of service."*

Unlike Our Lord's disciples, my dear Sisters, you will not ask for an explanation of the parable. Only let me add this. You rightly give much thought and prayer to sharpening your vision of seeing Christ in the poor. The choice of the theme for this Encounter would seem to reflect a certain need that exists in the Company of intensifying the search for the Messiah that is present, not only in the poor, but in each member of the Community. Let not the words *fraternal community* obscure from you the truth that what is in question is charity, that personal sharing in the agape of God which all of us enjoy because of our baptism. *"The love of God is poured forth in our hearts by the Spirit of God."* (Rom 5:5). What is in question is the reality that a tiny spark of the love that is in the heart of Christ has been lodged in each of our hearts through baptism. Too often the agape or charity of God that is in our hearts has been taken hostage by vanity, jealousy and selfishness. The challenge that faces us is to liberate the agape of God in our hearts, so that the members of our local communities and of our Provinces will be the first to benefit from its joyful warmth and healing power.

In closing this Encounter which has been blessed by God in a thousand hidden ways, my prayer is that you will grow in respect and love for each of the Sisters of your Province. Assemblies, meetings, projects, revision of works, all will be of little avail if the communities of our Provinces are not glowing points of that charity which is patient, is kind, is not jealous, not irritable; that *agape* that hopes the best of everyone, that endures all things. My prayer is that the Sisters of your Provinces in turn will follow your example of being a shining light of charity, and that in your search for the hidden Messiah within the Community, you will draw many others to the Community. I ask this grace through the Father, the Son, and the Holy Spirit. *"May God in His goodness,"* prayed St. Vincent, *"be pleased, my dear Daughters, to pour forth His Spirit on you in abundance, which is nothing but love, sweetness and charity so that by the practice of these virtues, you may do all things in the manner He wishes you should do them, for his glory, your own salvation and the edification of your neighbors."* (Coste IX, Fr. ed., p. 279).

Conferral of Doctoral Degree

10 June 1988   Niagara University, New York

Your Excellencies and my dear Friends,

I do not know if the records of this University keep note of visitors who pass through Niagara and pay courtesy calls on the community here. Should such records exist, I would be deeply interested to turn back the pages to the year 1884. Sometime in the course of that year Father Thomas McNamara, a seventy-five year old Vincentian from Ireland, crossed the Atlantic and visited some houses of the Community in the United States. He made his way also across the border into Canada and met with the sixty-eight year old Archbishop of Toronto, John Joseph Lynch. It was a meeting of old friends. Almost fifty years had passed from the time they had first met. It was in the year 1835 in the city of Dublin that these two men first became acquainted with each other. There was only a seven year difference in age between the two men, but that was sufficient to make one the teacher of the other. The seventy-five year old Vincentian priest, who in 1884 had crossed the Atlantic and who was visiting with the Archbishop of Toronto, was meeting one of his former pupils. Archbishop Lynch, the first President and Superior in this University was, historical records tell us, the first pupil to enter St. Vincent's College, Castleknock, Dublin. The year was 1835 and one of the priests who received him and taught him was Father Thomas McNamara who now, almost fifty years later, was meeting his former pupil, presumably for the last time, in Toronto.

The group of priests who taught the young John Joseph Lynch was a very small group, and they formed the nucleus around which the Irish Province of the Vincentian Congregation grew. Very likely it was the dedication to the work of education and the preaching of missions, which this group of priests carried on, that inspired John Joseph Lynch to join them in 1839. Three years after his ordination in 1843, and with the permission of his Superiors, he left the shores of Ireland to join the relatively young Province of Vincentians who were working here in the United States. The story of his life after that is familiar to a number of you who are listening to me today. It was in 1856 that John Joseph Lynch opened the doors of the seminary that grew into the University we know today. Father Lynch guided and directed it until the Holy See named him Bishop of Toronto in 1859.

The year 1856 was and will remain a very significant year in the history of this University. It was the beginning of a chapter in the history of the Congregation in the United States, which can rightly be described as a glorious one. It is not for me to read the role of honor of the Alumni of this University, of priests, Sisters and lay people who have at a national and an international level made notable contributions to the well-being of the Church and the State. Allow me just in passing to congratulate the Board of Trustees on the representative character of those whom they have chosen to honor at this convocation. We, who have been honored today, are a diverse group, but all of us rejoice in sharing in some small way the vision of St. Vincent de Paul, a man who studied in two universities during his lifetime. St. Vincent did not easily forget the years he passed in two of France's universities. It is noteworthy that he kept the parchment of his degrees until the end of his life, even if he hid them from the eyes of his Confreres, who would only discover them in his room after his death. We who are being honored here today are indeed grateful to St. Vincent de Paul. We are also grateful to the University of Niagara. May Niagara continue to push back the frontiers of knowledge, shedding all the time, on the territory acquired, the light of the Catholic Faith.

In 1856 while the University of Niagara was receiving its first students, another Catholic University in Ireland was struggling to be born. At the request of the Irish hierarchy John Henry Newman, later Cardinal, had in the 1850s worked to launch a university in Dublin, commuting between England and Ireland no less than seventy-two times. The university would be Catholic in ethos and would offer to its students an education of the highest academic standards. The difficulties that Doctor Newman encountered were very formidable and he did not judge his efforts to have been notably successful. However, the years of Cardinal Newman's labors in Dublin were fruitful in many respects. It was thanks to his experience in Ireland that today we have his work, *The Idea of a University*, a book that will for centuries to come challenge all who are engaged in the task of university education. Doctor Newman was an Englishman in Ireland. Like many other Englishmen in Ireland of yesterday and of today, he found it difficult to understand what the poet Tennyson called, *"The blind hysterics of the Celt."* So it was that the Archbishop of Dublin, later Cardinal Cullen, advised Doctor Newman that, if he wanted to acquire some background knowledge of the social and political scene in Ireland, he would do well to consult two Vincentian priests, Father Thomas McNamara and Father Philip Dowley. (cf. *Letters and Diaries of J.H. Newman*, vol. 16, p. 272). From the correspondence of Doctor Newman we know that he did consult them. The Vincentian Community was not unknown to John Henry Newman. After his reception into the Catholic Church he gave some thought to joining St. Vincent's Community. In the last decade of his life, when he was a Cardinal, he wrote to a Vincentian in Dublin: *"I recollect well how, when I became a Catholic, the first religious body which attracted my reverend notice was yours."* (Letter 15 Nov. 1882 to Rev. M. O'Callaghan. Original in C.M. Archives, Dublin.)

He chose St. Philip's Oratory. He retained, however, until the end of his life what he called *"sympathy and interest in the Congregation of St. Vincent."* (Ibid.). He would undoubtedly have been pleased to learn that the new university which was rising within earshot of the great Niagara Falls was being placed under the patronage of the Virgin Mary. For only two months before he was received into the Catholic Church in October 1845, John Henry Newman had begun to wear as an Anglican the Miraculous Medal.

Of these three men, John Joseph Lynch, Father Thomas McNamara and John Henry Cardinal Newman, it is the latter who is the most celebrated. For us, however, of the Vincentian Community, and particularly of the local Vincentian community here in Niagara, it is gratifying to think that the Founder of this Seminary-University was taught by a man who was guide and friend to Newman, during the years when the latter was launching the Catholic University in Dublin.

It was while he was in Dublin that Cardinal Newman wrote: *"A great university is a great power and can do great things; but unless it is something more than human, it is but foolishness and vanity in the sight and in the comparison of the little ones of Christ." (Univ. Sermons,* p. 58).

The little ones of Christ, that last phrase evokes St. Vincent de Paul. Perhaps it may surprise some of you to learn that the great patron of the poor considered evangelical simplicity to have been his gospel. *"Simplicity, "*he said, *"is my gospel."* (Conf. Eng. ed., 24 Feb. 1653, p. 538). Universities speak to us much more of complexity than of simplicity. Yet G.K. Chesterton remarked: *"The chief object of education is not to learn things; nay, the chief object of education is to unlearn things. The chief object of education is to unlearn all the wickedness of the world and get back into that state of exhilaration we all instinctively celebrate when we write by preference of children."* (*All Things Considered,* p. 53).

I would like to think that any Vincentian university has inherited from St. Vincent de Paul two distinguishing features; first, a love and practical concern for the neglected people of this world. Does not the word *neglected* mean unchosen, a concern for the unchosen people, that is, for those who are not singled out by governments and other agencies for favor? Second, a university that has St. Vincent de Paul as its inspiring patron will have a certain stamp of evangelical simplicity about it. At its deepest level simplicity is the policy of acting always with only God in view, or to quote St. Vincent, *"to see and judge things from Christ's point of view."* (CR II, 5).

Evangelical simplicity is an indispensable condition for graduating in that great university in which at present we are all undergraduates and whose Chancellor is Jesus Christ. He confers degrees after years of meritorious work, but the degrees we all hope to receive at the end of the day of our life's work will be, in the last analysis, degrees Honoris Causa.

Ladies and gentlemen, I thank the University for the honor accorded me in conferring a Doctorate of Letters, Honoris Causa. I presume to voice the thanks also of those who are being honored with me today and who with me belong in different ways to the great spiritual family of St. Vincent de Paul. I salute Niagara University, its President, its Faculty members, its Board of Trustees. I greet its first President, John Joseph Lynch, whom because he was born in the county next to my own in Ireland, I feel free to call my neighbor's child. And to Father Thomas McNamara, what shall I say? Well, I will let you into one of my family secrets today. *"Thank you, Uncle Thomas."*

Faith

My dear Sisters,

There was a celebrated Scottish poet of the last century who one day was plowing his field and, in doing so, disturbed a little field mouse. The poet felt sorry for the mouse, and he went on to reflect that the mouse was in a sense more fortunate than he. The mouse, he said to himself, cannot look back on the past nor look forward to the future in the way that we human beings can. We look back on the past and experience much regret. We look at the future and, according to the poet, we can *"only guess and fear."*

When I was asked to talk to you on the subject, *The Daughters of Charity in 1988*, I felt a little like the mouse, limited to the present. While there is much to be said for living totally in the present, the reality is that we have a past and we do think about our future. So I began to think about your past in the Community and about your future. The past has made you what you are today; the future, at each moment of your lives you are advancing into it.

When I heard, my dear Sisters, that you are celebrating twenty-five years of vocation, my mind traveled back to the year 1963. What a memorable year that was for all of us! It was the year of the two Popes. The month of June saw the death of John XXIII and the election of Paul VI. It was the year of the second session of Vatican Council II. It was the year which saw the beatification of Elizabeth Ann Seton and the publication of the encyclical, *Pacem in Terris*.

In 1963 the Superioress General, Mother Guillemin, had been in Rome and wrote for the Company a refreshing account of her impressions of the Council. She asked a priest how long the Council would last and the priest answered: *"It will never finish."* He went on in a

prophetic manner to say that *"A new way of working had been discerned, a new way of thinking and reflecting together. "* Taking up the
idea, Mother Guillemin applied it to the lives of the Sisters and she
continued: *"We also should be at work: we must not imagine that we
shall one day have finished our formation, that one day we shall have
attained perfection, and declare we are satisfied with ourselves. We
shall always be on the way; on the way towards the only perfection:
God Himself. It is only at the moment when we shall be united to God,
penetrated by Him, that we shall have reached the degree of perfection
that is to be ours. We must keep this thought well in mind: that we should
always be at work, work upon ourselves without being discouraged if
we perceive that we have not yet the perfection we wish to attain. "*
(Echo, Eng. Ed. 1963, p. 16).

"To be on our way . . . . " You, my dear Sisters, have been on your
way in the Community now for twenty-five years. As you throw a
backward glance on these twenty-five years, I am sure a vast variety of
memories will jostle together: memories of your months in the Seminary; of your being sent on mission; of your first Sister Servant; of the
poor you have met; of some retreats you have made; of your taking of
vows; of crises you met and surmounted; of changes of apostolates; of
misunderstandings; of tears; of family bereavements. What a book each
one of you could write! St. Thèrése of Lisieux wrote her autobiography
which was entitled: *"The Story of a Soul."* We are all not as gifted as
St. Thérèse, to be able to write with such lucidity and wonder about our
relationship with Our Lord, but each of us has the material for the
writing of a book on our experience of God's loving invitations to us
and of our responses. We may never write a spiritual autobiography,
but we will one day see the complete story of our lives in video. We
and everyone else will be in admiration of it. Yes, for as St. Paul remarks
in his letter to the Ephesians: *"We are His (God's) workmanship, "* (Eph
2:10) or as it can be translated, *"masterpiece".* When we will have
reached Heaven and when all trace of sin will have been purified, we
will be a masterpiece of God's creative and redeeming love. Through
God's loving mercy, even our sins, our defects, our mistakes will have
been used and transformed in such a way that we will praise from our
hearts the glory of God's grace.

To return for a moment to 1963, there was much hope in people's hearts. In that year the world had been saddened by the death of Pope John XXIII. Elected Pope in 1958 at the age of seventy-seven, the world had looked upon him as a caretaker Pope, until the Spirit of God used Pope John to convene Vatican Council II. A new springtime for the Church seemed to have dawned. Worldwide renewal and dialogue had begun to sound as new themes in the great symphony which is the life of the Church. Pope John himself had spoken shortly before his death of a new Pentecost. There was an air of expectancy in the Church. Something momentous was about to happen. For that reason I imagine that you were buoyed up by much hope when you entered the Company and began your formation in the Seminary.

I am almost hesitant to ask you: *"How do you feel about your vocation today?"* Yet I should not be hesitant. The fact that you are still in the Company and that for now almost two decades you have on the 25 March renewed your Vows, should be a sufficient response to my question. I have little doubt that most of you, if not all, would say to me: *"I am happy to be a Daughter of Charity. I feel privileged to serve the poor in the Company."* What reaction could I have to such a reply but that of St. Vincent who so often exclaimed in the presence of the first Sisters: *"May God, Sisters, be praised. May God be praised."*

When a few moments ago I said I was almost hesitant to ask if there was in your hearts the hope that was in them in 1963, I had in mind some factors which, humanly speaking, would tend to drain hope from your hearts. As year succeeded year after 1963, the numbers entering the Community began to diminish. The median age of the Community began to rise. Houses had to be closed. Cherished apostolates to the poor had to be given up. At times the dialogue, which had at the Church's recommendation been introduced into our Communities, seemed to make for confusion rather than clarity. Certain experiments, made in the name of renewal, seemed to lead in uncertain directions. These factors and others have undoubtedly left some Sisters thinking, like the two disciples on the road to Emmaus who in their disillusionment said to the Risen Christ: *"But we had hoped...."* (Lk 24:21). Visiting different provinces of the Company, particularly in countries where vocations are scarce, I have been much impressed by the joy and the hope that is evidenced in the Sisters' outlook on the Community. Such joy and hope come, I am convinced, directly from the Spirit of God. We must never allow ourselves to forget that the Company itself is the work of the Holy Spirit, nor must we ever overlook the fact that the vocation of a Daughter of Charity is in itself an expression of hope. When you devote yourselves to the education of the poor, you mediate hope. When you alleviate the sufferings of the sick and dying, you mediate hope. When you devote yourselves to the care of mentally or spiritually handicapped people, you mediate hope. If you are to continue to serve the poor, then there must be hope in your hearts. At every Mass we are invited to lift up our hearts, *sursum corda*. That is not an appeal to assume any artificial gaiety or false optimism. It is an appeal to lift up our hearts after we have lifted up our eyes to Christ crucified and reflected on His sufferings, death and resurrection. That was the way of St. Louise. When at Mass we are invited to lift up our hearts, we are asked to do so because of Our Lord's promise that He will be with the Church until the end. *"I am with you always."* (Mt 28:20).

It is a healthy spiritual practice to allow our minds to dwell on the grounds of our hope. I have sometimes wondered how many people must suffer some form of depression through their daily intake of gloomy news from our televisions, radios and newspapers. The daily diet of conflicts, crises and tragedies must leave many of our elderly and nervous people with grounds for pessimism and depression. For that reason, if you are to be, as St. Vincent wanted you to be, angels of light to the poor, it is essential that you fill your minds with the thought of God's goodness to you in the past and His continuing goodness each day in giving Himself to you in Holy Communion.

I have been casting a backward glance at the past twenty-five years. What of the years ahead? How do you feel about the prospect that is opening up before you now? I think immediately of a hymn which Cardinal Newman wrote when he was in the midst of a spiritual crisis:

"Lead, kindly light, amid the encircling gloom.
Lead Thou me on . . . .
Keep Thou my feet. I do not ask to see
the distant scene; one step enough for me."

We do not ask to see *"the distant scene."* Our Lord Himself has counseled us to live one day at a time. (cf. Mt 6:34). How many times did not St. Vincent exhort us to have confidence in Divine Providence. Perhaps for the years that lie ahead, the ideals which Pope Paul VI proposed and discussed in his first encyclical, *Ecclesiam Suam*, might shed light on our path.

First, Pope Paul was convinced that, if the Church deepened its own self-awareness, it would become a still greater force for good in the world. We in our Community have reason to be grateful to God for the deeper self-awareness which it has gained over the past twenty- five years. The Sisters throughout the world have, through the experience of the General Assemblies and through the new Constitutions, been enabled to share more profoundly in the vision which God gave to St. Vincent and St. Louise, when they established the Community more than three centuries ago. Through greater self-awareness provinces have been able to commence the formidable task of revising the works of the Company, a task made necessary by the rapidly changing social needs of today's world. What your Constitutions state in one of the opening paragraphs must continually be the topic of prayerful reflection: *"The call heard by the first Sisters is ever the same. Throughout the world it continues to raise up and assemble the Daughters of Charity, who try to rediscover at the source the inspiration and intuitions of their Founders, so that they may respond with ever renewed fidelity and availability to the needs of their time. "* (C. 1.3).

Second, Pope Paul proposed to the Church in his first encyclical the ideal of renewal. We have lived with that concept now for twenty-five years. What Mother Guillemin said of formation in 1963 is also valid for renewal today: *"We must not imagine that we will one day have finished . . . and declare that we are satisfied with ourselves."* (Echo, Eng. ed., 1963, p.16). From Pope Paul's encyclical I take his observation that we must be on our guard against a growing tendency to prune away from the Christian life everything that requires effort or causes inconvenience. This observation is particularly relevant for our living of the consecrated life today. (cf. *Ecclesiam Suam*, §49). The Community, like the Church, *"will rediscover its youthful vitality, not so much by changing legislation as by submitting to the obedience of Christ and observing the laws which the Church lays upon itself for the intention of following in Christ's footsteps."* (Ibid. §51).

Third, Pope Paul VI proposed to the Church the ideal of dialogue, an ideal which he developed at some length. It suffices here to recall those qualities of dialogue which the Pope considered to be particularly necessary if it were to be effective. Dialogue within our Community, and particularly with our Superiors, should be characterized by 1) clarity, 2) gentleness, 3) trust, 4) prudence. *"Before speaking,"* remarked the Pope, *"we must take great care to listen, not only to what people say, but more especially to what they have it in their hearts to say. Only then will we understand them and respect them and even, as far as possible, agree with them."* (*Ecclesiam Suam*, §87).

I cannot bring this talk to a close without thanking you, my dear Sisters, for all that you have done for the Church, for the poor and for the Company. It is now twenty-five years since you heard Our Lord say to you: *"Come and see."* (Jn 1:30). You did come and you did see and you have remained with Him, living your life according to the ideals our Founders proposed for Daughters of Charity. The river of years has flown over you. You have lived through many vicissitudes. Perhaps you think back to the beginnings of your vocation when the water was pure, springing up from the ground. You look back, too, on the later years when the water seemed to be meandering a little aimlessly. You might even think that the present waters of your vocation are somewhat slow and sluggish. In a sense, that does not matter, provided you are trying to get back to Jesus Christ, Who is the source of life and holiness for us all. We have to make up our minds repeatedly to be with Him and to follow Him.

Following Him means yielding ourselves up to Him. It means living in Him and allowing Him to live in us. *"You did not choose Me, but I chose you and appointed you that you should go and bear fruit, and that your fruit should remain."* (Jn 15:16). As you pass these days together, you would do well to reflect on the words of the prophet Hosea: *". . . Behold, I will allure her, and bring her into the wilderness and speak tenderly to her . . . .And there she shall answer as in the days of her youth."* (Hos 2:16,17). I am certain that the Lord is speaking tenderly to you, my dear Sisters. May you be able to respond to Him as in the days of your youth in the Seminary.

Let me leave the final word to St. Vincent. Were he with us today, I do not think he would change much in the letter which he wrote to Sister Jeanne Lepintre, Sister Servant at Nantes, at the end of November, 1651:

> *I ask Our Lord to be Himself His own thanks for this and for the calm you are enjoying after all the storms and troubles that have buffeted your little bark. We must love Our Lord deeply and, along with that, keep ourselves in readiness to endure other upheavals and additional setbacks. Man's condition is never the same; he is humbled, then exalted; sometimes at peace, sometimes persecuted; enlightened today and plunged into darkness tomorrow. What is to be done? As I said, let us be prepared for whatever may happen. When we suffer, hope that God will deliver us; when He treats us gently, store up the gentleness and patience in order to make good use of the trials that will ensue. In a word, Sister, we must give ourselves to God in all respects, and hope that His Will may be done. We must conform ourselves to it in both unpleasant and pleasant circumstances, which constantly succeed one another. This requires us to be ready for anything and completely detached from ourselves. O my God, who but You alone will give these things to us? We humbly ask them of You through Your Son Jesus Christ. May God grant us the grace to be always faithful to His lights and to our little spiritual exercises. I recommend myself humbly to your prayers.* (Coste IV, Eng. ed., ltr. 1428, pp. 281-282).

That last request of St. Vincent, his unworthy successor today also makes to you, my dear Sisters. Thank you.

Blessed Ghebre Michael

15 July 1988   Naples, Italy

My dear Friends of Jesus Christ,

I would like to introduce you this evening to our special guest who is celebrating his two hundredth birthday. Before he left this life for heaven, he was aware that the Vincentian family was a large one, comprising priests and Brothers of the Congregation of the Mission, Daughters of Charity, the Vincentian Volunteers, the Society of St. Vincent de Paul, and other religious sisters and groups of laity who look to St. Vincent de Paul today as their special heavenly Patron. Our guest is a priest, dark-skinned, with the features of an Ethiopian, and his name is Ghebre Michael. In greeting us, he might begin by first clarifying a small point of truth. All his life, from the time he was a young student, Blessed Ghebre Michael had a passion for the truth and at times suffered much for it. *"The truth,"* Blessed Ghebre Michael might say, *"is that although I wanted to join the Vincentian Community and had been told I could, I was taken away to prison before I could formally enter it."* Our Beatus might also go on to explain to us that it was only in the final years of his life that he had come to know St. Vincent's Community. He would describe himself as a late vocation to the Vincentian Community, for he was a man in his late fifties when he experienced the call of God.

Ghebre Michael had been attracted to the Vincentian Community, not by anything he had read about St. Vincent de Paul nor by anything he had heard about the large Vincentian family. He was drawn to the Community by a man who was a living commentary on what it meant to be a Vincentian.

It was in Cairo in the year 1841 that Blessed Ghebre Michael first met St. Justin De Jacobis, a Vincentian of the Province of Naples. By that time Blessed Ghebre Michael was a monk, belonging to the Coptic Church which was separated from the Roman Catholic Church. Some years were to pass and through his contact and conversations with St. Justin De Jacobis, Blessed Ghebre Michael was to discover, not only that the fullness of truth was to be found in the Roman Catholic Church, but he was to experience also a strong desire to live his life according to the spirit of St. Vincent de Paul. He had found that spirit incarnated in the humble Vincentian, St. Justin De Jacobis. It was from St. Justin De Jacobis, who had been ordained a bishop in January 1849, that Blessed Ghebre Michael received the priesthood on New Year's Day, 1851. It was the first ordination to the priesthood which St. Justin had performed.

Looking around at us all this evening, this gentle Ethiopian priest might go on to say to us: *"I appreciate very much the place you have chosen for this celebration of my two hundredth birthday, for within the walls of this church there has gone up to heaven the incense of countless prayers which many saintly Vincentian priests and Brothers have in the past two hundred years offered to God. The walls of this church have seen also countless Daughters of Charity and other members of the Vincentian family come here on the feast days of St. Vincent and St. Louise. I know, too, that the walls of this church have seen the youthful Justin De Jacobis at prayer. They have also seen a steady stream of hard-working diocesan priests come here to make retreats and to receive the Sacrament of Penance and spiritual direction from such saintly Vincentians as Father Micalizzi. For all that I am deeply grateful to God, to His Mother and to St. Vincent de Paul."*

Were we to ask Blessed Ghebre Michael how he felt as a priest and convert to Roman Catholicism, he might reply: *"It is like Ethiopia."* He would then go on to explain that his country is one of great natural beauty. It is also one through which travel is very difficult because of the high mountains that crisscross the land. *"The Catholic faith,"* he might say, *"is like that. It has special beauty and brings with it an indescribable joy and peace. But in living the Catholic faith, I met mountains of difficulties. Because I adhered fully to everything that the Roman Catholic Church teaches, I had to undergo torture and public floggings on numerous occasions. But I can assure you that, despite the pain, I experienced an extraordinary inner strength which only God could have given me. To you all, I can say with St. Paul, 'You have observed . . . my sufferings, what persecutions I endured; but from them all the Lord rescued me.'"* (2 Tim 3:10-11).

Looking at the color of the vestments I am wearing this evening, Blessed Ghebre in his passion for truth could say gently: *"Are you sure you are wearing the right color? I mean, I did not actually die from soldiers' bullets, even if on one occasion I was sentenced to death and would have died were it not for the kind intervention of an English official. I died in chains all right, and from exhaustion. However, I think I could say I died a natural death. "* When we would tell Blessed Ghebre Michael that the Church considered him, because of his sufferings, to have been a martyr, he would accept that judgment because the Church, for Blessed Ghebre Michael, was the pillar of truth. I think Blessed Ghebre Michael might appreciate a distinction that was made in my country during times of persecution. The people would speak of red martyrdom and white martyrdom. Every baptized person is called to martyrdom, that is, to give witness to others of his faith. Some are called to red martyrdom, that is, to shed their blood because of their Christian convictions. Others, and they are in the majority, are called to white martyrdom, that is, to witness by the good quality of their lives that Jesus Christ is real, that He is risen and that He lives on in His Church. Sometimes it is more difficult to be a white martyr than a red martyr, because white martyrdom can last for decades. The Church and the Vincentian Family have need today of authentic white martyrs. The Church and the Vincentian Family have need of men and women who have the courage to live profoundly what each of us professes every Sunday of the year: *"I believe in one holy, Catholic and apostolic Church."*

At the present time, perhaps more so than at any time in recent centuries, the Church has been the subject of much criticism, not only from those who are its professional enemies, but also from men and women within it. The Church today has many enemies within its own household. It is a phenomenon of our times and one which Blessed Ghebre Michael, who suffered so much for one single article of the Catholic creed, would find hard to understand. His exhortation to us on his two hundredth birthday might very well be: *"Be faithful to Jesus Christ, true God and true man. Be loyal to the visible head of the Church on earth, the Pope. Defend the doctrinal and moral teaching of the Church, the pillar of truth, and lastly, remember that 'you have not yet resisted,' as I and so many others have done, 'to the point of shedding your blood.'"* (cf. Heb 12:4).

For the life, death and beatification of Blessed Ghebre Michael, we rejoice and are glad. For the example, zeal and holiness of St. Justin De Jacobis, we rejoice and are glad. For the blessings and graces given to all who prayed in this Church, we rejoice and are glad. Through the intercession of Mary, the Mother of God, of St. Vincent de Paul, St. Louise de Marillac and all the Saints of the Vincentian Family, may each of us be a witness on earth to the Resurrection of Christ and share in His glory in heaven.

Patience

23 July 1988   Salzburg, Austria

My dear Sisters,

The stories or parables which Our Lord told to His audiences can, for the most part, be understood by a child, and yet the greatest Christian intellects could reflect on these stories and draw from them much nourishment for their minds and for their spiritual lives. The parable in today's Gospel is simplicity itself, but there is a mine of spiritual riches in it. One could say that, like a mine, there are different strata in it. You could say that it centers on the theme of patience.

The first stratum is the patience of God. We often hear people ask: *"Why does God allow this or that to happen?"* In asking the question there is sometimes a note of reproach, almost blaming God for the evil in the world. Sometimes we put too many questions to God, when we could be devoting more time to reflecting upon and admiring His great patience. Each moment of the day there are people gravely insulting God, provoking Him, shaking their fists at him, and all the time our God remains silent. He does not retaliate by destroying this tiny, almost insignificant planet of the universe, which we call earth. Were the earth to disappear from the universe, it would hardly be missed. God does not destroy the planet, because He has told us that He *"so loved the world that He gave His only Son, that whoever believes in Him should not perish but have eternal life.* " (Jn 3:16). *"Love,"* says St. Paul, *"is patient."* (1 Cor 13:4). Our silent, loving God is a patient God Who waits. Our Lord makes that clear in today's parable.

The second stratum in today's Gospel is patience with others. Most of us are experts at seeing the weeds that grow in our neighbor's field. We have a sharp eye for the defects in our neighbor's character. We have an instinctive desire to pluck the weeds out of our neighbor's character. Sometimes our motives for doing so are not pure. We wish to correct our neighbor because his way of acting merely irritates us. Our Lord's advice is that we should be patient. Above all, we should not correct our neighbor when we are angry or impatient. You will recall what St. Vincent said. In his lifetime he had on three occasions corrected people in anger, and his corrections, he tells us, achieved nothing.

The third stratum in today's Gospel is patience with ourselves. Each of us is conscious that there are wheat and weeds in our characters. There is the wheat of our virtues and there are the weeds of our defects. As long as we live in our present human condition, there will be weeds in the field of our souls. The final eradication of all the weeds will come only after our deaths. It is true that we must continually keep cutting back the weeds, even if we cannot pull them up by the roots. We must cut back the weeds, and that is where mortification must come in. We mortify ourselves in order that the wheat of God's love, which is in our hearts, may be able to grow stronger day by day.

So, my dear Sisters, Our Lord's message for us today is that we be patient with Him, patient with others, and patient with ourselves. Our Lord does not wish that we be discouraged by His slowness in acting nor by our neighbor's defects, nor by our own weakness. Let me end by quoting a little advice which St. Vincent gave to a Superior who was suffering because of differences that had arisen among the different characters of his community: *"The remedy for all that is patience, support and prayer to God . . . .I hope you will find by all these means peace and joy for yourself and for your community. (I hope) that these means will be a help to all in general and to each in particular in order to advance in virtue. But remember that patience is as necessary for us to support each other as charity is to support the neighbor. May it please God to give us both one and the other. I am in His love, Your humble servant, Vincent de Paul, unworthy priest of the Mission.* " (Coste VII, Fr. ed., pp. 275-276).

Pilgrimage to Jerusalem

15 August 1988   Paris, France

Mother Duzan, Father Lloret and my dear Sisters,

How many pilgrimages did Mary, the Mother of God, make, I wonder, during her lifetime? One can easily count twelve for certain, for does not St. Luke in his Gospel refer to that annual pilgrimage which she made with her husband, Joseph, and her Child, Jesus, to Jerusalem. *"Now His parents, "* writes St. Luke, *"went to Jerusalem every year at the feast of the Passover. And when Jesus was twelve years old, they went up according to custom. "* (Lk 2:41, 42). Mary would seem to have kept up that custom of going every year on pilgrimage to Jerusalem, because twenty or twenty-one years later we know that she was in Jerusalem for the feast of the Passover. Presumably she had made the pilgrimage to Jerusalem from her home town of Nazareth. That was the pilgrimage which ended in tragedy, for it was while she was in Jerusalem that year that she learned of the arrest of her Son, and some hours afterwards watched Him put to death on a cross outside the walls of the city. As had happened twenty years previously, she lost her son for three days, but was to find Him again in the glory of the Resurrection.

Mary's pilgrimage to Jerusalem that year would seem to have been prolonged, for we know that seven weeks later she was still in Jerusalem. With her Son's disciples she was waiting to be endued once more with power from on high through the coming of the Holy Spirit on Pentecost Day. That was the day which saw a new sort of pilgrimage inaugurated. The starting point of the pilgrimage was Jerusalem and its destination the ends of the earth. From Jerusalem the apostles set out, making their way through Judea and Samaria and beyond that to the most distant parts of the known world, as they had been asked to do by Jesus.

That particular pilgrimage is not over yet. It has not yet reached its destination. More importantly, you and I are making that pilgrimage and, as the Pope has reminded us in His Encyclical *Redemptoris Mater*, Mary, the Mother of God, is accompanying us on that pilgrimage. The idea that Our Lady is accompanying the Church on her pilgrimage of faith is one of the central ideas of the Pope's encyclical.

Let us come back to Mary and her pilgrimages. Difficult as her pilgrimages to Jerusalem must often have been—there were no buses or trains in her day—she would have rejoiced as she approached Jerusalem and caught sight of the Temple gleaming in the sunlight. For her, as for the disciples of Jesus, the Temple was not only a hallowed place, but it was *"a thing of beauty and a joy forever." "Look, Teacher, what wonderful stones and what wonderful buildings,"* (Mk 13:1) exclaimed the disciples as they contemplated with pardonable pride the beauty of their Temple.

Mary would have sung the psalms which are familiar to us, as she entered the Temple. *"To You our praise is due in Sion, O God. To You we pay our vows. You will hear our prayer."* (Ps 65:1). Looking back on her journey to Jerusalem, Mary would have prayed the final verse of that psalm with a special depth of feeling. *"The hills are girded with joy, the meadows are covered with flocks, the valleys are decked with wheat, they shout for joy. Yes, they sing."* (Ps 65:13,14). That psalm, as do so many others, celebrates the beauty of God, and we are certainly not stretching our imagination when we reflect that she, who is the most perfect human masterpiece of God's hands, must have had a particular and special appreciation of God's beauty.

There was a Russian writer of the last century who wrote: *"The world is saved by beauty."* Perhaps we react immediately and say, *"No, we are saved by the death of Jesus on the cross."* That is true, but even in the pain and horror of the crucifixion, is there not an awesome beauty? Is there not a beauty in Jesus' entrusting all of us to the care of His mother in the final moments of His life? In the words of Pope John Paul II: *"Mary's motherhood, which becomes man's inheritance, is a gift which Christ Himself makes personally to every individual."* (*Redemptoris Mater*, §45) Is there not a pathetic beauty in His prayer for His executioner and in His words of comfort to the dying thief?

When we reflect upon the Beatitudes, on the Sermon on the Mount, and on Jesus' farewell words to His disciples, can we not say that the world has been saved by the beauty of Our Lord's wisdom? And what of His healing of the sick, of His acceptance of sinners, of His tenderness to the poor? Must it not have seemed to these simple people that the world was being saved by the power and spiritual beauty of a man who spoke with authority and authentic love?

The world will continue to be saved by beauty. As you move around in the world of the poor, my dear Sisters, and as you see the countenances of so many people, torn by sufferings, and see, too, the face of evil, you must wonder where beauty is to be found. Must a Daughter of Charity content herself with the thought that she will see the beauty of God only after her death? No. To use a metaphor of St. Vincent, she must think of herself as a ray of sunshine which *"gives both light and warmth and is undiminished even when it beams on what is not clean."* (CR IX, 2). It should be a source of encouragement to you that for thousands of poor people, the presence of a Daughter of Charity, offering humble and loving service, is an education in the meaning of spiritual beauty. If every human being is searching at every moment for what is good and true and beautiful, then a Daughter of Charity who is living her vocation authentically must be considered as one of the greatest gifts God can give to the poor in this life.

The beauty of God keeps breaking into our lives, like the sun piercing through the clouds. Apart from the many traces of His beauty, which God has left us in His mountains and seas, in His trees and in His flowers—and does not the Spirit of God through the Creation Canticle at Sunday Lauds invite us to lift up our eyes to see the beauty of the world?—there is the beauty of gratitude, of friendship, of fortitude, of faith which the poor so often share with you in most unexpected ways. In your lives you should be open and sensitive to beauty, for where there is true appreciation of beauty, there will be thanksgiving. And thanksgiving is the highest form of giving.

What of today's feast? Is it not a sign post on our road of pilgrimage that, when we have reached our destination, we will be made beautiful in body and in soul, so that we can live fully in the presence of that beauty which, to quote St. Augustine, is *"ever ancient and ever new?"* (*Confessions*, Book 10).

Meantime, however, we are traveling on the road of pilgrimage. The road to God's city is not like a modern highway. It is not straight and it is not built for speed. There are many unexpected twists and turns on our pilgrim route, and one can only cover so much ground in a day. He, Who is the Way, has counseled us to live only one day at a time. To rush ahead with excessive speed is to drain ourselves of energy. *"Do not be anxious about tomorrow, for tomorrow will be anxious for itself. Let the day's own trouble be sufficient for the day."* (Mt 6:34). At different points of the road there are signs which read: *"Mary, the Virgin of Nazareth, was here."* At times we read the signs through the mist of tears, and at other times in the bright sunshine of joy and hope. At all times, however, the Daughter of Charity sees Mary, as your Constitutions state, as *"the Immaculate one, the Mother of God, Mother of Mercy, and hope of the lowly."* (C. 1.12). On the road of pilgrimage we do not travel alone. Indeed the vocation of the Daughter of Charity is to accompany *"those who suffer, those stripped of human rights and dignity, those in poor health."* (C. 2.1).

Today, my dear Sisters, we lift up our eyes to the mountain of God where Mary, His Immaculate Mother, with glorified body, now dwells. As we look back on that year which was specially dedicated to her, we can sing with the Psalmist the words which Mary herself would have sung in the Temple: *"You have crowned the year with Your goodness."* (Ps 65:12). Yes, it has been a year crowned with the goodness of God, a year that has brought us closer to His Mother, a year that has given us a clearer insight into her beauty as a person and as a mother.

May the contemplation of Mary's beauty strengthen within you the conviction of St. Peter who wrote to the Christian women of his day: *"Your beauty must be the beauty of your inner character and personality. It must consist of the beauty of a gentle and serene character, a beauty which the years cannot wither, for in God's sight that is what is really precious."* (1 Pt 3:4).

May the closing of this year, dedicated to Mary, be for you, Mother Duzan, on this your feast day, an occasion when the treasury of God's graces will be opened for you in a special way. May the beauty of God and His Mother be your inspiration and strength in your pilgrimages to the Provinces of the Company. May you be to them what Mary is to the entire Church, *"a sign of hope and comfort for your people on their pilgrim way."* (Preface for Feast of Assumption).

Movement from Activity to Solitude and Prayer

6 September 1988   Celbridge, Ireland

The passage of St. Luke's Gospel to which we have just listened this evening, is one of movement. Jesus, Who had spent the whole night in prayer, moves from the mountain down to what St. Luke calls *"a level place."* (Lk 6:17). Jesus has moved from prayer to action. It is a characteristic feature of St. Luke's Gospel that there is what you might describe as a pendulum-like swing in Our Lord's activities. St. Luke accentuated the fact that Our Lord moves from involvement with people, healing and preaching and teaching them, to long periods of solitude when He devotes Himself to communing with His Father in heaven. From the mountain or desert place of prayer He will then descend again to continue the mission which He has received from His Father in Heaven, so that all may come to the knowledge of the one true God and Him whom He has sent.

This evening all of us gathered here are thinking of movement. The community which has lived here for ten years or so, is on the move. By no stretch of the imagination can we think of this locality as a mountain, nor as a desert place. However, it is appropriate to recall this evening that, when an alternative location to Blackrock was being sought twelve years ago, one of the factors that influenced the decision to choose this particular locality was its tranquillity. A certain distance from the din and bustle of a city facilitates growth and appreciation of that interior silence without which we cannot hear God speak. If we humans are to hear the voice of the living God, then there must be a measure of stillness and silence in our lives. *"Be still and know that I am God."* (Ps 46:11). That is a truth which Jesus Christ has taught us by word and by example. It is a truth to which St. Vincent also subscribed. When setting forth the ideal of prayer for his Community, he evoked the scene of this evening's Gospel. He wrote: *"Christ, the Lord, in addition to his daytime meditations, sometimes used to spend the whole night in prayer to God. We cannot fully follow his example in this, though we should try to do so while making allowance for our weakness."* (CR X, 7).

In the present day Constitutions of the Vincentian Congregation that ideal finds expression in this phrase: *"Through the intimate union of prayer and apostolate a missioner becomes a contemplative in action and an apostle in prayer."* (C. 42).

We are on the move. Our celebration this evening, however, is tinged with a certain regret. The stay of the Community here in Celbridge has been short. Buildings, however, do not make a Community. Indeed St. Vincent reminds us in our Rule that *"we should not have a disproportionate liking for any ministry, person, or place, especially our native land, or for anything of that sort."* (CR 2, 10). It is significant, too, that the name which he gave the members of his Congregation was that of missioners. He had a fondness for that word, mission. Missioners do not settle down. They are always on the move so that they may proclaim Jesus Christ, crucified and risen, particularly to the poor.

We are on the move. It is with regret that we leave this locality. The principal reason that prompted the Visitor and his Council to take this decision has been the fewness of vocations. Rather I should say, the fewness of applications. For it is salutary for us all to think that the truth may very well be that God has called and is calling men to our Congregation, but for one reason or another these men are diverted, distracted or, let us face it, even discouraged from joining us by what they see of the quality of our community life and apostolates.

We move with regret, but our lives must not be lived with regret. Our lives must be lived forward. With St. Paul, we do not look back to what is past, but rather press forward to the upward call of our vocation in Christ Jesus. (cf. Phil 3:14). The decision has been taken by the Provincial, not solely because of the fewness of applicants. It has also been taken in the hope that in the present circumstances the work of formation will be carried on more effectively elsewhere. The ideal of formation itself is unchanging. Those whom God calls to our Community must be formed to become apostles in contemplation and contemplatives in action.

We are on the move. As we go, we are accompanied by a host of friends and well wishers, a fraction of whom are here this evening. The

Daughters of Charity, the friends of the Vincentians, and the Holy Faith Sisters, are more than well-wishers to us. They share with us the vision of St. Vincent. So this celebration is an occasion for thanking God and also for thanking that wide Vincentian family for the spiritual, material and financial support they have given us so constantly and generously over the years.

Towards the end of his life—two years precisely—St. Vincent was forced to give up a property as a result of a law suit. He felt the loss of it acutely. He capitalized on this experience to reinforce in his Community the need of adhering lightly to things in order to practice what he called *holy indifference.* I would like to end this homily by quoting a short letter St. Vincent wrote to a layman, a good friend of his, on that particular occasion:

Good friends share the good and the bad that comes to them; and as you are one of the best we have in the world, I cannot but let you know of the loss we have suffered in the affair you know of (the loss of the farm at Orsigny). However, I don't mean it is something bad which has come upon us, but rather a favor God has done us, so that you may kindly help us to thank God for it. I call the afflictions God sends a favor from Him, especially those that are well received. For, His infinite goodness, having prepared us for this deprivation before it was decreed in law, has also made us acquiesce in this unexpected result with extra resignation, and I venture to say, with as much joy as if it had been in our favor. This would seem to be a paradox to one who was not versed, as you are, in heavenly affairs, and who did not know that conformity to God's good pleasure in adversities is a greater good than all temporal interests. I beg you very humbly to allow me to put into your heart the sentiments of my own.

(Coste VIII, Fr. ed., pp. 252-253).

May the sentiments of serenity and confidence which St. Vincent expressed in this letter be ours this evening.

Attitude of Servant

22 October 1988   Albany, NY

My dear Sisters,

I am happy to have this occasion of reflecting briefly with you on the particular vocation which is yours at the present moment, of Sister Servants, that is, servants of the Servants of the Poor. The topic which has been chosen for this particular talk is the attitude of servant. That topic goes to the heart of the matter. If we really understood what it means to be a servant at all times, we would be excellent leaders of our communities. Since all Christian activity is presented to us by Christ as service, it follows that, if the members of our local communities really understood what it means to be a servant at every moment of the day, to be servants of the poor, servants of each other, servants of the Sister Servant, then our communities would be little paradises on earth. But this earthly paradise is, as we all know only too painfully, overgrown with thorns and briars, which the sinfulness of humanity has sown in that earth which God saw as good. So we suffer in Community. However, we must work with Him Who came to restore all things and, as far as it is possible, to make our community lives resemble more the life of union which is the life of the Blessed Trinity. In that work of restoration to which we are all called by our baptism, you have a vocation within a vocation. You are called to be servants of the Servants of the Poor.

In addressing you I am conscious that many must have spoken to you of this or similar topics relating to your vocation as Sister Servants. It is for that reason that I feel that we are nowadays a little like the Athenians in St. Paul's time. They liked to have new speakers so that they could have new ideas of the universe and about life. I wonder sometimes, too, whether future generations will not think of us as a paper generation. We have turned out enough miles of paper during the past twenty years to carry us to the moon and back. It makes me wonder how much of it has really been read and, more importantly, how much of it has been assimilated and how much of it has influenced us and made us change our lives profoundly.

In making this last observation, I am not opposing that *aggiorna-mento* which the Spirit of God through the Council called for, nor am I opposed to the revision of our works, based on a study of the charism of our Founders. However, before we achieve the revision of our works, we must set about the revision of our lives. Continual daily conversion in our personal lives will inevitably lead to that revision of works desired by the Spirit of God and the Church.

We are certainly not without a sufficiency of books, articles, reviews, documents, memoranda, and plans. From time to time I think of the rather pessimistic author of Ecclesiastes who said in his own day that *"of making many books there is no end."* (Ecc 12:12). I think, if he lived today, he might have decided against writing even his own short work.

All that I have been saying is a digression and a personal opinion, but I am convinced that we must try to keep a proper proportion between the time we give to reading or listening to conferences and the time we devote to reflection and prayer. Perhaps we need to return to St. Vincent's celebrated little method which he adopted in preaching. According to that little method, St. Vincent advised us to consider the nature of the topic, the motive for action and the means of putting into practice the conclusions reached. Perhaps I could apply St. Vincent's little method to the subject which has been proposed to me, "The Attitude of Servant."

First, to be servants. One of the first observations to be made is to remark upon the distinction between service and servant. We give service, but we are servants. It is one thing to serve the poor, and another to be a servant of the poor. Politicians and government officials work in what we sometimes call the public service. They will tell you that they serve the public. Airlines will tell you of the services which they offer to travelers. All these people, however, would not like to be considered as servants of the public. The air hostesses would not like it if, on your entry into a plane and after having greeted them, you said to them: *"During this flight you will be my servant."* No, they are happy to offer their services, but they would not like to be considered our servants.

One could say that the Christian vocation is at once to be a servant and to offer services. It is certainly the vocation of a Daughter of Charity. She is called to serve the poor in the Company, but what is more important, she is called to be a servant, to have the mentality of a servant, and that is to have the mentality of Jesus Christ. *"Have in you,"* wrote St. Paul, *"the same sentiments which were in Christ Jesus....He emptied Himself....He humbled Himself, becoming obedient unto death, even to death on the cross."* (Phil 2:7-8). The mentality of a servant is one of being humble and of being obedient. Only after we have learned to be humble and obedient after the manner of Jesus Christ can we offer service to the poor in His name.

The motive for being a servant, then, is that Jesus Christ chose to be a servant, and He is our way, our truth and our life. He lived His life as a servant of all whom He met, particularly of the poor. The means of being a servant is to carry out faithfully day in and day out the work that our Superiors ask us to do, however humble and insignificant that work may be.

Our vocation is to be servants in collaboration. Those two words, *in collaboration*, evoke for us the Community. It is *through* the Community that we serve the poor. It is also *with* the Community that we serve the poor. At times we see and hear about poor people who are living in great distress. We experience a strong desire to help them. That may be good, but we have to ask ourselves if the Community is asking us to serve these people. Our vocation is to collaborate with the Community in serving the poor. That calls at times for much self-sacrifice, for we may not find it easy to work with others in the Community for the service of the poor. Those two words, *in collaboration*, are important.

Our Founders emphasized very much the need of union and unity among the Sisters. Without union and unity it would be impossible to work in collaboration with others. Union and unity are the means of achieving practical collaboration in the service of the poor.

What is our motive for working in collaboration with others? Nothing less than Jesus Christ; the whole mystery of the Incarnation is a mystery of collaboration of God with humanity. St. Vincent liked to contemplate Our Lord's collaboration with the Apostles in the work of announcing the Kingdom of God. It must not have been very easy for Our Lord to work with the twelve Apostles at times. Our Lord Himself always sought the fulfillment of His Father's Will, while the Apostles on many occasions sought selfishly their own promotion and were intent on following their limited and often selfish vision which they had of Him and of their own prospects in life.

Collaboration itself is a form of service. More to the point, the person who sincerely and humbly collaborates can be said to have an attitude of a servant. I have stressed the importance of collaboration because one of the challenges that faces the Sister Servant is to secure that collaboration from the Sisters of her community. The Sister Servant may be most willing to collaborate with the community, but not each Sister willing to collaborate with her. There is a continuing challenge for the Sister Servant to try, while manifesting an attitude of servant, to secure the maximum collaboration for the apostolates of the community and for living life in accordance with the letter and spirit of the Constitutions and Statutes. Much of your work as Sister Servants is a work of persuasion. Your task is to persuade the Sisters that their peace lies in a joyful acceptance of the simple message of the Gospel, that is, in a faithful carrying out of the Constitutions. Persuasion is not always easy, but it succeeds more often than direct commands. The foundation of all effective persuasion is humility. It is humility that helps us to respect the dignity of the individual Sister, while at the same time giving us the strength to put forward to her the ideals of our vocation.

Up to this point I have not evoked St. Vincent. So let me introduce him. For many years I have often reflected on an appointment he made in the year 1656. In that year, when he was already seventy-five years of age, he appointed Superior of a seminary a young man twenty-seven years of age. That says a lot for St. Vincent's confidence in youth. The young priest went to St. Vincent and asked him for some advice on being a Superior. St. Vincent commenced to offer him some counsels, at the end of which the young man had the good sense to go to his room and write what St. Vincent had just said to him. We still have this jewel of writing among St. Vincent's works. It is not a very long piece but it is full of spiritual and practical wisdom. Let me just quote a few sentences from it:

> It is therefore . . . essential for you to empty yourself of self
> in order to put on Jesus Christ . . . If a Superior is filled with

God, if he is replenished with the maxims of Jesus Christ,
all his words will prove efficacious and a virtue will go out
from him which will edify . . . .An important point, one to
which you should carefully devote yourself, is to establish a
close union between yourself and Our Lord in prayer. That
is the reservoir from which you will receive the instructions
you need to fulfill the duties on which you are now about to
enter. You will in doubt have recourse to God and say to
Him: 'O Lord, You Who are the Father of light, teach me
what I ought to do in this circumstance.' I give you this
advice, not only for those difficulties which will cause you
pain, but also that you may learn from God directly what
you should have to teach . . . .You should also have recourse
to prayer in order to beseech Our Lord to provide for the
needs of those entrusted to your charge. Rest assured that
you will gather more fruit in this way than by any other.
(Coste XI, Fr. ed., p. 342).

Perhaps I should continue along that line of St. Vincent in offering you some counsels which perhaps might be of help to you. Let me offer you one negative and one positive one.

Negatively, do not force the growth of your community too much. A farmer cannot force the growth of wheat in the field. We cannot force the spiritual growth of other people. It is important for a Sister Servant, as it is for everybody, to accept people as they are and to help them to grow, but not to force them to grow. It is significant that Jesus said: *"And I, if I am lifted up, will draw all things to Myself." "I will draw all things to Myself."* (Jn 12:32). He did not say: *"I will force all to do as I want them to do."* Positively, try to create around you the conditions that will help people to grow in faith, and in hope, and in love of God and the poor. The gardener can remove obstacles that prevent the growth of the seed in the ground. He can shelter, and when necessary water the ground, to assist the growth of the seed. So, too, with us, we should try to create around us the conditions that will enable people to come out of themselves into the light and sunshine of God's grace. I sometimes think that all of us underestimate what we can do to create within our communities the atmosphere that will allow, not only ourselves, but others to mature in the love of the Community and of our vocation to serve the poor.

One of the most practical pieces of advice any of us could receive in authority is to start by taking things and people as we find them, and not as we would wish them to be. Apropos of that, one of the most practical pieces of advice in the New Testament is the letter of St. James. You will find much in it to help you in your task. *"My brothers, you will always have your trials, but when they come, try to treat them as a happy privilege."* (Jas 1:2). All of us know that Sister Servants have often much to suffer, precisely because they are Sister Servants. St. James speaks of suffering as a happy privilege. I think it is important that, whatever our sufferings are, we try not to talk too much about them, at least to our communities. If we speak too much to our communities about our difficulties as Superiors, our communities will not be happy ones. An air of gloom will settle down upon them. I am not saying that a Sister Servant should not confide her difficulties to a prudent person. Indeed this meeting should afford you an opportunity of talking in general about some of the difficulties that you experience in guiding your communities, always respecting the law of charity. St. James would say that whatever your sufferings are as Sister Servants, through them you are becoming *"fully developed and complete."* (Ibid., v. 4).

To be a servant, to have the attitude of a servant at all times, is not easy. You have much need of the grace of God and of mortification. Mortification, does the word sound a little outdated to you? It certainly is not one of the mode words in today's spirituality. Yet I feel that it must be rediscovered if religious life is not to be emaciated and devoid of relevance in today's world. All of us need to reflect more on some of those great sayings of Christ: *"I came, not to do my own Will but the Will of Him Who sent Me."* (Jn 5:30). *"He that saves his life will lose it."* (Jn 12:25). *"Unless you deny yourself and take up your cross daily and follow Me, you cannot be My disciple."* ((Ibid., v. 24). *"Unless the grain of wheat falls into the ground and dies, itself will remain alone."* (Mt 16:24).

If our local communities are not meditating on these great utterances of Christ and concretizing them in our personal and community lives, we will slowly and almost imperceptibly seek more and more comforts.

We will become less and less interested in the poor. We will become, within the walls of our little community houses, ever seeking to expand our personal enterprises. We will hardly avert to the fact that proprietors are not servants.

That is a rather downbeat note which I have just sounded and I do not wish to conclude with it. I would like rather to end on a note of appreciation and thanks to each of you personally for what you are doing in enabling the Sisters of your communities in the Province of Albany to be what St. Vincent would like them to be and to do at the present time. Let me say here that during the last eight years I have admired the spirit of humility which I have noted among the Sister Servants throughout the entire Company of the Daughters of Charity. Many times in visiting communities, I could not guess who was the Sister Servant, which is proof that Sister Servants in the Company are authentically humble people. For that with St. Vincent I say, *"Blessed be God!"*

Let me end by reading you a few sentences from a letter which St. Louise wrote to a Sister Servant: *"I praise God with all my heart for the graces He has bestowed on you . . . . Those to whom God gives the charge of others must forget themselves entirely and in all things, but especially in spiritual matters and in the little satisfactions that may assist our Sisters to advance toward perfection. Remember that those in authority must be the pack-mules of the Company. Please join with me in asking Our Lord for this spirit for you and for me."* (*Spiritual Writings of Louise de Marillac*, ltr. 376, p. 458).

To that prayer of St. Louise de Marillac all of us here can say, Amen.

Advent Letter—Poverty

14 November 1988   To Each Confrere

My dear Confrere,

May the grace of Our Lord Jesus Christ be with us forever!

More than once when I sat down to write a personal letter to you in Advent time, the thought came to me: *"Why not write about poverty?"* Who can ignore the fact that the Word of God, when He chose to be born of the Virgin Mary, could find no room in the inn at Bethlehem? Until now a host of reasons seemed to justify my not taking up the subject. Our vow of poverty, I reasoned, cannot be adequately treated in a short letter; conditions in provinces vary greatly; older Confreres see poverty differently from the young. I would venture to say that these were excuses rather than reasons. I suspect that the true motive for my reluctance to write to you on the topic of our vow of poverty has been a certain unease about my own manner of living this vow. It is so much easier to write or speak about the poor and the misery and injustice of their condition, than to write or speak about the reality of the vow of poverty as it impinges on my own life. The experience of being comfortably housed and well fed, along with the security that I will be cared for in old age, has a way of making the words *personal poverty* sound unreal as they fall from my lips or my pen.

Often, too, I have noticed that reflections on my manner of living my vow of poverty are prefaced by such considerations as: *"You are not a religious. Your vow is special. It is taken for the purpose of mission. This is the twentieth, not the seventeenth century."* *"True"*, replies St. Vincent. *"We are not religious; it has been considered necessary that we should not be religious. We are less worthy than religious although we live in community. However, it may be said that poverty is the bond of Communities and especially of ours which has greater need of it than others."* (Coste XI, Fr. ed., p. 223).

That greater need of personal poverty to which St. Vincent refers, must lie in the particular vocation which is ours in the Church. In a letter to Father Codoing, St. Vincent remarked: *"We are not sufficiently virtuous to be able to carry the burden of abundance and that of apostolic virtue and I fear we may never be, and that the former may ruin the latter."* (Coste II, Eng. ed., ltr. 718, pp. 517-518). There is a continual tension, often not fully recognized, between affluence and apostolic virtue in our lives. Expressing the idea in another way, one could say that there is an interior logic between the following of the poor Christ in my personal life and my proclamation of Him to the poor. Identification with the poor Christ in my personal life must precede the work of evangelizing the poor, if my preaching is to be fully authentic. For it is in the name of the poor Christ that I speak to and for the poor.

It is precisely to further identification with the poor Christ that we take a vow of poverty. To quote Pope Paul VI on evangelical and religious poverty: *"It is on this point that your contemporaries challenge you with particular insistence."* (Evang. Test.§16).

Our Constitutions, Statutes and Provincial Norms set forth the detailed means for living according to the letter and spirit of our vow. Read them meditatively and you will find that they are at once a stimulus to apostolic virtue and a defense against the incursion of affluence in our lives. It is the inner sanctuaries of our hearts, however, that need most vigilance. *"Be on your guard,"* said Our Lord, *"against greed of every kind."* (Lk 12:15). The Greek word for greed *pleonexia* is most expressive. It signifies a desire to have more. It is that *more* which needs attention. Securing more leisure time, more superfluities, more travel, more personal comforts can and often does mean less for the poor, as well as a distancing of myself from the person of the poor Christ. The slow, silent growth of affluence in my life can mean the slow death of genuine love for others and the slow extinction of that zeal which is the flame of the love of God in my heart. *"We are not sufficiently virtuous to be able to carry the burden of abundance and that of apostolic virtue."* (Coste II, Eng. ed., ltr. 718, pp. 517-518).

For many people in the Western world, the feast of Christmas is a feast of affluence, divorced from the event that gave it meaning originally in Bethlehem of Juda. Not so for us who believe that the poverty of Christ's birth and life is a mysterious but real manifestation of the *"power of God and the wisdom of God."* (1 Cor 1:24). If we are to be effective apostolic agents and communicators to the poor of the power and wisdom of God, then we must enter personally into that experience of Christ Who, *"though He was rich . . . yet became poor so that by His poverty you might become rich."* (2 Cor 8:9). Without such an experience, our words and even our actions for the poor will be those of hollow men.

The prayer of Christ, Who lived and died a poor man, was that his joy would be in us. He Himself could rejoice in the beauty of the lilies of the field and in the contentment of the birds of the air. *"Whatever is true, whatever is honorable, whatever is lovely, whatever is gracious,"* (Phil 4:8) rejoiced the heart of the man Christ Jesus. May it be so for us. May your celebration of the feast of Christmas be a joyful one, and bring you a new measure of apostolic virtue. It is the wish and prayer of all of us here in the Curia.

Asking you to remember me in your prayers, I remain in the love of Our Lord, your devoted confrere.

1989

Lighted Candles in the Darkness

1 January 1989   Paris, France

Mother Duzan, Father Lloret and my dear Sisters,

When darkness falls on Christmas Eve in the country from which I come, there is an old custom of placing a single lighted candle in one of the windows of the house. The custom of doing so originated among the simple peasants of the countryside, long before electricity was invented. Leaving the lighted candle in the window on Christmas Eve was a gesture of faith. In doing so the simple people wished to let Mary and Joseph know that, wherever they saw a candle in the window, there was to be found a room and a welcome. When the custom started I do not know, but it is certain that the people who first did so had much faith, but very little of the goods of this world. As so many of our Sisters have discovered, the poor often have a highly developed sense of generosity and are ready to share the little they have with those who have even less.

The custom of placing a lighted candle in the window on Christmas Eve spread in time to towns and cities. A lighted candle, even in an age with electricity, has a certain magic. Perhaps for that reason well-to-do families in towns and cities began to place a candle in one of the windows of their house, simply because they considered it an appropriate Christmas decoration. It was artistic. On occasion, passing through the wealthy residential parts of cities and seeing some decorative candles in windows, I have often asked myself the question: What would be the reaction if Mary and Joseph called at that particular house and asked for a room for the night so that Mary could give birth to her child? What would be the reaction if anyone, apart from a very close friend of the family, called and asked for lodgings there on Christmas night? I do not think it is presuming too much to say that the reply at the door would be the same as that of the inn keepers of Bethlehem: *"I'm awfully sorry, but try somewhere else."* For the dwellers in those

422

wealthy houses, the lighted candle in the window on Christmas Eve has lost its original significance.

For our Founders, our Community is seen as one great house that has a lighted candle in its window, not just on Christmas night but at all times. With their vision of faith St. Vincent and St. Louise saw each local community and each individual Daughter of Charity as so many lighted candles, assuring the poor that if they approached, they would find light and warmth and shelter amid the darkness, the coldness and the inhospitality of this world. Thank God, the Community continues to shine on all continents of the world, giving assurance to the poor that, where Daughters of Charity are to be found, there the poor will find friends who are true reflections of Christ, the Light of the world.

Each individual local community faces the challenge every day of not only keeping the flickering flame of charity alight, but also of making sure that it is not an empty sign. A family can become closed in on itself; so too can a local community. Almost without knowing, a community can be saying what the inn keeper in Bethlehem said to Mary and Joseph: *"Sorry, there is no room here."* The periodic but regular revision of a Province's works is undertaken for the purpose of making sure that the Company does not drift into suburbia, where the candle in the window is a pleasant, seasonal decoration and no more. *"Fraternal charity,"* your Constitutions remind us, *"extends beyond the local community. The Sisters are hospitable and gracious, they are aware that priority must be given to the needs of the mission and to those periods of time necessary for community living."* (C. 2.22).

Not only must our communities be lighted candles in the darkness of this world, but each of us individually must be a sign of welcome to all who knock at the door of our hearts. We can only do this if we are convinced that, at every moment of our day, Christ Himself stands at our door and knocks.

Yes, my dear Sisters, that is one of the great truths of our faith, that Christ is seeking the hospitality of our hearts, not just on Christmas Eve but on every day of the year. Perhaps you will recall that beautiful reading of the Song of Songs, which the Church proposes for our meditation a few days before the feast of Christmas. The passage is part of a love story, and the lover is presented as standing outside the house of the girl he loves. *"There he stands, gazing in at the windows . . . .My beloved speaks and says to me: 'Arise, my love, my fair one, and come away' . . . ."* (Sg 2:9-10).

That is an image of the relationship between God and His Church, between God and the individual soul. Often Our Lord is addressing us in the words of the Song of Songs: *"You are like a dove that hides in the crevice of a rock. Let me see your face, let me hear your voice."* (Ibid, v. 14). Yes, too often we are curled up in ourselves, in the crevices of our own selfish preoccupations, avoiding the gaze of the lovely face of Christ and failing to hear his enchanting voice.

In the heart of Him who is our tremendous lover, there is the hope that we will open the door of our hearts so that we can meet more fully His loving gaze. The enchanting voice of Christ is heard through the accents of the poor, through our Superiors, through those whose lives we touch in Community. His voice is to be heard even in the most insignificant events of our daily lives. As day succeeds day in this new year of grace, we can make only one of two responses to the voice of Christ. Either we can respond by opening the door of our hearts fully or we can close or only leave half open that door at which He stands and knocks at each moment. If He can share our lives with us, it means that He has been invited into the intimacy of our hearts. The lighted candle in the window has meaning. When Christ cannot share our thoughts, our words, our actions, then He is turned away from our door. The lighted candle is an empty sign. It is but a decoration.

At the beginning of this new year, Our Lord invites us in the words of the Song of Songs *"to arise, my fair one, and come away."* (Ibid., v. 14). It is an invitation to close loving union with Him without whom we can do nothing. *"Arise, my fair one, and come away."* It will be the invitation that we will receive when all our years will have run their course. Then, at the moment of our deaths, what will dismay and pain us most will not be our sinfulness, but the feeble response we made to the persistent intensity of His love. *"Behold I stand at the door and knock: if anyone hears my voice and opens the door, I will come in to him and eat with him and he with me."* (Rv 3:20).

At the beginning of this new year, I pray through the intercession of the Mother of God that each of us will be to each other and to the poor *"a burning and a shining lamp"* (Jn 5:35) of love. From his place in heaven I am sure St. Vincent's wish is no different from that which he expressed to St. Louise in January 1638: *"I wish you a young heart and a love in its first bloom for Him who loves us unceasingly and as tenderly as if He were just beginning to love us."* (Coste I, Eng. ed., ltr. 288, p. 408).

Being Occupied is Different from Being Busy

17 January 1989   Lisbon, Portugal

My dear Sisters,

The Saint whom the Church is honoring today is very distant from us in time, and the sort of life he led will not serve as a very practical model for a Daughter of Charity. St. Anthony, the Abbot, spent many years of his long life in the desert, and that is not the vocation of a Daughter of Charity. However, he did have contact with a number of people who recognized him to be a man very close to God and for that reason a source of practical wisdom. Even in the remoteness of the desert, people used to flock to him, thus making it difficult for him to have that solitude which he so much desired.

Many years ago I recall hearing a story told about St. Anthony. He lived to a very old age, and at the end of his life someone came to him and said: *"Anthony, you have had a very long life, and in the course of it you must have had very many worries and anxieties."* To which Anthony replied: *"Yes, I had, but most of them never happened."* Anthony was confessing that he had anticipated in his mind many difficult situations which never arose. Anthony was confessing to have failed to take Our Lord at His word when He advised His disciples to live one day at a time. *"And do not be anxious about tomorrow, for tomorrow will be anxious for itself. Let the day's own trouble be sufficient for the day."* (Mt 6:34). Certainly we would be spared much worry and anxiety in our lives if we could fully put into practice that counsel of Him Who is our wisdom and our sanctification.

St. Anthony is distant in time, not only from us but also from St. Vincent, for St. Anthony lived and died in the third century of the

Christian era. However, St. Vincent in his writings quotes him four times, twice in his conferences to the Daughters and twice to his Community of missioners. On the first occasion when St. Vincent quoted St. Anthony in his conference to the Sisters, he did so in support of the advice he gave them that they should be always occupied. (cf. Conf. Eng. ed., 22 Jan. 1645, p. 195). That is not a counsel one hears too often nowadays. The trouble with us modern people is that we are too occupied; we are too busy. Many of us have what I might call the *St. Martha syndrome.* We are busy about many things and are not sufficiently centered on the one thing that is necessary.

However, it must be said that it is one thing to be occupied and it is another thing to be busy. St. Vincent's advice and that of St. Anthony is that we should always be occupied. These two Saints do not advise us that we should always be busy. Being occupied does not necessarily mean being busy. I can be occupied in taking recreation, but I should not be busy about taking recreation, and if I am, it is no longer recreation. If I am always busy and give other people that impression, then it means that I have not properly understood the meaning of the Sabbath in my life, and God intends that there be a Sabbath in the rhythm, even of my daily life.

In today's Gospel Our Lord reminds us that the Sabbath has been made for man, and not man for the Sabbath. In giving us a Sabbath in our lives, God is proposing to us that we should not allow ourselves to be dominated by work, but rather that we should dominate it. We can only dominate our work if we can leave it and detach ourselves from it. Certainly dedication to the service of the poor holds a primacy in your lives as Daughters of Charity, but you should not allow your dedication to become a despot, so that you reduce the time you give to prayer, to spiritual reading, to sleep, and to recreation. If we allow ourselves to become too busy, then we will lose our serenity and, more often than we realize, it is serenity which the poor seek from us when they come to speak with us. I have heard it said that some elderly Sisters find great difficulty in accepting old age and retirement. The cause of their difficulty could be a failure to understand the distinction between being occupied and being busy. There is a very relevant paragraph in your Constitutions which calls for much reflection. Let me read it to you. *"The Sisters strive to maintain a balance between work, recreation and rest, ordering their lives according to the prudent advice given by their Founders and reiterated by the Church."* (C. 2.6).

The second occasion when St. Vincent cited St. Anthony was when he was speaking to the Sisters about prayer. St. Vincent alluded to recollection and said that it was *"St. Anthony's greatest prayer."* (Coste X, p. 604). Recollection is the capacity or ability to make oneself aware of the presence of God, and that is not limited to the periods of formal prayer or meditation. In one of her letters St. Louise wrote to a Sister: *"A practice which our Most Honored Father taught us at one of his recent conferences will prove useful to you. It is, my dear Sister, to turn to God at the beginning of each action; to make an act of humility, recognizing that we are unworthy to perform it."* (*Spiritual Writings of Louise de Marillac*, ltr. 461, p.493).

In the Seminary we were taught about the importance of recalling the presence of God frequently. We in St. Vincent's Communities must not forget the emphasis which St. Vincent put on the virtue of simplicity. Simplicity is speaking and acting always with God alone in view. God is touching our lives at every moment of the day, and we are touching Him. He is particularly close to us in the Church, in the Sacraments, in the Community, in the poor. If we wish to be sensitive to the presence of God in our lives, we have to recall His presence frequently. We have to give ourselves moments of stillness and reflection in the midst of our work, so that we can become more conscious of the reality of God. We must become more conscious that it is in God that we live and move and have our being at all times.

The God in Whose presence we live is not a cold deity. He is the God of the first reading of today's Mass. *"God,"* wrote the author of the letter to the Hebrews, *"will not forget your work and the love you have shown him by your service, past and present, to his holy people."* (Heb 6:10). That truth should give us hope. *"Our hope,"* to quote again the first reading, *"enters into the inner shrine behind the curtain, where Jesus has gone as a forerunner on our behalf, having become a high priest forever according to the order of Melchizedek."* (Heb. 6:20).

Called by Name to Be with Him

20 January 1989   Porto, Portugal

My dear Confreres,

For a number of years now the passage from St. Mark's Gospel to which we have listened, has impressed two truths on my mind each time I reflect on it. The first truth is this: in this morning's Gospel St. Mark gives us the reasons why Our Lord chose the twelve Apostles who were to be His close friends and collaborators. He chose them so that they could be with Him, so that they could have power over evil spirits, and so that they could go out and preach and make Jesus Christ's message known. What is interesting for us is the first reason which St. Mark gives for the choice of the twelve Apostles. Jesus chose these men so that they could be with Him.

That is very important for all of us who have received a special vocation from God. Certainly He has chosen us to do some special work for Him during our lives. But the first reason He has chosen us is so that we can be with Him, so that we can be His special friends. Good friends share everything. So before we think of serving the needy and the poor, we must share everything with Jesus Christ. In practice that means that we spend time with Him in prayer, talking to Him about everything that is in our minds and hearts, and also being ready to sit silently in His presence, so that by His Holy Spirit He can speak to us about His love and His concern for us. We must seek Jesus Christ in prayer, before we go out to seek Him in the poor. For the twelve apostles, casting out devils and preaching the good news of Jesus Christ was important, but it was more important still that they keep close to Jesus Christ and that they share everything with Him.

Second, I am sure you noticed how St. Mark gives us the names of all the Apostles. We can be certain that Jesus Christ called each of them by his name. Often reflect on the fact that Our Lord has called us by name to the Church and to our Community. Jesus Christ would like us to reflect often on the words of the prophet Isaiah, in which he tells us that the names of God's friends are written on the palm of God's hand. When you have grasped something with your hand, it is very close to you. God has grasped us by His hand, but He did not stop at that. He has engraved our names in His hand and in His heart. Each of us matters enormously to Him, however small and insignificant we may feel ourselves to be in this great world.

I recall some years ago an English Cardinal appearing on British television. He was being interviewed by a non-Catholic man who always used his skills to put awkward questions to the prominent people whom he invited to undergo an interview of forty-five minutes. The program was immensely popular and watched by millions of people. Part of the attraction of the program was that it was possible to see very closely the reactions of the interviewee to the questions put by the interviewer. Cardinal Heenan was asked by the interviewer which point of Catholic teaching he found hardest to accept. The interviewer was hoping that he would say, perhaps, *Humanae Vitae*, Papal infallibility or the Assumption of Our Lady. When the Cardinal was asked the question, he paused for a moment and then he replied: *"The point of Catholic teaching which I find hardest to accept is that God should be concerned about me."* It was a brilliant reply and one which was totally unexpected by the interviewer.

I think it is important that we often reflect on the fact that Jesus Christ is always thinking of us as individuals. In recent years we have been asked to think about the social responsibilities which flow from our celebration of the Eucharist. However, we must never forget that we receive all the Sacraments as individuals. We were baptized as individuals; we were confirmed as individuals; we are fed one by one with the Body and Blood of Christ every day. When we receive the Sacrament of Reconciliation, we do so normally as individuals, and when we will receive, please God, the Sacrament of the Sick, we will receive it as individuals. We need to reflect often on the fact that we are loved personally by Jesus Christ. To each of us He still says: *"I know mine and mine know Me."* (Jn 10:14).

I seem to have come to the end of this homily without making any reference to St. Vincent. The person of Jesus Christ was everything to Him. The Rule of the Mission, he said, was Jesus Christ. Here are his celebrated words: *"Remember, Monsieur, we live in Jesus Christ through the death of Jesus Christ and we must die in Jesus Christ through the life of Jesus Christ, and our life must be hidden in Jesus Christ and filled with Jesus Christ, and in order to die as Jesus Christ, we must live as Jesus Christ.''* (Coste I, Eng. ed., ltr. 197, p. 276).

Let us not forget that the great monument of his works for the poor can be said to have been built on his priesthood, which according to the Vatican Council Decree on Priestly Formation, is at the heart of the Renewal in the Church of today. *"The wish for renewal of the whole Church,"* declares Vatican Council II, *"in great part depends on the priestly ministry, animated by the Spirit of Christ."* (Introduction to Decree on Priestly Formation).

"Jesus went up the mountain and summoned the men He himself had decided on, who came and joined Him." (Mk 3:13).

Moral Courage

21 January 1989   Portugal

My dear young People,

You will have noticed the color of the vestments which I am wearing—red. It is the color of blood. Today the Church is honoring a young girl who poured out her blood for the faith many centuries ago in Rome. Her name was Agnes. She was a martyr for the faith. To be a martyr one has to be a person of courage, great courage. St. Agnes was a person of courage. She poured out her blood because she was convinced of the value of the Christian faith. For us men it is good to be reminded that young girls can have more courage at times than we men have. St. Agnes, though young, showed a courage which many men, older and physically stronger than she, did not have.

We men like to think of ourselves as courageous. None of us would like to be considered a coward. The truth is that at times we do not say what we believe to be right because we fear that we will become unpopular. We do not say what we believe to be true, because we fear that others will laugh at us and say that we are not modern. We do not defend what is good and beautiful, because we fear that others will judge us to be narrow-minded and old-fashioned. Such attitudes show that we are not as courageous as we might think ourselves to be.

It is from Jesus Christ that we must look for moral courage. He was a remarkably courageous man by any standards. He is ready to communicate this moral courage to us who are his friends. We get courage to be strong followers of Christ and loyal Catholics by contact with Jesus Christ Himself. When we read the pages of the Gospel, when we receive the Sacraments, Jesus offers us courage.

The world and the Church have need today of persons of moral courage. We admire the present Pope for his moral courage. We recognize that the Church and the world have need of such moral courage. The Church has need, not only of the moral courage of the Pope, of Bishops and priests, but in a special way of young people. It is the young especially who must show moral courage to the young. Young people can show great courage in sports. That courage is physical courage. Young people can also show great courage in war. It is often more difficult to show moral or spiritual courage. Try to be a person of courage to those of your own age. Be courageous, not only with your words, but with the actions of your life. Fight to eliminate hunger and misery, as did St. Vincent de Paul. Fight to persuade others to bring about a more just society in the world. Do all this with the courage that comes from thinking about and speaking to Jesus Christ.

In speaking to you this morning, my dear young people, I am aware that you are passing through very important years in your life. It is in youth that we set about choosing the highway that is going to take us into the heart and into the happiness of God for all eternity. God in His goodness has planned not just one highway, but a special one for each of us. For one person the route will be marriage, for another the priesthood. Yet another will reach God by serving Him in the poor as a Sister or as a Brother.

Many of you are now on the approach roads which will lead you into the highway which God wants you to take. That is why it is so important that at this point in your lives, you should listen carefully to the directions which the Spirit of God is giving you quietly and lovingly.

Often in the course of the day ask the Spirit of Jesus Christ to help you make wise choices, even in small things. By doing so you will be honoring Jesus Christ Who has sent the Holy Spirit to be our guide along the road of life. If we make right choices in small things, then we

will make right choices in big things. If we allow the Spirit of God to
assist us in making small choices every day, He will not abandon us at
the moment when we must make a big choice, such as a decision about
what vocation we will choose in life. In a word, my dear young people,
every day say to Our Lord what St. Paul said when he was struck down
by God on the road to Damascus. St. Paul's first words after his
accident, which God Himself had caused, were: *"Lord, what will You
have me to do?"* (Acts 22:10). May the strength and courage of the light
of God, our Father, of our Lord Jesus Christ, and of the Holy Spirit, be
with you always.

Foundation of the Congregation of the Mission
25 January 1989   Lisbon, Portugal

My dear Confreres,

Let me begin by addressing a word of welcome to the laity who are
present here this morning. In welcoming them I would like to explain
to them that the 25 January is a special day for us priests and Brothers
of the Congregation of the Mission. It is the day on which we celebrate
the foundation of our Congregation. It was on the 25 January 1617 that
St. Vincent preached a sermon in a little country church in the north of
France, a sermon that moved many of the people present to change their
lives through sincerely confessing their sins in the Sacrament of Penance or Reconciliation.

Eight years would pass before St. Vincent would formally establish
his Congregation. When he preached his sermon on the 25 January, he
had not the slightest idea of founding a Congregation. That would come
eight years later. Decades later he would consider that in reality his
Congregation owed its origin to that sermon preached in the little
country church at Folleville, France, on 25 January 1617.

It is the way of old men to look back and muse on the significant
events of their lives, and St. Vincent was no exception. It is in the last
decade or less of his life that we find the most frequent references to
the event of 25 January 1617.

Unlike old men who often look back on the past with nostalgia, St.

Vincent looked back at Folleville, not with nostalgia, but with wonder and gratitude for what the grace of God had done. Being a man who loved to share with others, St. Vincent wished that his Community would share in his wonder and his gratitude by celebrating in a special way each year the 25 January, the Feast of the Conversion of St. Paul. So it is that when the 25 January comes around, we find ourselves dividing our attention between St. Paul on the road to Damascus, and St. Vincent mounting the steps of the pulpit in the little chapel at Folleville.

It was only in later years that both saints would see the full significance of these events in their lives. Years were to separate Damascus from Antioch, Jerusalem, Corinth and Rome. Years, too, were to separate Folleville from Algiers, Madagascar, Scotland and Poland. What was given to both saints in later years was the perception that the fall from the horse or the mounting the steps of a pulpit in a country church were no chance happenings.

On this anniversary of the Foundation of the Congregation, we Vincentian priests and Brothers feel particularly grateful to our Community. We speak of our Community in a broad sense as being a family. To our parents we owe an enormous debt of gratitude, as we do also to the other members of our family with whom we were brought up. So many of our good qualities—and let us not with false humility deny them—have come to us from God through the home into which we were born. After our natural family, I feel it is our Community that has given us much more than anybody else in this world. It is the Community that has given us the spirit of St. Vincent. It is the Community that has helped us to form our spirituality. It is the Community that has supported us in our work. It is the Community which in the end will support us in our old age, if we live that long. It is the Community which after our deaths will go on pleading to God for His mercy for us. All of us have received much from the Community and will continue to receive much from this family of St. Vincent into which, by God's Providence, we have been led. On occasions in our lives we may feel resentful, angry and impatient with authorities in the Community. My prayer for all of us is that such moods may not blind us permanently to the goodness and kindness of God, which He is showing us daily through the family of St. Vincent.

What I have been trying to say has been expressed marvelously by St. Vincent himself in a paragraph of our Common Rules: " . . . *we should think of other congregations as being far worthier than our own, though we should have greater affection for ours, just as a well brought up child will have far greater love for his own mother, poor and unattractive as she may be, than for any others, even if they are outstanding for wealth and beauty.* " (CR XII, 10).

To us today St. Vincent would like to repeat what he said of the Folleville sermon to the community of St. Lazare on 6 December, 1658: *"See, I beg you, the many reasons we have for praising God, for having sent us to remedy this evil; and reasons, too, for kindling in our hearts love for the work of helping the poor and of doing that work wisely and well, because their needs are great and God is counting on us."* (Dodin: *Entretiens*, p. 498).

With all our Confreres in heaven and on earth, *"Let us rejoice and be glad, for this is the day which the Lord has made."* (Ps 117:24). For the future of the Congregation, can I pray a better prayer than that of St. Paul, that *"having the eyes of your heart enlightened, you may know what is the hope to which He has called you"*? (Eph 1:18).

Jesus Christ Casts Out a Demon

30 January 1989   Rome, Italy

My dear Sisters,

The Gospel to which we have just listened, at first sight might not seem to be a very appropriate one for a retreat meditation, but you will find in the incident recorded by St. Mark a wealth of spirituality that could enrich us greatly, particularly during these days of special grace.

When St. Mark recorded this incident in the life of Jesus, he wished to emphasize one particular point for his readers, namely, that there was, and still is, an immense power present in Jesus Christ. You will have noted how much St. Mark insists on the fact that the demonic power that had taken possession of the poor man was very strong. The man was violent, violent with himself and violent with others. He lived in a cemetery. Today we would say that he was a marginalized person.

Then this lonely, mentally disturbed man met Jesus Christ. In a moment he is cured and he becomes tranquil and normal. Jesus Christ gave him no tranquilizing tablets, nor did He have a lengthy interview with him as a modern psychiatrist might do. St. Mark stresses that it was the divine power, radiating from Jesus, which instantly cured this mentally deranged man.

We accept that fact easily, but we tell ourselves, that we are not mentally deranged people. That may be true. However, we must acknowledge that there are forces of evil at work all around us and within us. The Spirit of God dwells within us through Baptism, but a sort of guerilla warfare is being carried on within our bodies by forces of evil which we have not yet completely dominated. We can sin by thought, by word, by actions and by omission.

During our retreat we lay ourselves open in a special way to the divine power of the person of Jesus Christ. We meet Jesus Christ as did the man in today's Gospel. Jesus Christ will meet you through the words of the Bible on which you will reflect during this retreat, through the conferences of Father Gaziello and through the conversations you will have with the Visitatrix and the Director. He will meet you, too, in a special way in the Sacrament of Reconciliation and each morning in the Eucharist. Wait for Him in silence and try to open wide the doors of your heart to Him.

At the end of this retreat Jesus Christ will say to each one of you what He said to the man in today's Gospel: *"Go home to your friends and tell them how much the Lord has done for you and how He has had mercy on you."* (Mk 5:19). Yes, you will go back to your communities to continue the work which the Community has asked you to do. You will continue to pray for the poor and to serve them as best you can. You will talk about the retreat to the Sisters of your community who are not here with you. If you want to know how successful your retreat has been, I think you will find it by measuring the gratitude that will be in your hearts. When Our Lord cured the man in today's Gospel, He gave him a mission, and his mission was to think upon and speak about the goodness and the mercy of Jesus Christ. He gives that mission to each one of us, particularly at the time of retreat. Yes, proclaim the goodness and the mercy of Jesus Christ in your prayers but, above all, by the goodness of your lives. If you return to your communities with a new realization of how much God has done for you and how He has had mercy on you, then you will have been healed during this retreat by the power of Jesus Christ, Who is the same yesterday, today and forever.

I make my own, my dear Sisters, these words of St. Vincent which he addressed to one of the first Daughters of Charity. He wrote: *"Yes, my Sister, I hope that in acting as true Daughters of Charity, as you have done up to the present moment, you will efficaciously invite Our Lord to bless and multiply the work of His hands for comforting and for the salvation of His poor members who are our masters."* (Coste VIII, Fr. ed., p. 297).

My dear Sisters, through the intercession of Mary, the Mother of God, may the peace of Jesus Christ be the healing of our minds and of our hearts.

Blessed Marie Anne and Odile

1 February 1989   Paris, France

My dear Sisters,

Each year the feast of Blessed Marie Anne and Odile is celebrated as a vigil of that day when the Mother General asks the grace of the Renovation of Vows for the entire Company. So it is that martyrdom and renovation go hand in hand. In a broad sense we can say that there can be no renovation without martyrdom. That is not to say that all Sisters are called to shed their blood, as did Sister Marie Anne and Sister Odile. However, we are all called to something of which martyrdom is the external sign. For at the heart of Christian martyrdom is a sharing in the total self-giving and offering of Christ. The very word *martyr* means witness. All of us are called to be, not only witnesses but also active participants in the offering which Jesus Christ continues to make of Himself daily to the Father in the Sacrifice of the Mass.

Martyrdom is a language which we are called to learn. It is a language that is learned slowly and painfully. To some it is given to speak the language of martyrdom with power, elegance and distinction. They are those who have, in witnessing to Christ, resisted, to quote a phrase in today's first reading, *"to the point of shedding blood."* (Heb 12:4). Among such are to be numbered our two Sisters Marie Anne and Odile.

The language of martyrdom, like any living language, is subject to subtle change with the passing of time. Living languages change with usage. New words are formed and incorporated into the language. No one speaks today in the idiom of the seventeenth century. The idiom has changed, but the language is the same. So it is with the language of martyrdom. For the Christian, for the consecrated person, the language will always be the language of the cross. The idiom, however, is subject to change. No Sister will be executed this morning at Angers, but the Sisters who live in the community of Angers, and in each community the world over, are being called today to proclaim by word and work and humble service that the Risen Christ is with them and that He is making all things new. Being a martyr today is to live in such a way that those who do not share our convictions with faith are led to ask the question, "Why?" Why does a man or woman forego the right to marriage? Why does a person voluntarily accept the restraints on doing what he or she would like to do? Why this submission to Rule and persons? Why this simple, uniform life style? Why this generous gift of self to those who are needy and destitute? A true renovation of vows is a martyrdom. It is a witnessing to the reality of that invisible world of God's grace and love, a world that has been opened up for humanity by the death and resurrection of Jesus Christ, Who is the supreme Martyr. *"If anyone wishes to be My disciple, let him deny himself, take up his cross daily and follow Me."* (Lk 9:23).

As Sisters Marie Anne and Odile walked to the field of martyrs at Angers on this morning one hundred ninety-five years ago, who knows but that the Spirit of God whispered to them the words of encouragement to which we listened in the first reading: *"Lift your drooping hands and strengthen your weak knees and make straight paths for your feet."* (Heb 12:12-13). May they intercede for us who are slow learners of the language of martyrdom. May they win for us the grace of continuing to speak courageously to the men and women of our time by our manner of life, as we walk on the narrow road to that city whose maker and builder is God.

St. Vincent the Educator

12 February 1989   Bathurst, Australia

My Lord Bishop, the Honorable Member for Clare, Ladies and Gentlemen,

It was G.K. Chesterton who remarked once that there is a Catholic way of teaching everything, even the alphabet, if only to teach it in such a way that those who learn it will not look down on those who don't. If that be a definition, however broad, of Catholic education, then St. Vincent de Paul was a superb educator, for he spent his life trying to teach and convince people, particularly those who had material goods or who were gifted in mind, that they should not only not look down on others, but that they should share their riches with those less fortunate. The true educator is one who starts with the conviction that the student is not a container into which one must pour information, but rather one who has inherent powers of reasoning and imagination that are waiting to be awakened. To be a true educator, one must be a humble person, and humility is an outstanding facet in the character of St. Vincent de Paul.

It was the humility of St. Vincent de Paul that lay at the root of his respect for persons. That respect was extended also to academic institutions. We have proof of that in the fact that he studied for degrees in two French universities and kept as a treasured possession to the end of his days the parchments attesting to the fact that he had obtained degrees in theology and canon law. His experience in the classroom was very limited. It could be said that he was a tutor rather than a professor. The two boys of the De Gondi family perhaps knew him best as an educator and that only for a short time.

St. Vincent, as an educator, was not bound by the walls of a classroom. In the large school of life he taught Queens and Princes, Cardinals and Bishops, simple country folk and children of the inner city of Paris. He taught all these people much more than the alphabet. He taught them the alphabet of charity which is the language of the kingdom of heaven, and he taught it humbly. The secret of learning that alphabet is to become a child, for only those who are children can enter the kingdom of heaven. For that reason, when St. Vincent listed the requirements for those who would join him in teaching others, the alphabet of charity, the virtues or values of simplicity and humility took first place.

Speaking to those whom we might describe as undergraduates in his school of charity, namely students of philosophy, he said: *"May the philosophy that you are going to learn help you to love and to serve the good God even more than you did previously; may it help to elevate you to Him by love; and while you study the science and philosophy of Aristotle and learn all his divisions, may you learn the science and philosophy of Our Lord and His maxims, and put them into practice with the result that what you learn will not serve to puff up your hearts but rather enable you better to serve God and His Church."* (Coste XII, Fr. ed., pp. 63-64).

What the students learn in the classroom must not *puff up* their hearts. They will not have learned Catholic philosophy if, in doing so, they are looking down on those who have never studied the works of Aristotle or Aquinas. Not that St. Vincent was simplistic in his approach to education. Towards the end of his life in one of his conferences he told the Daughters of Charity: *"Now, it is necessary for Daughters of Charity to teach the poor . . . and, therefore, Sisters should first of all be instructed before they can teach others."* (Conf. Eng. ed., 16 March 1659, p. 1183).

He agreed, even though a little diffidently, with a proposition made by St. Louise de Marillac, that the Sisters should be sent to the Ursuline Nuns to learn the art of teaching, for the Ursuline Nuns were the most professional of women teachers in the France of the seventeenth century. (cf. Coste I, Eng. ed., ltr. 279, p. 427). Two months before he died, St. Vincent said to the Sisters at a conference: *"A few days ago I had a letter from Narbonne in which I was told of the wonderful things our Sisters are doing. Sister Frances has been to a city, far away from Narbonne, to which she was sent by the Bishop of Narbonne to learn an excellent method that is practiced there for the education of the young. She learned it and is now applying it to the great edification of all."* (Conf. Eng. ed., 24 July 1660, p. 1278).

In an age that was dominated by the study of the ancient classics, it is interesting to note how open St. Vincent's mind was to other fields of learning. He was sensitive to the fact that there is a wide diversity of talents in the young, and he recognized that a student who may not have a gift for languages and literature may be richly endowed to work in the area we would call today technology. Writing to Father Coglée, Superior of the Mission at Sedan, he remarks:

I think it is inadvisable to continue the special money grant, because as a rule it is of very little use for boys to begin the study of Latin when there is no opportunity of going on with it; and this is the case when their parents cannot supply what is required. An exception, perhaps, could be made in the case of an intelligent boy who might excite the interest of some charitable person to help him on. Apart from that, most of these boys stop halfway. It is far better for them to learn some craft or other as soon as they can. You should do this kindness to these poor boys of Sedan by urging their parents to apprentice them to some trade or other . . . . (Coste V, Fr. ed. p. 491).

In a letter to St. Louise de Marillac, written in February or March 1641, he refers to a past pupil of the Ursuline nuns of the parish of St. James, in Paris, who had learned to weave tapestry in the convent. He suggested to St. Louise that this girl should reside with the Daughters of Charity in La Chapelle for two or three months in order to teach the Sisters tapestry-weaving so that they might, in turn, instruct the children in their schools. (cf. Coste II, Eng. ed., ltr. 517, p. 186).

More could be said about St. Vincent as an educator, but I must end. So let me close this brief reflection on St. Vincent and education by inviting you into one of his classrooms which he frequented much in the later decades of his life. He is seated, surrounded by a number of Daughters of Charity. He is educating these girls in the fundamentals of spirituality that will help them in their vocation of serving the poor. Quite a few of his auditors are unable to read or write. So St. Vincent, the teacher, does not deliver a lecture. He is Socratic in his method, respectfully and humbly inviting the Sisters to share with him and with the other participants whatever insights the Lord may have given them on the subject under discussion. A supreme educator, he recognizes the principle that students will learn and retain more easily the truths which they discover through guidance. In one word, perhaps the supreme discovery that St. Vincent, the educator, made in his lifetime was that there is, after all, a Catholic way of teaching even the ABCs.

Jesus Christ Cures the Paralytic

7 March 1989   Paris, France

My dear Sisters,

I am sure some of you here this morning have entertained sympathy for the paralytic in this morning's Gospel. He had spent, remarks St. John, no less than thirty-eight years waiting for his turn to reach the pool of water after the angel had touched it with healing power. Perhaps there are some of you here who have been waiting that length of time to be invited to come to the Mother House to participate in a Vincentian Session. Now at last you have reached this source of grace, which does so much to heal and strengthen Sisters in their vocation as Daughters of Charity. I have no doubt that there are many Sisters in the provinces who would treasure the experience you have had, but somehow, like the man in today's Gospel, someone else gets to the pool before them.

There is no record in today's Gospel that, after the paralytic had been cured by Our Lord, he thanked his Healer. In fact, he seems to have gone to the leaders of the people and, prudently or imprudently, told them that it was Jesus who had cured him. I would suggest that your final prayer, before leaving the Mother House and its Chapel, be a prayer of thanksgiving to God and His Mother for bringing you into the pool of grace where so many others, like you, have found strength to continue giving themselves to the service and to the healing of the poor.

It is a paralyzed man who lies before Our Lord in this morning's Gospel. Our Lord heals him and later He tells him not to sin again. There would seem to be a certain similarity between paralysis and sin. Was Jesus suggesting to us that sin is a form of paralysis, an inability to feel guilt, an insensitivity to the need of forgiveness from God?

It was Pope Pius XII who said: *"The sin of the century is the loss of the sense of sin."* Paralysis is, according to the dictionary, *"a partial inability to move or feel."* We could almost define sin as an inability to move and feel with Jesus Christ. The saints are those who developed to the greatest degree the ability to move and feel with Jesus Christ. It is in this that St. Vincent's greatness lies. The saints are those who are least paralyzed by sin. The paralysis of sin is a widespread epidemic today. There are those who will tell us that they are not convinced that abortion, euthanasia and divorce are wrong. Perhaps we do not suffer from that degree of paralysis, but we can suffer from what St. Vincent in the C.M. Common Rules calls *"attaching no great importance to either God's honor or the salvation of others."* (CR II, 15). We can find ourselves saying that we do not feel the need of the Sacrament of Penance, and that we do not know what sins to confess. All that could be a symptom of a certain spiritual paralysis which is sin.

What therapy can be recommended for the paralysis of sin from which we may suffer? To begin with, it is a good practice at the end of every day to spend some moments thanking God for His goodness to us and reflecting on how we have failed Him and our neighbor during the day. Second, a Christian who can humbly and regularly make an act of faith in the Sacrament of Penance will come to see and feel the presence of sin and imperfection in his life. That experience can be a little painful, but the pain itself is a sign of receding paralysis. When St. Paul wrote to the Romans, he spoke of being *"alive with a life that looks towards God through Christ Jesus."* (Rom 6:11). Part of the power of the Sacrament of Penance is to make us more alive with the movements and the feelings of Jesus Christ. In the ritual of the Sacrament of Penance the Church suggests to the penitent this prayer: *"Lord Jesus Christ, Lamb of God Who takes away the sin of the world, reconcile me with your Father by the grace of the Holy Spirit. Wash with Your blood all my faults and make of me a new creature to the praise of Your glory. Amen."*

More frequently in recent years we have been referring to the Sacrament of Penance less as confession and more as a Sacrament of Reconciliation. The season of Lent is preeminently the season of reconciliation. If we are paralyzed spiritually to a greater or lesser degree, then it is due to some failure to be reconciled with God, with the Church, with the Community, with ourselves. The Sacrament of Reconciliation can effect for the better our whole experience of living. Pope John Paul II has made that precise point in his apostolic exhortation on Penance and Reconciliation: *"It has to be added that this reconciliation with God leads, as it were, to other reconciliations, which repair the breaches caused by sin. The forgiven penitent is reconciled with himself in his inmost being, where he regains his own true identity. He is reconciled with his brethren whom he has in some way attacked and wounded. He is reconciled with the Church. He is reconciled with all creation . . . .Every confessional is a special and blessed place from which, with divisions wiped away, there is born new and uncontaminated a reconciled individual, a reconciled world!"* (III, chap. 2, §5).

My dear Sisters, you have come to the end of your Session. I wish you a safe return to your provinces. You have gathered much fruit from this meeting here in the Mother House. May that fruit, to quote the words in the final sentence in this morning's first reading, *"be good to eat and the leaves medicinal."* (Ez 47:12).

The Least of Christ's Brethren
13 March 1989   Egypt

My dear Sisters,

Whenever I read the Gospel for Monday in the first week of Lent, I think of a diocesan priest who is working in London, and who told me on one occasion of how a group of priests were discussing the topic of the experience of dying. In the group there was a priest who had a rather sharp tongue and who tended to be very critical of both priests and people. This particular priest said in the course of the discussion that he hoped he would see Our Lord face-to-face immediately after his death. One of the priests in the group immediately said to him: *"Even if you do see Our Lord immediately after your death, you would not be able to recognize Him, for you cannot recognize Him at present in the persons of those with whom you live."* Perhaps this was a rather hard saying, but it did express the truth that Our Lord puts before us in today's Gospel, namely, that He is present in the sick, in the prisoner, in the hungry, in the thirsty, that He is present in the least of His brethren. *"As long as you did it for one of My least brothers, you did it for Me."* (Mt 25:40).

Let me ask you: who do you consider to be the least of Christ's brethren? Immediately we think of the categories mentioned in today's Gospel. A Daughter of Charity will think at once of the poor. Yes, the poor are among the least of Christ's brethren, because they are suffering, because they have little money or are very sick in body or are mentally handicapped. Suppose someone were to say to you: *"The least of Christ's brethren is to be found in your Community."* Would you be surprised at that statement? Our first reaction would be to say: *"No, that is not true. The Community provides for us well during our lives, takes care of us when we are sick and prays for us when we are dead. So it is difficult for us to think that anyone in our own Community is the least of Christ's brethren."*

However, we can look at it another way. The least of Christ's brethren in my eyes is the person to whom I am showing least love. So it is quite possible that I am showing more love to the poor than to one or two or more of my own Community. If that is so, the least of Christ's brethren are within my Community. Our Lord could be very well saying to me: *"Show more love to the person whom you love least."* Often it happens that the person we show least love to is someone in our own Community.

It is difficult to see Christ in the poor. It is even more difficult to see Him in a person whose weaknesses of character or whose ill will towards me is all too apparent. Still Our Lord keeps saying to me: If you find it difficult to see Christ in the poor or in the person who annoys you in your own Community, begin by trying to be Christ to such people: to say nothing, to do nothing which Christ would not say or do. That calls for faith. Your Constitutions express magnificently in one single phrase all that I have been trying to say: *"The service of the Daughters of Charity is at the same time a vision of faith and the concrete expression of that love whose source and model is Christ."* (C. 2.1).

Let us not be discouraged at our failures in our service of the poor or by our failures in fraternal charity. With the grace of Jesus Christ we must keep trying. Let us draw confidence from these words of St. Vincent: *"If God gives a happy eternity to those who have only given a glass of water to a poor person, what will He not give to a Daughter of Charity who leaves everything and dedicates herself to the service of the poor throughout her entire life . . . . She has good grounds for hoping to be among those to whom He will say 'Come, blessed of My Father, possess the Kingdom which was prepared for you.'"* (Coste IX, Eng. ed. p. 252, 13 Feb. 1646).

Source of Strength and Energy

17 March 1989   Egypt

My dear Sisters,

Some months ago when preparing for this visit with you, I noticed that today is the Feast of St. Patrick. As you know, St. Patrick is the national Patron of Ireland, and he is also honored as a great missionary. Perhaps I would surprise you by saying that St. Patrick was not an Irishman. Possibly he came from France or from Wales. He was taken as a hostage by some Irish terrorists (we have some still in Ireland today) and passed some years as a slave in Ireland. Then he ran away, back to his own country, but in a dream he heard the voices of the Irish inviting him to come back again and walk once more among them. He came back as Bishop and began a program of evangelization which was blessed with success. He died probably about the year four hundred sixty.

What manner of man he was, we can learn from a short autobiography which he wrote at the end of his life. He was not a scholar and he knew it. In fact, he describes himself *"like a stone which was lying in the mud and which God took up and used for the building which He wished to make."* In his very short autobiography he shows himself to be familiar with the pages of the New Testament. He expresses a very personal pain, but without bitterness, because of some people who broke confidences which he had given to them and which had made life difficult for him. From his autobiography one can see that he was saturated by the thought of Christ. In the Irish language there is a rather beautiful hymn called *St. Patrick's Shield*:

Christ be with me,
Christ within me,

Christ behind me,
Christ before me,
Christ beside me,
Christ above me,
Christ in the hearts of all that love me,
Christ in mouth of friend and stranger.

St. Patrick was first and foremost a man of intense, prolonged and genuine prayer. He could honestly confess that he prayed daily and *". . . as often as a hundred times and at night almost as frequently, even while in the woods and on the mountains. Before daybreak I used to be awakened to prayer in snow and frost and hail . . . and there was no sloth in me, as I now perceive, because the spirit was then fervent in me."*

Whenever I read the very short autobiography which the aged St. Patrick left us, I am always struck by that last phrase. *"There was no sloth in me, as I now perceive, because the spirit was then fervent in me."* Those of us who have been many years in the religious life feel age creeping up on us, taking a toll from our bodies. But what of our spiritual energy? Is a decline in spiritual energy inevitable with the passing of years? I do not think so. St. Paul tells us what his experience was: *"Though our outer nature is wasting away, our inner nature is being renewed every day."* (2 Cor 4:16).

It is certain that there will be dark days in our lives, when we will seem to have no relish for spiritual things, for our apostolates, for our Community. At such times we can only do as St. Vincent did in his period of darkness and trial—hold fast to the Credo and keep contemplating the experience of Christ on the cross. We can also find strength in that assurance of St. Paul that *"our nature is being renewed every day."* (Ibid.). Yes, it is every day that we feed on the Body and Blood of Jesus Christ. It is every day, even in old age, that we are being nourished and renewed by the Bread of eternal life. It is from our daily participation in the Holy Eucharist that we will receive the strength to remain fervent to the end. Nor should we overlook the continuing presence of Christ in the Blessed Sacrament as a source of strength and energy, at every stage and at every crisis in our lives, to enable us to continue to show forth, by our words and, above all, by our example, the love of Christ to others, first to the members of our own Communities and then to the poor to whom we are sent. St. Leo the Great reminds us in the office of Readings for Thursday in the fourth week of Lent that *"Jesus Christ performed and suffered everything necessary for our salvation, so that the power which was in the head might also be found in the body."*

Let me end by quoting some words of St. Vincent with which St. Patrick would easily identify: *"Our vocation is, then, to go, not into one parish nor into one diocese, but to go throughout the world. And to do what? to set fire to the hearts of men, to do what the Son of God did, He Who came to cast fire on the earth in order to inflame it with His love. What must we wish for, if not that it burn and consume everything? My dear brothers, please let us reflect on that. It is true, I have been sent, not only to love God, but to make Him loved. It is not sufficient to love God if my neighbor does not love Him. I must love my neighbor as the image of God and the object of His love."* (Coste XII, Fr. ed. pp. 202-203).

Through the prayers of Mary, the Mother of God, St. Patrick and St. Vincent, may that grace be ours.

Our Lady, Reflect her Light and Love

19 March 1989   Alexandria, Egypt

Your Excellency and my dear Brothers and Sisters in Christ,

Let me begin by expressing my joy and happiness in being with all of you this evening. For almost a week now I have been visiting different centers in this country, where the Daughters of Charity and the Vincentian Fathers are working. I have been greatly impressed by what I have seen of their work in this country which had the privilege of offering hospitality to the Saint whom the Church is honoring today. For us Christians the most glorious page in the history of Egypt must be that in which it is recorded that it hosted for some time the Word of God, His Virgin Mother, Mary, and her husband, Joseph. We can say with some degree of certainty that St. Joseph would not have come willingly to Egypt. Most refugees, and St. Joseph was a refugee, leave their own countries unwillingly. But when St. Joseph did come to Egypt, he found it to be a secure place where he could shelter the two great treasures entrusted to his care, the Virgin Mary and her Child, Jesus.

We honor him because of who he was and what he did, not because of anything he said. Search the New Testament and you will not find record of any word spoken by St. Joseph. When St. Matthew tells us that St. Joseph was a "just man," he is telling us that, not only was he honest and paid his bills, but that he was thoroughly good.

St. Joseph was a man whose role in life seemed to be that of one who was used by others. Open the Gospel of St. Matthew, and the first thing that meets your eye is the genealogy of Joseph. You have not gone very far in the Gospel when you realize that the genealogy of Joseph is there, not for his own sake but merely that St. Matthew may prove that Jesus Christ is the son of David, the son of Abraham. As you read on through those first two chapters, you seem to be constantly running across the same thing. No sooner does St. Matthew tell you something that St. Joseph did, than he hastens to add that in so acting, he was merely fulfilling something which had been foretold centuries before, that Divine Providence was merely using this man to accomplish a greater purpose.

Allowing himself to be used, that is one of the many traits which we admire in the character of St. Joseph. It should be one of the characteristics of our lives that we be prepared to allow ourselves to be used in unspectacular ways.

In allowing himself to be used by God, St. Joseph was reflecting an attitude which he must have admired in Mary of Nazareth. She had allowed herself to be used by God also when she replied to the angel, *"Be it done unto me according to thy word."* (Lk 1:38).

This evening we are honoring St. Joseph. We have also gathered to honor Mary who was conceived without sin, a title with which Daughters of Charity and Vincentian priests and Brothers like to greet her. No doubt Mary, the Mother of Jesus, could tell us many stories of how she protected billions of people from all sorts of dangers down through the centuries. She could tell us stories about how she has protected each one of us, not only from danger such as accidents on the road or in the air, but the more serious danger of falling into sin. In Mary's eyes, as in the eyes of her Son, the greatest tragedy that can happen is not an air crash, not failures in examinations, not even death. The greatest tragedy that can happen is that we reject what her Son and His Church want us to do, for when we reject the voice of her Son and of His Church, and the voice of our consciences, we are committing sin. It is sin alone that can keep us distant from God, from Jesus Christ and from Mary herself. If it is serious sin, it could, if we do not repent, separate us from God for all eternity, and that would be a story with a tragic ending.

I have no doubt that you have confidence in the intercession of our Lady. Honor her also by imitating her. Our world today has a deep need of people who will reflect in the darkness, and in the violence of this world, the light and the love of Our Blessed Lady. Our world has need of people who believe and who manifest by their lives that their bodies are the temples of the Spirit of God, Who, by His power, brought forth from the womb of the Virgin Mary, Jesus Christ, true God and true Man.

My dear people, beloved by Jesus Christ and beloved by Mary, the Mother of God and our Mother also, may you experience in your lives the intercession of Our Lady at all times and in all places. Let me now address a short prayer to her who is the Mediatrix of all graces:

> *O Mary, Virgin Mother of God, you were preserved, as no other human being has been preserved, from original sin. You never committed sin during your life. We praise and thank God for that great privilege. Pray for us, for we know ourselves to be sinners. Above all, through your powerful intercession may the story of our lives have a happy ending so that with you we may praise and thank God, Father, Son and Holy Spirit, for all eternity. Remember us, therefore, Blessed Joseph, and pray for us to your Son. Bid the Blessed Virgin, your Spouse, to look favorably upon us, the Mother of Him Who with the Father and the Holy Spirit lives and rules forever.* (St. Bernardine of Siena, 2nd Reading of March 19 Office).

Every Sin Has Its History

21 March 1989   Abruzzo, Italy

My dear Brothers and Sisters in Jesus Christ,

Over and over again in the pages of the New Testament, we have proof of that impetuous enthusiasm which characterized St. Peter and which so often led him into trouble, or at least into embarrassing situations. We cannot but admire his impetuous enthusiasm when he said to Our Lord during the Last Supper: *"I will lay down my life for You."* (Jn 13:37).

Peter was a friend of Jesus Christ both before and after His death on the cross. He felt so attached to Jesus Christ that he could not conceive of ever betraying Him. There is great sincerity in Peter's protest that even if all others would betray Jesus, he would not. Yet, when *"the maid who kept the door said to Peter, 'Are not you also one of this man's disciples?' He said: 'I am not.'"* (Jn 18:17). That was Peter's moment of weakness. Out of fear, out of human respect, he denied that he ever knew Jesus Christ. We know that Peter's denial of Christ did not run deep. Despite his denial, Peter really believed in Christ, for how else can we explain the fact that after his denial, he went out and, as St. Mark, who probably heard it from Peter himself, says: *"He broke down and wept."* (Mk 14:72).

On one occasion Cardinal Newman said that *"every sin has its history."* By that he meant that we don't suddenly become alienated from Jesus Christ. We don't suddenly fall into serious sin. In any history of serious infidelity in our lives, we will find that it was preceded by a slow lessening of our love for the person of Jesus Christ.

We can draw great encouragement in our lives from Peter's experience. All of us fail Jesus Christ in many ways, but I think there are very few of us who fail Him by losing all faith in Him. No matter what sins we commit, no matter how low we may stoop, no matter how far we may stray from Christ, all of us can still retain one prayer, namely, the utterance of Peter: *"Lord, you have the words of eternal life."* (Jn 6:69).

Some time ago I was visiting the Provincial House in Rome and I was asked to go to visit a Sister in the Infirmary who was at the point of death. As we stood around her bed, I listened to a Confrere reading the prayers of the dying, and I was struck by that phrase which the Church suggests to us, that *"no matter what sins your servant has committed, he or she has not lost faith in the mystery of the Blessed Trinity, Father, Son and Holy Spirit."* That was Peter's experience. He may have failed Christ by denying Him, but he never lost faith in the goodness and tenderness of Jesus Christ.

There is another point in Peter's life history upon which it is worth reflecting. He knew about his failure in the past, and his failure was widely known in the Church of his time. All four Evangelists record his denial of Christ. Yet Peter could accept that failure and still move on to work for Jesus Christ and for the coming of His Kingdom. Peter could accept the failures of his past because he had enormous confidence in the power of Christ to forgive. Peter often made his meditation on what Our Lord had said about forgiveness, that he must forgive seventy times seven times. We can imagine Peter saying to himself: *"My Lord Jesus Christ taught me how and how often I should forgive, and I know that He practiced every word He preached. So I draw confidence from the sincerity of His words to me: 'Feed My sheep.'"* Undoubtedly St. Peter would have interpreted that as that all was forgotten and all was forgiven.

My dear brothers and sisters in Jesus Christ, let us go forward, like St. Peter, confident in the fact that we have said to Jesus Christ, if not in words, at least in our hearts, *"Lord, to whom shall we go? You have the words of eternal life."* (Jn 6:69). Whatever may have happened in the past, we will make our own the sentiments of St. Vincent, who encouraged us: *"to ask His divine goodness for a great confidence in all that is happening to us. Provided only that we remain faithful to Him, we shall not be wanting for anything. He Himself will live in us. He will guide us, defend us and love us. All that we will say, all that we will do, everything will be pleasing to Him."* (Coste XII, Fr. ed. pp. 141-142).

Let me conclude by quoting some words of the present successor of St. Peter. Speaking to us, Fathers and Brothers of the Congregation of the Mission, the Pope expressed a Vincentian ideal which I consider valid for the entire family of St. Vincent:

*The advent of science and its applications, industrial devel-
opment and the often haphazard growth centers have begot-
ten a new class of poor who suffer as much as and,
undoubtedly, more than the rural and town populations of
past centuries. Without monopolizing charity and social
action, Monsieur Vincent would move heaven and earth to
go to the aid of today's poor and to evangelize them . . .
search out more than ever, with boldness, humility and skill,
the causes of poverty and encourage short and long term
solutions; adaptable and effective concrete solutions. By
doing so, you will work for the credibility of the Gospel and
of the Church. Without waiting further, however, live close
to the poor and see to it that the Good News of Jesus Christ
is never lacking to them. "* (Discourse of 30 June 1986).

May the peace of Our Lord, which comes from the good news of
Jesus Christ, be with you all forever.

Betrayals

22 March 1989   Abruzzo, Italy

My dear Sisters and my dear Nurses,

The Gospel this evening is a sad one, for it tells the story of how a
man, who was a close friend of Jesus Christ and who, for some obscure
motives known only to himself, facilitated the arrest and execution of
Jesus Christ. The whole of the Christian world condemns Judas for what
he did. For the Christian, Judas will remain for all time the classic
example of what it means to betray a friend. Mention the name of Judas
Iscariot to any Christian, and the word *betrayer* will enter his or her
mind at once. When listing the twelve Apostles, all the evangelists place
his name in the last place and rather sadly add the phrase, *"who also
betrayed Him."*

St. Vincent often said, quoting St. Francis de Sales, that if an action
of a person presented one hundred different interpretations, we should
try to take the most favorable one. Reflecting on Judas, who figures so
prominently in the Gospel of this evening, could I say something in his

defence or, if not in his defence, at least to help us to better understand him and his dismal betrayal of Jesus Christ, *"to know all is to forgive all"?*

Is there anything we could know about Judas Iscariot that would make it easier for us to forgive him for what he did? Sometimes I reflect on the priest character in a novel I read once: the priest as he sets out on his bicycle to do his parish rounds always prays a Hail Mary for the soul of Judas Iscariot. Certainly Our Lord used no harsh words against Judas when they met each other for the last time in the Garden of Gethsemane. Jesus just posed one simple, searching, question: *"Dost thou betray the Son of Man with a kiss?"* That question is not the utterance of an unforgiving person. These are the last recorded words that Jesus addressed to Judas, words that are less terrifying than those He had spoken earlier about the sin which Judas would commit in betraying the Son of God.

"To know all is to forgive all," we say. Once I read an article by a psychologist who was using his skills on the twelve Apostles. This author made the suggestion that, of all the apostles, Judas alone was from the south of the country, all the others were from the north of Palestine. Perhaps because of this, the author suggested, Judas felt himself a little bit outside the community and, to compensate for his sense of isolation, he began with petty thefts first and ended by asserting himself in the betrayal of Jesus to His enemies. Regardless of the correctness of the psychologist's report on Judas, we would do well to reflect on what we might be doing to someone whom we tend to ignore or isolate, simply because we consider her odd or because she sees things differently from the way we see them.

As for our own betrayals of Jesus Christ, they are in the last analysis an assertion of ourselves against Him or against others or against what we know to be His Will for us. We want this or that, so we make things difficult for this or that person. Often, while we may have an uneasy feeling that our motives are basically selfish, we press ahead nonetheless.

Whatever our betrayals in the past have been, great or small, they can be the experience out of which conversion comes. It was so with Peter. For Peter, his betrayal of Jesus Christ spelled out repentance and a deeper attachment to the person of Jesus Christ. For Judas, betrayal spelled out only remorse.

Remorse and repentance, there is a world of difference between them, a difference of heaven and of hell. My prayer for all of us this evening is that we will see more clearly that in betraying Jesus Christ, we betray ourselves. We hand ourselves over to something that is of much less value than the upward call of our vocation in Christ Jesus. In betraying Him, we are betraying much more than the material purse He entrusted to Judas. For He continues to hand Himself over to us in Holy Communion. He continues to give us a privileged vocation of special service to the sick poor: privileged because He gives it only to a minority of the baptized, and specialized because your service is to His poor, whom He regarded and still regards as a special category of people in His Kingdom.

My prayer this evening is that all our betrayals in the past may bring us closer to, rather than withdraw us from, the loving Person of Jesus Christ.

Love and Obedience

3 April 1989   Paris, France

Mother Duzan, Father Lloret and my dear Sisters,

On Good Friday evening Italian television presented a program on the topic of suffering. In the studio there was a panel of serious-minded Christians, a bishop, two priests and a few prominent Catholic lay people. A cloistered nun was also a participant in the discussion, but from her convent where a TV camera had been set up. Viewers were invited to phone in questions on the topic of suffering and, as you could well imagine, there was a wide variety of questions on a subject which is as complex as it is mysterious. The panel of speakers did not resolve the question of human suffering, but, as it was Good Friday, there were frequent references to the experience which Jesus Christ had of suffering, as He passed through the gates of death on the Cross. Perhaps the most refreshing and touching of the questions which the viewers presented was one from a little child, eight years of age, who picked up his parents' phone and asked the distinguished panel how Jesus Christ was able to bear such great sufferings on the Cross.

The child's question was clear and transparent, but I am not so sure that the reply of the adults was as full and adequate as it might have been. I have no way of knowing if the child was satisfied with the reply of the learned grown-ups. The particular speaker who answered the child's question seemed to stress very much the fact that Jesus Christ was not only man, but He was also God, and as God was capable of enduring the excruciating pain that is experienced in death by crucifixion.

That is true as far as it goes, but it does not go far enough. The child's mind had been focused on the experience of Jesus Christ and particularly on the physical sufferings of Jesus Christ crucified. Perhaps the child had not been told that many other men have suffered the pain of crucifixion and lived for two or three days hanging on a cross. What was not unfolded for the child was the mental outlook, the vision which Jesus Christ had as He gave Himself over to the leaders of the people, to Pilate and to the rough hands of the soldiers who executed Him.

Had St. Paul been a member of the TV panel, he would surely have interrupted and said: *"Excuse me, but I would just like to say that Jesus Christ was able to endure so much suffering, not so much because He was God (though He was), nor for that matter because He was a particularly strong man (though He was), but because of something that was burning within Him. You are eight years of age, so you know what obedience is, and because presumably you have good, kind parents, you know what love is. There lies the secret of Jesus Christ's strength to sustain so much suffering."*

What the Company on each continent of the world is celebrating today is the call that each Sister has received to enter into that mysterious world of love and obedience to His Father which was the life experience of Jesus Christ on earth. In reflecting on and contemplating the Person of Jesus Christ, the apostle Paul does not dwell on the historical details of Jesus' life in his writings. He alludes to the crucifixion and death of Jesus. What seems rather to fascinate St. Paul is the intensity and depth of the love and obedience of Jesus Christ. *"He loved me and delivered Himself up for me."* (Gal 2:20). *"He was obedient unto death, even death on the Cross."* (Phil 2:8). All else in the life of

Jesus Christ—the healing of the sick, the feeding of the hungry, the hours spent teaching by the Lake of Galilee, the concern for children, the interest in and respect for the marginalized people of society—was an expression of those two deep, inner attitudes in the mind of Jesus Christ. Just as the atmosphere of the earth breaks up the pure white rays of the sun into myriads of colors which delight our eye, so did the love and obedience of Jesus Christ flower in a profusion of gestures that enlightened the spirits and comforted and healed the bodies of those who discovered that virtue went out from him. (cf. Lk 8:46).

The day of Renovation in the Company is the day when new virtue, new strength, bursts forth from the Daughters of Charity the world over. That virtue and that strength is the virtue and strength of the Risen Christ. It is the strength of the loving and obedient Christ. The essence and foundation of your four vows are the two attitudes of love and obedience. Without love your lives will be, to quote St. Paul, like *"a noisy gong or a clanging cymbal."* (1 Cor 13:1). Without obedience you will wander, imperceptibly perhaps at first, into a desert and lose live contact with Him Who is your Way, your Truth and your Life. (cf. Jn 14:6).

The love that impels us to give ourselves to the service of the poor has its origin in the love that we have for the living Person of Christ. In devoting ourselves to the poor, we live with the conviction that we are giving back to Jesus Christ a morsel of that love which He has shown and continues to show to us as the days of our lives unfold. More difficult than loving the poor is the living of obedience. Often we can accept the poor more easily than we can accept our Superiors or those in the Community with whom our Superiors ask us to live. Yet the Christ Who was sent to preach good news to the poor and Who loved them in word and in action is the Christ Who was obedient unto death, even death on the Cross. We cannot divorce the loving Christ from the obedient Christ. It is love and obedience that underpins not only your service of the poor, but your practice of evangelical poverty and chastity.

The obedience of Jesus Christ was a total surrender of Himself to His Father and to His Father's permissive Will. It was a loving surrender, not a calculated adaptation. We can adapt to situations in Community and persuade ourselves that we are obedient. Adaptation, however, does not always express obedience, for to be obedient is to allow oneself to be vulnerable, as Jesus Christ allowed Himself to be vulnerable. Jesus Christ did more than adapt Himself to the Will of His Father. He fully accepted that Will, even in Gethsemani. It is through obedience, and not through mere adaptation, that we are sanctified. The author of the letter to the Hebrews reminds us that *"when Christ came into the world, He said . . . 'I have come to do Thy Will' . . . and by that Will we have been sanctified through the suffering of the Body of Jesus Christ."* (Heb 10:5,9,10). Our sanctification, a modern Anglican has remarked, is achieved through *"an intense desire not to have one's own way."*

Today our thoughts reach out to the Company on every continent of the world. Hour by hour, from the rising of the sun to its setting, Sisters are renewing the offering of themselves to God for the service of His poor. *"This is the day which the Lord has made. Let us rejoice and be glad."* (Ps 118:24). However, let not countries and continents distract us from the relevance of Pope Paul VI's words: *"The purpose of the Church is not confined to preaching of the Gospel in ever extending territories, proclaiming it to ever increasing multitudes of men. She seeks by virtue of the Gospel to reflect and, as it were, recast the criteria of judgment, the standard of values, the incentives and life standards of the human race which are inconsistent with the Word of God and the plan of salvation."* (*Evangelii Nuntiandi*, §19).

Yes, the Renovation centers on recasting our criteria of judgment and our standards of values which are inconsistent with the Constitutions and Statutes and hence inconsistent with *"the Word of God and the plan of salvation."*

"The Vows have their origin in the death of Our Lord on the Cross," wrote St. Louise, *"through which He won us entirely for God, His Father. That is one of the effects of the enigmatic promise which He made when He said: 'If I be lifted up from the earth, I will draw all things to Myself.' (Jn 12:22) . . . . Most Holy Virgin, you are the model in everything, but principally in that which concerns the vows. You were the first who consecrated your virginity to God and you have merited by this virtue to attract Him into your womb. Let me from now on honor you as my holy Mother and learn from you the fidelity which I owe to*

my God for the rest of my days." (*Sainte Louise*, Fr. ed. 1961, pp. 845-846).

On the March to the Year 2000

24 April 1989   Loreto, Italy

My dear Young People,

I do not know if anyone has remarked upon the fact that today is the birthday of St. Vincent de Paul. He is 408 years old today, or should I say 408 years young. The presence of you young people here today is proof of the fact that, for you, Vincent de Paul is still relevant to the young generation. His words, his activities, his life and especially his interest in and love for the poor and the marginalized of the society of his time speak to you, the youth of Italy, and to the youth of the world. So we wish St. Vincent a very happy birthday. That is hardly necessary, for his degree of happiness could not be greater, immersed deeply in the happiness and joy of God Himself which will go on uninterruptedly for all eternity.

Our Lord said that there were many rooms in His Father's house. So I can imagine that many have left their rooms in heaven today to wish St. Vincent a happy birthday. St. Louise de Marillac, St. Catherine Labouré, and St. Justin de Jacobis will be among the first callers. As they are leaving, they will undoubtedly see millions and millions of poor people lining up to wish St. Vincent a happy birthday. As they queue up at his door, the poor, who are now no longer poor, are saying to one another, *"Well, no, I did not know him personally on earth, for he lived long before my time, but I knew some of his friends—Priests of the Mission, Daughters of Charity, members of the Vincentian Volunteers, members, too, of another Society which bears his name— and it was they who spoke to me about him. It was they who came and relieved my sufferings and lightened my pain of loneliness in life. Sometimes they would say that they learned from Vincent de Paul the importance of looking for the presence of Jesus Christ on earth in our faces, in our suffering bodies, and in our aching hearts."*

As we think of that long line of men, women and children in heaven, of many nations and tongues, that stretches back three centuries and who wanted to wish St. Vincent a happy birthday today, we think also of ourselves. We, who are the most recently born into St. Vincent's family, are at the end of the line. Those in heaven are of yesterday, and we of today have our minds set on tomorrow. As members of the Vincentian Volunteers, you are setting out for the year 2000. It is the theme of this national congress. You are on the march. You are on pilgrimage. So, will you allow me to say something to you about the route?

On the highway which your group has taken towards the year 2000, you will find the usual signs which we read on all the highways of Italy. Each of these signs has a message for you. Let me select some of them. You may select others and apply them to the progress of your journey together. You are traveling in a large pullman coach.

First, large coaches have a speed limit to respect. Perhaps some of you would like to go faster and will try to persuade the driver to do so. But there is wisdom in respecting the speed limit. St. Vincent de Paul never liked to do things in too much of a hurry. Driving at an excessive speed may result in loss of control. For St. Vincent de Paul, doing things slowly and methodically enabled him to see more clearly in what direction God's highway was leading. *"I see nothing more common,"* he wrote one day, *"than the bad results of things done hastily."* (Coste I, Eng. ed., ltr. 295, p. 424). So observe the speed limits, working always within the framework of your Statutes.

Next, on the highways there are tolls to be paid. Driving on highways is pleasant, but the tolls at the exit are often expensive. It is the price one pays for comfort in driving and for the saving of time. You, the drivers, do not think of your own personal comfort so much as the advantages, the blessings, and the benefits you will bring to the poor. You have undertaken this journey, not for pleasure but to bring the light and joy of Christ to the poor. You have undertaken it together. The toll is what it costs in the efforts you make to collaborate with each other, to give of your time, not only to the poor but to the group. It costs a lot at times to give up your own personal interests in preference to those of others. All that costs you much, but remember the words of Our Lord that even if you give a cup of cold water to the least of His brothers, you will not go without a reward. (cf. Mt 10:42). From his room in heaven St. Vincent would like to repeat the advice he once gave to some missionaries setting out on a journey: *"Be united and God will bless you, but let your union be through the charity of Jesus Christ, for no other union that is not cemented by the blood of this Divine Saviour can last."* (Abelly, bk. I, ch. I, pp. 145-146).

On the great highways of your country there are signs such as: *"No Stopping."* Only in emergencies is one allowed to stop by the side of the road. You are an active member of the Youth Group. Everyone expects you to continue being so, unless for some special reason or emergency you must drop out. Remember that the group does depend to some extent on your presence, on your contribution to the program. Perhaps you feel you would not be missed if you dropped out. But what would become of the Group if everyone felt the same. If every car on the highway decided to pull over to the side to have a few winks of sleep or to admire the scenery, there would be chaos on the road. So keep on moving and do not allow yourself to be distracted by the scenery or by the traffic that is overtaking you.

On our highways there are long tunnels. Perhaps some of you passed through them on your way here, long tunnels like that which winds under the Gran Sasso. Tunnels are built to find convenient ways around obstacles, as great as the Gran Sasso. The terrain which you will have to pass over between now and the year 2000 will be rocky and mountainous. The growing number of young people who are using drugs, the fragility of family life, the lack of honesty and justice in society, are like so many large mountains. They seem irremovable and you seem powerless before them. However, with the grace of God something can be done. They must not be obstacles to your journey forward. You must find a way through them, but especially you must try to take care of some of those who are lying on those mountains, like the robbed man in the Gospel, badly wounded and half dead. (cf. Lk 10:25-37).

Can I say lastly a word about the service stations on the highway? You will find them there, and you will need to stop there for refueling, if you are to continue on your journey towards the year 2000. The energy that keeps you going is the love of God in your heart. That love has been poured into your heart by the Spirit of God at baptism. You must keep in contact with the Spirit of God. Every day try to give yourselves ten or fifteen minutes of quiet, reflective prayer on the Gospels, speaking to Jesus Christ and His Spirit Who dwells in your heart. You will have need, too, of the food of the Eucharist. Every Holy Communion is Viaticum, for is that not the food which Our Lord Himself has given for life's journey? You will need the Sacrament of Penance or Reconciliation. Too easily on the journey our vision can get clouded over with the dust and mud of sin. Periodically we need to clear the windshield of our minds, if we are to see clearly the way ahead. The Word of God in the Sacrament of Penance is always a light for our faltering steps.

When you drive on the highway, you need patience. Not all drivers are considerate. On the journey to the year 2000 you must be patient. Be prepared to stop to help others who have been badly injured on the road of life. The Youth Group must consider itself as a sort of mobile First Aid that is interested, not only in reaching the year 2000 but also in helping the casualties that lie on the road, and who are suffering physical or mental or spiritual wounds.

My dear young people, I congratulate you on the work you are doing and I am happy to be with you today. We may not have 408 candles to put on St. Vincent's heavenly birthday cake, but you have something more valuable and pleasing to offer him. You have those countless gestures of love which you have shown and continue to show to those whom St. Vincent loved, namely, the poor of Jesus Christ. At the end of this Congress, as he looks at you, setting off for the year 2000, I am certain that he would say to you what he wrote to St. Louise de Marillac on the 6 May 1629: *"Go, therefore, Mademoiselle, go in the name of Our Lord. I pray that His Divine Goodness may accompany you, be your consolation along the way, your shade against the heat of the sun, your shelter in rain and cold, your soft bed in your weariness, your strength in your toil, and, finally, that He may bring you back in perfect health and filled with good works. "*(Coste I, Eng. ed., ltr. 39, pp. 64-65).

What more can I say to you as you take the highway for the year 2000, if not, "Buon Viaggio!"

Spiral of Violence

15 May 1989   Armagh, Northern Ireland

When I visit foreign countries and am asked my nationality by lay people, and I reply, Irish, another question invariably follows. Are you from the North or from the South? When I reply that I was born in the South, while receiving some of my education in the North, I notice that no further question is put to me. On these occasions I have asked myself: What is the unspoken question in the person's mind? I have often felt that, when I have been asked whether I am from the North or from the South, the questioner is thinking about some of those episodes of violence in northern Ireland, about which he has read in the newspaper or seen on TV. Fratricidal violence did not start in 1969, nor even three centuries ago, but in the episode recounted in the first reading of today's Mass, the violence done by Cain to his brother, Abel. It is recounted in Chapter 4 of Genesis and follows immediately on the account of man's fall and his rebellion against God. That fact seems to underline the truth that the consequence of a revolt against God is a revolt against one's brother.

As you listen to that first reading, it must have seemed all too familiar to some of you, particularly those of you who are working in some of the troubled areas on this side of the border. *"The Lord said: 'What have you done! Listen, your brother's blood cries out to Me from the soil.'"* (Gn 4:10). Abel's blood on the soil . . . and what an amount of blood the soil of the North has soaked up these last twenty years. The violence Cain did to his brother, Abel, revolts us, and often you have been revolted by the violence that has taken place, sometimes in your parish, before which you felt powerless.

Cain's motivation for murdering his brother, Abel, is somewhat obscure. It would seem to proceed from jealousy, rather than from a sense of injustice. As so often happens nowadays, after the foul deed is done, then there is an attempt on Cain's part to justify it. Asked by God what he has done to his brother, Abel, Cain makes the very feeble defensive reply: *"I do not know. Am I my brother's keeper?"* (Ibid., v. 9).

Cain is sentenced by God to be a wanderer on the face of the earth.

He is fearful, as he thinks of the murder of revenge to which he himself may now fall victim. The tit for tat killings in the land of our time are not a new phenomenon. It is in the face of Cain's fear that God guarantees him protection. *"The Lord put a mark on Cain, lest anyone kill him on sight."* (Ibid., v. 15).

In guaranteeing Cain his safety, God was in effect bringing about a reconciliation between Cain and Himself and also between Cain and the descendants of Abel. The priest in northern Ireland—or for that matter anywhere in the world—is an agent of reconciliation. You will recall the thought of St. Paul: *"God,"* he writes, *"was in Christ, reconciling the world to Himself . . . and He gave us the ministry of reconciliation. So we are ambassadors of Christ, God making His appeal through us."* (2 Cor 5:19, 21).

I recall the title of a book, written on the priesthood by an American Cardinal of the last century. It was, *"The Ambassador of Christ."* Some of you may remember how Tom Cleary in Maynooth years ago used to present that title as an ideal of the living of our priesthood. An ambassador finds himself in delicate situations, caught often between two fires. I imagine some of you here must have found yourselves on occasion between two fires, when some incident of violence has taken place and you must celebrate a Requiem Mass and preach a homily. You have to choose your words very carefully and, even when you do, you are not sure that they will not be taken out of context and twisted to give a meaning other than you intended. You may experience the pain of being misunderstood by one or both of our Communities. The pain of misunderstanding so often begets the pain of isolation. In such circumstances you can fall back on the thought that you are a minister of reconciliation, that you are an ambassador of Christ, that He has confidence in you, and that He is at work within you and through you by the grace of ordination which is in you, through the imposition of the hands of the Bishop who ordained you.

In this morning's reading we have an account of the first steps God took to halt what today we call the spiral of violence. The past twenty years in northern Ireland have sadly been the story of a spiral of violence. Thank God, in many ways priests have tried to halt that spiral which, like a tornado, has been passing over our land. *"What's the use,"* you must be tempted to say after so many vain attempts to halt the violence. Let me just end with those words of Pope John Paul II, spoken almost ten years ago at Drogheda: *"I appeal to all who listen to me; to all who are discouraged after the many years of strife, violence and alienation—that they attempt the seemingly impossible to put an end to the intolerable . . . .In the years to come, when the words of hatred and the deeds of violence are forgotten, it is the words of love and the acts of peace and forgiveness which will be remembered. It is these which will inspire the generations to come . . . .Christ, Prince of Peace; Mary, Mother of Peace, Queen of Ireland; St. Patrick, St. Oliver, and all the saints of Ireland; I, together with all those gathered here and with all who join with me, invoke you. Watch over Ireland. Protect humanity. Amen.*

Genesis

16 May 1989   Armagh, Northern Ireland

It is exactly sixty years ago this year that there was quite a stir in present-day Iraq when some biblical excavators thought they had come upon on traces of a large flood which they thought might very well have been the historical basis of the narrative in the sixth and seventh chapters of Genesis. Things have moved on since then, and today the news would be less exciting for us because we do not interpret the chapters of Genesis so literally as was done formerly. We accept the sixth chapter of Genesis as a lesson in theology, rather than as one in history or geography. The theological point is clear to us: namely, that when man sins, he displeases God and his sin has disastrous cosmic effects. The infinite mercy of God, however, intervenes to repair the consequences of man's disobedience. *"I say,"* wrote the poet Hopkins, *"we are wound with mercy, round and round, as if with air."*

Reading and reflecting on this second reading, it struck me that the passage in Genesis has gained a certain new relevance in recent years for two reasons: first, the chapter speaks of a cosmic disaster, the destruction of all life on the earth. That has become a very uncomfortable possibility in our generation. Now it is not God alone who can destroy our planet. Man, as we are all only too painfully aware, has found the means to extinguish all life on this globe. Second, which one of us has not heard in recent years of "the greenhouse effect"? With the heating up of the atmosphere, the polar ice caps will begin to melt, which in turn will cause the ocean levels to rise. Large tracts of low-lying land the world over will be inundated with, presumably, loss of life and property, as in that flood described in today's first reading.

Present-day ecologists think of the future of the planet and of generations to come. The author of Genesis is more far-seeing because he sees and recognizes that the danger to the planet is ultimately rooted in man's sinfulness and selfishness, in his failure to respect the law of God. The older theology books and catechisms used to treat of the seven deadly or capital sins: pride, covetousness, gluttony, lust, anger, envy, and sloth. That terminology may be out of vogue in today's catechetical language, but it is still valid for categorizing the sources of all our sins and of all our danger and fears for the future of life on this planet.

Where do we priests come in on this scenario? As priests we are special ambassadors of Christ to the world. From St. Paul's letter to the Colossians we know that *"all things were created through Him and for Him and in Him all things hold together."* (Col 1:16-17). In a special way we are, to use St. Paul's phrase, *"stewards of the mysteries of God."* (1 Cor 4:1). Among the mysteries of God are the works of His hands. As stewards of the mysteries of God we are appreciative of the beauty of this world and of the goodness of all material things. Is not every created thing a mystery of God? The simplest thing in existence might not have been. Because we are in a special way stewards of the mysteries of God, we should not only be appreciative of creation but, as far as possible, concerned that the good things of the world are equitably distributed. To those who see the way we live and hear what we say and observe our actions, there should be manifest in everything that *"preferential option for the poor"* of which the Church and the Pope have so often spoken in recent times. The bishops here in Ireland through their statements have given us a lead. The Pope has reminded the Church that this preferential option for the poor *"is essentially based on the Word of God, not on criteria offered by human sciences or adverse ideologies which often reduce the poor to abstract sociopolitical or economic categories.* "(Address to Cardinals, Christmas 1984). Recently I read that one-third of the population of Ireland is living below the poverty level. The question naturally suggests itself, how many of that one-third come under my direct pastoral care?

In an era that is clouded and shadowed by the prospect of the extinction of all life on this planet, I would like to encourage you to maintain your confidence in the power of that Mass which you celebrate daily. In the fourth Eucharistic Prayer we are reminded that it is this Sacrifice which *"brings salvation to the whole world."* It will be only in the light of the Beatific Vision that we will see how many evils and disasters were turned aside by the power of this Sacrifice, which *"brings salvation to the whole world."* As you stand at the altar each day, gather all the people of the earth into the great Ark which the Son of God has left us in the Mass, so that by its power the world *"may have life and have it more abundantly."* (Jn 10:10).

To quote the poet Hopkins:

"Generations have trod, have trod, have trod;
And all is seared with trade; bleared, smeared with toil;
And wears man's smudge and shares man's smell . . . . "

(God's Grandeur)

The Two Great Commandments
8 June 1989   Niagara University, New York

My dear Confreres,

I was at my desk preparing this homily one evening last week, when Father Baylach, Editor of *Vincentiana*, came to my room with a large sheet of statistics of the Congregation. Each year he devotes many weeks to compiling a list of statistics on the basis of the returns we receive from the Visitors. Father Baylach picked out two or three points in the statistics which he thought would be of particular interest and significance to me. First, only a little over 5% of the total number of Confreres of the Congregation are engaged in the apostolate of popular missions. Second, 12% of our personnel are engaged in the formation of future priests in our own seminaries and in diocesan seminaries. Third, close to 10% are engaged in the apostolate of suffering, that is, those who are sick, aged and infirm. Fourth, the highest percentage of Confreres, almost 28%, are engaged in parochial ministry.

When Father Baylach made his observations, I was poring over the text of today's Gospel, and particularly over the question which the Scribe had put to Our Lord: *"'Which is the first of all the Commandments?' 'This is the first,' replied Our Lord .... 'You should love the Lord, your God, with all your heart, with all your soul, with all your mind and with all your strength.'"* (Mk 12:30). When Father Baylach left my room, I continued to reflect on the Gospel, but I was distracted by the statistics. Each Confrere accepts the two great Commandments of the law. Each Confrere tries to live by them to a greater or lesser degree of perfection. Then the question came to my mind: Would any change be effected in the statistics of the Congregation if for one day or three days, each Confrere tried to maximize by one degree his living of the two great Commandments of the law? You will remember the scene, an imaginary one but very much in character, in the film, *Monsieur Vincent,* when Queen Anne of Austria, is talking to our Founder towards the end of his life. She is listing some of his great achievements. He listens pensively and then mutters: *"I have done nothing."* She continues to catalogue the works he has initiated and again St. Vincent mutters: *"I have done nothing."* The Queen becomes a little impatient with him and says: *"Monsieur Vincent, if you say you have done nothing, what must we do if we are to save our souls?"* Monsieur Vincent slowly raises his head and with his piercing black eyes looks at the Queen and utters the one word: *"More."* Could this Province do more about loving God? Could it love God with more of its strength, with more of its mind, and with more of its soul? Would that change the columns of the statistics? I do not pretend to answer the question with any precision, but I think there would be some movement in those columns. They say that a pebble thrown into the sea raises the level of the oceans around the world. What would happen to the Congregation, to this Province of Philadelphia, if over the next few days each of us came out of ourselves just one degree more to meet the God of love, Who created us and Who gave Himself up to death on the cross because He loves each one of us?

What shall I say about St. Vincent and the two great Commandments of the law? The spiritual genius of St. Vincent, as with so many other saints, lies in the success he had in marrying so happily in the texture of his life the two great Commandments of the law. I like very much the observation of the French historian, Bremond, in his work on the history of religious sentiment in France of the sixteenth century: *"It is not his love of mankind which led him to sanctity, but it is rather that sanctity made him truly and efficaciously charitable. It is not the poor who gave him to God, but God Who gave him to the poor."* (H. Bremond, *Histoire du sentiment religieux de France*, III, p. 219).

The dynamism, the energy, the love which St. Vincent manifested to the poor did not come from any doctrinaire views on politics or sociology. The source of his energy and the clarity of his spiritual vision came from his contemplation of the words and actions of Jesus Christ in the pages of the Gospel and from his daily contact with Jesus Christ in the quietness of prayer. He became convinced that, once men and women are made new through their personal dedication to Jesus Christ, a new world will follow.

I would like to think that your Convocation and Assembly will have as one of its principal consequences a check on the balancing or realignment of the two great Commandments of the law in the lives of the Confreres. The idea is that we would be men of God, men with experimental knowledge of God and of Him Whom He has sent, yet not so heavenly-minded as to be of no earthly use. The whole idea is lucidly presented by St. Vincent in a letter which he wrote to one of his priests. He appeals to him to exercise: *"... the two great virtues of Jesus Christ, that is, religion towards the Father and charity towards men. So then, Father, is there any other task in the world more necessary or more desirable than yours ... ? Humble yourself unceasingly and have full confidence in Our Lord so that He will unite you with Himself."* (Coste VI, Fr. ed., pp. 393-394).

Through the intercession of Mary Immaculate and of St. Vincent, may that grace be given to each of us for the glory of God and the salvation of humanity.

St. Joachim and St. Anne

26 July 1989   Salvador, Brazil

My dear Friends in Jesus Christ,

I do not think that there is any married couple, apart from St. Joachim and St. Anne, who have the distinction of being honored by the Church in her universal calendar as saints and as a married couple. Individual married people are to be found in the Church's feast day cycle, but on no other day of the year does the Church honor two people together who were married and who are now proclaimed saints. The parents of the Blessed Virgin Mary, St. Joachim and St. Anne, alone have this distinction in the course of the Church's cycle of feast days.

When I was reflecting on that, I thought that it is a pity that the Church's calendar does not offer us one or two more feast days of married couples, in order to underline the truth that, not only is it possible for individual married people to reach the heights of holiness, but that both partners in marriage together can reach eminent holiness. After all, a good married couple pray and plan and work and suffer together. It is surely possible and is a fact that many married couples reach holiness together in and through their vocation.

We hear much today about marriages that break down, of infidelity within marriage. Would it not be desirable to have a day or two in the year when the Church would focus our minds on some married couples who became saints through their relationship with each other in marriage? Married couples have been the ministers to each other of the Sacrament of Matrimony. In my own home I often heard it said that, if all the sacraments give as much grace as does the Sacrament of Matrimony, then there must be very great grace to be received in the sacraments. The grace of the Sacrament of Matrimony must be capable of bringing, not only one, but two partners in marriage to the heights of holiness.

Since Vatican Council II, the family has often been referred to as the domestic Church. The family has a special mission in the Church. Rather like the Church, it is called to be one, holy, catholic and apostolic. Thanks to the domestic Church in the house of Joachim and

Anne, God was able to find one whom He could make worthy to be the Mother of Our Lord Jesus Christ. Blessed indeed were the eyes and the ears of Joachim and Anne.

Although the term, domestic Church, was not used in St. Vincent de Paul's day, he did much in his lifetime to strengthen the stability of individual families. Through his foundation of the Confraternities of Charity in France, he helped many lay people to become aware of what they could do for those domestic Churches which were suffering from poverty. It is rather remarkable, too, that the Society which bears his name today, should have been founded by a group of laymen some one hundred fifty years ago in Paris, the most distinguished of whom will hopefully be beatified in the future. As the years pass, the memory of Frederic Ozanam, a devoted husband and dedicated father, instead of fading, seems to be becoming fresher. Interest in him as a human character has grown. It would seem, too, that the Spirit of God has been whispering gently to us that here was a man, not only of profound intelligence and of great heart, but also a man of great personal holiness. I like to think that Frederic Ozanam chose St. Vincent de Paul as Patron of his Society, not only because St. Vincent was a man of great charity, but because he showed real sensitivity to the importance of the vocation of the laity.

Of the family, the document of Puebla makes this observation: *"It was not abolished, either by the penalty of original sin or by the punishment of the flood, but it continues to suffer from the hardness of the human heart."* (Puebla, §581).

Yes, the family suffers from the hardness of the human heart outside the home and from within it. Speaking to societies and associations that take their inspiration in part from the life of St. Vincent de Paul, I feel confident in asking all of you to do what you can to give stability to the Christian family in your society. The hardness of the human heart of which Puebla speaks is a consequence of original sin. The heart of an infant is tender. It only grows hard when it encounters coldness, indifference, lack of understanding, first within the family and then outside it. If the domestic Church is properly supported by those who live within it and those outside it, the spiral of violence, drug addiction and injustice in the world would be, if not exactly halted, at least considerably weakened and reduced.

So my prayer for all of us on this day, when we are honoring the domestic Church which gave us Mary, the Mother of God, is that we will not lose faith in the possibilities for good that can be realized by each baptized person and by each family.

When I speak to members of Vincentian societies or Marian Associations, one of my prayers for them is that they will not lose heart in their vocation to be the salt of the earth and the light of the world. My prayer for them is that weariness will not overtake them, that they will see the light around them, rather than the darkness. May you take comfort in these words of St. Vincent: *"Rarely is any good done without difficulty; the devil is too subtle and the world too corrupt not to attempt to nip such a good work in the bud. Courage . . . .It is God Himself who has established you in the place and duty where you are. If His glory is your goal, what can you fear or, rather, for what should you not hope?"* (Coste IV, Eng. ed., ltr. 1487, p. 361).

"Jesus said to His disciples: 'Blessed are your eyes because they see and blessed are your ears because they hear.'" (Mt 13:16).

The Lord's Prayer

30 July 1989   Campino Verde, Brazil

My dear Friends in Jesus Christ,

When the late Pope Paul VI lay dying on an August evening in 1978, he prayed over and over again the opening words of that prayer which Jesus taught His disciples: *"Our Father, Who art in heaven; Our Father, Who art in heaven."* It seems that he did not wish to pray the rest of the prayer, because he found so much theology, so much comfort and so much meaning in just those few opening words. It was the same with St. Teresa of Avila in her lifetime. Often she could not finish the Our Father because she, too, found that the first few words said everything.

What a rich word is the word, *father.* It brings to our minds what our own human fathers have done for us. When you say *father*, you think of one who provides, and the great provider for us all is God, Our Father, Who is in heaven. We can see many things wrong with the world, but it is also good to think of what is right in the world. Who made the sun to rise this morning? God, Our Father, Who is in heaven. Who is giving us the air we breathe at this moment? God, Our Father, Who is in heaven. Who gives us the fruits of the earth and the rains to soften the soil? God, Our Father, Who is in heaven. Who feeds the birds of the air and clothes the lilies of the field? God, Our Father, Who is in heaven. We could continue making a long list of the good and beautiful things we can see with our eyes or hear with our ears in this world of ours, and all of them have come from God, Our Father, Who is in heaven.

Who has told us all this? Jesus Christ Who is Himself also God. There are people who say that the most important truth that Jesus Christ has taught us in the Gospels is that we have a Father in heaven and He is God. It is Jesus Christ Who taught us to call God *our Father*. The word He used when He was praying at that most difficult moment in His life, in the Garden of Gethsemane, was an intimate tender word that a child would use to his father, *Abba*. Our human fathers, whom we have known on earth, are very faint shadows of that loving, caring and providing Father, Who is in heaven and Who night and day watches over us as a father does his child.

When we pray the Our Father, Jesus has taught us to think of God first before ourselves. *"May Your name be praised, may Your Kingdom come, may Your Will be done."* It is only then that we present our own needs to Our Father, Who is in heaven. First we ask for bread. *"Give us this day our daily bread."* We ask for bread; we do not ask for luxuries. We ask for bread for today, because Jesus has reminded us, *"Do not be anxious about tomorrow, for tomorrow will be anxious for itself. Let the day's own trouble be sufficient for the day."* (Mt 6:34). When we ask Our Father in heaven for bread, we cannot but think also of the bread of the Eucharist. May Our Father in heaven make us worthy to eat of the Bread of Heaven on earth, so that we may be worthy to take our place at God's great banquet table in heaven. We ask for pardon. We need it. Do not convince yourself that you do no wrong and hence have no need of God's pardon. Do not allow others to convince you that sin does not exist, or that God does not mind when we do wrong. In the Sacrament of Reconciliation and often throughout the day, we need to pray the prayer of St. Peter who fell down at Jesus' knees in the boat saying, *"Depart from me for I am a sinful man, O Lord."* (Lk 5:8). At the end of the Our Father we ask Our Father in heaven to free us from the danger of being unfaithful. Each of us can be unfaithful in different ways: married people, priests, Sisters, young people, all of us can be unfaithful to the teaching of the Church of Jesus Christ. We know that Jesus Christ prayed before He died that His friends would not be unfaithful. Infidelity can have serious consequences for us in this life and in the next. If not, why did Jesus Christ place the request to deliver us from the temptation to be unfaithful, in the prayer which He so kindly taught us?

The Gospel of today tells us that it was the example of Jesus praying that made His disciples want to pray like Him. In their lifetimes they would have come to the conclusion that St. Vincent de Paul reached in his lifetime: *"If we persevere in our vocation, it is thanks to prayer. If we have success in our tasks, it is thanks to prayer. If we do not fall into sin, it is thanks to prayer. If we remain in charity and save our souls, all this is thanks to God and to prayer."* (Coste XI, Fr. ed., p. 407).

May Mary, the Virgin Mother of God and our Mother, St. Vincent and St. Louise obtain for us all the grace of praying from our hearts that prayer which Jesus taught to His friends.

Laborers in the Vineyard

4 August 1989   Curitiba, Brazil

My dear Friends of Jesus Christ,

A few months ago Pope John Paul II published a document for the Church on the subject of the vocation of lay people. It was the fruit of his reflection and that of the Bishops, priests and laity who had met in Rome for a month in 1987 to discuss the role of the laity in the Church and in the world today. On the opening page of this pastoral exhortation the Pope recalls Our Lord's parable about the man who had a vineyard. The owner of the vineyard wanted workers, and so at different hours of the day he went out into the market place and hired those who were unemployed. Each time he gave the same orders to the workers: *"You go into my vineyard too."* (Mt 20:4). The Pope goes on to say: *"From*

*that distant day the call of the Lord Jesus, 'You go into my vineyard
too,' never fails to resound in the course of history: it is addressed to
every person who comes into this world." (§2).*

Each of us here today has received a personal invitation to work in
the Lord's vineyard, and your very presence here is an indication that
you have accepted that invitation. All of us are united through baptism,
but we are also united through our love for St. Vincent de Paul and his
spiritual family. As members of that spiritual family—and it is a large
family—we have been given a particular piece of that vineyard of the
Lord to cultivate. We have been asked to take particular care of those
who are needy or poor, who are without the means to live a life that is
worthy of a child of God. We have been asked to work in a neglected
part of the Lord's vineyard. When I speak of a neglected part of the
Lord's vineyard, I am thinking of neglected people. A person who is
neglected is a person who has not been chosen, who is left aside and
rejected. The rejection is not on the part of God, but on the part of society
today.

Our vocation as members of the Vincentian family is to recall the
parable of the Good Samaritan often, and not only to recall it, but to
live it and to *be* the Good Samaritan. That is what St. Vincent de Paul
was. He walked down the road of life, and in his early years he was
rather like the Priest and the Levite in that parable. You will recall that
the Priest and the Levite passed by the poor man who was lying on the
road after the robbers had mugged him and had stolen his money. In
the early part of his life Vincent de Paul was not distinguished by his
love for the neglected of this world. Then he changed and by the grace
of God came to realize the importance of being like the Good Samaritan.
He had eyes for every form of human suffering, physical and spiritual.
He was unwilling to pass by those who were suffering deprivation of
any kind. Not only would St. Vincent cross the road and look at the poor
and deprived, but like the Good Samaritan, he took practical action to
heal and rehabilitate the wounded forms of humanity which he found.
St. Vincent says to each one of us what Our Lord said to the lawyer
who drew forth from Him the parable of the Good Samaritan: *"Go and
do likewise."* (Lk 10:37).

The heart of St. Vincent's message to his large family is summed up aptly in a phrase of a homily which Pope John Paul II preached when he celebrated Mass in honor of St. Vincent in St. Peter's Square on the 27 September 1987: *"With the testimony of his life completely dedicated to Christ present in the poor and needy, Vincent seems to speak to the men of his epoch and to those of today with the same words which St. Paul uses in his letter to the Philippians, '. . . Let each of you look not only to his own interests but also to the interests of others.'"* (Phil 2:4, *L'Osservatore Romano*, 28 Sept. 1987).

The interests of others, individual or familial, open up for us a field of immense work. They can appeal to our sense of charity and also to our sense of justice. The Church in our day has been focusing our attention on the claims which the poor have been making in the name of justice. Often we feel powerless in the face of unjust structures in society. However, even in the face of such powerlessness we must ask ourselves if there are any steps, however small, that we can take. It is towards the end of his pastoral exhortation on the *Vocation of the Laity* that the Pope remarks: *"Each person is called by name to make a special contribution to the coming of the Kingdom of God. No talent, no matter how small, is to be hidden or left unused."* (§56).

My dear members of the Vincentian Family, I thank you for coming here today to celebrate this Eucharist with me. May all of us draw strength from the Bread of Life. May each of us receive an increase of joy and peace through the intercession of the Immaculate Virgin Mary, St. Vincent, St. Louise and all our Vincentian Saints in Heaven. May we all find new heart to heed the Lord's command: *"You go into my vineyard, too."* (Mt 20:4).

Vincentian Principles in Education

7 August 1989   Rio de Janeiro, Brazil

My dear Friends,

It is a joy and a pleasure for me to have this opportunity of speaking to you this evening. I feel that you are not total strangers to me, because now for a number of years I have felt that I knew the professors and students of this college. That may surprise you. The truth is that from the first time I met Father Almeida in Rome a number of years ago, he spoke to me about this college and of its importance to our Vincentian Province of Rio. I was aware, too, of the great volume of work which Father Palú dedicated to the animation and administration of this college, before he was elected Assistant General in July 1986. Father Almeida returned in that year and once more Divine Providence assigned him to the Directorship of this large and prestigious college. May it grow from strength to strength.

Through Fathers Almeida and Palú I have come to know something of the achievements and the problems of this college. I praise and bless God for the good education that has been imparted to so many thousands of students in the classrooms of the college. As for the problems of the college, I must confess my inability to shed much light on them. Nor do you expect me to do so. As a Congregation in the Church, we have a fairly extensive commitment to the apostolate of education. How many members of our Congregation throughout the world are engaged full time in teaching, it would be difficult to say. I do know, however, that the largest Catholic university in the United States, St. John's University, is in our care, as also a large university in Chicago and in Manila, and a smaller one at Niagara in the United States. On all continents there are some Vincentian priests and Brothers engaged in the apostolate of education. They are in partnership with hundreds of lay men and women, forming the minds of the young. I like to think that, although the numbers of Vincentian priests and Brothers engaged in the apostolate of education are small in proportion to the numbers of laity who collaborate with them, something of the philosophy and spirituality of St. Vincent de Paul impregnates our educational establishments. Your very presence here this evening is indicative of the interest you have in St. Vincent de Paul, whose unworthy successor I am presently.

The world which St. Vincent de Paul knew best was the world of the poor. It was to the poor that he dedicated the mature years of his life. He was not unfamiliar, however, with lecture halls and classrooms. As a young priest he was a private teacher to two young boys, one of whom later became a distinguished, if not a particularly saintly, Cardinal. Earlier still he had studied at two universities in France. As a mature priest he was deeply interested in the educational system of seminaries in France. So, if he were here with us this evening, I think he would mix easily with you who are engaged in different ways in the work of educating the young.

Let me present three appeals which St. Vincent might make, were he speaking to you this evening:

First, in your work of education lift up the minds of the young to what is good, true and beautiful. Often when I visit educational institutes today, I get the impression that their programs of education are orientated too exclusively to examinations. It is true that it is difficult that it be otherwise. Still, it is healthy and wholesome to pause often and to reflect on the challenge which faces us in education to form young people's minds to an appreciation of what is good and true and beautiful in all human experience.

Second, in your work of educating the young, lift up their minds to the condition of those in society who do not receive an education such as is being given in this college. Lift up their minds to those who are suffering from hunger for food, hunger for justice, hunger for understanding, hunger for God. I cannot help thinking that, were St. Vincent de Paul among us, he would greet each successive generation of students who graduate from this college with the question: *"And what, my brothers and sisters, are you now going to do for the poor with your newly acquired qualification in the human sciences?"*

Third, lift up the minds of the young to the life that awaits them beyond the frontiers of death. An education that limits the horizons of the young to the present life and ignores the eternal truths and the revelation of God, is not worthy of being called a Christian education. We must not form our young so that they become experts in building the city of man but give no thought to building the city of God. We must, to quote St. Paul, *"all stand before the judgment seat of God."* (Rom 14:10). St. Vincent de Paul lived with a burning conviction that without a knowledge of the central truths of Christianity, along with a life that conformed itself to Christian teaching, one would be irreparably lost after death. (cf. Coste XII, Fr. ed., p. 80). That conviction was a strong motivating force in all that he did for the poor.

The education that is being imparted in this college must be an evangelizing education, an education that gives prominence to the values of the Gospel of Jesus Christ. Anything less is a betrayal of Jesus Christ and unworthy of the Saint who is the patron of this College. The document of Puebla issues a formidable challenge to us when it states that: *"Catholic education must produce the agents who will effect the permanent organic change that Latin American society needs. This is to be done through a civic and political formation that takes its inspiration from the Church's social teaching. "* (Puebla §1033).

My dear friends, I thank you for the welcome you have given me this evening. I pray God's blessing on you and on your families. If I were to ask one special grace for this college, it would be that the union that exists between teacher and pupil, between religious and lay teachers, between parents and teachers, would be strengthened and deepened, for education is primarily the formation in love of the young, and to form the young is to renew the world.

Live the Mystery of the Assumption
15 August 1989   Paris, France

Mother Duzan, Father Lloret and my dear Sisters,

At Christmas 1987 a Daughter of Charity here in Paris gave me a present of a small paperweight for my desk. It is rather unusual in that it has been fashioned out of a heavy metal that had been used for a purpose very different from that of keeping papers firm on the top of a desk. The metal was once a weapon of war. It was a piece of shrapnel that had been gathered somewhere in the north of France: a relic from the second World War.

The shrapnel had been collected by a Benedictine monk, and from it through fire and heat he chiselled out the features of the Virgin Mary with the Infant Jesus nestling in her bosom. As one looks at the metal now, one is reminded both of war and peace; of destruction and salvation; of violence and gentleness; of sin and innocence. The metal that once was a symbol—and more than a symbol—of death has become a symbol of life. For did not Jesus Christ come into the world so that humanity might have life, true life, and have it more abundantly. (cf. Jn 10:10). Did He not enter the world through the womb of the

Virgin Mary, whom we salute in the Salve Regina as *"our life, our sweetness and our hope"*? The metal paperweight speaks of a past that is marred by sin and of a future that is pregnant with hope, for Christ has come not to condemn the world but to save it.

The transformation that has taken place in the metal has been wrought by human hands, but before human hands etched out the features of Mother and Child, there was the inspiration that came to the Benedictine monk to make a weapon of war and destruction proclaim a message of peace and salvation. One cannot look at the paperweight without thinking of the sinfulness of humankind and the forgiveness of God, the selfishness of humans and the unselfishness of God, the hatred that lurks in the human heart and the love that abides in the heart of God and in the heart of her who was conceived without sin.

The paperweight is a masterpiece created through the inspiration of an artist. The Incarnation is a masterpiece created by the inspiration of Him Whom we call the Holy Spirit. *"And the angel said to her: the Holy Spirit will come upon you and the power of the Most High will overshadow you; therefore the Child to be born of you will be called holy, the Son of God."* (Lk 1:35).

Two great and unique transformations were worked in the person of Mary by the Divine Artist. The first we honor on the 8 December and the second on the 15 August. The metal of the paperweight was created good. It was human perversity that twisted it towards dealing death to people. All of us are born with original sin, which is a bias that deflects us towards evil. Mary, we believe with the certainty of faith, was preserved from original sin and that bias towards evil, through the foreseen merits of her Son. The Divine Artist, however, continued to work on her through life, and through the fire and heat of suffering shaped her into that person of holiness than which no greater has ever been or will ever be created. That is the first transformation worked in the human person of Mary of Nazareth.

The second transformation we contemplate today. Because we see now by faith, as St. Paul remarks, in a dark manner, we cannot penetrate fully the mystery of the reality that Mary is now body and soul in heaven. We rejoice and are glad that the Divine Artist has put His finishing touch to one human person. All others must wait until the Day of the Lord has come, and her Divine Son will appear *"in a cloud with power and great glory."* (Lk 21:27).

However deep and impenetrable the mysteries of God are, they have been made known to us for a purpose. Each mystery of God is a beam of light shining in the darkness of this life and lighting up the path of pilgrimage that leads us back to our Father's house. When the angel Gabriel announced the mystery of the Incarnation to Mary of Nazareth, Our Lady was perplexed. (cf. Lk 1:34). God's mystery was too incomprehensible for her human mind. But in accepting and, above all, in living the mystery of the Annunciation, Mary found light and strength to go forward through the joyful, sorrowful and glorious mysteries of her own existence. So, too, with us as we contemplate today the mystery of Mary's Assumption, body and soul, into heaven, our minds will ask: *"And how can this be?"*

Yet, by the grace of faith we can accept the mystery of the Assumption, but what of living it? The mystery of the Assumption of Our Lady carries a message and invitation to our minds and to our bodies. For our minds the message and invitation is one of hope. The work of being transformed into more perfect images of Christ goes on in us daily. Often it is a painful process, a purification, as it were, by fire and heat. It is in preparation for the finishing touch of God when we will fully share, body and soul, in the Resurrection of Christ, and in His joy, which, He assures us, *"no one will take from us."* (Jn 16:22). Hope is a flower, but it is a flower, according to St. Thomas Aquinas, that can be blighted by two diseases, namely, lack of humility and lack of greatness of soul. That is a sentiment that is echoed in the writings of our Founders, but more so in the actions of their lives. Is the flower of hope withering in any of our communities? We would do well to look to our humility and to how we are manifesting greatness of soul daily.

What about the mystery of Our Lady's Assumption and our bodies? From our childhood we have been taught that our bodies are temples of the Spirit of God, and each day of our lives we cradle on our tongues the living body of Jesus Christ, our Lord and God. That is a great mystery which fails at times to cut into our consciousness, as we go about our daily work of serving others. Recently I read an observation of a celebrated and saintly Jewish Rabbi who wrote: *"There are three ways in which we may respond to the reality of the world around us: we may exploit it, we may enjoy it, we may accept it with awe."* (A. Heschel, *God in Search of Man*, p. 34).

The mystery of the Assumption of Our Lady into heaven invites us to accept our bodies with awe, knowing that we have been bought with a great price and knowing, too, that we are destined to be with the Risen Christ, Who has gone before us to prepare a place for us.

The paperweight of the Mother and Child on my desk keeps letters and loose pages from being blown hither and thither by chance breezes. How many times has the Mother of God stabilized us, when storms of one kind or another threaten our human and spiritual equilibrium. The thought is never far from my mind that, in placing paper under the metal image, Our Lady will take care of her Son's business. May the Divine Artist, Who created her, be praised, and may she be thanked.

May you, Mother Duzan, on this, your feast day, find new joy and strength in your vocation of stabilizing the Company as it gives glory to God and brings hope and comfort to the poor of the world. May the Mother and Child continue to protect you, guide you and give you that peace which is one of the fruits of the Spirit of God, Who is the Divine Artist.

Money, A Good Servant but a Bad Master

24 September 1989   Buenos Aires, Argentina

My dear Friends,

It is a joy for me to set foot in your country once again. I am passing through Argentina on my way, first to Paraguay and from there to Colombia. So I am in a real way a true pilgrim. Pilgrims are always on the move. Pilgrims pass through many towns and cities, and everyone who knows that they are pilgrims, knows also that they have only a very limited time to pass in any one particular place.

Our whole life is a pilgrimage. We are on our way to that city whose Maker and Builder is God. We are on our way to take our place at a great celebration to which we have been invited. Jesus Christ has assured us that He has gone before us to prepare a place at the great festive table in our Father's house.

Admission to that great celebration is something that money cannot buy. The only currency that has any value to secure an entry to the celebration in heaven is that of love. In a world where so many things can be bought with money, often our minds center more on money than upon love. Jesus Christ, when He was on earth, had little or no money. In fact, in today's Gospel He tells us that we cannot give ourselves to God and to money. He gave Himself entirely to doing the Will of His Father in heaven and He did so by using the currency, not of money but of love.

Jesus Christ, however, was not so impractical as to despise utterly the use of money. He paid the Temple tax, and He graciously accepted food and drink that others provided for Him with hard-earned money. What Jesus Christ is saying to us in today's Gospel is that money, like fire, is a good servant but a bad master. Fire serves us well to cook our meals and to light and warm our houses. It is a good servant. But when fire rebels and dominates us, it can kill us and destroy the work of centuries.

It is likewise with money. When money is employed as a servant, it can bring joy and comfort to millions and especially to those who have little or none of it. But let money take the first place in our lives and it can become a tyrant. It can harden our hearts and blind our vision of the supreme realities of our existence. For many, it is only at the end of their lives that they realize that money, valuable as it may be, cannot be taken to the grave. *"There are,"* as I once heard an old man express it, *"no pockets in a shroud."*

Money is a good servant, but a bad master. St. Vincent de Paul recognized that truth. Millions of dollars, or écus, passed through his hands and he made every cent a good servant. The only question he posed himself was: *"Where can this servant be used best?"* The money which his two Communities received or possessed, he regarded as *"the patrimony of the poor."* It was to be used in the interests of the poor.

Jesus Christ has said that the poor will always be with us. This is true. So, too, you might say, is money, sometimes more, sometimes less. When we find ourselves thinking much about money, it is at that moment we must also begin to think of the poor. In being generous to the poor, trying, when we can, to secure more justice for them, then we are, to quote Our Lord's words in today's Gospel, *"making friends for ourselves through our use of this world's goods."* It will be the poor, whom we have helped during our pilgrimage through life, who will be the first of our friends to welcome us to God's table in heaven. At times we worry about money. Sometimes we have reason to, and at other times our worry about money is groundless. Parents of families often worry about having sufficient money to pay their bills, sufficient money to educate their children. It is a justifiable worry. However, Our Lord encourages all of us to live only for the day, not to think too much about the problems of tomorrow. When we are concerned about money or the loss of it during life, we will find peace in these words, written by St. Vincent eighteen months before he died: *"If by chance we have ever seen or heard, on any occasion, persons who serve God and trust in His goodness being without what they need for their condition in life, then we would have reason to be concerned for our own needs. The only thing we must do is to commend ourselves to His Providence, be faithful to our obligations and be certain that sooner or later God will provide that which He knows to be necessary for the accomplishment of the designs He has for us. Can we do anything else?"* (Coste VII, Fr. ed., p. 543).

True Liberation

26 September 1989   Buenos Aires, Argentina

My dear Sisters and Confreres,

The author of a short book of the Bible, that of Ecclesiastes, takes a special delight in reminding us that there is nothing new under the sun. If he were alive today and heard us talking about the importance of liberation theology, he might shake his head and say: *"Did I not tell you more than two thousand years ago that there is nothing new under the sun . . . ?"* Liberation theology is not new. One of the most important books of the Old Testament is taken up largely with that idea. The Book of Exodus is an account of how the Israelite people were liberated from the Egyptians, and the remainder of the Old Testament is a celebration of that liberation which was repeated again and again

throughout their history. For centuries the Israelites celebrated it faithfully each year in the Feast of the Passover. The first reading of today's
Mass tells us how, after their return to Jerusalem from Babylon, they
dutifully celebrated the Feast of the Passover in the new temple. The
Feast of the Passover will always remain significant for the Christians,
for it was in the course of celebrating the Passover, or the great
liberation from Egypt, that Our Lord instituted the Sacrifice of the
Mass. Our Lord's own sacrificial death is the great liberation of
mankind and each Mass is a celebration of that event.

When we speak of liberation today, our minds center upon the poor.
We think, not only of the sufferings of the poor, but in a special way of
sufferings that are caused to them through the injustice of others. When
we think about how they can be liberated, we think in a particular way
how we could achieve greater social justice in our society.

All of us are aware of the immense work which in his lifetime St.
Vincent de Paul accomplished to liberate the poor of his day from their
sufferings. It must be said that explicit references to injustice, as being
the cause of their sufferings, are few in his writings. He was a man of
his time and the demands of social justice, as well as the responsibilities
of ownership, had not been spelled out as clearly as they have been in
our day. If St. Vincent de Paul was a man of his time, it must not be
forgotten that he was also a man of the Church. Listen to this: *"The sort
of liberation we are talking about, knows how to use evangelical means,
which have their own distinctive efficacy. It does not resort to violence
of any sort or to the dialectics of class struggle. Instead, it relies on the
vigorous energy and activity of Christians, who are moved by the spirit
to respond to the cries of countless millions of their brothers and
sisters."* (Puebla §486).

Take out the word 'dialectics' from that quotation and it would fit
quite easily in almost any of St. Vincent's letters. It is, in fact, a
quotation from the document of Puebla. St. Vincent would be the first
to agree that *"whatever the miseries or sufferings that afflict human
beings, it is not through violence, power plays or political systems, but
through the truth about human beings that they will find their way to a
better future."* (Puebla §551).

St. Vincent de Paul was, above all, a man of the Gospel, and in his correspondence, in his contacts, he was never far from the Person of Jesus Christ. The pages of his correspondence and of his conferences are penetrated by the Gospel. It is for that reason that it can be confidently asserted that on the theme of liberation, he would remind us, as the Document of Puebla does, that *"we must try to read the political scene from the standpoint of the Gospel, not vice versa."* (Puebla §559).

For St. Vincent de Paul—as for all the Saints of the Church—the formula for reaching sanctity is the same, namely, the accomplishment, at every moment of the day, of the Will of God. It is the formula proposed by Our Lord Himself in the Gospel of today. *"My mother and My brothers are those who hear the word of God and act upon it."* (Lk 8:21). It is a very simple formula, so simple that we can fail to see it, or if we see it, we can distort it by putting our own personal interpretations on what we think God *should* want. A young Vincentian priest did a doctoral thesis in Rome three years ago on St. Vincent's spirituality. The title of his dissertation was: *"The Fulfillment of the Will of God was the Unifying Principle between Action and Prayer in St. Vincent de Paul."* Yes, we accomplish the Will of God through action in our lives. It must, however, be action that springs from prayer. It is only in that way that we can feel certain that our action is an expression of God's Will in our lives.

Let us allow St. Vincent to speak. To a young priest of his Community, who sought his advice one day, St. Vincent said: *"Jesus Christ, Who should be the exemplar of all your conduct, was not content with employing sermons, labors, fasts and even His blood and death itself, but He also added prayer to all that. He had no need whatsoever of prayer for Himself, and hence it was for us that He prayed so fervently, and also to teach us to do the same, both in regard to all that concerns ourselves and all that concerns those of whom we should be, with Him, the saviors."* (Coste XI, Fr. ed., pp. 345-346).

Through the intercession of the Virgin Mary, St. Vincent and St. Louise, may God give to each one of us here and to the two Communities of St. Vincent a true understanding of liberation. May He give us all the grace of being intent always on freeing ourselves from the oppression of sin in our personal lives. May He give us grace to accomplish lovingly at all times and in all places His Will, which is our peace.

Messages and Messengers

29 September 1989   Asuncion, Paraguay

My dear Sisters,

Today the Church is honoring three principal angelic messengers of God. These messengers find a place in the litany of God's Saints, even though they do not have bodies like ours nor have to live their lives on this planet. We may find it difficult to imagine other beings that have not bodies like ours. But we should not allow our difficulties, or imagining other creatures that are totally different from us, to put limits on what God is able to create. The trouble is that we humans are so much centered on ourselves and on our world that we find it difficult to think about others, and particularly to think that God could create creatures that have intellects more powerful than ours, but that do not have flesh and blood and bones like ours. There are people who deny the existence of angels, but who at the same time like to think that there may be life on other planets.

When we think about angels in our lives, we can think of them as special messengers of God to us. In the very early Church there was such a devotion to angels that St. Paul had to remind Christians that the principal messenger of God to mankind was Jesus Christ. That remains true now and will always be so. It is Jesus Christ by His words, His life, His sufferings and His death, Who has shown us how God wants us to live on this earth. When St. Vincent said that *"nothing pleases me except in Jesus Christ,"* he was expressing a profound truth. It is good to ask ourselves often, *"Could Jesus Christ share this thought, this remark, this experience with me?"* He is the first and principal messenger of God to each of us.

The existence of angels can remind us that God sends His messages to us in all sorts of ways. We will never know in this life how many times and on how many occasions God sent His angels to us with messages. Besides angels, God uses many other ways of communicating with us. Perhaps that was a reason that made St. Vincent have such devotion to Divine Providence. St. Vincent was not a superstitious man, but he trained himself to be sensitive to the signs by which God transmitted His messages to him.

St. Vincent's insistence on the importance of being faithful to our Rule came from his devotion to the Providence of God, for he saw the Rule of the Community as a clear message from God. He saw the events of his life also as so many messages from God, which he accepted with the reverence one would show to an angel. In the cries of the poor he heard the voice of the suffering Christ, and he interpreted the message as an appeal for help. When he saw the Sisters going out to help the poor, he thought of the angels: *"Ah! my God, how many angels are now busily occupied in counting your footsteps! Those you have taken in coming here have already been counted and so, too, will those you are about to take, because a Saint tells us that 'All the steps taken by the servant of Jesus Christ for His love are reckoned unto them.'"* (Conf. Eng. ed., 25 Dec. 1648, p. 413).

Yes, we are receiving messages from God at all times and in a diversity of ways. May we not be so busy and so distracted that we do not hear them. Above all, may we ourselves become in turn good messengers of God to our communities and to the poor. May we be messengers of faith and hope and love. May we be messengers of God, not only in words, but in deeds also. May we be messengers who bring light and encouragement into the lives of all whom we meet. In one word, may we be Christ to others, for He is *"full of grace and of truth."* (Jn 1:14).

May the angels of God bring God's blessing and protection on all those who will live and work in the house which we bless today. May this Provincial House be a sign of that unity which exists among the Sisters of this Province, a unity so much desired for the Company by our Founders. May that Community prayer which we recite find its realization in this house and every house of the Province. *"This house, O Lord, is Thine; this house is Thine. Let there not be found in it a single stone which Thy sacred hand has not placed therein. Keep them in Thy name whom Thou has called and sanctify them in truth."*

Priest—A Messenger of God

3 October 1989   Ibague, Colombia

My dear Friends in Jesus Christ,

In the country from which I come, we have in our language a very old phrase to translate the word, *priest,* a phrase not used nowadays, but in past centuries it was commonly used. A priest was called a *teachtaire Dé,* which means *messenger of God.* I like the expression very much, for that is what a priest is, no matter what he is doing. If he stands at the altar to preside at the Eucharist, he is a messenger of God. If he preaches, baptizes, absolves or anoints the sick, he is a messenger of God. Because a priest is a priest, not only when he performs sacred functions, but is a priest at every moment, so he is a messenger of God at all times. As priests we have to convey the message of God to the people of our time. The people to whom we speak, particularly during the celebration of the Eucharist, are thirsty for the word of God. As messengers of God, we priests have to make sure that we are transmitting the message of God and not just our own personal opinions. The message we preach is the message of Jesus Christ and His Church. What we preach must be what Jesus Christ and His Church want us to preach. If I preach my own Gospel, I am betraying the trust that God has put in me when He ordained me priest. All of us know that Vatican Council II stated that the primary work of the priest is to preach the Gospel.

What has prompted me to reflect on the priest as the messenger of God? It is a little phrase in today's Gospel. Jesus, on his way up to Jerusalem, sent, according to St. Luke, *"messengers on ahead of Him."* (Lk 9:51). He has also sent messengers on ahead of Him to prepare the world for His second coming. Among His principal messengers must be numbered the priests of His Church.

If we are to be faithful messengers of Jesus Christ, then we must have grasped well the message of God. One cannot give a message to another person unless one knows clearly what the message is. So, too, with us who are messengers of God; we must be familiar with and know well what it is God wants to say through us. There is a very rich expression in St. Paul's letter to the Colossians in the third chapter: *"Let the word of God dwell in you richly.* " (Col 3.16). Think well on each of those words. St. Paul is saying that the message of God should be living within us, that through reflection and prayer the message of God should be producing much fruit in our own lives. *"Let the word of God dwell in you richly. "* (Ibid.). It is the fruit which the word of God bears within us that we share with others when we preach or speak or collaborate with God's people.

The message of Christ is caught rather than taught. Certainly, the message of Christ is not to be communicated by fire and sword, that is, by violence. In today's Gospel the Apostles, James and John, wanted to call down fire on those who were not prepared to welcome the message of Christ. Our Lord made clear to them that that was not His way. Jesus Christ had said on another occasion: *"Learn of Me because I am gentle and humble of heart. "* (Mt 11:29). When Our Lord refused to call down fire from heaven on the town that would not receive Him, He was manifesting that gentleness which we, as His followers, must try at all times to show.

Three months or so ago the Pope visited some Scandinavian countries. In some of these countries he was received coldly by religious leaders who were not Catholic. In one Protestant Church to which he was invited, he was told he could be present but that he would not be allowed to speak in the Church. He could speak outside the Church in a hall but not within the Church. The Pope accepted this restriction, and many people, particularly journalists, commented on the gentleness and humility of his bearing. The gentleness and humility of the Pope in the face of a lack of hospitality was a reflection of the attitude of Christ in today's Gospel. What we might call the Pope's silent homily, perhaps achieved more than a spoken one.

So, my dear priests and seminarians, may each of us become a trustworthy messenger of God. Through the intercession of the Virgin Mary, who welcomed the messenger of God in the person of the angel Gabriel, may the word of God dwell in each of us richly, and may we be at all times gentle and humble messengers of God.

Devotion to the Sacred Heart of Jesus

6 October 1989   Medellin, Colombia

In celebrating Mass with you today, I am conscious of the fact that it is the first Friday in the month of October. All over the world many Catholics recall and honor in a special way the Sacred Heart of Jesus on the first Fridays of the month. Both the Sacred Heart of Jesus and the thought of Mary, the Virgin Mother of God, bring to our minds the immense love which both Jesus and Mary have for each one of us. When we see so much suffering, so much poverty, so much pain in the world, we are tempted to doubt if God or Jesus Christ cares for us. In such dark moments, it is good for us to think that God said that even if a mother could forget the child of her womb, He could not forget us. (cf. Is 49:15). Each time your eye catches the crucifix, each time you look at a picture of the Sacred Heart of Jesus, God is saying to you through His Son, Jesus Christ, that He cares. An infant, sleeping in the arms of its mother, may not be conscious of the care that it is receiving. So, too, with us in this life, we are sleeping, very often unaware of the unceasing care and love which God has for each one of us.

When we pray to the Sacred Heart of Jesus, we try to make ourselves more conscious of that personal love which Jesus Christ has for each of us. Remember, He knows us all by our Christian names and thinks of us as individuals.

Devotion to the Sacred Heart, however, does not stop at that. Jesus Christ has said to us: *"This is My commandment; love one another as I have loved you."* (Jn 15:17). Jesus Christ had a very big heart. We know many big-hearted people. Devotion to the Sacred Heart means that we, in turn, must try to be big-hearted persons. To be big-hearted means to be generous to others. When we think of generosity, we think of money, but there are many things other than money with which we can be generous. We can be generous in forgiving. We can be generous in trying to understand others. We can be generous with the time we give to others, and I am sure you can think of many other ways in which we can be generous to those whom we meet in life. Jesus Christ was generous with all that He had to give and He had little or no money. He was generous in the end in giving His life for all of us.

Reflecting on the generosity of Christ, I often think of an observation made by Pope Pius XII in his encyclical, *Haurietis Aquas*, on devotion to the Sacred Heart. He said that the three great gifts of the Sacred Heart to us were: the Eucharist, the Priesthood and His own Mother. When I reflect on this, I feel that if Pius XII were writing today, he might say that there are five great gifts, corresponding to the five wounds of Christ. Since the death of Pope Pius XII, the Church has become more conscious of the importance and place of the Holy Spirit in the life of the Church, and we have during the past two decades come to perceive more clearly the mission of the Church in today's world. So the Spirit of God and the Church itself are two further gifts of the Heart of Christ.

These five gifts of the Heart of Christ are like five pieces of a beautiful mosaic. Take away one and the beauty of the masterpiece is spoiled. We cannot be truly devoted to the Eucharist without reverencing the Priesthood, Our Lady, the Church and the Holy Spirit. If we do not see Christ in the Eucharist and show reverence to Him there, we will find difficulty in seeing Him in a poor man and, consequently, we will have difficulty in showing that deep reverence which our Founders ask us to show to the poor. It is appreciation of the five gifts of the Heart of Christ which will lead us to the center of God. St. John the Evangelist, who in his Gospel writes of each of these gifts in turn, had at the end of his life only one message to give to the Christians, which he repeated over and over again. *"God is love—God is love."* May each one of us be convinced of that truth and, because we are made in the image of God, reflect it in what we do and say to those with whom we live and to the poor.

Let me end by quoting from a letter of St. Vincent to Sister Nicole Haran: *"From God I ask only two things for you and for your Sisters: the first is that He give you a great concern for the salvation and for the relief of the poor; and the second, that He give you the grace to love one another and to bear with one another; for, if you have one and the other, you will practice the virtues Our Lord recommended most to us! You will give edification to everyone and you will enjoy great peace."* (Coste, VII, Fr. ed., ltr. 2512, p. 52).

Most Holy Rosary

7 October 1989   Santa Rosa de Cabal, Colombia

My dear Friends in Jesus Christ,

Whenever I visit our sick, aged and dying in hospitals or in our infirmaries, my eye invariably catches sight of rosary beads in their hands, or protruding from under their pillows, or resting on their bedside tables. I have noticed almost always that the sick and aged members of our Vincentian family have their rosary beads within easy reach of the grasp of their fingers. I recall visiting a priest in the hospital over a protracted period of time. When he entered the hospital, at first he kept beside his bed a number of history books in which he was very interested, his breviary, his watch and his rosary beads. All of these kept company with each other for a time. Then one by one he took leave of them as he became progressively weaker, until there remained only his watch and his rosary beads. These two personal objects alone witnessed his passing from time into eternity.

Neither a watch nor a rosary is essential for human existence. Some of us are rather heedless of time, unpunctual, and often wasteful of time, so that one wonders what purpose a watch serves. As for rosary beads, one can count the Hail Marys on one's fingers or on a rosary ring. But it is a common experience that, when we have a taste for no other forms of prayer, we will reach for our rosary beads, or rather move towards reflecting on the life, death and resurrection of Jesus Christ as we see it through the eyes of His Mother, Mary.

Pope Paul VI said on one occasion in speaking of the rosary: *"It is at this school that we become Christian . . . ."* Mary herself was the first to move slowly through the school which brought her ever more deeply into the mystery of the Incarnation and of the Church. Meditatively she passed through the Joyful, Sorrowful and Glorious Mysteries of her Son's life and work. We must not suppose that it was only the Joyful Mysteries she *"kept in her heart."* (Lk 2:51). We can be certain that the Sorrowful and Glorious Mysteries of her Son's life, and her participation in them, were pondered by her as profoundly as she meditated on her Son's birth and all the circumstances surrounding it. (Lk 2:19).

Now she joins us as we in turn reflect on these mysteries in that school of the rosary *"where we become Christian."* She joins us as we in our turn move towards the final glorious mystery of our existence through the joyful and sorrowful mysteries of our own human lives. Through our contemplation of the Joyful, Sorrowful and Glorious Mysteries of the rosary, we are slowly learning to cope, not only with the joys and sorrows of our lives, but are being prepared to bear what St. Paul calls *"the weight of glory."* (2 Cor 4:17).

The rosary is a simple and humble prayer, for centuries beloved by simple and humble people, the *anawim* of God. If the Miraculous Medal can be considered the catechism of the *anawim* of today, then the rosary must be considered one of their most cherished prayers.

We, who are members of St. Vincent's family, must never allow ourselves to forget that on the same occasion when Our Lady told St. Catherine Labouré that she loved the two Communities of St. Vincent, she also referred to the fact that we were not praying the rosary very well. Some people say that the rosary is not suited for modern people. Do not let them persuade you to give up the practice of praying the rosary daily. Our Lady is pleased when we pray the rosary, and that is enough.

However distracted we may be when we frequent the school of the rosary, we are in the company of Mary who of all our race has seen furthest into the Mystery of God, Father, Son and Holy Spirit. Of all humans, it is she who will best teach us how to show to the world and to the poor *"the blessed fruit of her womb, Jesus."* Of all humans, it is she to whom we will turn when we begin to feel the things of earth slip from our grasp. Of all humans, it is she who will deliver us safely from the womb of time into the light of eternity. *"Holy Mary, Mother of God, pray for us at the hour of our death. Amen."*

Characteristics of a Saint

1 November 1989   Manila, Philippines

My dear Confreres,

When Pope John XXIII canonized St. Maria Goretti, the man who had murdered her was sitting in the front row of those participating at her canonization ceremony. When Pope John Paul II canonized St. Maximilian Kolbe, seven years ago, an aged man was sitting close to the papal altar during the Mass of canonization. He was the man whose place St. Maximilian Kolbe took in the death cell in the concentration camp of Auschwitz. When, at the close of the last century, a Vincentian priest and martyr, John Gabriel Perboyre, was beatified, his brother, who was also a Vincentian priest, had the joy of celebrating Mass the following day in honor of his martyr brother. All these people I have mentioned must have felt particularly close to those who were being raised to the honors of the altar.

Today's feast should be a reminder to us that we also are very close to the saints and the saints to us. You will remember how, shortly before her death, St. Theresa of Lisieux said that she would spend her life in heaven in doing good on earth. That sentiment could be shared by all the saints in heaven. They are contemplating the beauty, the truth and the goodness of God and, because they see more clearly the immensity of the love He has for us poor, fragile sinners, they are spending their time, as St. Theresa expressed it, in doing good on earth, through interceding for us with Christ to the Father from Whom all good things come.

The saints are close to us and we can feel close to the saints, even when we fall short of their achievements. Saints differ very much in character and temperament. With the exception of Mary, who was conceived without sin, the saints have, like the rest of us, their faults and limitations. If you ever found yourself in the presence of a very saintly person, the overall impression you would have is that you are being accepted by that saintly person. You would feel that even if you told that saintly person the worst things about yourself, you would still be accepted and your weaknesses would be understood. It is not that the saint considers sin to be of no importance; quite the contrary. The saint has an unusually highly developed sense of sin. The saints' power of accepting people, so much less worthy than they, is nothing other than the holiness and the love of God breaking through their personalities. The holiness of the saints is not their own. It is God's. In the Eucharistic prayers we acknowledge that *"all life, all holiness, comes from You . . . ."* Certainly we must cooperate with God to become holy, but the holiness we see in others, and in ourselves, is God's holiness. It is His love, His justice, His goodness, like the sun, breaking through the clouds.

St. Vincent de Paul remarked on one occasion that we should be like the rays of the sun that penetrate into dark and murky places, yet remain uncontaminated by the dust and the dirt. A saint is like a ray of sunshine that enlightens and warms and is unaffected by the dust of sin.

I have been concentrating on the saints on earth. Today the Church is thinking of that great crowd from every nation and race and people and tongue who stand before the throne of the Lamb of God in heaven. Whether the saints are on earth or in heaven does not really matter, for we are all one in Christ Jesus. A saint in heaven is but continuing what he saw as his vocation on earth, the loving of God with his whole heart and his whole soul, with all his strength and with all his mind, and loving all on earth who have been redeemed by the Blood of the Lamb. St. Theresa of Lisieux did not wait until she got to heaven to devote herself to doing good on earth. Listen again to St. John's words in the second reading: *"Beloved, we are God's children now . . . . When He appears, we shall be like Him for we shall see Him as He is, and everyone who thus hopes in Him purifies himself as He is pure."* (1 Jn 3:2-3).

On the 1 November 1658 St. Vincent wrote to one of his missionaries, and I make my own the sentiments he expressed on the feast of All Saints that year: *"I pray the Saint of saints, whose feast we are celebrating today, that He will make you one of their number. You are following in their footsteps by His mercy. Continue to elevate your heart from this earth to Heaven through works and good practices which lead to God and which are best suited to draw down Divine grace . . . .It is by that road that Our Lord and our Master calls all His missionaries after Him . . . .May it please His goodness to animate you with His spirit and with the virtues which accompany it."* (Coste VII, Fr. ed., ltr. 2702, p. 327).

Purgatory

2 November 1989   Manila, Philippines

My dear Sisters,

On this day when we are thinking about the souls in purgatory, it is good for us to reflect on the two truths that we know are certain about purgatory. The first truth is that purgatory exists, and the second truth is that those who are undergoing purification in purgatory are helped by the prayers of the faithful on earth, and particularly by the offering of the Sacrifice of the Mass. We know that these two truths are certain, because the Church has given us an infallible assurance that this is so. The Church does not ask us to believe anything more than that. She does not tell us how long purgatory may last, or what kind of suffering the souls endure there. In telling us that there is such an experience of purgatory after death and that we can help the souls in purgatory by our prayers and good works, the Church has told us enough to encourage us to pray for those who are undergoing that purification which is necessary before they can enter into the banquet hall of heaven.

Suppose you are coming into a city after a long walk on a dusty road, and somebody asks you to accept an invitation immediately to a banquet with all the important people of the country present. You would excuse yourself for a few moments, saying that, as you are covered with dust, you would like to freshen up before entering the banquet hall. You would be glad to have the opportunity of making yourself worthy to take your place at the table. Now at the end of our lives, there is a great likelihood that some of the dust of sin will be still clinging to us. No one can enter the banquet hall of heaven with sin still clinging to him. So purgatory is there to cleanse and purify us before we take our place at the table of God in heaven.

Perhaps you have heard someone saying to another: *"You cannot take your money with you to the grave."* That is true. Even if we cannot take our money to the grave, our hearts can be unduly attached to money and to other things. We can enter heaven only when we can fully surrender ourselves to God. So God has to cleanse our hearts and make them pure, and that experience can be and is very often painful.

The Church does not tell us what form that purification takes. Sometimes I imagine it must rather be like the experience that Peter had when Jesus looked on him after Peter had denied Him. Peter felt the pain of that loving look and went out and wept bitterly. His tears came from the remembrance of the great personal love which Jesus had shown him. We can console ourselves that, whatever form of purification there may be in purgatory, it does not come from the hands of a vindictive God. In the Bible we read: *"The souls of the just are in the hand of God. In the sight of the unwise they seem to die, but they are in peace."* (Wis 3:3).

The second truth, which the Church has made clear to us, is that we can help the souls in purgatory by our prayers, our good works, and especially by the Sacrifice of the Mass. When St. Monica was dying and was surrounded by her son, St. Augustine, and his brother, she told them that it did not matter where they buried her body. *"All I ask of you,"* she said, *"is that you remember me at the altar of God."* No, it does not matter greatly where they place our bodies after we have died, but it does matter greatly that people will pray for us after our death. No Mass is ever celebrated without the dead being remembered. No Mass is ever celebrated without it touching the souls in purgatory.

In praying for the souls in purgatory daily and commending those we have known in this life by name to the mercy of God, we are uniting ourselves, not only with our departed friends and relatives, but with Jesus Christ Who said: *"I go to prepare a place for you."* (Jn 14:2). Praying every day for the souls in purgatory, we are cooperating with Jesus Christ in the preparation of that place which He is preparing for those who love Him. To us, as to all the souls in purgatory, Jesus Christ keeps saying: *"Let not your hearts be troubled . . . .I will come again and will take you to Myself, that where I am, you may be also . . . .I will see you again and your hearts will rejoice and no one will take your joy from you."* (Jn 14:1, 3; 16:16).

Priests Must Be Gospel Men

4 November 1989   Angono, Philippines

St. Vincent was an infant of three years of age when St. Charles Borromeo died. The contrast between the two family backgrounds is striking. St. Charles came from a wealthy, long established, noble family; St. Vincent from poor peasant stock. St. Charles was made a Cardinal at the age of twenty-two. This early elevation of Charles to the dignity of Cardinal is explained by the fact that his uncle was Pope Pius IV. He assumed the post of being an administrator of the Diocese of Milan. Today one would say that he was a governor. Then sometime later he was nominated Archbishop of Milan, thus filling a See which had lain vacant for some eighty years.

St. Charles Borromeo concentrated his energies on bringing about the reform of the clergy and of religious life. In that he did work similar to the work to which St. Vincent devoted himself in France. Let us listen to St. Charles as he speaks at the last Synod of his lifetime: *"Is your duty preaching and teaching? Concentrate carefully on what is essential to fulfill that office faithfully. Make sure in the first place that your life and conduct are sermons in themselves. Do not give people cause to purse their lips and shake their heads during your sermons, since they have heard you before preaching one thing, then seeing you doing the exact opposite . . . .Or is your task the care of souls? Then do not neglect your own. Do not spend yourselves so completely on other people that you have nothing left for yourself. Of course, you have to look after the souls you have been put in charge of but not to the extent that you forget your own. Brothers, do understand this: there is nothing quite so necessary to all churchmen as mental prayer, prayer that paves the way for every act that we do, that accompanies it and follows it up."* (Office of Readings).

St. Charles Borromeo devoted much time to reforming the clergy. He saw clearly, as the Council document on the formation of priests reminds us, that the heart of the renewal of the Church is the priesthood. That is true of yesterday and of today. We must be Gospel men. Our preaching must issue forth from a heart that has meditated and reflected on Christ and His Gospel. As priests, we seek after and work for greater justice in the world. However, in seeking after greater justice for society, we must always interpret the political situation in the light of the Gospel and not vice versa.

Through the intercession of St. Charles Borromeo and of St. Vincent, may the Church in our day be renewed through the dedication of those called to be priests. May the Church, in the words of the prayer of the Mass, *"bear the image of Christ and show His true likeness to the world."*

An Urgent Invitation

7 November 1989   Jaro, Philippines

My dear Confreres,

Whenever I read the Gospel to which we have just listened, I think of it as the Gospel of excuses. *"A man was giving a large dinner and he invited many . . . but they began to excuse themselves, one and all. The first man said that he had bought some land and had to go to see it, the second man that he had bought some cattle and he wanted to go and inspect them, and the third man said he had married a wife."* (Lk 14:16-20). Now all three made excuses for not accepting the invitation. The excuses were polite and they seemed, on the face of things, to have been genuine. Perhaps the most genuine is the third. Could you get a more genuine one than a man who was newly married and did not want to leave his wife alone during their honeymoon? He was a man who was socially concerned. He understood the value of the person. What is interesting—and perhaps a little frightening—about this parable is that the man who gave the banquet did not accept the excuses. The host was not only disappointed, but was angry. That would seem to indicate that the excuses were not fully valid. The excuses seemed reasonable, but they were rejected. Those invited had not understood—or chose not to understand—the urgency of the invitation.

This parable is a parable about an urgent invitation. Have you ever noticed how many of Our Lord's parables are about invitations? That should not surprise us, because you will notice from the Gospels that the little word *come* was often on the lips of Jesus. *"Come to Me, all you who labor and are burdened."* (Mt 11:28). To Peter in the darkness of the night across the waters, He addressed the word, *come. "Allow the little children to come unto Me."* (Mt 19:14). It is the word *come* that is at the heart of the vocation of the disciples, and of all our vocations.

Not only is the word *come* at the heart of our vocations, but it could be said to be the word that God is speaking to us at each moment of our day. It is His *come* that invites us to prayer. It is His *come* that invites us to give ourselves to the apostolate. It is His *come* that we hear in the cries of the poor. Even in those difficult situations in which we find ourselves, Jesus Christ is still uttering His *come*. When we find ourselves in difficulties, we waste much time saying to ourselves that if things were different, if I had been given more opportunities, if I had been given greater talents, if, if! When I indulge in regrets about what God has not given me, I am making it more difficult for myself to hear His *come*, for His love is present in all circumstances of my day. Even when things go wrong and I am surrounded by the rubble of my failures, His invitation to come is still there. Even when we fail Him through sin, He continues to invite us to rise again, to come to Him as the prodigal son did to his father.

I began this homily by suggesting that the three men who rejected the invitation to come to the banquet did not perceive or understand the urgency of the invitation. God loved us so much that He was not content to send His invitation in writing nor through the silent inspirations of the Holy Spirit. Rather, His beloved Son, though He was in the form of God, emptied Himself, becoming obedient unto death, even to death on a cross. Perhaps, at some time in your life, you received an invitation printed in letters of gold. The invitation that God presents to each of us comes not written in letters of gold, but through the living Person of Jesus Christ, Who has loved us and delivered Himself up for us. That it why it is so important that we provide time for frequent meditation on our crucifixes, why it is so important that we find time occasionally to make the Way of the Cross. It is through reflection on the humility and obedience of Jesus Christ that we will most securely respond to God's personal invitation to us that we come to the banquet which He has prepared for us. *"My daughters,"* exclaimed St. Vincent, *"there is nothing so worthy to be loved by you as your vocation, and that for the reason I have just given, namely, that God Himself is its author."* (Conf. Eng. ed., 25 Dec. 1648, p. 408).

Living Sanctuaries

9 November 1989   Cebu, Philippines

My dear Seminarians,

Man's urge to erect buildings for God has resulted in many edifices, from the Temple in Jerusalem to the colossal new Church, as big as St. Peter's, built by a President in Africa. The Temple in Jerusalem meant much to Mary and Joseph, for does not St. Luke remind us that they were accustomed to make the journey each year from Nazareth to Jerusalem? It must have meant much to Jesus as a boy. What young boy is not impressed by the great national monuments of his country and of its capital?

In his adult years the Temple was for Jesus not only the goal of many of his pilgrimages to the Holy City, but also the place where, as St. John notes, He so often gave expression to some of the most profound truths that mankind has ever heard. Yet, for all that, the Temple of Jerusalem was not to have for Jesus lasting significance. The time would come, as He predicted, when there would not be a stone left upon a stone of that building whose walls had heard the voice of the Son of God.

Let me speak to you of another shrine, not of stone and marble but of flesh and blood. Each one of us, who has been baptized, is a sanctuary. Before Christian churches were built and there were only ornate pagan temples to be seen in cities, St. Paul reminded those who had been baptized that they were temples. *"Your body,"* he wrote, *"is a temple of the Holy Spirit."* (1 Cor 6:19). Each of us is a sanctuary, prepared and decorated lovingly by God, so that our bodies could be the temples of the Holy Spirit. It is a truth of our faith that the Spirit of God lives within each of those who are His friends. The Spirit of God living within us is active and is prompting us all the time with ideas that will lead us to the truth, and suggesting to us ways in which we could manifest the love of Jesus Christ to the world.

One of the principal activities of the Spirit of God, living in the sanctuary of our body, is assisting us in prayer. *"The Spirit, too, helps us in our weakness,"* wrote St. Paul, *"for we do not know how to pray as we ought, but the Spirit Himself makes intercession for us with groaning which cannot be expressed in speech.''* (Rom 8:26). We cannot pray as we ought because we cannot see the future. We cannot see a year ahead or even an hour ahead. Left to ourselves, we might pray for things which would harm us ultimately, or fail to pray for things which would be for our good. So the Spirit of God is helping us to pray all the time. He does not force Himself upon us. Rather he is like a welcome guest in our homes. He will not intrude but is glad to help, when asked, with some task or other.

Not only does the Holy Spirit help us to pray as we ought but, in the words of St. Vincent de Paul, He gives to the person in whom He resides, *"the same inclinations and dispositions which Jesus Christ had on earth and will make the person act in the same way, I do not say with the same perfection but, according to the measure of the gifts of this Divine Spirit.''* (Coste XII, Fr. ed., conf. 196, p. 108).

We are the shrines of the Holy Spirit, that same Holy Spirit Who entered into Mary at the Annunciation and brought about the conception of Jesus Christ, through Whom all things were made and through Whom all good things come to us.

May Our Lady's powerful intercession with God keep us all safe as we make the pilgrimage of life, and at the end may we be found worthy to take our places in the great Shrine of Heaven with the Father, Son and Holy Spirit, Who live and reign forever and ever.

Advent Letter—Identify with Christ

15 November 1989   To Each Confrere

My dear Confrere,

May the grace of Our Lord Jesus Christ be with us forever!

The feast of Christmas is the feast of *God made young.* The feast of Christmas brings us back to the moment when the eternal Word, through whom the stars and all things were made, came forth from the womb of the Virgin Mary as an infant whom *"she wrapped in swaddling clothes and laid in a manger.''* (Lk 2:7). Because Christmas is the feast of God made young, we speak of it as the children's feast. It is St. Luke who reminds us of the growth of the Word made flesh as He passed through youth and adolescence into the maturity of manhood. *"And the child grew and became strong, filled with wisdom, and the favor of God was upon Him."* (Lk 2:40).

There is a youthful Christ and a fully adult Christ, and throughout our lives we are called upon to identify with both. We are called upon to identify with the youthful Christ, for is it not one of the great truths of our faith that Christ has made each one of us through baptism an adopted son of His heavenly Father? Is not that the reason why He reminds us that *"unless you turn and become as little children, you shall not enter the kingdom of heaven?"* (Mt 18:3). It is the adult Christ Who calls us forth from the security of our homes to follow along the road of renunciation, which challenges us to live obedience, poverty and celibacy, so that we can transmit the life of Christ to others—and that they may have it in abundance. There is the youthful Christ and the adult Christ. Our own lives pass inevitably from youth to adulthood and, as they do, we try to marry the simplicity, humility and gentleness of a child to the more manly and demanding virtues of self-denial and zeal for the salvation of others. (cf. CR II, 14). The tide of youth recedes from us and, as it does, we of an older generation may feel content enough to listen to its distant roar. Feeling less secure about youth, we may lose contact with the young. The succeeding generations of youth may seem to some as of another world, culturally different and with alien values.

It is for that reason that I suggested to the Visitors at Rio de Janeiro last July that during the year 1990 the entire Congregation would try to draw closer to the world of the young, within the general project of evangelization. Every new generation is a new continent to be conquered for Christ by offering to it a listening and a loving heart. To that continent we of an older generation must carry *"the unfathomable riches of Christ,"* (Eph 3:8) the wisdom of the Church's experience, and the precious heritage that we receive from St. Vincent, preserved for us by the fidelity of those who have during more than three centuries lived the Vincentian vocation.

Do not lose heart in trying to conquer this new continent for Jesus Christ. You are not alone. Jesus Christ is with you. Let no Confrere think he is too old to advance into the new continent of youth. Let him take heart from the fact that, as Pope Paul VI wrote: *"The men of our day are more impressed by witness than by teachers. And if they listen to these, it is because they also bear witness." (Evangelii Nuntiandi,* §41). We have, too, the encouraging words of St. Vincent: *"So let us work courageously and lovingly for such a good Master as ours; let us imitate Him in His virtues; above all, in His humility, gentleness and patience. Then you will see good results in your manner of directing."* (Coste III, Eng. ed., ltr. 914, p. 154).

As individuals, could we during 1990 devote more time to praying for youth, to listening to youth, to sharing our convictions of faith with youth, all after the manner of St. Vincent, courageously, humbly, gently and lovingly? As a community, could we make our houses more open to youth, manifesting a readiness to share from time to time the experience of our community prayer with youth?

In making these suggestions to you, I do so because old and young are all *"one in Christ Jesus."* (Gal 3:28). I do so, too, because the young have much to tell the not-so-young about the new world which is emerging, while the old from their experience of life have much to tell the young about those Christian values which will never change. With such a meeting of minds and hearts, new expressions of wisdom and truth can be fashioned. It is these new expressions of wisdom and truth that will help us all to proclaim to the poor of today the mystery of Christ. It is the mystery of a God who so loved the world that He became young, that He then grew in age and wisdom, and that He finally through love and obedience gave His life on the cross for the life of the world.

May each of you, be you old, middle-aged or young, receive from the *God made young* an increase of His life this Christmas. Such is the wish and prayer of all of us here who work in the Curia.

Evangelization of Peoples

24 November 1989   Rome, Italy

My dear Brothers and Sisters in Christ,

It is very appropriate that during our three days here we should celebrate a votive Mass for the Evangelization of Peoples. For is it not a fact that it is the Orders, Congregations and Societies of Apostolic Life that are in the vanguard of evangelizing the nations of the world? What would happen if tomorrow the Superiors General were to withdraw all their men who are working in the mission fields of the Church? The missions *ad gentes* would virtually collapse. It is true that during Vatican Council II the Spirit of God moved the Bishops of the Church to assume greater responsibility for the missions of the Church. They were encouraged to look beyond the boundaries of their own dioceses and to share their personnel and resources with the countries and regions that are designated as missionary. Much has been accomplished. However, it is still the Orders, Congregations and Societies of Apostolic Life that are today shouldering the heaviest burden of evangelizing the peoples of the world.

Dare I say that the work of evangelizing peoples may have been somewhat easier fifty or a hundred years ago? The colonial era may have had many unattractive features, but it cannot be denied that at times and in some places missionaries were able to avail of facilities that assisted them in the task of preaching the good news of Christ. The colonial era has passed and the proclamation of the Gospel in mission countries faces challenges today which could be described as new.

There is the challenge for missionaries to be particularly sensitive to the cultures of the countries to which they go. In missionary seminaries today there are courses in inculturation. We would hardly have found such formal courses in seminary programs of a hundred years ago. There is, too, the growth of nationalism in many countries, which can be an impediment to the work of missionaries.

The fanaticism also of some Islamic countries has closed the door to the Christian missionary. Perhaps, too, the theology of the anonymous Christian may have cooled the ardor of some Christians to go forth from their homeland to proclaim the Gospel among religions than antedate Christianity.

Notwithstanding these difficulties, we must press ahead with the evangelization of peoples, for the command of Christ, *"Go, therefore, and make disciples of all nations,"* (Mt 28:19) is for all time. We must allow it to echo again and again in our own hearts and make it echo in those of the members of our Institutes. We must open ourselves to be strengthened by Our Lord's assurance, *"I am with you always."* (Mt 28:20). I knew an eminent professor of Church history who on several occasions remarked to me that he thought the great heresy in the Church today was Pelagianism. I ask, do we try to do too much on our own and, in doing so, magnify the difficulties of evangelization? We can be forgetful of Our Lord's silent presence and of the strength He is lending unceasingly to those whom He calls to the task of evangelization in countries other than their own. *"I am with you always."* (Mt 28:20).

When we reflect on evangelization, the masterful document of Paul VI, *Evangelii Nuntiandi*, comes to mind. There are those who consider this document the finest of Pope Paul's writings. You will recall how the Pope states in that document that the first person to be evangelized is the evangeliser himself. (cf. §41). The truth is that there are acres and acres of territory in my own heart where the Gospel of Christ has not yet been preached. A reflection on my actions and reactions of a single day in my life can bring home to me the realization of how much evangelization has yet to be done in the territory of my heart. Let us not, however, be cast down in spirit. The work of evangelization of peoples, as well as the continual evangelization of my own heart, is ultimately the work of the Spirit of God. Evangelization is our response to the imperative of Jesus Christ, *"Go forth."* It is an imperative, however, that is always lightened by the promise, *"I will be with you,"* (Ibid.) and if God is for us, who is against us?

Freely Have You Received, Freely Give

9 December 1989   Quercianella, Italy

My dear Deacons,

There is a point in this morning's Gospel which has special relevance for all priests and deacons. St. Matthew makes a clear allusion to the hierarchy in this morning's Gospel. According to the evangelist Jesus called the twelve disciples and gave them certain powers. When we examine the parallel text in St. Mark's Gospel, we find clearly expressed the purpose for which Jesus set up the hierarchy. In the third chapter of St. Mark's Gospel we read: *"Jesus called to Him those whom*

He desired, and they came to Him and He appointed twelve to be with Him and to be sent out to preach and to have authority to cast out demons. " (Mk 3:13-15). Have you noted the order? The hierarchy was set up first of all in order that those chosen may be able to be *"with Jesus. "* The second purpose, for which the hierarchy has been instituted, is the ministry of preaching and the casting out of demons.

Your service as deacons covers three areas: the liturgy, preaching and charity. The foundation of these functions, however, must be a close personal union with Jesus Christ. No matter how busy our lives may be, it is necessary, if we wish to discharge well our functions as deacons or priests, that we find time to be *"with Jesus"* in the silence of reflective personal prayer. In the western world we can become so taken up with the work of the Lord that we forget the Lord of the work. The three general functions of the liturgy, preaching and charity, can so absorb a man's energies and his time that he becomes unable to speak to Our Lord in the silence of deep prayer.

In the Gospel of today Our Lord reminds us of the truth, *"freely have you received, freely give. "* (Mt 10:8). We can communicate the power of Christ and His consoling word to others only if we ourselves have laid ourselves open to receive the power and consolation of that word of Christ in the intimacy of prayer every day. In a word, our first response to the invitation of Our Lord to become members of His hierarchy is summed up in the response to today's psalm: *"Blessed are those who wait on the Lord. "* (Ps 146). It is by waiting on Our Lord in the silence of prayer, that we will receive an outpouring of His Spirit, that spirit of wisdom, of understanding, of counsel, of knowledge, of fortitude, of piety and of fear of the Lord.

Through the intercession of Mary, the Mother of God and Mother of the Church, may each one of us here be able to receive the grace of waiting on Our Lord in the silence of prayer.

The Stooping of God

25 December 1989   Rome, Italy

My dear Sisters,

Some years ago when I was visiting our communities in the Province of the Middle East, I went to Israel for some days. I made the journey from Jerusalem to Bethlehem, where our Sisters had a small hospital. With some of our Fathers and Sisters we went around to the church which marks the spot where tradition says Jesus Christ was born. One of the features of this church is that the door of entry into it is very low. One has to stoop to enter the church. If I remember rightly, I was told that the door was made very low centuries ago to prevent men from riding on their horses right into the church.

When you think of the mystery of Christmas and of the Incarnation, it is the feast of the stooping of God. Think of this great universe of ours. Our planet, the earth, is but a tiny speck among the stars and planets of the universe. The God Who made them all chose to be born as a helpless infant from the womb of a young Jewish girl. That was the beginning of the stooping of God, which would continue until the day He stooped to be nailed to a cross and to die.

When God stooped and was born in Bethlehem, He did so gently. Everything in Bethlehem suggests gentleness. Mary and Joseph accepted gently the refusals that they received at the inn, and went off to seek a cave in which Mary could bring forth the Blessed Fruit of her womb, Jesus. The shepherds listened to the song and message of the angels, and then gently made their way to Bethlehem to find the Child and His Mother. The Magi gently received the answer of the jealous Herod and continued their journey from Jerusalem to Bethlehem until they found the newborn King with His Mother. There would be so much more peace in our lives, if we knew how to be truly gentle—gentle and patient with ourselves, gentle and patient with others. When the Infant of Bethlehem had grown up, He asked His followers to learn from Him to be gentle and humble of heart. (cf. Mt 11:29).

The mystery of the birth of Jesus is supremely a mystery of love. The purpose of the coming of Christ was to speak to us humans about the love which the great, eternal and all-powerful God has for us short-lived, weak, fragile and sinful human beings. Think of any newborn infant. Would you be afraid of it? An infant is the least frightening of all humans. The language of a newborn infant is one that invites us to draw close and to help. A newborn infant calls forth from our hearts love. A newborn infant is helpless. Its language is that of humility. A newborn infant is uncomplicated. The cries of an infant are simple. Its needs, too, are simple and elemental. The language of an infant is simplicity.

My dear Sisters, the language of God at Christmas is one of love, of humility and of simplicity. Your vocation is to continue learning that language, not only at Christmas but throughout your lives. It is the language that you must learn to speak if you wish to draw near to the poor. For your vocation as Daughters of Charity is to stoop to serve the poor in simplicity, humility and charity.

The feast of Christmas is the feast of the stooping of God. To enter into the feast we, too, must learn to stoop. If we want to penetrate into the mystery of the Incarnation, we must learn to stoop in humility before God and before humans, and to stoop before humans is much more difficult than to stoop before God. It is at Christmas that we wish each other peace. If we wish to experience peace in our personal lives, then we must learn to stoop in humility. *"In humility,"* writes St. Paul, *"count others better than yourselves."* (Phil 2:3). It is St. Vincent who assures us that the person who has humility will enjoy peace, but the person who has it not will be subject to continual anxieties. (CR II, 7).

All that I have been saying has been expressed marvelously by St. Louise in a letter which she wrote a few days after Christmas in 1659: *"You will learn from Jesus, my dear Sisters, to practice solid virtue, as He did in His holy humanity, as soon as He came down upon earth. It is from the example of Jesus in His infancy that you will obtain all that you need to become true Christians and perfect Daughters of Charity."* (*Spiritual Writings of Louise de Marillac*, ltr. 647, p. 666).

For all of us here I make my own the prayer of Cardinal Newman: *"May each Christmas as it comes, find us more and more like Him, Who at this time became a little child for our sake, more humble, more holy, more happy, more full of God."*

1990

Someone Looked On Me Differently

1 January 1990   Paris, France

Mother Duzan, Father Lloret and my dear Sisters,

Shortly before Christmas a Sister Servant wrote to me and in her letter she described some of the apostolates of the Sisters of her community. Among the poor whose lives were being touched by the love of the Sisters was an alcoholic man, Peter, who had been struggling to be cured of his weakness. Speaking to the Sisters on one occasion, Peter said: *"If I have tried to change, it is because one day someone looked on me differently."* Very likely Peter—as so often happens to alcoholics—was acutely aware that in his weakness he had lost much respect for himself and had also forfeited the respect of his family and friends. Then someone entered Peter's life who, to use his own phrase, looked on him differently. Someone succeeded in seeing more in Peter than his particular weakness, and succeeded, too, in transmitting lovingly to Peter the message that he could be different. That experience gave Peter the courage to begin to change.

Reflecting on the Sister Servant's letter in the days before Christmas, I found myself saying, *"Is that not the story, too, of the Incarnation?"* For is not the mystery of the Incarnation the story of how God at a point in human history began, as it were, to look on humanity differently? From the moment when Mary gave her consent at the Annunciation, God began to look differently on the humanity which He had created. Just how differently God looks on humanity since the Incarnation becomes clear by simply contrasting the experience of Moses on Mount Sinai and the experience of the shepherds and the Magi, as they drew close to the pathetic weakness of a God Who was an infant nestling in the arms of the Virgin Mary. In their wildest dreams, the people of the Old Testament did not think that the Messiah, Who would come, would be the person of God Himself. Even if they did, they could hardly have imagined that God

510

would have chosen to be born of a Virgin and should make His entry into the world in such a humble and natural way. For us who live after the event, our minds will never penetrate to the depths of the mystery that the God who made the stars, could lie behind a pair of human eyes and reach out with infant hands to the mother who nourished Him. A mystic poet expressed the wonder of the Incarnation when he wrote:

> *"Little Jesus wast thou shy Once,*
> *and just so small as I?*
> *And what did it feel like to be*
> *Out of heaven and just like me?*
> *And didst thou sometimes think of there*
> *And ask where all the angels were*
> *. . . . Thou canst not have forgotten all*
> *That it feels like to be small."*

> (F. Thompson, *Ex ore infantium*)

God certainly looked differently on humanity when He began to look at it through the eyes of an infant, who would grow up to be that man who would look on the crowds with compassion because they were hungry, and who would be deeply distressed by the many faces of suffering which is the heritage of sinful and broken humanity. What can we say of God's way of looking at our weakness when He viewed it from the Cross? As He died, there was one man close to Him who could say with Peter, the alcoholic: *"If I have tried to change, it is because one day someone looked on me differently."* *"Truly, I say to you, today you will be with Me in Paradise.* (Lk 23:43).

When God looked at humanity differently through the Incarnation, He was passing a vote of confidence in us sinful, fragile humans. Zacchaeus, Matthew, Peter, Mary Magdalene, Paul of Tarsus—all had deep experiences of God's vote of confidence. Each of them and a host of other people in the pages of the New Testament were changed when God looked on them differently through the eyes and person of Jesus Christ. There has been no century since then that has not produced men and women whose lives have been profoundly and radically changed through their experience of meeting Jesus Christ and of having firsthand experience of being looked at differently by Him.

We must put ourselves among that number, even if we do not consider ourselves to be heroic in the practice of virtue. For has not Christ looked at us and made us adopted children of His Father in Heaven? Does He not by His spirit abide in us and we in Him? Is He not through His Spirit the delightful and unobtrusive guest at all times of our souls? Is not His daily approach to us in Holy Communion a sincere assurance on His part that, whatever others may think of us, He sees us so differently that He surrenders Himself to us totally—body, blood, soul and divinity? Perhaps it is that, in these days when our attention and energies are so much directed outward, we can lose sight of the activity of God within the temples of our bodies. *"Do you not know that your body is a temple of the Holy Spirit within you, which you have from God?"* (1 Cor 6:19).

It was a favorite idea of St. Vincent that each of us is called in our own particular way to continue the mission of Jesus Christ on earth. If so, each of us is called to look on every person differently, that is, to share with Jesus Christ the vision He has of each individual person. If we wish to try to change society and to better the conditions of life for the poor, then we must start out with the vision of Jesus Christ. It is through an ever-deepening personal partnership with Christ that we will most securely change society and be authentic servants of the poor. *"Without Me,"* He has told us, *"you can do nothing."* (Jn 15:5). Acting in partnership with Jesus Christ, we will frequently discover that we release love when we reveal to others their own particular spiritual beauty.

This spiritual principle holds good also for life within our Community. During these weeks and the coming months, you will be focusing your thoughts on assemblies, domestic and provincial. In the coming months your minds will be centered on the topic: *The Daughter of Charity in and for the World of Today.* You will be giving much thought to and engaging in much discussion on how you can make your presence and service more effective in the world, particularly in the world of the poor. Let us not forget, however, that the first world in which we live is that of our local community. If we desire that the Company be a more effective force in the universal Church, then we must commence with our local communities, by bettering and refining the quality of the love we show to one another within the Community. A Sister's power for loving others will often be called forth in a new way when she receives a word of sincere encouragement from her Sister Servant or a companion. Each of us can say with Peter, the alcoholic, *"If I have tried to change, it is because one day someone looked on me differently."* We can, unfortunately, be very economical and sparing with our words of encouragement and commendation to the members of our community. It is an economy which is often motivated by feelings of resentment or of jealousy although we may be slow to acknowledge that we shelter such feelings in our hearts.

The Company will have achieved much if, over the coming months, each Sister comes to acknowledge in a practical way the presence of Christ in those with whom she lives. The work of your assemblies could be reduced to a challenge to look on persons differently, that is, through the eyes of Jesus Christ. Too often we lock ourselves into the room of our own personal prejudices and cannot look on people differently. We do not succeed in climbing through the wounds of Jesus Christ and peering out through His eyes on the world, on the poor and on those with whom by Divine Providence we are called to live our lives in community.

May each day of this New Year be a day of change for us, as we grow steadily into a greater likeness to Jesus Christ. May we, to quote St. Paul, be *"changed into His likeness, from one degree of glory to another; for this comes from the Lord Who is the Spirit."* (2 Cor 4:18). May you, to quote St. Vincent, *"Continue, dear Sisters, to do the Divine Will in all things. Entrust yourselves to God, call upon Him, and rest assured that He will be your strength, your consolation and, one day, the glory of your souls."* (Coste IV, Eng. ed., ltr. 1330, p. 169).

The Women's Christmas

6 January 1990   To Each Daughter of Charity

My dear Sister,

May the grace of Our Lord Jesus Christ be with us forever!
In the country from which I come, the feast of the Epiphany is known

as *"Little Christmas"* and also as *"The Women's Christmas."* There is a tradition that on the feast of the Epiphany it is the men who prepare the main meal, and the women are left free to enjoy the feast day more fully. Hence the day is known as *"The Women's Christmas."* I need hardly say that the tradition of men preparing the dinner has long since lapsed, even if the name, *"The Women's Christmas,"* still remains.

It is on the evening of *"The Women's Christmas"* that I write to thank you for your letters, your gifts, your assurance of Masses and prayers that have been reaching me over the past few weeks. During the Christmas season I have been reading your letters. Some were written by hand, some by typewriter, but all issued from hearts that speak fluently the language of self-sacrifice and of love of the poor and needy. It is costly to speak that language, and so it is for that reason I would like to think that on the evening of *"The Women's Christmas"* you are enjoying a little rest, and that you are refreshing yourselves so that you can give yourselves to your apostolate, whatever it be, with renewed energy and love.

It may seem at first sight an unusual grace to ask for, but the grace or the art of being able mentally and physically to blend in proper proportions work with rest, is a precious one in an era of agitation, overwork and frayed nerves. *"There is a time to keep and a time to cast away,"* writes the author of the Book of Ecclesiastes (3:6). Some of us can be so intent on keeping time for work that we lose the art—or leave undeveloped—our faculty of casting away time through rest, reflection and recreation. Some such idea seems to have been in St. Vincent's mind when he wrote to St. Louise: *". . . be careful not to do too much. It is a ruse of the devil by which he deceives good people, to induce them to do more than they are able, so that they end up not being able to do anything. The spirit of God urges one gently to do the good that can be done reasonably, so that it may be done perseveringly and for a long time. Act, therefore, in this way, Mademoiselle, and you will be acting according to the Spirit of God."* (Coste I, Eng. ed., ltr. 58, 7 Dec. 1630, p. 92).

This little reflection of mine has been prompted by the celebration today of *"The Women's Christmas."* It is my prayer that she, who through her generosity first gave us and still gives us Christmas, and who could quietly ponder all things in her heart, may win for you the grace of being still and knowing that God is God (cf. Ps 45) and that He hides today behind the faces of the poor.

With a most grateful heart for all the good you are doing and for all the kindness you show me, I remain in the love of Our Lord, devotedly yours.

Sense of Proportion in Our Lives

24 January 1990   Cologne, Germany

My dear Sisters,

First, let me greet you as I think St. Vincent would greet you. Whenever he wrote a letter to a missioner, he began with the words with which, in one form or another, we now commence the Mass: *"May the grace of Our Lord Jesus Christ be with us forever!"*. It is a beautiful greeting, for it is the grace of Jesus Christ that has brought us every good thing and is bringing us every good thing today. It is the grace of Jesus Christ that brings us the love of friends, the love of Sisters, the love of the Community, the love of the poor. It is the grace of Jesus Christ . . . yes, all of us could spend this entire day composing a litany of those good things that come to us through the grace of Jesus Christ. So, while greeting you with St. Vincent's favorite greeting, I am also praying with you that you will experience in a new and special way the grace of Our Lord Jesus Christ in the living of your lives with Him for the service of the poor in the Community.

All of us here are called to live out our lives in Community. In the vision of St. Vincent and St. Louise, the Daughters of Charity were to devote themselves to Jesus Christ in the service of the poor, but they intended that this be done in and through the Company. So the tradition has always been strong that we serve the poor through and in the Community.

For us the Community has been a source of support and of strength. It is not always easy to live life in Community, but I think it is true to say that after what we have received from our parents and family, there is nobody on this earth who gives us more than the Company to which

God in His goodness has called us. It is the Company that has passed on to us the rich spirituality of St. Vincent and St. Louise. It is the Company that passes on to us the traditions of three hundred years of Community experience. It is the Company that offers us the opportunities of working for the poor, and it is the Company that supports us in doing so. It is the Company that will look after us in our weakness, sickness and old age. It is the Company that will pray God to be merciful to us when we have left this life and are experiencing the purifying process of Purgatory.

It is important that in our service of the sick and of the poor we keep a sense of proportion in our lives. That sense of proportion is touched upon by St. Vincent when he wrote in one of his letters: *". . . The works of God have their moments. His Providence arranges that they take place then and not sooner or later. The Son of God saw the loss of souls, and nevertheless He did not anticipate the hour ordained for His coming."* (Coste V, Fr. ed., p. 396).

If I mention the importance of keeping a sense of proportion in our lives, even in the service of the poor, thus avoiding excessive or indiscreet zeal, I do so because I feel that the urgency of your work must weigh heavily upon your hearts. That word *urgency* evokes for us St. Louise's motto: *"CARITAS CHRISTI CRUCIFIXI URGET NOS."* Yes, through prayer, reflection and obedience, let us make sure that all sense of urgency in our lives is coming from the *"CARITAS CHRISTI CRUCIFIXI." "And so there are many poor Daughters of Charity,"* observed St. Vincent, *"who lose a great deal by their own fault. They serve the poor, they come and go, they wear themselves out, and all for nothing when they follow their own will. Sisters, you may do all you please, but the best of your actions will not be meritorious without this virtue (of obedience)."* (Conf. Eng. ed., 23 May 1655, pp. 704-705).

The charity of Christ presses us at all times. It presses us not only to serve the poor, but it is the same charity that keeps us linked to each other in love within the Community. I have already stressed that our vocation is to serve the poor in and through the Community. What is a Community, in a Christian sense, if it is not animated by charity?

Over the past twenty years the General and Provincial Assemblies have put much emphasis on the service of the poor. The revision of works has been done and continues to be done in the light of the criterion that the vocation of a Daughter of Charity is to serve the poor. Much has been done to direct the energies of the Sisters towards the service of the poor. In saying that, I do not wish to imply that the Sisters before Vatican Council II did not serve the poor. They did so with much dedication. The number of the poor in the world has, however, increased in the last two decades, and the whole Church itself has become more conscious of her mission to manifest *"a preferential option"* for the poor. Answering this call of the Holy Spirit, the Company has been intensifying its work for the poor and seeking the most abandoned of the poor. Thanks be to God for what the Company has succeeded in doing for the poor by revising its works.

Recently I have thought that perhaps now the call of the Spirit is to intensify the life of charity within the Community. In the vision of our Founders, a Sister should carry to the poor a spark of that fire of charity at which she warms herself within the Community. That is the ideal. Read the conferences of St. Vincent and you will see how frequently he returns to topics like *Fraternal Charity in the Community*, the need to forgive the little injuries and slights we may receive in the Community. All of us recognize that at times it is more easy to show love and understanding to a poor person who calls at our house than to show love and understanding to a member of the Community who kneels beside me in the chapel or sits beside me in the refectory. Yet the truth is that, the more I try to be a radiating center of love within my Community, the more effectively will I serve the poor outside the Community. The more brightly the flame of charity burns within our houses, the more will it attract vocations. Where there is division within a Community, where individuals are selfishly pursuing their own projects, where there is constant criticism of the conduct of other members of the Community, a young aspirant will not feel at ease and will not remain with us. So, as you prepare for your Domestic and Provincial Assemblies, could I appeal to you to give some thought and reflection to the quality of your charity within the Community? If it is good, then your mission to the poor will be authentic and will be blessed by God.

Let me leave the final words to St. Vincent himself. They are words which he spoke toward the end of a conference on the topic, "The

Preservation of the Company": *"Well now, my Saviour, that is enough. May Our Lord Jesus Christ grant us the grace to realize the importance of what has just been said, so that we may put it into practice, and that we may not, by our sins and infidelities, be the cause of the ruin of this beautiful Company which He Himself has formed according to His own wishes. We ask this grace of Thee, O Lord, by the merits of Thy holy Mother and by the services Thou dost wish to derive from the Company. Grant us, O my Saviour, Thou Who art the light of the world, the grace of which we stand in need to detect the wiles by which the enemy desires to seduce the souls of those who have given themselves to Thee, and prevent him from entering into and overturning the work of Thy hands."* (Conf. Eng. ed., 25 May 1654, pp. 618-619).

Lenten Letter—Celibacy

28 February 1990   To Each Confrere

My dear Confrere,

May the grace of Our Lord Jesus Christ be with us forever!

Over the years in my letters to you I have touched on some of the subjects which are at the heart of our vocation in the Church and in the Congregation. Of the four vows which we take, I have already written to you about three of them. Now at the beginning of Lent allow me to offer you a thought on our vow of chaste celibacy.

Meditating on the person of Our Lord, I have often wondered how striking and almost paradoxical He must have seemed to those who saw the works of His hands and listened to the words of His lips. Here was a man Who loved life, Who came eating and drinking, Who appreciated the beauty of creation as He saw it in the birds of the air and the lilies of the fields, Who, more significantly, was highly sensitive to and accepting of those for whom celibacy was anything but a value. He himself was a celibate. He announced that He had *"come that they (people) may have life and have it more abundantly,"* (Jn 10:10) and He was a celibate. Clearly He was speaking of a life that was deeper and more mysterious than that which physical generation produces.

Of all the evangelical values that Christ left us and is still offering us,

I would dare to say that the one which is hardest to understand and accept is the value and meaning of celibacy. When Our Lord made clear and explicit reference to celibacy, He hinted that not all men would grasp this: *"Jesus said to them: 'Not all men can receive this precept, but only those to whom it is given.'"* (Mt 19:11). I think it can be said that there will always be a deep mystery surrounding celibacy, for Our Lord linked this value directly with the growth of the kingdom, which is one of the deep mysteries of the New Testament. All Our Lord's stories about the growth of the kingdom have the element of mystery in them, and something of that mystery must also surround the value of evangelical celibacy. Some of the difficulty in discussions about celibacy as a value arise from the fact that it is seen more as a problem than as a mystery, and there is a profound difference or distinction between a problem and a mystery.

Celibacy is about life. It was that life to which St. John, at the end of His Gospel, refers when he expresses the hope that those who read what he has written may believe in Jesus Christ and have life in His name. (cf. Jn 20:31). To be celibate is to transmit that life which has its source in the loving heart of the celibate Christ. Our vow of chaste celibacy is about loving. We live among God's people as special signs of His loving care. For all that, the pain of loneliness can at times gnaw sharply at our hearts. We are acutely conscious of what we have sacrificed. What we have assumed, however, is even greater than what we have given up. The hearts of celibates are a shelter for *"the joy and hope, the grief and anguish of the people of our time, especially of those who are poor or afflicted in any way . . . .Nothing that is genuinely human fails to find an echo in their hearts."* (Gaudium et Spes, §1).

The task that we have taken on through our vow of chaste celibacy is to give life to others and to give it to them more abundantly. The question that we can pose to ourselves at the end of any day is: To whom have I given life today? Whose life have I enriched by prayer, by word, by action, by understanding, by patience, by compassion? Caring is at the heart of the celibate's vocation. One who is celibate for the sake of Christ and for the Gospel (cf. Mk 10:29) is eminently a man who cares for the world in which he lives, and cares, too, that those to whom he is sent will reach the city that lies beyond the horizons of life and of time. Indeed, the temptations that come to all of us celibates may sometimes stem from a diminishment of our sense of caring for others. Where our sense of caring for others diminishes, we become less celibate and more distant from the celibate Christ, Who saw himself as the good shepherd Who gave His life for His sheep.

"No man or woman," wrote Cardinal Newman, *"can stand alone."* His words highlight the importance for the celibate of prayerful union with the Eucharistic Christ. These words also could be said to evoke the importance for us of authentic community life, if we are to support each other in giving fruitful expression to the charism of celibacy which we have received. Intimate union with Christ and true fraternal communion are two of the four means which our Constitutions suggest to us as helpful, if we are to be *"a living source of spiritual fecundity in the world."* (C. 30).

My prayer for all of us is that, not only will we be faithful to our vow of chaste celibacy, but that we will have confidence in the goodness of our lives and in celibacy as a hidden, silent power that is mysteriously at work within us for the growth of the kingdom of God in the world. With kind greetings to you and asking a remembrance in your prayers, I remain in the love of Our Lord and of His Virgin Mother, your devoted confrere.

Providence of God

5 March 1990   Eastern Europe

I need hardly tell you what a joy it is for me to visit your country and the countries of your neighbors, which for so long lay behind what we called the Iron Curtain. There were chinks in that curtain, so that from time to time we could penetrate and come to see you. Always, however, we came with the consciousness that a great weight lay upon the souls of your people. The human spirit is indomitable and even in those dark years there were always rays of light shining in the darkness. They were the men and women in whose souls dwelt the Spirit of God. If the faith is alive in your country today after decades of systematic attempts at eliminating it, it is because the Spirit of God is stronger than the powers of darkness. If the Community of St. Vincent lives on in your country, it is because that same spirit, which inspired St. Vincent to establish it, has been at work among you, enlightening you, guiding you, strengthening you.

When we pray to the Holy Spirit, we speak of Him as renewing the face of the earth. We think of Him as moving across the world and drawing order out of chaos, harmony out of discord. If we have been astounded at the rapid changes that have taken place in these last few months here in Eastern Europe, it is because the Spirit of God has moved across these countries and with His quiet strength has melted down that Iron Curtain and caused the wall in Berlin to fall, as did the walls of Jericho.

The Spirit of God has not ceased His activities. He continues to speak to us through a succession of events. I imagine that St. Vincent, if he were with us today, might point out two appeals which the Spirit of God may be making to us at the present time.

First, I think the Spirit of God is inviting all of us to renew our confidence in the Providence of God. St. Vincent had a profound devotion to the Providence of God. He believed that God in His kindness was leading us all the time. As St. Vincent saw things, it was important that we should allow God to lead us and not rush ahead of Him. It is God Who leads us, not we Him. *"The works of God have their moments,"* wrote St. Vincent, *"His Providence brings them about at one particular point in time, neither sooner nor later."* (Coste V, Fr. ed., p. 396).

It is the Providence of God that has led you through the dark tunnel of fear, of suspicion and apprehension into the new light of day that is presently dawning. It is the Providence of God that has preserved you until now. It is the Providence of God that has given you new freedom. The Providence of God may have led you through a dark valley, but now you have been brought into a place of fresh and open pastures.

Second, St. Vincent might remind you of the importance of unity among yourselves, as you enter now upon a new chapter of your history. St. Vincent spoke much about serving the poor and about evangelizing the poor. I would say that he was equally concerned that the members of his Communities would be united with each other. He was convinced that, if his Communities were to do good work in the Church, it was essential that they be united closely in love with one another. His message to you today might very well be to deepen the unity among yourselves. It will be your concern for unity that will help you to be obedient to the Church and to the authorities in our Community. It will be your concern for unity that will enable you to do much work for others. Where unity is, there Christ will be and *"if God is for us, who is against us?"* (Rom 8:31). *"And where do you think God dwells on earth?"*, said St. Vincent, *"In hearts filled with charity and in Companies that are always united."* (Conf. Eng. ed., 1 Jan 1644, p. 139).

May God be praised and thanked for His goodness in bringing us here together today. May His grace and His peace accompany you on every step of the road you are now taking into the future, and may Mary, the tender, loving Mother of God, be the inspiration of all that we do for the Church, which is the Body of her Son.

Renewal of Vows

24 March 1990   Paris, France

Mother Duzan, Father Lloret and my dear Sisters,

When the angels and saints in heaven celebrate the feast of the Annunciation of Our Lord, it is only natural that the Angel Gabriel should be a center of attention. Each year the celebration of the feast revives a rumor that the Angel Gabriel had a special difficulty with the commission that was given to him by the Most High. It seems that, when he was asked to go to the planet Earth to a town called Nazareth, he set out obediently and promptly. He went out into the great vastness of the universe which God had created. He traveled from one galaxy of stars to another but could not find the planet Earth. His angelic intelligence had never failed him before, but now it seemed to do so. At last he decided to return to heaven. *"Could it be,"* he asked himself, *"that the planet Earth no longer exists"*? Humbly—for angels esteem humility as the greatest wisdom—he spoke of his difficulty to the Most High. *"Yes, indeed,"* replied the Creator, *"the planet Earth is scarcely visible in the universe. It is but a speck of dust. For my part, I know where it is from the sound of the beating of the human heart."*

So the Angel Gabriel set out once again, and this time he found the planet Earth and the town called Nazareth, but again he was perplexed. Which of the young girls in Nazareth who bore the name Miriam or Mary (for there were a few) was the one the Lord intended? Angels do not make mistakes, so Gabriel returned once again to heaven and humbly asked the Most High for more enlightenment. *"It is she,"* the Eternal Father replied, *"whose heart is beating in perfect harmony with Mine. And you will find that there is only one such in Nazareth, or indeed in the whole of the universe."* The Angel Gabriel went once again to Nazareth and, having found the Virgin Mary who was betrothed to Joseph, greeted her, *"Hail, O favored one, the Lord is with you."* (Lk 1:28).

The vows that we take have everything to do with our hearts and with bringing them into unison with the heart of Jesus Christ, truly God and truly man. It is as clear as daylight to us that the heart of Jesus Christ was not set on money or on what money could buy. He had not whereon to lay His head, and He died deprived of every material thing. Nor was His heart set on doing His own will, but on that of His Father. He lived as a celibate so that others might have life and have it abundantly. As for service, He assured us that He had not come to be served but to serve.

Candid reflection in prayer on our own lives can reveal to us how well or how ill our hearts are beating in unison with the heart of Christ. The day of renovation and the preparation that leads up to it are designed to bring our lives into harmony with the heartbeat of Jesus Christ, chaste, poor, obedient and serving. Is there an echo in our lives of the chaste love of Christ? Does the note of the humble obedience of Christ sound a chord in our actions and reactions to authority? Does the simplicity of Christ's lifestyle harmonize easily with ours? Is His servant mentality a theme that runs through the entire composition of our lives?

The vows which we make are music to the ears of God. When we look at a musical score of a symphony by Beethoven or of a Mass by Johann Sebastian Bach, it does not look particularly inspiring. There are a series of strokes and dots and lines on a succession of pages. But give those pages to the members of an orchestra under the direction of a musical conductor and we will be ravished by the beauty of the sound.

The music of Christ's life was written with blood and tears, and He has told us that at all times He studied to do the Will of His Father in heaven. To make music in our hearts to God we need the written score of lines and strokes and directives of interpretation. It is one of the graces of the day of renovation that Sisters come to a fresh realization that their lives are singing a new hymn to God. *"Sing a new song to the Lord,"* (Ps 98:1) wrote the psalmist. A Daughter of Charity who has revised the score of her life in preparation for this day of renovation, is enriching the harmony of heaven, while bringing new gladness to the poor she serves.

The heart of Mary of Nazareth beat always in unison with the heart of God, her Creator and Savior. It was always pure and authentic. Vows are designed to eliminate what is false and unauthentic in the living of our vocation, so that when we are living our vows, our lives resonate to that of the chaste, poor, obedient and serving Christ. *"Batter my heart, three-personed God,"* prayed the poet, *"Take me to you, imprison me, for I, except you enthrall me, never shall be free, nor ever chaste, except you ravish me."* (John Donne: *Divine Meditation*).

Our vows give stability to us in our ascent to God, for we are ever subject to the gravitational pull of what St. Paul refers to as *"the desires of the flesh."* (Gal 5:16). Visiting recently our Communities in Eastern Europe, I reflected much during those days on the damage which for forty years the powers of darkness caused to the Body of Christ. I marveled at the fidelity of Sisters and Confreres to their vocation and at the strength of their desire to rebuild the walls of Jerusalem. More than once during my visit to these European countries, I found myself wondering if the powers of darkness may not be at work in more subtle ways among us, who have not lived under political systems that are oppressive of religious values. Perhaps we would do well to ponder Our Lord's words that a person's enemies may well be living within his own household. When the tempter stands on our doorstep here in countries where there is political freedom, he prefers to assume the guise of a plausible salesman, who will try politely to persuade us that we are not truly free unless we are seeking to eliminate discomfort, to discard restraints and to secure greater independence. From such specious freedoms, our vows, understood and lived, will deliver us. *"One may say that if the Son of God was tempted He was all powerful to resist it,"* remarked St. Vincent, *"but what can a poor Daughter of Charity do to prevent herself yielding to temptations? Courage! You will conquer in Jesus Christ. Rest assured, there is no happier state than that which renders us conformable to Our Lord."* (Conf. Eng. ed., 20 Aug. 1656, pp. 827-828).

On this feast day the Angel Gabriel in heaven is always a focus of attention. He is wont, however, to remind his friends that it is a busy day for him. It is a day when he is continually descending to earth in his search for new Nazareths where the Word of God can take flesh again in the hearts of Daughters of Charity and through them, in their service of the poor, make music to our Father in heaven.

Vincentian Ministry to Clergy

24 April 1990   Northampton, PA

I do not know if Father Kehoe and the faculty of this seminary, when planning and selecting the date for this talk, were aware of the fact that the 24 April is the birthday of St. Vincent. Today the Saint is a healthy 409 years old, and I imagine that in our Father's house, where there are many mansions, he is receiving many callers from his numerous friends and admirers of many nations and tongues. What the heavenly birthday greeting is, I do not know. It cannot be *Happy Birthday,* for happiness in fullness is already possessed. As for *Many happy returns of the day,* an eternity of them is already assured. I doubt if Vincent de Paul celebrated his birthday in any marked way when he was on earth. He lived into his eightieth year, and four days before he died he celebrated the sixtieth anniversary of his ordination to the priesthood. Father Jean Gicquel, a priest who kept an eye on St. Vincent's mortality, wrote a little diary of community events during the last few weeks of the Saint's life. He makes no allusion to the diamond jubilee of St. Vincent's ordination to the priesthood. We have no way of knowing what St. Vincent's personal sentiments were on the sixtieth anniversary of his ordination. It is likely that they would not have been very much different from those he expressed earlier in one of his letters to a priest: *"For me, if I had known what the priesthood was when I had the temerity to enter into it, as I know it now, I would have preferred to work on the farm than give myself to such a tremendous state in life. I have said this a thousand times to the poor people of the countryside . . . and indeed, the older I get, the more I am confirmed in this opinion, because I discover every day how far I am from the perfection which I ought to have as a priest."* (Coste V, Fr. ed., p. 568).

The Bishop who ordained Vincent de Paul was aged. Very probably Vincent was the last priest he would ordain, for a few weeks later the Bishop would close his eyes on this earthly scene. His eyes were already weak. One can legitimately surmise that he would have had difficulty in reading the text of the Pontifical on the morning he ordained young Vincent de Paul. There was nothing wrong with the eyesight of the ordinand, but he suffered from a certain shortsightedness in his spiritual vision. He himself testifies to that in the confession which he made in the letter from which I have just quoted.

The cataracts, that blurred Vincent de Paul's spiritual vision of the priesthood on the day of his ordination, would be removed, not through any rapid surgery but rather through a therapy that would be prolonged and gradual. It would, however, be some years before the therapy would commence under the direction of the Divine Therapist.

Search as they may, biographers of St. Vincent are unable to glean any insights which Vincent de Paul may have had into his priesthood during those early years. If one of the salient points in the theology of the diocesan priesthood was that a benefice was attached to or was an accessory of the office of priesthood, it could be said that Vincent de Paul thought more about the *beneficium* than the *officium.* His various travels within and outside France, as well as the contacts he was making with influential people in the early years of his priesthood, bear out the point. It is little wonder that in that first decade of his priesthood, when the pursuit of a benefice had caught his imagination and was absorbing much of his energy, there should be no indication of a desire to offer a ministry to his fellow priests. Perhaps the first and certainly a very significant spiritual service which St. Vincent offered to a fellow priest was when he met a professional theologian in Paris, whose mind had begun to be tortured with scruples and doubts of the most excruciating kind. The priest sought counseling and direction from St. Vincent, who then experienced what a modern psychologist might call transference. An encircling gloom descended upon the mind of St. Vincent, and he was led out of the darkness only when he began to visit the sick in the charity hospital close to the place where he resided. In the words of St. Vincent's official biographer: *"After three or four years of unspeakable mental anguish, he made a promise to God to consecrate the rest of his life to the service of the poor. The taking of this resolution immediately banished the temptation and banished it for life; never afterwards was he troubled in regard to the faith, the truths of which were in his mind as indisputable as the most evident facts, since they were based on the very words of God Himself."* (Coste: *The Life and Works of Saint Vincent de Paul,* vol. I, p. 49).

The success which St. Vincent had in alleviating the mental distress of the Parisian theologian, who died with much peace and serenity of soul, did not lead St. Vincent to set up a counseling service for the clergy of Paris. He was then too intent on following the kindly light of God's Spirit directing his steps to the poor. It would be the poor themselves who would lead him back to priests whose difficulties were more spiritual than psychological. It would be the poor who would guide him along the path that led him to see the truth which more than three centuries later would find expression in the document of the Second Vatican Council, *Optatam Totius*: *"The desired renewal of the whole Church depends in great part upon a priestly ministry animated by the Spirit of Christ."* (Introduction).

The Spirit of Christ works gently in the Church. Three or four years of experience in preaching the Gospel to the poor would pass before Vincent and his first associates would be led to turn their attention to the clergy. As an old man he would look back and say to his Community: *"In the beginning the Company concerned itself only with itself and the poor, but in the fullness of time God called us to contribute towards the formation of good priests, of giving good pastors to parishes and teaching them what they should know and practice .... Who would have thought of the exercises for ordinands and of seminaries? This undertaking never occurred to our mind until God showed us that it was His pleasure to devote us to it."* (Coste XII, Fr. ed., p. 84).

The fullness of time to which St. Vincent refers dawned in a rather undramatic way. The year was 1628 and the occasion was a coach journey Vincent was making with the Bishop of Beauvais on a July day. The two men were discussing what today we might term the ongoing formation of the clergy. The term, *ongoing formation*, however, would be rather a pretentious, if not an inaccurate, description of what the two men were thinking about, for regrettably in the case of many of the clergy of the time, no initial formation had been given. The Bishop of Comminges, for instance, quite a pious man himself, demanded of candidates that they should turn up at his residence the night before ordination and listen to a sermon, and that they should avoid gambling and all forms of debauchery for that one night in their lodgings. (cf. J. Duquesne, *Les Prêtres*, p. 184, Paris, 1965). As the coach in which the Bishop and M. Vincent were travelling jogged along, the Bishop closed his eyes. It seemed that he had nodded off to sleep, as Bishops sometimes do during clerical discussions. But no, he was thinking. Opening his eyes, he told M. Vincent that he had been reflecting on what would be the most effective and practical way of improving the formation of the clergy, a topic which had often been broached by M. Vincent. From the discussion was born the retreat for ordinands, a project which was launched shortly afterwards in the Diocese of Beauvais. (cf. Abelly, bk. I, pp. 117-118).

The retreat for ordinands could be described as a workshop or seminar of ten days to two weeks duration, consisting of some lectures on basic spirituality and on the administration of the Sacraments, particularly that of Penance. The format was simple and practical. It was soon adopted in other dioceses and became a requisite for ordination to the priesthood. St. Vincent himself planned and conducted a number of these retreats. Some thirty years later the ordinands of the diocese of Rome were required by Pope Alexander VII to go to the house of the Congregation of the Mission to follow there the retreat course which was given by the members of the Vincentian Community.

From the retreats for ordinands two other innovations issued from the mind and heart of St. Vincent, both of which orbited around the pastoral priesthood. Understandably some of the men, who had been enlightened by the experience of a retreat with M. Vincent and his priests before ordination, sought further enlightenment after ordination. So it was that a number of priests would gather on Tuesdays in M. Vincent's spacious community house to share their insights on the priesthood with him and with each other, while giving expression also to some of their needs as pastors. These in-service training courses became known as the Tuesday Conferences and were attended by professors of theology at the Sorbonne, like M. Duval; by Founders of Congregations, like Father Olier; and by future bishops, like Bossuet. These Conferences in time came to have an influence on the French clergy, far greater than that on the small original group.

It would be years later in 1642 that M. Vincent would launch a more protracted course of pastoral and spiritual formation for candidates for the priesthood. It would be a residential course for men in the four years immediately preceding ordination. The emphasis would be on the practical, rather than on the speculative, in the formation of men who would, immediately after ordination, assume responsibilities for parishes. The seminaries of M. Vincent would be centers of spiritual and pastoral formation of future priests, rather than complete schools of philosophy and theology. In launching this project in 1642, St. Vincent was giving a firm and practical shape to the decrees of the Council of Trent on seminaries. His project must be considered as one of the antecedents of the major seminary as we know it today.

With the passing of the years, a conviction, which may seem to us somewhat exaggerated, crystallized in St. Vincent's mind. It was that the failure of priests to live up to the ideals of their vocation was the cause of all the evils in the Church. *"So, then, it is we priests,"* he remarked at a conference, *"yes, we priests, who are the cause of the desolation which ravages the Church, of the deplorable losses she has sustained in many places."* (Coste XI, Fr. ed., p. 309).

Writing to a layman in 1659 he remarked that there were some men who had entered the priesthood by the window and not by what he called *"the door of a legitimate vocation,"* that these men sought rest rather than work, and that to priests must be attributed the ignorance, sins and heresies which were desolating the Church. (cf. Coste VII, Fr. ed., p. 463). These convictions of St. Vincent about the damaging potential of the priesthood, when it is not being lived in accordance with the mind of Christ and His Church, surfaced in my thoughts when I read an observation of Cardinal Ratzinger, which he made recently in Philadelphia in the course of a talk on "Some Perspectives on Priestly Formation Today." The Cardinal observed: *"It is probable that all the great crises in the Church were essentially connected with a decline in the clergy, for whom intercourse with the Holy had ceased any longer to be the fascinating and perilous mystery it is of coming close to the burning presence of the All-Holy One, and had become instead a comfortable craft by which to secure one's daily needs."* (L'Osservatore Romano, Supplement, Eng. ed., 26 Feb. 1990).

All St. Vincent's work for the preliminary and ongoing formation of priests in the France of the seventeenth century may be said to have had as its practical aim the dislodging of the image of the priesthood as being, in Cardinal Ratzinger's phrase, *"a comfortable craft."* Although he was not alone in working to give new lustre to the priesthood in the France of the seventeenth century, the personality of M. Vincent, with his vision and conviction that the poor must be the first beneficiaries of the spiritual riches which a priest dispenses, made him stand out among his contemporaries. *"History teaches,"* wrote Pope Pius XII, *"that when a saintly and zealous priest has arisen, wherever he has lived, all things around him have been as if by magic renewed and quickened; just as when in the desert a joyous fountain unexpectedly bursts forth, at once freshness and verdure triumph over aridity and desolation, and the caravans come to rejoice and to rest and rebuild their strength amid the enchantment of the new oasis."* (Pius XII, 22 March 1956).

The oases of new seminaries multiplied with the growth and expansion of the Congregation. In the lifetime of St. Vincent some twenty communities of the Congregation in France and three in Italy were engaged in the formation of candidates for the Priesthood. It has been estimated that in the lifetime of the Saint some thirteen or fourteen thousand *Ordinandi* made retreats in the Mission centers. In Madagascar, Father Nacquart, a Priest of the Mission, in a very lengthy letter to St. Vincent, etched out in broad strokes a program of priestly formation for indigenous vocations in that country. (cf. Coste III, Eng. ed., p. 538).

How much the formation of the clergy engaged the thought and the energies of the members of the communities in the decades following the death of St. Vincent is illustrated by the number of decrees on the topic that were promulgated by successive General Assemblies of the Congregation. In the period before the French Revolution there were some 160 seminaries in Europe directed by Vincentian communities, with one also in Goa, in Macao and in Peking. Among the letters of our Confrere martyr, Blessed John Gabriel Perboyre, there is one to his uncle in which he describes the work that was being done by the Portuguese Vincentians in the seminary of Macao.

The 150 years that followed the French Revolution saw a steadily increasing number of seminaries, minor and major, entrusted to the care of the Priests of the Mission in the Americas, in Africa and in Asia. Their very proliferation is a testimony to the success of the formula for formation which the Community over the years had elaborated and developed. Not that the formula was above criticism. Many of you will be familiar with the considered judgment of Msgr. John Tracy Ellis who, while appreciating the magnitude of the contribution made by the Vincentian Community to the formation of priests in your country, considered that the program of these seminaries laid too heavy an emphasis on the spiritual and pastoral elements and too little on the intellectual. (cf. *Essays in Seminary Education*, Notre Dame, 1967, p. 55). If the criticism be valid, then the lack of vision must be attributed, not to St. Vincent, who responded effectively to an immediate and urgent need of his time, but to successive authorities in the Congregation who clung too tenaciously to a life raft instead of boarding and manning a larger skiff. Be that as it may, a tree is known by its fruits, and the fruits of Vincentian seminary formation have been good and abundant, as the humble lives of hundreds of priests testify in countries as diverse as Poland and Paraguay, Ireland and Iran.

Now let me leave behind all our yesterdays and come into the land of today. Writing to the entire Congregation on 25 January 1979, Father James Richardson, Superior General, remarked that *"our role in certain seminaries has ceased, and that for various reasons. Often dioceses and their seminaries have sufficient learned and holy priests, capable of assuring their priestly candidates a suitable formation. If they tell us they no longer need us, let us humbly recognize this."* (*Vincentiana* 1979, pp. 85-86). The past thirty years have undoubtedly seen Vincentians, as a Congregation, take their departure from many seminaries, minor and major. Our presence in centers where candidates for the priesthood are formed has assumed new forms with an obviously smaller concentration of numbers and bearing less administrative burdens. On 1 January 1988 some 404 Confreres of the Congregation in the world were working in seminaries for the formation of diocesan priests or of candidates for our own Congregation. The demands for Vincentians to engage in the seminary apostolate come principally from the African continent. Regretfully we have had to decline many invitations. It is encouraging, however, to know that in one of the largest seminaries in Africa—or for that matter, in the world today—we have an African Confrere acting as one of the spiritual directors of the seminarians.

Our ministry to priests has found expression in the preaching of retreats to the clergy and acting as confessors and spiritual directors to them. The history of this work—much of it hidden—has not been chronicled as has the history of the work in seminaries. The Recording Angel, I am sure, has filled many pages of the Book of Life with the names of Vincentian priests of different nations who have been to their fellow priests what the old Irish monks liked to call a *soul friend*.

At this point I would like to make two rather personal observations about our Vincentian charism of forming seminarians and of our ministry to priests.

There can be no doubt that, in the optic of St. Vincent, the foreground was occupied by the poor. It was the poor who, under the guidance of the Holy Spirit, had led him to labor for the priesthood and for its greater efficacy in the Church. It was to the poor that he sent the priests of his own Congregation to proclaim the good news of Christ. For Vincent de Paul, a priest of his Community was a man who, through his constant efforts to chisel into his character the humility and charity of Christ, is humble about himself and his abilities, has a deep respect for the dignity of others, and makes it his principal mission to manifest genuine love, especially to those who for any reason have lost the sense of their own dignity and worth in the sight of God. The world of the poor was, in St. Vincent's vision, to be penetrated by priests, messengers of God, who in turn were to be penetrated by a love of the poor. For St. Vincent the great world of the poor and the smaller world of ordained priests were like two concentric circles. The living person of Jesus Christ was *"the still point of the turning world."* During the last thirty years of his life St. Vincent moved easily in these two worlds, introducing one to the other. Two years before he died, he wrote in his Rule for missioners: *"Though our preference is for missions, giving them should not mean omitting our work for the clergy, whenever we are asked to do this by Bishops or Superiors. The reason is that by the nature of our Congregation, we are bound almost equally to both."* (CR, XI, 12).

"Almost equally to both..." In the General Assembly of the Congregation in 1968-69 and in the successive Assemblies of 1974 and 1980, the Congregation expressed its mind that the end of the Congregation is the evangelization of the poor. Official approbation of this statement was given by the Holy See through its approval of the Constitutions in 1984. As one of the criteria for evaluating our works, evangelization of the poor has been consistently invoked by Provinces throughout the world. Personally I have frequently thought that in recent years the Congregation has allowed its apostolate to the clergy to be eclipsed by its concern—albeit a just and a valid one—to evangelize the poor.

It is evident that the scenario of priestly formation has greatly changed over the last three decades. During this period academic standards in the seminaries of your country have risen notably. The obtaining of accreditation has demanded greater professionalization and has resulted in the development of high quality programs. The locus of theological studies, too, has changed. There has been an unprecedented growth of theological activity outside the traditional seminary (cf. Rev. Robert Wister, "The Teaching of Theology 1950-1990: The American Catholic Experience." AMERICA Feb. 3, 1990). Apart from the academic study of theology, the concept of personal formation and development has acquired new depths. Spiritual direction itself has become more complex. All these developments are formidable, demanding a high degree of specialization and of broad collaboration with agencies outside a particular Congregation. Facing such a changed scenario, has our Congregation quietly retreated before these demands, insisting that its end is the evangelization of the poor? However understandable such a retreat may be, and indeed to some degree inevitable, it is to be regretted that in a period in the history of the Church, when the priesthood is being challenged to make adjustments in the manner in which it exercises and expresses itself in the post-Vatican II Church, our Congregation should not be more prominent in its ministry to priests.

The spiritual needs of priests have been well articulated in recent years. There comes to my mind the address which Father McNulty made to the Holy Father on the occasion of the Pope's meeting with priests in Miami in September 1987. Like a refrain running through Father McNulty's address were the words: *"If priests could open up their hearts and tell you of their priesthood, they would speak of . . . "* and Father McNulty listed a number of priestly hopes and concerns. Our Vincentian ministry to priests will address itself to such hopes and concerns. Supreme among a priest's hopes and concerns today, and in any era of history, must be holiness of life. Do we priests talk less nowadays about the primacy of personal holiness in the priest's life and much more about self-fulfillment—an expression, incidentally, that is not to be found in the pages of the New Testament? Valuable as the sciences of psychology and sociology are to a priest today, they are not a substitute for holiness. *"No, Monsieur,"* St. Vincent advised the young Superior of the Seminary of Agde, *"neither theology nor philosophy nor discourses can act upon souls. It is necessary for Christ to intervene with us or we with Him: that we act in Him and He in us, that we speak as He does and in His Spirit."* (Coste XI, Fr. ed., p. 343).

The Vincentian ministry to priests will have as its highest purpose the assisting of priests to grow in all things into the likeness of Christ, the great high priest. It is only when priests are earnestly trying to climb the mountain of the all-holy Lord that they will have the wisdom and experience necessary to speak with the accents of the Good Shepherd to the people they are called to lead. For that reason St. Vincent did not hesitate to set forth in his Rule holiness of life as a first requisite for his priests: *". . . the whole purpose of the Congregation is: 1. to have a genuine commitment to grow in holiness, patterning ourselves as far as possible on the virtues which the great Master Himself graciously taught us in what He said and did."* (CR, I, 1).

As for helping clerics to grow in holiness, St. Vincent saw it as a challenging work that was *"the most difficult, most elevated and most important for the salvation of souls and the advancement of Christianity."* (Coste XI, Fr. ed., pp. 7-8). In accepting that challenge we, his spiritual heirs, must, to quote the Irish poet, Patrick Ravanagh:

> *". . . . . . .lie down again*
> *Deep in anonymous humility and God*
> *may find us worthy material for His Hand. "*
> (*Collected Poems*: "Having Confessed")

As spiritual heirs of St. Vincent de Paul, we continually accept the challenge to be men who are intent on growing in personal holiness, intent, too, on sharing with the poor *"the unsearchable riches of Christ,"* (Eph 3:8) eager also to assist the clergy in their pursuit of holiness. I cannot think of any better gift to offer M. Vincent on his birthday. Can you?

Seventy-Fifth Anniversary

26 April 1990   Bangor, Pennsylvania

Bishop Welsh, my dear Fathers, Sisters and Parishioners,

When I was a young boy, I lived within the shadow of an Augustinian Church. We often went to Mass there. The Augustinian Fathers who served the Church frequently spoke of Mary, the Mother of God, and invoked her intercession under the title of Our Lady of Good Counsel. On one of the two side altars there was an illuminated picture of Mary holding the Child Jesus in her arms, the original of which is to be found in a shrine of Our Lord at Genazzano, some thirty miles or so outside of Rome. I cannot remember now anything particular that the Augustinian Fathers said about Our Lady of Good Counsel, but I do remember the last two lines of a simple hymn that was sung from time to time in the Church and which my mother in our home would sometimes quote: *"O Mother of Good Counsel, tell me what I ought to do. "*

For us who believe in the power of Mary's intercession at all times, it is natural that we should in moments of perplexity call upon her to help us in making right decisions. It is natural that we should ask her for advice and counsel, when we cannot see clearly ahead on the road of life. I like to think that she herself, when she was a pilgrim on earth, appealed often to God's wisdom and knowledge in her moments of perplexity. We know that she was perplexed momentarily at the Annunciation, and she must certainly have prayed in her heart before she replied to the angel: *"Tell me, tell me what I ought to do."* When she was reaching the term of her pregnancy and was searching with Joseph in Bethlehem for a lodging house in which she could bring forth her child, and to her dismay found all doors closed, she must have appealed to God, her Father, praying: *"Tell me, tell me what I ought to do."* Did she repeat that prayer, I wonder, when twelve years later she lost Jesus in Jerusalem? *"Tell me, tell me what I ought to do."* At Cana in Galilee, when she saw the embarrassment of her hosts when the wine had run out, would she ask her Son, the Wonderful Counsellor, to anticipate His hour by working a miracle? *"Tell me, tell me what I ought to do."* She had, too, to make a decision when she learned that they had condemned her Son to execution in Jerusalem. Would she go to Calvary to see the brutal death that was being meted out to her Son? *"Tell me, tell me what I ought to do."*

Every Christian is continually faced with decisions to make, if he or she is to live according to the Gospel of Jesus Christ. We have the indwelling Spirit of God to guide us to make right decisions that are in conformity with what God wants us to do. In such moments of decision we would do well also to appeal for counsel to her who is the Mother of Him Who is called the Mighty Counsellor.

Does a parish face moments of decision? Pastors, assistants and people in the living of their individual vocations certainly do. Are parishes, as a whole, asked to make decisions? They are and perhaps since Vatican Council II with the introduction of local parish councils, the parish as a unit is being invited to make more decisions as a group of Christians than it did previously. Last year in his Apostolic Exhortation on *The Vocation of the Lay Faithful in the Church and in the World*, Pope John Paul II reminded the world that the *"laity ought to be ever more convinced of the special meaning that their commitment to the apostolate takes on in their parishes.* " (*Christi Fidelis Laici,* §27). The Pope goes on to remind the laity of what Vatican Council II stated: *"The laity should accustom themselves to working in the parish in close union with their priests, bringing to the Church community their own and the world's problems as well as questions concerning human salvation, all of which need to be examined together and solved through general discussion. As far as possible the laity ought to collaborate in every apostolic and missionary undertaking sponsored by their own ecclesial family.* " (*Decree on Apostolate of Laity, Apostolicum Actuositatem,* §10)

The celebrations of parish jubilees, be they of twenty-five, fifty, seventy-five or one hundred years, are occasions when we not only look back on the past, but look forward to the future. On the occasion of a jubilee such as that which we are celebrating this evening, we look back gratefully to the priests who worked here and to the parishioners who collaborated so generously with them in building up the Kingdom of God here in Bangor. We rejoice that this parish has been during its seventy-five years, a nursery of heaven. Within its boundaries hundreds of its members have grown up to be strong, convinced Catholics, some of whom undoubtedly are now in high places in our Father's house. For all that the parish has received, we give thanks and praise to God from Whom all good things come.

We must not only look back. We must also look forward. A jubilee celebration is a halt on the road so that decisions may be made about the journey ahead. What decisions face the people of this parish as a parish at the present time? Is God calling it to embark on any project for the poor (and surely a Vincentian parish must be characterized by its love for the poor), on a project for the diocese, for the third world, for greater justice in society? Does the parish plan on commemorating this jubilee in ways other than tonight's ceremony? These are questions which call for decisions by the parish. In taking them, I am sure you will not fail to turn to her who is the Patroness of your parish, Our Lady of Good Counsel, for it has never been known that anyone who fled to her protection, or sought her intercession, was left unaided.

May Mary, the Mother of Good Counsel, draw closer to you all as you enter upon the quarter century that will culminate in the centenary of this parish in the year 2015. May she help you in the years that lie ahead to shape your decisions as individuals and as a parish, so that they will be in full harmony with the teaching of Her Son and of His Church.

"O Mother of Good Counsel, tell me, tell me what I ought to do."

Disciples on the Road to Emmaus

29 April 1990   Emmitsburg, Maryland

My dear Sisters,

The Emmaus incident, as recounted by St. Luke, could be described as one of the finest short stories in all literature. It is a story which begins in sadness and ends in joy. It is a story which begins in a mood of disillusionment and ends in one of hope. It is a story that describes how Christ gently put light where there was darkness and faith where there was unbelief. Above all, it is a story that speaks volumes about the humility, sensitivity and gentleness of Christ.

The incident opens in a mood of depression. The two disciples are walking away from Jerusalem, sad and disheartened. They are joined by the Risen Christ, who perhaps noticing their sadness, sympathetically asks them, *"What matters are you discussing, as you walk along?"* (Lk 24:17).

Often the best help we can offer a person who is depressed is to afford them an opportunity of talking. And Jesus Christ does exactly that when He encounters the depression of the two disciples. So often depressed people seek only a listening ear, or rather I should say—a listening heart. By listening attentively and lovingly to them, He drained the depression out of them.

I am sure that many of you here have discovered in your work for the poor that, while their material needs are often great, their spiritual needs may be greater still. I am sure, too, that many of you have discovered that on many occasions, when the poor present a problem to you or seek your advice, you come eventually to realize that their real need is not your advice, but rather the sympathy of your listening heart. Often I feel that I have given advice to people when what they were really asking for was understanding and compassion. They were seeking rather a listening heart than a speaking bureau of information. Perhaps words like *"What you ought to do is . . . "* come too easily to our lips when people are sharing their pain or their difficulties with us.

In the dialogue between Our Lord and the two disciples, did you notice the slight note of sarcasm used by the disciples? *"You must be the only person staying in Jerusalem who does not know the things that have been happening there these days. "* (Ibid., v. 18). Jesus ignored the note of sarcasm and simply asked, *"What things?".* It is always wise to ignore sarcasm, and more wise never to employ it, for it is a very wounding weapon.

When Jesus had by His loving and attentive listening lifted the disciples out of their depression and thus given them joy, He went on to open the meaning of the Scriptures to them. Did you notice, too, the delicacy of Christ? *"He appeared to be going further, but they constrained him, saying 'Stay with us, for it is towards evening and the day is now far spent.'"* (Ibid., vv. 28-29). If Our Lord's ignoring of the sarcasm of the two disciples was an indication of his gentleness, then His unwillingness to force His company on the disciples was a manifestation not only of his respect for their persons, but also of that humility of heart which He asked us to learn from Him.

Gentleness and humility of heart are the only two virtues which our Lord asked us to learn from Him. He may have told us to be charitable, to forgive those who offend us and so on, but there are only two virtues He asked us to learn from Him, that of gentleness and of humility.

Some time ago the thought occurred to me that all our failings could be traced back to a lack of gentleness or a lack of humility. List any of the defects you recognize in yourself, and see if they be not rooted in a lack of gentleness and humility: our impatience, our aggression, our stridency, our rudeness, our jealousy, our boastfulness. All these flourish in the garden of our souls because we have failed to learn gentleness and humility from the shepherd of our souls, Jesus Christ.

The gentleness I speak of is not weakness but rather it is strength controlled. The world has much need of that gentleness which is strength controlled, which is the gentleness of Christ. Strong public protest about one issue or another is a phenomenon of our day. Marches of angry men and women are a familiar sight on our streets. I like very much St. Peter's counsel to the Christian women of his day: *"Your adornment is rather the hidden character of the heart, expressed in the unfading beauty of a calm and gentle disposition."* (1 Pt 3:4). That is an ideal for any Daughter of Charity in the living of her vocation, expressing at all times *"the unfading beauty of a calm and gentle disposition."* (Ibid.).

Humility is not the most spoken of virtues today. Our age places much value on self-expression and on what each person thinks, and humility often finds itself relegated to a back place in the Christian scale of values. It merits, I think, more frequent meditation on our part, for it is humility that marked so forcefully the entry of Our Lord into life, and it was humility that distinguished His passing from this world. St. Paul saw the point clearly when he wrote: *"Christ humbled himself, becoming obedient unto death, even to death on a cross."* (Phil 2:8).

So let me end this homily by simply and humbly asking for us all from the Christ of Emmaus that we would come to know more deeply the value of gentleness and humility on the journey of life which we are making in His company at the present time towards the Heavenly Jerusalem. May we not only know what gentleness and humility are, but may we also, through God's grace, give proof of them to those whose lives, inside or outside the Community, we daily touch.

"May God be pleased," prayed St. Vincent, *"to grant the Company the grace to study especially and above all the means of acquiring this holy virtue of humility . . . . Yes, my brothers, I repeat it, we should run after the acquisition of this virtue of humility. May His Divine Majesty be pleased to grant us this grace."* (Repetition of Prayer, 1 Nov. 1657).

Vocation and Mission of Women

10 May 1990   Assisi, Italy

Your President, Signora Dilde Grandi, has very kindly invited me to greet you at the opening of your Assembly (International Association of Ladies of Charity—AIC). I am very grateful to her and to the members of the executive committee, for this opportunity of expressing in the name of the whole Vincentian family my good wishes to all of you and to assure you that, during these days of your Assembly, you will have a special place in my prayers.

In inviting me to greet you this morning, I see in your President's gesture an expression of her desire to bring you back to your origins as an Association or Confraternity of Charity. The genius and the holiness, the vision and the practical sense of St. Vincent de Paul must always be allowed to permeate your policies and your programs. In doing so you will be assured, not only of his patronage and intercession, but also of continued success in meeting some of the needs of the poor, who turn to you daily for direction and collaboration in their efforts to rise above their conditions of poverty.

Since your last General Assembly, Pope John Paul II has given to the world two documents which have much significance for the Church. They are two documents which directly or indirectly will influence the deliberations of your Assembly. I refer to the Apostolic Letter, *Mulieris Dignitatem*, on the dignity and vocation of women, and the Apostolic Exhortation, *Christifideles Laici,* on the vocation and the mission of the lay faithful in the Church and in the world.

In his letter on the dignity and vocation of women, the Pope, treating of how, throughout Christian history, women have contributed notably to the apostolic mission of the Church, evokes *"Monica, the mother of Augustine, Macrina, Olga of Kiev, Matilda of Tuscany, Hedwig of Silesia, Jadwiga of Cracow, Elizabeth of Thuringia, Birgitta of Sweden, Joan of Arc, Rose of Lima, Elizabeth Ann Seton and Mary Ward."* (§27). Clearly, thousands of other women could be added to that list. What, however, might merit mention in this context—and certainly deserves further study—is the gift which St. Vincent de Paul had of placing a high degree of confidence in Christian women for the realization of a variety of projects, which he judged would be carried through and sustained more effectively by women than by men. Vincent de Paul had an unusual degree of insight into the spiritual energies that lay hidden in the feminine soul. Moreover, he had the gift of releasing those energies and channeling them into what was the passion of his life, namely, the poor and the suffering members of the Body of Christ. In that way St. Vincent de Paul opened up for the women of his day new vistas of apostolic action, so that they were no longer confined to the option of either the cloister or the hearth. (cf. M. Marocchi, in *Actes du Colloque International d'Etudes Vincentiennes*, ed. Vincentiana, Roma 1983, p. 41). There is something of the challenge of the prophet in what St. Vincent said to your predecessors on 11 July 1657. *"It is eight hundred years or so since women have not had some public office in the Church. They had it previously and they were called deaconesses . . . but around the time of Charlemagne, by a secret disposition of Divine Providence, this ceased, and your sex was deprived of all office . . . .And now this same Providence addresses itself to some of you today to supply what is lacking to the sick poor of the Hotel Dieu. They are responding to this plan . . . .These good souls have responded by the grace of God to these designs with ardor and constancy."* (Coste XIII, Fr. ed., p. 810).

Your Founder, then, must be seen as a herald, in some degree, of the riches which the Church in our day is now drawing forth from her treasury on the vocation of women in the world.

Your reflections during this Assembly will also be made in the light of the document on the laity, *Christifideles Laici.* In that document the Pope gives much attention to the vocation and mission of women in the Church and the world. I see your Assembly as a challenge to finding ever more effective means of enhancing the dignity of the poor, of securing greater justice for them and of serving them. There is an external challenge, and there is also an internal one for you as members of this Assembly. In his forceful appeal to the developed nations of the northern hemisphere on the 29 January this year, the Pope observed that: *"Justice makes more progress when a spirit of understanding prevails and each person gives of his or her best."* (Address at Ouagadougou, 29 Jan. 1990).

With a spirit of mutual understanding prevailing in this Assembly, and with each delegate offering her best to the discussions, the cause of justice in the world will be effectively, if not dramatically, advanced. In the words of the Holy Father: *"As a person with a truly unique life story, each is called by name, to make a special contribution to the coming of the Kingdom of God. No talent, no matter how small, is to be hidden or left unused."* (*Christifideles Laici*, §56).

My hope and prayer is that in the treasury of experience, of spiritual gifts, of practical expertise, that is represented in this Assembly, no talent, no matter how small, may be left hidden or unused. *"Such is your office, Ladies, such is your portion,"* exclaimed St. Vincent. *"Let us grasp the feet of Our Lord and pray Him to pour forth more and more life, energy and warmth into your spirit so that you may continue to the end that which you have begun."* (Coste, XII, Fr. ed., p. 815).

Three Graces of Mary

13 May 1990   London, England

My dear Confreres and my dear Sisters,

The date, 13 May, reminds most of us that it is the feast of Our Lady of Fatima and, were it not a Sunday, we might reflect a little on the person of the Mother of God and of her place in heaven and on earth today.

The date also recalls the attempt that was made on the life of the Pope nine years ago today. It was a coincidence that the Pope should have suffered this attempt on his life on one of the feast days of the Mother of God to whom he is deeply devoted. It reminds me of St. Catherine who, on the 8 December in the last month of her life, on coming out from the rue du Bac, slipped and broke her wrist. Her reaction to the pain was: *". . . my bouquet of flowers. Every year the Blessed Virgin sends me one like this."* A Sister said to St. Catherine, *"Look what happens to you when you take the trouble to go to pray to her at the Mother House."* Catherine replied very calmly: *"When the Blessed Virgin sends suffering, she is imparting a grace to us."* (R. Laurentin, *The Life of Catherine Labouré*, Eng. ed., p. 225).

Reflecting on the three readings of today's Mass, I think we can select three graces which were given to Mary and that shine out in her life.

The first reading centers on the idea of service. In the daily distribution of food it seems that some widows in the church of Jerusalem were being neglected. So a resolution was taken to remedy the situation. Deacons were appointed and sent on mission. The mission they were given was one of humble service—the distribution of food to needy people.

For you who work here in London, it is interesting to note that, even in the first years of the Church, differences in language and culture gave rise to pastoral problems. The pastoral difficulty, mentioned in today's first reading, was one that arose between people who spoke Hebrew and those who spoke Greek. Your presence here in London is to achieve what the first deacons were ordained to do, to assure that a difference in language and culture does not deprive a section of the people of the care and love that Our Lord and His Church wish to offer to all. You are giving service, and service distinguished her who called herself the servant or, more accurately, the slave of the Lord.

The second reading highlights the dignity of a Christian. *"You are a chosen race, a royal priesthood, a consecrated nation,"* (1 Pt 2:9) writes St. Peter. Mention the word *royal* to any English person and he will immediately think of the royal family. The members of the royal family are wealthy people. It is almost impossible for an English person to think of a royal person who is not wealthy.

Although Mary of Nazareth was a member of the royal house of David, she was certainly not wealthy. Nevertheless, she was royal and had the dignity of royalty. What a changed place the world would be if all Christians could think of themselves and others as members of a royal family and of the need, therefore, to behave with the dignity of royal persons. The royalty of Christians is derived, not from the house of David but from the family of God Himself, Who has adopted us as His children. Our royalty stems from our baptism, a point made clear by St. Peter in his letter to the people to whom today's reading was addressed. St. Paul in his letters to the Romans and Galatians stresses the point that baptism has made us adopted children of God, our Father.

The Gospel of today's Mass is an exhortation to faith. *"Do not let your heart be troubled. Have faith in God and faith in Me."* (Jn 14.1). We know of at least three occasions when the heart of Mary was troubled. When the angel spoke to her at the Annunciation, she was troubled by the greeting that was offered to her. Mary's heart was also troubled when she lost Jesus in Jerusalem and when with Joseph she sought Him sorrowing. Her heart must have been almost broken as she watched His life drain away on the cross on Calvary. Yet we know that she lived her life with the conviction that the fruit of her womb was the

Son of the Most High and that the Holy Spirit had, at the moment of the Incarnation, overshadowed her.

So I pray, through the intercession of the Mother of God and of St. Vincent and St. Louise, that each of us may come to appreciate the value of our service to God in the Community, to realize, too, more fully the dignity that is ours through baptism, and to have an unwavering faith in the goodness of God, Who has called us out of darkness into light. We make this prayer through Christ, Our Lord.

Mountain of Joy

3 June 1990   Santiago, Chile

My dear Young People,

We are standing on the Mountain of Joy. The first sentiment I would like to express to you is the joy that is in my heart to see so many of you gathered here. You rejoice together because you have received into your hearts the Holy Spirit, Him Who is called the first gift of God to those who believe in Jesus Christ. It is a coincidence that we should be gathered here together on Pentecost Day, the feast day of the Holy Spirit. Let us greet Him together with the salutation which the Church likes to use as a welcome to the Holy Spirit, *"Come, Holy Spirit."* With our hearts and lips let us three times make Him welcome: *"Come, Holy Spirit."*

When the Holy Spirit comes into a person's heart through baptism, He does not come with empty hands. When you visit a friend's house on a special occasion, you will bring a gift. The Spirit of God brings not one gift, but seven gifts. He also brings a variety of fruits. St. Paul in one of his letters lists some of the fruits. They are: joy, peace, patience, kindness, faithfulness, gentleness, love and self-control. (cf. Gal 5:22).

So you see that one of those fruits is joy. If you have joy in your heart, that is a sign of the presence of the Holy Spirit in your heart. You yourselves have discovered that, for I was impressed when I heard you say that a Christian who is sad is a sad Christian. That phrase reminded me of a prayer which one of the great saints of your nation, St. Teresa of Avila, a very joyful person, once made. She wrote: *"May the Lord deliver us from sad saints."* I think, too, of another person, not from Spain, not a saint, and not a Christian by conviction, who said once with acidity: *"If Christians really believe that they have been redeemed by Christ, they certainly do not show their joy in the way they live."*

The joy of which I speak is not a superficial thing. Some of the people who present advertisements on our television screens will smile at us and tell us that with this or that new commodity we will experience new joy in our lives. Often we do not believe them and often, too, we know that the smile on their faces is somewhat artificial. It is not necessarily an expression of joy.

There is another curious thing about joy: it can live quite peaceably with suffering. Have you ever visited someone in the hospital who was suffering much but whose presence radiated a quiet joy? No doubt some of you have visited poor and needy people who had not much more than the essentials of life, but who communicated to you contentment and joy. Clearly, such people have received from the Spirit of God a generous portion of that fruit which we call joy.

In the market of life you will meet many vendors of joy. All of them will offer to increase joy in your life. Unfortunately, many of the vendors will offer you spurious articles, a species of joy which is not authentic or lasting. The joy they offer is like a fruit which looks ripe and attractive, but when tasted is bitter and perhaps already decayed. Drugs can give a momentary sensation of joy; so, too, can the gratification of sexual powers outside the loving relationship of marriage. In our hearts, however, we know that such joy is not authentic nor lasting. It is not one of the fruits which has the authentic mark of the Holy Spirit upon it.

If we wish to increase joy in our hearts, there is no market in this world where it can be bought. We cannot even borrow it from another person, even when we meet someone who seems to have a plentiful supply of it. The truth is that joy is a by-product. If you want to make plastic material, you must first have oil. If you want to have joy in your life, if you want to increase joy in your life, then look to charity. For joy and peace are two by-products of charity. Throw away a little bit of yourself for the sake of another person, and you will find that you will slowly be suffused by a glow of joy. I do not say that it will not cost you something to do this. Often it will be painful and difficult to help another person who is needy or poor or unreasonable or selfish. Sometimes you will feel that you have lost something of yourself. And so often you have. But did not Jesus Christ say that the person who loses his life, because of the love he has for Christ, will find it? What you will find will not be what you have thrown away in love, but will be an increase of joy in your heart. That increase of joy will come directly from Jesus Christ, working through the Holy Spirit, His first gift to those who believe in Him. *"These things,"* said Jesus Christ on the night before He threw away His life for us, *"I have spoken to you, that my joy may be in you, and that your joy may be full."* (Jn 15:11).

My dear young people, we stand on the Mountain of Joy—so called, as you have told me, because of the joy the pilgrims of old experienced when they caught their first sight of the Cathedral after months, perhaps, of travel. Strengthened by the Spirit of God, be pilgrims of joy as you move along the road of life. You will have joy in your heart if, on your pilgrim ways, you keep your eyes and your hearts open to those who, because of injustice, poverty, sickness, or addiction, are lying on the road, wounded and half-dead. Try to lift them up and find them shelter. In doing so, you will be acting as did that good Samaritan whom we know as Jesus Christ. May He, with our Father in Heaven and the Holy Spirit, be praised forever.

Shaping our Eternity

5 June 1990   Orense, Spain

My dear Friends of Jesus Christ,

First, let me say how honored I feel that so many of you have come here today to celebrate the Eucharist with me. You are a diversified group of people. Some are young; some are less young. Some are married; some are single. Some are strong and healthy and some are less so. There is a diversity of nationality also. You are Spanish and I am Irish, but we are all united in Jesus Christ, Who has called us here today to offer with Him the Sacrifice of the Mass, in the unity of the Holy Spirit to the glory of God, the Father in heaven.

In today's first reading St. Peter turns the minds of his people towards the distant future. He writes: *"Look for the coming of the day of God and try to hasten it. Because of it the heavens will be destroyed in flames and the elements will melt away in a blaze. What we await are new heavens and a new earth . . . . You are forewarned, beloved brothers. Be on your guard lest you be led astray by the error of the wicked and forfeit the security you enjoy."* (2 Pt 3:12-13, 17).

It is good for us from time to time to reflect on the only two alternatives that await us after our deaths—everlasting life or a state of everlasting death which is separation from God and from all whom we have loved in this life. It is certain that the urgency of salvation, the urgency of the choice that each individual adult person must make of one or other of these alternatives, was a strong motivating force in the life of St. Vincent. He loved the poor and did an enormous amount of work to relieve their sufferings. Let us never forget, however, that St. Vincent's eyes were always on the horizons of eternity and of what follows after our death. What we call the eternal truths—death, judgment, hell and heaven—were very real for him and constantly before his mind. He has told us that for twenty years before his death, he never retired to rest without preparing himself to meet Our Lord as judge.

In recent years we have not heard people talk or write so much about hell as they did in previous centuries. What has been emphasized for us is the infinite mercy and goodness of God which He shows to us sinners. That emphasis is good. However, it is important that we should not lose sight of that which is an eternal truth, namely, the existence of hell. The Church does not tell us that anybody is there, but she does clearly teach that there is a possibility that people may find themselves in hell for all eternity. If a person should have the frightful misfortune to find himself or herself in hell, that would not be the choice of God for the person, but rather the person's own choice. During our lives we are shaping—by what we do or leave undone, good or evil—the sort of eternity which we wish to have. St. Peter in today's first reading reminds us that we are awaiting *"a new heaven and a new earth."* (Ibid., v. 13). The truth is, although we cannot see it, that every good action of ours is constructing those new heavens and a new earth. Jesus Christ is working in and through us to bring about His Kingdom which, when completed, will be a *"new heaven and a new earth."* (Ibid.).

There is a story told of a man who in this world had been used to every luxury. He died and he arrived in heaven. An angel was sent to conduct him to his home. They passed many beautiful houses, and the man thought that each one, as he came to it, must be the one allotted to him. When they had passed through the main streets of heaven, they came to the suburbs and a part of the city where the houses were much smaller. At last they came to a house which was little more than a hut. *"That is your house,"* said the angel. *"But I cannot live in that,"* said the man. *"I am sorry,"* said the angel, *"but that is all we could build for you with the material you sent up."* Heaven and hell are consequences of what we choose for ourselves during our lives, and God respects those choices. Jesus Himself has said: *"The hour is coming when all who are in the tombs will hear His voice and come forth; those who have done good things into a resurrection of life, and those who have done evil to the resurrection of judgment."* (Jn 5:28-29).

Perhaps you feel that what I am saying is very depressing. If so, we should reflect on what Jesus said the night before He died: *"I am the way, the truth and the life."* (Jn 14:6). Through the Church and through the Sacraments, Jesus is trying to coax us and persuade us to accept that life which He is offering to us, and not the condition of everlasting dying which is hell.

When we pray the first Eucharistic Prayer and when we have almost reached the consecration, the Church places on our lips the prayer: *"Save us from final damnation and count us among those whom You have chosen."* Yes, may God save us all from final damnation. May we be found worthy to take our place at the banquet table in heaven, a foretaste of which we have when we eat the bread of life in the Eucharist, that bread of life which He promised one day when He spoke outside the synagogue in Capernaum. *"This is the bread which came down from heaven . . . . He who eats this bread will live forever. This He said in the synagogue as He taught at Capernaum."* (Jn 6:58-59).

May Mary, the Mother of God and our Mother, St. Vincent, St. Louise and all the saints keep whispering directions into our ears, so that we will at the end of our lives be able to enter into the *"new heavens and the new earth"* and take our places at that table which God in His love has prepared for those who love Him.

Fatima

23 June 1990   Machel, Mozambique

My dear Confreres and my dear Sisters,

Today is the feast of the Immaculate Heart of Mary. When I think of the Immaculate Heart of Mary, I immediately think of Fatima, and that calls up Portugal, a country which over the centuries has sent priests and brothers, sisters and laity, to the ends of the earth, proclaiming Jesus Christ and sharing with millions the riches of our Christian faith. Let me, in the name of St. Vincent and of his Communities, pay tribute to those Confreres and Sisters who fifty years ago came to this great land to preach the good news of Christ after the mind and heart of our two Founders, St. Vincent and St. Louise. It is a joy for me to be with you for this festive celebration. May our prayers today bring down a new outpouring of grace on each member of the Vincentian family, and bring, too, the gift of a new justice and a new peace to this country, so long tried by violence and war.

Let me bring you back to Fatima. It is a remarkable coincidence that when Our Lady appeared to the three children in Fatima on the 13 May 1917, a young priest was being ordained bishop in the Sistine Chapel in Rome, the Chapel in which the Cardinals elect the Pope. That young bishop was to become Pope twenty-two years later and was to be known as Pope Pius XII. It was he, three years after he had become Pope, who was to fulfil the wish Our Lady had expressed to the three children at Fatima, namely, that the world be consecrated to her Immaculate Heart. When Our Lady appeared at Fatima in 1917, a world war was raging. When Pope Pius XII first consecrated the world to Our Lady, a second World War was causing immense suffering to people of many nations. Ten years later in 1952, this same Pope again consecrated the world to Mary's Immaculate Heart.

On the 13 May, too, nine years ago in St. Peter's Square in Rome about 5 p.m., an attempt was made to assassinate Pope John Paul II. It was a miracle that his life was saved and on the feast of Our Lady of Fatima the following year, he himself made a pilgrimage to Fatima, in Portugal, to thank God and Our Lady for having preserved his life from the bullet of the man who tried to kill him. During his prayer of thanksgiving, the Pope consecrated the world to Our Lady's Immaculate Heart.

On the 25 March in 1984, when the Church celebrated the feast of the Annunciation, Pope John Paul II consecrated the world again to the Immaculate Heart of Mary, and he asked all the Bishops of the Church (in their different Cathedrals), to join him in praying the act of consecration of the world to Our Lady, which he had used a year earlier at Fatima. The Pope, like so many others today, can see the threat, not just of a war, but of the destruction of life on this planet. It is a threat that hangs over *"the poor banished children of Eve."* Yes, *"the poor banished children of Eve."* That is a phrase from that beautiful prayer, the "Salve Regina." In that prayer we appeal to Our Lady to *"Turn then, O most gracious advocate, thine eyes of mercy towards us."* The Popes in our times have been asking Our Lady to turn her eyes towards us who are poor and are wounded by sin. We must not be content with asking Our Lady to turn her *"eyes of mercy towards us."* We must turn our eyes towards her. Above all, we must turn our hearts towards her, so that they may become hearts that are tender, gentle and humble, as was hers and that of her Son, Jesus.

The Popes have consecrated the world to the Immaculate Heart of Our Lady, because that has been Mary's wish, and because in doing so they were promoting and securing peace in *"this valley of tears."* Each one of us can do something to bring a little more peace into this world. It is not only governments that have the responsibility of promoting justice and peace in the world. We are being invited all the time to be instruments of God's peace by our words, or our silence, or our acts. *"Lord, make me an instrument of Your peace,"* prayed St. Francis of Assisi. *"Where there is hatred, let me sow love; where there is sorrow, joy."*

Be peacemakers, not troublemakers, among those whose lives you touch. Be an instrument of peace and reconciliation and you will be a true child of Mary. Be a peacemaker and you will be consecrating the world to the Immaculate Heart of Mary. Be a peacemaker, work for justice, show love, and you will be, like Mary, an agent of life, of sweetness and of hope. You can be certain that, if we are instruments of peace during our humble lives, she will *"after this, our exile, show us the blessed fruit of her womb, Jesus."*

Youth: Each One a Missionary

23 July 1990   Benagalbon, Spain

My dear Young People,

The character of Jonah would hardly figure among the ten most interesting characters of the Old Testament. It could be said that he probably never existed. The story of Jonah is just a story, but a story with a point to it. Jonah received a missionary vocation from God and he tried to avoid it. Instead of going to the country for which he received a vocation, he tried to go somewhere else. What happened? He was shipwrecked. Then, the story goes, he was swallowed by a whale and after three days, thrown up on a seashore, alive. Jonah got the message and straightaway set out for the city of Nineveh, the city to which God from the very beginning had intended him to go as a missionary.

It would seem that Jonah at first did not want to be a missionary, and the reason seems strange to us. He did not want a pagan people to share in the privilege of the Israelite faith. He was like a Christian who says, *"charity begins at home"* and then lets it end there. Jonah was a little like the elder son in Our Lord's parable of the Prodigal Son, and we know that the love of the elder son in that parable was narrow and selfish.

To be a missionary one must have a strong love in one's heart for Jesus Christ and His Church. It was his personal love for Jesus Christ and His Church that pushed St. Paul to go from country to country— sometimes at great personal risk—to proclaim that Christ had come, that Christ had died, that Christ had risen, and that Christ would come again. Today, as always, it will be true that, unless the love of Christ overwhelms the heart of the contemporary Christian, missions will remain an *optional extra* for those who like that sort of thing.

I once heard a man say that the first question each of us will be asked by Jesus Christ after our deaths will be: *"And where are the others?"* We don't go to heaven alone. Every Christian is a missionary: some in mission lands, others in the wide circle of national life, others in the narrower circle of parish life and others again in the inner circle of family life. Every Christian is a Public Relations Officer for Jesus Christ. It is hard to realize this in a country where almost everyone at least bears the name Christian. Jesus Christ does continue to count on each of us Christians setting out every day from that little independent island that is one's self, and touching down on the shores of other peoples' lives with His gifts of understanding, compassion and support, and with the gift of faith in Jesus Christ and His Church.

One half of the world does not know how the other half lives. Whoever first made that statement was exaggerating. We scarcely know how the family in the next block lives, much less half the world. Yet it is one definition of a Christian that he is one who is interested, not in how half the world lives, but in how the whole world lives. *"Go, make disciples of all nations."* (Mt 28:19). That was the final message given by Jesus Christ to His friends before He ascended into heaven. If He asked us to do it, then it must be possible.

The Marian Vincentian Youth has taken that final message of Jesus Christ seriously. Tonight I salute those of your members, thirty-four of them, who set out this summer for Honduras and Santo Domingo. I greet, too, those young people who have already spent three years working in Honduras and who now have asked to remain a further two years.

Let us who remain here at home, however, never forget that every Christian at every moment is called to be a missionary. Make no mistake about it. You are proclaiming a message at every moment of the day, even when you are not speaking. Your message must be authentic. It will be so, if you are authentic. Your authenticity as a Christian comes from your personal relationship with Jesus Christ, truly God and truly man, and with His Mother Mary. Often ask yourself: *"Could Jesus Christ and His Mother Mary share what I am going to say or what I am going to do?"* If you can reply *yes*, then you are authentic. You are transmitting a message that will have an effect, not only on those who hear and see you, but you will also be building up the Body of Christ, which is the Church.

All that I have been saying to you, my dear young people, can be marvelously summed up in the final phrase of the first reading of today's Mass: *"God has shown you, O man, what is good; and what does the Lord require of you but to do justice and to love kindness and to walk humbly with your God."* (Mi 6:8).

Yes, do justice, love kindness and walk humbly with your God. Do that and you will be a missionary; you will be a disciple of St. Vincent de Paul; you will be a true devotee of Mary Immaculate, and you will live in Jesus Christ Who is the life of our life.

Holiness

4 August 1990   Confort, France

My dear Sisters,

I do not wish to leave you without expressing in the context of the Eucharist my thanks to you for the hospitality and kindness you have shown me during the past few days. More than once I said to myself during these days: the spirit of Sister Rosalie Rendu lives in this house. I give thanks to God for that and pray that His protection will surround you as the mountains surround your house.

In the course of our lives in the Community we make many retreats and, as time goes on, it is inevitable that we forget much that was said to us by those who preached to us during our annual retreats. That does not matter a great deal. What matters is that our retreats would change us and make us a little more like Jesus Christ in our thoughts, in our words and in our actions. Little phrases from various retreats we have made in our lives will lodge in our minds and remain there. I recall making one of my first Community retreats almost forty years ago and a saintly Confrere, perhaps a little dramatic in the way he put things, said: *"Be a saint and the world will wear a path to your door."*

This sentence always comes to my mind when we are celebrating the feast of St. John Mary Vianney or, as perhaps he is better known, the Curé of Ars. Before the end of his life, the world had begun to wear a path to the door of his rectory. The attraction, which this simple parish priest had, was nothing other than great personal holiness.

The Curé of Ars has a great deal in common with St. Vincent. They both came from peasant families. They both were experienced parish priests and they are now both saints. St. John Mary Vianney is patron of all pastors and St. Vincent is patron of all works of charity.

The lives of both these priests and saints were marked by much mortification. The life of the Curé of Ars was marked by an extraordinary degree of self-denial and austerity. The grace to carry out the penances which he did is an extraordinary one and not given to everybody. While St. Vincent would probably protest if we said he assumed the sort of penances as the Curé of Ars, it is certainly true that in his writings and conferences, he places much stress on the need for mortification in our lives. He stressed the importance of mortification of our wills, judgments, and senses with as much emphasis as he urged us to serve the poor.

If we are to grow in the love of God and our neighbor, mortification must be a reality in our lives. It is not a question of imposing mortification on ourselves for its own sake. Being mortified means saying *no* to ourselves. We say *no* to ourselves so that we may say *yes* to God and His Will. For St. John Vianney, and for all the saints, it is doing the Will of God which lies at the heart of all holiness. Doing the Will of God means saying *yes* to Him. However, the reality of original sin in this world and my own personal sins have biased me towards putting my own will in the first place and God's in the second. For that reason, I must constantly cut back those little shoots of selfishness which prevent the tree of my life from bearing fruit. What particular acts of mortification should be in the lives of each of us will vary from person to person. This, however, is certain, that according to St. Vincent's teaching, my judgment, my will, my heart and my senses must feel the touch of the pruning knife, so that, to quote St. Paul, *"the life of Jesus may be manifested in our bodies."* (2 Cor 4:10).

Jesus Christ described Himself as *"the light of the world."* That light shines through the lives of His friends, in the way that the sun shines through the stained glass windows of a church. Hundreds of colors will make up one stained glass window and each will admit a special quality of the sun's light. So it is with the holiness of the saints. Each of them lets in a special quality of Him Who is the light of the world. The holiness of St. Vincent de Paul is different from the holiness of St. John Mary Vianney, but it is the light of Jesus Christ that penetrated brilliantly through both of them. That same light penetrates through us and illuminates Christ's Church in our time. Perhaps the difference between the great saints, like St. Vincent and the Curé of Ars, and myself is that I have allowed the dust and grime of sin and selfishness to settle on my window so that the light of Christ cannot reach into my Community as it should, or touch the poor as it might.

Let me not end, however, on a negative note. I make my own the sentiments of St. Vincent: *"God be blessed, my dear Sisters. I beseech the Divine Goodness to grant you all the grace to love holy obedience, to practice it in imitation of His Son towards your Superiors, your Rules and Holy Providence, and to this end to bestow on you the blessing of the Father, Son and Holy Ghost."* (Conf. Eng. ed., June 1642, p. 69). To that prayer of St. Vincent I have no doubt that the Curé of Ars would utter a full hearted Amen.

A Tiny Speck of Blue

15 August 1990   Paris, France

Mother Duzan, Father Lloret and my dear Sisters,

At the beginning of June it was announced that a satellite, which had been launched thirteen years ago, had now reached the extremity of the solar system and, before leaving it and travelling out into interstellar space at the speed of almost two million kilometers a day, it had sent back some photographs of enthralling beauty. The photographs showed the whole solar system with the sun and its surrounding planets. Our planet, the earth, could be seen just as a tiny speck of blue and white against an immense background of black darkness.

It is only yesterday—for what is four hundred years in the history of the universe?—since those who lived on this planet of ours believed that the sun and the stars revolved around the earth. We humans thought that our planet was at the center of God's universe. Then slowly the truth dawned on humanity that it was not so, and now we not only know, but we can see, that our planet, with ourselves on it, is but a tiny speck of blue in the immensity of the universe.

The explosion of science, however, has not changed the fact that, for all our smallness, we are at the center of God's personal love. Today as yesterday and tomorrow, it will remain true that *"God so loved the world that He gave His only Son, so that whoever believes in Him should not perish, but have eternal life."* (Jn 3:16).

To one looking at this earth of ours from beyond the solar system, a person could be forgiven for thinking that the earth was no more than a tiny speck of blue. Such a person could not even guess that this tiny speck of blue holds myriad forms of life, nor could an interstellar traveler glean a hint of the rich variety of human civilizations that our globe contains. What could such a traveler know of any one human mind which, we are told, holds within it a million times more pieces of information than there are stars in the universe? What must we say of the nobility and sanctity of so many of God's people on this earth?

No one from the vastness of space could hear the cries of the millions of poor people who live on this earth, nor the groans of the oppressed, nor the pain of the sick, nor the despair of the depressed. Nor from interstellar space could one guess that God Himself had for a few passing years taken on in person a human form and walked on the surface of this tiny speck of blue.

That dark world of suffering is shot through with the light of charity. Think of the sum of human suffering which at this very moment is being lightened by the love, the care, the tenderness, the self-sacrifice of the thirty thousand Sisters of your Community. The charity that shines out in your Company could be magnified billions of times and yet fall short of reflecting in its totality that mysterious reality which we call Christian charity. Before this mystery of human suffering, alleviated by Christian charity, *"the Church,"* to quote Pope John Paul II, *"bows down in reverence with all the depths of her faith in the Redemption."* (Apostolic Letter, *Salvifici Doloris*, §24). All this spiritual beauty, inspired and sustained by the Spirit of God, is enclosed within this tiny speck of blue.

We know with the certainty that comes from faith, that God has not yet finished His work on this tiny speck of blue. The Kingdom of God in its fullness has not yet been realized. *"We wait,"* writes St. Peter, *"for new heavens and a new earth."* (2 Pt 13). We know also—again with the certainty of faith—that the Divine Artist has already put the final touches to that masterpiece of His creation whom we recognize as Mary of Nazareth, His Immaculate Mother and now ours. Alone among the children of men, Mary of Nazareth can claim to have celebrated the mystery of Easter in its fullness and perfection. It is the uniqueness of that event which led Carl Jung, the celebrated psycho-analyst and not a Catholic, to say that the definition of the Assumption of Our Lady into heaven in 1950 was the most important religious event since the Reformation.

With the God whose hands have shaped this marvelous universe, we rejoice that in one, simple, loving and humble woman—so often imaged to us in colors of white and blue—we can see a tiny speck of the new heavens and the new earth. She is not distant from us, as are the stars. How could she be? Is not her vocation in heaven to be mother to each of the children of God? No mother worthy of that name is distant from her children.

The feast of Mary's Assumption into heaven projects us to the future and lifts our hearts in hope. In the short-term future there is for us the General Assembly of 1991. A General Assembly is a point in the history of the Community when, through the brooding of the Holy Spirit over the Community, a new vision of faith, of hope and of love is given to our Sisters.

Already you are praying in Community that the light and the fire of the Holy Spirit will descend anew upon the participants of the General Assembly. As you await a new Pentecost, reflect often on those words in the first chapter of the Acts of the Apostles, which describe the spiritual preparation of the disciples for the first Pentecost: *"All these with one accord devoted themselves to prayer."* (Acts I:14). The little words, *with one accord,* merit special attention. Let your prayer issue from a heart that can answer *yes* to St. Vincent's questions in his letter to Sister Nicole Haran: *"Are you in peace with those within and those outside the Community and, above all, are you truly united together? Do you really love each other? Do you show forbearance with each other?"* (Coste VI, Fr. ed., p. 95).

Let these months of preparation for the General Assembly be distinguished by a high and refined quality of mutual charity in each local community of the Company. It is through such charity that the Spirit of God will draw closer to us and will brood over us *"with warm breast and ah! with bright wings."* (G.M. Hopkins, *God's Grandeur*).

To you, Mother Duzan, on this, your feast day, I offer you in the name of the whole Company our greetings and our gratitude, along with the assurance of our daily remembrance of you in our prayers. For all of us you hold much significance. Dare I say it? A tiny speck of blue!

Humility

3 November 1990   Rome, Italy

My dear Sisters,

The final sentence in today's Gospel is magnificently illustrated by the life of the Saint whom the Church is honoring today. *"He who humbles himself shall be exalted."* (Lk 14:11).

In our own day St. Martin de Porres has undoubtedly been exalted. I am sure you have been struck by the number of statues of him one finds in different churches of the world. His exaltation has taken place in our day. It is only twenty-eight years ago that he was canonized and given a feast day, a memorial, in the universal calendar of the Church. Over the past thirty years people have made novenas to this humble lay Brother of the Dominican Order, who was born two years before St. Vincent and who died some twenty years before him. He resembles St. Vincent in his great love for the poor and also in the practical measures he took to relieve the sufferings of the poor of Lima. Like St. Vincent, he was a man of action. Unlike St. Vincent, he wrote little or nothing. If he were to have written a spiritual testament, there is little doubt but that he would have emphasized the importance of those two characteristically Vincentian virtues, humility and charity.

St. Martin de Porres is what we call a popular saint. It is difficult for us to explain why some saints are popular saints, who find that great numbers of people pray to them for a vast variety of favors. We can be certain, that it does not worry the saints in heaven whether one is more popular than another. They would very much share the sentiments of St. Paul in the opening sentence of the first reading of today's Mass. What matters is that Christ be preached, what matters is that people turn to the saints so that they may find their way more easily to their Father in Heaven.

The humble shall be exalted. By all accounts St. Martin de Porres was illegitimate and was a deeply humble person. Because he was so humble, people perhaps feel at ease in his company and, feeling at ease in his company, they speak to him about what is closest to their hearts and ask him to pray for them.

St. Martin de Porres exemplifies well what St. Vincent asks a Daughter of Charity to be—a humble loving servant of the poor. We know that St. Vincent gave much importance to humility in all that we do for the poor. He did so because that was his conviction and the fruit of his own meditation on the manner of life lived by the Son of God when He came on earth. St. Vincent must also have been convinced that it was all-important that the poor would feel at ease in the presence of a Daughter of Charity. What a Daughter of Charity does for the poor must come, not only from a loving heart but from a humble heart. In a very striking sentence at the end of a conference to his missionaries, St. Vincent shares with them his own conviction that, however charitable a man may be, if he is not humble, he does not have real charity. (cf. Coste XII, Fr. ed., p. 210).

As Sister Servants, would you agree with me that to be in authority today can create difficulty in the exercise of humility? Community meetings are a feature of our Community life today and I have known some Superiors within and outside our Vincentian family who have told me that these community meeting often cause them special anxieties.

You, as Sister Servants, are conscious of your role of being servants, of being open to listening to what each Sister may have to share. That openness on your part calls for humility. True humility is a strong virtue, as both Our Lord and His Mother Mary have shown us in their lives. You may often be called upon to point out to a Sister during a community meeting that her opinion, however strongly held, is not in accordance with the Constitutions and traditions of the Company. To do this with humility, with love and with firmness may not be easy. Nowadays, more than in the past, you may be told by the Sister that it is you who are wrong. Then you feel hurt. The hurt may prompt you to force your opinion strongly, or perhaps to do nothing. It is humility which will enable you to proceed along the road quietly, presenting the ideal, while being sensitive to the feelings and views of the Sister.

May the Lord continue to strengthen you in your work so that you can persevere, to paraphrase St. Paul in the first reading, for the joy and progress in the faith of all the Sisters of this Province.

Foolish Virgins

11 November 1990   Arezzo, Italy

My dear Sisters,

Many years ago I recall a very saintly Confrere saying on his deathbed that he was not so much preoccupied by the evil he had done during his life, but by the good he failed to do. That was many years before the Church changed the wording of the Confiteor in our Mass. When the liturgical changes were made fourteen or fifteen years ago, there was a little phrase inserted into the Confiteor in which we ask God's pardon, not only for our sins of thought, word and deed but also for our sins of omission. When we find ourselves at the end of a day saying: *"Well, I cannot recall any wrong I have done to anybody in the Community today,"* it is well to spend a little more time asking ourselves, *"What more good could I have done today?"* Perhaps we have not hurt anyone's feelings, but have we given them much encouragement in their work; have we positively promoted unity in the Community; have we offered a word of praise to anyone during the day; how much time have we spent reflecting on the hidden needs of those with whom we live in Community? Yes, we have need of God's pardon for failing to do the good we could do.

I have been reflecting on our sins of omission because the failure of the five foolish virgins was caused by sins of omission. The failure was not that they fell asleep, not that they failed to awaken at midnight, not that they were unwilling to accompany the bridegroom. No, their failure lay in this: that they had not provided sufficient oil for their lamps, that they had not sufficient foresight in the living of their lives.

The foolish virgins should have thought and planned a little for the future. Perhaps you might say that Our Lord has advised us to think only of today and its needs. *"Do not be anxious about tomorrow, for tomorrow will be anxious for itself."* (Mt 6:34). However, to worry is one thing, and to plan is another. Foresight is one thing; anxiety is another. Our Lord encourages us to reduce anxiety in our lives. He does not discourage us from prudently planning for the future. Towards the end of St. Vincent's life he appointed a very young man Superior. He was only twenty-six years of age. This priest, Father Durand, had the good sense not only to ask St. Vincent for some advice on how he should behave as a Superior, but also to commit St. Vincent's words to writing. As you would expect, the advice St. Vincent gave him was both spiritual and practical. After St. Vincent had treated of the importance of prayer and humility, he reminded the young Superior that he had to attend to the temporal needs of his community. Let me quote a sentence or two: *"If in the Gospel the Son of God directed us not to take thought for the morrow, this should be understood as deprecating too much anxiety and worry about worldly goods. It certainly does not mean neglecting the means of livelihood . . . . Give yourself, then, to God, for the purpose of ensuring the temporal welfare of the house to which you are going."* (Coste XI, Fr. ed., p. 350-351).

Prudent planning for the future is part of our Community life. In recent years the Provincial Project and the Project of the local community have assumed importance in the Company. The Community Project is, your Constitutions state, a means of vitality in its service of Christ (cf. C. 3.46). If the Community is to advance securely into the future, it needs a plan. It needs to exercise foresight. The Community must be numbered among the wise virgins of the parable. If we are to have a good Community Project, it is necessary that each Sister try to contribute in simplicity to the making of it and to contribute to its implementation by a humble acceptance of it.

May you, my dear Sisters, live your lives sharing the conviction of St. Vincent, expressed in one of his letters, that *"the works of God have their opportune moment."* His Providence arranges that they take place then and not sooner or later. Through the intercession of Mary, the

Mother of God, the Virgin most prudent, may you work faithfully and wait patiently in joyful hope for the coming of the bridegroom, Jesus Christ.

The Problem of Hunger

17 November 1990   Rome, Italy

One could say that satisfying hunger in its many forms is the principal role of every Religious Community in the Church. The word *hunger* evokes in our minds the distress and pain, which those experience whose bodies are starved, deprived or undernourished because there is no food to hand.

There are, however, other forms of human hunger to whose alleviation Religious Communities all over the world dedicate themselves. There is the hunger for God, the hunger for Christ, the hunger for truth, the hunger for justice, the hunger for acceptance. With each of these forms of human hunger Religious Communities are concerned. Enriched by a wide variety of charisms by the Holy Spirit, Religious Communities pledge themselves to alleviate all forms of human hunger after the manner of Christ Himself, Who manifested practical compassion for the hunger that gnaws at the human heart, the human mind and the human body.

For our present purposes we focus on the pain and problem of the millions who see the sun rise and set without having swallowed a mouthful of sustaining food. Let me quote from a work of Arthur Simon: *"Imagine ten children at a table dividing up food. The three healthiest load their plates with large portions, including most of the meat, fish, milk and eggs. They eat what they want and discard the leftovers. Two other children get just enough to meet their basic requirements. The remaining five are left wanting. Three of them—sickly, nervous, apathetic children—manage to stave off the feeling of hunger by filling up on bread and rice. The other two cannot do even that. One dies from dysentery and the second from pneumonia, which they are too weak to ward off. These children represent the human family . . . ."* (Arthur Simon, *Bread for the World*, New York, Paulist Press, 1975, p. 14).

Religious Communities must be considered as sitting among the three healthiest children, for Religious Communities have in the main adequate nourishment to sustain them in their work. It is right that it should be so. The role of Religious Communities is not to place themselves in such a condition that they would become *"sickly, nervous and apathetic children of God."* Rather their role is to alert their companions, who are close to them, about the condition of those further down the table who have little or nothing to eat: those who are sitting below the salt. Their role is not only to alert others about the phenomenon of an unequal distribution of wealth and food in the world, but to rise from the table and to the best of their ability provide for and serve those whose hunger is only too obvious from the lines which the pangs of hunger have traced in their faces.

To the problem of hunger in the world there is a theological and scriptural dimension. Any solution to the problem of hunger which would ignore this dimension will inevitably be short-term and inadequate. Men and women live, not only by bread but also by the word of God. (cf. Mt 4:4). Religious Communities are well-placed to present and explain this particular dimension to the problem of alleviating hunger. In the history of the Church Religious Orders and Congregations have shown themselves to be particularly aware of the centrality for Christian lives of Chapter 25 of St. Matthew's Gospel: *"I was hungry and you gave me food."* (Mt 25:35).

At the level of social communications Religious Communities are strategically placed to sensitize people to the problem of hunger. Many Orders and Congregations have an international and missionary character, so that the problem of hunger that exists in a third world country, is often graphically brought home to a first-world country by returning missionaries. Through personal contacts and through appeals for funds in religious bulletins, a process of awakening people's consciences to the claims of justice and charity is continually taking place. Among Christians, who has not listened to and been moved by some returned missionary, as he or she spoke of vast areas of other continents where the breaking of the word of God goes hand in hand literally with the breaking of bread to fill empty stomachs? Every Religious Community has as an ideal, that which was proposed by Vatican II in its decree, *Ad*

Gentes, namely, it tries to *"expand the range of its charity to the ends of the earth and to have the same concerns for those who are far away as for its members."* (§37).

The role of the Religious Community in sensitizing the world to the problem of hunger could be said to be carried out on two levels; first, at the level of information and education. Information: Religious Communities have through their members first-hand information about the reality of hunger in the world. It is information which can be and frequently is shared. Education: Religious Communities are, particularly through their apostolates of education, well-placed to open the minds of people to the seminal ideas contained in Paul VI's document, *Populorum Progressio,* and in the numerous appeals which Pope John Paul II has made on behalf of the hungry millions who are forced today to exist rather than to live.

Second, at the level of deep commitment to their specific vocation as religious in God's Church. By living their vocation with authenticity and a certain radicality, Religious Communities can open the minds and the hearts of people to the unselfish compassion of Jesus Christ, Who showed such concern that people should be hungry, and Who taught His disciples to ask the universal Father of the human family to give us all (for no exceptions were made) our daily bread.

Forgiveness

20 November 1990 Rome, Italy

My dear Brothers and Sisters in Jesus Christ,

When I was a seminarian in the National Seminary in Ireland, there was a stern old man in charge of the young boys who worked in the kitchen of the College. Every night he would gather the young members of the staff around him in order to pray the Rosary. At the end of the Rosary he used to add various petitions, one of which was: *"Now, let us pray for our enemies, if we have any."* This was rather amusing to the young boys who thought that the old man considered each of them to be his personal enemy, at least to judge from the remarks he would make in the course of the day's work. The old man for his part thought that all his remarks were made with the best of intentions, namely, to make sure that the work of the kitchen was properly done. The old man had no difficulty about praying for his enemies because he did not think he had any. Others did not see it that way. They felt that he needed a lot of forgiveness from them.

Most of us think that we have more forgiveness to give than to receive. We like to think that more people are unfair or unjust to us than we are to them. Because we think in that way, we find it hard to offer forgiveness, real forgiveness, to others. We think much more of how hard it is for us to forgive than we do about the difficulty that others may have in forgiving us. We measure out our forgiveness like money, very carefully and with much calculation. I doubt if we use the same care when we come to measuring the cost of that forgiveness which we expect and receive from others. If we spent more time thinking about what it cost others to forgive us, rather than about what it costs us to forgive others, we would be more successful in taking resentment out of our hearts.

I have been reflecting on our personal experience of offering and receiving forgiveness. What about forgiveness as experienced by a group, a society, a nation? We have witnessed in recent years some apologies being offered by one nation to another for wounds inflicted in the course of a war, though many decades have passed. The world would be a happier place if such collective apologies were made more often. But, as with individuals, forgiveness is measured out meagerly and with much calculation.

For us, members of COR UNUM, who think much about the poverty and hunger in Third World countries, and of what we could do to alleviate it, how much thought have we given to forgiveness? Not that the Third World has hurt us, but perhaps the peoples of the Third World think, at least some of them, that it is we who have need of much forgiveness from them. Leaving aside the facts of history and the injustices that colonial powers may have done in the past, it is probably true that the very fact of the present unequal distribution of wealth among the nations, causes resentment in the hearts of many in Third World countries. Where there is resentment, there is need for offering forgiveness. So we in the First World may be in more need than we realize of receiving forgiveness. St. Vincent de Paul is reputed to have said to the first Daughters of Charity that it would only be through the evident love in their hearts that the poor would be able to forgive them for the bread which they, the Sisters, were offering to them. Today, as in St. Vincent de Paul's day, people do not live by bread alone. The bread we offer must be seasoned well with the condiments of justice and of love.

May the Lord through the intercession of His Virgin Mother Mary give us the grace of seeing more clearly the need we have of offering and receiving daily forgiveness. May He strengthen the love in our hearts, so that we may be more generous in offering and more gracious in receiving forgiveness. May He enlighten our minds to accept the truth that a loving and forgiving heart is the womb of justice and of peace.

Feast of Christ the King

25 November 1990   Santurce, Puerto Rico

My dear People,

First, let me say how happy I am to be celebrating Mass with you this morning. Every Sunday of the year is like a little Easter day, for on Sundays we rejoice in a special way as we reflect on the great truth that not only did Jesus Christ, truly God and truly man, die, but on the third day after His death He rose again. In rising from the dead Jesus Christ has given us all hope and a reason to be joyful, for we know that it is His wish and desire that we share with Him the joy of surmounting the unpleasant experience of death.

The Resurrection of Jesus Christ was a triumph. Today's feast also suggests triumph, for we are celebrating the feast of Jesus Christ, Universal King. Jesus Christ is King, but He is a very special sort of King. When Jesus Christ was born, He did not look like a King and He looked even less like one when He died. Kings are not born in stables and they do not die writhing in pain on a cross at the outskirts of a city. There were some hints, when He was born, that He was a King. Wise men came from far away, looking for Him Whom they said was born *"King of the Jews."* So, too, when He was dying, there was written over

His head the words, *"Jesus of Nazareth, King of the Jews."* (Jn 19:19). These were only hints and the last one was not intended to be really serious. But we know that Jesus Christ was and is a King.

Today in the world we do not have as many kings as we had at one time. Sometimes governments will give prizes or awards or decorations to people who during a year have distinguished themselves by a work for peace or their devotion to others or outstanding services they have rendered to the State. For a while people will talk about these people, but then they are forgotten. That is not so with Jesus Christ, Who is the Universal King. Since He rose from the dead, there has never been a day in the history of humanity when His name and His memory were not on people's minds, on their lips and in their hearts. So it will be until the end of time. Today we are reminding ourselves that it was *"through Him all things were made and without Him was made nothing that was made."* (Jn 1:3). We are reminding ourselves that in Jesus Christ made man, we find all that we admire, all that we love, all that attracts us in the individual people whom we meet and love. It is because, not only all things were made through Him, but because all things were made for Him, that we salute Him as Christ, the Universal King. We salute Him as King, too, because He has bought us with the price of His Blood. (cf. 1 Pt 1:19).

We are citizens of His kingdom because He had made us so through Baptism. He makes us guests at His royal table every time He feeds us with His own Body and Blood in Holy Communion. He gives us a royal pardon every time we approach Him in the Sacrament of Penance, after we have said and done things that are unworthy of one who is a citizen of His kingdom. He has honored us by asking us for our cooperation in establishing in this world *"a kingdom of justice, of love and of peace."* (Preface). He has also invited us to share with Him finally the dominion which He has over all things.

Kings today are surrounded with security. They have around-the-clock bodyguards. Jesus Christ does not need that sort of security, for He has risen and death cannot touch Him any more. What He does ask of us, citizens of His kingdom, is not so much to guard His Person, but to guard what He said and what He did. He wants us to keep that secure for Him until He comes again in glory. That is what loyalty to Jesus

Christ, Universal King, means. It is very easy for us to sing hymns in honor of Christ, our King. When He was on earth, people did so, too, but one day He quoted from the Old Testament the words: *"This people honors Me with their lips, but their hearts are far from Me."* (Mt 15:8). Perhaps there are times when He feels just like that about us. This man, this woman, honors Me with their lips, but their hearts are far from Me.

Devotion to Christ the King means loving those people whom, when He was a king on earth, He liked to have close about Him—the poor. Devotion to Christ the King means loving and being servants of the poor in the way and in the spirit with which He served them when He was on earth. Devotion to Christ the King means opposing and rejecting violence in all its forms. Devotion to Christ the King means working for peace and reconciliation in our society, for His kingdom is one of love and justice and peace.

My dear Sisters, on this feast of Christ, the Universal King, I pray that He will bless all of you with His gifts of peace and of love. I pray, too, that Mary, His Mother, whom we will be honoring under her title of Our Lady of the Miraculous Medal, will protect you and your families now and at the hour of your death.

Advent Letter—Church on the Mountain and in the Market Place

1 December 1990   To Each Confrere

My dear Confrere,

May the grace of Our Lord Jesus Christ be with us forever!

A little over a month has passed since the conclusion of the Synod in which I was privileged to participate. Throughout the days of listening and discussing I often reflected on the joy the event must have given to the heart of St. Vincent. For three decades of his life he spent himself not only planning and discussing the topic of the formation of priests, but man of action that he was, organizing means and structures to secure that priests be well formed for the task of leading God's people. How St. Vincent would have rejoiced if the Pope of his day had called together a representation of the Bishops of the world and invited them to reflect on the topic of the formation of priests. How he would have rejoiced even more if the Pope of his day had assisted at the general sessions of such a meeting, as did Pope John Paul II at the recent Synod.

The theme of this Synod was linked to that of the preceding one in 1987 on the Christian Laity. Indeed it seems that the strength of the voice of the laity, as expressed at that Synod, influenced greatly the choice of the topic for the 1990 Synod. That in itself is an indication of how central to the life of the Church is the ministerial priesthood. It is the priest who stands at the heart of the renewal of the Church in our day and indeed always, a truth that St. Vincent saw so clearly. Lay people will never come to achieve the full potential of their vocation as laity, if priests are not living to the full their vocation. Within the context of our own Community, we can say that it will be difficult for our Brothers to enter fully into the mission of the Community, if we priests are not aware of the dignity of the priesthood, and express that dignity in a life that is distinguished by its humility, its prayerfulness and its loving concern for the poor, oppressed and suffering members of Christ's body. Just as in the Church the vocations of priest and lay person are complementary, so, too, within the Congregation. When as priests or Brothers, we accept, value and appreciate each other's particular vocation within the Community, the life of the Congregation is greatly strengthened and its mission in the Church made more effective.

One day during the Synod, when our language group was discussing a rather lengthy summary of what had been said during the previous ten days in the presence of all the Synodal Fathers, one of the Bishops expressed surprise that no mention had been made of eternal life in the particular position paper. It was an oversight on the part of those who drafted the document. But did it not reflect a way of thinking that makes us sometimes focus our attention on horizons that are too limited?

The Church lives at once on the mountain and in the market place. One could say that during the past three decades particularly she has lived in the market place, where she has been pained by the sight of an increasing number of poor people who are also being made to suffer many injustices. In her loving concern the Church has not only raised her voice in protest, but has encouraged us to translate that concern into concrete actions. (cf. *Sollicitudo Rei Socialis*, §43).

The Church also lives on the mountain from which she can see, though in a dark manner, the vast vistas of eternal life that stretch beyond the frontiers of time. Indeed the eternal life the Church proclaims and to which she calls humanity is more than the perfection of life as we know it on this earth. The life she proclaims and to which she invites humanity to share is the eternal life of God. *"The eternal life which was with the Father and was made manifest to us,"* (1 Jn 1:2) found its fullest and most adequate expression in Jesus Christ, Who was born of the Virgin Mary.

The mystery of Christmas is the celebration of the call of humanity to share that eternal life of God. As we are reminded each day at Mass, the invitation is *"to share in the divinity of Christ, Who humbled himself to share in our humanity."*

Both from the mountain and from the market place the Church proclaims the good news that all are called to share in the life of God. As Pope Paul VI expressed it: *"Evangelization, then, will include a prophetic proclamation of that other life which is man's sublime and eternal vocation. This vocation is at once connected with and distinct from his present state; it is the vocation of a life to come which transcends time and history and all the transient circumstances of this world of which the hidden significance will one day be revealed . . . . But evangelization will not be complete unless it constantly relates the Gospel to men's actual lives, personal and social."* (*Evangelii Nuntiandi*, §28-29).

Between the mountain and the market place there is the cave of Bethlehem. It speaks to all of us of new life. It also speaks sadly to us of the selfishness of humanity. The poignancy of St. Luke's phrase, *"because there was no place for them in the inn,"* (Lk 2:7) reminds us that, then as now, there is a great gap between *the haves* and *the have-nots* in society and among the nations. The celebration of Christmas challenges each one of us to close, even by a millimeter, that wide gap.

May that faith with which we have been gifted, lift our minds anew to *"the things that are above."* (Col 3:2). May each one of us, priest, Brother and seminarian, find fresh confidence this Christmas in the power of Mary, the Mother of Our Lord, to nurture the divine life that we carry within us and to express that life in salvific action for the world. That is my prayer and my hope. With kindest greetings from all of us here in the Curia and commending the Congregation and myself to your prayers, I remain in the love of Our Lord, your devoted confrere.

Meekness and Humility

12 December 1990   Santiago, Chile

My dear Sisters,

A saintly Christian poet, who lived three centuries ago, wrote a very short poem in which he imagined how God made the first man. He pictured God as having beside him a large *"glass of blessings"* which He intended to pour into man. He first gave man beauty, then wisdom, honor, pleasure. Then God noticed at the bottom of the glass one blessing left. It was rest. So God said: *"If I give My creature this jewel of rest, he will adore my gifts instead of Me. He will take his rest in nature and not in the God of nature."* God then decided not to pour into man this last blessing. Because he would be weary and tired, man will seek rest and if goodness does not lead him to his Creator, his lack of rest will *"toss him into My breast."* With that phrase the poem ends.

Many centuries earlier a great saint and theologian had, after he had tried everything which he thought might give him rest, been forced to accept the truth which he expressed in a sentence which has since become famous: *"Lord, You have made us for Yourself and our hearts are restless until they rest in You."* The saint and theologian was Augustine of Hippo.

I have been reflecting on the restlessness of our hearts because of the words of Our Lord to which we have just listened in the Gospel. *"Come to Me all you who are weary and find life burdensome, and I will refresh you."* (Mt 11:28). It is true that we will not rest fully until we see and possess our God and Creator in heaven. When a Christian dies, the prayer which the Church puts on our lips for him is, *"Eternal rest grant unto him, O Lord.* " What keeps the souls in Purgatory from attaining full rest in God is their undue attachment to those things which in their lifetime they believed would give them rest. The experience of Purgatory is rather like separating an already tired child from the toy or the game that he keeps clinging to, when it is past the hour of sleep.

Our hearts will only find their rest when we rest with God in Heaven. Meantime we are on our way to that final rest. On the way God has thoughtfully provided for us in the person of His Son and in His Church and especially in the Eucharist, wherein we can find not only some rest but, as Our Lord Himself assures us, refreshment also. *"And I will refresh you . . . your souls will find rest."* (Mt 11:28-29).

Not only will we find rest and refreshment in Christ as we move along the road of life, but He would have us learn from Him gentleness and humility of heart. Gentleness and humility of heart contribute much to our peace and rest on our journey to heaven. It was St. Vincent de Paul's conviction that, if we had humility of heart, we would have much peace, while if we were without it, we would be subject to continual anxieties. It is remarkable that in the life of St. Vincent de Paul, the more he heard the cries of the poor and tried to answer them, the more convinced he became of the need of gentleness and humility in his own life and in the lives of those who were helping him to serve the poor. Towards the end of his life he wrote these lines on the importance of gentleness: *"All shall likewise study with great diligence this lesson, taught us by Christ: 'Learn of Me because I am meek and humble of heart.' We shall consider, too, as He Himself has said, that it is by meekness that we possess the land, because by the practice of this virtue we gain the hearts of men to convert them to the Lord, which those fail to do who deal harshly with the neighbor."* (CR, II, 6).

St. Vincent would wish us to be sacraments of the gentleness of Christ. Not only do the Sacraments bring us strength, but they put us in contact with the Risen Christ. Not only must we bring strength and help to the poor, but we must put them in contact with the gentleness of Jesus Christ. That is why it is important that we should not be angry people. If there is anger in our hearts, it will be difficult for us to help the poor effectively because we will not bring to them the gentleness of Jesus

Christ. It was that conviction which led St. Vincent de Paul to say that, *"however charitable a man may be, if he is not humble, he does not have real charity."* (Coste XII, Fr. ed., p. 210).

May God give all of us this grace of accepting the invitation of Christ to draw close to Him in the Eucharist, especially when our hearts are troubled. May we learn from Him to be gentle and humble of heart, so that a measure of rest may be ours during life's pilgrimage, and at the end may we have so lived in charity that He can pour into our beings *"that jewel of rest"* for which He made us.

First Holy Communion

13 December 1990   Punta Arenas, Chile

My dear Sisters and my dear Friends,

During the course of my life I have seldom had the joy of celebrating a Mass during which some children received the Body and Blood of Our Lord for the first time. First let me say a word to you children, for this is a very important day in your lives. All of you know what it is like to be hungry and thirsty. Perhaps you have played a game and at the end of it, you want to drink something, because you have perspired. Or perhaps you had a long walk and you came home hungry, looking for something to eat.

One day Jesus Christ had gone on a long walk and many people followed Him. As Jesus Christ was a very thoughtful person, He saw that the people were hungry and He asked his closest friends to do something. They did not know what to do, for there were no shops in the area. There was one boy who had a few pieces of bread and a few fish. They thought that was no use among a large crowd of grown-up men and women. Jesus, because He was God, took the little bit of bread, broke it and then told His close friends to share it with the people. A wonderful thing happened. That little piece of bread kept coming and coming until thousands of people had eaten of it and had had enough. It was a miracle.

Next day Jesus told the people that He would give them another sort of bread which would help them to live forever. That bread would be Himself. The people found that hard to understand. Today, by a miracle, that bread which Jesus promised is still available. You, my dear children, are going to taste that bread, which is the Body of Jesus Christ, for the first time during this Mass. It will give you strength to be a person like Jesus Christ—kind, good and unselfish. In the little white host is Jesus Christ Who is God. Jesus, although we cannot see Him, is giving you everything in Holy Communion. He does that so that you will be able to grow up into a person like Him. He wishes you to live close to Him, and He wishes to live close to you in this life, and after your death He wishes you to live with Him forever in heaven and be happy in a way that you have never been or ever will be during your life. And so, my dear children, when you receive the Body and Blood of Jesus Christ in some minutes, give Him a warm welcome into the home of your hearts.

Now let me speak to you adults. None of us can recall our coming into the world, nor can we recall the celebration of our first birthday, but is there anyone of us here who cannot remember the first occasion when we received the Body and Blood of Christ? Somebody once told me—and I do not know if it is a historical fact—that towards the end of his life Napoleon was asked what was the greatest day in his life, and he replied: *"The day I made my first Holy Communion."* Even today in a secularized age, the occasion when a child makes its first Holy Communion is an event in the child's life and in the life of the family. How much time is devoted to preparing children for their first Holy Communion. How much money is still spent on new clothes for children on the occasion of their first Holy Communion. So much work and so much expense for the first Holy Communion, and must we say that it stops there? There is a second Holy Communion and a third Holy Communion. There was the Holy Communion of yesterday and there is the Holy Communion of this morning.The excitement of the first Holy Communion has passed into our memories, but it is still the same Lord, Who is giving Himself, as we were taught, body and blood, soul and divinity, to be the food of our souls. It is still the same Lord, Who is providing us with the food for our journey towards eternity. *"Jesus Christ is the same yesterday, and today and forever."* (Heb 13:8).

The word, Eucharist, means thanksgiving. Each Holy Communion should make us more grateful to God for all the gifts He has given us. There is a beautiful prayer of St. Thomas More who always kept his heart detached from the things of this life, even when he was rich and enjoyed much favor from King Henry VIII. In the end the King took everything from St. Thomas, even his life. Nevertheless, St. Thomas continued to pray: *"Thanks be to You, Lord Jesus Christ, for all that You have given me. Thanks be to You, Lord Jesus Christ, for all that You have taken from me. Thanks be to You, Lord Jesus Christ, for all that You have left me."*

On this day when we rejoice to see children receive the Eucharist for the first time, may God give us the grace to be grateful for everything He has given us in Christ, and to show our gratitude by generosity to others, especially those who have received so much less than we have.

Let me end this homily by praying the prayer which St. Louise de Marillac used to pray before Holy Communion: *"Sweet Jesus! Gentle Jesus! My God and my All! Have mercy on all souls redeemed by Your precious blood. Inflame them with the arrow of Your love in order to make them grateful for the love that urged You to give Yourself to us in the Blessed Sacrament. To this end, I offer You the glory which You enjoy within Yourself from all eternity, and all the graces that You granted the Blessed Virgin and the saints, together with the glory that they will eternally render You by this same love. Amen."* (*Spiritual Writings of Louise de Marillac*, A. 49, p. 834).

1991

Dance of Life

1 January 1991   Paris, France

Mother Duzan, Father Lloret and my dear Sisters,

A little over three weeks ago, when I was visiting a number of our Provinces in Latin America, a small group of Sisters, accompanied by a number of blind children in their care, came to the house of our Fathers where I was staying.

The children had brought with them a number of musical instruments and they wished to play, to sing and to dance, as an expression of their welcome. Quite some time passed before I was called down to the hall to find the little orchestra all set up with three Sisters discreetly standing at the side. Then one of the children, fingering sensitively a little card with Braille lettering, made a speech of welcome after which the music and the songs began. A little later came the dances. It was then that the expressions on the children's faces assumed an air of greater concentration. Clearly, when one is blind, one's movements are made more cautiously. There were some daring spirits who tried to pivot, often successfully but occasionally unsuccessfully which resulted in a momentary loss of balance and a fall. From time to time during the necessarily limited movements of the dancers, the Sisters, ever so gently with a touch, guided the children back to their correct places when they had strayed somewhat or had fallen. It was a touching scene, watching the interested and loving concern of the Sisters in the background and the faces of the children, joyful in the darkness in which they spend their lives.

It all seemed to me as a parable of our own lives. The mystery of life and death, the darkness of a future that opens out before us and which with certainty or accuracy we cannot predict. The mystery of suffering, the problem of poverty in a world that is rich in resources, all confirms St. Paul's observation that *"we see now in a dark manner."* (1 Cor 13:12).

The dance of life, however, continues. Our steps falter often and we even fall and must be assisted to rise again. Watching lovingly from the side and from above is our Father in heaven. His presence to us is invisible, but His touch is there to keep the movement of life's dance steady and according to pattern. Like the Sisters, He watches lovingly and silently, entering into the joy of the dance, for *"His delights are to be with the children of men."* (Prv 8:31).

God not only looked on lovingly at the dance of His blind children, but the Word Himself joined the dance, not as an adult teacher but as a child. It was Mary, His Virgin Mother, who taught Him His first steps in the dance of life, and it was the Spirit who led Him to respond fully to the movements of His Father's Will.

The dance of life is not always easy. Some steps are painful, but none so painful as those that the Word Incarnate took along the path that led to Calvary. The gentle touch of our Father will continually guide us along that path so that the figure of life's dance may reach its ending in our Father's house where our joy will be complete and our vision will be no longer partial, for then we will see the beauty, harmony and love of God with unimpaired vision.

When the children had finished dancing and it was time for some refreshments in the refectory, they were lost. The house was strange to them. So in little groups of three, hands linked one to another with the first in line holding on firmly and trustingly to a Sister's hand, they began to move along the corridor to the refectory. Was this, I asked myself, what ascetical writers of the past had in mind when they wrote and spoke of blind obedience? Are we so enlightened today that we like to dispense, as far as we can, with that guidance which obedience provides? *"Far from diminishing the dignity of the person,"* we read in the Constitutions, *"obedience enhances it by increasing the freedom which belongs to the children of God."* (C. 2.8).

Perhaps it is not the blind children who so much reminded me of God as the Sisters who were caring for them. For the Sisters, the achievement of the children was everything. Is it not true that humanity, even in all its frailty and sinfulness, is that which gives most joy to the heart of God? The children danced with joy, but in their blindness they could not see the love and interest shining in the faces of the Sisters who were giving their whole selves to their care and education. Is it not so with us who cannot see, or but very faintly see, the height and the depth of *"the love of God in Christ Jesus, Our Lord"?* (Rom 8:39).

It was, however, when a Sister ever so gently with her hands moved a dancing child back onto the stage when she had lost her direction, that I was most reminded of God's guidance of the world and of our own individual lives. For the children, the hands of the Sister were not visible, but they had long come to trust the touch of such loving hands. The hand of the living and loving God is touching our lives at every moment. The saints are those who can respond with utter trust to the most delicate touches of the Spirit of God and who live with the conviction that *"for those who love God all things work together unto good."* (Rom 8:28). The saints are those who, like St. Louise, can say: *"I beg Him with all my heart to let you know how good it is to trust in Him . . . . Look to Him often as children do to their father and mother for their needs."* (*Spiritual Writings of Louise de Marillac*, ltr. 234, p. 277).

For the blind children, the Sisters were sacraments of the Providence of God. The vocation of a Daughter of Charity is deeply rooted in the Providence of God. We know that St. Vincent remarked on one occasion that, if the Daughters of Charity had not received the title, Daughters of Charity, they would be known as Daughters of Divine Providence. In all the varied apostolates of the Community which are directed to the poor, I like to think of the Sisters as angels or messengers of God's Providence.

The Providence of God is silent and loving. He makes the fruits on the trees grow, but silently. So, too, with a Daughter of Charity; she silently and lovingly serves the poor, anticipating their needs. The Providence of God does not force His love on His creatures. He makes the seasons produce wheat and rice in the fields. Humans can use it, abuse it or waste it. So, too, with a Daughter of Charity; she does not force herself on the poor, for she respects their dignity, nor is she strident or aggressive in her service. The Providence of God is patient. He allows the cockle and the wheat to grow together until the harvest time when the separation will be made. So, too, with a Daughter of Charity; she exhibits in her Community life the tolerance or support so often recommended by St. Louise to her correspondents: *"The support we owe to one another,"* she wrote to a Sister Servant, *"should prevent us from noticing the weaknesses of our Sisters, except if we are able to help them."* (*Spiritual Writings of Louise de Marillac*, ltr. 355, p. 112).

On this day, my dear Sisters, when, with the comforting presence of the Mother of God, we stand on the threshold of a new year and wonder what the Providence of God may hold for us in the months ahead, we can be sure that the dance of life, whatever its movements, will be directed by One whose love is beyond comprehension and Who will accompany and guide all our steps with the harmonious music of His grace. *"I said to the man who stood at the gate of the year, 'Give me a light that I may tread safely into the unknown', and he replied, 'Go out into the darkness and put your hand into the hand of God. That shall be to you better than light and safer than a known way.'"* (N.L. Haskins).

Lenten Letter—Sacraments of Eucharist and Reconciliation

1 February 1991   To Each Confrere

My dear Confrere,

May the grace of Our Lord Jesus Christ be with us forever!

The weeks of Lent and Paschal Time are in a special way sacramental weeks. Holy Thursday celebrates the institution of the Eucharist and the Priesthood, and the blessing of the holy oils on that day evokes the Sacrament of the Sick. Who could assist at the vigil ceremonies on Holy Saturday without reflecting on baptism and on that *second baptism* which is the Sacrament of Penance? Pentecost will recall the Sacrament of Confirmation, and since Pentecost is the birthday of the Church, the feast may also suggest the Sacrament of Marriage of which the Church is a symbol.

Sacramental weeks. In the country from which I come, there are in the mountainous areas large rocks which today are pointed out as *Mass Rocks*. These rocks were the altars on which the Mass was celebrated during the years when Catholics were persecuted for their faith. It was around these rocks in the remote areas of the country that the faithful would gather and a hunted priest would celebrate the Sacrifice of the Mass. Participation in the Eucharist on these occasions involved high risk for both priest and people. The *Mass Rocks* remain today as eloquent witnesses to the meaning and cost of evangelization and of the sacraments in another epoch.

On occasion over the past few years I have reflected on those *Mass Rocks* when I have participated in discussions on the relationship between evangelization and the sacraments. Today we emphasize the truth that evangelization must not be thought of as exclusively sacramental. *"Action on behalf of social justice,"* declared the Synod of 1971, *"and participation in the transformation of this world, are constitutive elements in the preaching of the Gospel."* However, have we, who celebrate the Eucharist in the relative comfort of our churches and oratories, lost something of that sense of privilege of those who participated in the Eucharist at risk to their lives? For it must be considered a privilege and not an obligation to be daily invited by the Principal Concelebrant of every Mass, the Risen Christ, to join with Him in offering to the Father in the unity of the Holy Spirit all honor and glory and to plead with Him for the evangelization and salvation of the world. That sense of being privileged to celebrate the Eucharist lies behind the sentiment which St. Vincent expressed in a letter to the superior of two candidates who were about to be ordained to the priesthood: *". . . I have begged Our Lord and will continue to beg Him to grant them always renewed dispositions for the [Holy] Sacrifice and the grace never to offer it through routine. I entreat them to remember me when they say,* 'nobis quoque peccatoribus.'" (Coste III, Eng. ed., ltr. 1028, p. 296).

And what of the prolonged presence of Christ in the Blessed Sacrament? Would I be right in saying that sensitivity to the reality of this presence (or to the presence of reality) has diminished over the past two decades? We have perhaps acquired a more heightened sensitivity to God's presence in the word of Scripture and in the person of the poor. Yet a long tradition in the Church, which St. Vincent himself greatly respected, teaches us that by cultivating a sensitivity to Our Lord's presence in the Blessed Sacrament, we will be enabled to recognize and respond more fully to Christ in situations where His presence may not be immediately obvious.

Sacramental weeks. What of the Sacrament of Reconciliation in our own personal lives? *"We priests,"* wrote Pope John Paul II in the Apostolic Exhortation after the Synod of 1984, *"on the basis of our personal experience, can certainly say that, the more careful we are to receive the Sacrament of Penance and to approach it frequently and with good dispositions, the better we fulfill our own ministry as confessors and ensure that our penitents benefit from it. And on the other hand this ministry would lose much of its effectiveness if in some way we were to stop being good penitents. Such is the internal logic of this great Sacrament."* (Reconciliatio et Paenitentia, #31).

Is the falling off in the frequency with which people avail of the Sacrament of Penance, related in any way to us priests not *"being good penitents"* ourselves? Have we priests too quickly abandoned our confessionals in recent years, telling ourselves that the faithful do not come and that they do not feel the need of the Sacrament of Reconciliation? Could it be that we do not present to the faithful clearly enough the patience of the Father in the parable of the Prodigal Son who waited lovingly and long for his son to return?

For us in the Congregation there is a further *"internal logic"* in the Sacrament of Penance. We can truthfully say that our Congregation was founded upon the experience of one penitent being reconciled with God and with the Church through the patient understanding of St. Vincent, shown in the Sacrament of Penance. It is logical, then, that in all our programs for evangelization, the Sacrament of Penance will have a prominent place and that we ourselves be known as men who are authentic ambassadors of Christ, sharing in His ministry of reconciliation.

I pray that in the coming weeks we may gratefully allow ourselves to be touched and embraced lovingly by Christ in the Sacraments of the Eucharist and of Reconciliation. Strengthened by this experience, we will in turn become ourselves sacraments of Christ's love, of His justice, of His compassion and of His peace to the men and women of our time. *"Now then,"* exclaimed St. Vincent, *"let us ask God that He give to the Company this spirit . . . this heart of the Son of God, the heart of Our Lord, the heart of Our Lord, the heart of Our Lord."* (Coste XI, Fr. ed., p. 291).

Commending myself to your prayers during these sacramental weeks, I remain in the love of Our Lord, your devoted confrere.

Do the Best We Can

14 February 1991   Ho Chi Minh, Vietnam

My dear Sisters,

During the past few days I have admired here in the sanctuary an arrangement of flowers in the form of a bird, looking towards the altar and tabernacle. The floral arrangement reminded me of a little story about a bird. One day a large horse was walking along the road and he saw a little bird lying on its back, looking up into the sky, with its legs pointing upwards. The large horse asked the little bird what it was doing. *"I heard a rumor,"* said the little bird, *"that the sky was going to fall today. So I am going to try to hold it up."* The large horse began to laugh and laugh. *"How can you,"* he said, *"with your little, tiny legs hold up the sky?"* The little bird replied: *"I know, but I am going to do the best I can . . . the best I can."*

"The best I can," that is what you, my dear Sisters, have been doing during the past fifteen years. Many times since 1975 you must have thought that the sky was falling on your little Community. Like the little bird on the road you decided as a Province that you were going to do the best you could to hold up the sky. And you have succeeded. The blessing and strength of God have been upon you. The Immaculate Mother of God has been at your side. You have continued to serve the poor and to be united among yourselves, and your Province today is experiencing a new hope and new life.

To each of you, my dear Sisters, I address the words of St. Vincent to Sister Anne Hardemont: *"Continue, my Sister, and you will see the glory of God, you will possess your soul by your patience . . . . It is for charity, it is for God, it is for the poor."* (Coste VII, Fr. ed., pp. 382-383).

"If you love the Lord, your God," the first reading of today's Mass reminds us, *"and follow His ways . . . . you will live and increase, and the Lord your God will bless you in the land which you are entering to make your own."* (Dt 30:16).

This afternoon Father Lauwerier and I will leave this land into which we entered ten days ago. You have offered us wonderful hospitality and numerous gifts, for which we are most grateful. The greatest gift which you have given us is the witness of your lives, which are clearly and deeply impregnated with the spirit of St. Vincent and St. Louise. For that gift neither of us could adequately express our thanks. We must resign ourselves to being like the little bird on the road and do the best we can in thanking you.

When the day comes at the end of time for the sky to fall, may all of us here this morning meet each other again around the table of Our Lord in the house of His Father, from Whom all good things come in time and eternity.

Pharisee and Publican

9 March 1991   Barquisimeto, Venezuela

My dear Confreres,

Some years ago I knew a priest who liked to put this question to people when he was talking to them about the parable to which we have just listened in the Gospel. *"If you were to enter the Temple and found the pharisee and the publican kneeling there, which of the two would you kneel beside?"* All of us would probably reply, *"The publican, of course."* We prefer the publican because he is a humble man and all the world feels at ease with humble people. We do not feel at ease with people who boast about themselves and make us feel inferior. The pharisee is boastful in his prayer and we would not feel too comfortable in his presence. We would draw close to the publican and pray with him: *"Lord, be merciful to me, a sinner."* Besides, we know from the story that Jesus Christ approved the publican, and we are always on the side of the good.

In saying that we are always on the side of the good, I am dangerously near to praying the prayer of the pharisee. For that reason, it might be good if we did not answer the question: *"Which of the two would you kneel beside?"* quite so quickly. If we like to think of ourselves as always on the side of the good people, and if we too quickly join the publican, there is a possibility that we could be despising the pharisee. It was precisely because the pharisee despised others that he was not accepted by God, nor his prayer either. *"Believe me, this man went home from the temple justified, but the other did not."* (Lk 18:13). It is very easy to despise others almost without knowing it. The next time we read this parable, we would do well at the end of it to stand for a moment at the door of the Temple and ask if we despise anybody. It is only when we have answered that question with a *no* that we can enter the temple and begin the prayer of the publican: *"God, be merciful to me, a sinner."*

The Church has learned the parable of today's Gospel very well, for whenever she prays her greatest prayer, the Mass, she always begins by making her own the prayer of the publican: *"Be merciful to me, a sinner . . . . Lord, have mercy. Christ, have mercy. Lord, have mercy."* Not only at the beginning but throughout the Mass, the Church makes us repeat the prayer of the publican in one form or another. *"Look not on our sins but on the faith of your Church . . . . Lord, I am not worthy that You should enter under my roof, but only say the word and I shall be healed."*

Not only has the Church learned this parable well, but so did St. Vincent de Paul. We could say that St. Vincent made two great spiritual discoveries in his lifetime. The first one was the presence of Jesus Christ in the person of the poor. The second one was that, if you wish to do something for Jesus Christ, you need His grace, and His grace is given only to the humble, only to those who can pray from the depths of their hearts, *"Lord, be merciful to me, a sinner."*

During his lifetime St. Vincent could be said to have built a great building to shelter the poor and suffering of this world. Like the good Samaritan, he spent a great part of his life lifting people off the roads and the streets and bringing them to a great inn where they could be healed and cared for. We have inherited that great inn, and its management is now in our hands. I think, however, that St. Vincent would remind us often, were he with us today, that the great building stands only because it has a good foundation, and that foundation is humility. In his writings and talks he comes back again and again to the importance of being humble. Humility is a grace of our Lord Jesus Christ. Perhaps we do not boast like the pharisee in today's Gospel, but that does not mean that we are humble people. Humility only comes when the light of Jesus Christ, Who Himself is humble of heart, penetrates deeply into our being and into all our thinking and reflection. When that light does penetrate into us, it transfigures everything, not only our opinion about ourselves but our attitude towards others. It is the light of humility that enables us to see the color and the variety of gifts that God has given to others and to praise Him for them in the way that we can praise Him for the variety of colors that we see in the flowers of the fields.

Let us listen to this appeal of St. Vincent: *"Let us give ourselves fully and wholeheartedly to God. Let us work solidly at virtue and principally at humility. Yes, humility. Let us ask God earnestly that He would kindly give us this virtue . . . humility, yes humility. I repeat it. Humility."* (Coste XI, Fr. ed., p. 389).

To all of us here who have the responsibility of maintaining the great inn of charity established by St. Vincent, and who have, too, the responsibility of evangelization, may the grace of humility be given to us, for without it we will do no lasting good. With humility God will be glorified, the poor will be served and made happy, and we ourselves will enjoy the grace and peace of Jesus Christ, Who is gentle and humble of heart.

Remembering

14 March 1991   Caracas, Venezuela

My dear Friends in Jesus Christ,

Let me talk to you about a word that I am sure is often on our lips when we pray and when we speak to our friends. It is a word which comes to our lips even more frequently, as the years of our lives pass. It is the word *remember*. As we lose friends through death and feel the pain of loneliness, we find a little consolation in remembering the good times of the past and speaking about them. How often we find ourselves saying, *"I remember when I was young . . . "* Sometimes we feel ourselves to be better people when we remember the goodness of others to us, their generosity, their unselfishness, their tenderness, their thoughtfulness.

That little word *remember* is at the center of the first reading of this evening's Mass. God was displeased with the Israelite people. He had done great things for them, but they had short memories. They became so absorbed in themselves that they forgot God and failed to remember His goodness to them in the past. There is one very frightening sentence in the reading to which we have listened. God said to Moses that He would let His anger blaze up against His people and that He would destroy them. (cf. Ex 32:10).

Then Moses, who was an arbitrator between God and His people, prayed and asked God to remember some of the very good people who had belonged to the nation in the past. They were not only national heroes but they were also saints and great friends of God. *"Remember, "* he prayed, *"your servants Abraham and Isaac and Israel."* (Ibid., v. 13). In recalling these great leaders, Moses was saying to God: *"Surely you could not destroy a nation that once had such great and holy persons as these, "* and God relented *"in the punishment He had threatened to inflict on His people."* (Ibid., v. 14). For us who live thousands of years later, it is interesting to think that that little word *remember* is at the heart of our greatest prayer, the Mass. The Mass is the great prayer in which along with Jesus Christ we ask God the Father to remember the life, sufferings, death and resurrection of His only Son: *"Remember the goodness, the perfection, the love which Your Son, Jesus Christ, had when He lived on earth and especially when He offered His life on the cross."* Since the first Pentecost, groups of Christians have gathered together and offered the Mass, renewing again and again the great act of remembering, while at the same time making present again the offering that Jesus made of Himself on the cross. In doing so, we, like Moses, are turning away the displeasure of God with the world and, more than that, we are bringing down upon the entire world, whether it knows it or not, an uncountable number of graces and favors and blessings.

Every day we hear some frightening things about the cruelty and the wickedness of men. What would the world be like if it did not have the Sacrifice of the Mass? Always remember that there is no grace, no joy, no good thing in this world that has not come to us through Jesus Christ, and particularly through the Mass. At the end of every Eucharistic prayer we are reminded that it is through Christ that all good things come.

Remembering is at the heart of the Eucharist. Let us not leave our remembering just to the time of the Mass. Outside Mass try to remember gratefully. We can spend much time remembering the wounds, the bruises, the injustices life may have given us. We can remember with bitterness the past, but that leads nowhere. Remembering the past with bitterness only makes us more bitter and a Christian should not be bitter, for there was no bitterness in Jesus Christ, notwithstanding the failures of His apostles and the betrayal of Him by Judas. Eucharist means thanksgiving. Give time to recalling the good things of the past, and give thanks to God for them. Thanksgiving at any time of the year, at any time of the day, is a good tonic. It will make you feel better.

May the Virgin Mary, who in her Magnificat remembered God's goodness to her people, help us also to be mindful of His goodness to us in the past and to praise Him for His kindness every day in the Eucharist. *"Praise to You, Lord Jesus Christ, King of endless glory."*

Choices

17 March 1991   Cumana, Venezuela

My dear Friends of Jesus Christ,

At the beginning of this century there lived in the country from which I come a young man who for his part in a rebellion was executed. He was a Christian and a Catholic, a gentle person, not very practical. Perhaps you would say he was a dreamer. Shortly before he died, he wrote a little poem, entitled, *"I see His Blood upon the Rose."* What this young poet wanted to say was that, when he saw a red rose, he thought of the blood of Christ. When it rained, he thought of the tears of Christ. The beauty of the sea reminded him of the heart of Christ. The final line of the little poem is, *"His cross is every tree."*

When Jesus Christ walked on this earth and looked at trees, He must have thought of the cross and crucifixion. Crosses were made of wood and were not ornaments, as they are today. The cross was a sign of shame, a sign of defeat. Wooden crosses would have spoken to Jesus Christ of death, a shameful death, a very painful death.

Whether red roses reminded Jesus Christ of His blood, which would be poured out on the tree of the cross, we do not know. We do, however, know that a grain of wheat spoke to Him about His death and His resurrection. Listen to His words as we have them in today's Gospel: *"Truly, truly I say to you, unless a grain of wheat falls into the earth and dies, it remains alone, but if it dies, it bears much fruit."* (Jn 12:24).

For a Christian, that is, for a follower of Christ, it is important that he or she knows how to die. I am not now thinking so much of death at the end of our lives, though dying is necessary, if we are to enter fully into the joy of living with Christ in heaven. I am thinking of the importance for a Christian to be able to say *no* to himself. One day Our Lord said: *"If anyone will come after Me, he must deny himself . . . "* (Mt 16:24). To deny oneself means to say *no* to oneself.

Supposing you are about to make a journey on foot and you are not too sure of the road. You will ask directions. You might consult a map. Then you set out. You reach a junction in the road. One road goes down into a valley and another road goes up a hill. You hesitate and wonder which road you will take. You know that the place to which you are going lies on the other side of the hill. The easier road goes down the hill, which will demand much less energy, but you know that it is round about and dangerous. The other road is a steep climb. You would like to go down the hill to save yourself effort, but your better judgment will suggest that you take the more difficult, uphill road, knowing it will bring you to the place to which you are going.

It is like that with us on the journey of life. We must make choices. Our instincts, our selfishness, our pride will often suggest to us to follow them. It is an easier road. But Christ, His Church and our consciences suggest another way. To follow that road, we must say *no* to our natural instincts. It may be difficult and demand much effort, but that effort will bring with it a peace and contentment that money will not buy. *"Unless a grain of wheat falls into the earth and dies, it remains a single grain of wheat; but if it dies, it brings a good harvest.* "Years after Our Lord had spoken those words, St. Paul told his converts: *"Those who belong to Christ have crucified their lower nature with all that it loved and lusted for."* (Gal 5:24).

Lent is a time when we think about doing some crucifixion of our lower nature. That does not mean that we banish all pleasure, all joy from our lives. Lent is a time when we check on the direction our lives are taking. Do we always take the easy, downhill road in every choice we make? Lent is a time when we apply the brakes to downhill movements in our lives and try to change direction and to change gear. We do that by allowing Jesus Christ to have a greater say in our lives, in our decisions, in our thoughts, in our actions. That will mean saying *no* to ourselves, perhaps many times a day. By saying *no* to ourselves, we are like the little grain of wheat that dies. Once we have said *no* to ourselves and have died a little, we will experience new life and a new peace.

Invite Jesus Christ, then, into your lives and He will help you on the uphill road, for, as He assures us in the final sentences of today's Gospel, *"If I am lifted up from the earth, I will draw all things to Myself."* (Jn 12:32).

May we, through the intercession of the Virgin Mary who denied herself and stood at the foot of the cross, be able to see more clearly the blood of Christ on every rose, the cross of Christ in every tree, and the life of Christ in every grain of wheat.

Living our Vows

8 April 1991   Paris, France

Mother Duzan, Father Lloret and my dear Sisters,

Two weeks ago I was in the Greek city of Salonika, where St. Paul preached to the Thessalonians. In that city today there is a small Vincentian presence of three priests and a Brother and four Daughters of Charity. On Sunday morning I celebrated Mass with them and with a number of people of the Vincentian parish. In the afternoon my Confreres and I made a brief tour of the city and our first stop was at a medieval Orthodox church.

When we entered it, a baptism was taking place. The Orthodox priest had just concluded the first part of the ceremony and was proceeding from the entrance of the church to the sanctuary, where a large font had been prepared. The subject of the baptism was a young boy about seven years of age. As the little procession made its way to the sanctuary, the boy's mother whisked him suddenly out of the church. A minute later they returned. The boy was wearing a bathrobe. The priest had already begun the prayers at the font, surrounded by the boy's family and friends. On entering the sanctuary the boy mounted a low pedestal and then the mother removed the bathrobe and there the boy stood, totally naked and totally unselfconscious, as the priest continued to read prayers from the Greek ritual. We did not wait to see the actual baptism which according to the Greek Orthodox rite would be one of immersion.

Coming out of the church, the implications of Christian baptism bore in upon me in a new and significant way. St. Paul's question seemed more penetrating: *"Do you not know that all of us who have been baptized into Christ Jesus were baptized into His death?"* (Rom 6:3) and *"all of you who have been baptized into Christ have put on Christ."* (Gal 3:27). For St. Paul, to be baptized is to surrender everything to Christ. To be baptized into Christ Jesus is to become as naked as a corpse that is being prepared for burial. It is to be totally immersed in the cleansing and life-giving waters of baptism and to emerge clothed with new life, the life of the Risen Christ. *"If anyone is in Christ,"* wrote St. Paul, *"he is a new creation."* (2 Cor 5:17).

To be a Christian, then, is to live costly, for total surrender to anyone, even out of love, is costly. To all who would be baptized, Jesus Christ has said, *"If anyone will come after Me, let him deny himself, take up his cross daily and follow Me."* (Lk 9:23). Those who died on crosses in Jesus' time, died naked.

If it is costly to live as an authentic Christian, to live with vows is even more so. That truth is put clearly to us in the document of Vatican II, *Perfectae Caritatis: "The members of each Institute should recall first of all that when they made profession of the evangelical counsels, they were responding to a divine call, for the purpose that, not merely being dead to sin (Rom 6:11), but renouncing the world also, they might live for God alone .... This constitutes a special consecration which is deeply rooted in their baptismal consecration and is a fuller expression of it."* (§5). To live our vows is to live naked before God. It is to allow ourselves to become so absorbed by His presence, so fascinated by His beauty and His love, that we become in time quite unselfconscious of what the world may think or say.

To live our vow of chastity is to live with our eyes and hearts firmly fixed on the living person of Jesus Christ, with whom we partner everything. What we cannot share in thought, word or act with Jesus Christ is to a greater or lesser degree a failure to live chastely. To live chastely is to live lovingly at every moment of the day with Jesus Christ. And that can be costly.

Our vow of poverty speaks of nakedness. The reality, however, is that I can clutter my life with so many things, with so many vain and worldly desires, that I am wearing protective clothing against the refreshing rain and warm sunshine of God's love and grace.

What of obedience? The nakedness of Christ on the cross was but an external expression of the nakedness of His Will before His Father in heaven. *"Not My Will but Yours be done,"* (Lk 22:42) was His prayer in the Garden of Gethsemane. In our day, freedom of expression has been encouraged in religious Communities with a view to arriving at a clearer knowledge of what God may be asking of a Community or of an individual. In itself it is good, but it can also be a stretching out for a robe that will cover that nakedness before God which is at the heart of our vows. Obedience is a condition of nakedness before God.

Service of the poor? As Daughters of Charity you live much in the light of that fourth vow. The poor are always close to the hearts of the Daughters of Charity. You, my dear Sisters, from your experience know that to serve the poor you must be continually divesting yourselves of comfort, convenience and prestige. And that is costly. St. Vincent expressed his thoughts on the maxims of the world in one of his conferences: *"'What do you say, Sister? Do you not think it reasonable to . . . keep this rule which teaches us to shun the maxims of the world and embrace those of Jesus Christ?' 'Yes, Father,' replied the Sisters. 'Do you intend to follow the maxims of Our Lord?' When they replied again, M. Vincent told them that they must ask this grace from Our Lord*

Jesus Christ. 'I beseech Him by the intercession of the Blessed Virgin, to grant it to this Company.'" (Conf. Eng. ed., 2 Nov. 1655, p. 766).

To come back to the ceremony in the Orthodox church. We did not have time to wait and see the actual immersion ceremony. We hastened on to visit the site where tradition has it St. Paul preached to the citizens of Thessalonica. Had we waited to see the conclusion of the baptismal ceremony, I have no doubt but that the naked boy would have been covered by a new robe to signify that he was now a new creation in Christ Jesus. I have wondered since, how ornate that robe might have been, probably more ornate than the little piece of white linen that is offered at the end of the ceremony to a person who is baptized in the Latin Rite.

Whether it be in an Orthodox church or in a Latin church, baptism is being stripped naked only in order to be clothed again. Listen to St. Paul as he writes forcefully and impatiently to the Galatians: *"For as many of you as were baptized into Christ have put on Christ."* (Gal 3:27). The metaphor is one of clothes. Old clothes have been thrown away and new ones have been acquired. St. Paul shows a fondness for thinking of the baptized as people who are very elegantly dressed, spiritually. To the Colossians he writes: *"Put on, then, as God's chosen ones, holy and beloved, compassion, kindness, lowliness, meekness and patience, forbearing one another and, if one has a complaint against another, forgiving each other . . . . And above all these, put on love which binds everything together in perfect harmony."* (Col 2:12-14).

Our vows, as a fuller expression of our baptism, must be seen as a condition of nakedness before God, so that He can clothe us with the stunning beauty of charity and a perfectly matching ensemble of virtues. Of the virtues that match or harmonize with charity, St. Vincent's eye was attracted very much by humility, and he said so on innumerable occasions. When I reflect on the virtue of humility (and it has been said that humility is not characteristic of twentieth century people), I like to think of a little phrase in St. Peter's first letter when he counsels Christians to *"put on the apron (or 'overall') of humility"* (1 Pt 5:5). Aprons are put on because there is work to be done and service given, or better, service to be offered. But the service offered must harmonize at all times with charity, for if service, however valuable it may seem inside or outside the Community, clashes with charity, then the harmony of the ensemble is spoiled. That may be the moment to present ourselves naked before God in prayer, so that He can clothe us with a robe that is pure love and not synthetic.

When you renew your vows each year, my dear Sisters, you once again immerse yourselves totally in Christ. *"Let us live, therefore, as if we were dead in Jesus Christ,"* wrote St. Louise when reflecting on her baptism. *"Henceforth, let there be no further resistance to Jesus, no action except for Jesus, no thoughts but in Jesus!"* (*Spiritual Writings of Louise de Marillac*, A23., p. 786).

Each year, on the day when the Virgin Mary surrendered herself totally to the designs of God for the saving of humanity, you surrender yourselves anew into the hands of the living and loving God. With the Virgin Mary's surrender a new dawn from on high shone upon humanity. With her a new chapter in the history of humanity opened, a chapter that is not yet closed. God's saving work continues in our world, and each of us through obedience writes a line in that chapter, which will only be closed when Christ will come again to hand the Kingdom over to His Father, and God will be all in all. Meantime let us live with the vision of St. Paul, who wrote to the Corinthians: *"Always, wherever we may be, we carry with us in our body the death of Jesus, so that the life of Jesus, too, may always be seen in our body."* (2 Cor 4:10). At once naked and clothed.

Servant of the Lord

25 April 1991   Czestochowa, Poland

My dear Sisters and my dear Confreres,

It is with joy and emotion that I make my second visit to this shrine of Our Lady, a shrine which holds in the hearts of all Polish people a special place of affection. In the long nights of suffering which your nation has experienced at different epochs of history, it was here in this shrine of the Mother of God that you and your ancestors found the grace to live the ideal of St. Peter of being *"fortis in fide,"* *"strong in faith."*

It has been here that in the words of the *Salve Regina* you sent up your cries *"mourning and weeping"* to the Mother of God who as a *"most gracious advocate"* has turned her eyes of mercy towards you.

So I give God thanks, and His Mother, too, that I have been given the privilege of revisiting this shrine that has been sanctified by the prayers of numerous generations of pilgrims, sanctified, too, by the presence and prayer of Pope John Paul II.

When I was a very young boy at school, my companions used to say that because 4,000 years had passed from the fall of Adam until the birth of Christ, it was a good thing to try to recite during the four weeks of Advent the Hail Mary 4,000 times. I have a vague memory of trying to do it on a couple of occasions, but cannot remember now whether I ever succeeded in reaching the number 4,000.

All of us here, even the youngest, will have saluted the Mother of God in the words of the Hail Mary many more times than 4,000. Not only do we recognize Mary's unique importance in the history of humanity, but we also love her. Have we not at some time in our lives felt that it was Mary, the Mother of God, who interceded and obtained from her Son some special grace that meant a great deal to us? Yes, she is full of grace, the Lord is with her. She has prayed in a very personal way for us and will continue to do so until that moment when the *"now"* and *"the hour of our death"* of the prayer of the Hail Mary are one and the same.

The power of Mary's intercession is great because of who she is, the Mother of God. That is her most glorious title. She would never have been the Mother of God if God Himself had not chosen her and if she had not spoken those very simple words that we repeat so often when we pray the Angelus: *"I am the servant of the Lord; be it done to me according to your word."* She would never have reached that depth of intimacy with Him who was her Creator, if she could not have spoken from her heart those simple words that close the account of the Annunciation.

Mary's final words to the Angel Gabriel reveal two attitudes which I think we must develop in ourselves, if we are to grow in intimacy with Our Lord. *"I am the handmaid of the Lord."* *"No, neither philosophy nor theology nor discourses,"* observes St. Vincent, *"influence souls.*

It is essential that Jesus Christ be intimately united with us, or we with Him, that we operate in Him and He in us; that we speak like Him and in His spirit, as He Himself was in His Father and preached the doctrine taught Him by the Father." (Coste XI, Fr. ed., p. 343).

I am the servant of the Lord. I am the servant, or *slave* which is the actual word Our Lady used. I am on the lowest rung of the hierarchy in any society. For anyone who is acquainted with the spirituality of St. Vincent, there is no need to say how central humility was in his approach to God and to the poor. The opening words of the first reading of today's Mass put before us the ideal of humility: *"In your relations with one another, clothe yourselves with humility, because God is stern with the arrogant but to the humble he shows kindness. Bow humbly under God's mighty hand, so that in due time he may lift you high."* (1 Pt 55-56).

And Mary's other phrase, *"Be it done unto me according to your word,"* is that not a perfect expression of the virtue of obedience? It was Mary's acceptance of God's invitation which brought God into the world and into our lives in the person of Jesus Christ. It will likewise be with us. Some time ago I came across these words of Cardinal Newman, whom the Pope recently declared Venerable: *"Any religion which does not bring you nearer to God is of the world. You have to seek His face; obedience is the only way of seeking Him. All your duties are obediences. To do what He bids is to obey Him and to obey Him is to approach Him."* (Newman, "Parochial and Plain Sermons").

May the humble and obedient Virgin of Nazareth, Our Lady of Czestochowa, win for us all from her Son the grace of being, as He was, humble and obedient unto death, even to death on the cross.

Courtesy

31 May 1991   Rome, Italy

My dear Sisters,

Forty years ago there lived in England a Catholic layman of great culture who was a strong apologist for the Church and a poet whose family roots were in France. One day he visited a monastery, and the monks brought him into one of their great halls where he noticed three large paintings on the walls. The first depicted the Annunciation, the second the Visitation, and the third the Nativity. *"Here,"* exclaimed the poet, *"are three paintings, and in each of them there shines out the light of courtesy."* That prompted the poet to write a poem on courtesy, the opening stanza of which is:

> *"Of courtesy, it is much less*
> *Than courage of heart or holiness,*
> *Yet in my walks it seems to me*
> *That the grace of God is in courtesy."*

Contemplating the Virgin Mary in the mural, as she rides out from Nazareth to visit her cousin Elizabeth, the poet remarks that:

> *"Her face was both great and kind,*
> *For courtesy was in her mind." (H. Belloc).*

Of all the mysteries of the rosary the second joyful mystery is that in which courtesy is foremost. The visit which Mary made to her cousin was a visit of courtesy. Elizabeth immediately recognized it as such, for she exclaimed in grateful wonder, *"And why has this happened to me, that the mother of my Lord comes to me?"* (Lk 1:43). Elizabeth thus responds to the courtesy of Mary in coming to visit her, and Mary matches Elizabeth's courtesy with yet another gesture of courtesy in allowing Elizabeth to speak. Mary simply greeted Elizabeth and then allowed her cousin to speak. Elizabeth for her part shows a delicate courtesy to Mary. She did not start talking about her child or about her good news. All her words were directed to the praise of Mary and of the Child she was bearing in her womb. *"Blessed is she,"* exclaims Elizabeth, *"who believed that there would be a fulfillment of what was spoken to her by the Lord."* (Ibid., v. 45). Mary's courteous reaction is not one of false humility, but a simple hymn of joyful thanksgiving to Him Who was ever mindful of the poor. It could be said that in praising God, her Saviour, for remembering the poor, Mary was anticipating by thirty years her Son's first beatitude: *"Blessed are the poor in spirit, for theirs is the Kingdom of Heaven."* (Mt 5:3).

How the feast of the Visitation of Our Lady came to be linked with the feast of the Visitatrixes of the Company, I do not know. Was it because there is a certain kinship between the words Visitation and

Visitatrix, or because Visitatrixes, especially nowadays, must undertake many journeys so that they keep in contact with the Sisters of their Provinces and support them in the living of their vocation? What is certain is that the office of Visitatrix calls for those qualities which Mary of Nazareth exhibits in the second joyful mystery of her Rosary: physical strength, authentic humility, openness to others, patient listening, joyful gratitude, and gentle courtesy. This is a formidable list of qualities which, like flowers, need careful cultivation, and which will not flourish without the living water of divine grace. Throughout the Company today and here at Jacob's Well, we ask the Lord to give our Visitatrixes that living water, while we for our part offer them the bread of our appreciation and thanks.

Relating the quality of courtesy to our Vincentian spirit, St. Louise with her emphasis in her correspondence on the importance of tolerance, gentleness and cordiality, offers us the ingredients of true Christian courtesy. These three qualities, so highly valued by St. Louise and which are the essence of courtesy, could be said to be close relations, if not daughters, of the three virtues that characterize all members of the Company.

Courtesy—the word itself almost evokes another age, another society. Be that as it may, it is certain that our society, marked as it is so often by anger and protest, has need of men and women who speak the living language of courtesy. Our society has need of people who will exemplify the qualities of tolerance, gentleness and cordiality. The Church and the world have need of guides who by their manner of living will point toward that more excellent way commended by St. Paul when he wrote that *"love is patient; love is kind; love is not envious or boastful or arrogant or rude. It does not insist on its own way; it is not irritable or resentful."* (1 Cor 13:4-5).

The most delicate flower of charity is courtesy.

> *"Our Lady out of Nazareth rode,*
> *It was her month of heavy load;*
> *Yet was her face both great and kind,*
> *For courtesy was in her mind."* (H. Belloc).

Something Lost

13 June 1991   Rome, Italy

My dear Sisters,

If you were able to visit all the parish churches in the world and see the statues that the faithful have placed in them, you might very well find that the statue which is most commonly found, after that of the Mother of God and St. Joseph, would be that of the saint whose feast we are celebrating today, St. Anthony of Padua or, if you prefer, St. Anthony of Lisbon.

We think of St. Anthony as the Saint who has a special interest in those who have lost objects and cannot find them. He is a very popular Saint and, although he is dead more than seven hundred fifty years, people talk to him in their prayers as if he had only died yesterday. He is the Saint who in heaven still seems to have the charism of finding things that have been lost.

Something that has been lost: those words were on the lips of Our Lord often enough. He said that He had come to save those who were lost. Jesus Christ loved to tell stories about finding things that had been lost. You will recall the parable of the woman who had ten coins and lost one. When Jesus told that story, was He thinking of His Mother Mary in Nazareth? Perhaps on some occasion He saw her seeking for a coin that had been lost. It is not always a sin, thank God, to lose or mislay things, and so Mary, like the rest of us, probably had that experience. You will recall, too, the parable of the man who had a hundred sheep and lost one; also the parable of the man who had two sons and lost one. Jesus Christ seems to have thought a lot about seeking and finding what was lost.

All our lives we are seeking something we have lost. Our hearts, whether we fully recognize it or not, are seeking the God Who made us and that paradise which Adam and Eve lost. We are, as we so often say in the Salve Regina, *"exsules Hevae," "poor banished children of Eve."* The experience of this Assembly is a seeking for something which in a sense we feel we have lost. Is there anyone here who would not like to have had the experience of being members of one of those communities which St. Vincent and St. Louise in their lifetime guided? We feel, perhaps, that we have lost the freshness and the simplicity and the openness of those first communities with whom our Founders conversed. Our search to find what we feel we may have lost, is made more difficult by the complexity and number of cultures in which today the Company now finds itself implanted.

The Church in our day has become more sensitive in its appreciation of the values it finds in the different cultures of our world. That must be considered a gain for our generation. It must, however, be recognized that the values of any particular culture are not supreme. Not all the values of a culture are Gospel values. Cultures are in need of evangelization. In his recent encyclical on the missions, Pope John Paul II has remarked that *"since culture is a human creation and is therefore marked by sin, it, too, needs to be healed, enobled and perfected."* (*Redemptoris Missio,* §54). It was Paul VI who stated in his apostolic exhortation, *Evangelii Nuntiandi, "the rift between the Gospel and culture is undoubtedly an unhappy circumstance of our times, just as it has been in other eras."* (§20).

To the person of faith the sociological values of a culture will always be subordinate to theological ones. Because sociological values are more apparent, there is always the risk that the theological values will be overlooked. St. Paul found a lost theological value when he discovered that his preaching of a powerless and crucified Christ was a barrier to belief for the Jews and sheer nonsense for the Gentiles, but ultimately a revelation to the people of his time of the power and the wisdom of God. (cf. 1 Cor 1:23-25). Perhaps it is that we, who live in an age that has lost to a degree a sense of the transcendence of God, must come to a fresh discovery of that truth and of that wisdom which comes from a loving contemplation of the poor, obedient and humble Christ on the Cross. Perhaps we stand in need of a revision course in what St. Paul calls *"the language of the Cross."* (1 Cor 1:18).

You may be saying to yourselves that I have lost St. Anthony. So let me end by telling you of a woman who once said to me that St. Anthony was fond of money. I asked her to explain what she meant. She told me that, when you ask St. Anthony to help you find something that you have lost, you must also promise him that you will give some money to the poor; otherwise he will do nothing for you. I don't believe that the saints in heaven can be bribed in such a crude way. But I do believe that there is no one in heaven who is not interested in seeing the poor helped. It cannot be otherwise, since everyone in heaven has passed the test set forth by Our Lord in the twenty-fifth chapter of St. Matthew's Gospel.

May God in His mercy, through the intercession of His Mother Mary, our Founders and St. Anthony, help us to find His Son, lost today, as always, in the persons of the poor.

Spiritual Testament of St. Louise de Marillac

24 June 1991   St. Louis, Missouri

My dear Friends of Jesus Christ,

In the large community dining room of the Vincentian Mother House in Paris there hang on the end wall of the wooden panelled room two sizeable portraits. One is of St. Vincent and the other of St. Louise. Both were painted in the last century by a Brother of the Community who was endowed with considerable artistic talent. In the portrait of St. Vincent, who then was already more than a hundred years canonized, he is depicted as standing in a warm glow of bright colors, holding in his hand a crucifix on which he is gazing intently. St. Louise is presented as a slight figure, dressed in widow's weeds and without a halo. She sits demurely with a book in her hand and wearing an expression of serenity tinged, however, with a certain sadness. The twin portraits are a study in contrasts: St. Vincent stands as a man of action, St. Louise sits as a woman of patient waiting. Perhaps it is the background of St. Louise's portrait, which is that of a parlor or waiting room, that lends the impression of patient waiting to the entire picture. Let me imaginatively suggest that St. Louise is waiting to be interviewed by a board of men who in seventeenth century Paris are seeking a Director for a number of social projects.

The applicant will be expected to initiate and supervise projects for the care of prisoners, infants of one-parent families, schools for the handicapped and poor, the staffing of hospitals, day centers for the elderly, and residential homes for low income groups. The projects are multiple, but one executive director is being sought. Although it is not explicitly stated, the interviewing board expects that only men will apply. To their surprise a woman comes forward and she is a widow. During the interview she comes across as a quiet and decidedly intro-spective character. She seems to be excessively absorbed in the welfare of her only child. The panel of interviewers confer. No, she is not the person for the post. To begin with, she is a woman. She would not have the required energy and organizational ability. Besides, how could a woman who seems to be so over-anxious about her only son be capable of transcending herself to be of assistance to the dozens of social workers whose work she will have to supervise, not to mention the hundreds of poor and deprived people with whom she will have indirect, and sometimes direct, contact. The board expresses their regret to the applicant.

You might well ask me when the imaginative interview took place. Let me say shortly after Christmas 1625. It had been a sad Christmas that year for Louise, for only four days before the feast, her husband, Antoine, had died, leaving her with a twelve-year-old son, Michel. She had presented herself for the interview because, although she was assured of a modest income, still she had to think of her son Michel and of his future. Besides, she was aware of her capacity to give service to others. Her husband's illness had been long and debilitating and she had devoted her energies to caring for him. Now there was a void in her life.

In the course of the interview she had been asked what previous experience she had of working in the social services. She had to admit with some embarrassment that she had none. What interests had she, apart from being a wife and mother? She could truthfully say that she liked to do a little portrait painting. Before the death of her father, she had received the benefit of an education in a rather high-class convent school. Her grand aunt, a member of that particular religious community, had tutored her in art and literature. The questioner was surprised when Louise had dropped the word *literature*, for women generally were not conversant with literature. Rather bashfully Louise explained that she liked to read some of the well-known modern spiritual authors, like Francis de Sales, who had died three years earlier, and the works of Benedict of Canfield, and the *Imitation of Christ.* *"The Imitation of Christ,"* remarked the interviewer. *"So you know Latin?"* Louise replied simply that she could read it with a certain facility, and then she was silent.

When she left the room, the interviewing board agreed among themselves that Louise had indeed received an education in the arts and humanities that was rather exceptional for any contemporary woman. They could see that the cast of her mind was more speculative than practical, and that consequently she was not suited for the rough and tumble of life among what the board rather smugly described as the *"lower classes."* *"A tearful widow,"* remarked one of them patronizingly, *"with aspirations to be a mystic."*

That she was a tearful widow in the early months of 1626 was evident, but that she had aspirations to be a mystic was a judgment that was not so evident. Her aspirations were to do the Will of God, for the teachers of the school of spirituality which she had frequented stressed over and over again that the fulfillment of the Will of God was the central and indispensable condition of all sanctity. Her aspirations were to sanctity and not to mysticism. Certainly her present confessor and spiritual director, Monsieur Vincent, did not speak of mysticism. Coming from the plains of the Landes district, he was a man who was content to point out to people fields which had rich soil, and then would leave them to open the furrows themselves, according as the Divine Landowner might suggest through His grace and inspiration.

To come back to the St. Lazare portrait of St. Louise and the impression of patient waiting that it communicates, it must be said that it is not the parlor or waiting room background that imparted that gift of patient waiting to St. Louise. The deeply spiritual experience which St. Louise had on Pentecost Sunday 1623 in the Church of St. Nicolas des Champs had at once tranquilized her spirit and schooled her to waiting patiently for the *Kairos* of God's Providence in the future. *"I was advised,"* she wrote years later, *". . . that a time would come when I would be in a position to make vows of poverty, chastity and obedience and that I would be in a small Community where others would do the same . . . . I was also assured that God would give me one whom He seemed to show me."* (*Spiritual Writings of Louise de Marillac*, A.2, p. 1).

Ten years were to pass before that design of God was to be realized, and Louise was blessed in having as Director a man who held it as a cardinal principle that one must always walk a pace or two behind the Providence of God on the road of life, and that to overtake Providence on that road was to risk collision with forces beyond one's powers. It was during that ten-year period that Monsieur Vincent, writing to St. Louise, had remarked that: *"one beautiful diamond is worth more than a mountain of stones, and one virtuous act of acquiescence and submission is better than an abundance of good works done for others."* (Coste I, Eng. ed., ltr. 46, p. 75).

Diamonds are not found on the surface of the ground. Their beauty is hidden in the darkness of the earth. So one could easily understand why an interviewing board in 1626 might have missed perceiving the deeper and more precious qualities of mind and will that lay hidden behind the features and demeanor of the young widow, Louise de Marillac. Had the interview taken place five or six years later, some of the qualities of a diamond would have appeared more easily. The Board would have learned how Louise had, in the course of a little over a year, not only visited but established and organized the Confraternities of Charity in a number of parishes. The journeys she had undertaken and her calm reaction to opposition, which on occasion she had encountered, revealed a diamond-like quality of hardness in her personality that was at once resistant and attractive.

Those years 1630 and 1631 brought Louise into contact with a wide circle of people. There were those passengers in the sometimes uncomfortable coach journeys which she was now taking. Not all of them were as educated and refined as Louise, and as for the coachmen, their language was not always that of the convent at Poissy where she had received a lady's education. There were, too, in the different parochial centers she was now visiting, the Ladies of middle and upper class society whom she was grouping and quietly organizing in the service of the poor. She would patiently explain to them the spiritual and practical directives which the Parisian priest, Monsieur Vincent, had drawn up. Then, there were the sick poor in their homes, some of whom in company with the Ladies, she would visit, suggesting practical advice on how the service could be best offered.

"Would to God," wrote Monsieur Vincent to Louise when she was in the city of Beauvais, *"that good Madame de la Croix could follow your advice! It would be worth as much to her as a good religious order would be. As for the drugs, you have done well to deliver them, but your treasurer should not have bought them; she does not realize where that may lead."* (Coste I, Eng. ed., ltr. 58, p. 93), and in another letter, *"You will be talked about at the St. Benoit meeting. Mademoiselle Tranchot is relating wonders about you. I do think it would be a good idea for you to take the trouble to visit the good woman in order to stabilize her spirit so that she can easily strengthen the others!"* (Ibid., p. 96).

This gift of leading others, or rather of collaborating humbly with others and thus unobtrusively helping them to develop their talents of service, must have given Louise a certain sureness of touch when on 29 November 1633 she gathered into her own house a small group of young girls. To these girls, coming in the main from rural France, she would impart a basic spiritual formation that would motivate them to give themselves fully to God for the service of the poor.

The work of forming the village girls in her house was time consuming and might well have given Louise a good excuse for remaining at home. Not so. Her delicate sense of responsibility led her to travel to the various parochial centers throughout France, where the Sisters had been placed. The little communities needed consolidation. Much could be done by letter, but her meditations on the Incarnation led her to appreciate the value of personal presence among those whom she wished to confirm in their vocation of serving Christ in the poor. What modern executives and personnel managers are now discovering about the importance of personal contact with employees, if the efficiency of a firm is to be improved, Louise de Marillac had adopted as normal practice more than three centuries ago. She could have enlightened and astounded our imaginary board of interviewers with her insights, but then they did not pose the question to her because it was beyond the horizons of their minds.

Travelling was costly for Louise, not so much in financial terms as in the expenditure of physical energy. On the 2 February 1640 Louise took the coach from the city of Angers to Paris. It would be several days before she would reach Paris. She had already spent three months in

Angers, where she had been negotiating the terms of a contract with the secular administrators of the hospital there. Only the day previously she had signed the contract according to which the Daughters of Charity would undertake the nursing of the sick poor in the hospital. It was winter time, and throughout the weeks she had spent in Angers, Louise's health had caused some concern. Back in Paris Monsieur Vincent was aware of the fact and somewhat worried about the effect which the rigors of the return journey would have on Louise's health. Monsieur Vincent contemplated hiring a special coach in Paris and sending it to Angers or, if not, he suggested that Mademoiselle should travel "Business Class." Three letters within ten days touched on the matter. He wrote:

"With regard to your return, I ask you to let it be as soon as possible. Hire a stretcher and rent two good strong horses. I would have sent you a litter, but I do not know which you need, a litter or a stretcher. I entreat you, Mademoiselle, to spare nothing and, whatever it may cost, to get what will be the most comfortable for you." (Coste II, Eng. ed., ltr. 420, pp. 11-12). Six days later he writes again: *"If you take a stretcher, as I wrote you to do, because the coach, especially on the cobblestones, from Orleans to Paris would be too hard on you, it will suffice to have one Sister with you. You can have the others come by water as far as Tours and by coach from there to here."* (Ibid., p. 12). Three days later the subject is raised again: *"But what are you saying about coming back by water, Mademoiselle! O Jesus! You must do no such thing! Please have a stretcher hired and rent or, rather, buy two good horses—we will pay here what they cost—and come home that way."* (Ibid., p. 15).

The Sisters at Angers might well have offered themselves to our Board of Interviewers as guarantors of Louise's ability to formulate clearly the theory and practice of good interpersonal relations. Four years after her return to Paris in 1644 she wrote to the Sisters there: *"If our Sister is depressed or forlorn, if she is too quick or too slow, what in the world do you expect her to do about it? This is part of her character. Although she often tries to overcome herself, nevertheless, she cannot prevent these inclinations from frequently appearing. And should her Sister, who is supposed to love her as herself, become annoyed with her, be rude to her or frown upon her? O my dear Sisters,*

*be on your guard against acting like this. Instead, pretend that you do
not notice it and do not criticize her, bearing in mind that it will soon
be your turn when you will want her to act this way toward you."*
(*Spiritual Writings of Louise de Marillac*, ltr. 104B, p. 114).

It is not surprising that a woman with such penetrating psychological
powers should have had a facility of collaborating easily with others. It
can be said that one of Louise's outstanding gifts was precisely that of
collaboration. She would undoubtedly put forward Monsieur Vincent as
her great collaborator in her projects for the needy, the destitute and the
sick poor of her day. To collaborate with one of Monsieur Vincent's
intellectual caliber and sensitive compassion, not to mention his holiness,
may not have been difficult. Clearly Louise had complete confidence in
his judgment on spiritual as well as on administrative and temporal matters.
What, perhaps, may easily escape observation are Louise's powers of
thinking independently of Monsieur Vincent and of taking on occasion a
longer view of a question. Such independence of thought served to
complement and enhance the collaboration between the two Saints.

Two incidents will suffice to illustrate the point. First, the project for
the care of the foundlings at Bicêtre. It would seem that Louise saw
more clearly than either Monsieur Vincent or the Ladies of Charity the
impracticality of placing the foundlings in a large rambling castle which
had been long vacant and which in Louise's words had become *"the
haunt by day and by night of all sorts of evil persons,"* (Coste II, Eng.
ed., ltr. 770, p. 596) and which would entail enormous expense to make
it properly habitable. (cf. Ibid., p. 597). Louise's letter to Monsieur
Vincent on this occasion sets out clearly and compellingly the reasons
for not acquiring the castle. Either Monsieur Vincent or the Ladies did
not see the force of her arguments; the Ladies pressed ahead and the
transfer of the foundlings was made, a move which was later recognized
to have been a very costly mistake. One happy consequence, however,
of the mistake was that it provided Monsieur Vincent with the occasion
of making, after being strongly prompted by Louise, one of his most
moving appeals to the Ladies of Charity. He begged them to give
generously and without counting the cost, so that the lives of the
foundlings might be saved. (Coste III, Eng ed., ltr. 1090, pp. 402-405).

A second example of Louise's tenacious independence of judgment can be seen in her determination to have the Company of the Daughters of Charity placed under the authority of Monsieur Vincent and his successors, rather than under that of the local bishops. Louise saw this arrangement as the best means of assuring unity of spirit and of direction in the Company. What was her dismay, then, when in November 1646 Monsieur Vincent seemed to acquiesce meekly in the decision of the Archbishop of Paris that the Company be subject to him. Almost nine years would pass before Louise would secure what she had long desired, prayed and worked for. It was on the 18 January 1655 that Cardinal de Retz, Archbishop of Paris, signed the document committing to his *"dear and beloved Vincent de Paul . . . the care and guidance of the aforesaid Society and Confraternity, during his life and after him to his general successors of the Said Congregation of the Mission."* (*La Compagnie des Filles de la Charité: Documents*, pp. 676-678, ed. Sr. Elisabeth Charpy, Paris 1989).

Louise's ability to collaborate with people was a grace she shared with others. Barbe Angiboust at Fontainbleau is offered some advice on how she should relate with the Queen, (cf. *Spiritual Writings of Louise de Marillac*, ltr. 435, p. 189), while Julienne Loret is counselled on how she might cope with a difficult pastor of Jansenist leanings (cf. Ibid., ltr.302, p. 349). Perhaps the most delicate tribute of all to Louise's powers of collaboration was something that happened a few hours after her death on 15 March 1660. She had expressed a wish in her Testament to Monsieur Vincent that she be buried close to the Priests of the Mission (*La Compagnie des Filles de la Charité: Documents*, p. 997). He agreed, but her wish was set aside when the pastor and people of the parish of St. Laurent, where she had lived and where she was known and loved, expressed their strong desire that her remains be interred in their parish church. And so it was done, a deft finishing touch to the portrait of one who was an artist of collaboration.

The spiritual gifts of Louise de Marillac were many and neither a portrait in oils nor the probing questions of an interviewing board could fully reveal them to us. *"No one comprehends what is truly God's,"* wrote St. Paul, *"except the Spirit of God."* (1 Cor 2:11). A remarkable feature of Louise's pilgrimage to God is that, as she advanced along the way, she became more aware of the guiding presence of the Spirit of

God in her own life and in that of the Company. The feast of Pentecost became for St. Louise a significant landmark in her pilgrimage. It was on Pentecost Sunday, the 4 June 1623, that she emerged from a dark night of spiritual purification. Twenty-one years later on the eve of Pentecost 1644, she and a sizeable group of Ladies of Charity were providentially saved from death or serious injury when the floor of a room, where they should have been present but were not, collapsed. The coincidence of that event with the vigil of Pentecost was not lost on Louise. In a new way she became conscious of the overshadowing and protective wings of Him Who is traditionally represented by a white dove.

It was, however, in the final decade of her life that her sensitivity to the presence and role of the Holy Spirit was most marked. The Spirit of God in the thought of Louise was the prolongation of the presence and action of Christ in the Church. One must, following the spirit of the final injunction of Christ, keep oneself, as did Mary and the first disciples, in a continual state of readiness for a fresh descent of the Holy Spirit. Such an attitude calls for a total and trustful surrender to the designs of God as they unfold themselves in the pattern of each day's events. *"Souls that are truly poor and desirous of serving God should place their trust in the coming of the Holy Spirit within them believing that, finding no resistance in them, He will give them the disposition necessary to accomplish the holy Will of God which should be their only preoccupation."* (*Spiritual Writings of Louise de Marillac*, A.25, p. 802).

A charming portrait of the spiritual gifts of Louise emerges from the reflections which Monsieur Vincent, along with the Sisters of the Mother House, made on two days during July 1660. Let us eavesdrop for a moment on what is being said by the Sisters gathered around the now aged and fragile Vincent in the Community Room of the Sisters' Mother House:

> *Father, I noticed that she was most careful and ardently desired that the Company should preserve the spirit of poverty and humility and often used to say, 'We are the servants of the poor; therefore, we should be poorer than they.' . . . . 'Your remark about her, Sister, is in my opinion*

most true, when you tell us that she loved poverty greatly.
You saw how she was dressed, clad in the poorest fashion,
and she loved this virtue so much that she asked me long ago
that she might live as a poor woman. She always urged that
the Company should preserve this spirit which is certainly
a sovereign means for its preservation.'" . . . . *'And you,*
Sister?' 'Father, I remarked that her letters were written in
a very humble style . . . . *She had great charity for the Sisters*
and was afraid of annoying them. She did her best not to
displease anyone and always excused the absent. This did
not prevent her from correcting faults, but she always did
so most skillfully and patiently. She always urged us to take
great care of the poor and looked on whatever was done for
them as done to herself. She often advised us in her letters
to observe the rule and to live in great union with one
another.' 'And you, my Daughter?' 'I have noticed, Father,
all that our Sisters have said is quite true. Moreover, she
had the patience of a saint, great charity and wonderful
humility.' Ah! Sisters, exclaims St. Vincent, what a picture
does God place before your eyes and painted by yourselves!
Yes, it is a picture which we possess and which we should
regard as a prototype that should animate us to do likewise,
to acquire her humility, charity, forbearance, firmness in all
her government, and that should also animate us to remem-
ber how in all her actions she tended to conform them to
those of Our Lord . . . . *This, Sisters, then, is a picture which*
you should gaze on, a picture of humility, charity, meekness,
patience in infirmities. Behold what a picture! And how are
you to make use of it, my dear Sisters? By striving to form
your life on hers . . . . *A beautiful picture, O my God! This*
humility, faith, prudence, sound judgment and always an
anxiety to conform all her actions to those of Our Lord.
(Conf. Eng. ed., 3 and 24 July 1660, pp. 1258-1281).

Perhaps it would be timely to commission another artist to present our Mother House in Paris with a new portrait of St. Louise.

A double title was suggested to me for this talk: *"The Gifts of St.*

Louise. The Future of the Legacy. " I must confess to have been puzzled by the second title and to have been at a loss about what I should say about the future of the legacy. Moreover, I experienced a certain reluctance to don the prophet's mantle and would prefer instead to heed Thornton Wilder's dictum that *"the future is the most expensive luxury in the world. "* Perhaps I should plead my poverty at this point and bow out.

I hope that you will excuse me if what I have to say about the future of the legacy is more in the nature of a simple postscript to what I have presented, rather than a full treatment of the topic. That we have received a spiritually rich legacy from St. Louise is certain. Perhaps we have not been fully aware of the size and value of that legacy she has left us. More than three centuries have passed since St. Louise died, and perhaps it is only in this decade, and more particularly during this year, that the Vincentian Family is discovering fully the gold of spirituality that St. Louise has left us as a legacy.

Let us listen to her spiritual Testament: *"My dear Sisters, I continue to ask God for His blessings for you and pray that He will grant you the grace to persevere in your vocation in order to serve Him in the manner He asks of you. Take good care of the service of the poor. Above all, live together in great union and cordiality, loving one another in imitation of the union and life of Our Lord. Pray earnestly to the Blessed Virgin, that she may be your only Mother. "*

This spiritual Testament was recorded by the Sisters who attended St. Louise during her final illness. We are indebted for this text to Don Nicolas Gobillon who in 1676 wrote the first biography of St. Louise. The Testament of St. Louise is more than a testament. It could be said to be a succinct spiritual autobiography and a summary of the principal themes on which she spoke and wrote to the Sisters during the almost three decades she guided the Company.

". . . To serve Him in the manner He asks you. " Discovering the Will of God moment by moment and a faithful and loving fulfillment of it was the pivot around which all St. Louise's actions turned. *"Courage then, my dear Sisters, "* she had written in June 1642. *"Seek only to please God by faithfully observing His commandments and evangelical counsels . . . . "* (*Spiritual Writings of Louise de Marillac*, ltr. 441, p. 75).

"Take good care of the poor . . . . " It was a counsel that St. Louise had lived herself. *"I have seen her,"* remarked a Sister after her death, *"gathering poor people round her who were coming out of prison; she washed their feet, dressed their sores and took great pleasure in serving them. "* (Conf. Eng. ed., 3 July 1660, p. 1259).

"Above all, live together in great union and cordiality . . . . " In the vision of St. Louise, the Sisters were to warm themselves at the fire of mutual charity within the Community before going out to offer a spark of that fire of love to the poor through their services of caring, teaching, supporting and comforting. All that humble and loving service was to be inspired by the example of Christ with whom they should remain intensely united at all times.

"Pray earnestly to the Blessed Virgin that she may be your only Mother." The phrase, *"only Mother,"* had been used on a number of occasions by St. Louise before she uttered it in her final testament. St. Louise, who had not known her natural mother, had clearly found a mother in the Immaculate Virgin Mother of God. St. Louise wished that the Sisters would experience something of that love and tenderness which she over seven decades of her life had found in Mary, *"the only Mother."*

The biographer, Gobillon, records that after St. Louise had left her testament to her Sisters, she said that *"if I were to live a hundred years, I would make the same recommendations to you. "* (Gobillon, *La Vie de Mme Le Gras*, Paris, 1676, p. 175). Thus we, who this year commemorate the four hundredth year of her birth, have from St. Louise herself a firm assurance that her Testament is still valid today, and indeed for the future, for:

"Time present and time past
Are both perhaps present in time future,
And time future contained in time past. " (T.S. Eliot "Burnt Norton" in *Four Quartets*).

Martyrs of Arras

26 June 1991   Montreal, Canada

My dear Sisters and my dear Confreres,

Today the two Communities of St. Vincent are honoring a group of Daughters of Charity who seventy-one years ago this year were beatified by Pope Benedict XV. In 1994 we will be celebrating the two hundredth anniversary of the martyrdom of these four Daughters of Charity. It was on this day that they witnessed for Christ by undergoing martyrdom in Cambrai in France.

When we think of martyrs, our minds probably travel back to the eras in the history of the Church when Christians were being persecuted in great numbers. We think of the decades of persecution that Christians suffered before Christianity was recognized by the Roman Emperor. Our minds will make contact, too, with Christians of the last century in China, notably two martyrs of our own Community, John Gabriel Perboyre and Francis Regis Clet, and the Daughters of Charity whom we are honoring today. In this century we will think of the excesses of Stalin against Ukrainian Catholics.

But what of the present? Is the present climate in the world such that we have seen the end of martyrdom? With the political changes in Russia and Eastern Europe, can we say that the age of martyrs is over? We may be inclined to think along such lines, but further reflection will show us that the age of martyrs has not passed. Eighteen months ago we had six Jesuits in San Salvador brutally murdered because they were strong witnesses for Christ and His Gospel.

During my visit to Czechoslovakia last year I talked with a Jesuit Bishop. He was ordained a priest in 1950 and then a year later secretly ordained a Bishop in the basement of a hospital. For eighteen or nineteen years he worked clandestinely, and then in the brief year of Dubcek he surfaced. With the advent of the Russians he was put into prison because he was known to be a Bishop. After his release in 1978 attempts were made on his life by agents of the secret police and he was subject to much harassment, until a year ago when his country became free. Following that he was officially named Bishop of one of the ancient dioceses of Czechoslovakia. Eight years in prison and then ten years of harassment by the police is a form of suffering that comes very close to martyrdom. That Bishop is among those who in two days' time will be created Cardinal by the Holy Father.

An element in the expression of most martyrs is that of resistance. Martyrs are Christians who, when asked to say *yes*, uttered a categorical *no* because of the convictions of their faith. They persisted in saying *no* under suffering that was inflicted upon them and brought them to death. They did this because of their loyalty to Jesus Christ and to His Church.

If the word martyr means *witness*—and all of us are called to be witnesses to Christ—where is the element of witness in our lives, and where is the element of resistance? For us, priests and Sisters, we should look for it first in the area of our vows. Where do others see resistance in our lives? For all Christians resistance will be shown by being obedient to the Gospel of Jesus Christ and to His Church. That is not always easy. It is always easy to do something that everyone else is doing, but that does not mean that it is always right. It takes courage to profess our faith in word and action. When courage is called for, resistance will be called for. Pilate had not the courage to go against the crowd when they asked that Jesus be crucified. He had no courage. He could put up no resistance.

Our Lord has said: *"You also are witnesses because you have been with Me from the beginning."* (Jn 15:27). It is the Spirit of God, as Our Lord reminds us, Who will support us and strengthen us in giving witness to Him, in being martyrs. *"If our perfection is to be found in charity, as is clear,"* wrote St. Vincent, *"then there is no greater charity than that of giving oneself for the salvation of souls and to be consumed for them in the way that Jesus Christ was."* (Coste VII, Fr. ed., pp. 292-293).

May Blessed Marie Madeleine and her companions intercede for us so that our charity may be perfected for the salvation of souls and for the glory of God.

Jesus Christ Cures the Leper

28 June 1991   Montreal, Canada

My dear Confreres and my dear Sisters,

I invite you to enter into the mind of the leper as he made his journey to meet Jesus. It is certain that he would have had to make a journey, for as we know, lepers were obliged to live away from the local community. So, let us enter into this poor man's thoughts as he hobbled along the road to meet Jesus. *"My condition is getting worse. I am growing weaker. My limbs are wasting away and are falling off. I do not see much hope for my future. If I am to live, I must do something. I must try something that I have not tried before. I have heard people talking about this marvelous man, Jesus of Nazareth. He has cured many people. I heard He cured ten lepers. Perhaps He would cure me. But how can I get close to Him? It means breaking the law if I go into a town to get close to Him. Then, even if I do get close to Him, perhaps He will repel me, in the same way as people repel and strike mosquitoes. However, I think He is a very compassionate man. He will feel sorry for my condition, and perhaps He will cure me—perhaps. Anyway it is worth trying. So I will keep on walking until I meet Him."*

The leper who came to Jesus should not have come to Him. When he did come, Jesus felt compassion for him as He did for all those who came to be healed. He stretched out His hand and touched him. That in itself was a courageous gesture. *"Be cured. And the leprosy left him at once."* (Mt 8:3).

Jesus asked the leper not to speak about it, but the leper in his joy and exultation could not keep quiet. St. Mark in his Gospel observes that the leper told everybody about it *"so that Jesus could no longer go openly into any town, but had to stay outside in places where nobody lived."* (Mk 1:45). We could say that, having cured a leper out of compassion, Jesus had to experience something of the solitude and loneliness which lepers experienced.

We here in modern cities do not meet people suffering from the physical disease of leprosy. We do, however, encounter very frequently nowadays people who suffer from the pain of solitude and loneliness.

For some of our elderly people, loneliness could be described as the disease of our times. For you, Daughters of Charity, who are devoted to the service of the poor, the loneliness and solitude of the aged must be one of the modern forms of poverty which you are trying to alleviate.

Speaking to members of St. Vincent's Communities, I would like to make a passing reference to the fact that, even within our own communities, there can be members who suffer acutely from loneliness and solitude. Perhaps it is that we do not find some of the members of our community attractive persons, but then Jesus did not find the leper of today's Gospel a particularly attractive person, and yet He stretched out His hand and touched him. May God give us the grace of sharing the sentiments of the human Heart of Jesus Christ, so that we can stretch out our hands to touch, not only the poor and the outcasts of our society, but those who, within our own community, feel alone and isolated.

Frequently I have the privilege of visiting the sick Sisters in the Infirmary. To them I always express my gratitude for the prayers which they offer, not only for the Mother General, for me and all others who hold authority in our Community, but also for the prayers and sufferings they offer for the two families of St. Vincent. In my own Province, I knew a very saintly and good-humored Confrere who used to tell us at table that the only hope we Vincentians had of getting to heaven was through the prayers of the Daughters of Charity.

I seem to have moved away from the Gospel of today. Let me say by way of conclusion: Jesus cured the leper, but He did not wish the fact to be made known. That is the way St. Vincent and St. Louise would like us to work in the Community and for the poor, quietly and without seeking praise. Such is the Vincentian way of working for God's Kingdom.

Story of a Soul

17 July 1991   Nanga Pinoh, Indonesia

My dear Confreres,

One of the great spiritual classics of our times is the autobiography of St. Thérèse of Lisieux which she entitled, *The Story of a Soul*. It is a book that is written with that simplicity which characterized the spirituality of her whom we know as the *Little Flower*. It is a book that is characterized by that simplicity for which Our Lord gives thanks in today's Gospel: *"Father, Lord of heaven and earth, to You I offer praise for what You have hidden from the learned and the clever, You have revealed to the merest children."* (Mt 11:25).

Each of us could write a book entitled, *The Story of a Soul*, recounting the way in which we found our vocation and the story of some of the great graces which God has given us since we entered the Community. Our book might not have the simplicity nor the depth of St. Thérèse's. Nevertheless, it is true that God calls each of us to the Community through different ways and different events. In our meditation it is good to reflect often on the fact that, while we share with others a common vocation, God thinks and deals with each of us individually. We can never forget Our Lord's parable of the lost sheep. The shepherd left the ninety-nine in order to seek out the one that was lost. *"I am the Good Shepherd and I know mine and mine know Me."* (Jn 10:14).

The first reading of today's Mass is about a shepherd and some lost sheep. However, it is much more than that. It is the story of the way in which Moses found his vocation. Moses was looking for some lost sheep when he noticed a bush which was burning but not being consumed. Out of curiosity he went over to see the strange sight. It was then that God called him to lead His people. *"Come, now! I will send you to Pharaoh to lead My people, the Israelites, out of Egypt."* (Ex 3:10). It was then that God gave him the assurance: *"I will be with you."* (Ibid., v. 12).

When you look back on the history of your own vocation, you will probably discover that it was a chance meeting with a person, a remark made about the missions, or a very casual contact with a Confrere, that led you to the Community. God used that event, that person, that happening, to say to you what He said to Moses: *"Come."* As time went on and the ideals of St. Vincent and the Community were put before you, you probably felt like saying, as Moses did: *"Who am I?"* And in the history of your soul, more than once you have heard the voice of God, saying to you as He said to Moses, *"I will be with you."*

When I think of the missions of the Congregation, I think of you here in Kalimantan as being among those who are in the front line. I can recall vividly my last visit here when I learned of some of the difficulties under which you work. Your vocation calls for great generosity of heart and I know that almost all of you have given more than ten years of your life to working in this part of the Lord's vineyard.

May the Lord continue to be your strength and your joy. My prayer for you is that in the midst of so much hard work, you may find time daily to rest in the Lord through time spent in meditation. Let me quote Pope John Paul II in his recent encyclical on the missions: *"The missionary must be a 'contemplative in action.' He finds answers to problems in the light of God's word and in personal and community prayer. My contact with representatives of the non-Christian spiritual traditions, particularly those of Asia, has confirmed me in the view that the future of mission depends to a great extent on contemplation. Unless the missionary is a contemplative he cannot proclaim Christ in a credible way. He is a witness to the experience of God, and must be able to say with the Apostles: 'that which we have looked upon ... concerning the word of life, ... we proclaim also to you.'"* (1 Jn 1:1-3). (*Redemptoris Missio*, §91).

Do Whatever He Tells You

23 July 1991   Kediri, Indonesia

My dear Sisters and my dear Confreres,

When St. John the Evangelist was finishing the writing of his Gospel, he knew that there were very many more things he could say about Jesus Christ, but it would take too long to put them down on paper. *"There are also many other things which Jesus did,"* wrote St. John, *"if every one of them were to be written, I suppose that the world itself could not contain the books that would be written."* (Jn 21:25). When we listen to the Gospels being read, we often think that we would like to have more information about the events or the words of Jesus. We can only resign ourselves to waiting until we get to heaven to learn more about the details of Our Lord's life, death and resurrection.

When you heard in today's Gospel that, while Jesus was addressing the crowds, His Mother came on the scene and wanted to speak with Him, did the question: *"I wonder what she wanted from Him,"* arise in your mind? St. Matthew, the Evangelist, does not tell us. As long as we are in this life, we can only guess what she wanted from her Son, Jesus. She was a mother, so perhaps she wanted to assure herself that He had sufficient food and shelter, or perhaps she wanted to know if she could be of any practical assistance to Him in His work of preaching to the people. Did she come to ask Him to do a favor for a neighbor of theirs in Nazareth who was sick? Had she heard of some family in distress and too embarrassed to ask for help? Remembering the miracle He worked at Cana, did she come to ask Him to relieve the embarrassment of this family in the way that He had relieved the embarrassment of the hosts at the marriage feast of Cana?

Before Our Lord spoke to His Mother, He reminded the people that the important thing in life, and particularly for those who wanted to be His friends, was doing the Will of our Heavenly Father. Because He was thinking of His Mother at that particular moment, did He add, *"There is one person who at every moment of her life has done perfectly the Will of our Heavenly Father, and that person is My Mother Mary?"* If He did not say that on this particular occasion, He has said it since. Jesus Christ said that He would be with His Church until the end of time. We know that His Church has said with infallible certainty that Mary, Mother of Our Lord Jesus Christ, was not only conceived without sin but lived a totally sinless, life and so she perfectly fulfilled the Will of God at every moment.

Today both Our Lord and His Mother are body and soul in heaven. Their bodies are changed, but they are the same persons that they were on earth. Mary is still a mother. She is mother, as we know, to each one of us and, because she is a mother, she has a heart and an ear for all our needs. It is still her vocation to be a mother. We know that the smallest needs of a child will always receive the attention of its mother, if she is a good mother. Our Lady's greatest concern for us is that we would do the Will of God, for she knows that is the way that we will reach the place where she and her Son are now. If you do not know the way to a place, you will ask directions. The directions which Mary offers us are the same as those which she offered to the waiters at the marriage feast of Cana. On that occasion she said to the servants: *"Do whatever He tells you."* (Jn 2:4). She is saying the same to you and to me today. Do whatever Jesus tells you. Jesus Himself has left this earth, but He lives on in His Church, in the Sacraments and in the pages of the New Testament. So if we are to do what He wants us to do, we must listen to the Church. We must listen to His voice as it is expressed to us through our Constitutions and through our Superiors. We must reverently approach Him in the Sacraments and we must take a little time every day to reflect on His words as we hear them proclaimed in the Gospel at every Mass.

May Our Lady obtain for us all the grace of doing the Will of her Son as perfectly as our frail nature will allow.

The Prodigal Son

25 July 1991   Kediri, Indonesia

My dear Sisters,

Perhaps the most touching of all the parables which Our Lord told is that of the prodigal son. It is the parable that speaks most loudly of the mercy of God. It is the parable, too, that tells us most about the meaning of conversion. The details of that conversion are very familiar to us. One person who reflected and prayed upon this parable remarked that the whole story of the conversion of the prodigal son is to be found in two verbs. The request the younger son makes to his father is this: *"Father, give me the share of the property that falls to me."* (Lk 15:12). Toward the end of the parable, when the younger son returns home, the request he makes of his father is this: *"Father . . . make me as one of your hired servants."* (Ibid., v. 19). Between the *"give me"* of the beginning of the parable and the *"make me"* at the end lies the story of the conversion. There is an altogether different attitude of mind expressed in the *"give me my money"* and *"make me one of your hired servants."* In the story of any conversion you will find that the starting point is a selfish demand, and the finishing point is a readiness to be a servant.

The parable of the prodigal son came to my mind when reflecting on the Gospel to which we have just listened. It is not a story of a conversion, but rather the foretelling of a conversion that would take place. St. James wants Our Lord to give him one of the principal places in His kingdom and Our Lord foretells that he will be treated as Jesus Himself would be treated. He would drink from the same cup as Christ, the suffering servant, would drink from. To make the point clearer, Our Lord underlines how important it is that His disciples would have the attitude of a humble servant. *"Whoever would be great among you must be your servant . . . even as the Son of Man came, not to be served but to serve."* (Mt 20:26,28).

When Paul VI wrote the document, *Evangelii Nuntiandi*, he made the point that the first person to be evangelized was the evangelizer himself. How much evangelization of myself has yet to be done can come home to me when I reflect on how far I am from having the mind and the attitude of a servant in all that I do. There is a very big difference between offering service and being a servant. There are millions of people who offer service of one kind or another, but the number of people who have the deeply Christian attitude of being a servant is much fewer. In our Communities we speak of devoting our lives to the service of the poor. That is a laudable ideal. It will not, however, be realized in depth unless we are really servants. St. Vincent was very enlightened when he called the poor *"our lords and masters."* We cannot be true servants of the poor, either as priests or as Daughters of Charity, unless we are first servants of Our Lord. That opens up the whole dimension of the quality of obedience which we offer to God through our Community. When Mary was asked by the Angel Gabriel to become the Mother of God, she gave her consent by saying: *"I am the servant of the Lord."* (Lk 1:38). She did not say: *"I place myself in the service of the Lord."* In fact, the word she used was *slave*. *"I am the slave of the Lord."*

If we are to devote ourselves to the service of the poor, we must become their servants. We cannot become servants of the poor unless we are slaves of the Lord. It is a difficult ideal to live, but all things are possible by the grace of God. Our growth in holiness will have much to do with the development in ourselves of this attitude of being servants and slaves of the Lord. *"Have this mind among you which was in Christ Jesus,"* (Phil 2:5) and the mind which was in Christ Jesus was that of a servant. Today's Gospel makes it very plain to us. *"Whoever would be first among you must be your slave, even as the Son of Man came, not to be served but to serve."* (Mt 20:27-28). If St. Vincent gave so much importance to the virtue of humility when speaking to his two Communities, I think that the reason was that in our preaching or in our work for the poor, we would have the mind of Christ Jesus, the mind of a servant.

Through the intercession of the Mother of God, St. James and our Founders, may God give us all the grace of continual conversion, making us as one of His servants.

Multiplication of Loaves and Fishes
28 July 1991   Garum, Indonesia

My dear Confreres,

When we decide to give gifts to our friends at Christmas or on other occasions during the year, we like to prepare the gifts carefully. We look for a nice box or some fancy paper in which to put our gift. Then we may place in the box or parcel a card on which we write some lines of greeting. All this preparation helps the recipients of our gifts to enjoy the sensation of wondering or guessing what the gift might be.

When Jesus Christ came to give us the greatest gift He could, He prepared that gift very carefully. First, He promised the gift. Then later He prepared the setting or the room in which He would present the gift to His disciples and to us.

Today's Gospel is an account of some of the preparations which Our Lord made for giving us the gift of the Eucharist. In this sixth chapter of St. John's Gospel, you will notice how carefully Our Lord prepares His disciples for the gift He is going to give them. He begins by asking Philip a simple question: *"Where can we buy some bread for these people to eat?"* (Jn 6:5). Before we hear Philip's answer, St. John himself interrupts. *"He only said this,"* observes St. John, *"to test Philip. He Himself knew exactly what He was going to do."* (Ibid., v.

6). That is a little point which St. John likes to bring out in his Gospel, namely, that Jesus is Lord and Master of every situation.

After that Andrew makes his contribution to the community discussion. He does so, however, without much confidence, and he admits it. *"There is a boy here with five barley loaves and two fish, but what is that among so many?"* (Ibid., v. 9). Andrew must have been the most surprised of all when he saw that his suggestion was accepted by Jesus. The only person who could have been more surprised was the little boy, who must have wondered if he was going to lose completely the bread and the fish his mother had given him that morning.

Jesus is Lord of every situation, and so He uses the lunch of a little boy to feed a great multitude of people. He does the same today. No matter what evil people do, no matter how depressed we may sometimes feel about the future of this world, Jesus Christ, as we say so often in our prayers, *"lives and reigns forever and ever."*

Jesus today uses our gifts, our talents, the strength of our arms and the sweat of our brows, just as He used the lunch of the little boy in today's Gospel. The little boy had to give away his lunch first, so that it could be brought to Jesus. So, too, with us. If we are to be of use to Jesus Christ, we must surrender to Him what we have and what we are.

All of us are like that little boy. We have something in our hands. For some it may be sickness and suffering. Jesus Christ invites the sick, the old, the lonely, to put their suffering in the chalice at Mass. He can use it for the salvation of the world. Christ sacrificed Himself on the cross. Christ and His members, the baptized, sacrifice themselves in the Mass. If in the course of our day we meet with suffering, disappointment, anything that hurts, we must try not to grumble. It is our Mass. People will be saved only by sacrifice. The only sacrifice of lasting value in the world is Christ's Sacrifice, the Mass. Only insofar as my life is a life of sacrifice, in which I have given all to God, will it be of use for the saving of the world. So with St. Ignatius I pray: *"Dear Jesus, teach me to be generous. Teach me to give and not to count the cost . . . to look for no reward except knowing that I am doing Your holy Will."*

A Gospel of Delicacy

29 July 1991   Surabaya, Indonesia

My dear Friends of Jesus Christ,

I am very happy to have this opportunity of meeting you and celebrating the Eucharist with you who share with me the precious gift of the faith which we have received from Jesus Christ through the one, holy, catholic and apostolic Church. I recognize, too, that you share with me admiration for St. Vincent de Paul who by his words and by his life has shown us how we ought to fulfil the two great commandments of loving God and of loving our neighbor. It is a marvelous experience for me to visit different continents of the world and to meet people of many nationalities, cultures and languages, who are united by their love and admiration of this Saint who is called the Apostle of Charity, the friend of the poor and animator of the laity.

The reading from St. John's Gospel is chosen by the Church today because of St. Martha whose feast we celebrate. It is a passage of the Gospel which we associate with funeral Masses and the final prayers which are recited at the gravesides. How often have we heard those words of Our Lord, *"I am the Resurrection and the life. He who believes in Me, though he die, yet shall he live."* (Jn 11:25). Young people do not spend too much time reflecting on death. When I was young, I used to cherish the hope that I would be among those people whom St. Paul tells us will be alive when Our Lord will come again and who will escape death. When we grow a little older, we come to accept the inevitability of death, and we live in the assurance of Our Lord's words that He is the Resurrection and the Life and that, if we believe in Him, we shall never die. We live in the hope that we will be, in the words of the first Eucharistic prayer, *"saved from final damnation and counted among those whom God has chosen."*

It is not, however, upon death and the enormous assurance and hope that Our Lord gives us about it in today's Gospel that I wish to reflect. The account of the raising of Lazarus could be described as a Gospel of delicacy. When Martha and Mary became aware of Lazarus' serious illness, they sent the news of it to Jesus. Quite clearly they wanted Him to do something for them, but He did not. Have you noticed how delicately they expressed their request? *"He whom You love is sick."* (Jn 11:3). There is no shrill demand, just a gentle manifestation of their concern and an expression of implicit confidence that Jesus will do something for His friend Lazarus. When Jesus reaches Bethany after the death of Lazarus, both sisters express the same regret, but in a most delicate way. *"Lord, if You had been here, my brother would not have died."* (Jn 11:21, 32). It is not exactly a reproach, but rather a delicate expression of regret. What a response it drew forth from Jesus! Martha and Mary did not dream that their brother Lazarus would be called back to life. But the impossible happened. Lazarus came forth from his tomb.

In his letter to the Philippians, St. Paul expresses the hope that he may come to experience in his life and work *"the power of the Resurrection"* of Christ. (Phil 3:10). Too often we forget that we are not on our own. The power of the Resurrection of Christ is breaking into our lives and through us into the lives of others, as surely as it penetrated into the darkness of Lazarus' tomb. We do not raise people from the dead, but we must not interpret Our Lord's words, *"I am the Resurrection,"* as words which will be fulfilled only at the end of time. The power of the Risen Christ is already at work through us.

In speaking to you today, I am aware that many of you offer yourselves to Jesus Christ through participating in the Conferences of St. Vincent de Paul. Through the work of the Conferences you are fulfilling Our Lord's command of sharing practical love and concern for the poor, of bringing to them a little of the life of the Risen Christ. Our Lord has told us that in visiting prisoners, in caring for the sick, in feeding the hungry, we are rendering service to Him personally. We know, too, that the great test which we must pass, if we are to enter heaven, is a test in love. At the end of our lives God will ask us if we have shown practical love to the poor and needy. Jesus Christ feeds us with His body and blood. He asks us to feed with practical actions the poor and all people whose lives we touch. Pope John Paul II has told us that: *". . . whatever association of the lay faithful there might be, it is always called to be more of an instrument leading to holiness in the Church through fostering and promoting 'a more intimate unity between the everyday life of its members and their faith.'"* (*Christifideles Laici*, §30).

As Catholics you are a very small minority among the millions of people who live in your country. Let not the smallness of your number discourage you. Think of yourselves as points of light in your society. The light is not yours. It is Christ's. He is at work through you, even when you are hardly aware of it. To you I address the words which St. Vincent wrote in one of his letters: *"I ask Our Lord . . . to redouble your strength, to sustain you with the essence of His Spirit, to gladden you with the hope of His glory and the success of your work."* (Coste IV, Eng. ed., ltr. 1368, p. 214).

A Great Figure of Human Perfection
30 July 1991   Surabaya, Indonesia

My dear Sisters and my dear Confreres,

After Pope Paul VI canonized St. Justin de Jacobis on 26 October 1975, he spoke of him briefly at the window of his apartment before reciting the Angelus. The Pope said that Justin de Jacobis today has only one fault, namely, that *"he is not better known."* Perhaps the reason St. Justin is not better known is because of his humility. It was the humility of St. Justin that most impressed the Capuchin Bishop (later a Cardinal) who ordained Justin Bishop in 1849. Repeatedly in his reports to Rome, this Capuchin Bishop speaks of the humility of Justin de Jacobis. With difficulty Justin was persuaded to be ordained Bishop and when he was, it was in the dead of night (because of persecution) and with little ceremony in a country shed. It was through his deep and authentic humility that St. Justin cut a path into the hearts of the Orthodox clergy and people. His humility enabled him to be patient with the Orthodox clergy who were through prejudice initially opposed to him. It was his humility that made St. Justin de Jacobis a genuine ecumenist one hundred years before Vatican II. *"God raised up this great figure of human perfection,"* wrote the Capuchin, Bishop Massaia, *"on a base of humility, to be a lesson to Ethiopia and to the apostles who would carry on the work he began."*

Some years ago a Vincentian priest from England made a visit to Ethiopia and to the region where St. Justin worked. On his return journey he visited me in Rome. What impressed this priest most was that the people of Alitena spoke of St. Justin as if he had died only yesterday. The priest went on to reflect that, although other missionaries had come and perhaps had worked as hard for the people, it was Abuna Jacob's memory which was most fresh. It was clear that St. Justin's personal holiness had left a fragrance among the people which had not yet vanished. St. Justin was a great evangelizer. He had a deep conviction that the person who first needed evangelization was himself, and he gave himself the task to preach the Gospel to himself every day. That conviction of St. Justin found expression in almost identical words in the masterly document, *Evangelii Nuntiandi*, written by Pope Paul VI in 1975. In that document one will find expressed many insights which St. Justin had already acquired and put into practice in this land of Ethiopia more than one hundred years ago.

Had St. Justin been alive and present at Vatican Council II, I imagine he would have spoken very eloquently from his own experience on such arguments as ecumenical relations among Christians, relations with non-Christians, the necessity of the Church presenting herself as poor to the world. He could have contributed excellent ideas to his fellow bishops when they were writing the document on the Church's Missions *Ad Gentes*. St. Justin as a missionary would have rejoiced at the title which Vatican Council II gave to what is its most fundamental document on the Church, *Lumen Gentium*. In one word, St. Justin was a man who lived before his time. He was in the best sense of the word a catholic man, a universal man. In one of his early addresses to the Ethiopian people we catch something of the earnest sincerity of this Vincentian priest and bishop. He said: *"If you ask me who I am, I will reply, 'I am a Roman Christian who loves the Christians of Ethiopia'. If anyone asks you, 'Who is this stranger?', reply, 'He is a Roman Christian who loves the Christians of Ethiopia more than his mother, more than his father, and who has left his friends, his relatives, his brothers, his father and his mother, in order to come here to visit us and to show his love for us.'"*

To the intercession of this humble Vincentian bishop and missionary I commend the Vincentian family of the entire world and especially the Vincentian family here in Indonesia. Perhaps the human and spiritual greatness of this man, Italian by birth but Ethiopian by adoption, will never be fully known until we meet him in heaven.

Today, my dear Sisters and my dear Confreres, I leave you to return to Rome, the center of our Christian world. My prayer for all of you is that you will be, as St. Justin was, always faithful to the successor of Peter, the Bishop of Rome. Until the end of time it will be the role of the successor of Peter to strengthen all Christians in their faith. You have strengthened my faith during this visit to your country. The Vincentian family here in Indonesia may be small. That should not trouble you, for we know that St. Vincent and St. Louise loved to be humble and small in the Lord. I thank you for all that you have given to me. Indonesia is always with me in Rome through the presence and excellent services of Father Victor Bieler, the Secretary General. To him I express my thanks and your thanks for the laborious work of translation which he has done throughout this visit. May the Lord be his and your reward, and may St. Justin, St. Vincent, St. Louise and all our Vincentian Saints obtain for us by their intercession the blessing and peace of God, Father, Son and Holy Spirit. Amen.

What are You Seeking?

15 August 1991   Paris, France

Mother Elizondo, Father Lloret and my dear Sisters,

Almost two months have passed since the General Assembly finished its work and the Visitatrixes and Delegates returned to their Provinces. During the intervening weeks there have been meetings in the Provinces during which the decisions of the Assembly have been explained to the Sisters. It is not difficult to imagine the scene in the Provincial Houses or in centers throughout the Provinces; Visitatrixes and Delegates being plied with questions: *"What was the Assembly like? Were all the Provinces represented? What of the Provinces that have been emerging from oppression? What decisions were taken? What matters were most discussed? How do you see the Inter-Assembly Document?"* and so on.

Yet, however urgent some of these questions may seem to us, they are not the most important. There is one question which should precede all other questions in our post-Assembly discussions and sessions. It is a question posed by Our Lord Himself and recorded in St. John's Gospel. The question, as recorded in the fourth Gospel, comprises the first words to fall from the lips of Christ. John the Baptist has just pointed out the Messiah to the assembled crowds. Jesus seems to walk away. Andrew and John are inspired to follow Him, and then the Evangelist notes: *"When Jesus turned and saw them following, He said to them: 'What are you seeking?'"* (Jn 1:38).

That question of Jesus Christ has echoed down through the centuries. In one form or another it has been put by the great Founders of monasticism to those who presented themselves as candidates at the doors of their monasteries. If our Founders did not formulate the question in the words of Jesus Christ, they did so by the emphasis both of them gave to the virtue of simplicity, which has held such a prominent place in Vincentian spirituality. To act always with God alone in view is to attempt to answer Christ's question: *"What are you seeking?"*

The question of Jesus Christ to Andrew and John has a depth to it much greater than Jacob's Well, and hence not so easily answered. Young students the world over will often deflect a teacher's question, which they cannot easily answer, by immediately asking one themselves. The ruse was known to Andrew and John, for instead of answering Our Lord's penetrating question, they put a question to Him themselves: *"They said to Him: 'Rabbi (which translated means Teacher), where are you staying?'"* (Ibid.).

The answer to the question, *"What are you seeking?"* may seem to lie on the surface of the well. *"Why, it is clear. I want to give myself to God for the service of the poor in today's world."* Yet perhaps I need to hear the voice of the Samaritan woman, reminding me that *"the well is deep."* (Jn 4:11). Not as deep as the human heart, however, which has an ingenious capacity for concealing from our minds the real object of our search, *"The heart,"* wrote the Prophet Jeremiah, *"is more devious than any other thing, perverse too: who can pierce its secrets?"* (Jer 17:9).

What our hearts are seeking will condition our interpretation of the Inter-Assembly Document, and of all else that took place during the Assembly. We could learn something about the well of our hearts if we monitored some of the reactions that the Assembly has called forth from us, and also some of the questions we are now posing to Visitatrixes and Delegates. Draw up some water from the well. How does it taste? Cool and refreshing? Good. That will call forth gratitude, and gratitude is always a sign of a healthy spiritual heart, as the opening lines of Mary's Magnificat testify. Or does the water seem tepid and flat? That could be a reflection of our own spiritual condition, calling for greater self-discipline and less self-gratification. Or does the water taste somewhat bitter? St. Vincent's terse comment would be that which he wrote in a letter to one of his Confreres: *"Bitterness has never served any purpose but to embitter."* (Coste I, Eng. ed., ltr. 368, p. 526).

How the water tastes will, whether we realize it or not, color our service of the poor. How can a heart that is brimming over with gratitude not bring light, joy and hope into the lives of the poor? And how can a heart that is weakened by worldliness or wounded by resentment conceal its condition from the poor? *"I beseech Our Lord Jesus Christ,"* prayed St. Vincent one day in the presence of the Sisters, *"Who came on earth to destroy it (spirit of the world), to make known to each one of you all the circumstances in which it will be necessary for you to fight it, to replenish you with His own divine spirit, which is a great spirit of charity, humility and poverty, contrary to the spirit of pride, covetousness and avarice, and that He may give it to the Company in general and to each one in particular!"* (Coste IX, Fr. ed., p. 449).

To the question, *'What are you seeking?'*, Mary, the Virgin Mother of God, alone among us humans could reply at any moment of her existence and with utter sincerity and truth: *"the loving Will of God, my Saviour."* That was her reply to the Angel Gabriel. It was the seeking and the perfect accomplishment of the Will of God, her Saviour, that made her great in and for the world of her day, even if her greatness was, like a frail flower of the field, *"born to blush unseen."* It is on her preservation from original sin, on her Motherhood of God and her personal fulfillment of God's Will at each moment of her existence, that her bodily Assumption into heaven can be said to rest.

Mary's Immaculate Conception and her Assumption into heaven are two unique graces, proper to Mary alone. She draws closest to us when she gently challenges us to seek and carry out *"amid the pots and the pans,"* to quote the phrase of St. Teresa of Avila, the loving Will of

God in our lowly lives. Let us be on our guard, in this age of free expression of opinion, against exalting our private judgment beyond its limits and mistakenly dignifying it by calling it God's Will.

Let us not be so corralled into the world of today that we lose sight of what we and the poor we serve are called to be in the tomorrow of God's eternity. To us who are so preoccupied with adapting to change today, Mary's Assumption into heaven opens for us a window that looks inward to the unchanging and eternal God.

Our God, however, is a God of life whose Son entered time and lived among us. Through Him we possess within us a particle of divine life that struggles to grow into beauty and to be a joy forever. *"To be dead is to stop believing in the masterpieces we will begin tomorrow,"* writes P. Kavanagh, a modern Christian poet. Our faith assures us that Mary, the Virgin of Nazareth, is a unique masterpiece of God's creation. If God has revealed so much to us about her greatness, even beyond this earthly life, it can only be to encourage us to believe in the masterpieces we are called to begin tomorrow. As individuals and as a Community in the Church, whatever be our limitations, whatever ridicule a secularist age may pour upon us, we are not dead as long as we are humbly and obediently striving, after the manner of Mary, to fulfill the Will of God in our lives and thus become masterpieces of His grace.

For you, Mother Elizondo, I can think of no more fitting prayer, on this, your first feast day as Mother General, than to ask God to strengthen your belief in the masterpiece which is the Company, in its goodness and holiness, in its dedication to the poor. May you find in the Company, and in the Provinces which you will visit, a pale reflection of that joy and hope which Mary, assumed into heaven, radiates to the Church and to the world.

Envy and Jealousy

29 September 1991 Paris, France

My dear Sisters,

When Jesus Christ was a young boy living in His home at Nazareth and learning about the religious and political history of His nation, Mary and Joseph would certainly have told Him much about Moses. Moses was one of the great characters in the religious history of the Israelite people. The lesson must have impressed itself very deeply on the mind of the young Jesus, for you will recall how, after His Resurrection, in walking on the road to Emmaus, He began to explain the whole religious history, starting with Moses. *"And beginning with Moses and all the prophets, He interpreted to them all the scriptures concerning Himself."* (Lk 24:27). Moses was a great leader. He was great in action, but he was also great in mind. You will notice how in today's first reading a young man told Moses that there were other people prophesying in the camp and, when even Moses' assistant, Joshua, asked Moses to stop these men from prophesying, Moses replied: *"Are you jealous for my sake? Would that all the people of the Lord were prophets. Would that the Lord might bestow His spirit on them all."* (Nm 11:29). Moses was secure in the knowledge that all gifts come from God. Moses liked to look up; lesser men liked to look down. To be a prophet is to be God's messenger. Lesser men around Moses felt threatened because their leader was not the sole proprietor of God's word.

In today's Gospel St. John is disturbed by the fact that another man, who was not among Jesus' disciples, was casting out devils. Jesus is serene and undisturbed and advises John and the other disciples to take a broader view of God's saving activity: *"He who is not against us is for us."* (Mk 9:40).

Both in the first and the third reading, there would seem to be evidence of jealousy. Moses' assistants and Jesus' disciples would, in all likelihood, have denied it. They would have said something like this: *"We don't really mind, but all the same, good order demands,"* and so on. Envy and jealousy have a way of seeming to be very reasonable virtues. Envy and jealousy use a lot of cosmetics to conceal the ugly green of their faces.

Envy and jealousy are like cancer. The primary site of the cancer is in the heart, but it will metastasize into speech and action. It was St. Thomas Aquinas who said that at the center of all envy and jealousy lies sadness and that sadness is sinful. When we indulge in sadness at the success of another, the joy that Jesus Christ prayed would be in us, the joy that He shares with His Father, suffers frostbite and dies. It was St. Thomas, too, who noted that we are not jealous of those who are removed by time and distance from us. The disciples of Moses were not jealous of the patriarchs, nor Jesus' disciples of the prophets of the Old Testament. We are envious and jealous of those who are our contemporaries or who are younger than we. Jesus Christ was sent to His death by the envy of His contemporaries: *"Pilate perceived that it was out of envy that the chief priests had delivered Him up."* (Mk 15:10). Envy and jealousy continue to wound the body of Christ which is His Church. Envy and jealousy are holding back the coming of the kingdom of God. Envy and jealousy are a scandal, that is, an obstacle to the growth of God's kingdom on earth. In today's Gospel Jesus Christ speaks in very hard terms of those who place obstacles in the way of the coming of God's kingdom.

The radium that can cauterize the cancer of jealousy is the grace to rejoice with those who rejoice. To rejoice and share in the joy of the success of another will not mean a diminishment of ourselves, however much we may feel that that is so. To enter into the joy of another whose success has been greater than our own, to be generous in measuring out our words of congratulations on their success, is to reflect the mind of Jesus Christ in today's Gospel. *"May Our Lord,"* prayed St. Vincent at the end of a conference on envy, *"grant us the grace to let us see and detest this accursed vice so contrary to charity. I beseech the Divine Goodness that the words of blessing I am now about to pronounce may be operative in your hearts and mine, so that the evil sin of envy may be driven out of them forever."* (Conf. Eng. ed., 24 June 1654, p. 631).

If that grace of which St. Vincent speaks, is given to us, my dear Sisters, the joy of Christ will be able to enter our hearts and with His joy the peace that surpasses all understanding.

On this, your feast day, Father Lloret, may the archangel Michael bring our prayer to the Most High and return bearing special gifts of joy and peace for you. May your patron Michael be accompanied by the archangel Raphael, whose name signifies *'God has healed,'* bringing with him the gift of health for you, so that you may continue to enlighten the Daughters of Charity of the world with your wisdom and experience for the glory of God and the salvation of the poor.

Limitations and Compensations

13 October 1991   Paris, France

My dear Confreres,

The Gospel this morning is one that centers on youth. St. Mark at the beginning of the passage seems to emphasize the rich man's youth, for he comes running up to Jesus. He is not only rich and young, but he also has high ideals. With utter sincerity he tells Our Lord that he has observed all the commandments, and St. Mark notes that Jesus loved him. At the end of the Gospel we have the young Peter who has left all things and followed Jesus and is anxious to know what he will have. Our Lord spells out to him the reward that comes to all who leave all for Christ.

Whenever I read the Gospel and encounter Peter, I find myself reflecting that in Peter we find the history of our own vocation. First, Peter was generous. He leaves everything to follow Christ. We think of our own years when we made big sacrifices to enter the Community. Then a little later we find ourselves asking, as Peter asked in this morning's Gospel, *"What shall we have?"* We look back on our early years in the Community or in the priesthood, marked by great generosity, and those years are followed by years in which we become more calculating. Our minds seem, perhaps, more intent on what we will get from the Community than what we can give it. There are also Peter's moral failures, and none of us would dare to throw any stone at Peter. In one way or another, we also have failed and denied the Christ whom, as young men, we left all things to serve.

How many years are on our shoulders! We may not have the same physical strength, the same enthusiasm for the cause of Christ that we had when we first entered the Community. I do not think, however, that we should let our minds dwell too much on that. The fact is that we have persevered in our vocation, even if we have had ups and downs. The fact is that God has kept us in life and, as long as He leaves us in life, He has work for us to do. Perhaps in the last years of our lives the scope of our activity may seem very narrow. We find that we are compelled by diminishment of strength to be passive rather than active.

We may even regret that we wasted the energies of our youth. Whether that be true or not, I like to think that the final years of our life may surprise us when in the vision of God we will see the entire panorama. St. Paul remarked in his letter to the Corinthians that when he was weakest, then he was strongest because the power of Christ was at work in him. Old age has great limitations, but it also has some compensations. Only age can bring a clearer vision of what is really essential in life. All of you here are given by Our Lord a fresh vision of the value of the Eucharistic Sacrifice of the Mass. Whether the world recognizes it or not, it is through the Mass that all good things come to humanity. If God has left you in life, it may be for no other purpose than to celebrate or assist at the Mass of each day. In that way, with Christ and through Christ and in Christ, you will be giving all honor and glory to the Father from Whom all good things come.

Let me end this little reflection by quoting one of my favorite passages from the writings of St. Vincent. It is his reflection on old age:

> *All our life is but a moment which flies away, disappears quickly. Alas, the seventy-six years of my life which I have passed seem to me but a dream and a moment. Nothing remains of them but regret for having so badly employed this time. Let us think of the dissatisfaction we will have at our deaths if we do not use this time to be merciful. Let us then be merciful, my brothers, and let us exercise mercy towards all in a way that we will never find a poor man without consoling him, if we can, nor an uninstructed man without teaching him in a few words those things which it is necessary to believe and which he must do for his salvation. O Saviour, do not permit that we abuse our vocation. Do not take away from this Company the spirit of mercy, because what would become of us if You should withdraw Your mercy from it. Give us, then, that mercy along with the spirit of gentleness and humility.* (Coste XI, Fr. ed., p. 342).

Yes, may that spirit of mercy, gentleness and humility be given to us all here and to the Congregation throughout the world.

The Dignity of Women

18 October 1991   Belletanche, France

My dear Sisters,

Of the four Gospels, it is that of St. Matthew which St. Vincent in his conferences would seem to have quoted most frequently. However, I think the evangelist who most resembles St. Vincent in his temperament and in his thought is St. Luke, whose feast we are celebrating today.

St. Luke presents Our Lord as one who has a special interest in and love for the poor. It is St. Luke who throws most into relief the mercy of God and the concern which Jesus had for those who were considered sinners and marginals in society. It is St. Luke who brings out the prominent place which women played in the saving work of Jesus Christ. Is it not one of St. Vincent's great achievements that he discovered or rediscovered the important role women could play in mediating the tenderness of Christ to the needy and the sick and the handicapped people of his time? The present Pope wrote an encyclical on women in the Church today, and he gave the encyclical the title, *Mulieris Dignitatem* or *The Dignity of Women*. St. Vincent and St. Louise succeeded in giving to the women of their time a new sense of their dignity, a new appreciation of their capabilities of helping the poor to regain their self-respect, thus enabling them to live in a manner worthy of persons who had become adopted children of a heavenly Father.

The woman, who of all generations has received the greatest dignity from God, is the Virgin Mary of Nazareth. It is thanks to St. Luke that we know something of Mary's spiritual outlook. It is St. Luke who has given us the description of the five joyful mysteries of our rosary, and it is St. Luke who has given us Mary's *Te Deum* for the Incarnation, the hymn of her *Magnificat*.

Jesus Christ and His Mother were gentle persons. When he wrote his Gospel, St. Luke emphasized for us the gentleness of Jesus Christ. He did so in such a way that three hundred years later St. Jerome, a Father of the Church, said that St. Luke was *"the scribe or the evangelist of the gentleness of Christ."* Our age needs to be reminded of the gentleness of Christ. People protest strongly about many things today. No doubt there are at times good reasons to do so. Jesus Christ also protested against social abuses. Still we must not forget that He asked us to learn gentleness and humility from Him. St. Vincent cultivated gentleness and humility in his own life, in order that he might resemble Jesus Christ and thus be of greater service to the poor.

It is not always easy to be gentle. As the years advance and our bodily pains increase, we can become impatient easily with people and especially with those who live in community with us. We feel the pain of being more limited in what we can do, and we can seek relief sometimes from the pain of limitations by showing annoyance with the imperfections and limitations of other people. When we pray that lovely hymn, *Ave Maris Stella*, we ask Mary to make us *"gentle and chaste."* Yes, I think the person who is really gentle will be chaste, and the person who is really chaste will be gentle.

The Gospel of St. Luke is the Gospel of prayer. It is the evangelist, St. Luke, who makes most references to the fact that Jesus used to spend much time in prayer. He moved from prayer on the mountain to the work of teaching and healing the poor and suffering. Here in Belletanche I know that you give much time to prayer, my dear Sisters. I have no doubt that through your prayers and sacrifices you are winning many graces for our Vincentian family throughout the world. At times you may feel discouraged that your prayers do not bring more vocations to our Provinces, particularly here in Europe. You must be like St. Peter and keep launching out into the deep, even if you have worked all night and taken nothing. Your prayers and your sacrifices are like incense in God's sight. Because of them, the mercy of God is daily descending on your Company and making you pleasing in His sight.

My dear Sisters, I thank you for all your are doing and recommend myself and St. Vincent's Communities to your prayers. May the peace and gentleness of Christ reign in your hearts and in your Community today and always.

Forbearance

My dear Sisters,

The two Apostles whose feast we are celebrating could be considered as the youngest in vocation of the community of the Apostles. Their names occur in the tenth and eleventh places in the list of Apostles which St. Luke presents in the Gospel to which we have just listened. Only Judas is placed after them, as he is also in the other Gospels. He is placed last in the list by the evangelists, because of his betrayal of Jesus.

We know almost nothing of Sts. Simon and Jude. Simon is called the *zealot* by St. Luke. It would seem to indicate that until Our Lord called him to be an Apostle, Simon was rather a fanatical person. All of us have met a religious fanatic some time in our lives. Usually, such persons are intolerant in their religious views and often are aggressive in the expression of their opinions. I doubt if Simon would be accepted by a bishop today as a candidate for the priesthood. Clearly Jesus Christ saw some special quality in his character that made him choose Simon to be one of His closest friends. Possibly, beneath the fanaticism Jesus saw a deep sincerity that would make his preaching effective, and for that reason and others, Jesus called him to be an Apostle.

When one reflects on the qualities and characters of the Twelve Apostles, one can easily imagine that it must not have been easy for Jesus to work with them. Simon was probably strong-headed and stubborn, as fanatics often are. Peter was impetuous, inclined to rush into action without reflecting on the consequences. James and John were called *the sons of thunder*. They were impatient, as we know, with the Samaritans who would not allow Jesus to pass through their town, and wanted to take revenge on them. All the Apostles would seem to have been ambitious and eager to get the top jobs in the kingdom of God. Judas was sly and certainly had not the virtue of simplicity. Thomas would seem to have been a man who did not trust the words of others easily. All Twelve could candidly admit that they were, to use an expression of St. Vincent, *"a wretched Company."*

When one lists the defects of character that we can see in the Apostles, we are inclined to say, *"Surely Jesus Christ could have made a better choice when he was establishing what must be considered the first Christian community."* Yet, as St. Paul reminds us in the first reading, these were the men who were to become the foundation of the Church which will last until Jesus Christ comes again. As we see things, the foundations are weak, but the building that we know as the Church has lasted now almost two thousand years. God saw and still sees the weakness of the foundations, but He continues to work in and through them.

In our local communities we may find ourselves saying that if one or two members, or even more, were not in it, we would be much happier, and we would serve the poor better. That may be true. But God asks us to accept the community in which His Providence places us. It cannot be more difficult for us to accept our community as it is, than it was for Our Lord to accept the Apostles He chose. He was perfect, the Apostles were not. We are certainly not perfect, nor are those with whom we live. The work of God, however, must go on. We must avoid wasting time and energy wishing that our superiors would make a few changes in our community. Rather, let us work at convincing ourselves that God is at work, not only in us, but even in and through our defects and limitations and through the defects and limitations of others. Continually we must try to convince ourselves that Our Lord sees good qualities in others that may be hidden from us, just as He saw the good qualities that were hidden in Simon, the fanatic. *"Give yourselves to God,"* said St. Vincent, *"to practice those two beautiful virtues of courtesy and forbearance . . . . Give yourselves to God to render yourselves conformable, as far as possible, to your Spouse by the practice of His virtues, so that the daughters may bear some relation to their Father. You call yourselves Daughters of Charity, that is to say, daughters of God."* (Conf. Eng. ed., 30 May 1658, pp. 1058-59).

My dear Sisters, I have said nothing about St. Jude. He certainly has many clients who pray to him, for he is known—and I do not know how he got the title—as Patron of Hopeless Cases. During the Last Supper he asked Our Lord why He showed Himself to the Twelve and not to the world. (cf. Jn 14:22). That question would seem to indicate that he was a man who wanted to share with others what he had received from

God. Our Lord rewarded St. Jude by answering his question with a magnificent revelation on what each of us is already sharing in the intimacy of our Christian beings: *"Jesus answered him: 'If anyone loves Me, he will keep My word, and My Father will love him. We will come to him and establish our home in him.'"* (Ibid., v. 23). Could anyone ever consider himself to be a *"hopeless case"* in the light of that assurance and of that promise?

Through the intercession of Mary Immaculate and the Apostles Simon and Jude, may we become more aware of the Divine Guests who live within us, and may we become true patrons of those who think of themselves as hopeless cases, for such is our Vincentian vocation.

God is Concerned about Me

31 October 1991   Paris, France

My dear Confreres,

Some years ago the late Cardinal Heenan of London was interviewed on television by a man who was certainly not a Catholic and perhaps not a very convinced Christian. He was, however, a very competent and skilled interviewer. To be interviewed on television by this man was to be exposed to some very searching personal questions. Millions of viewers could see the reactions to the questions in the expression of the person being interviewed. It was entertainment that millions enjoyed for years.

The Cardinal was asked what point of Catholic teaching he found hardest to accept. The interviewer had quite clearly prepared himself for a number of possible replies, and from the reply given, he would proceed to probe further into that particular point. Perhaps it would be Papal infallibility, abortion, birth control, euthanasia or divorce. The Cardinal, before answering the question, paused for a moment and reflected. Then with striking simplicity and sincerity he remarked: *"The point of Catholic teaching that I find most difficult to accept is that God should be concerned about me."* It was a reply the interviewer did not expect and one could see that he was quite perplexed by the reply.

For us who are Catholics, it is easy to accept the Cardinal's reply.

Each of us believes and accepts, at least with our heads, that God is concerned about us, as we have been told so hundreds of times in homilies since we were children. But it is a little more difficult to grasp that truth, not just with our heads but also with our hearts.

That truth was grasped by St. Paul. It was a truth that burned itself into his being. How else can you explain those burning words of his in the first reading of today's Mass: *"Who shall separate us from the love of Christ? Shall tribulation or distress or persecution or famine or nakedness or peril or sword? . . . I am sure that neither death nor life . . . nor height nor depth nor anything else in all creation will be able to separate us from the love of God in Christ Jesus, Our Lord."* (Rom 8:35ff.).

To be convinced of the truth that God is concerned about us, that God loves us, is itself a grace. There are millions of people who are not aware of the truth. There are millions more who have heard the truth stated and have not believed it. There are still millions of others who have heard it but doubt it and are not fully convinced about it. If we want to be convinced of the truth that God is concerned about us, that He loves us personally, we must humbly and simply ask Him often for that favor or grace.

It is a grace well worth asking for, because once we are convinced of it, we will blossom and open out as a flower in the sun of springtime. Watch how an infant responds to real love when it is lavished upon it. The infant cannot speak, but from the expression on its face, you know that it is pleased and happy and confident. When the child experiences constant love, it will grow up serene and content and become, in turn, capable of showing love to others. If we wish to show love to others, particularly to the poor, we must be convinced that we ourselves are loved by God personally and that He is concerned about us personally.

As members of the Provincial Council you are aware of the personal problems of a number of Confreres. I think it would be true to say that our problems in the Congregation or in the Province would be very much less, if Confreres were really convinced that they were loved by God, and that they were precious in His sight. We would seek much less for recognition from others if we could realize that we were really loved and cherished by God. Then we would find it much easier to show love and concern for others in the Community. We erect barriers between ourselves and others because we feel that we are alone in this world. We are not, for the Lord of today's Gospel is brooding over us as a hen does over its chickens.

St. Vincent could not have done what he did for the poor, if he had not been convinced that God personally loved him and loved the poor. So, with St. Vincent I offer you the advice he gave to St. Louise as he worked to build up her confidence in the truth that God was concerned about her: *"Relieve your mind of all that is troubling you: God will take care of it. You cannot become involved in this without saddening (so to speak) the heart of God, because He sees that you are not honoring Him enough by holy confidence. Put your trust in Him, I beg you, and your heart's desire will be fulfilled. Once again I repeat, cast aside all those mistrustful thoughts which you sometimes allow to invade your mind. And why would your soul not be full of confidence, since you are, by His mercy, the dear daughter of Our Lord."* (Coste I, Eng. ed., ltr. 53, p. 90).

May God in His mercy and through the intercession of His Mother Mary, give us all the grace of being convinced that He is concerned about us and that He wishes that nothing would separate us from the love which is in His Son, Christ Jesus.

Advent Letter—Community Life

11 November 1991   To Each Confrere

My dear Confrere,

May the grace of Our Lord Jesus Christ be with us forever!

Two or three years ago an English Jesuit published a spiritual book to which he gave the title, *"The God of Surprises."* It could very well be the title of our Bible, for is not the history of our salvation a series of surprises which culminate in that greatest of all surprises which we know as the Incarnation? What greater surprise could we humans experience than that *"Christ, though He was in the form of God... emptied Himself and consented to be born in human likeness."* (Phil 2:7). Almost equally astounding for us was the manner of His coming.

He stole into our world *"while gentle silence enveloped all things and night in its swift course was half spent"* (Wis 18:14) and was born of the Virgin Mary in a cave. A medieval poet caught the spirit of His coming among us when he wrote:

> *You shall know Him when He comes,*
> *Not by dint of drums,*
> *Not by anything He wears,*
> *Not by the vantage of His airs,*
> *Not by His gown,*
> *Not by His crown,*
> *But His coming known shall be*
> *By the holy harmony*
> *That His presence makes in thee.*

The mystery of Christmas is the mystery of God's breaking into the human community in a new and totally astounding way. The cave in which He chose to be born is in itself an expression of that hollowing or emptying which has been God's experience in the Incarnation. All that we call the Christmas atmosphere of joy and festivity is something like a lingering fragrance or a glowing fallout of that exultant underground explosion which took place in a cave in the Judean hills some two thousand years ago.

God's entry into our human community, however, was a harsh experience for Him. Beyond the circle of Mary and Joseph, with the shepherds and the wise men, people were unwelcoming or, at best, indifferent. St. John can be said to have captured the pathos of the occasion when he remarked that *"He came unto His own and His own people did not accept Him."* (Jn 1:11). The *kenosis* or self-emptying of God did not begin with His experience of suffering death on a cross. As the hymn, *Te Deum*, expresses it: *"When You took our nature to save humanity, you did not shrink from birth in the Virgin's womb."*

For Jesus Christ the experience of the Incarnation was an experience in community living. It had for Him, as it has for us, its agreeable and its less agreeable features. It is Jesus Christ who, through His loving acceptance of a life lived in a community, has given to it a new dimension and a new value. Every baptized person has received from Jesus Christ a personal invitation to the community of His Church that was born from His side on the cross. Every Christian is a community person. Those, however, who have been gifted with a call to a Congregation such as ours, are invited to live their lives with a particular consciousness of the value of community and of its God-given power of strengthening the wider Christian community.

For us in the Congregation, community life, to quote our Constitutions, *"has been a special characteristic of the Congregation and its usual way of living from its very beginning. This was clearly the will of St. Vincent."* (C. 21,§1). The Congregation organizes its community life so as *"to prepare its apostolic activity and to encourage and help it continually."* (C. 19). For us evangelization of the poor is colored and receives a certain tonality from our community living, while our community living itself is orientated towards evangelization. Evangelization, for all its importance, must not be invoked lightly as a cause for dispensing ourselves from the demands of community living, nor community sought as a means of sound-proofing us from the cries of the poor.

What needs attention perhaps in our living of community life at the present time is an increased sensitivity to the importance of sharing together regularly the spiritual ideals that are inherent in our vocation as Vincentians. Have we yet succeeded in revitalizing, or reviving for present-day circumstances, the repetition of prayer and the regular weekly conference, which have been features of life in the Congregation since its beginning? Without searching and sharing our common spiritual ideals, community living will be superficial and will inevitably sprout shoots of undesirable individualism which will weaken the apostolic thrust of the works of our Congregation. Our community life should be a continual and communal searching into the mine of those spiritual riches which are our family heirlooms, come down to us from St. Vincent. Such searching together will draw us closer to each other and unite us in the task of bringing to the poor the good news that God is not beyond the stars, but has been born of a Virgin in a cave and that we are already alight with His brightness.

Let me suggest to each community of our Congregation that, as an Advent exercise, it should come together and spend some time reflecting upon and assimilating the content of what is a particularly rich chapter in our Constitutions, chapter II, *Community Life.* Such an exercise will enhance our appreciation of our particular vocation and stimulate us to go out and surprise with good news some of those people who feel lost and abandoned in the waste lands of the world.

For our God remains, even today, a God of surprises. May He surprise you this Christmas with a new measure of His joy and peace. That is my wish and prayer, as it is of all who live and work here in the Curia. Commending myself and the Congregation to your prayers, I remain, your devoted confrere.

Service to God

11 November 1991   Siena, Italy

The saint whom the Church is honoring today may seem a long way from us in time, but not so far in distance, for as a young boy he spent some time in Pavia. St. Martin lived towards the end of the fourth century, and the scene of his apostolic labors was for the most part in France. Let me introduce him to you. Martin is a young soldier, a conscript doing his military service. He is not baptized. One night in a dream he sees Jesus Christ, dressed in half the cloak which he had given to a poor man. He hears a voice saying: *"Martin has covered Me with his cloak."*

Martin spent ten years as a monk in the desert. Then one day, moving into the city, he found the people were looking for a Bishop and they tried to persuade Martin to accept the office. He refused. Then the people played a trick on him. They called him out to see a sick person. Martin went and the crowd swept him along to the Cathedral where the Bishops of the Province were gathered to choose a new Bishop for the city of Tours. When the Bishops saw Martin, they were not impressed by the people's choice. His hair was unkempt and he was poorly dressed. The priests and people insisted and their wishes prevailed. Martin became Bishop of Tours. We, like the Bishops of St. Martin's day, tend to judge by appearances. We meet people in fine clothes and discover that they are in reality poor persons, while we meet people clad in very poor clothes and discover them to be very fine and rich persons. Martin proved to be a very good Bishop. By boat, by donkey, by foot, he visited the most remote areas of his diocese. He encountered many difficulties. When his health failed him and he was near death, the people gathered round and said to him: *"Martin, do not leave us."* Martin's prayer was: *"Lord, if I am still needed for your people, I do not refuse the work and may Your Will be done."* Martin died on the 8 November 397.

St. Martin's prayer is a very sensible one. Often we meet elderly people who ask: *"Why does God leave me in life, when I am becoming such a burden to myself and to other people?"* The only answer that we can give is to be found in St. Martin's prayer: *"Lord, if I can be of service to You . . . ."* God leaves us in life only as long as we can be of service to Him, not a moment more, not a moment less. We tend to judge by appearances, and we can be so mistaken at times. When we are young, strong and active, we seem to accomplish much. People may speak in admiration of what we achieve. All appearances seem to indicate that we are rendering much service to God and to His Church. When we are old, all appearances seem to indicate that we are largely useless to God and to His Church. We could be wrong in thinking that we are offering God little service when we are suffering from what Father Teilhard de Chardin calls *"the diminishments of sickness and old age."*

At the end of his life St. Vincent reflected much on the mercy of God, and on the importance of showing mercy and compassion to each other in our weaknesses. In both St. Vincent and St. Martin love and mercy shone out in their characters and, as with so many saintly people, the older they grew, the more tender they became.

Through the intercession of St. Martin and St. Vincent may each of us come to see more clearly the presence of Christ, not only in the poor but in all people, and may we be convinced that until we draw our last breath, we are being of service to God and to His people.

Acceptance—Non-Acceptance

19 November 1991   Antananarivo, Madagascar

My dear Sisters and Confreres,

My first thought must be one of gratitude to God who has brought me once more to this country that was so dear to the heart of St. Vincent. I am grateful, too, to God for the safe journey, walking, as the psalmist might express it, on *"the wings of the wind."* (Ps 104:3).

The passage from St. Luke's Gospel, to which we have just listened, is one of the slightly humorous passages in the New Testament. If humor is the ability to see the incongruous, then we have it here. Zacchaeus may have been an important figure in Jericho, but when it came to public meetings, he was lost. He had to run along the road ahead of the crowd and climb a tree if he wanted to see Jesus of Nazareth passing by. Zacchaeus was rich, remarks St. Luke, but even in 30 A.D. there were things that money couldn't buy. No money could bring it about that Zacchaeus could add a cubit to his height. It was the sight of this important but tiny little man, looking out through the leaves of a tree, that seemed to have been incongruous to St. Luke and to Our Lord.

Humor is refreshing, but it can turn sour. Then you have derision. It was, perhaps, the derision of the crowd that first attracted the attention of Our Lord to Zacchaeus. They were laughing at the sight of Zacchaeus up in the tree. Then the courtesy of Christ intervened, and He turned the vinegar of derision into the warm wine of acceptance. *"Come down quickly, Zacchaeus, for I must remain in your house this day."* Two questions arise here. First, is this the only place in the Gospel that Our Lord invited Himself to another man's house? Second, is this the only place in the Gospel where Our Lord hurried a person? *"Come down quickly . . . . "* Perhaps that was only the courtesy of Christ, Who suited His invitation to Zacchaeus, for St. Luke depicts Zacchaeus as a man in a hurry, running along ahead of the crowd and running home so that he could receive his distinguished guest.

This passage of St. Luke's Gospel is a study in attitudes, the attitudes of acceptance and non-acceptance. Zacchaeus accepts Our Lord joyfully and the sign of his acceptance is his open house and his resolution to give half of his goods to the poor. Outside the house of Zacchaeus we have non-acceptance, the crowd protesting and murmuring because Jesus had accepted Zacchaeus with all his defects, physical and spiritual. This evening we are inside the house of Our Lord. We are sitting around His table here. We have been accepted by Him. We accept the poor. There may, however, be particular people whom we do not accept, or to whom we manifest an attitude of coldness and reserve. In this we are not like Christ. The meaning of our Holy Communion is that we accept, not only the Christ of the Eucharist, but the whole Christ, the Christ of the domestic situation, of the community situation into which St. Luke puts Our Lord in today's Gospel.

So often in our contacts with others we set up in our minds conditions for accepting people and, because we do, we are unable to change them. Have you ever noticed how Our Lord always seemed to make people conscious of their strengths before He made them aware of their weaknesses? He accepted Zacchaeus, even though in the past he had been dishonest. You will notice often in the letters of St. Vincent that he will begin by praising a Confrere before he draws attention to his faults. Very often it is prejudice in our minds that prevents us from accepting people.

May Christ, through the power of the Eucharist, lower the barriers of prejudice in our minds and open our hearts to give hospitality, not only to the poor, but to those whom we would exclude through personal dislike. *"And Jesus said to him, today salvation has come to this house because this man, too, is a son of Abraham. The Son of Man has come to seek out and save what was lost."* (Lk 19:9-10).

Taking Risks

20 November 1991   Madagascar, Atananarivo

My dear Confreres,

I never read the parable of the talents in the Gospel without feeling some sympathy for the man who was given only one talent and who went off and buried it for safety's sake. In telling you that, I am probably telling you a lot about myself; that I am slow to take risks, and am overcautious. The man who received one talent seemed to be doing a very prudent thing, especially when he knew that his master was an *"exacting man"* (Lk 19: 21). It is easy to understand the reason why the servant of one talent was condemned. He was condemned for a sin of omission. He was a man who had probably been told to be careful about taking risks in life. He was afraid of risking the investment of his one talent.

There is an element of risk in every decision we take in life. We risk our lives when we decide to enter a car or take a plane. Each decision we take, great or small, carries an element of risk. Clearly some decisions carry more risk than others. It may not have been the direct intention of Our Lord in His parable to encourage us to take risks. But His own life and message are a stimulus to us not to eliminate all risk from our lives. Did He not say: *"He who saves his life will lose it, and whoever loses his life will save it?"* (Lk 9: 24). He risked His own life for the salvation of every human being. That certainly is an encouragement to us to take risks because of our love for Our Lord. Mary, His Mother, took a risk when she drew Jesus' attention to the shortage of wine at Cana. She risked saying to Him: *"They have no wine,"* (Jn 2: 3) when she probably knew that *"His hour had not yet come."* (Jn 2: 4).

Pope John XXIII risked calling an Ecumenical Council, and four years ago Pope John Paul II risked inviting the leaders of the world religions to Assisi. I am sure there were people who told both Popes beforehand that their actions were risky and imprudent. Too easily I identify all risk with imprudence. At times I fail perhaps to risk expressing an opinion to others lest it would be considered imprudent. I tend to identify prudence with inaction and silence. Yet prudence should lead to action and speech as often as it leads to inaction and silence. The man who hid his one talent was, I am sure, convinced that he was doing the prudent thing. Yet, how severe was the reproach he received for his inaction.

It is the Spirit of God dwelling within us whom we must allow, as Our Lord indicates in another passage of the Gospel, to enlighten us about the moment when we should speak and when we should keep silence; when we should act and when we should refrain from action.

Yes, the Spirit of God is with us, but we have relegated Him to live in the basement of our house. We live for the most part in the upper apartments and because of our own chattering and our constant dialoguing with passersby, we cannot hear His voice. We want to live solely off our own resources, and so we become too calculating in our decisions and too fearful in action. We are often without light and without courage to take the risks He suggests, because we forget about the guest we have left in the basement. *"God did not give us a spirit of timidity,"* wrote St. Paul, *"but a spirit of power and love and self-control."* (2 Tim 1:7).

Through the intercession of the Virgin Mother of God and of St. Joseph, who knew how to take prudent risks, may we obtain the gift of being courageous enough to step out of our boats when Christ calls to us across the waters.

Contemplatives in Action

22 November 1991   Fianarantsoa, Madagascar

My dear Confreres,

The two passages to which we have just listened, could be described as a study in contrasts that meet at a focal point. In the first reading from Maccabees we were given a description of the spirit of joy and exultation after the victory won by Judas. The reading pulsates with a sense of enthusiasm and of hope. The Israelites had found a new sense of purpose in their lives which generated a deep sense of gratitude to God. All that culminates in the dedication of the Temple. Perhaps you noticed that the word *joy* occurs no less than four times in that first reading. In the second reading there is a marked contrast. Jesus discovers that the Temple is being profaned. There is buying and selling. There is, quite clearly, a loss of a sense of direction, a loss of a sense of purpose, a loss of vision, and the mood is not of joy, but of anger. The focal point for these two events is the same: the Temple. It was into this same Temple, where Judas and his men had rejoiced, that Jesus and His disciples entered and found the scene that is described in this evening's Gospel. There is a time difference of some one hundred seventy or one hundred eighty years.

What, you might say, had happened in the meantime that there should have been such a loss of vision? Nothing very dramatic. The years had passed; the Romans had annexed Judea, but they respected the religious convictions of the people. There seemed to have been an imperceptible contraction of vision. The sense of genuine religion had weakened, or rather, had been warped. Our Lord reminded the woman at the well that a time would come when people would worship God in spirit and in truth. It would seem that many who entered the Temple in Our Lord's day worshiped God with their lips, but their hearts were far from Him.

If we are to maintain vision in our lives; if we are not to be men who worship God with our hearts and not only with our lips, we must give attention to our mental prayer. To give attention to mental prayer means being ready to waste time, so to speak, in prayer. By wasting time in prayer I mean being ready to set aside time from work and vocal prayer. It means being ready to sit still in the presence of God, allowing His presence to seep into us and quietly challenge us. The psalmist had the correct idea when he exhorted us to *"be still and know that I am God."* (Ps 46:11). It is through such prayer that we slowly make Jesus Christ increasingly a point of reference in our lives, for decisions great and small. I like very much what Pope John Paul II has written in his encyclical:

> *The missionary must be a 'contemplative in action'. He finds answers to problems in the light of God's word and in personal and community prayer. My contact with representatives of the non-Christian spiritual traditions, particularly those of Asia, has confirmed me in the view that the future of mission depends to a great extent on contemplation. Unless the missionary is a contemplative he cannot proclaim Christ in a credible way. He is a witness to the experience of God, and must be able to say with the Apostles: 'that which we have looked upon . . . concerning the word of life, . . . we proclaim also to you.'* (1 Jn 1:1-3) (*Redemptoris Missio*: § 91).

It is in our own Constitutions that the way to becoming a contemplative in action is indicated: *"Through the intimate union of prayer and apostolate a missioner becomes a contemplative in action and an apostle in prayer."* (C. 42).

Through the intercession of Mary, our Mother and Queen of the Missions, may each of us become contemplatives in action and apostles in prayer. May we become daily more like to Christ in word and in action, thus giving glory to God Who lives and reigns forever and ever.

Look Forward and Backward

23 November 1991   Fianarantsoa, Madagascar

Let me speak to you about the two Saints whom the Church is honoring today. You will forgive me if I speak first of St. Columbanus, for he is the only Irishman to be found in the universal calendar of the Church. Perhaps some of you want to spring to your feet and ask me about St. Patrick. Well, St. Patrick was not born in Ireland. He was only Irish by adoption. St. Columbanus is a latecomer to the universal calendar of the Church. It was only when the calendar was being revised after the second Vatican Council, that he found himself honored by a place in it. St. Columbanus was a monk and a missionary, moving from Ireland to France where he founded the celebrated monastery of Luxeuil. From there he moved to Switzerland and finally to Bobbio in the north of Italy, where he died early in the seventh century. His tomb is to be found there today. St. Columbanus was a man of great energy and had a rather fiery temperament. Fiery temperaments are not uncommon in Ireland today! It would seem that on a number of occasions he clashed with local authorities, both civil and ecclesiastical. Perhaps it was for that reason that he felt himself obliged to move on from place to place. He was a strong, austere and authoritarian character. That may not appeal to us today, but then we must always remember not to judge people out of their times. St. Columbanus would impose rigorous penances on his monks for violations of the monastic rule. The monks, however, recognized him to have a great heart. He taught them that they would find joy in obedience, that through evangelical poverty they could make other people rich, and that through celibacy they would give life to those who looked for the grace of Our Lord Jesus Christ. He may have been austere but he was also tender, as his prayer, which is quoted in the Divine Office, shows: *"We pray, Lord, for nothing other than Yourself to be given to us, for You are our all, our life, our light, our salvation, our food, our drink, our God. Inspire our hearts, I beg You, our Jesus, with that breath of Your Spirit and wound our souls with Your love.*" (Divine Office, Week 21, Thursday).

Separated by five centuries from St. Columbanus is St. Clement, who lived at the end of the first and at the beginning of the second century. Those of you who have visited Rome, may have been brought to the very interesting Church of San Clemente, where you found yourself in a Church that was built in the twelfth or thirteenth century. Over one hundred years ago when the Dominicans, who have charge of the Church, were making some alterations in the sacristy, they chanced upon a staircase that they did not know existed. It led down into a fourth century Church. Further excavations revealed that this fourth century Church stood upon some buildings, including the remains of a pagan temple, of the first century and earlier. It would seem that it was here where St. Clement, the third successor of St. Peter, lived.

If you were to ask St. Clement in heaven today what was his greatest concern during his Pontificate, he might very well reply: *"Divisions in the Church of Corinth."* We all know that in his day St. Paul was also concerned about divisions in that Church. There were those who were supporters of Paul, others of Cephas, and others of Apollus. Were we to put modern names on them, we might speak of them as conservatives, progressives, and devotees of liberation theology. What worried Paul and what worried Clement was the threat that these divisions posed to the unity of the Church, which is the Body of Christ. Perhaps if St. Clement were allowed to address one sentence to us today, he might ask us to think of his Church in Rome. *"If you twentieth century people,"* he might say, *"like to walk off your busy modern streets into the twelfth century Church, remember that it is standing on a fourth century one and that in turn on a first century one."*

All of us have been exhilarated by the new things which Vatican Council II, prompted by the Spirit of God, presented to us. Let us not, however, forget the old. Keep in mind the man of whom Our Lord spoke, who could from his treasury bring forth both new things and old. Do not forget what you are standing upon. We are standing upon the shoulders of the generations that have gone before us. Look always in both directions. Look forward but also look backward. Remember, you advance along the road by keeping one foot on the ground and moving forward with the other. To the young among us, allow me to say that it is good to remember that the Church did not begin with the second Vatican Council and will not end with it. Be grateful for the past. And to us older men, we are asked to be open to what is emerging in the Church, and not to close our minds firmly against everything that is new. We, too, must be grateful.

Let me end by reading some sentences from a prayer of St. Clement, which the Church puts into the Office of Readings on Monday of the first week in ordinary time:

> *Lord, we entreat you to help us. Come to the aid of the afflicted, pity the lowly, raise up the fallen, show your face to the needy, heal the sick, convert the wayward, feed the hungry, deliver the captives, support the weak, encourage the fainthearted. Let all nations know that you alone are God; Jesus Christ is Your Son and we are your people, the sheep of your pasture .... Give peace and concord to us and to all mankind, even as You gave it to our ancestors when they devoutly called upon You in faith and truth. Lord, You alone are able to bestow these and even greater benefits upon us. We praise You through Jesus Christ, our High Priest, and the champion of our souls. Through Him be glory and majesty to You now and throughout all generations, forever and ever. Amen.*

Giving Without Measure

25 November 1991   Vangaindrano, Madagascar

My dear Sisters and Confreres,

The Gospel of St. Luke has a number of distinguishing features, one of which is the prominence which St. Luke gives to the place of women in the story of our salvation. First of all, we have read and reread those exquisite first two chapters of St. Luke's Gospel where women figure prominently, Our Lady, Elizabeth and Anna, the Prophetess. It is St. Luke who recalls gratefully the kind services which women gave to Our Lord as He went around preaching the Gospel. It is St. Luke who presents us with the grief of a widow who had lost her only son in death. In today's Gospel St. Luke draws our attention to the poor, generous widow who had put into the Temple treasury *"all the living that she had."* (Lk 21:4).

St. Luke does not give us the name of this widow. It would appear that Our Lord did not speak to her. All unnoticed she was doing what the love of God asked of her, as an expression of her devotion to Him. She did not realize the good she was doing. For that reason, I think that she could be declared the patroness of those who go about their work silently and unobtrusively, who receive little or no praise from anybody for what they do, and who do not realize the depth of the goodness of the heart which God has given them.

Our Lord did not seemingly say a word to the widow, but He did use the occasion to impress upon the Apostles the importance of generosity, of acting with God alone in view, which according to St. Vincent is the essence of simplicity. This widow of today's Gospel did not measure what she was doing. On occasion, I have thought that we have a passion for measuring things today. We measure the success of policies through questionnaires and assessments. We measure the achievements of people. We measure the time we devote to projects. The only thing we don't measure seems to be the time we give to measuring and assessing. Certainly, measure and assessment have their places: they can be valuable and necessary for planning the future. However, let us never forget that the ultimate and all important measure for us in our individual lives is the purity of heart with which we do the actions that make up our days. It was such purity of heart that Jesus Christ saw in the widow and by that He measured the depth of her generosity and goodness. We could say that, if we wish to measure our generosity at any time, we should do so by counting not so much what we have given away, but how much we have kept for ourselves.

The widow of today's Gospel, I suggested, could be the patroness of those who do not realize the good they are doing. I am quite certain that many missionaries do not realize the extent of the good they do, both inside and outside our Communities. Perhaps it is just as well. We are thus more easily helped, in St. Vincent's phrase, to remain *"humble and hidden in the Lord."* (CR XII, 10).

In your moments of discouragement about the value of your own work, think of the widow of today's Gospel who, until she met Christ in glory, never realized the extent of her generosity. *"Your life is hidden with Christ in God."* (Col 3:3). Be content that it be so. He knows, He sees your heart as He saw the generosity of the widow's heart. He will use your generosity in a way that you do not suspect, just as He used the generosity of the widow in a way of which she was totally unaware, for the instruction of the Apostles, His first missionaries.

Our generosity, however, needs careful cultivation. As the years advance and perhaps as our grip on life is loosened by age and a diminution of our forces, there grows up within us a desire to acquire more material things and to hold fast to them. Imperceptibly our hearts can become somewhat hard, and we become less generous towards others. The cultivation of generosity in our lives can be an expression of our vow of poverty. Let us frequently ask Our Lord to keep us generous and willing to heed the counsel of a priest-poet: *"On Christ throw all away."* (G. Hopkins).

In celebrating Mass with you today I am very conscious, as you are too, that we are recalling gratefully the fifty years of Sister Anne Marie's vocation in St. Vincent's Community. She has, through living her vows, *"on Christ thrown all away."* Sister Anne Marie, may the Lord give you much peace on this day, and may He continue to rejoice your heart until you see Him face to face in heaven.

A Council of Change

26 November 1991   Farafangana, Madagascar

My dear Confreres and Sisters,

The theme of the two readings today is change; the change of kingdoms foretold in the first reading and the change in the Temple foretold by Our Lord in the Gospel. What a shock it must have been for the disciples to hear Our Lord speak about the destruction of what they considered to be the indestructible Temple. It must have been like someone forecasting the destruction of St. Peter's Basilica in Rome.

Cardinal Newman of England, who lived in the last century, once wrote these two sentences: *"To live is to change. And to live perfectly is to have changed often."* Cardinal Newman knew what it was to change, for he had lived many years of his life as an Anglican pastor before becoming a Catholic. When he did become a Catholic—and it was a very big sacrifice for him to leave the Anglican Church which he greatly loved—he had much experience in his long life of the truth of his assertion that *"to live is to change and to live perfectly is to have changed often."* The Cardinal was a profound thinker and he wrote a great deal. His thought influenced many of the bishops who assisted at the Council and that is why he is sometimes called the hidden presence at Vatican Council II.

There is no need for me to say that Vatican Council II was a Council of change. It is only as the years pass that we are seeing more clearly how profound has been the change introduced to the Church by what the Holy Spirit inspired the Bishops of the Council to do. Change has affected the lives of us all. To change has been more difficult for some people than others. Many people have welcomed the changes of Vatican II, but for some it has been a cause of great suffering and some people have resisted change. Most people in the Church have accepted change, even if we are not too clear where change is leading us.

This little reflection on change has been prompted by the change to take place in the Temple in Jerusalem as foretold by Our Lord in today's Gospel. The disciples did not wish to accept the idea of change, even though it was the Spirit of God Who was the author of it. To calm them, Our Lord said: *"Neither must you be perturbed . . . . "* (Lk 21:9).

Change that is suggested to us by the Spirit of God through the Church is an advance into truth. You will recall that Our Lord promised us the Holy Spirit so that He could lead us into all truth. (cf. Jn 16:13). Because we are living at a time of great change, we need to be devoted to the Holy Spirit, Who is the one Who presides over all change. It is good to know by heart one of the Church's hymns to the Holy Spirit and to recite it every day. If we are troubled by the changes in the Church or in the world, we should call upon the Holy Spirit Who is, in the words of the Sequence of the Holy Spirit, *"the best of all Consolers."* If we find that we are resisting the changes that the Church or Community is asking of us, let us call upon the Holy Spirit Who is capable of softening our hearts.

To accept change does not mean that every interpretation of change suggested by the Church has been fully correct. The Synod in Rome in 1985 made it clear that some interpretations of Vatican II Council had not been correct. That is why we have to pay attention to the authorities in the Church and to our Superiors *"in whose hands,"* to quote a phrase of St. Vincent, *"our souls are, by a disposition of Divine Providence, placed."* (CR II, 3).

In these days of change, we do well to remember Our Lord's advice in today's Gospel: *"Neither must you be perturbed . . . ."* (Lk 21:9). By cultivating a certain silence in our lives, by making Jesus Christ in the Blessed Sacrament the center of our lives, by looking to Jesus Christ, Who is wisdom itself, we will come to accept with serenity the changes which the Spirit of Truth is asking us to accept. May Mary, the Mother of God, through her intercession, enable us to live with the truth that *"to live is to change and to live perfectly is to change often."*

Hidden with Christ in God

28 November 1991   Farafangana, Madagascar

My dear Sisters and Confreres,

When I raise my eyes from my desk in Rome and look across at the book shelves in my room, there stand the two rather large volumes of the definitive biography of Saint Catherine, written by Father René Laurentin. The first volume, giving the text, comprises almost four hundred pages, and the second volume, giving us the footnotes to the text, has more than six hundred pages. One thing is certain, neither Catherine herself nor those who lived with her ever dreamt that such a lengthy and scientific biography could have been written about such a simple Daughter of Charity, who lived her life *"hidden with Christ in God."* (Col 3:3). Two other certainties present themselves to us from a study of this definitive biography: first, the authenticity of the apparitions of Our Lady to St. Catherine and, second, the authenticity of St. Catherine's own sanctity.

Today we are thinking about St. Catherine and her sanctity. Father Laurentin, commenting on the sanctity of St. Catherine at the end of his work, states that it all could be summed up in this phrase: *"God in everything,"* and also *"everything in God"* and *"everything for God."* After St. Catherine's death, one of her superiors remarked that Catherine frequently, at the Community confession of faults, accused herself of failing to perform those acts which recalled to her the Presence of God. Catherine not only saw God in everything, but everything in God. That program of sanctity was not of Catherine's own making. It was another expression of that fundamental virtue which St. Vincent recommends to both his Communities, the virtue of simplicity, the virtue which enables us to act always, as St. Vincent expressed it, *"with God alone in view."* I think it is important for us all to remind ourselves that it was not seeing Our Lady with her physical eyes that made Catherine a saint. Rather, it was seeing God with her spiritual eyes that brought her to the heights of holiness. Catherine, to quote one of her companions who was later to become Mother General, showed that *"her pure and limpid gaze looked only to God."*

It was during the month of November 1876 that Catherine made her last retreat, just a few weeks before her death. As she made her retreat in the Chapel of the rue du Bac, she had hardly need of a preacher. She would have looked at the altar and recalled what Our Lady had said to her forty-six years earlier: *"You will have much to suffer, but come to the altar. There you will receive all the graces you need." "You will have much to suffer . . . ."* She had. There were misunderstandings in her life as there are in the lives of all of us. There was the Sister Servant who felt urged to humiliate Sister Catherine, and she noticed that the characteristic reaction of Catherine was to bite her lips and be silent in order that one word might not borrow another in anger. She had learned, like Jesus, to give *"no answer, not even to a single charge."* (Mt 27:40). Talking of biting lips, St. Catherine must have had to bite them on other occasions as well so that she could keep her secret. For forty-four years St. Catherine kept her secret, and that called for much silence and self-control. When Pius XI beatified Sister Catherine in 1933, he remarked: *"We know of no more striking example of the hidden life than that of this soul of whom everyone was speaking during her lifetime for such a number of years, but who remained in the shade, hidden."*

On this feast of St. Catherine when we think of the Daughters of

Charity throughout the world who find in St. Catherine's life much inspiration, I would like to quote the encouraging words of Pope John Paul II in his recent encyclical on the missions. He wrote:

> *I extend a special word of appreciation to the missionary Religious Sisters, in whom virginity for the sake of the Kingdom is transformed into a motherhood in the spirit that is rich and fruitful. It is precisely the mission ad gentes that offers them vast scope for 'the gift of self with love in a total and undivided manner.' (Mulieris Dignitatem, §20). The example and activity of women who through virginity are consecrated to love of God and neighbor, especially the very poor, are an indispensable evangelical sign among those peoples and cultures where women still have far to go on the way towards human promotion and liberation. It is my hope that many young Christian women will be attracted to giving themselves generously to Christ, and will draw strength and joy from their consecration in order to bear witness to him among the peoples who do not know him." (Redemptoris Missio, §70).*

On the day before St. Catherine died, her Sisters in the community asked her if she was going to leave them without telling them anything about the Blessed Virgin. Catherine replied: *"The rosary must be said better . . . .The Immaculate Conception must be honored and that purity, of which it is the most beautiful symbol, must be dear to our children . . . . Did she (Our Lady) not promise: I shall grant special graces every time that people pray in the Chapel of the rue du Bac, especially for an increase of purity, that purity of the spirit, of the heart and the will which is pure love?"* May St. Catherine Labouré obtain for us all that purity of heart, of mind and of body, which is pure love.

Beginnings are Almost Imperceptible

29 November 1991   Baraketa, Madagascar

My dear Sisters,

When we look at a river as it flows through one of our cities, we realize that it is the same river which, as a little stream, trickles over the ground at its source. It is the same river with a difference, however. At the source the water is pure and fresh. In the city, the water is broad and deep, but it is less pure than it is at its source.

This morning our minds are centered upon the source of that great river which is the Company, and which now for 358 years has been giving joy to the city of God which is His Church. Today our hearts and voices rise in thanksgiving to God for what He has done in and through the Company in His Church, which is the Body of Christ. Our minds pass in review the 358 years of the life of the Company. We think of the thousands and thousands of Sisters who have been called to it and the millions of poor who have been helped and saved through it. *"How can I repay the Lord for His goodness to me? The cup of salvation I will raise. I will call on the Lord's name."* (Ps 116:12-13). We can only do as the psalmist did when he reflected on the succeeding epochs of the history of his nation. Each meditation ended with the same refrain: *"Eternal His merciful love . . . eternal His merciful love."* (Ps 136).

The beginnings or sources of great rivers are almost imperceptible; so, too, the beginning of the Company. Its rising out of the ground was watched lovingly by Vincent de Paul and Louise de Marillac and the small group of village girls whom St. Louise welcomed to her house on this day 358 years ago. We would wish to know so much more of what happened on that day, but it has gone unrecorded. It is, however, hardly possible that that day closed without prayer. Knowing St. Louise, we can easily surmise that she would have begun the evening prayer by thanking God, Father, Son and Holy Spirit, for what had come to pass that day. Devotion to the mystery of the Most Holy Trinity was a prominent feature of her spirituality. Nor would she have failed to honor the mystery of the Immaculate Conception: *"I believe and confess thy holy and Immaculate Conception."* Since their purpose for coming together was to serve the poor of Jesus Christ, the poor would have been commended to God in that evening prayer. It is almost certain that St. Louise would have prayed earnestly for Monsieur Vincent, who was known to each of them, for it was he who entrusted the little group of village girls to her care and formation. Surrounded by these simple village girls, St. Louise would have remembered to breathe a prayer for the repose of the soul of her who some months earlier had left this earth to found the Community in heaven, Marguerite Naseau. So the first day of the life of the Company ended, and God saw that it was good.

In the course of its journey to the ocean, a river changes but never so much as to be separated from its source. So, too, the Company. Dedication to God for the service of the poor, simplicity, humility, charity—this was the fresh spring water that trickled into the life of the Church on the 29 November 1633. It would not be long before Monsieur Vincent would be among them to reinforce the formation St. Louise was now giving to the group. *"I shall now say, my dear Daughters, that the spirit of true village girls is extremely simple, no cunning, no double meaning words . . . .Country girls are remarkable for their great humility . . . .I must tell you, my dear Sisters, that I feel greatly consoled whenever I see those of you who really possess this spirit . . . .Yes, I repeat, my Daughters, when I meet you in the streets . . . I experience an inexpressible joy. May God be blessed."* (Conf. Eng. ed., 25 Jan. 1643, pp. 75-76).

Rivers are pure in their source, but they lose some of their purity as they pass through the cities built by men. They become impure through what people, through carelessness, thoughtlessness, and selfishness, throw into them. It is so with our Community. Its purity and freshness is ever threatened by what we, through laxity, lack of mortification and selfishness, cast into it. It is only when we are pure that we can give life to the poor; purity in thought, in word and in deed, purity of intention, purity of heart. *"The Sisters,"* wrote St. Louise in a letter, *"must often renew their purity of intention which causes them to perform all their actions for the love of God. This will enable them to preserve the spirit which true Daughters of Charity must possess. Finally, I beg all of you not to allow the distance which separates you from us to cause you to forget the care with which you must observe of your Rules and the virtues which the Daughters of Charity must possess."* (*Spiritual Writings of Louise de Marillac*, ltr. 400, p. 432).

May the Lord in His mercy continue to bless and strengthen the Company throughout the world, so that the poor may be served and He be glorified.

Leading Others to Christ

30 November 1991   Baraketa, Madagascar

My dear Confreres,

I cannot now remember which of the Popes had a special personal devotion to St. Andrew, the Saint of today. His devotion seems to have been quite intense, for, by a decree, he had St. Andrew's name inserted into that prayer which followed on the Our Father of the Mass. Some of us here will remember how in the opening lines of that prayer, *Deliver us, O Lord,* the intercession of Our Lady, St. Peter, St. Paul and St. Andrew were invoked. Then the revision of the liturgy was made, and it was deemed good that at that point in the Mass no reference should be made to the intercession of the saints. I have speculated on the reason why this particular Pope had such a profound devotion to St. Andrew. Could it have been for the reason that it was St. Andrew who introduced St. Peter, the first Pope, to Jesus Christ? You will recall from St. John's Gospel that it was Andrew who first met Jesus Christ, but as Andrew was a full partner in Peter's fishing business, the next day he thought it only fair to share his great find with his brother, Peter. Both Peter and Andrew were not long in the company of Jesus, when the natural qualities of leadership which Peter enjoyed asserted themselves. It was Peter who became the undisputed leader in the apostolic group, a leadership which was to be confirmed in a very solemn way by Jesus Himself. After that Andrew seems to have lost his identity. He became known to the evangelists, not so much for his own qualities but by the fact that he was the brother of Peter.

It was Andrew who brought Peter to Jesus. It was Andrew, too, who in a sense brought the little boy to Jesus when they were in a remote place, and Jesus had posed the question how the crowd could at a late hour of the day be fed. It was Andrew who said: *"There is a boy here who has five barley loaves and two fish, but what are they among so many."* (Jn 6:9). To Andrew, then, must have fallen the task of bringing the little boy to Jesus. I have sometimes wondered how that little boy must have felt about Andrew when he began to take the lunch which the boy's mother had carefully prepared for him that morning. There must have been a certain sense of panic, if not injustice. Then, when the boy saw what Jesus did with the five loaves and two fish, forever afterwards he must have treasured the memory of St. Andrew, who had made it all possible.

Again, it was on Palm Sunday evening that some Greeks came to Jerusalem and wished to see Jesus. They went to Philip. Possibly Philip felt uneasy about them, as being in some way undocumented persons. For that reason he went to Andrew. So you see that Andrew was regarded by the Apostles as a very good liaison officer. I have sometimes thought of Andrew as a good director of vocations, or a patron for those engaged in the work of directing vocations.

All that I have been saying about persons leading others to Jesus Christ is brought out in St. John's account of Andrew's own vocation. You will recall how, in the first chapter of St. John's Gospel, Andrew heard John the Baptist refer to Jesus Christ. Equivalently he said: *"There he goes, the Lamb of God."* The words penetrated deeply into Andrew, conveying not only the idea of victimhood but of gentleness. So he followed Jesus Christ until Jesus, turning around, said to him and his companion: *"'What do you seek?' And they said to Him, 'Teacher, where are you staying?' He said to them, 'Come and see.' They came and saw where He was staying and they stayed with Him that day, for it was about the tenth hour."* (Jn 1:38-39).

We speak much about evangelizing the poor and about pastoral programs and community projects. They are important topics. However, let us never forget that in the last analysis we bring people to Jesus Christ most effectively by our own willingness to allow Him to act through us. We allow Him to work through us when we surrender our wills to Him. After all, the only gift we can give back to God is our wills. It is through constantly surrendering our wills to Him that we become more transparent, thus allowing the light of God's love to flow unimpeded through us. And it is only the light of God's love that will bring about the conversion of people. It is, to quote a phrase of St. Vincent, *"through being filled with God,"* that we become efficacious missioners. *"By being united to Him,"* and again I quote St. Vincent, *"as the branches to the vine, we do the same as He did on earth, I mean we bring about the same divine action and beget children of Our Lord like St. Paul did, filled with His spirit."* (Coste XI, Fr. ed., p. 344).

Through the intercession of St. Andrew may we come closer to Christ and so lead others to Him Who is the way, the truth and the life.

The Centurion

2 December 1991   Antanimora, Madagascar

My dear Confreres,

I do not think we would be far off the mark if we said that the attitude of Our Lord's disciples towards the centurion of today's Gospel was ambiguous. To begin with, he was a centurion, an army man. Perhaps he was a centurion in the Roman army and, if he was, he was part of an army of occupation. Is an army of occupation popular anywhere in the world? I doubt it. So deep down in the breasts of Our Lord's friends there would very likely have been sentiments of antipathy towards him. On the other hand, St. Luke's version of this event underlines the point that this centurion was rather unusual; he had built a synagogue at his own expense, even though he was a gentile. So people thought well of him, and they supported the request he made to Our Lord.

What can we say of Our Lord's attitude towards the centurion? He showed respect and compassion for him. More than that, Our Lord manifested admiration for the simplicity and authenticity of the centurion's faith. Our Lord's gaze penetrated behind the military uniform into the heart of the centurion, who was concerned about the health of his servant or slave. Our Lord was capable of detaching the centurion from his cohort and of seeing him as a sensitive, compassionate individual.

When we immerse ourselves in the social problems of our day, we tend to draw up armies of people and label them, so that we may command them. It may facilitate our planning to a certain degree, but we run the risk of seeing people only in categories of good and evil. We run the risk, too, of dividing the world into well-intentioned people and badly-intentioned people. The reality is that there is evil in the hearts of good men and good in the hearts of evil men. I often feel that there is need to tune more finely our assessments of people, so that we will not divide the world into two categories: of black and white, of good and evil.

What an extraordinary exhibition of the mind of Our Lord we find in today's Gospel! He was truly God, yet He could stoop down in admiration of the faith of the centurion. Quite simply and sincerely and humbly, he expresses admiration for the goodness and faith of the centurion.

It is a wonderful grace to be able to see and admire real goodness in other people. Our Lord did not hesitate to express to others His admiration at the faith and goodness of the centurion. Speak to others more often about the good you see in them. It is a grace of God to be able to admire good qualities in others which, perhaps, we do not have ourselves. It is a grace of God to be able to admire and wonder, and it is wonder that keeps us young. It is wonder that we see in the eyes of a child and, unless we become as little children, we shall not enter into the Kingdom of Heaven.

So let me end with some words of St. Vincent which, were he with us today reflecting on Jesus Christ and on the centurion, he might address to us as he did to one of his priests: *"We should help and support one another and strive for peace and union among ourselves. This is the wine which cheers and strengthens the travelers along this narrow path of Jesus Christ. I recommend this to you with all the tenderness of my heart."* (Coste IV Eng. ed., ltr. 1414, p. 265).

Security—Insecurity

3 December 1991   Ambovombe, Madagascar

My dear Confreres and Sisters,

I would like first of all to greet the Pastor of the Cathedral Parish and to thank him for having invited me to preside at this Eucharistic celebration in the Cathedral, which is the Mother of all the churches in the diocese. It is this church which in a special way is the Church of the Bishop, and the Bishop is the father of the diocese. It is the Lord Himself who has invited us and encouraged us to collaborate always with the Bishop of the diocese, each of us according to our particular vocation. When a family is united, all its members are happy. When the people of a diocese are united with the Bishop, and when each person respects the special vocation of others, then that diocese will be, not only happy, but it will also be effective in establishing here the Kingdom of God. We must often remind ourselves that our work, whatever it may be, is to establish God's Kingdom, not ours. It is by collaborating well with the Bishop that we can have the assurance that it is God's Kingdom and not ours that we are building. I am happy to greet the Vicar General, who is the Bishop's representative at this celebration, and to assure the Bishop, through him, of our respect and of our prayers.

Some years ago I had the joy of visiting the castle near Pamplona where St. Francis Xavier was born. It is a very well preserved castle, and one can still see the living quarters of the family and the oratory where the saintly mother of the future saint taught her young child to pray. In that oratory, too, one can still see the large crucifix before which the family prayed. The expression on the face of the suffering Christ is a smile. The artist wished to convey the joy of the Resurrection breaking through the sufferings of Christ. The castle itself is a sort of fortress. To the young Francis it must have seemed impregnable. Everything in the castle speaks of security.

The greatness of St. Francis Xavier lies not so much in the immense missionary labors as in his ability to exchange the security of such a home for the insecurity of life on the missions. Had he not been able to make that exchange, he would not have been able to bring so many to Christ. It was that initial sacrifice which made all the rest possible and what an achievement was his. The list of countries which St. Francis touched in his lifetime is impressive, even by the standards of a jet age: India, Sri Lanka, Indonesia, Malaya, Japan, the shores of China—all these in a lifetime of forty-seven years. Estimates vary about the number of people he baptized, and possibly some today will question the principle of baptizing so many people without deeper catechesis. That may or may not be true. We must, however, always resist the temptation to devalue success stories, for in devaluing the achievements of others, we may be only excusing our own lack of generosity and courage.

St. Francis exchanged the security of his castle for the insecurity of life in a world totally different from that which he knew. Security! How conscious we are of security today. We make provision for security in our old age. Violence has made us conscious of the need for security on planes and even in our own homes. Has all this left us less prepared to take risks in life? I am not thinking of foolish risks, but have we become too security conscious? Has it left us overcautious, overconcerned about what people or society will think of us? Our vocation is an invitation to take risks for Christ.

Taking vows is a risk. Our vow of Obedience implies that we will go where others will ask us to go, and to each of us Our Lord may be saying what He said to St. Peter about his future: *"You will stretch out your hand and another will gird you and carry you where you do not wish to go."* (Jn 21:18). The very process of consultation, which the Church has recommended to us as a means for discovering more clearly the Will of God, can, if it is not seen in the perspective of faith, empty our vow of Obedience of that sense of risk. We can use the process of consultation to build up fortifications around ourselves that protect the heart, like the castle which St. Francis Xavier left to answer the call of Christ. The risks we take in Community must be taken in the context of obedience. It is interesting to note that in the adventurous life of St. Francis Xavier, he wrote long letters to St. Ignatius, some of which he wrote on his knees in order to express his sense of obedience. The thousands of miles that separated Francis from Ignatius, and the wide diversity of conditions in which the two men were working, did not weaken the sense of obedience in Francis Xavier. St. Francis Xavier would have understood very clearly what the Constitutions of the Sisters state, that *"far from diminishing the dignity of the person, obedience enhances it by increasing the freedom which belongs to the children of God."* (C. 2.8).

Even when we do take what we can call prudent risks, we are faced so often with the indifference of those who are not concerned and the cynicism of those who are not convinced. Do not lose heart. Above all, do not be afraid to be known as people who have received a special vocation from God. Do not be disheartened by the poor results that come from tasks which you have undertaken because of your generous heart. To a missionary who was somewhat discouraged by the situation in which he worked, St. Vincent wrote: *"A long time passes before a laborer sees the results of his work. Sometimes he does not see at all the abundant fruit which his sowing has produced. This happened to St. Francis Xavier, who did not see in his lifetime the admirable fruits which his holy work produced after his death, nor the marvelous progress of the mission which he had commenced. This consideration ought to keep your heart strong and elevated to God, confident that all will be well, even though it may seem the contrary to us.* " (Coste V, Fr. ed., ltr. 1951, p. 457).

Through the intercession of Mary, the Mother of God, who in Pope Paul's phrase is the *"star of evangelization,"* through the intercession of St. Francis Xavier and our Holy Founders, may our hearts be kept strong and elevated to God as we wait in joyful hope for the coming of Our Savior, Jesus Christ.

God's Generosity

7 December 1991   Tolagnaro, Madagascar

My dear Sisters,

The Gospel passage to which we have just listened is one of the most beautiful in St. Matthew's Gospel. It brings out magnificently the compassion of Christ. Jesus Christ was compassionate in His Heart, *". . . and when He saw the crowds, He felt sorry for them because they were harassed and dejected, like sheep without a shepherd."* Jesus Christ was not only compassionate with His heart, but He was compassionate also with His tongue and with His hands. *"Jesus made a tour through all the towns and villages . . . proclaiming the good news of the Kingdom and curing all kinds of diseases and sickness."* Not only was He compassionate in His heart, with His tongue and with His hands, but He willed that the compassion should reach the people until the end of time. For that reason, He said to His disciples, *"The harvest is rich, but the laborers are few. So ask the Lord of the harvest to send laborers into His harvest."* (Lk 10:2). We are His laborers today. We are His heart, His tongue and His hands.

At the end of the passage of today's Gospel, Jesus asked His disciples to be generous. *"The gift you have received, give as a gift."* (Mt 10:8). There are millions who watch pictures of poverty on our television screens and feel generous towards the poor. Their reaction, so often, goes no further than feeling. You, however, imitate God, our Father, in that you are not content to feel generous, but you show your generosity at a particular time and place.

What we need to do is to reflect on the infinite generosity of God as expressed in St. John's Gospel: *"God loved the world so much that He gave His only Son so that everyone who believes in Him may not be lost but may have eternal life."* (Jn 3:16). *"God so loved the world that He gave His only Son."* One could say that this is the central declaration of the Christian faith. The heart of the Gospel is not *'God is love.'* That indeed is a precious truth, but it does not imply any divine act for our saving. The words, *"God so loved the world that He gave,"* indicate the cost to the Father's heart. *"He gave."* It was an act, not just a continuing mood of generosity. It was an act at a particular time and place. That is why I say that we could consider the phrase, *"God so loved the world as to give His only Son,"* as the heart of the Christian Gospel. A Daughter of Charity is a sign of God's love, a Daughter of Charity is a sign of God's generosity, a Daughter of Charity is a sign of God's service, of His service in a special way to the poor.

But before a Daughter of Charity can be a sign of God's love, a sign of God's generosity, a sign of God's service, she must have personal experience of God's love, God's generosity, God's service. The most unfortunate people in society are those who have not had the experience of being loved. Before loving others, we must come to the realization that we are at every moment of our lives being loved by God. If we do not reflect often in prayer on the fact that the love of God is flowing down upon us at each moment of the day, it will be difficult for us to show love to others, to show love to the poor.

My prayer for you today is not only that you will have a love for the poor and be generous to the poor and be of service to the poor but, more importantly, that you will have each day a fresh experience of God's love, of God's generosity and of God's service, for Jesus Christ still stoops to serve our needs, Jesus Christ Who is yesterday, today and the same forever.

The Immaculate Conception

9 December 1991   Madagascar

My dear Sisters,

You may remember in the life of St. Bernadette how, when she asked Our Lady who she was, Our Lady replied: *"I am the Immaculate Conception."* Young Bernadette had difficulty, not only in understanding the phrase, but in remembering it. All the way home she kept repeating it, lest she would forget it: *"I am the Immaculate Conception."* As a child, these two words, *Immaculate Conception*, were big words, difficult for her to understand and difficult to remember. Bernadette had no difficulty, however, in understanding the message which Our Lady gave her, nor would she ever forget the beauty of Our Lady's person, her smile and her gentleness.

It is not difficult for us to remember the two words, *Immaculate Conception*, nor do we find it difficult to accept the mystery proposed to us by the Church, that Mary alone of all human creatures was conceived free from original sin through the merits of her Son's life, death and resurrection. Perhaps it is difficult for us to find a way in which this great mystery can have an effect in our little lives. God does not reveal mysteries to us only that we may praise Him; all the mysteries of our faith are intended to shape the way in which we live our daily lives.

Of all the saints who have drawn out for us the practical implications of the mystery of the Immaculate Conception in our lives, I think St. Louise must be placed in first rank. You know how devoted she was to this mystery. When you enter the chapel of the rue du Bac, you see up over the high altar the first words of her prayer: *"I believe and confess thy holy and Immaculate Conception."* That prayer is very beautiful. Note how St. Louise has made it concrete for you. It is St. Louise who spells out for you the practical meaning of the Immaculate Conception: *"Obtain for me from your Divine Son humility and charity, great purity of heart, mind and body, perseverance in my holy vocation, the gift of prayer, a good life and a holy death."* In those few phrases, St. Louise spells out for you what practical devotion to the Immaculate Conception should mean.

Mary could say at all times with perfect truth the words which the present Pope has as his motto: *"Totus tuus." "I am fully yours."* That is the meaning of her Immaculate Conception. She was fully God's property at all times, and He knew He could use her freely for His purposes. Her whole life was an expression of what she said to the Angel Gabriel at the Annunciation: *"I am the slave of the Lord. Be it done unto me according to your word."* The mystery of Mary's Immaculate Conception is the marvel that one human person, by the grace of God, was at every moment of her life completely open to God, as the mountains are to the sun and the wind and the rain. May Mary, conceived without sin, pray for us sinners who have recourse to her today, so that we can exclude sin from our lives. May she pray for us so that we may become fully hers and fully God's.

On this beautiful feast day some Sisters will pronounce their vows for the first time. By your vows you yield yourselves totally up to the love of God, as do the incense grains to the fire. Through your vows of chastity, poverty, obedience and service of the poor, you overcome the resistance which the selfishness of your hearts opposes to the love which God has for you. By living your vows faithfully, you become more free and, although your lives may seem to be small, like the little grains of incense, they are in fact giving forth much fragrance in the Church of God. You are, in St. Paul's phrase, *"the good fragrance of Christ."* (2 Cor 2:15).

Your vows put certain limits on your freedom. You accept those limits lovingly and gladly. If your vows limit your freedom, they also give you a new freedom. Your vows keep you from being over absorbed in things, so that you may be more concerned about people. They are a wall of fire and the fire has its origin in the love which God has for you and for the poor whom He wishes you to serve. Ask often from God the grace of being able to see *fidelity* to your vows as a response to the love He has shown you in calling you into the Company. Reflect often on the fact that because relatively few are called in the Church to pronounce vows of chastity, obedience, poverty and service of the poor, your vows must be considered as a privileged way of loving God. Your vows are about loving God with your minds and hearts and bodies. Your vows should help you to become loving persons. Often ask yourselves the question: Into whose lives am I bringing love? A married woman who lives her vocation brings love into the lives of her husband and children. To whom does the Daughter of Charity bring love? The poor, but also into the lives of those with whom she lives in Community. At the end of a day it can be helpful to reflect on the way we have touched other people's lives and ask ourselves the question: What person has been enriched by the love I have shown through the living of my vows today?

To a Sister who had told him of her appreciation of the vows she made in the Company, St. Vincent wrote: *"My Sister, I praise God for the good dispositions He gives you to make yourself more and more agreeable in His eyes. You will reach this happy state if you practice well humility, gentleness and charity towards the poor and towards your Sisters. I pray Our Lord, Who has given us the example of these virtues, to gift you with this grace."* (Coste VII, Fr. ed., pp. 454-455).

The prayer of St. Vincent, my dear Sisters, is also mine for you. May the peace of Our Lord be with you always and may the Immaculate Mother of God always be your inspiration.

God With Skin On

25 December 1991   Rome, Italy

My dear Confreres and my dear Sisters,

A few years ago I recall a teacher telling me of a discussion which she was having with a group of young children about God. She was asking the children to tell her how they thought of God, what images of God they had in their little heads. Then one child put up its hand and said, *"I want my God to have skin on . . . ."*

The feast of Christmas is the celebration of the fact that we have a God Who *"has skin on"* and Who took that skin, along with blood and bones and all that makes up a human body, from the womb of the Virgin Mary through the power of the Spirit of God. We are rejoicing tonight that the God Who made the stars emerged one night from the womb of a Palestinian girl who, because there was no room in the inn, was obliged to lay Him in a manger. We are gathered here tonight to celebrate the birthday of our God Who *"had skin on."*

Birthdays are always happy events. When the birthdays of our close friends come around, we wish them a *Happy Birthday*. When we wish someone a happy birthday, we wish to say that we are glad that he or she was born. We wish to say that he or she means something to us. That is why, perhaps, we can remember best the birthdays of our parents and closest friends. They mean so much to us. Tonight we have come to wish Our Lord a happy birthday. By our presence here in the chapel at an unusual hour for Mass, we wish to say that we are glad that He came into the world and that His coming has meant a lot to us. When His birthday was first announced to the shepherds on the hills of Palestine, the angel said to them that they had reason to be glad because *"there is born this day in the city of David a Saviour who is the Messiah, the Lord."* (Lk 2:11). That is what Our Lord means to all of us tonight and always. He is our Saviour. It will be through Him, and only through Him, that all of us, please God, will safely reach the end of our pilgrimage on earth and see in all His glory Him Who is our Saviour, the God *"who has skin on."*

Birthdays are joyful events. When we celebrate anyone's birthday, we don't expect the person who is being honored to give gifts. It is the people who are invited to the celebration who are expected to give presents. But at Our Lord's birthday party, He Himself offers a gift to all who will accept it. The gift that He offers to each of us individually is a share in the life of God. The Infant who was born of the Virgin Mary was like any other infant. He needed all the care that any infant needs, and Mary gave it to Him. But He was different from all other infants in that within that tiny Body, the life of God Himself lay hidden. Later on, when He would have grown up into manhood, He would give to all those who would receive Him a share in that life of God. In the simple and magnificent words of St. John the Evangelist, *"To all who received Him and believed in His name He gave power to become children of God."* (Jn 1:12). Jesus Christ is already within us through sanctifying grace, but the Church wishes that the grace be renewed and that we live with a new life more independent of sin, more free from imperfections and undue attachment to creatures and to the things of this passing world. That is one of the special graces offered to us by God in our celebration of the feast of Christmas each year. So we rejoice tonight, for not only was our Saviour born, as each of us was born into this world, but He is offering to all of us the gift of a new and deeper share in that life which was His from all eternity.

The birthday gift, then, that Our Saviour gives us is Himself. We should not come to the birthday celebration empty-handed. What gift can we give Him Who is the Lord of all? The psalmist puts into the mouth of God the words, *"I own all the beasts of the forest. . . . I know all the birds in the sky . . . . Were I hungry, I would not tell you, for I own the world and all it holds."* (Ps 50:10-12). The only gift we can offer our newborn Saviour, and which He does not yet possess, is our hearts, within which lie our wills. Aligning our wills ever more closely with His Will, at all times and in all circumstances, is the only gift we can offer Our Saviour on Christmas day and every other day throughout the year. It is the gift we try to place on the altar each time we celebrate the Eucharistic Sacrifice. It is the gift which Jesus Himself offered to His Father. *"When Christ came into the world, He said, 'Sacrifice and offerings you have not desired, but a body you have prepared for me;'* . . . *Then I said, 'See, I have come to do your will, O God.' "* (Heb 10:6).

So, my dear Confreres and my dear Sisters, in the words of Cardinal Newman: *"May each Christmas as it comes find us more and more like Him who at this time became a little child for our sake, more humble, more holy, more happy and more full of God."*

1992

Discovery of Shepherd of Jericho

1 January 1992   Paris, France

Mother Elizondo, Father Lloret and my dear Sisters,

One day in the year 1947 a shepherd who lived near the town of Jericho went out to look for some lost sheep. He wandered into a cave in search of his sheep, and there in a cavity he made a remarkable discovery. He found some manuscripts that had lain there untouched for nearly two thousand years. The manuscripts dated back to the first century of the Christian era, among which was almost the complete text of the book of the prophet Isaiah. It was not the first remarkable and historical discovery that shepherds have made in the lands of the Bible. When Moses was out searching for some lost sheep, he noticed a bush that was burning. Out of curiosity he went to see what was happening and found his vocation. *"When the Lord saw that he (Moses) had turned aside to see, God called to him out of the bush, 'Moses, Moses!' And he said, 'Here I am.'"* *(Ex 3:4)*. What shall we say of that little group of shepherds who, while watching their sheep one night, were surprised by the singing of a chorus of angels and were given clues as to how they would discover in a cave *"a Saviour, who is the Messiah, the Lord."* (Lk 2:2). This discovery made by the shepherds of Bethlehem on that night will remain until the end of time humanity's greatest and most astounding discovery, unequaled by any mystery of science uncovered by the men and women of our time or any future time. The child in the cave of Bethlehem was the Word of God *"without whom was made nothing that was made."* (Jn 1:3).

A few months ago a certain stir was created among scripture scholars when an expert claimed that among the papyri discovered by the shepherds of Jericho was a tiny fragment of the Gospel of St. Mark. He asserted that it dated back to the year 50 A.D., about twenty years after Our Lord's death and resurrection. The tiny fragment in question is but two verses of the Gospel, and even those two verses are hardly complete. The fragment reads: *"They did not understand about the loaves, but their hearts were hardened. And when they had crossed over, they came to land at Gennesaret, and moored to the shore. And when . . . ."* (Mk 6:52-53).

Reflecting on this tiny phrase from the Gospel of St. Mark, I asked myself if most of the difficulties which I encounter in living my Christian and Vincentian vocation could not be said to have their origin in a failure to *"understand about the loaves."* When we read the New Testament and come across the word *bread*, our minds instinctively think of the Eucharist. Can we ever forget the astounding claim of Our Lord, *"I am the bread of life; he who comes to Me will never hunger,"* (Jn 6:35) and of His invitation to eat of that bread so that we may have eternal life? Nor could the Christian of St. Paul's day have failed to be impressed by the strong reminder of St. Paul to the Corinthians when he wrote: *"Because there is one bread, we who are many are one body, for we all partake of the one bread."* (1 Cor 10:17).

Coming down to our own day, we have in the documents of the Church repeated reminders that *"the Eucharist is the source and the summit of all preaching of the Gospel."* (*Pres. Ord.* §5; *Evang. Nunt.* §29). Our work for the poor is a proclamation to the world that we have understood *"concerning the loaves,"* while our failures in that apostolate and in the living of our vows are an acknowledgement to the world that we have failed *"to understand about the loaves."*

One of the most memorable occasions in the lives of all of us is the day when we made our first Holy Communion. Everything on that day conspired to impress on our childish minds the awesomeness of the occasion. Indeed, it might very well have been the first time in our lives when we made a profound act of adoration and grasped in a very limited way the meaning of adoration. There followed a second and a third Holy Communion and perhaps we have had already the experience of Holy Communion ten or twenty thousand times. What of adoration in our lives today? Could it be that its importance impinges less upon us? Prayer of intercession often occupies the foreground of our minds, yet the prayer of adoration must be the foundation stone of all our prayer. Without the prayer of adoration there will be a certain shallowness and superficiality about our prayers of intercession, and that superficiality and shallowness will reflect itself in our words, in our interests, in our relationships, in the quality of our work.

Opening ourselves to the experience of profound adoration in the silence of prayer is closely linked with the practical living of that virtue which St. Vincent described as *"the basis of all holiness in the Gospels and a bond of the entire spiritual life,"* humility. (CR II,7). To be humble one must first have had the experience of adoration in prayer that goes beyond any formula of words.

Today in the Church we hear expressed a wide variety of opinions— some informed, some less so—on a range of topics that touch both faith and morals. In religious Communities an enhanced importance is being given to the opinions of individuals, and a collaborative and corespon- sible style of government has been encouraged. How does all this affect my understanding and living of humility today? Is it feeding my ego to the point that I am giving an inflated value to my own opinions so that yielding to others becomes a more rare experience in my life?

It has been said that until Christ came philosophers knew nothing of the virtue or value of humility. Could it be that in our age, which is now often described as a post-Christian age, we have lost our appreciation of that virtue which Our Lord asked us to learn from Him, and which St. Vincent considered at once so essential and yet so elusive? It is authentic and deep adoration in prayer that will be the first step on that ladder of humility which leads upward into the heart of God, and outward to the service of others.

The presence of Christ in the Blessed Sacrament can be an effective aid to deepening within ourselves an attitude of attentive adoration. A sensitivity to the presence of Christ in the Blessed Sacrament can be a school of sensitivity. In our relations with others, in our service of the Gospel and of the poor, it is not always easy to recognize the presence of Christ. We need a training in sensitivity to His presence. It is precisely through the presence of Christ in the Eucharist that we can learn to recognize and respond to Him in situations and persons where His presence is not so obvious. The streets may be, to quote St. Vincent's celebrated phrase, the cloister for the Daughter of Charity, but she will still need time in order to retire into the Upper Room where, like Mary of Bethany, she can give herself to attentive adoration of her Lord and her God. To do so is to come to *"understand about the loaves."*

Each one of us from personal experience can subscribe to St. Augustine's confession: *"Our hearts are restless, Lord, until they rest in Thee."* In our living of community life, in our service of the poor, in coping with stress, it is easy to lose our poise, and then our hearts become even more restless. That is the moment to halt and attend to that fundamental relationship with our Father in heaven which is one of adoration and of confidence. It is only when our hearts are able to rest in peaceful and self-forgetful adoration before God that we can effectively mediate to others *"the goodness and loving kindness of God, our Saviour."* (Tit 3:4).

"To understand about the loaves" and to eat of the bread of life is to commit ourselves to be bread for others, and that means allowing ourselves to be devoured by others. It is the invitation of Our Lord to all whom He nourishes with His body and blood, His soul and divinity. *"We must be like good bread,"* wrote Ida Gorres. *"Our Lord became bread, we too must become bread for others . . . . To be bread, to allow ourselves to be eaten by others, devoured, to be wholesome, nourishing, strength-giving, satisfying and furthering growth."*

Long before Our Lord gave Himself in the Eucharist, He had been bread for the people. Think of the scenes in the Gospels when the people pressed about Him and when He and His disciples had not even time to eat. He was being devoured by others. Think of the sick He healed and the crowds whom He taught. He was nourishing and helping others to have life and to have it more abundantly. It is St. Luke who observes that *"a power came forth from Him and healed them all."* (Lk 6:19). The total giving of herself to Christ, to the Community and to the poor is the vocation of a Daughter of Charity. In doing so she becomes bread for others and in living that ideal she will more clearly *"understand about the loaves."*

We have reached, my dear Sisters, the shore of another year. Each day of it will bring its invitation to us to discover in the caves of our daily lives the Word of God and to *"understand about the loaves."* To a member of his Community who was unsettled and wavering in his vocation, St. Vincent wrote: *"If we want to find the manna hidden in our vocation, let us restrict and confine all our desires within it. Let us esteem and love it as a precious gift from the hand of God, and try to accomplish His holy Will in it always and in all things. This is my prayer to Him and what I ask you to ask of Him for the whole Company and for me . . . ."* (Coste IV, Eng. ed., ltr. 1537, p. 443).

May Mary, the Mother of the Word of God, on this, her feast day, show unto us the fruit of her womb, so that we may, as did the shepherds after their discovery of the Word of God in a cave, make known *"the saying which had been told concerning the child."* (Lk 2:17).

Typical Day in the Life of Jesus

15 January 1992   Rome, Italy

My dear Confreres,

The passage from Mark's Gospel, to which we have just listened, is one of particular interest, because it enables us to follow Our Lord for twenty-four consecutive hours. We could say that this passage gives us a description of a typical day in Our Lord's public life. This particular day happened to be a Sabbath, and Jesus spent the morning in the synagogue. Today's Gospel begins with the words, *"After leaving the synagogue, Jesus entered the house of Simon and Andrew."* (Mk 1:29). Peter might have been a little embarrassed because *"his mother-in-law lay ill with a fever."* (Ibid., v. 30). I suspect that she was the cook, for St. Mark tells us that when she had been healed by Jesus, she *"began to serve them."* In other words she got the lunch ready; there was no lunch ready when they arrived.

All afternoon Jesus would spend in recreation with His little community of disciples, for it was forbidden to do any work on the Sabbath. Then, when the first star appeared in the sky, the Sabbath was over. *"The crowds of sick people came to the door of the house to be cured of their diseases."* (Ibid., v. 34). From the few phrases St. Mark uses, you will get the impression that this work of healing went on into the night. *"All who were sick were brought . . . the whole town was at the door . . . . and many were cured."* (Ibid.).

Presumably Jesus then took some sleep but, if He did, He did not sleep long. St. Mark notes that Jesus rose very early in the morning and went off to a quiet place to pray, where St. Peter and the disciples found Him later. (cf. Mk 35-36). So we are again at the beginning of another day in Our Lord's life.

What is very interesting in that description is the balance that one sees in the activity of Jesus. There is prayer: liturgical prayer in the synagogue, and that is balanced by private prayer. There is hard work, and that is balanced by rest and relaxation with His little community. We, in our Community, have that same balance in our day. St. Vincent wanted us to pray privately and to pray together: to work and to take recreation. In our Constitutions we will find all those elements. If we blend the ingredients properly, then we will be balanced and effective missionaries after the heart of St. Vincent.

The first reading is also of particular interest to us, for it is the story of how Samuel found his vocation. Samuel was a youth serving his apprenticeship under a man named Eli who was an Old Testament priest. One night Samuel thought he heard Eli calling him. Three times during the night he arose, but Eli said that he had not called him. Then Eli suspected that the voice was that of God and he suggested to the young Samuel that, when next he heard his name being called, he should reply by saying: *"Speak, Lord, your servant is listening."* (1 Sm 3:9). Samuel did just that and he immediately received from God a clear message about what he was to do.

Samuel did not immediately recognize the voice as that of the Lord. We might be tempted to say, *"Why did not the Lord make it clear to Samuel in the very beginning that it was He who was calling?"* That remains God's secret. It took time for Samuel to discover his vocation. It is so with you. You are presently in the Internal Seminary of our Community. You have reason to think that the Lord is calling you to the priesthood in St. Vincent's Community. Some of you may have been a little like Samuel, who did not recognize the Lord's call at once, and you may have started out on another path of life, until it became clear to you that Our Lord was inviting you to the priesthood. Sometimes, too, the Lord seems to call a man to the priesthood, and then in the seminary He makes clear to him that it is not to the priesthood that

He is calling him. For that reason, I have for many years thought that a seminary is a place where a man discovers his true vocation in life. If that is so, then it is important that in the seminary a man must be very intent on listening to the voice of the Lord. In practice that means doing as perfectly as you can at each moment of the day what God is asking of you. When I was in the seminary, we were told to live the axiom, *"Do what you are doing. "* It means taking one thing at a time and giving it your undivided attention, considering the particular task as God's invitation at that moment to do His Will. If you live that axiom for the love of Our Lord, I have no doubt that you will hear the voice of the Lord clearly and you will know what to do with your life.

My dear Seminarians, I thank you for coming here this morning to celebrate with me the Eucharistic Sacrifice, which is our greatest and most efficacious prayer. Through the intercession of Mary, the Mother of God and the Mother, too, of our Congregation, and through the intercession of St. Vincent, may you be enlightened to see the hope of your calling, and may you be generous in responding to the voice of the Lord. May you at all times be ready to reply with the sincerity of Samuel: *"Speak, Lord, for your servant is listening. "*

Marriage at Cana

19 January 1992   Rome, Italy

My dear Confreres,

One afternoon during my recent visit to Madagascar I was resting in a room of a Confrere during the siesta hour. This Confrere had a collection of modern commentaries on each of the New Testaments, translated from German into Spanish. To induce a little sleep, I took one of these volumes, the commentary on the first twelve chapters of St. John's Gospel, and at random I selected the Cana incident in order to see what interpretation the author might have given to it. The particular commentator had many interesting insights on the significance of the marriage at Cana. He dwelt on the abundance of the wine provided by Our Lord, six hundred liters of it, as expressing the richness and gratuitousness of grace in the Messianic era. He had also some fascinating insights into the new covenant and on the union between Christ and His Church to which St. John alludes in the second chapter of his Gospel. But of Mary's place in the incident he had little to say beyond emphasizing the fact that Our Lord had replied to His mother in brusque terms which indicated a certain tension in their relationship. I felt a little disappointed that a commentator, who had otherwise shown a fine spiritual sensitivity to some of the truths that lie hidden in these verses of St. John's Gospel, could miss or ignore the power of Mary's delicate and sensitive pleading with her Son in order to spare the blushes of the host and hostess of the feast.

Whatever difficulties Catholics may have with what seems like a cold reply of Jesus to His mother, it does not shake their belief that Mary of Nazareth holds a singular and privileged place in God's plan of salvation in the Church. It is also our belief that her power of intercession with God is unique among the saints. Some of the early Fathers of the Church did not hesitate to speak of Mary as an *"all-powerful intercessor."* I have wondered how some Protestant theologians react on reading the rich and almost extravagant passages in the writings of the early Fathers on the Mother of God. The only conclusion I reach is that to see the importance of the role of Mary in my own life and in that of the Church is a very special grace. I often reflect on the conclusion that Karl Rahner reaches after several pages of theologizing on Mary: *"Thus at the beginning and end of all praise of Mary and of all Marian theology,"* he writes, *"all one really can do is to ask one's hearers very quietly and simply to pray for the grace to be able to love Mary."* (*Theological Investigations*, Vol. III, pp. 130-131).

"To be able to love Mary...." All of us claim to love Mary. We would be embarrassed and hurt if anyone questioned our personal devotion to the Mother of God. What needs investigation from time to time is the depth and practicality of that love. St. Thérèse of Lisieux wrote that she would like to be a priest in order to be able to preach about the Virgin Mary. In that same context she remarked with realism that sermons on the Blessed Virgin Mary that elicit only reactions of *Ah, Ah, Ah,* from the congregation are not of much use. They may only alienate people from Mary by making her too remote from our world of struggle and of suffering. Could the criticism made by St. Thérèse

of some sermons on the Mother of God be leveled at my devotion to the Mother of God? My devotion must go beyond salutations and acknowledgement of her unique privileges. My devotion to the Mother of God must be characterized by something of that practicality of which Mary gives proof in today's Gospel. Mary displayed real feminine intuition in anticipating the embarrassment the hosts of the wedding would experience when the wine would run out. Not only did she perceive the need, but she immediately took practical steps to meet the need. Those simple but poignant words, *"They have no wine,"* express a remarkable degree of sensitivity for her hosts and for her Son. Our devotion to Our Lady must have something of that practical character which St. Vincent indicates in our Common Rules: *"Confreres, therefore, both individually and collectively, should, with God's help, try to carry out this devotion perfectly: 1. by specially honoring every day this preeminent Mother of Christ who is also our Mother; 2. by putting into practice, as far as possible, the same virtues as she did, particularly humility and chastity; 3. by enthusiastically encouraging others, whenever opportunity and means permit, to show her the greatest reverence and always to serve her loyally."* (CR X, 4).

"At Cana in Galilee," writes Pope John Paul II in his encyclical *Redemptoris Mater, "there is shown only one concrete aspect of human need, apparently a small one and of little importance (they had no wine), but it has a symbolic value. This coming to the aid of human needs means at the same time bringing those needs within the radius of Christ's messianic mission and salvific power. Thus there is a mediation. Mary places herself between her Son and mankind in the reality of their wants, needs and sufferings."* (§21).

May it be given to us all to accept that truth, not only with the eyes of our minds but with our hearts. May Mary of Cana through her intercession change the water of our little efforts into the rich wine of love for her Son and His Church.

The Balance of the Cross

28 January 1992   Manila, Philippines

My dear Confreres,

I consider it a special grace that by the Providence of God I should have been invited to celebrate the Eucharistic Sacrifice with you on the feast of one of the world's greatest philosophers and theologians.

There are many aspects of the work of St. Thomas, many sides in his character that could be taken for consideration. When I set about preparing a homily on St. Thomas, I found myself thinking of what the Pope who canonized him said when there was some question of an insufficient number of miracles: *"There are as many miracles as there are articles in his works."* I have chosen just one, because I think it is fundamental to the appreciation of the man and his work, and because it is something which comes from the source that St. Thomas took to be central in his life, namely, the cross and Him Who hung upon it. The question of balance is something that is important for us. Truth is being presented to us in many fragmentary forms today. We are hearing and reading a great deal these days, perhaps a great deal more than men did in St. Thomas' day, for ours has become an age of great specialization. It is becoming increasingly difficult to see where all fits in. Yet we must try to coordinate it all and press it into the service of Him Who is the true light and to Whom we are to give testimony. In the priesthood we are going to see and hear human nature at its worst very often. We will tend to become pessimistic and discouraged about everything. We will need the balance of the cross to keep us right, the balance of Him Who amid the jeers and taunts of His enemies knew that He was reconciling everything to the Father.

Then there is the balance in our own lives of work and prayer and recreation. Psychologists and psychiatrists are telling the world today that the way one maintains mental health consists largely in the right blending of work and recreation. One of them has spoken about the great cross of love and adoration and work and play, which he considers to be essential for mental health. It is nothing new. St. Thomas taught it all seven hundred years ago—not only taught it but lived it, having learned it from that cross of Our Lord Jesus Christ in Whom is *"our salvation, life and resurrection."*

Then there is the balance, too, in our judgments about men and things. *"I judge just judgments,"* said our divine Lord. When we make judgments, we have to remember, like St. Thomas, that there is no error so great that may not have its grain of truth. The balance of the cross will make us respect the opinions of others, and reflect with St. Thomas that, after the Magisterium of the Church, we should think more of what is said than of who it is that said it.

Lastly, there is the balance to be maintained in our estimation of the work that we do, keeping a proper sense of proportion about it. *"I have seen such things,"* St. Thomas said at the end of his life, *"that make my work look like a little straw."* I somehow think that the vision was not for him the shock that it would have been for a lesser man, for a man not so saintly as St. Thomas. For St. Thomas all through his life had what Chesterton called a sort of huge humility which was like a mountain, or rather like the immense valley which is the mould of a mountain. He had that sense of proportion about his work and his achievements. His friend Reginald told him one day, as they were walking along, that he was going to be made a Cardinal. *"No,"* replied St. Thomas, *"I will never hold any great position in the Church or in our Order. I could not serve our Order better in any other state than the one I am in."*

St. Paul said of our Divine Lord that He reconciled all things to God through Himself, making peace through the blood of His cross. It was St. Thomas' glory to have reconciled with the grace of Christ all things in himself, first to God, and then set about reconciling others to God. We who share, or will share, in the same priesthood in which St. Thomas shared, must do the same, reconciling all things in ourselves to God, and then reconciling others to God. It is the continuation of the work of the Incarnation. *"Star differs from star in glory . . . ."* We are not gifted with an intellect such as St. Thomas enjoyed. But at least we can start at the same point that he started from, the foot of the crucifix, referring much more frequently than we do to the crucifix for the solution of the difficulties we may be having in reconciling ourselves to God and His Will. We should look to the crucifix for the strength which we need to continue the writing of our *Summa* which is our lives as theologians or as priests. St. Thomas has left it on record that he obtained more wisdom from the foot of the crucifix than from all his books, and that invariably when trying to solve a problem, the solution would come to him at the foot of the crucifix. At the end of his life, it was a figure from a crucifix which spoke to him and said: *"Thomas, thou hast written well of Me, what reward wilt thou have?"* And his reply was: *"None other than Thyself, Lord."* That would lead us to think that the cross is really the key to the man and his work.

Ronald Knox was speaking once to the Dominicans on the feast of St. Thomas. He reminded them that what we honor on his feast is not the profundity of the genius of St. Thomas. Rather we thank God for the life of a religious man who scrubbed his cell, kept his rule, said his office, and loved our Blessed Lady like the rest of us. If he had never put pen to paper, the world would have been poorer, but heaven would not have missed one of her citizens. He entered the kingdom of heaven like a little child; it is the only entrance. Let us ask him to win for us his purity, his humility, his love of obedience, before we ask him for a tincture of his learning.

Significance of Candles

2 February 1992   Paris, France

My dear Sisters,

I do not suppose that there has ever been a time in the history of the world when there has been so much light in it. Compare the amount of light which any of our houses has at night time now, and what the Sisters had a hundred years ago. The lights of any modern city are reflected in the night sky and can be seen for many miles before one approaches the city. Think of what Our Lord said to the people of His time: *"The night comes when no man can work."* (Jn 9:4). Because we can create and use artificial light today, the candle has almost been forgotten. The Church, however, retains the candle. You can say that the life of a Christian is lit by a candle, or rather, a series of them. When we received a share in the life of God Himself at baptism, a candle was lit and we were told to *"take this burning light and keep your baptismal innocence blameless throughout your life."* It is a candle that we hold in our hands when on Holy Saturday we celebrate the rising of Christ Who is our head. It is a candle that the Church burns on our altars when Christ with His Church offers Himself to the Father in the Eucharist. It is the Paschal candle that will be lit when the Church is saying farewell to us at our funeral Mass.

The Church keeps the candle, even in this age of artificial light, as a gentle reminder to us of the difference between the light of reason and the light of faith. The light of reason can give us much but, like artificial light, it can sometimes fail. When our electricity fails, we fall back upon the candle. In the life of a Christian, the light of reason is not sufficient. There are truths which flesh and blood will not reveal to us and are only made plain by the soft, gentle light of faith which is a gift of our Father in heaven.

A candle gives forth its light but only at the cost of being consumed. Jesus Christ said He was the light of the world. He gave forth light by being consumed to the point of death on a cross. So a candle speaks to us, not only of the light of faith but of the life and sacrifice of Jesus Christ. With that life and sacrifice Mary, His Mother, was closely associated, and a shadow of that sacrifice falls across the pages of today's Gospel.

When the aged Simeon and Anna met the young couple, Mary and Joseph, they shared the sentiments of wonder together. Mary and Joseph *"wondered at the things that were being said about the child,"* (Lk 2:33) while the wonder of Simeon and Anna expressed itself in thanksgiving. The capacity to wonder is one of God's greatest gifts. When we are young, our minds are filled with wonder. Then as we grow older, we seem to lose our capacity for wonder, and that is a great loss for us. When Jesus said that we must become as little children if we wish to enter the kingdom of heaven, He may have been saying to us: *"Unless you have the capacity to wonder at the deeds of God as a child does, you will not be able to enter heaven."* I imagine that a great part of our happiness in heaven will be the wonder which we will experience when we will be fully open to the intensity of God's love for us, to the depth of His wisdom and to the purity of His beauty. I read once of a

Jewish rabbi who was dying and who was suffering a great deal. One of his prayers was: *"Lord, you can take away everything from me, but do not take away from me the gift of wonder."*

"Ask for the only thing you need," wrote George Bernanos, *"a star and a pure heart."* Today's feast could be said to be a celebration of the star in Mary's life and of her pure heart. In the Temple she was told that the Infant in her arms would be the joy of her people and the light of the nations; she would nurture and care for her Son, knowing that His future would be a glorious one and, in a mysterious way, piercingly painful for herself. The white light of some stars carry mysterious tints of red in them. *"Ask for the only thing you need, a star and a pure heart."* Mary's offering of the fruit of her womb in the Temple came from a pure heart. It was a further expression of her surrender to her God and Saviour of all that she was and possessed, a prolongation of her *Fiat*.

In living our own vocation all that we need is a star and a pure heart. A star that will keep leading us to find Christ in the poor and in the happenings of our daily lives; a star whose light will be such that in all circumstances and eventualities we can say with the beloved disciple. *"It is the Lord."* (Jn 21:7). And a pure heart: *"The Sisters must often renew,"* wrote St. Louise to Sister Anne Hardemont, *"their purity of intention which causes them to perform all their actions for the love of God. This will enable them to preserve the spirit which true Daughters of Charity must possess."* (*Spiritual Writings of Louise de Marillac*, ltr. 400, p. 432).

Perhaps we would see the star in our lives more clearly if our hearts were more pure, for the beatitude of purity of heart is linked to the vision of God. It is through daily prayerful, but not anxious, reflection on our motivations for action, through spiritual direction and regular use of the Sacrament of Reconciliation, that we can come to that greater purity of heart which will enable us to see more clearly the star in our lives and prepare us for the face-to-face vision of God in the heavenly Jerusalem. *"Who shall climb the mountain of the Lord? Who shall stand in His holy place? The person with clean hands and pure heart, who desires not worthless things."* (Ps 24:3-4).

Centenary of Vincentian Presence

3 February 1992   Dublin, Ireland

My dear Friends of Jesus Christ,

The two readings from Scripture to which we have just listened would not be your choice for an occasion such as this, when we are gratefully celebrating the Centenary of the Vincentian presence here in All Hallows College. In the first reading the fortunes of David have sunk to their lowest point. He is in flight from his own son. Only a handful of trusted servants remain with him. The news is broken to him that *"the hearts of the men of Israel are now with Absalom."* (2 Sm 15:13). The narrative continues: *"David then made his way up the Mount of Olives, weeping as he went and his feet bare . . . .* (Ibid., v. 30). *As David was reaching Bahurim, out came a man of the same clan as Saul's . . . and as he came he uttered curse after curse and threw stones at David and at all King David's officers."* (2 Sm 16:5). This is a sad story of a loss of loyalty with the inevitable divisions that such a loss always entails and is certainly not a festive reading.

What of the passage from St. Mark's Gospel? To begin with, it is one of the strangest of episodes recorded in St. Mark's Gospel. Were we at Speaker's Corner at Hyde Park in London, we would feel a trifle embarrassed if a fanatical ecologist in the audience challenged us to explain the rather arbitrary destruction of those two thousand pigs, even if pigs cannot be exactly described as an endangered species. Again, this is hardly an appropriate reading for an occasion when we are recalling that legion of priests to whose formation the Vincentian Community has been privileged to contribute for a hundred years.

The two particular readings, however, of this evening's Mass are what the Providence of God through His Church offers us as pabulum for our nourishment today, Monday of the fourth week of the year. Taking them as they are, we must consider them as an invitation to interpret events by the Word of God and not the Word of God by events. The events that are foremost in our minds this evening are the arrival of those three Vincentian priests, Father James Moore, Father Daniel Walsh and Father Joseph Geoghean to this College exactly one hundred years ago today. We gratefully recall their arrival and the unbroken presence of members of St. Vincent's Community in this missionary College, which lays claim on all the Saints of God as Patrons for the work that goes on within its walls.

I referred to the Providence of God. Four years after his death the first biography of Monsieur Vincent was published. Its author was a retired Bishop who had lived as a guest in St. Vincent's Community for some years. Observing Monsieur Vincent over a number of years, he remarked that he thought that devotion to the Providence of God was a distinctive characteristic of the personal spirituality of Monsieur Vincent. Even if the Bishop had written his work without having personally known St. Vincent, he would have come to that conclusion from a study of his correspondence and writings. Over and over again he counseled his priests to keep always one step behind, rather than one step ahead of Divine Providence. *"We have as a maxim,"* he wrote to his priest agent in Rome, *"never to establish ourselves in a place to which we have not been invited . . . . We must be convinced that God will be more honored by submission to His Divine Providence, waiting on Him and awaiting His orders, rather than by taking the initiative to anticipate them."* (Coste V, Fr. ed., p. 164).

The point had been well taken by the Vincentian authorities here in Dublin and in Paris when, some years before 1892, the fortunes of All Hallows College, for a variety of reasons, were at a low ebb. A clash of temperaments and of viewpoints seems to have divided the staff with a consequent undesirable effect on the formation of the students. In October 1891 it was the Conference of Irish Bishops who recommended to the authorities in Rome that the direction of All Hallows be entrusted to the Vincentians. Less than four months later the Irish Provincial had chosen and appointed the first three priests to assume the direction of the College, already a half century old.

It is easy for us to imagine that a certain sense of trepidation must have existed initially between the group of priests already resident in All Hallows and the three newcomers. Neither group could foretell what the reaction of the student body might be. Both sides might have very well feared what is described in the opening sentence of this evening's first reading: *"A messenger came to tell David that the hearts of the men of Israel are now with Absalom."* (2 Sm 15:13). By all accounts, however, the transition of administration was harmonious and smooth. More than half the former staff remained, and relations between the new and old administration were cordial. The ideals of Father Hand, the Founder of the College, continued to be respected, but they were now shot through with the spirituality of a Saint who has been described by Daniel Rops as a *"Builder of the Modern Church."* What both sides may have feared, happily did not come to pass. *"So David and his men went on their way"* (Ibid., v. 14). The community of Vincentian priests, always with a representation of diocesan priests on the staff, have continued for one hundred years, and for that, *"Blessed be the name of the Lord."*

It is not for me to assess or evaluate the work of the Vincentian community here in All Hallows over the past century. I am strongly discouraged from doing so by St. Vincent himself, for in the final sentence of the Rule which he wrote for his Community two years before his death, he said: *"We must get it firmly into our heads that when we have carried out all we have been asked to do, we should, following Christ's advice, say to ourselves that we are unprofitable servants and that we have done what we were supposed to do, and that, in fact, we could not have done anything without Him."* (CR XII, 14).

If St. Vincent would have me be silent, perhaps with his profound respect for Bishops, he will listen humbly to a distinguished Archbishop whose text book of apologetics was once studied in all the secondary schools of Ireland. It was Archbishop Sheehan of Sydney who forged out the Latin inscription on the tombstone of the first Vincentian President of All Hallows, James Moore. Recalling the fact that James Moore was the sixth President of All Hallows, (and in the past one hundred years there have only been six others), he described him as a priest who was *"outstanding in prudence, distinguished by kindness, and luminous in his integrity of life."*

Prudence with its sister virtue of simplicity was placed first in the hierarchy of those virtues which Vincent de Paul wished to be a distinguishing characteristic of his priests. Humility and gentleness, which beget kindness, came next, while mortification and zeal lend a solid integrity to a priest's life. James Moore seemingly had learned well at the school of St. Vincent de Paul. With greater or lesser degree of success, the generations of Vincentians who have worked in the formation of priests in All Hallows have, by word and example, tried to share those values with the students whom Divine Providence entrusted to their care on the way to the sanctuary of ordination.

Most of the Vincentians who labored here for a number of years lie buried in the little cemetery a hundred yards or so from this chapel and equidistant from those wooden gates that have kept eye on the comings and goings of priests, students and laity over the past century. If there be an All Hallows Community Room in heaven, the topic of the growing number of laity passing through the All Hallows gates in recent years will have come up for discussion frequently enough. Should they seek the view of Monsieur Vincent—he lives in a nearby Mansion House known to them all—he would show enthusiasm for the new courses in laity and pastoral formation that are now a feature of the College's curriculum. He might gently remind his Confreres in the words of George Bernard Shaw that *"all the professions are conspiracies against the laity,"* and that in his lifetime he had as many friends among the laity as among the clergy. On being interviewed, he would admit to having tried to form and mobilize the laity for the kingdom of God and for the service of the marginalized in the society of his day. Perhaps with one of those subtle twists of humor that characterized him, he might ask us who was the first missionary sent out by Our Lord according to the Gospel of St. Mark. He himself would have the answer: the man out of whom a legion of devils had been cast. *"Go home to your people,"* Jesus said, *"and tell them all that the Lord in His mercy has done for you. So the man went off and proceeded to spread throughout the Decapolis all that Jesus had done for him. And everyone was amazed."* (Mk 5:19-20). The man in question was one of the laity.

The Vincentians who came here a hundred years ago would not claim to have been savants. They were humble, holy and experienced priests who had thrown their hearts away on Christ, the eternal High Priest. They and the Vincentians who have succeeded them have tried to live their lives under the gentle influence of St. Vincent de Paul. We Vincentians might appropriately seize the words of the poet, Patrick Kavanagh, to express what is in our hearts:

I can never help reflecting
Of coming back in another century
From now and feeling comfortable
At a buzzing coffee table,
The students in 2056
With all the old eternal tricks.
The thing that I most glory in
Is this exciting unvarying
Quality that withal
Is completely original . . . . . .
  What wisdom's ours if such there be
Is a flavor of personality.
  I thank you and I say how proud
That I have been by fate allowed
To stand here having the joyful chance
To claim my inheritance
For most have died the day before
The opening of that holy door.
With that same poet, we Vincentians today sing:
  "So be reposed and praise, praise, praise,
  The way it happened and the way it is."

Lenten Letter—Mortification

10 February 1992   To Each Confrere

My dear Confrere,

May the grace of Our Lord Jesus Christ be with us forever!

Among the many bulletins and periodicals that arrive here in the Curia from the different Provinces, a little anecdote in one of them recently caught my attention and interest. It was a story of an old, wise and simple peasant who spoke little. When asked one day what he was doing, the old man replied: *"I am busy dying. A man has a lot of dying to do. Today is a good day for dying."* And he continued: *"One thing a man must learn is how to say goodbye . . . . Some people never learn that, and it is important. Some people never throw anything away and their possessions are so many that instead of owning their possessions, their possessions own them . . . . To enjoy life, travel light. You have to say goodbye to a lot. You have to die a lot."*

In St. Vincent's vision of us, he would see us as men who are busy dying, not once in a lifetime but many times a day. Being a man who is busy dying every day is a salient characteristic of a Vincentian priest, Brother or seminarian, for mortification (how old-fashioned the word sounds!) is one of those five virtues or values which we, as members of the Congregation, pledge ourselves to cultivate and express in our manner and style of living. Our modern Constitutions remind us that *"The Congregation tries to express its spirit in five virtues drawn from its own special way of looking at Christ."* (C. 7). We are reminded, too, that *"our spirit and our ministries ought to nourish one another."* (C. 8).

Would it be true to say that in our day mortification has become the Cinderella of our five virtues? Somehow it is easier to talk of the importance of zeal for evangelization of the poor than of mortification, which seems to have a negative connotation. It is not that we deny a place to mortification in our lives, but over the years mortification tends to become diluted by the little compensations which we award to ourselves. St. Peter knew all about it. He left his boat and fishing nets to follow Our Lord. For him it must have been a costly sacrifice. It was his all and he left it. Time passed, and later he seems to have become more calculating: *"We have left everything and followed You. What, then, shall we have?"* (Mt 19:27). St. Peter's mind was running along the lines of compensation.

Into our lives, too, there slip imperceptively little self-gratifications which in an earlier period we may have outlawed. We tend to invoke the principle of occult compensation. We find pretexts for having this and enjoying that. We can even do so in the name of greater efficiency in carrying out our apostolates, but honesty and sincerity in prayer will alert us, at times, to the possibility that such concessions may be deflecting our hearts from Christ and insulating us against the cries and the pains of the poor. The truth is that we can drive out selfishness by the front door, but it has a way of sneaking silently in by the back door.

If mortification of our senses (and St. Vincent stresses the importance of both interior and exterior mortification) seems negative and repellent to us, it may very well be that our vision of mortification is too narrow. We may be giving emphasis to the principle of dying without looking further into the life that mortification can generate. The dying, which was the experience of Christ, led into His Resurrection, and the dying which He proposes to all His followers has no other purpose than that they may become more *"alive for God in Christ Jesus."* (Rom 6:11).

For St. Vincent, as for all other saints, holiness meant doing the Will of God as perfectly as one could at all times. The reality, however, of original sin in the world, along with my own personal sins, has biased me towards putting my own will in the first place and God's in the second. For that reason I must constantly cut back those little shoots of selfishness, sensuality and vanity that prevent or retard the tree of my life from bearing fruit. A man has to be busy dying. What particular forms of dying he should choose may vary somewhat from person to person. This, however, is certain, that according to St. Vincent's teaching our judgment, our wills, our hearts and our senses must feel the touch of the pruning knife so that, to quote St. Paul, *"the life of Jesus may be manifested in our bodies."* (2 Cor 4:10). Thus the daily Eucharistic Sacrifice will have depth and meaning for us.

Let no one, then, persuade us that the mortification of our senses, interior and exterior, is now outmoded. We have *"passions and desires"* that run contrary to the law of the life of Christ within us. It is humility to acknowledge them, and it is charity to crucify them. Only thus can we belong fully to Christ Jesus. Only thus can we proclaim with authenticity the good news of Christ to the poor. Only thus will our vows remain a living reality.

"To the modern science of psychology," writes a present-day Catholic philosopher, *"we owe the insight that the lack of courage to accept injury and the incapability of self-sacrifice belong to the deepest source of psychic illness. All neuroses seem to have as a common symptom an egocentric anxiety, a tense and self-centered concern for security, the inability to 'let go', in short, that kind of love for one's own life that leads straight to the loss of life."* (J. Pieper, *Fortitude and Temperance*, p. 40).

"One thing a man has to learn is how to say goodbye." Let me avail

of this Lenten letter to say goodbye to you as Superior General. As you are aware, a new Superior General will be elected in July, to whom you will give the same love and respect that you have given to me over the past twelve years. I gladly lay down this office with a heart full of gratitude for all that I have received from you, while conscious of so much that I have done imperfectly and so much left undone. At the end of a calendar year we feel urged to pray the "Te Deum" along with the "Miserere." I pray both and once again commend the Congregation, the forthcoming General Assembly and myself to your prayers. In the love of Our Lord I remain, your devoted confrere.

Conversion

17 February 1992   Guatemala

My dear Sisters,

In a sense we have reached the summit of our meeting today when we celebrate the Eucharistic Sacrifice of the Mass. For, as many of the Council documents and those issued after the Council keep reminding us, the summit and source of all evangelical activity is the Eucharist. In celebrating the Eucharist with you, each of us will be embraced personally by Jesus Christ in the gift of Himself in Holy Communion, and it is He who at that moment asks us to accept each other with understanding, forgiveness and love. So our Eucharistic celebration is an intense moment of union with Christ and with one another. *"Holy Communion with the Body of Jesus Christ,"* wrote St. Louise, *"causes us truly to participate in the joy of the Communion of Saints in Paradise."* (*Spiritual Writings of Louise de Marillac*, A. 15, p. 713).

The Lord has already nourished us by His word in the two readings to which we have just listened. Our Lord in today's Gospel speaks about signs. Some of the people of His time were too demanding in asking for signs, and so St. Mark observes: *"With a sigh from the depths of His spirit, He said, 'Why does this age seek a sign? I assure you, no such sign will be given it'."* (Mk 8:12).

Jesus had already given the people hundreds of signs in the miracles He had worked and, in so doing, He was asking them to change their way of living. He does not perform signs and miracles merely to satisfy people's desire for the unusual happening, much less to satisfy their curiosity.

When Jesus worked His miracle at Cana at the request of His Mother, St. John in his Gospel remarked that this was *"the first of Jesus' signs,"* (Jn 2:11) and then he added, *"and His disciples believed in Him."* (Ibid.). That change in the hearts and minds of His disciples was a true conversion. It was a new turning towards Christ. Jesus continues to work signs down to the present day and in all of them Mary, His Mother, is interested. The greatest of His signs today are being worked in the human heart. By that I mean the conversion which by His grace He causes to take place in human lives. Conversion of the human heart will always be considered one of the Lord's greatest signs, and one that God most earnestly desires. In today's Gospel Jesus indicates that conversion is one of His greatest signs, one that He most earnestly desires. Has not Mary, His Mother, repeatedly made known to us in her various apparitions that we should pray for our own conversion and for the conversion of the world?

The story of the saints' lives is a story of continual conversion; that is, a story of continual turning towards Someone. That Someone is the person of Jesus Christ as He is made known in the Gospel. The story of St. Vincent's life is the story of how he kept turning towards Jesus Christ and towards the poor. That must also become the story of our lives. In his direction of people St. Vincent often gave them as a guiding principle the practice of frequently stopping during the day in order to answer the simple question: *"What would Jesus Christ do or say if He were in the circumstances in which I find myself now?"* In trying to answer that question and act upon the answer, a conversion is taking place. St. Vincent gave much thought and time and energy to answer another simple question which he often asked himself, *"What can I do for the poor?"* In doing so, he was experiencing a further conversion.

Conversion for us in St. Vincent's Communities will mean allowing Jesus Christ and the poor to invade the citadels of our minds and of our hearts. Our minds and our hearts are like fortresses. We live within them, but are reluctant to admit Jesus Christ and His poor into the very center of them. We will allow Him in just so far, but we often by our action or inaction show Him that we don't wish Him to take us over completely. He is continually asking us to surrender to Him. He is asking us continually to let go, and we insist on holding on. Conversion or repentance is about surrender. Most of us are a little like St. Augustine who, when he was living a sinful life, used to pray: *"Make me chaste, O Lord, but not yet."*

In treating of the Sacrament of Penance, your Constitutions, my dear Sisters, state that this sacrament is a *"source of personal conversion."* (C. 2.13). If you wish to sustain your efforts of turning towards Jesus Christ and His poor, approach Our Lord in this sacrament frequently. Perhaps you find it difficult to do so and feel that you are not drawing much benefit from it. Do not be discouraged. Think not so much of what you are getting from it, but rather on what Jesus Christ wishes to give you on each occasion that He meets you in this sacrament. It is rather remarkable that in the Inter-Assembly Document there is a strong call to conversion. In each section of the document we are struck by the phrase, *"We are called to conversion."* Let me end by recalling for you the third of those appeals for conversion: *"We remember that the Community is OUR PRIMARY PLACE OF BELONGING. We do not live Community life 'only for the sake of being together' but rather, to find STRENGTH there for service. We want to receive each Sister as a GIFT from God, to strive for UNITY while regarding DIFFERENCES and COMPLEMENTARITIES as sources of enrichment. We want to intensify our attitude of servant toward our Sisters, manifesting cordiality, support and gentleness."* (Inter-Assembly Document, p. 10).

May the Lord, through the intercession of His Immaculate Mother Mary and of our Founders, give to all of us the grace of personal and ongoing conversion.

Blessed Francis Regis Clet

18 February 1992   Guatemala

My dear Sisters and Confreres,

One hundred and seventy-one years ago today Blessed Francis Regis Clet was put to death in China by strangling. He was an old man of seventy-two years, and he had spent the last thirty of those years working as a missionary in China. He suffered death for the faith and was beatified by the Pope ninety-one years ago.

Blessed Francis Regis Clet had worked as a Vincentian in a seminary in France for some years before he asked his Superiors to be sent to China. He was a teacher of theology, and he was so brilliant that other priests and students used to refer to him as a *"walking library."* Even though he could have remained a teacher, he preferred to go to China to make Jesus Christ known in that vast country. Blessed Francis Regis Clet, for all his intellectual brilliance, was a simple, humble priest of St. Vincent's Congregation.

He was at the time of his death Superior of a little group of missionaries, and from prison very shortly before he died he sent a letter to his Confreres, asking them to remain united among themselves. Here is a sentence from that letter: *"'A cord that has three strands in it is not easily broken.' These words of the Holy Spirit found in the Bible tell us that unity and concord are the most secure way to bring any undertaking to its desired end."* (Breviary Lesson of the feast).

St. Vincent would be in full agreement with that. He wished both Sisters and priests to work for the poor as members of a community, and he knew that a community cannot exist unless each person is ready to cooperate with the other members. That calls for mortification of our judgment and our will which, at times, can almost be as painful as martyrdom. It is good to ask ourselves at the end of the day: *"Did I do anything to break up community life today?"* We can also ask ourselves a second question every night: *"Did I do anything to build up my community today?"* In other words, did I contribute anything towards helping the community to be a more pleasant place to live, and in that way help it to serve the poor more easily?

We may not be, like Blessed Francis Regis Clet, *"walking libraries."* But all of us can, by the grace of Our Lord Jesus Christ, become *"walking invitations to unity and peace"* within our local communities and in our Provinces. If each of us tries to become *"walking invitations to unity and peace"* within our communities, then each local community will become, according to St. Vincent, *"a paradise on earth."*

On many occasions I have been asked if there is any news about our Confreres and Sisters in China. There is scarcely any. We know a little about some Sisters, and some tenuous contact was made with a small number of them. It seems certain that in the last two years the oppression of those loyal to the Holy Father has been intensified. These heroic men and women have need of the support of our prayers. The words of Pope John Paul II in his encyclical on the missions, *Redemptoris Missio*, are very much to the point: *"Internal and external difficulties must not make us pessimistic or inactive. What counts here, as in every area of Christian life, is the confidence that comes from faith, from the certainty that it is not we who are the principal agents of the Church's mission, but Jesus Christ and His Spirit. We are only co-workers, and when we have done all that we can, we must say; 'We are unworthy servants; we have only done what was our duty.'"* (Lk 17:10). (§36).

The words of the Pope towards the end of his encyclical are a real challenge: *"We must increase our apostolic zeal to pass on to others the light and joy of the faith, and to this high ideal the whole People of God must be educated . . . . We cannot be content when we consider the millions of our brothers and sisters, who like us have been redeemed by the blood of Christ but who live in ignorance of the love of God. For each believer, as for the entire Church, the missionary task must remain foremost, for it concerns the eternal destiny of humanity and corresponds to God's mysterious and merciful plan."* (Ibid. §86).

Through the intercession of Mary, the Virgin Mother of God, Queen of the Missions, and of Blessed Francis Regis Clet, may we daily bring *"the light and joy of the faith"* to all whose lives we touch.

Opinion Polls

20 February 1992   Guatemala

My dear Sisters and my dear Confreres,

I don't suppose a week passes but we read or hear about the results of some opinion poll that has been taken on some topical question. Presidents, prime ministers and politicians are being continually subjected to scrutiny by those professional organizations that sample public opinion on their political performance. We, too, have had surveys or polls on the moral attitudes of people at the present time. We tend to think of such surveys or opinion polls as a phenomenon of our time.

In today's Gospel, however, we have Our Lord presented as a person who was interested to know the results of an opinion poll which He thought some of His disciples might have carried out. *"And Jesus asked His disciples, 'Who do men say that I am?'"* (Mk 8:27).

The disciples gave the results quickly, even if they did not give exact percentages. They replied, *"Some John the Baptist, others Elijah, still others one of the prophets. "* (Ibid., v. 28). The fact that Our Lord probed further with the question, *"But who do you say that I am?"* (Ibid., v. 29), is proof that the opinion polls were completely wide of the mark. With a blinding flash of intuition—or should I say faith?—St. Peter stepped forward with his *Credo*: *"You are the Messiah. "* (Ibid.). How grateful we are to Peter for getting it so right and for expressing the truth so simply and so profoundly.

St. Peter's *Credo* was not, however, as Our Lord assures us, his own composition entirely, as St. Matthew records the incident. It was an enlightenment which he had received from our Father Who is in heaven. It is one of the marvelous facts of our experience that each one of us here has been transfused by the same light from the same source, even if in different degrees of intensity.

When St. Peter was an elderly man, he compared that light to a flickering lamp in the darkness of this world. *"You will do well, "* he wrote, *"to pay attention to this as to a lamp shining in a dark place until the day dawns and the morning star rises in your hearts. "* (2 Peter 1:9).

In our increasingly secularized society it is more difficult to keep alight the flickering lamp of faith than it was some decades ago. The variety of different opinions on questions of morality and of faith that seem to have cropped up in the last two or three decades can have the effect, if not of shaking our belief, at least of increasing the darkness that seems to surround us. To whom shall we turn and what shall we do?

When you are groping along a dark passage by the light of a single candle, it is wise not to peer too much into the darkness, but rather to look at the light which will enable you to take the next step. What I think is important for each of us is to let the light of faith fall fully on the simple immediate steps we must take, the simple immediate actions we must do in our lives. I think that it is very significant that Our Lord said that it will be the pure of heart who shall see God. (cf. Mt 5:8). The more pure our hearts, the more clearly will we penetrate the truths of God and be less likely to be carried away by merely human opinion polls. When St. Vincent placed such importance on the virtue of simplicity, he did so in order to strengthen in us the light of faith. That faith will enable us to take little but sure steps towards Jesus Christ, the light of the world, and at the same time to take steps towards meeting Him in the persons of the poor.

When the celebrated Cardinal Newman of England was experiencing much difficulty on the road of his conversion to the faith, he wrote a hymn entitled, *"Lead Kindly Light."* One of the lines of that beautiful hymn reads: *"The distant scene I do not ask to see. One step enough for me."*

I have come almost to the end of this homily without making any illusion to the first reading from St. James' letter. St. James was not a speculative theologian, but rather a man who would have subscribed to a proverb in your language which reads: *"Obras son amores y non buenas razones."* (Love is action and not just good reasons.) Certainly his remarks about favoritism of the rich in today's world do not call for any elaborate exegesis. St. James' message is simple and as clear as daylight.

Allow me to just make one comment. We must, by all means, have a preferential option for the poor in our apostolates. Let us opt for the poor, however, without despising the rich. If we wish the rich people to be converted so that the poor may receive greater justice, we will not do so by despising and closing our hearts entirely to them. St. Vincent gives us a marvelous example. He passionately loved Jesus Christ in the person of the poor without, however, despising the world of rich people among whom he moved in a simple, non-judgmental manner. No one could question St. Vincent's preferential option for the poor. In his 2,500 letters you will not find a single line that expresses disdain for the rich. He knew that to bring about the conversion of persons, we must not only love them, but show that love in word and action. If we are to be reconcilers, agents of reconciliation (and during this visit to Central America I have heard many references to reconciliation), we must love and cherish both parties that are to be reconciled. May the Lord in His mercy give each of us this grace.

Social Justice

24 February 1992   El Salvador

My dear Lay Vincentians,

When in Rome I begin to reflect on the great social problems that confront the Church in Latin America and the violence that at times erupts in society in this continent, my mind seems to travel first to El Salvador. Perhaps it is that the murder of Archbishop Romero and of the six Jesuits, with their two housekeepers, captures my imagination more quickly than other deeds of violence. Then, too, the long struggle that has gone on here and the prominence given to the recent truce focuses my mind more on this country than on others.

The sufferings of your people have been long and protracted, and only the Lord knows the extent and depth of sorrow that must have filled thousands of hearts here in El Salvador. The night of suffering has been long indeed, but there is no night so long that the dawn does not come slowly and silently. I like to think that, during my short visit to your country, I am privileged to share with you the new hope that for the past two months is struggling to see the light.

The truth is that the solution to all the social problems of this country and of the world is to be found in the first reading of today's Mass. St. James diagnoses the ills of society with acute psychological insight: *"for where there is envy and ambition there will also be disorder and wickedness of every kind,"* (Jas 3:16) and the final sentence is very apt for the situation in El Salvador today: *"Peacemakers, when they work for peace, sow the seeds which will bear fruit in holiness."* (Ibid., v. 18).

Sensitivity to the claims of justice has grown notably in the last two decades. It could be said that in that time we have come to recognize injustice as the sin of the world. The documents of the Council, Church Synods, Bishops Conferences, have encouraged all Christians to interest themselves in the questions of justice in our world and, within the limits of individual vocations, to take appropriate action. Has this development devalued the term *charity*? Perhaps it is for that reason that Pope John Paul II, in his encyclical, *Dives in Misericordia* poses the question: *"Is justice enough?"* In answering it he remarks: *"The experience of the past and of our own time demonstrates that justice alone is not enough, that it can even lead to the negation and destruction of itself, if that deeper power, which is love, is not allowed to shape human life in its various dimensions. "* (§12).

St. Vincent's name conjures up in our mind the poor and also charity. Of justice, however, St. Vincent has little and almost nothing to say. That need not surprise us, for social justice was not discussed by theologians in his time as it is today, and St. Vincent was a man of his time. He was also a man of the Church and so he would have no difficulty in accommodating himself to the Church's insistence today on justice. He will, however, always remain the Apostle of Charity. Perhaps he would not be greatly interested in speculative discussion on the relationship between justice and charity. When the Ladies of Charity felt themselves discouraged before the difficulties of the apostolates that they had undertaken for the poor, he said simply to them: *"I will say to you what St. Paul said: 'Have you given something beyond what you have of surplus? Have you resisted even to the point of pouring out your blood?'"* (Coste XIII, Fr. ed., no. 194, p. 796).

In the same vein he asks: *"But how can we love God, if we do not love that which He loved? There is no difference between loving Him and loving the poor, between serving well the poor and serving Him."* (Coste XIII, Fr. ed., no. 198, pp. 811-812).

The point I have been making is that a Vincentian in search of justice will never lose sight of the fact that love always holds the primacy. We are realistic enough to recognize that charity, at times, can conceal an injustice, but it must be said also that not all legal justice is objectively just. The Synodal Document of 1971 expresses it clearly: *"The love of the neighbor and justice are inseparable."* Justice is measured; love is unmeasured. Love is a sign of something that is unmeasured. The Vincentian must be not only one who seeks justice, but one who by his life speaks to the world of the boundless fecundity of God's love. He is one who by his activity proclaims to the world not so much that God is just, important though that be, but that God is love. In the Christian and Vincentian vision of things one cannot practice justice without love. The sin of the world may be injustice. The great commandment of Christ, Who came to take away the sin of the world, is love.

Through the intercession of Mary, Mirror of Justice, Seat of Wisdom, and Mother Most Amiable, may we, by our manner of life, contribute to building up a civilization of justice, of love and of peace.

Patron Saint Should Not be a Signboard
26 February 1992   Managua, Nicaragua

Dear Friends in Jesus Christ,

First of all, I thank you from my heart for coming here this morning to greet me and to tell me a little about the works which, by the grace of God and through the generosity of your hearts, you are doing. The variety of the works are like the flowers of your country, varied and rich in color. My hope is that you will attract others, especially the young, to work with you for the glory of God, for the good of the Church and for the well-being of the needy, the sick, the elderly and the poor.

On occasions like this, when I speak to a group of people who have a common interest in St. Vincent de Paul, I find myself wondering what St. Vincent's reactions would be, if he were to join us physically and to speak to us. Knowing a little about his character, I feel his first reaction would be one of wonder and exclamation. Even during his lifetime, expressions of wonder and exclamation at what God was doing through him were often on his lips. The two Communities which he founded were not very large at the time of his death, but the fact that they existed at all was, for St. Vincent, a wonder in itself. To the first Daughters of Charity he often said: *"I never thought of founding the Company, neither did Mademoiselle Le Gras nor Father Portail."* And he expressed similar sentiments to his group of missioners.

It is not difficult to imagine that, on coming here this afternoon, he would marvel at the fact that his Communities were to be found in the five continents of the world; that there were about 200,000 Ladies of Charity, that his own name was being used by a Society of lay men and women who worked to alleviate the sufferings of the poor in countless parishes all over the world. He would be lost in admiration, too, that Mary, the Mother of God, had chosen to appear to a Daughter of Charity in the rue du Bac, Paris, and to entrust her with the mission of promoting devotion to her Immaculate Conception through the Miraculous Medal; from that sprang other groups of Christians, young and old, who were devoting themselves to living a deeper Christian life and who had special interest in serving the poor. *"Serving, yes, "* he might say, *"that is what Our Lord Jesus Christ did when He was on earth. He served the poor, He served the sick when He healed them. He served the hungry crowd in the desert by miraculously providing bread for them. He served rich and poor alike by telling them about the coming of God's Kingdom and the life of the world to come.*

"Service of, or serving the poor, " St. Vincent might continue, *"is a more delicate task than we sometimes imagine. To be a servant one has to be humble, for a servant has to think all the time of the needs of those whom he serves. When I was a young priest and lived in the great house of the De Gondi family at Folleville in France, I used to watch the servants in the dining room. During the meal the servants at table hardly spoke at all. They observed the guests and offered them just the portions of food which they (the guests) chose. Their attention was given fully to those whom they were serving. They had to forget themselves. And that is what humility is about. So, for that reason, I say that to be a servant of the poor, one has to be humble, one has to forget oneself. That is what Jesus Christ, Who was truly God, did when He was on earth. Did He not say that He had come on earth, not to be served but to serve?*

"The world in which you are living has changed greatly since my time. There are millions more poor people on the face of the earth than there were three centuries ago. It is a grace of God that you have not allowed yourselves to become discouraged by the sheer numbers of poor who need help, millions more than in my time. Political systems seem so much more complex now than they did in the Europe I knew. My attempts to mediate between politicians of my time were not successful. When we have done everything in our power to mediate between people, we should preserve our tranquillity and peace, whether we are successful or not. It is only when we have emptied ourselves of self that God will fill us with Himself. Do not give up in the face of difficulty. 'The doctrine of Christ,' I remember writing two years before I died, 'can never deceive, while that of the world is ever deceitful.' (CR

2:1). *Do not lose your nerve, but make sure that you refer all your projects, great or small, to Jesus Christ and to the Will of His Father. Don't forget that it is the earth which revolves around the sun, not the sun around the earth. Christ is the center, not we, however dazzling our projects may appear. Christ is the light of the world. We must allow that light to penetrate the crevices of our minds so that we may at all times do, as He did, the things that are pleasing to His Father in heaven."*

As you have been listening to my imagining how St. Vincent might speak to us were he with us today, you may be saying that it is too spiritual, that you would prefer practical suggestions about what you should do for the poor today. Yes, you are right to ask that St. Vincent would suggest some practical programs of action for the poor, for he was a man of action. He was not a mere theorist. His thirty years in the countryside marked him for life. St. Vincent de Paul was a man of the earth. For that reason he might ask us today: what are your roots? Or let me put the question in another way. Listening to our discussions and keeping at the same time one ear open to what the politicians of our day are saying, he might make this observation: *"The politicians of your day seem to be greatly concerned about the poor. Thank God for that. I spent much of my life trying to convince politicians of my day of the existence of the poor. The politicians of your day seem happiest when they are denouncing the inequalities in your society. What then, I ask, is the difference between a politician today and a member of one of the groups that claims me as Patron?"* I do not propose to answer that question, but simply to offer it to you as a point of further discussion and reflection. You may find the beginnings of an answer in a few phrases which I came across in a modern biography of Frederic Ozanam: *"A Patron Saint should not be a mere signboard to a Society, like St. Dennis or St. Nicholas over the door of a tavern. A Patron Saint should be regarded as a type on which we should try to pattern ourselves, as he patterned himself on the divine type which is Jesus Christ."* (J.P. Derum, *Apostle in a Top Hat*, p. 112).

To that profound thought of a great layman who loved St. Vincent de Paul, let me add some words from the document of Puebla: *"The required change in unjust social, political and economic structures will not be authentic and complete, if it is not accompanied by a change in our personal and collective outlook regarding the idea of a dignified, happy human life. This in turn disposes us to undergo conversion."* (Puebla §1155).

Through the intercession of the Virgin Mary and all our Vincentian Saints may the grace of conversion be given to each one of us.

Every Christian Should be a Preservative

27 February 1992   Léon, Nicaragua

My dear Sisters,

The presence of Mary, the Mother of God, in the pages of the Gospels can sometimes be evoked and felt in a way that is not immediately apparent. The passage of the Gospel to which we have just listened is one such. Our Lord speaks about salt. In the home of Nazareth as a young boy, He would have watched His mother using salt as a preservative of food. Now, in His adult years, Jesus finds a new and metaphorical use for salt. His followers are to be the salt of the earth. His disciples are to act as preservatives of the values that Jesus proposes.

Today we do not need salt to preserve food. We have frigidaires and deep freezes, common at least in first world countries. In a spiritual sense, however, we have to give much importance today to the idea of preservation. How often do we not say that we are living in an age of change? In an age of change, therefore, preservation assumes a new importance, for although change is often a sign of the movement of the Spirit of God, we must not forget that there are values which do not change and which we must strive to preserve. Change is like a river. In its movement a river can irrigate and make fertile the country through which it passes. A river at once renews and conserves. A river, however, can become swollen and become a flood. It is then a destructive force as it carries away with it trees and houses and people.

Every Christian in the world is, or should be, a preservative. A Christian is called to preserve the truths revealed by God and Jesus Christ and proposed to us by His Church. A Christian is called to be a preservative of the joy that comes with the conviction that we are called to happiness in and through Jesus Christ. A Christian is called to be a preservative of that love which is unselfish, is patient, is kind, but is not envious. A Daughter of Charity for her part is called to be a preservative of those values which shone clearly in the person and in the life of Jesus Christ, namely, His poverty, His chastity, His virginity, His obedience and His service and love of the poor.

So much for the closing sentence of today's Gospel. Let us reflect for a moment now on the opening sentence. *"Jesus said to His disciples, 'Whoever gives you a cup of water to drink because you bear the name of Christ, will by no means lose the reward.'"* (Mk 9:41). Last December I was in Madagascar, where the poverty of the people is great. During my visit I heard of a Daughter of Charity who was working in a hospital where a very poor boy of eight years was brought in as a dying patient. The little boy had remarkable faith. He received Holy Communion and spoke to the Sister about going to heaven. After a little pause he said to the Sister: *"And, Sister, in heaven there will be clear water to drink."* It would seem that the child's idea of heaven was a place where there would be limitless quantities of clear water to drink. For that child a cup of clear water was heaven itself.

In a certain sense it can be said that to give a cup of water to a person who is really thirsty is to give that person heaven. In doing such a small act of kindness to a person in need, we are bringing heaven down to earth. More important still, as all are reminded in today's Gospel, Christ becomes more present in our lives and in the world by the smallest act of kindness we do to anyone inside or outside the Community. I say inside the Community, because we can at times be so intent on serving the needy outside the Community that we can overlook offering to the members of our own Community those little services which can do so much to make life easier, and can do so much to make Christ more present in our Community.

So, my dear Sisters, with St. Vincent: *"I implore God with all my heart to pour forth on your Company the spirit of union and cordiality by which you will honor the Divine Unity in the Trinity of Persons, and the cordial respect that reigned in the family of His Son in His human life;"* (Conf. Eng. ed., 1 Jan. 1644, p. 142).

Three to Get Married

28 February 1992   Central America

My dear Friends in Jesus Christ,

There was a very popular television personality in the United States some years ago. He was a Bishop and this Bishop was also a writer. To one of the books which he wrote, he gave the title, *"Three to Get Married."* The point of the title was that, besides having a man and a woman for marriage, something else is necessary. It is as important as the man and woman, and it is love. Perhaps you will say that this is obvious, but I am quite sure there are many people who, because of their experience in marriage, would say that love in marriage is a much deeper and more complex reality than they realized when they decided to marry.

It is about marriage that Our Lord speaks to us this morning in the Gospel. Let us leave aside for a moment what Our Lord has said to us about marriage in the New Testament, and let me ask you to reflect on what you would say if you were invited up here and asked to speak for a few minutes on the importance of love in marriage.

A couple who have been married for thirty or forty years might stand here and say: our children are now grown up. We had much joy in rearing them, but experienced many difficulties and anxieties about them from time to time. They are now reared and we are back where we started. We are united still and we love each other. We see love in marriage differently from the way we saw it in the weeks before we got married. We have had our differences, but we would never wish to be separated.

An engaged couple would tell us of the joy and the hopes that are in their hearts as they look forward to their wedding day and of building a home together. They are so much in love with each other that they cannot see on the horizon of their lives a single cloud that could sadden their hearts.

A divorced man and woman would speak with sorrow in their voices. All began well, but then the marriage broke up. Little difficulties became great ones. Tension grew. There was a failure to understand each other, and perhaps one or the other was unfaithful to the promises made in marriage.

A widow and widower would look back on marriage and recount some of the joys and sorrows of those years. Uppermost in their minds would be the pain of separation that was brought about by the death of their partner.

Yes, and a child can speak of marriage. Perhaps we might be surprised at what a child could tell us about marriage. Children observe with great penetration the relationship they see between their father and mother. More perhaps than any social assistant, a child can detect a strain in the relationship between its father and its mother.

What will a priest and a Sister have to say about marriage? They will speak in favor of marriage and of the importance of lifelong fidelity to the promises given in marriage. Priest and Sister will acknowledge gratefully what they have received from their parents and family and will explain why they have chosen the priesthood and religious life in preference to marriage.

We have allowed a number of people to express their views on marriage. What matters most, whether we are married or not, is the view of Jesus Christ. If you were asked to say in one sentence what Jesus Christ has told us about marriage, would I be wrong in saying that the first reply we would all make is this: Jesus Christ said that marriage is for life and that divorce is wrong?

Yes, marriage is for life and, if it is, love must be for life. Love is for life. There is a phrase that all of us can think about and use, whether we are married or single, priest or religious. Love is for life. Each of us, throughout our lives, is called to manifest love, each in a different way, according to his or her vocation and condition of life. Often ask yourself the question: what persons have been enriched by my life? Jesus Christ was a celibate, but think of the billions He enriched by His life. A mother and father enrich their children in hundreds of ways. A widow and widower can continue to show love to others in ways different from the way they showed it to their deceased marriage partner. The vocation of a priest or Sister is about love, showing love particularly to the poor and those who have been deprived of all that human love brings. For all of us, love is for life, and it is on love that each of us will be examined at the moment of our deaths. St. John of the Cross put these words into the mouth of God: *"At evening time I will examine you on love."* More important still are the spoken words of Jesus Christ. He has told us that a surprise will await us in death. The surprise will be a pleasant or an unpleasant one, and that will depend on the love we have shown to others during our span of years on this earth. *"I was hungry and you gave me food; I was thirsty and you gave me drink; I was a stranger and you welcomed me; I was naked and you clothed me; I was sick and you visited me; I was in prison and you came to me."* (Mt 25:35-36).

May all of us be strengthened to share with others the love God has put into our hearts. Love is for life, and love is to be shared. Through the intercession of Mary, the Immaculate Mother of God, may we be made worthy of the promises of Christ, Who lives and reigns forever and ever.

Rich Young Man

2 March 1992   Panama

My dear Friends of Jesus Christ,

First, let me say how happy I am to have this opportunity of speaking to you who have taken St. Vincent de Paul to be your patron and inspiration. You are not alone among the laity of the world who find in St. Vincent de Paul an example of what it means to live the Gospel of Jesus Christ, of what it means to take to heart, day after day, the command of Jesus Christ to love God with one's whole heart and soul, and to love one's neighbor as oneself. It is to you lay people that Pope John Paul addresses this appeal in the special exhortation he wrote to the laity of the world three years ago: *". . . . The Church cannot withdraw from her ongoing mission of bringing the Gospel to the multitudes . . . who as yet do not know Christ the Redeemer of humanity . . . . The activity of the lay faithful . . . is revealed in these days as increasingly necessary and valuable."* (*Christifideles Laici*, §36).

Today, as lay Vincentians, your witness and your fidelity to the Church and to the Pope are of supreme value. Here in the countries of Central and South America many are leaving the Church and becoming members of small sects. That is sad, because the Catholic Church has the fullness of the truth that Jesus Christ preached. To abandon the Catholic Church is to leave a house and a home and to act like a child who lives in a comfortable home, but who, because he has a difference of opinion with his parents, walks out into the darkness, attracted by some lights he sees on the street. To be a Catholic in the world today is to be a privileged person. To abandon the Catholic Church is to throw away an inheritance of inestimable value.

I invite you now to meet the young man in today's Gospel a few hours after he had talked with Jesus Christ. You find him sitting in the comfort of his home, *"for he had great possessions."* (Mk 10:22). The expression on his face is a little sad. A few hours earlier he had come away from Jesus Christ, as the evangelist remarks, *"sorrowful."* Let us imagine asking the young man why he is sad and the reply he would give to our question.

Well, he might begin: "I had heard a lot about Jesus of Nazareth, and not only heard about Him, but I had listened to Him and had seen the love and compassion He had for people, particularly the poor, the blind and the lame. I admired, too, His strength of character, His wisdom and His tenderness. In one word, I recognized Him as a man of holiness, a man who was close to God. I seized my opportunity today and I ran up to Him and posed the question: *'What must I do to inherit eternal life?'* (Mk 10:17). He replied, as good teachers often do, by putting a question to me: *'Why do you call Me good?'* (Mk 10:8). Before I had time to answer His question, He remarked: *'No one is good but God alone.'* (Mk 10:18). He then referred to a few of the commandments, and I was able to say truthfully that I had kept them all. He believed me fully and I will never forget the depth of love that was in His expression when He said: *'You lack one thing. Go, sell what you have and give to the poor, and you will have treasure in heaven, and come, follow Me.'* (Mk 10:21). I felt He was absolutely right, but I could not part with my money. I could not give up the comfort of this home to follow Him, for He seems to have nothing and His closest friends are in the same condition . . . . I cannot forget Him, and yet I cannot follow Him. It is not that He is a hard man, this Jesus of Nazareth. I cannot say that He asked the impossible of me, but I could not rise to His invitation. That is why I feel sad since I went away and left Him."

We cannot pass any final judgment on this rich young man because we cannot enter into the mysterious world of God's grace. Perhaps we could ask the question: Did the young man tend to rely too much on negative goodness? He had not broken the commandments, but how much good had he done for others? Was Our Lord saying to Him: "With all your possessions, with your wealth, with all that you could give away, what positive good have you done to others? Have you gone out of your way to help and comfort and strengthen others as you might have done?" Perhaps Our Lord was saying to him: "Stop looking at goodness as consisting in *not* doing things. Take yourself; take all that you have and spend yourself and your possessions on others. Then you will find true happiness in time and in eternity."

To be a close friend of Jesus Christ one has to be poor. That is clear from this morning's Gospel. St. Vincent grasped that message clearly. Each one of us has to live according to the vocation which we have received from God. We are asked to think often of the style of life which Jesus Christ adopted on coming into the world, and above all, as St. Paul suggests, to be always *"mindful of the poor."* (Gal 2:10).

So, my dear friends, may you continue to be apostles of Jesus Christ in your homes and at your work. He is counting on you to make Him known and to extend His Kingdom here in Panama. Be a person who is just and who is loving, and Jesus Christ will be with you, and He will use you to proclaim His message to the men and women of our time.

Our Table of Values

7 March 1992   Lima, Peru

My dear Sisters,

This evening's Gospel, describing the call of Levi or Matthew, suggests a question to us, and it is this: Would St. Matthew have invited you and me as his guests to that dinner which he gave to a few of his friends to celebrate his new vocation? Before answering the question, let me raise another: Would you like to be invited to St. Matthew's dinner? Our instinctive reaction is to say *yes*, for there is an instinct in all of us which makes us wish to be known and appreciated by important people. Matthew is certainly a very important man. He has been so ever since he published that brief work of his on the life, death and resurrection of Jesus of Nazareth. It immediately became a best-seller and will remain so until the end of time. So, as I said, our instinctive reaction is to be pleased that Matthew, an important person, invited us to his party, and we are happy to accept his invitation.

Our instincts do not always guide us honestly, and a little reflection might lead us to doubt the honesty of our reactions to Matthew's invitation. I am quite certain that I would not have accepted Matthew's invitation, if Jesus Christ had not first met him and had spoken two words which utterly changed him. *"Follow me,"* Jesus said to him, and St. Matthew's perspective on life was totally changed.

The tax collectors in Jesus' time were notorious for their greedy appetites for money and for their injustice. Zacchaeus' confession to Our Lord tells us a little about the sins and temptations of tax collectors at that time.

So, for the reason that I would not like to be associated with unjust and unpopular people, and because of consideration of personal honesty, on second thought I would probably decline Matthew's invitation. But in doing so, I find that I am now coming into conflict with Jesus Christ, Who chose Matthew to be a close friend, even with his hardened heart and grasping fingers. Jesus chose Matthew as he was, and for what he would become. Very often I accept people for what they can become, while refusing to accept them for what they are. It is there that I come into conflict with Jesus Christ. Jesus did not overturn Matthew's money table, but He did overturn his table of values. As a result, Matthew, the tax collector, became the friend and apostle of Jesus.

Now, if I am to become a closer friend and a more zealous apostle of Jesus Christ, I must continually invite Jesus Christ to overturn my table of values. The greatest difficulty in doing so is my conviction that my table of values does not need to be overturned. It is only when someone provokes me by some word that hurts my sensibilities and I react strongly, that I will come, after some later reflection, to realize that my values are not those of Jesus Christ and that I have put my own values at the top of the list, and His at the bottom.

At times I can be frightened by my own classification of those poor whom I will help. I want the poor whom I select for helping to be respectable and to come up to my standards for them. It is possible that my standards do not correspond with those of Jesus Christ. To express the idea in another way, how much at home would I feel with those other guests at Matthew's dinner, guests who had not been invited by Jesus Christ, but with whom He willingly and lovingly sat down to eat?

To come back to that first question I raised: Would St. Matthew have invited you and me to his dinner? To judge from the list of his other guests, I hardly think so. St. Matthew might have judged us too good to be asked. That is a little frightening in the light of Our Lord's statement in today's Gospel: *"I have come, not to call the righteous, but sinners."* (Mt 9:13). I remember reading a scriptural commentator's observation on that sentence. He said that the point of Our Lord's phrase was this: *"The only people I can call are sinners, people who genuinely recognize themselves as such. If you think yourself virtuous, then I have not come for you. Or rather, you have put yourself by your smugness outside the circle of those who can benefit from my coming."* That interpretation should certainly urge us to pray for what the psalmist calls a humble and contrite heart.

Today's Gospel is very much a Vincentian Gospel, for it underlines the importance of conversion, of humility, of gentleness and of love for the poor, however difficult at times they may be.

Through the intercession of Mary, conceived without sin, of St. Vincent and St. Louise, may we become each day more like Jesus Christ, Who came to call sinners to conversion and to serve the poor in their needs.

Altar of Sacrifice

25 March 1992   Paris, France

Mother Elizondo, Father Lloret and my dear Sisters,

During a recent month-long visit to a number of our missions and communities in Latin America, it was suggested to me one afternoon by my Confreres and our Sisters that I visit one of the most celebrated, historical sites that lies within the territory of our Apostolic Vicariate of El Petén in Guatemala.

The site is historical because it was the seat or capital of the Maya civilization which mysteriously vanished many centuries ago. Of this city nothing was known until some 150 years ago, when it was discovered in the midst of hundreds of acres of tropical forest. The intensive growth of tall tropical trees and dense undergrowth had, over the centuries, grown up and concealed it. What stand now revealed—and only a part of the city has been uncovered—are a number of tall and massive constructions in stone with broad, steep steps mounting to a height of thirty or forty meters. To mount them can leave even the youngest person rather breathless, and a person who has not a head for heights possibly dizzy. These majestic monuments were built solely for the purpose of sacrifice and could be described as altar-temples. Today they command and inspire awe, as they silently witness to an ancient people's desire and need to speak to an unknown god in the language of sacrifice, even of human sacrifice.

As I contemplated these massive altar-temples, built with the strength of thousands of arms and with the sweat of countless human brows, I began to reflect on what the builders of these great altars might say to us moderns and what we might say to them. Clearly the heart of their religion was sacrifice. For them sacrifice was the only language which they could speak to a deity or a power which they recognized to be immeasurably greater than themselves. Whatever we might say about the confused notions they had of God, they certainly had a highly developed sense of the transcendent and of the sacred.

For our part, we would speak to them of the beauty and the wonder of what took place in Nazareth when the one true God asked a Virgin, whose name was Mary, if she would consent to be overshadowed by the Most High and thus conceive and bring forth a Child, Who would be the Saviour of the world and Who would be none other than God Himself.

That announcement to this ancient people would take their breath away, but their astonishment would be all the greater when we would go on to tell them that now there was only one sacrifice in the world, that of Jesus Christ. For, to quote from the letter to the Hebrews: *"When Christ came into the world, He said: 'Sacrifices and offerings you have not desired, but a body you have prepared for Me . . . .' Then I said, 'Lo, I have come to do your Will, O God.'"* (Heb 10:5-7).

There is now, we might continue, only one sacrifice in the world, that of Jesus Christ, and His sacrifice had everything to do with the fulfillment of another person's will, that of the eternal Father of Jesus Christ. It was through the perfect accomplishment of that Will which brought Jesus Christ to death on the altar of the cross wherein lies the salvation of the world.

The ancient people of the Maya civilization might then ask how we today offer sacrifice. We would explain to this highly intelligent people the meaning, uniqueness and centrality of our Eucharistic Sacrifice, pointing out to them that only insofar as our lives reflect and are in harmony with the sentiments of Christ, the High Priest, can they become an acceptable offering to the one true God. We might tell the Maya people that, if all the civilizations of the world disappeared in some nuclear holocaust, what people from another planet thousands of years later might discover most often in the ashes, would be the cross, not in one massive form in one place, but in millions of forms in a diversity of metals on all the continents of the globe. The cross speaks the language of sacrifice: humility, poverty, obedience, forgiveness and love. We would further go on to tell them that a tiny minority of Christ's followers are continually invited to learn and speak proficiently the language of Christ's sacrifice through the vows of chastity, obedience, poverty and service of the poor. A Daughter of Charity could fittingly quote the words of the Inter-Assembly Document and say that: *"Immersed in the world, we belong to Christ. Through the radicality of our total gift to God, confirmed by our vows, we want to be for this world a prophetic voice that witnesses to the living God. We want to live the Evangelical Counsels."*

Our vows are indeed the language of sacrifice, but it is a language that has no meaning apart from its relationship to the person of Jesus Christ. Some time ago in Rome, two Moslems stopped me on the street, asking for directions to their hotel, and as I walked a little bit of the way with them, they began to speak about religion. They asked me how Jesus Christ could be God if He died on a cross, for God cannot die. I tried to answer them as best I could. Later in the day when reflecting on the experience, I wondered how convincing I would have been if they had followed up their question by asking me to explain my vows to them.

Would my explanation be interpreted as a lived experience of devotion to the person of Jesus Christ, poor, chaste, obedient and a servant of the poor? To live with vows is, in the words of St. Vincent, to live in that condition of life *"which Our Lord embraced on earth . . . and which consists, among other means, of living in poverty, chastity, obedience and stability in one's vocation."* (Coste V, Fr. ed., p. 316).

To live a vowed life is to climb day by day the steep steps that lead to the altar of sacrifice where we take our stand on that *"living stone, rejected by men, but in God's sight chosen and precious . . . to offer spiritual sacrifices to God through Jesus Christ."* (1 Pt 2:4-5). To live fully a vowed life is to take a stand on a height that can make one dizzy. To counteract such dizziness one must always look up and not down. It is only by constantly lifting up our gaze to Jesus crucified that we will succeed in not panicking nor losing our balance. To look down is to compromise and to take back, at least partially, what once had been placed on the altar of sacrifice. Perhaps the ancient Mayan people would have difficulty in understanding us as we tried to explain compromise in sacrifice, for sacrifice with them would seem to have been not only costly, but absolute and irrevocable.

It is not that the world has lost the idea of sacrifice: thousands daily sacrifice themselves for ends and purposes unrelated to religion. What our modern world may have lost sight of is the uniqueness of the sacrifice of Christ and the urgency of our personal participation in it through a life lived with *"Jesus, the apostle and high priest of our religion."* (Heb 3:1).

To live a vowed life is to live continually in an attitude of surrender and submission to the will of another. Let us recall frequently that it is the same Father in heaven Who invited Jesus Christ to accept His Will, Who now invites us moment by moment to surrender to Him. The agents who manifest that Will and the circumstances in which we live our lives may be different, but it is the same Father. *"I am ascending to My Father and to your Father, to My God and your God."* (Jn 20:17). The greatest obstacle to living the vowed life is our reluctance to place on the altar of sacrifice our own will and judgment. It was Mary's readiness to place her will and judgment on the altar of sacrifice that made the Incarnation possible, and through it the immeasurable riches of grace lavished on humanity.

The day of the Renovation of your vows, my dear Sisters, is a day of rediscovery. In the forest of your lives you come to see with fresh eyes the beauty of that temple of which you are *"living stones."* (1 Pt 2:4). Perhaps with the passing of time the undergrowth of selfishness, independence and vanity has been allowed to climb up and conceal the altar of sacrifice. The grace of renovation is a grace to cut back all that is hiding the simple and majestic features of Christ which His Spirit is tracing out in your characters and in your lives.

Today I address to each of you the words which St. Vincent wrote in a letter to the community of Sisters at Nantes: *"I never think about you and the happiness you have to be Daughters of Charity and the first to be engaged in assisting the poor where you are, without feeling consoled. However, when I hear that you are living as true Daughters of Charity, which is to say, as true daughters of God, my consolation is increased to the extent that only God alone can make you realize. Keep this up, dear Sisters, and strive more and more toward perfection in your holy state .... a state which consists in being true daughters of God, spouses of His Son and true mothers of the poor."* (Coste III, Eng. ed., ltr. 939, p. 181).

Countering Atheism and Agnosticism
26 April 1992   Rome, Italy

My dear Confreres,

It is St. Thomas, the Apostle, who shares the stage with the Risen Christ in today's Gospel. Of the Twelve Apostles, perhaps St. Thomas is the man who could most easily understand the mentality of so many whom we meet today. Which of us here has not met people who are honest, responsible and kind, yet who say quite frankly that they are not practicing believers. They are people who, although they may have been baptized Catholics, say that they are agnostics and are unmoved by the Church's credal formulae and its claim to be *"the pillar and foundation of truth."* (1 Tim 3:15).

The good agnostic—and I use the word in its popular sense—is often a generous, concerned person. Generosity and concern for the person of Jesus was a feature of St. Thomas' character. We can recall the generosity with which he offered to go along with Our Lord into Judea, into the danger of death. *"Thomas . . . said to his fellow disciples, 'Let us also go that we may die with Him"* (Jn 11:16). Well-meaning agnostics will often challenge us to present the Church's teaching more convincingly and in a clearer light. It was Thomas who said to Our Lord at the Last Supper: *"Lord, we do not know where you are going. How can we know the way?"* (Jn 14:5).

The agnostic features of St. Thomas stand out most clearly, however, in that statement of his recorded by St. John in today's Gospel: *"Unless I see in His hands the print of the nails and place my finger in the mark of the nails and place my hands in His side, I will not believe."* (Jn 20: 20). Thomas, the agnostic, became a believer and we will always be grateful to him for that magnificent expression of his surrender to believing in the divinity of Our Lord, recorded in today's Gospel: *"Thomas answered Him: My Lord and my God."* (Jn 20: 28).

We, who carry in earthen vessels the priceless gift of faith and who feel the urgency of our vocation to proclaim the good news of Christ to the poor, often feel almost paralyzed by the agnosticism which we encounter in the modern world. The phenomenon of the non-practicing Christian is a very ancient one in the history of Christianity. However, today we meet a new phenomenon, the non-practicing Christian who, more than in the past, will justify his situation in the name of personal independence or authenticity. (cf. *Evang. Nunt.* § 56). The proclamation of the word of God in popular missions seems often to fall on deaf ears, or on indifferent hearts that question the relevance of our message today. We who live in Europe have heard the Pope in recent years call Catholics to commit themselves to the re-evangelization of this continent, while we are all aware of the growing number of people who are to be evangelized in Latin America, Asia and Africa.

Significant also for us is the explicit reference in our Statutes to the challenge which atheism throws down to us who are called to proclaim the good news of Christ to the poor. We read: *"2. - In the modern world atheism and materialism hold a challenge to the faith and to the traditional means of evangelization. Therefore, Confreres should carefully study the causes of this phenomenon, realizing that in this situation they are called upon to give witness to a strong personal faith in the living God and also to seek out new ways of fulfilling their vocation to evangelize.*" (Statutes, I, § 2).

Important though it be to proclaim and call for greater justice for the poor, we would do well in our preaching to be equally sensitive to the present day corroding currents of atheism that menace the spiritual responses of those whom we evangelize. Perhaps you will recall the public confession which the Church made at Vatican Council II in the document on the Pastoral Constitution, *Gaudium et Spes*. Treating of the phenomenon of atheism, the Fathers of the Council confessed that: *"Believers can have more than a little to do with the rise of atheism. To the extent that they are careless about instruction in the faith, or present teaching falsely, or even fail in their religious, moral or social life, they must be said to conceal, rather than to reveal, the true nature of God and of religion.*" (§ 19).

If, as individuals or as a Congregation, we have contributed to the growth of atheism in our world, the cause must ultimately lie in our failure to take Our Lord at His word and to look to Him daily and hourly as the Way for us, the Truth for us and the Life for us. This was one of St. Vincent's most profound convictions. *"Nothing pleases me,"* he wrote, *"except in Jesus Christ."* (Abelly I, p. 78) and *"Jesus Christ is the Rule of the Mission."* (Coste XII, Fr. ed., p. 130).

Faced with the immensity of the task of countering currents of atheism and agnosticism, of re-evangelizing continents, the question of Thomas is a very apt one: *"Lord, how can we know the way?"* It is a question, too, with which we priests can easily identify. Living in a new welter of questionings and opinions, witnessing the breakup of an old culture, experiencing the growth of secularism in our society, we can at times feel less sure of ourselves as we sound the trumpet call. We do well in such moments of hesitancy to pray: *"Lord, how can we know the way?"* Only when with Thomas we have prayed that prayer deeply and humbly, will we hear again the answer: *"I am the Way and the Truth and the Life"*. St. Vincent's conviction on this point was deep. *"If we cannot do anything of ourselves, we can do everything with God. Yes, the Mission can do everything because we have within us the seed of the omnipotence of Jesus Christ. Hence no one can excuse himself on the grounds of not being able. We will have always more strength than is necessary, especially when we will need it, because on the occasion one will feel as a new man.* " (Coste XI, Fr. ed., p. 204). Only then will we be able to move out confidently into the light, for if He is with us, who can be against us.

To each one of us may this grace be given, to exclaim in the darkness, but with the certainty of faith: *"My Lord and my God." "Thomas said to Him . . . . 'How can we know the way?' Jesus said to him, 'I am the Way and the Truth and the Life.'"*

New Hope

27 April 1992   Miren, Yugoslavia

My dear Sisters,

You have been making your annual retreat and you have come to the end of those days of special grace which all of us experience each year when making our retreat. When we make our retreat, we are like Nicodemus in today's Gospel. We do not come secretly or by night to make our retreat, but we do resemble Nicodemus in that we wish to come to know Our Lord better. We, more than Nicodemus, are convinced that Our Lord is a *"true teacher come from God,"* (Jn 4:2) and, like Nicodemus, we lay ourselves open to listen to what Jesus Christ may wish to say to us.

What Jesus said to Nicodemus was that he must be regenerated or born again. Nicodemus took Our Lord's words literally and asked Him to explain something which Nicodemus considered to be impossible. *"How can anyone be born after having grown old? Can one enter a second time into a mother's womb and be born?"* (Jn 3:4). What Our Lord had in mind was the new life of grace which all the baptized would receive.

A new life means new action. For the baptized the new life of grace means a new way of living, a way of living which is different from the natural way of living. *"What is born of the flesh is flesh, and what is born of the Spirit is spirit,"* said Our Lord. *"Do not be astonished that I said to you, 'You must be born from above'."* (Jn 4:6-7).

In the early Church baptism would have only been given to adults after a period of preparation as catechumens. Christians, then, would have realized that a new line of conduct was called for by reason of their baptism, a line of conduct that would be costly. St. Paul made it very clear to the Romans when he wrote: *"Put on the Lord Jesus Christ and make no provision for the flesh to gratify its desires."* (Rom 13:14).

During our annual retreat we try with the grace of God to reflect on the reality of our baptism and on its implications. Our vows are but a refinement of our baptism. If to every baptized person the Church addresses the words of St. Paul, *"Put on the Lord Jesus Christ,"* the Church can say to us who have taken vows, *'You have been privileged, for to you has been given the call and the grace to live more closely to Jesus Christ in His poverty, in His obedience, in His chastity and in His love for the Poor.'*

Reading a modern commentary on St. John's Gospel when I was preparing this homily, I came across the observation that, while St. John speaks of regeneration through baptism, he might, if he were writing today, speak rather of liberation. Certainly baptism is a liberation, just as our vows, when lived fully, are a liberation. The vow of obedience can liberate us from seeking selfishly our own work and our own places and conditions of work. The vow of chastity can free us from the domination of an instinct which, while good in itself, can divide our hearts and thus make them less available for the work of the Lord and for the building up of His kingdom. The vow of poverty can liberate us from the dominion that money can exercise over our desires and our lives. The vow of service of the poor can liberate us from attachment to people who by their favor or their social prestige, might lure us away from those who are rejects of society or who, because of their poverty or their social class, are unattractive company.

Baptism and our vows are, my dear Sisters, a liberation. During the past year, you who live and work here in Slovenia must have come to a new appreciation of what liberation means. The liberation you have experienced has brought you new hope, a new reason for living, a new sense of appreciation of the history of your country and a new sense of gratitude to those who through their sufferings and struggles have achieved that liberation. It is so with baptism and our vows. When we live our baptism and our vows, we experience new hope. We come to a greater appreciation of the Community and its traditions. We gain a new appreciation of the riches and the graces of our vocation, all of which were bought at the price of the blood of Jesus Christ. *"You were bought with a price,"* wrote St. Paul to the Corinthians, *"therefore, glorify God in your body."* (1 Cor 6:20), while St. Peter reminds his converts that they were *"ransomed . . . with the precious blood of Christ, like that of a lamb without defect or blemish."* (1 Pt 1:19).

The final sentence in today's first reading describes an experience of the first Christians after they had prayed together. *"And they were all filled with the Holy Spirit and spoke the word of God with boldness."* (Acts 4:31). As you go forth from your retreat, my dear Sisters, may you be filled with the Holy Spirit and continue to live your vocation with courage and with hope, proclaiming by your lives the word of God. In the words of St. Vincent: *"I pray Our Lord that He will be the life of your life and the only desire of your hearts."* (Coste VI, Fr. ed., p. 562).

Martyrdom

28 April 1992   Zagreb, Yugoslavia

My dear Friends of Jesus Christ,

I am very happy to have this opportunity of celebrating the Eucharistic Sacrifice with you. When we come together to celebrate the Mass, we cannot but think of the mystery of Our Lord's death on the cross. The Mass is, as our faith teaches us, the re-enactment of the sacrifice which Our Lord made of Himself on the cross. The mystery of the Eucharist and of Christ's sacrifice is presented, in accordance with Our Lord's command, under the appearances of bread and wine. When Jesus Christ offered His sacrifice on Calvary, it must not have been a pleasing sight. Fresh blood would have stained the ground.

Fresh blood has stained the soil of Croatia in recent months and there must be at present many aching hearts among your people. Hundreds of your people are mourning those who have died in battle; thousands, have seen their homes damaged or destroyed. Croatia, your Fatherland, has been transformed into a Golgotha. My prayer for your country and for you is that the Good Friday through which you have been passing, will give place to a Resurrection that will bring peace and consolation to all who live in this Christian land.

Today the Church is honoring a priest who shed his blood for the faith. He was Peter Chanel, a French priest who lived in the last century. He began his priestly life as a diocesan priest, but some years later, because of his desire to preach the Gospel in countries where Christ had not been proclaimed, he joined the Marist Congregation. In 1836 he set out to one of the islands in the Pacific Ocean, where he worked for five years. A tribal chieftain grew jealous of the success which this priest was having in preaching the Gospel and he had him murdered. The martyrdom of this generous priest on the 28 April 1841, at the age of thirty-eight brought about the conversion of the people of the island. Pope Pius XII thirty-eight years ago canonized Peter Chanel, allocating this day as his feast in the Church's calendar.

All martyrs for the faith are distinguished by their generosity. Did not Our Lord say: *"Greater love than this no one has, to lay down one's life for one's friends."* (Jn 15:13). Not every Christian is called to shed his blood for the faith, but every Christian is called to be generous towards all and especially to the poor and suffering members of Christ's Body.

The message of this evening's first reading is one which encourages us to be generous. The author of the first reading, St. Luke, tells us that the first Christians were so generous that no one among them experienced dire poverty. *"The community of believers were of one heart and one mind . . . nor was there anyone in need among them, for all who owned property or houses sold them and donated the proceeds. They used to lay them at the feet of the Apostles to be distributed to everyone according to his need."* (Acts 4:32, 34-35). St. Luke also singles out one particular parishioner for special mention because of his generosity. He was Barnabas, who later would become St. Paul's companion as he went from town to town, proclaiming Jesus Christ to be God and Saviour of the world.

Perhaps you have not too much money with which you can be generous. Do not be disheartened. Jesus Christ had no place on which

He could lay His head. Yet can you think of anyone who was more generous than He, Who although He was God, emptied Himself and took the form of a servant when He lived among us? There are many things with which you can be generous:

"The best thing to give ....
to your enemy is forgiveness;
to an opponent, tolerance;
to a friend, your heart;
to your child, a good example;
to a father, deference;
to your mother, conduct that will make her proud of you;
to yourself, respect;
to all men, charity." (Lord Balfour).

All that was precisely what Jesus Christ did. That, too, was what His Mother did. It was what St. Vincent de Paul and all God's saints did. May we, dear brothers and sisters in Christ, be strengthened to do likewise.

God's Work of Art

29 April 1992   Ljubljana, Yugoslavia

My dear Sisters,

The Italians today are celebrating the feast day of one of their national Patrons, St. Catherine of Siena. The whole Church today is honoring this remarkable woman, whose love for God was so intense that in the short span of thirty-three years she reached the heights of mystical union with God. St. Catherine, however, was no cloistered nun. As a Dominican tertiary, she undertook difficult and dangerous journeys in the interests of Church unity and of peace in her nation. She was a strong-minded woman, and did not hesitate to tell the Pope of her day, Gregory XI, that he should leave France, where he and his predecessors had resided for seventy-four years, and return to Rome. Pope Gregory accepted the advice of this young lady of twenty-nine years of age and at once set out for Rome. Catherine became, a year or two later, one of the advisors of Pope Gregory's successor, Pope Urban VI, and she tried strenuously through negotiation to reconcile the political leaders of her time, so that the people could enjoy a measure of peace. St. Catherine was a strong woman, but because her heart was full of the love of God, she always showed the highest respect for the Popes and Bishops of her day, and acted with simplicity, a virtue which St. Vincent loved so much and which he wished should shine out in the character of every Daughter of Charity.

All the great saints had deep insight into a truth that is expressed in today's Gospel: *"God so loved the world that He gave His only Son that whoever believes in Him should not perish, but should have eternal life."* (Jn 3:16).

In that one sentence you have an answer to the questions: who, how, why and what of our Christian convictions. Who? God, the eternal, Creator of the universe. How? Jesus Christ, truly God, truly man, born of the Virgin Mary. Why? God loved humanity, even in its sinfulness and rebellion. What? Eternal life. It is eternal life that Jesus Christ is offering to those who will accept it, a share forever in the joy and happiness of God.

The tragedy of the world is that it does not see the gift of God. Humanity does not know, or chooses not to know and recognize, the depth of God's concern and interest in the welfare of the men and women He has created, and of His personal love for each one of them.

When you see a mother caring for and caressing her sleeping infant, that is a feeble image of what God is doing for us at each moment of our lives. The infant accepts the love and care, but is not able to say thanks. The infant cannot appreciate the love and care that is being poured out on it. So, too, with us. We are blind and insensitive to the intense love which God has for us and which reaches its high point in this life when He gives Himself to us in Holy Communion. *"O love of my Saviour,"* exclaimed St. Vincent in the middle of a conference, *"O love, Thou art incomparably greater than the Angels could, or ever will, comprehend."* (Coste XII, Fr. ed., p. 109).

God so loved the world that He gave His only Son so that the world might share eternal life in the intimacy of the Father, Son and Holy Spirit. Because God loved the world and because He loves each one of us, as if we were the only human being on this earth, there must be in each one of us a special quality of beauty which rejoices the heart of

God. St. Paul understood this when he wrote to the Ephesians and told them that they were *"God's work of art."* (Eph 2:10).

I, a work of art? With all my physical blemishes and moral defects? Yes, each one of us is God's work of art. It is true that we are defective. Still, each of us is unique and God sees in each one of us a special beauty which He sees in no other person. And He rejoices as He contemplates us, just as a father will rejoice as he looks on his infant child, even if it should be handicapped or devoid of good looks.

Because each of us is God's work of art, we must respect our own bodies and our minds and the bodies and minds of others. When you go into an art gallery, you would not dare touch the portraits, lest you damage them. So with God's art gallery, which is His Church, we must respect and not damage the masterpieces which God in His love has created. Masterpieces can be flawed and still remain masterpieces. We are flawed by sin, but we are nonetheless God's masterpieces.

May Mary, the Virgin Mother of God, conceived without sin, the only perfect human masterpiece, enable us to appreciate the beauty and the value of our own persons and those whose lives touch ours. *"God so loved the world that He gave His only Son so that whoever believes in Him should not perish, but have eternal life"* .... *"We are God's work of art."*

Good Shepherds

10 May 1992   Rome, Italy

My dear Confreres,

In December 1990 I spent two days in what is sometimes called the last city of the world, Punta Arenas in Chile. It is from this city that expeditions set forth for the Antarctic. The land around the city is poor and rather barren. The winter is long and bleak and cold. During the lunch in the house of the Sisters I was sitting beside the local Bishop, and in the course of the meal I asked him how many Catholics were in the extensive territory of his diocese. He replied, *"about a hundred thousand"* and then he added, *"and three million sheep."* Here, I said to myself afterwards, is one bishop in the world who must meditate a lot on what it means to be a shepherd, and who would hardly need to explain a word of today's Gospel to his people. There would be no risk that his people would interpret the metaphor of sheep and shepherd incorrectly, as might well happen in an inner city parish. Sheep are not our favorite image for Christians, for sheep are considered to be overly submissive. Sheep do not lead, they follow.

It is not so much what the sheep do, nor even what the shepherd does, that the key to understanding the metaphor is to be found. It is rather on the quality of the shepherd that we must center our attention: on his heart and mind rather than on his functions. Think of the occasions when Our Lord spoke of the shepherd. The shepherd is a man who protects; the hireling does not do so in moments of danger and crisis. The shepherd is a man who searches; he leaves the ninety-nine alone in order to search out the one sheep that is lost. The shepherd is a man who speaks and calls the sheep by name; the sheep recognize the authentic voice of the shepherd.

However unfamiliar we may be with shepherds, the image was a favorite one of Our Lord, because it conveyed to His hearers the idea of one who cares and who does not take to flight when danger threatens. The image of a shepherd continues to be used by the Church for the same reason that Our Lord used it. In the latest Apostolic Exhortation on the formation of priests, *Pastores Tibi Dabo*, the Pope repeats over and over again that the priest in the Church is: *"a sacramental representation of Jesus Christ, the Head and Shepherd. . . . Priests exist and act in order to proclaim the Gospel to the world and to build up the Church in the name and person of Christ, the Head and Shepherd. . . . The priest's fundamental relationship is to Jesus Christ, Head and Shepherd."* (§ 15-16).

The functions of a shepherd are to protect, to search, to speak. They are among the functions of Jesus Christ, the Good Shepherd. They are among the functions of every priest today who by Ordination represents Christ, the Shepherd, in and for His Church, each according to his particular calling as a priest.

As a priest what do I protect? If a persecuting secular authority were to arrest me as a priest, what evidence would it have to condemn me as a priest? Would it be evident that I am a man who by my manner of life protects the values of Christ, the Good Shepherd, and is prepared to suffer in order to uphold them?

As a priest, what do I search for? St. Vincent might well phrase the question in this way: Have you zeal for the salvation of souls, like Christ, the Good Shepherd, who came to search out the lost? Given St. Vincent's sensitivity to fulfilling the Will of God in the smallest details of his life, he might well ask: Do you as a priest consistently search out the Will of God, not only in the crisis points of your life, but day by day and hour by hour?

As a priest, what do I speak or proclaim? Are my words, my observations, my judgments in harmony with the voice of Christ, the Good Shepherd? *"My sheep hear my voice. I know them, they follow Me."* (Jn 10:27). Does my life, which is the most powerful evangelizing word I can speak, attract others or repel them from Christ, the Good Shepherd?

As representatives of Christ, the Good Shepherd, in the world today, one of our responsibilities is to find other shepherds, for with the eyes of Christ, the Head, we see that *"the crowds are harassed and helpless, like sheep without a shepherd."* (Mt 9:36). I like very much the idea proposed by Pope Pius XII that every priest should try to leave behind him a successor in the priesthood. Today the Church is praying particularly for vocations to the priesthood and to the religious life. The whole theology that underpins the work of securing vocations has been very succinctly expressed by St. Vincent when he wrote to Father Pierre de Beaumont on 2 May 1660: *"It belongs only to God to choose those whom He wishes to call to the Community. We are assured that a missionary, given by His fatherly hand, will do alone much more good than many others who do not have an authentic vocation. It is up to us to pray that He will send good workers into His harvest and to lead such good lives that, by the force of our example, we would attract, rather than repel, them to work with us."* (Coste VIII, Fr. ed., p. 287).

The harvest indeed is great and the laborers are few. There are many more than three million sheep seeking a shepherd. May the Lord in His mercy and through the intercession of His Immaculate Mother Mary make us worthy of the vocations He is calling to the Community.

Encouragement

My dear Sisters and my dear Confreres,

I am very grateful to God who has brought Father Lauwerier and me here so that we could greet you and listen to you as you describe the apostolates in which you are at present engaged. For Father Lauwerier this visit must be a very special one. It was he who sent the first Vincentians here when he was Visitor of the Province of Paris. For that reason I am sure that, as Assistant for the Missions, he has a special place in his heart for the Cameroon. We could say that he has a *preferential option* for this country and its people.

The first reading of today's Mass has a decidedly mission character. The Church at Antioch sends Paul and Barnabas on a new mission. St. Luke is more precise, for he makes it clear that it was under the inspiration of the Holy Spirit that the two Apostles left on what we now call the *second missionary journey*.

A study of the relationship between Paul and Barnabas can prove very interesting and in many ways relevant to missionary relationships today. When you read the Acts of the Apostles carefully, you will notice that, when they started on their journey, it was Barnabas who led the mission. Then gradually the natural leadership qualities of Paul took over, and St. Luke reverses the order of the names. It is quite clear that it is Paul who was taking the initiative. Barnabas did not resent this. He seems to have been an outstandingly humble man.

It is true that later he disagreed with Paul about John Mark. Paul was perhaps overdemanding in what he looked for in John Mark as a missionary, while Barnabas seems to have pleaded along the lines of *"Give him another chance."* Paul refused, and so Barnabas and Paul went their separate ways. But we do know that towards the end of Paul's life, he wished to be united with the man for whom Barnabas had pleaded. (cf. 2 Tim 4:11). In one word, the character of Barnabas is summed up by St. Luke who remarks on the significance of his name, *"The Son of Encouragement."* Barnabas wished to give encouragement to the young John Mark.

In the Irish language there is a proverb which goes: *"Praise the young, and they will come along with you."* All of us hopefully will remain young in heart until the end, and so a little word of praise and encouragement can go a long way in helping others along life's road. Sometimes we may be tempted to say, *"If I praise him or her, the result will be a swelled head."* In my experience, however, the swelling, if it does occur, will not last long. The knocks people receive in life will reduce such swellings very fast.

All of us could learn much from Barnabas. We talk a great deal about the pastoral care for vocations. Like Barnabas, we have to keep our eyes open for talents or, rather, for goodness in the characters of people who could, like Paul, become *"servants of Jesus Christ."* (Rom 1:1). Like Barnabas, we could learn not to be upset if those whom we bring to the Community may outshine us and serve Christ and the poor in a more striking way than we do. What matters for us today and every day is that we remain united closely to Jesus Christ, that we allow Him to abide in us and we in Him. It is only in this way that He can use us for His purposes, which will never be fully clear to us in this life. What matters is that we be people of profound humility.

St. Barnabas teaches us, not so much by his words but by his attitude, to be people who not only work for unity, but who also are humble and loving enough to encourage others. All of us need encouragement in our apostolates, and no one more than those who are in the front line of the Church's missionary endeavor. We are encouraged by the words of Pope John Paul II in his encyclical, *Redemptoris Missio: "The Church needs to make known the great Gospel values of which she is the bearer. No one witnesses more effectively to these values than those who profess the consecrated life in chastity, poverty and obedience in a total gift of self to God and in complete readiness to serve man and society after the example of Christ."* (§69).

To each of you I address the words which St. Vincent wrote to Jacques Pesnelle: *"Provided missionaries are truly humble, truly obedient, truly mortified, truly zealous and full of confidence in God, His divine goodness will make good use of them everywhere and will supply for the other qualities which perhaps they lack."* (Coste VII, Fr. ed., p. 237).

May the Lord through the intercession of Our Lady of Fatima, whose feast we celebrate today, make us humble agents of encouragement for the building up of His Kingdom.

Fear Not

15 May 1992   Cameroon

My dear Sisters,

It would be an interesting exercise to list the phrases which most frequently came to the lips of Our Lord. *"Do not let your hearts be troubled,"* Jesus says in today's Gospel. He is trying to cast out fear from the hearts of the Apostles on the night before He is to suffer death. When the disciples, on the Lake of Galilee in the darkness of the night, saw Jesus walking on the waves, they were terrified. They cried out *"for fear."* Immediately Jesus said to them: *"Take heart. It is I. Have no fear."* (Mt 14:27). We know that several times during his life Jesus said to people: *"Fear not."* After His resurrection, when He met His disciples in the upper room, He first wished them peace and then told them not to fear. Jesus Christ is interested always in trying to lighten our fears. When He comes to us in Holy Communion, He assures us that He is giving us everlasting life. That is a great assurance because the greatest natural fear which we have is the fear of death. Jesus Christ in every Holy Communion is assuring us that, as He can take care of that greatest natural fear, namely, death, He will also take care of those many other smaller fears which are hidden in our hearts. Some of these fears are known to us, others are not. To us, however, as to the frightened disciples, Jesus Christ keeps saying: *"Take heart. It is I. Have no fear."* (Ibid.). *"Do not let your hearts be troubled."* (Jn 14:1).

A phrase like *"Fear not"* will often be on the lips of anyone who is a close follower of Jesus Christ. St. Vincent and St. Louise spent much of their lives casting out fear from the hearts of the poor. They spent much of their lives encouraging and consoling the poor, inviting them to come to Jesus Christ and place their confidence in Him. Our Lord is always whispering into our ears, *"Fear not."* He does not wish us to keep that message to ourselves. He wants us to pass on the word to others. He wants to use us so that we can help others to cast out some of the fears that may be in their hearts. He wants to use us to invite others to come to Him. By the kindness of our words and the thoughtfulness of our actions, each of us can do much to lessen the fears that are in the hearts of our friends. Each of us can do much to bring our friends closer to Jesus Christ.

There is one other phrase in today's Gospel which could be the summary of everything Jesus said and did. To St. Thomas Jesus said: *"I am the Way and the Truth and the Life."* (Jn 14:6).

Christ is the Way. If you wish to go somewhere, you ask the way. We are pilgrims on our way to heaven. Jesus Christ is our way. We are following the right way if Jesus Christ can at all times share our thoughts, our words, our actions. St. Vincent often proposed to people as a program for their lives the simple question: *"What would Jesus Christ do, if He were in my place now?" "Christ"*, he said one day, *"is the rule of the Mission,"* and the Constitutions of the Daughters of Charity take that sentiment and state: *"Christ is the Rule of the Daughters of Charity."* (C. 1.5).

Christ is the Truth. Many people have spoken the truth and taught the truth. Only Jesus Christ could say: *"I am the Truth."* Truth is reality. To desire truth is to desire direct contact with reality. When we touch Christ in prayer or in the Sacraments, we are touching the fullness of reality. We are touching the truth and our minds are seeking reality and truth.

Christ is the Life. St. Paul has a marvelous phrase in his letter to the Colossians. *"Christ,"* he writes, *"Who is your life . . . ."* (Col 3:4). It is Christ Who has given us in baptism a spark of His risen life. We cannot see it, but it is there, just as we cannot see the life that is in the darkness of the earth and which shows itself in the beauty of spring flowers and in budding leaves. *"Christ, Who is your life . . . ."* (Ibid.).

"May my life be solely for Jesus and my neighbor," prayed St. Louise, *"so that by means of this unifying love, I may love all that Jesus loves . . . and may obtain from His goodness the graces which His mercy wills to bestow upon me."* (*Spiritual Writings of Louise de Marillac*, A.23, p. 786).

The *Poor* Poor

31 May 1992   Rome, Italy

My dear Volunteers,

You have kindly invited me to participate in the meeting which you are holding in Madrid on the 5, 6 and 7 June. I greatly appreciate your gesture and, although I will be in Spain during those days, I have already accepted engagements which would make it difficult for me to assist at your National Meeting. From my Confreres and from the Daughters of Charity, I have learned how vibrant your Association is throughout Spain and how vigorously you are working for the poor. If that fact rejoices me, how much more must it lift the hearts of the poor who in so many diverse ways you discreetly and lovingly serve.

Recently I have been reflecting on an ordinance which a bishop in the United States made for his diocese. Last year he asked that over a period of three months every meeting held under diocesan auspices begin with the question, *"How shall what we are doing here affect or involve the poor?"* At the end of three months the Bishop had some interesting observations to make on the experiment that had taken place. One of them was the following which I transcribe from his letter to the diocese:

"We tend to forget the *poor* poor.

A typical scenario: The chairperson begins the meeting by saying something like, 'Well, the Bishop has asked that we begin each meeting with a discussion about how this affects or involves the poor. So we're going to spend a few minutes doing that. I'll throw it open for anyone who would like to say something.' Silence.

Then someone says, 'Well, people can be poor in a lot of different ways. There are some people, for example, who don't have friends, and they are poor.'

I interrupt. 'I agree with you. But this decree has to do with the *poor* poor. They are the ones who get left out because they're not part of what I did yesterday or today. The other kinds of poor people are part of our lives, and we need to be concerned about them. But I want us to connect with the *poor* poor. If we deal with them, all the rest will follow. The *poor* poor are the ones who rarely if ever are first on an agenda. So let's talk about them.'

Mental note: Always start with the *poor* poor." (cf. Bishop Untener in *Origins*, 1 Aug. 1991).

I think the Bishop's observations could give us all much to reflect upon. In his original question, "How shall what we are doing here affect or involve the poor?" I like the two verbs, *affect* and *involve*. Both are important. We can spend much time discussing problems about the poor without ever—or at least only after much time—affecting the lives of the poor. Involvement of the poor: that is an ideal which we must try to realize in the programs we elaborate to relieve need and redress injustice. You try to involve the poor in the projects which you organize. We try to help the poor in such a way that they will be able to help themselves and thus rise out of their poverty in a way that is in harmony with their human dignity.

The work we do for the poor is a work of faith. Activated by the grace of Our Lord Jesus Christ and inspired by the example of St. Vincent and St. Louise, we try to bring the healing hand of Christ to those in need and the courageous voice of the prophet to those in power. This is the challenge that faces Vincentian Volunteers in your country today.

Praying God's blessing on your meeting and greeting each of you in the name of St. Vincent, I remain, in the love of Our Lord, devotedly yours.

Beatitudes

8 June 1992   Granada, Spain

My dear Sisters,

If the entire New Testament were lost and the only fragment that remained for humanity were the verses of the Gospel to which we have just listened, we would have quite a clear idea of what manner of man Jesus Christ was. The remainder of the books of the New Testament are but an illustration and explanation of the Beatitudes that Our Lord pronounced when, sitting down on the mountain side, He began to teach His disciples. The Beatitudes have been described as the Charter, the

Constitutions of the Kingdom of Heaven. They have also been described as a self-portrait of Jesus Christ. For Jesus Christ was a man who was poor in spirit. He was, too, one who showed Himself to be infinitely merciful. He was pure of heart. *"Which of you,"* he asked, *"will convince Me of sin?"* (Jn 8:46). He was a man who mourned. *"As He came near and saw the city, He wept over it, saying, 'If you, even you, had only recognized on this day, the things that make for peace'."* (Lk 19:41). And what volumes does not the Cross speak about a man who was insulted, persecuted and slandered, all for the cause of right and of truth. Apart from Our Lord and His Mother, no one ever lived the Beatitudes fully. The Beatitudes are a mountain which we must continue to climb, even if in this life we will never reach the summit.

The Beatitudes are a new scale of values. We might say that the Beatitudes are an invasion of God's madness into the world of what humanity considers to be good sense. Have you ever tried to make a list of what you would consider to be your eight beatitudes? This could be very revealing and, when set down on paper, might show a very deep chasm between the values of Our Lord and those by which we daily live. Let me ask another question. Do you feel comfortable with Our Lord's Beatitudes? Or has it been your experience, as it has been mine, that when you start to think or talk about one beatitude, you prefer after a short time to drop it because of its difficulty, and move on to another which you would consider more simple and easy? The beatitude that makes you feel most uncomfortable is probably the one that is most relevant to you personally.

The first beatitude, by reason of its position, could have a claim to being the most important and fundamental for a disciple of Christ. *"Blessed are the poor in spirit"* or, as St. Luke calls it, *"Blessed are the poor."* It may be a fundamental beatitude, for at its heart is the virtue of humility. A person cannot be poor in spirit without being humble. A person who is genuinely humble will also be poor in spirit. So the first beatitude may be the most important beatitude for, if we are poor in spirit, then we will be humble, and if we are humble, then all good things that we need will be given to us. In the Rule that St. Vincent wrote for his missioners, he remarks that to the man who possesses humility, all good things will come, while the man who has not humility, will be subject to continual anxiety. (CR II, 7). An aunt of mine, who was a religious, used often to say to my mother, *"If you have humility, you have everything."* It is true. If we have humility, we will certainly have peace and serenity. And with the peace and serenity of Jesus Christ, who Himself was gentle and humble of heart, we can endure much and find the courage and strength to do much for the building up of others in faith, hope and love. If we asked St. Vincent how he succeeded in making his charity blossom to such a remarkable degree in his life, he might very well reply, *"by cultivating humility."* It was humility that created within him that void which God was able to fill with the fire of divine love. St. Vincent's first biographer, Bishop Abelly, quotes the Saint as saying, *"Let us strive after humility, for the more humble a man is, the more charitable he will be to his neighbor."* (Abelly, Book I, ch. 21).

The truth of St. Vincent's teaching about humility and its relationship to charity was confirmed recently for me, when I read of someone who asked a friend of Mother Teresa of Calcutta what he thought of her. The reply was short and simple. *"She is a person who has lost her ego."* The end of all genuine mortification is the cutting back of all those excrescences of pride, vanity, envy, jealousy, and sensuality which spring from our ego. It is the selfish ego, and not our gifts or talents, that must be denied and mortified. It is such mortification that Our Lord had in mind when He told us that a person must lose his life or ego, if he is to preserve his life. It is the exaltation of my ego which impedes my growing more and more into the likeness of Jesus Christ Who is the life and the light of the world.

St. Vincent spoke and wrote frequently about what he called the evangelical maxims. The Beatitudes are a succinct summary of all the evangelical maxims, and the Beatitudes have been described as the "gospel of the Gospel." The following sentences from a letter of St. Vincent reveal his profound convictions about the value and importance of the evangelical maxims: *"Let people think and say whatever they wish. Rest assured that the maxims of Jesus Christ and the examples of His life are not misleading; they produce their fruit in due time. Anything not in conformity with them is vain and everything turns out badly for one who acts according to the contrary maxims. Such is my belief and such is my experience."* (Coste II, Eng. ed., ltr. 606, p. 316).

May Mary, who lived the Beatitudes so perfectly, assist us through her maternal intercession, as we climb the mountain of the Lord, striving always to attain greater poverty of spirit.

My Face is My Fortune

12 June 1992   Seville, Spain

My dear Sisters,

When I was a young boy, there was a popular song whose opening line was, *"My face is my fortune."* While it was a popular song, not everyone could sing that song with sincerity and conviction. Many preferred to sing it only when there was a large chorus of other voices! Within the Bible there is no such song, but there are, however, many references to the human face and to the Divine Face.

The Divine Face fascinated the people of Israel, but, of course, it inspired awe and even fear. Only by way of exception did God allow His friend, Moses, to see His face. *"Thus,"* writes the author of Exodus, *"the Lord used to speak to Moses face to face, as one speaks to a friend."* (Ex 33:11). One can interpret the phrase as an experience of a very intimate, personal communion with God.

The same must be said of the experience of Elijah, as described in today's first reading. The Lord was present, not in the strong wind nor in the earthquake, nor in the fire, but in the gentle breeze, and Elijah *"hid his face in his mantle and went out and stood at the entrance of the cave."* (1 Kgs 19:13).

"My face is my fortune." Yes, hopefully it will be some day, because as St. Paul assures us, we will find our supreme happiness in seeing God, not as now in a somewhat obscure and confused way, but we will see Him *"face to face."* Meantime we move along the way of pilgrimage and are subject to change of experience and also to change of mood. Where do we normally register our change of mood more than in the expressions on our faces?

If a person is not telling the truth, we say that he or she cannot look us in the face, while, when we are assured that we are telling the truth, we say, *"I can look anyone in the face and say what I am saying."*

Perhaps St. Vincent had that image in his mind when he said that to act with simplicity is to act with God alone in view.

In this life our faces sometimes reflect the face of God, and sometimes they do not. In the faces of the poor we can see the face of Christ on the cross. When we ourselves suffer personally, we can pray with a new sincerity the prayer of the psalmist, *"Do not hide your face from me in the day of my distress."* (Ps 102:3). Our faces in moments of joy will express the serenity of Christ. *"Let your face shed its light upon us,"* (Ps 67:2) prayed the Psalmist. When through instructing others or comforting the sick and the weak, we draw close to them, we are letting the light of God's face shine on them.

The light of God's face does not shine through ours, when we manifest a cold and distant attitude to others. We may feel, and rightly so, that others have wronged us, or perhaps we feel irritated or annoyed by them. Then our sentiments express themselves in our faces. At times we may be justified in showing displeasure, but anger and sadness are emotions that must be carefully controlled. It is all too easy to allow our emotions to usurp the place of reason and of our nobler Christian sentiments.

When we pray, we are in a certain sense trying within the limits of our human condition to see God face to face. All prayer is an expression of faith, and in this life it is by faith that we see God. To pray is to turn our faces towards the face of God. In prayer we not only try to look on the face of Christ, as we have come to know Him in the pages of the New Testament, but we expose ourselves to Him so that He may change our hearts. We are privileged as Christians when we pray. St. Paul recalls in his second letter to the Corinthians that in Old Testament times, the people had to put a veil over the face of Moses after he had encountered the Lord on Sinai. To look on the glory of God was too great to bear. In New Testament times St. Paul reminds us that *"all of us with unveiled faces, seeing the glory of the Lord, as though reflected in a mirror, are being transformed into the same image from one degree of glory to another."* (2 Cor 3:18).

That sentiment of St. Paul should encourage us in being faithful to daily meditation. We may seem to achieve little; we may be subject to many distractions, but all the time we are slowly being transformed inwardly and being made more like Christ in the sentiments of our minds and hearts. It is sometimes said that a husband and wife, who love each other over a long period of years, tend to resemble each other in their physical appearance. It is so with us in prayer. We come to know and love Our Lord more deeply, and as we do, we will represent Him more faithfully in our lives. In sustained prayer and meditation the light of the face of Christ shines on ours and we are made more ready for the experience of seeing Him face to face. In that experience we will find our happiness, not for a moment, as did the disciples on the mountain of the Transfiguration, but for all eternity. May the prayer of the psalmist one day be fulfilled in us: *"As for me, in my justice I shall see Your face and be filled, when I awake, with the sight of Your glory."* (Ps 17:15).

Then indeed our faces will be our fortunes.

Interview At the End of a Twelve Year Mandate

11 July 1992   Rome, Italy

    1. What are your sentiments at this time? Have you any regrets?

The sentiment that is uppermost in my heart at this particular moment in my life is one of profound gratitude to God. Over the past twelve years God has mediated to me through my Confreres, the Daughters of Charity and lay members of our Vincentian Family a torrent of refreshing graces and blessings. They have introduced me to a series of worlds of human poverty, and it has been one of the joys of these twelve years to see the almost infinite variety of human poverty to which members of the Vincentian Family are present and are striving to alleviate. I have often thought that there is no form of human poverty or pain in the world to which at least one member of the Vincentian Family is not bringing some assistance. The members of our Communities have been very considerate, kind and patient with me, so how can I have any other sentiment but one of gratitude to God for His goodness shown to me throughout these twelve years?

Regrets? The only regret I have is that I have left so much undone and so much done imperfectly. I can say that I regret now that I have not given myself more fully and wholeheartedly to the tasks of every day throughout these years. I feel that when I appear before God in judgment, my hands may look full of grain, but on closer inspection, there will be found much chaff. For that reason, I feel I have much need of the mercy of God and the prayers of others to win for me that mercy.

2. *What has pleased you most during the period of your term of office as Superior General?*

What has pleased me most during my period of office was to discover the goodness and holiness of so many members of our Vincentian Family. We have many Vincentian Saints in heaven, relatively few beatified or canonized. We have also many Vincentian Saints on earth and I have been privileged to meet a number of them. The faith of many members of our Communities has impressed me greatly, as indeed also has the charity and concern for the poor that exists among the members of our Vincentian Communities. The evangelical simplicity, humility and charity evidenced in so many priests, Brothers and Sisters, as well as in the laity, have been to me personally a stimulus to seek a deeper relationship with God from Whom all good things come. There have been natural joys also during these years. Visiting the various provinces and countries with the diversities of cultures and languages, customs and traditions, has been very enriching. It has been a source of joy to me also to find so many members of our Family ready to meet community, as well as my own personal, needs, once they recognized them. The cooperation I have received from those who worked closest with me here in Rome has also been a source of happiness to me. It would take me many pages of your review to set down an adequate list of all that has given me joy during these twelve years.

3. *Now how will you insert yourself into your Province of origin?*

I have placed myself at the disposal of the Father Provincial or Visitor of the Province of Ireland, expressing my readiness to assume whatever work in whatever place he would judge best. After some time, and having discussed the question with his Council, he suggested that I would go to a small community of ours in the city of Dublin. It is a college for third level education. The idea proposed to me is that in the coming months I would have some time to read and reflect and, I hope, pray more and at the same time be available for the preaching of retreats.

I hope also on my return to Ireland to work a little with the members of the St. Vincent de Paul Society in Dublin city, who are constantly asking us for priests who would act as spiritual guides to the many Conferences which exist in the city. I jokingly have told my friends in Dublin that I am but a poor immigrant now, coming from Italy and seeking employment. It would seem, then, that for a little time I will be somewhat "unemployed," but the prospect does not disturb me.

4. *What do you look for in the Community for the coming years?*

There exists in the two Vincentian Communities and in the different lay organizations a great desire to serve the poor more effectively. Much has been done in the past few years to draw closer to the world of the poor. I hope that the movement, if one may call it so, will continue. However, I would like to see in our Communities a greater and deeper dedication to prayer. Many times during these years I have asked myself and others if we have not been too busy, too active and too horizontal, in our approach to the problems of society today. It may be that we are so busy about the work of the Lord that we forget the Lord of the work. I would like to see in our Communities a greater sensitivity to the presence of Christ, not only in the poor but in our tabernacles. Visiting many churches and oratories throughout the world and admiring the great artistic beauty of some of them, most often what I have found missing in them is a priest, a Brother, or Sister engaged in quiet contemplation and adoration of Our Lord and Master Who, as our faith teaches us, is really, truly and substantially present there. Perhaps it is a question of achieving a balance between acknowledging the presence of Christ in the poor and His presence in the Blessed Sacrament. We must not lose sight of the importance of adoring Him in the Blessed Sacrament. I have heard it said that we cannot really recognize Christ in the poor if we have not first recognized Him in the Eucharist. In a word, we may be overactive, hence less contemplative, and action that is not rooted in contemplation of God and the humanity of Christ will inevitably be shallow and will not be fruitful for eternal life.

Epilogue

Father McCullen left to our absolute discretion the choice or selection of his writings for this volume. Only one paragraph of all his writings did he tentatively suggest be included. It is the final paragraph of his personal reflection on the state of the Congregation of the Mission at the close of his twelve-year mandate as Superior General. It was delivered on 3 July 1992.

> *In a moment of intimate self-disclosure Saint Vincent remarked one day: 'There are two things in me: gratitude and an inability not to praise the good.'* (Abelly, III, p. 208, 1st edition). *At the end of my mandate as Superior General, I find much gratitude in my heart for all the good I have seen in Saint Vincent's two Communities, and even more gratitude for all that I have received from the members of our Vincentian Communities. It has not been difficult for me to praise the good that I have seen and that I have experienced. My difficulty has been in not being able to see its full extent and to find adequate expressions of gratitude, and I continue to labor under that difficulty. In those who worked closest with me I have seen great depths of goodness. To the Assistants, then, and particularly to the Vicar General, Father Miguel Pérez Flores, whose competency and loyalty during a span of twelve years has carried me at times over difficult terrain, I owe an incalculable debt of appreciation. Let me also express my gratitude to the Sisters and Confreres who worked with me in the General Curia and of whose goodness I have been a daily witness and beneficiary. It was G.K. Chesterton who said that 'we choose our friends, but God gives us our neighbors.' In the neighbors God gave me in the Curia, I found excellent friends.*
>
> *How better can I end than with the words with which Saint Vincent concludes our Common Rules: "We must get it firmly into our heads that, when we have carried out all we*

have been asked to do, we should, following Christ's advice, say to ourselves that we are useless servants, that we have done what we were supposed to do, and that in fact we could not have done anything without Him. " (CR Xll, 14).

Index